ADDITIONAL BOOKS ON MANY OTHER
SUBJECTS ARE AVAILABLE

Accounting Desk Book
(4th Edition)

Estate Planning Desk Book
(3rd Edition)

Forms of Business Agreements With Tax Ideas: Annotated
(4th Edition)

How To Raise Money To Make Money
(2nd Edition)

How To Use Tax-Free
And Tax-Sheltered Investments
To Pyramid Your Capital

Lawyer's Desk Book
(4th Edition)

Life Insurance Desk Book
(3rd Edition)

Professional Corporation Desk Book
New

Real Estate Desk Book
(4th Edition)

Successful Techniques That
Multiply Profits and Personal Payoff
In The Closely Held Corporation

Real Estate Investment Tables

Real Estate Investments and How To Make Them
(4th Edition)

REAL ESTATE
FINANCING DESK BOOK

Joseph R. Bagby

President

Property Resources Co.

INSTITUTE for BUSINESS PLANNING, Inc.

IBP Plaza • Englewood Cliffs, N.J. 07632

©1975 *by*

Institute for Business Planning, Inc.
IBP Plaza, Englewood Cliffs, N.J. 07632

Library of Congress
Catalog Card Number
75-10420

Third Printing . . . . . August, 1976

Printed in the United States of America

ISBN 0-87624 495 9

About the Author

For many years, Joseph R. Bagby was a key figure on the real estate management team of Burger King Corporation. During this period, this relative unknown, with assets of only about $1 million, grew to become one of the leading fast food chains in the nation. At Burger King he acquired and leased real estate at a rate of $30 million a year.

Today, he is founder and president of another miraculous success story, Property Resources Co., a real estate financing firm that started with an initial $40 thousand investment and today has financed over $200 million worth of properties.

Widely sought as a financial and real estate consultant, Mr. Bagby has worked with such nationally known businesses as Gino's Inc., General Mills, Pillsbury, and Meridian Investing and Development Company, to name just a few.

Mr. Bagby is founder and president of the National Association of Corporate Real Estate Executives (NACORE), an "Association of Corporate Real Estate Executives in American Commerce, Industry and Government."

Having been an investment adviser, real estate salesman, property manager, and real estate appraiser himself at one time or another during his career, Mr. Bagby knows everything there is to know about real estate and how to finance it. His new book presents a complete picture of what this critical game of dollars and cents is all about, in easy to understand language.

No topic is too small or too big to discuss — a home — a lot — a condominium — a shopping center. The *Real Estate Financing Desk Book* is truly the first of its kind. Through it, Mr. Bagby gives men and women all over the country the full benefit of his real estate experience and know-how, in one compact edition that's indexed so you turn to answers instantly.

How to Make Best Use
of this Desk Book

Real Estate Financing Desk Book is intended as a handy, everyday tool for any person involved in real estate, a practical reference for any individual or group hoping to enter the fascinating world of property ownership and development.

To accomplish these purposes, the text is divided into three main sections. Part 1 leads you through every phase of successful financing, for just about any kind of property. Here you will find fast, dependable answers on the latest ideas and techniques being used to finance residential, commercial and industrial properties, nursing homes, motels and hotels, mobile home parks. Whether you're working on a $20,000 condominium or a shopping center worth millions of dollars, you'll quickly find one or more methods that can pay off big for you.

Part 2 puts at your fingertips every known, practical source of financing — together with the names and addresses of hundreds of individuals and institutions, many of whom are eager to lend right now. All told, there are almost 30 of these financing sources — including some that most real estate men may not have dared touch before. Now, however, you'll know exactly how to approach pension funds, insurance companies, foundations, money managers and all the other sources to get the money you need.

Part 3 provides a complete glossary of important financing terms, to help make even the most complex financing arrangements mere child's play. And the special help on tax considerations makes it simple to achieve the greatest tax savings whether you're using a tax-free exchange, a sale-leaseback, or any other financing technique.

Yes, with this remarkable Instant Answer Book you'll be able to pry funds loose from even the most reluctant lender — finance any deal in any money market — dramatically increase sales, commissions, and profits. Never again need you watch helplessly while deals take unbearably long to complete — or, worse — fall through entirely. You now hold in your hands the Master Key to closing deals quickly and successfully.

Heartfelt appreciation goes to my wife, Martha, for her extraordinary contributions to this work and to Paunee Rigsby Bagby for her exceptional research. To Louise and Hampton Green for their sustaining support and encouragement — unending gratitude. Many thanks also to Elaine Rigsby for her assistance.

The author is indebted as well to C.W. Kilpatrick and Richard M. Brown for their expertise and guidance in preparing this book, and deeply appreciates the research contributed by Carolyn Joslin. Special bouquets go to Betty Ritzler for her continued interest and excellence in compiling this material.

CONTENTS

Other Groups of Lenders and Brokers *(Continued)*

Foreign Funds . . . .

PART 1 — STEP-BY-STEP GUIDE

1. — What Makes Financing Tick

FIRST, THE FRAMEWORK

Financing does not stand as an isolated function of monied institutions or individuals. In fact, it is so interdependent and interrelated to the national and international economies that it must be viewed as a product of outside conditions rather than as a force shaping events.

One of the major influences on financing of housing and other properties is the federal government. It directly affects building and mortgage placements by providing actual funds or insurance for loans through its various agencies, departments, and programs.

Indirectly, the United States government can have astounding impact on the money supply for real estate projects. The government often becomes a competitor of private institutions, which traditionally make mortgage loans, by raising money to meet its existing loans or to finance present or planned operations.

For instance, when government spending is high or money is needed to pay off national debt, the government offers short-term Treasury bills at rates higher than those of other institutions which traditionally attract small investors' savings. As savers dip into their accounts, say, at savings and loan associations, these institutions find themselves drained of money for mortgages and other loans for residential and commercial real estate in their individual communities.

Not only does the government bid vigorously for savers' and investors' dollars, so do other members of the institutional lending family. In recent years for example, holding companies of large commercial banks have issued floating rate securities whose interests vary at a fixed rate above that of Treasury bills.

All of this scrambling for funds creates heavy money pulls in one direction and then in another so that there is a great imbalance of cash available for the various needs of borrowers.

The government will undoubtedly continue to stabilize money supply by legislation aimed at cutting down this kind of tugging between sources. It will also persist in clearly defining roles of the various institutions.

1

More flexibility in long-term interest rates charged is in the offing, with some institutions already using variable rates tied to cost-of-living increases or prime rate, that short-term interest rate charged the best customers of large commercial banks. Shorter-term, renewable mortgages will probably become more popular to combat inflationary dwindling of the long-term committed dollar. These charges will all serve the consumer and the saver more efficiently when there is rapid inflation, and will ultimately, in such an economy, make more cash available for loans.

Other countries, long troubled by vacillating monetary values, have been using floating interest rates for a while. But America, which has enjoyed a rather stable economy over many years, has not had to worry about its dollars losing substantially over long-term loan periods. Now we do, and we are meeting the crisis with new financing tools.

OTHER FACTORS AFFECTING THE MONEY MARKET

Of course, readiness of money also fluctuates with the general economy such as inflationary trends, prospects for business, government policies, and control of flow of dollars to banks and indirectly to other institutions.

The money market is linked above all to the law of supply and demand. Although it is basically the Federal Reserve System that controls the supply of currency through the banking system of this country, funds available for real estate investment come mainly from the savings of the population.

Investors, whether they be individuals, savings institutions, or insurance companies, look for the greatest possible return or rent for their money. This search for profit, which after all is the basis of our system, explains in part why the person seeking a mortgage may or may not be able to obtain it.

TIGHT MONEY

When there is ample money in circulation for loans or mortgages, we see liberal lending with high percentages of appraised property values applied towards mortgages. In this climate, there is usually no problem in obtaining 80, 90, or even 100 percent loans, and most lenders are able to make a large number of the loans applied for.

In what is known as a tight money market, there is extremely keen competition for the investors' funds since less money is in circulation but the demand for it is high.

One must remember that the money picture can change rapidly and should not be discouraged by a turndown on a mortgage if the general economic atmosphere is clouded.

Knowing the reasons for these ups and downs can help the investor master his timing for acquiring loans.

Here is a basic lesson in helping to understand whatever economy the individual may find himself facing:

The government ideally prints enough money to represent all the goods, services, and productivity of its people. If the government responds to great pressure to pump more dollars into the economy, it may do so quickly and with too much thrust and create inflationary trends. When it realizes inflation has hit, it may put a stop on money supply, causing businesses to be hurt and to cut planned expansion and payroll. At the same time, the government may be selling its own securities to clear its indebtedness or deficit spending, thereby putting further demands on the supply of money in the well.

If the government is too slow in putting cash into circulation, recession results. If government overreacts and throws too much currency into the mainstream immediately after halting it, recession and inflation will sit side by side.

In such a situation, the economy must cope with devalued money as it works its way through the system. Businesses may abandon long-range planning based on recessionary factors they were experiencing and adapt to more available dollars. The business community cannot respond immediately and usually requires one to three years to come back to full operational strength. What we experience then are lag time effects in adjusting to abrupt government changes in economic policy.

Consider that companies with a $7-million net worth are usually required by their lenders to show five-year plans, and these are often recast as dollars swell or diminish on the open market. If money does become available in large measure after a brief tight period, some firms will choose initially not to borrow and if a number of them pass up funds this may help force prime interest rates down further because then there may be an over supply of currency.

More consistent and better planned monetary and fiscal policy by the federal government in the future is essential.

THE FUTURE

Need for funds to build homes and buildings is enormous now and will be staggering in the future. Today, approximately 3.5 billion people live on this planet. By the year 2000, the world may almost double in population to about six billion.

During this time, there will be rising middle classes throughout the world who will demand housing and supporting plants, offices, factories, and new kinds of health, educational, recreational, and convenience facilities.

In addition to providing for this new population increase, at least 50 percent of the existing dwellings and business and industrial properties all over the globe will have to be rebuilt, and 25 percent or more of them will have to be substantially remodeled and upgraded.

Let's take a look at what these figures could mean in terms of dollars and cents to housing alone. With a world of six billion people, and an average family of five, there must be 850 million homes or residences of some kind. This would mean the world would have 500 million new family groups plus 350 million existing housing units which will have to be replaced for a total of 850 million in new residences to be built by the year 2000.

Of course, many people of the world live in meager surroundings today, and it is probably unrealistic to assume that each family could have a decent place to live by 2000.

To build 850 million new dwelling units in the next 25 years at an average cost of $30,000 per dwelling unit (allowing for the cost of inflation during this period) it would take $2 trillion, 550 billion. This amount is greater than the combined gross national products of Europe, the United States, and Japan which, in 1972, was approximately $2.5 trillion.

Certainly such a sum may seem a fantasy now and impossible to supply. Surely, current financing know-how will undergo strengthening and change to meet such demands. Money and material needs are sure to alter our concepts of housing and other buildings.

Today, for instance, many Americans feel a great strain in trying to buy the simplest kind of single-family home. A family must save money for a down payment for three, four, or five years or more. Many of them realize they may never be able to own a home and are turning instead to mobile home parks, condominiums, and modest townhouses.

The single-family home is simply beyond the reach of an ever-increasing number of American families. This, of course, is tragic for a nation that has considered home ownership almost a basic for some years.

In the early 1970's, the MIT Harvard Joint Center for Urban Studies completed an extensive study which pointed out that the nation would need 23 million new housing units by 1980 plus 13 million homes which either needed to be remodeled or modernized in some way. New programs provided by the government are simply inadequate to meet the huge demands of Americans. Creative and aggressive new financing techniques and vehicles are needed by lenders in order to provide housing and industrial and commercial properties called for in coming years.

Government programs must be more realistic regarding today's costs of construction and structure loans which the income of the people can support without subsidy.

One suggestion would be to provide 40-to-50-year mortgages as found in England on homes of up to $60,000 with two to three percent cash down.

This would allow a young family to buy a nice home with $1,200 to $1,800 cash as long as its income would support the mortgage payments. With a 40-to-50-year mortgage the payments of the loan would be substantially low.

To handle the huge demand for remodeled homes the government might provide up to $25,000 for any remodeling on long-term second mortgages, insured with savings and loans and other institutions, similar to long-term first mortgages if the owner of the property were able to meet these payments based on earnings. This type of program would immensely stimulate the housing industry and put many people to work.

Only a superficial look at real estate needs has been taken here, but ways to finance present and near future properties of all kinds are presented in detail in the pages to follow.

AMORTIZATION TABLES

The following tables are those most used in real estate financing. Utilizing these tables one can obtain information on mortgage financing as well as net lease or leaseback financing.

Each table ranges from one to 40 years and shows interest ranging from 7 to 13 percent. Payments can be figured on an annual, semi-annual, quarterly, or monthly basis. (The tables are on pages 6 to 21.)

ANNUAL PAYMENTS MADE IN ADVANCE

A table of the constant annual percent which is needed to amortize a principal amount calculated on an annual basis figured in advance.

Interest Rate	2 YEARS	3 YEARS	4 YEARS	5 YEARS	6 YEARS	7 YEARS	8 YEARS	9 YEARS	10 YEARS	11 YEARS	12 YEARS	13 YEARS	14 YEARS	15 YEARS	16 YEARS	17 YEARS	18 YEARS	19 YEARS	20 YEARS
7	51.70	35.62	27.60	22.80	19.61	17.35	15.66	14.35	13.31	12.47	11.77	11.19	10.69	10.27	9.90	9.58	9.30	9.05	8.83
1/8	51.72	35.66	27.64	22.85	19.66	17.40	15.71	14.41	13.37	12.53	11.84	11.25	10.76	10.34	9.97	9.65	9.37	9.12	8.90
1/4	51.75	35.70	27.69	22.90	19.72	17.46	15.77	14.47	13.43	12.59	11.90	11.32	10.83	10.40	10.04	9.72	9.44	9.20	8.98
3/8	51.78	35.74	27.73	22.95	19.77	17.51	15.83	14.53	13.50	12.66	11.97	11.39	10.89	10.47	10.11	9.79	9.52	9.27	9.05
1/2	51.81	35.78	27.78	23.00	19.82	17.57	15.89	14.59	13.56	12.72	12.03	11.45	10.96	10.54	10.18	9.87	9.59	9.35	9.13
5/8	51.84	35.82	27.82	23.05	19.88	17.62	15.94	14.65	13.62	12.78	12.10	11.52	11.03	10.61	10.25	9.94	9.66	9.42	9.21
3/4	51.87	35.86	27.87	23.10	19.93	17.68	16.00	14.71	13.68	12.85	12.16	11.59	11.10	10.68	10.32	10.01	9.74	9.50	9.28
7/8	51.90	35.89	27.92	23.15	19.98	17.73	16.06	14.77	13.74	12.91	12.23	11.65	11.17	10.75	10.39	10.08	9.81	9.57	9.36
8	51.93	35.93	27.96	23.20	20.03	17.79	16.12	14.83	13.80	12.98	12.29	11.72	11.24	10.82	10.47	10.16	9.88	9.65	9.44
1/8	51.96	35.97	28.01	23.24	20.09	17.84	16.18	14.89	13.87	13.04	12.36	11.79	11.30	10.89	10.54	10.23	9.96	9.72	9.51
1/4	51.99	36.01	28.05	23.29	20.14	17.90	16.23	14.95	13.93	13.10	12.43	11.85	11.37	10.96	10.61	10.30	10.03	9.80	9.59
3/8	52.01	36.05	28.10	23.34	20.19	17.96	16.29	15.01	13.99	13.17	12.49	11.92	11.44	11.03	10.68	10.38	10.11	9.87	9.67
1/2	52.04	36.09	28.14	23.39	20.25	18.01	16.35	15.07	14.05	13.23	12.55	11.99	11.51	11.10	10.75	10.45	10.18	9.95	9.74
5/8	52.07	36.13	28.19	23.44	20.30	18.07	16.41	15.13	14.11	13.29	12.62	12.06	11.58	11.17	10.82	10.52	10.26	10.03	9.82
3/4	52.10	36.17	28.23	23.49	20.35	18.12	16.46	15.19	14.18	13.36	12.68	12.12	11.65	11.24	10.90	10.60	10.33	10.10	9.90
7/8	52.13	36.21	28.28	23.54	20.40	18.18	16.52	15.25	14.24	13.42	12.75	12.19	11.72	11.32	10.97	10.67	10.41	10.18	9.98
9	52.16	36.25	28.32	23.59	20.46	18.23	16.58	15.31	14.30	13.49	12.82	12.26	11.79	11.39	11.04	10.74	10.48	10.26	10.06
1/8	52.19	36.29	28.37	23.64	20.51	18.29	16.64	15.37	14.36	13.55	12.88	12.33	11.86	11.46	11.11	10.82	10.56	10.33	10.13
1/4	52.22	36.33	28.41	23.69	20.56	18.34	16.70	15.43	14.43	13.61	12.95	12.39	11.93	11.53	11.19	10.89	10.63	10.41	10.21
3/8	52.24	36.37	28.46	23.74	20.61	18.40	16.75	15.49	14.49	13.68	13.02	12.46	12.00	11.60	11.26	10.97	10.71	10.49	10.29
1/2	52.27	36.40	28.50	23.79	20.67	18.46	16.81	15.55	14.55	13.74	13.08	12.53	12.07	11.67	11.33	11.04	10.79	10.56	10.37
5/8	52.30	36.44	28.55	23.84	20.72	18.51	16.87	15.61	14.61	13.81	13.15	12.60	12.14	11.74	11.41	11.11	10.86	10.64	10.45
3/4	52.33	36.48	28.59	23.89	20.77	18.57	16.93	15.67	14.67	13.87	13.21	12.67	12.21	11.81	11.48	11.19	10.94	10.72	10.53
7/8	52.36	36.52	28.64	23.94	20.83	18.62	16.99	15.73	14.74	13.94	13.28	12.73	12.28	11.89	11.55	11.26	11.01	10.80	10.60
10	52.39	36.56	28.68	23.99	20.88	18.68	17.05	15.79	14.80	14.00	13.35	12.80	12.35	11.96	11.62	11.34	11.09	10.87	10.68
1/4	52.44	36.64	28.77	24.09	20.98	18.79	17.16	15.91	14.93	14.13	13.48	12.94	12.49	12.10	11.77	11.49	11.24	11.03	10.84
1/2	52.50	36.72	28.86	24.18	21.09	18.90	17.28	16.03	15.05	14.26	13.61	13.08	12.63	12.24	11.92	11.64	11.40	11.18	11.00
3/4	52.56	36.79	28.95	24.28	21.19	19.01	17.39	16.15	15.18	14.39	13.75	13.21	12.77	12.39	12.07	11.79	11.55	11.34	11.16
11	52.61	36.87	29.04	24.38	21.30	19.12	17.51	16.28	15.30	14.52	13.88	13.35	12.91	12.53	12.21	11.94	11.70	11.50	11.32
1/4	52.67	36.95	29.13	24.48	21.41	19.23	17.63	16.40	15.43	14.65	14.02	13.49	13.05	12.68	12.36	12.09	11.86	11.65	11.48
1/2	52.72	37.03	29.22	24.58	21.51	19.35	17.74	16.52	15.55	14.78	14.15	13.63	13.19	12.82	12.51	12.24	12.01	11.81	11.64
3/4	52.78	37.10	29.31	24.68	21.62	19.46	17.86	16.64	15.68	14.91	14.28	13.77	13.33	12.97	12.66	12.39	12.17	11.97	11.80
12	52.84	37.18	29.40	24.77	21.72	19.57	17.98	16.76	15.81	15.04	14.42	13.90	13.48	13.11	12.81	12.55	12.32	12.13	11.96
1/4	52.89	37.26	29.49	24.87	21.83	19.68	18.10	16.88	15.93	15.17	14.55	14.04	13.62	13.26	12.96	12.70	12.48	12.28	12.12
1/2	52.95	37.33	29.58	24.97	21.93	19.79	18.21	17.01	16.06	15.30	14.69	14.18	13.76	13.41	13.11	12.85	12.63	12.44	12.28
3/4	53.00	37.41	29.67	25.07	22.04	19.90	18.33	17.13	16.19	15.43	14.82	14.32	13.90	13.55	13.26	13.00	12.79	12.60	12.44
13	53.06	37.48	29.76	25.17	22.14	20.01	18.45	17.25	16.31	15.57	14.96	14.46	14.05	13.70	13.41	13.16	12.94	12.76	12.60

6

Interest Rate	21 YEARS	22 YEARS	23 YEARS	24 YEARS	25 YEARS	26 YEARS	27 YEARS	28 YEARS	29 YEARS	30 YEARS	31 YEARS	32 YEARS	33 YEARS	34 YEARS	35 YEARS	36 YEARS	37 YEARS	38 YEARS	39 YEARS	40 YEARS
7	8.63	8.45	8.30	8.15	8.02	7.91	7.80	7.71	7.62	7.54	7.46	7.39	7.33	7.28	7.22	7.17	7.13	7.09	7.05	7.02
1/8	8.71	8.53	8.37	8.23	8.11	7.99	7.88	7.79	7.70	7.62	7.55	7.48	7.42	7.37	7.31	7.27	7.22	7.18	7.14	7.11
1/4	8.78	8.61	8.45	8.31	8.19	8.07	7.97	7.87	7.79	7.71	7.64	7.57	7.51	7.45	7.40	7.36	7.31	7.27	7.24	7.20
3/8	8.86	8.69	8.53	8.39	8.27	8.15	8.05	7.96	7.87	7.79	7.72	7.66	7.60	7.54	7.49	7.45	7.41	7.37	7.33	7.30
1/2	8.94	8.77	8.61	8.47	8.35	8.24	8.14	8.04	7.96	7.88	7.81	7.75	7.69	7.63	7.58	7.54	7.50	7.46	7.42	7.39
5/8	9.02	8.85	8.69	8.56	8.43	8.32	8.22	8.13	8.04	7.97	7.90	7.84	7.78	7.72	7.68	7.63	7.59	7.55	7.52	7.49
3/4	9.09	8.92	8.77	8.64	8.51	8.40	8.30	8.21	8.13	8.06	7.99	7.92	7.87	7.81	7.77	7.72	7.68	7.65	7.61	7.58
7/8	9.17	9.00	8.85	8.72	8.60	8.49	8.39	8.30	8.22	8.14	8.07	8.01	7.96	7.91	7.86	7.82	7.78	7.74	7.71	7.67
8	9.25	9.08	8.93	8.80	8.68	8.57	8.47	8.38	8.30	8.23	8.16	8.10	8.05	8.00	7.95	7.91	7.87	7.83	7.80	7.77
1/8	9.33	9.16	9.01	8.88	8.76	8.65	8.56	8.47	8.39	8.32	8.25	8.19	8.14	8.09	8.04	8.00	7.96	7.93	7.89	7.86
1/4	9.41	9.24	9.09	8.96	8.84	8.74	8.64	8.56	8.48	8.41	8.34	8.28	8.23	8.18	8.13	8.09	8.05	8.02	7.99	7.96
3/8	9.48	9.32	9.17	9.04	8.93	8.82	8.73	8.64	8.56	8.49	8.43	8.37	8.32	8.27	8.23	8.18	8.15	8.11	8.08	8.06
1/2	9.56	9.40	9.26	9.13	9.01	8.91	8.81	8.73	8.65	8.58	8.52	8.46	8.41	8.36	8.32	8.28	8.24	8.21	8.18	8.15
5/8	9.64	9.48	9.34	9.21	9.09	8.99	8.90	8.82	8.74	8.67	8.61	8.55	8.50	8.45	8.41	8.37	8.34	8.30	8.27	8.25
3/4	9.72	9.55	9.42	9.29	9.18	9.08	8.98	8.90	8.83	8.76	8.70	8.64	8.59	8.54	8.50	8.46	8.43	8.40	8.37	8.34
7/8	9.80	9.64	9.50	9.37	9.26	9.16	9.07	8.99	8.91	8.85	8.79	8.73	8.68	8.64	8.59	8.56	8.52	8.49	8.46	8.44
9	9.88	9.72	9.58	9.46	9.35	9.24	9.15	9.07	9.00	8.93	8.88	8.82	8.77	8.73	8.69	8.65	8.62	8.59	8.56	8.53
1/8	9.96	9.80	9.66	9.54	9.43	9.33	9.24	9.16	9.09	9.02	8.96	8.91	8.86	8.82	8.78	8.74	8.71	8.68	8.65	8.63
1/4	10.04	9.88	9.74	9.62	9.51	9.42	9.33	9.25	9.18	9.11	9.05	9.00	8.95	8.91	8.87	8.84	8.81	8.78	8.75	8.73
3/8	10.12	9.96	9.83	9.71	9.60	9.50	9.41	9.34	9.27	9.20	9.14	9.09	9.05	9.01	8.97	8.93	8.90	8.87	8.84	8.82
1/2	10.20	10.04	9.91	9.79	9.68	9.59	9.50	9.42	9.35	9.29	9.23	9.18	9.14	9.10	9.06	9.02	8.99	8.97	8.94	8.92
5/8	10.28	10.13	9.99	9.87	9.77	9.67	9.59	9.51	9.44	9.38	9.32	9.27	9.23	9.19	9.15	9.12	9.09	9.06	9.04	9.01
3/4	10.36	10.21	10.07	9.96	9.85	9.76	9.67	9.60	9.53	9.47	9.41	9.37	9.32	9.28	9.24	9.21	9.18	9.16	9.13	9.11
7/8	10.44	10.29	10.16	10.04	9.94	9.84	9.76	9.69	9.62	9.56	9.51	9.46	9.41	9.37	9.34	9.31	9.28	9.25	9.23	9.21
10	10.52	10.37	10.24	10.12	10.02	9.93	9.85	9.77	9.74	9.65	9.60	9.55	9.50	9.47	9.43	9.40	9.37	9.35	9.32	9.30
1/4	10.68	10.53	10.40	10.29	10.19	10.10	10.02	9.95	9.89	9.83	9.78	9.73	9.69	9.65	9.62	9.59	9.56	9.54	9.51	9.49
1/2	10.84	10.70	10.57	10.46	10.36	10.27	10.19	10.12	10.06	10.01	9.96	9.91	9.87	9.84	9.80	9.78	9.75	9.73	9.70	9.69
3/4	11.00	10.86	10.74	10.63	10.53	10.45	10.37	10.30	10.24	10.19	10.14	10.10	10.06	10.02	9.99	9.96	9.94	9.92	9.90	9.88
11	11.16	11.02	10.90	10.80	10.70	10.62	10.54	10.48	10.42	10.37	10.32	10.28	10.24	10.21	10.18	10.15	10.13	10.11	10.09	10.07
1/4	11.32	11.19	11.07	10.97	10.87	10.79	10.72	10.66	10.60	10.55	10.50	10.46	10.43	10.39	10.37	10.34	10.32	10.30	10.28	10.26
1/2	11.49	11.35	11.24	11.14	11.05	10.97	10.90	10.83	10.78	10.73	10.68	10.65	10.61	10.58	10.55	10.53	10.51	10.49	10.47	10.45
3/4	11.65	11.52	11.41	11.31	11.22	11.14	11.07	11.01	10.96	10.91	10.87	10.83	10.80	10.77	10.74	10.72	10.69	10.68	10.66	10.64
12	11.81	11.69	11.57	11.47	11.39	11.31	11.25	11.19	11.14	11.09	11.05	11.01	10.98	10.95	10.93	10.90	10.88	10.87	10.85	10.84
1/4	11.98	11.85	11.74	11.65	11.56	11.49	11.42	11.36	11.31	11.27	11.23	11.20	11.16	11.14	11.11	11.09	11.07	11.06	11.04	11.03
1/2	12.14	12.02	11.91	11.82	11.73	11.66	11.60	11.54	11.49	11.45	11.41	11.38	11.35	11.32	11.30	11.28	11.26	11.24	11.23	11.22
3/4	12.30	12.18	12.08	11.99	11.91	11.84	11.77	11.72	11.65	11.63	11.59	11.56	11.53	11.51	11.49	11.47	11.45	11.43	11.42	11.41
13	12.47	12.35	12.25	12.16	12.08	12.01	11.95	11.90	11.85	11.81	11.78	11.74	11.72	11.69	11.67	11.65	11.64	11.62	11.61	11.60

ANNUAL PAYMENTS MADE IN ARREARS

A table of the constant annual percent which is needed to amortize a principal amount calculated on an annual basis figured in arrears.

Interest Rate	2 YEARS	3 YEARS	4 YEARS	5 YEARS	6 YEARS	7 YEARS	8 YEARS	9 YEARS	10 YEARS	11 YEARS	12 YEARS	13 YEARS	14 YEARS	15 YEARS	16 YEARS	17 YEARS	18 YEARS	19 YEARS	20 YEARS
7	55.31	38.11	29.53	24.39	20.98	18.56	16.75	15.35	14.24	13.34	12.60	11.97	11.44	10.98	10.59	10.25	9.95	9.68	9.44
1/8	55.41	38.20	29.61	24.48	21.07	18.64	16.83	15.44	14.33	13.42	12.68	12.05	11.53	11.07	10.68	10.34	10.04	9.77	9.54
1/4	55.51	38.28	29.69	24.56	21.15	18.72	16.91	15.52	14.41	13.51	12.76	12.14	11.61	11.16	10.77	10.43	10.13	9.86	9.63
3/8	55.60	38.37	29.78	24.64	21.23	18.80	17.00	15.60	14.49	13.59	12.85	12.23	11.70	11.25	10.86	10.52	10.22	9.95	9.72
1/2	55.70	38.46	29.86	24.72	21.31	18.89	17.08	15.68	14.57	13.67	12.93	12.31	11.78	11.33	10.94	10.61	10.31	10.05	9.81
5/8	55.79	38.55	29.95	24.80	21.39	18.97	17.16	15.76	14.66	13.76	13.02	12.40	11.87	11.42	11.03	10.70	10.40	10.14	9.91
3/4	55.89	38.63	30.03	24.89	21.47	19.05	17.24	15.85	14.74	13.84	13.10	12.48	11.96	11.51	11.12	10.79	10.49	10.23	10.00
7/8	55.99	38.72	30.11	24.97	21.55	19.13	17.32	15.93	14.82	13.93	13.19	12.57	12.05	11.60	11.21	10.88	10.58	10.32	10.10
8	56.08	38.81	30.20	25.05	21.64	19.21	17.41	16.01	14.91	14.01	13.27	12.66	12.13	11.69	11.30	10.97	10.68	10.42	10.19
1/8	56.18	38.90	30.28	25.13	21.72	19.29	17.49	16.10	14.99	14.10	13.36	12.74	12.22	11.78	11.39	11.06	10.77	10.51	10.29
1/4	56.27	38.98	30.37	25.22	21.80	19.38	17.57	16.18	15.08	14.18	13.45	12.83	12.31	11.87	11.48	11.15	10.86	10.61	10.38
3/8	56.37	39.07	30.45	25.30	21.88	19.46	17.65	16.26	15.16	14.27	13.53	12.92	12.40	11.96	11.57	11.24	10.95	10.70	10.48
1/2	56.47	39.16	30.53	25.38	21.97	19.54	17.74	16.35	15.25	14.35	13.62	13.01	12.49	12.05	11.67	11.34	11.05	10.80	10.57
5/8	56.56	39.25	30.62	25.46	22.05	19.62	17.82	16.43	15.33	14.44	13.71	13.10	12.58	12.14	11.76	11.43	11.14	10.89	10.67
3/4	56.66	39.33	30.70	25.55	22.13	19.71	17.90	16.52	15.42	14.53	13.79	13.18	12.67	12.23	11.85	11.52	11.24	10.99	10.77
7/8	56.76	39.42	30.79	25.63	22.21	19.79	17.99	16.60	15.50	14.61	13.88	13.27	12.76	12.32	11.94	11.62	11.33	11.08	10.86
9	56.85	39.51	30.87	25.71	22.30	19.87	18.07	16.68	15.59	14.70	13.97	13.36	12.85	12.41	12.03	11.71	11.43	11.18	10.96
1/8	56.95	39.60	30.96	25.80	22.38	19.96	18.16	16.77	15.67	14.79	14.06	13.45	12.94	12.50	12.13	11.80	11.52	11.27	11.06
1/4	57.04	39.69	31.04	25.88	22.46	20.04	18.24	16.85	15.76	14.87	14.15	13.54	13.03	12.59	12.22	11.90	11.62	11.37	11.16
3/8	57.14	39.77	31.13	25.96	22.55	20.12	18.33	16.94	15.85	14.96	14.23	13.63	13.12	12.69	12.31	11.99	11.71	11.47	11.25
1/2	57.24	39.86	31.21	26.05	22.63	20.21	18.41	17.03	15.93	15.05	14.32	13.72	13.21	12.78	12.41	12.09	11.81	11.57	11.35
5/8	57.33	39.95	31.30	26.13	22.71	20.29	18.50	17.11	16.02	15.14	14.41	13.81	13.30	12.87	12.50	12.18	11.91	11.66	11.45
3/4	57.43	40.04	31.38	26.22	22.80	20.38	18.58	17.20	16.11	15.22	14.50	13.90	13.40	12.97	12.60	12.28	12.00	11.76	11.55
7/8	57.53	40.13	31.47	26.30	22.88	20.46	18.66	17.28	16.19	15.31	14.59	13.99	13.49	13.06	12.69	12.38	12.10	11.86	11.65
10	57.62	40.22	31.55	26.38	22.97	20.55	18.75	17.37	16.28	15.40	14.68	14.06	13.58	13.15	12.79	12.47	12.20	11.96	11.75
1/4	57.82	40.39	31.72	26.55	23.13	20.71	18.92	17.54	16.45	15.58	14.86	14.27	13.77	13.34	12.98	12.66	12.39	12.16	11.95
1/2	58.01	40.57	31.89	26.72	23.30	20.88	19.09	17.72	16.63	15.76	15.04	14.45	13.95	13.53	13.17	12.86	12.59	12.36	12.15
3/4	58.20	40.75	32.07	26.89	23.47	21.06	19.26	17.89	16.81	15.94	15.22	14.63	14.14	13.72	13.36	13.06	12.79	12.56	12.36
11	58.40	40.93	32.24	27.06	23.64	21.23	19.44	18.07	16.99	16.12	15.41	14.82	14.33	13.91	13.56	13.25	12.99	12.76	12.56
1/4	58.59	41.10	32.41	27.23	23.81	21.40	19.61	18.24	17.16	16.30	15.59	15.01	14.52	14.10	13.75	13.45	13.19	12.96	12.77
1/2	58.79	41.28	32.58	27.40	23.99	21.57	19.78	18.42	17.34	16.48	15.78	15.19	14.71	14.30	13.95	13.65	13.39	13.17	12.98
3/4	58.98	41.46	32.76	27.57	24.16	21.74	19.96	18.59	17.52	16.66	15.96	15.38	14.90	14.49	14.15	13.85	13.59	13.37	13.18
12	59.17	41.64	32.93	27.75	24.33	21.92	20.14	18.77	17.70	16.85	16.15	15.57	15.09	14.69	14.34	14.05	13.80	13.58	13.39
1/4	59.37	41.82	33.10	27.92	24.50	22.09	20.31	18.95	17.88	17.03	16.34	15.76	15.29	14.88	14.54	14.25	14.00	13.79	13.60
1/2	59.56	42.00	33.28	28.09	24.67	22.27	20.49	19.13	18.07	17.22	16.52	15.95	15.48	15.08	14.74	14.46	14.21	14.00	13.81
3/4	59.76	42.18	33.45	28.26	24.84	22.44	20.67	19.31	18.25	17.40	16.71	16.15	15.68	15.28	14.95	14.66	14.42	14.21	14.03
13	59.95	42.36	33.62	28.44	25.02	22.62	20.84	19.49	18.43	17.59	16.90	16.34	15.87	15.48	15.15	14.87	14.63	14.42	14.24

8

Interest Rate	21 YEARS	22 YEARS	23 YEARS	24 YEARS	25 YEARS	26 YEARS	27 YEARS	28 YEARS	29 YEARS	30 YEARS	31 YEARS	32 YEARS	33 YEARS	34 YEARS	35 YEARS	36 YEARS	37 YEARS	38 YEARS	39 YEARS	40 YEARS
7	9.23	9.05	8.88	8.72	8.59	8.46	8.35	8.24	8.15	8.06	7.98	7.91	7.85	7.78	7.73	7.68	7.63	7.58	7.54	7.51
1/8	9.33	9.14	8.97	8.82	8.68	8.56	8.45	8.34	8.25	8.17	8.09	8.02	7.95	7.89	7.83	7.78	7.74	7.69	7.65	7.62
1/4	9.42	9.23	9.07	8.92	8.78	8.66	8.55	8.44	8.35	8.27	8.19	8.12	8.05	7.99	7.94	7.89	7.84	7.80	7.76	7.72
3/8	9.51	9.33	9.16	9.01	8.88	8.76	8.65	8.54	8.45	8.37	8.29	8.22	8.16	8.10	8.05	8.00	7.95	7.91	7.87	7.83
1/2	9.61	9.42	9.26	9.11	8.98	8.85	8.75	8.65	8.55	8.47	8.40	8.33	8.26	8.21	8.15	8.10	8.06	8.02	7.98	7.95
5/8	9.70	9.52	9.36	9.21	9.07	8.95	8.85	8.75	8.66	8.58	8.50	8.43	8.37	8.31	8.26	8.21	8.17	8.13	8.09	8.06
3/4	9.80	9.62	9.45	9.31	9.17	9.05	8.95	8.85	8.76	8.68	8.61	8.54	8.48	8.42	8.37	8.32	8.28	8.24	8.20	8.17
7/8	9.89	9.71	9.55	9.40	9.27	9.15	9.05	8.95	8.86	8.78	8.71	8.64	8.58	8.53	8.48	8.43	8.39	8.35	8.31	8.28
8	9.99	9.81	9.65	9.50	9.37	9.26	9.15	9.05	8.97	8.89	8.82	8.75	8.69	8.64	8.59	8.54	8.50	8.46	8.42	8.39
1/8	10.08	9.91	9.75	9.60	9.47	9.36	9.25	9.16	9.07	8.99	8.92	8.86	8.80	8.74	8.69	8.65	8.61	8.57	8.54	8.50
1/4	10.18	10.00	9.84	9.70	9.57	9.46	9.35	9.26	9.18	9.10	9.03	8.96	8.91	8.85	8.80	8.76	8.72	8.68	8.65	8.62
3/8	10.28	10.10	9.94	9.80	9.67	9.56	9.46	9.36	9.28	9.20	9.13	9.07	9.01	8.96	8.91	8.87	8.83	8.79	8.76	8.73
1/2	10.37	10.20	10.04	9.90	9.78	9.66	9.56	9.47	9.39	9.31	9.24	9.18	9.12	9.07	9.02	8.98	8.94	8.91	8.87	8.84
5/8	10.47	10.30	10.14	10.00	9.88	9.77	9.66	9.57	9.49	9.42	9.35	9.29	9.23	9.18	9.13	9.09	9.05	9.02	8.99	8.96
3/4	10.57	10.40	10.24	10.10	9.98	9.87	9.77	9.68	9.60	9.52	9.46	9.40	9.34	9.29	9.24	9.20	9.17	9.13	9.10	9.07
7/8	10.67	10.50	10.34	10.21	10.08	9.97	9.87	9.78	9.70	9.63	9.56	9.51	9.45	9.40	9.36	9.32	9.28	9.25	9.21	9.19
9	10.77	10.60	10.44	10.31	10.19	10.08	9.98	9.89	9.81	9.74	9.67	9.61	9.56	9.51	9.47	9.43	9.39	9.36	9.33	9.30
1/8	10.87	10.70	10.54	10.41	10.29	10.18	10.08	10.00	9.92	9.85	9.78	9.72	9.67	9.62	9.58	9.54	9.51	9.47	9.44	9.42
1/4	10.96	10.80	10.65	10.51	10.39	10.29	10.19	10.10	10.03	9.96	9.89	9.83	9.78	9.74	9.69	9.65	9.62	9.59	9.56	9.53
3/8	11.06	10.90	10.75	10.62	10.50	10.39	10.30	10.21	10.13	10.06	10.00	9.94	9.89	9.85	9.81	9.77	9.73	9.70	9.67	9.65
1/2	11.16	11.00	10.85	10.72	10.60	10.50	10.40	10.32	10.24	10.17	10.11	10.06	10.01	9.96	9.92	9.88	9.85	9.82	9.79	9.76
5/8	11.26	11.10	10.95	10.82	10.71	10.60	10.51	10.43	10.35	10.28	10.22	10.17	10.12	10.07	10.03	10.00	9.96	9.93	9.90	9.88
3/4	11.37	11.20	11.06	10.93	10.81	10.71	10.62	10.53	10.46	10.39	10.33	10.28	10.23	10.19	10.15	10.11	10.08	10.02	10.02	10.00
7/8	11.47	11.30	11.16	11.03	10.92	10.81	10.72	10.64	10.57	10.50	10.44	10.39	10.34	10.30	10.26	10.22	10.19	10.16	10.14	10.11
10	11.57	11.41	11.26	11.13	11.02	10.92	10.83	10.75	10.68	10.61	10.55	10.50	10.45	10.41	10.37	10.34	10.31	10.28	10.25	10.23
1/2	11.77	11.61	11.47	11.35	11.23	11.14	11.05	10.97	10.90	10.83	10.78	10.73	10.68	10.64	10.60	10.57	10.54	10.51	10.49	10.47
1/2	11.98	11.82	11.68	11.56	11.45	11.35	11.26	11.19	11.12	11.06	11.00	10.95	10.91	10.87	10.83	10.80	10.77	10.75	10.72	10.70
3/4	12.18	12.03	11.89	11.77	11.66	11.57	11.48	11.41	11.34	11.28	11.23	11.18	11.14	11.10	11.07	11.03	11.01	10.98	10.96	10.94
11	12.39	12.24	12.10	11.98	11.88	11.79	11.70	11.63	11.57	11.51	11.46	11.41	11.37	11.33	11.30	11.27	11.24	11.22	11.20	11.18
1/4	12.60	12.45	12.32	12.20	12.10	12.01	11.93	11.85	11.79	11.73	11.68	11.64	11.60	11.56	11.53	11.50	11.48	11.45	11.43	11.42
1/2	12.81	12.66	12.53	12.42	12.31	12.23	12.15	12.08	12.02	11.96	11.91	11.87	11.83	11.80	11.77	11.74	11.71	11.69	11.67	11.65
3/4	13.02	12.87	12.74	12.63	12.53	12.45	12.37	12.30	12.24	12.19	12.14	12.10	12.06	12.03	12.00	11.97	11.95	11.93	11.91	11.89
12	13.23	13.09	12.96	12.85	12.75	12.67	12.60	12.53	12.47	12.42	12.37	12.33	12.30	12.27	12.24	12.21	12.19	12.17	12.15	12.14
1/4	13.44	13.30	13.18	13.07	12.98	12.89	12.82	12.76	12.70	12.65	12.61	12.57	12.53	12.50	12.47	12.45	12.43	12.41	12.39	12.38
1/2	13.66	13.52	13.40	13.29	13.20	13.12	13.05	12.98	12.93	12.88	12.84	12.80	12.77	12.74	12.71	12.69	12.67	12.65	12.63	12.62
3/4	13.87	13.73	13.62	13.51	13.42	13.34	13.27	13.21	13.16	13.11	13.07	13.04	13.00	12.97	12.95	12.93	12.91	12.89	12.87	12.86
13	14.09	13.96	13.84	13.74	13.65	13.57	13.50	13.44	13.39	13.35	13.31	13.27	13.24	13.21	13.19	13.17	13.15	13.13	13.12	13.10

SEMI-ANNUAL PAYMENTS MADE IN ADVANCE

A table of the constant annual percent which is needed to amortize a principal amount calculated on a semi-annual basis figured in advance. Divide by 2 to determine the semi-annual payment.

Interest Rate	2 YEARS	3 YEARS	4 YEARS	5 YEARS	6 YEARS	7 YEARS	8 YEARS	9 YEARS	10 YEARS	11 YEARS	12 YEARS	13 YEARS	14 YEARS	15 YEARS	16 YEARS	17 YEARS	18 YEARS	19 YEARS	20 YEARS
7	52.61	36.27	28.12	23.24	20.00	17.70	15.98	14.66	13.60	12.75	12.04	11.45	10.94	10.51	10.14	9.81	9.53	9.28	9.05
1/8	52.66	36.32	28.17	23.30	20.06	17.76	16.05	14.72	13.67	12.82	12.11	11.52	11.02	10.59	10.22	9.89	9.61	9.36	9.14
1/4	52.71	36.37	28.23	23.36	20.12	17.83	16.11	14.79	13.74	12.89	12.18	11.59	11.09	10.66	10.29	9.97	9.69	9.44	9.22
3/8	52.75	36.43	28.29	23.42	20.19	17.89	16.18	14.86	13.81	12.96	12.25	11.67	11.17	10.74	10.37	10.05	9.77	9.52	9.30
1/2	52.80	36.48	28.34	23.48	20.25	17.95	16.24	14.92	13.88	13.03	12.33	11.74	11.24	10.82	10.45	10.13	9.85	9.60	9.39
5/8	52.85	36.53	28.40	23.54	20.31	18.02	16.31	14.99	13.95	13.10	12.40	11.81	11.32	10.89	10.53	10.21	9.93	9.69	9.47
3/4	52.89	36.58	28.45	23.60	20.37	18.08	16.38	15.06	14.02	13.17	12.47	11.89	11.39	10.97	10.61	10.29	10.01	9.77	9.55
7/8	52.94	36.64	28.51	23.66	20.43	18.15	16.44	15.13	14.09	13.24	12.54	11.96	11.47	11.05	10.69	10.37	10.09	9.85	9.64
8	52.98	36.69	28.57	23.71	20.50	18.21	16.51	15.20	14.16	13.31	12.62	12.04	11.55	11.13	10.76	10.45	10.18	9.93	9.72
1/8	53.03	36.74	28.62	23.77	20.56	18.27	16.58	15.26	14.23	13.38	12.69	12.11	11.62	11.20	10.84	10.53	10.26	10.01	9.81
1/4	53.08	36.80	28.68	23.83	20.62	18.34	16.64	15.33	14.30	13.46	12.76	12.19	11.70	11.28	10.92	10.61	10.34	10.10	9.89
3/8	53.12	36.85	28.74	23.89	20.68	18.40	16.71	15.40	14.37	13.53	12.84	12.26	11.78	11.36	11.00	10.69	10.42	10.18	9.98
1/2	53.17	36.90	28.79	23.95	20.74	18.47	16.77	15.47	14.44	13.60	12.91	12.34	11.85	11.44	11.08	10.77	10.51	10.27	10.06
5/8	53.21	36.95	28.85	24.01	20.81	18.53	16.84	15.54	14.51	13.67	12.99	12.41	11.93	11.52	11.16	10.86	10.59	10.35	10.15
3/4	53.26	37.01	28.91	24.07	20.87	18.60	16.91	15.61	14.58	13.74	13.06	12.49	12.01	11.60	11.24	10.94	10.67	10.44	10.23
7/8	53.31	37.06	28.96	24.13	20.93	18.66	16.97	15.68	14.65	13.82	13.13	12.56	12.08	11.68	11.32	11.02	10.75	10.52	10.32
9	53.35	37.11	29.02	24.19	20.99	18.73	17.04	15.74	14.72	13.89	13.21	12.64	12.16	11.75	11.40	11.10	10.84	10.61	10.41
1/8	53.40	37.16	29.08	24.25	21.06	18.79	17.11	15.81	14.79	13.96	13.28	12.72	12.24	11.83	11.49	11.18	10.92	10.69	10.49
1/4	53.45	37.22	29.13	24.31	21.12	18.86	17.18	15.88	14.86	14.04	13.36	12.79	12.32	11.91	11.57	11.27	11.01	10.78	10.58
3/8	53.49	37.27	29.19	24.37	21.18	18.92	17.24	15.95	14.93	14.11	13.43	12.87	12.40	11.99	11.65	11.35	11.09	10.86	10.67
1/2	53.54	37.32	29.25	24.43	21.24	18.99	17.31	16.02	15.00	14.18	13.51	12.95	12.47	12.07	11.73	11.43	11.18	10.95	10.75
5/8	53.58	37.37	29.31	24.49	21.31	19.05	17.38	16.09	15.07	14.25	13.58	13.02	12.55	12.15	11.81	11.52	11.26	11.04	10.84
3/4	53.63	37.43	29.36	24.55	21.37	19.12	17.44	16.16	15.15	14.33	13.66	13.10	12.63	12.23	11.89	11.60	11.35	11.12	10.93
7/8	53.68	37.48	29.42	24.61	21.43	19.18	17.51	16.23	15.22	14.40	13.73	13.18	12.71	12.31	11.98	11.68	11.43	11.21	11.02
10	53.72	37.53	29.48	24.67	21.50	19.25	17.58	16.30	15.29	14.48	13.81	13.26	12.79	12.40	12.06	11.77	11.52	11.30	11.11
1/4	53.81	37.64	29.59	24.79	21.62	19.38	17.72	16.44	15.43	14.62	13.96	13.41	12.95	12.56	12.22	11.94	11.69	11.47	11.28
1/2	53.91	37.74	29.70	24.91	21.75	19.51	17.85	16.58	15.58	14.77	14.11	13.57	13.11	12.72	12.39	12.11	11.86	11.65	11.46
3/4	54.00	37.85	29.82	25.03	21.87	19.64	17.99	16.72	15.72	14.92	14.27	13.72	13.27	12.88	12.56	12.28	12.03	11.82	11.64
11	54.09	37.95	29.93	25.16	22.00	19.77	18.12	16.86	15.87	15.07	14.42	13.88	13.43	13.05	12.72	12.45	12.21	12.00	11.82
1/4	54.18	38.06	30.05	25.28	22.13	19.91	18.26	17.00	16.01	15.22	14.57	14.04	13.59	13.21	12.89	12.62	12.38	12.18	12.00
1/2	54.27	38.16	30.16	25.40	22.26	20.04	18.40	17.15	16.16	15.37	14.73	14.20	13.75	13.38	13.06	12.79	12.56	12.36	12.18
3/4	54.36	38.27	30.27	25.52	22.38	20.17	18.54	17.29	16.31	15.52	14.88	14.36	13.92	13.55	13.23	12.96	12.73	12.53	12.36
12	54.46	38.38	30.39	25.64	22.51	20.30	18.68	17.43	16.45	15.67	15.04	14.52	14.08	13.71	13.40	13.14	12.91	12.71	12.54
1/4	54.55	38.48	30.50	25.76	22.64	20.43	18.81	17.57	16.60	15.83	15.19	14.68	14.24	13.88	13.57	13.31	13.09	12.89	12.73
1/2	54.64	38.59	30.62	25.88	22.77	20.57	18.95	17.72	16.75	15.98	15.35	14.84	14.41	14.05	13.74	13.49	13.26	13.08	12.91
3/4	54.73	38.69	30.73	26.01	22.89	20.70	19.09	17.86	16.90	16.13	15.51	15.00	14.57	14.22	13.92	13.66	13.44	13.26	13.10
13	54.82	38.80	30.85	26.13	23.02	20.84	19.23	18.01	17.05	16.29	15.67	15.16	14.74	14.39	14.09	13.84	13.62	13.44	13.28

10

Interest Rate	21 YEARS	22 YEARS	23 YEARS	24 YEARS	25 YEARS	26 YEARS	27 YEARS	28 YEARS	29 YEARS	30 YEARS	31 YEARS	32 YEARS	33 YEARS	34 YEARS	35 YEARS	36 YEARS	37 YEARS	38 YEARS	39 YEARS	40 YEARS
7	8.85	8.68	8.52	8.37	8.24	8.13	8.02	7.92	7.83	7.75	7.68	7.61	7.55	7.49	7.44	7.39	7.34	7.30	7.26	7.23
1/8	8.94	8.76	8.60	8.46	8.33	8.21	8.11	8.01	7.92	7.84	7.77	7.70	7.64	7.59	7.53	7.49	7.44	7.40	7.36	7.33
1/4	9.02	8.85	8.69	8.55	8.42	8.30	8.20	8.10	8.02	7.94	7.87	7.80	7.74	7.68	7.63	7.59	7.54	7.50	7.47	7.43
3/8	9.11	8.93	8.78	8.64	8.51	8.39	8.29	8.20	8.11	8.03	7.96	7.90	7.83	7.78	7.73	7.68	7.64	7.60	7.57	7.53
1/2	9.19	9.02	8.86	8.72	8.60	8.48	8.38	8.29	8.20	8.13	8.06	7.99	7.93	7.88	7.83	7.78	7.74	7.70	7.67	7.64
5/8	9.28	9.10	8.95	8.81	8.69	8.57	8.47	8.38	8.30	8.22	8.15	8.09	8.03	7.98	7.93	7.88	7.84	7.80	7.77	7.74
3/4	9.36	9.19	9.04	8.90	8.78	8.67	8.56	8.47	8.39	8.31	8.25	8.18	8.13	8.07	8.03	7.98	7.94	7.91	7.87	7.84
7/8	9.45	9.28	9.13	8.99	8.87	8.76	8.66	8.57	8.48	8.41	8.34	8.28	8.22	8.17	8.13	8.08	8.04	8.01	7.97	7.94
8	9.53	9.36	9.21	9.08	8.96	8.85	8.75	8.66	8.58	8.51	8.44	8.38	8.32	8.27	8.23	8.18	8.14	8.11	8.08	8.05
1/8	9.62	9.45	9.30	9.17	9.05	8.94	8.84	8.75	8.67	8.60	8.54	8.48	8.42	8.37	8.33	8.28	8.24	8.21	8.18	8.15
1/4	9.70	9.54	9.39	9.26	9.14	9.03	8.93	8.85	8.77	8.70	8.63	8.57	8.52	8.47	8.43	8.38	8.35	8.31	8.28	8.25
3/8	9.79	9.63	9.48	9.35	9.23	9.12	9.03	8.94	8.86	8.79	8.73	8.67	8.62	8.57	8.53	8.48	8.45	8.42	8.39	8.36
1/2	9.88	9.71	9.57	9.44	9.32	9.22	9.12	9.04	8.96	8.89	8.83	8.77	8.72	8.67	8.63	8.59	8.55	8.52	8.49	8.46
5/8	9.96	9.80	9.66	9.53	9.41	9.31	9.22	9.13	9.06	8.99	8.92	8.87	8.82	8.77	8.73	8.69	8.65	8.62	8.59	8.57
3/4	10.05	9.89	9.75	9.62	9.50	9.40	9.31	9.23	9.15	9.08	9.02	8.97	8.92	8.87	8.83	8.79	8.76	8.72	8.70	8.67
7/8	10.14	9.98	9.84	9.71	9.60	9.50	9.40	9.32	9.25	9.18	9.12	9.07	9.02	8.97	8.93	8.89	8.86	8.83	8.80	8.77
9	10.23	10.07	9.93	9.80	9.69	9.59	9.50	9.42	9.34	9.28	9.22	9.17	9.12	9.07	9.03	9.00	8.96	8.93	8.90	8.88
1/8	10.31	10.16	10.02	9.89	9.78	9.68	9.59	9.51	9.44	9.38	9.32	9.26	9.22	9.17	9.13	9.10	9.07	9.04	9.01	8.98
1/4	10.40	10.25	10.11	9.99	9.88	9.78	9.69	9.61	9.54	9.47	9.42	9.36	9.32	9.27	9.24	9.20	9.17	9.14	9.11	9.09
3/8	10.49	10.34	10.20	10.08	9.97	9.87	9.78	9.71	9.64	9.57	9.52	9.46	9.42	9.38	9.34	9.30	9.27	9.24	9.22	9.20
1/2	10.58	10.43	10.29	10.17	10.06	9.97	9.88	9.80	9.73	9.67	9.62	9.56	9.52	9.48	9.44	9.41	9.38	9.35	9.32	9.30
5/8	10.67	10.52	10.38	10.26	10.16	10.06	9.98	9.90	9.83	9.77	9.71	9.67	9.62	9.58	9.54	9.51	9.48	9.45	9.43	9.41
3/4	10.76	10.61	10.47	10.36	10.25	10.16	10.07	10.00	9.93	9.87	9.81	9.77	9.72	9.68	9.65	9.61	9.58	9.56	9.53	9.51
7/8	10.85	10.70	10.57	10.45	10.34	10.25	10.17	10.09	10.03	9.97	9.91	9.87	9.82	9.78	9.75	9.72	9.69	9.66	9.64	9.62
10	10.94	10.79	10.66	10.54	10.44	10.35	10.26	10.19	10.13	10.07	10.01	9.97	9.93	9.89	9.85	9.82	9.79	9.77	9.75	9.72
1/4	11.12	10.97	10.84	10.73	10.63	10.54	10.46	10.39	10.32	10.27	10.22	10.17	10.13	10.09	10.06	10.03	10.00	9.98	9.96	9.94
1/2	11.30	11.15	11.03	10.92	10.82	10.73	10.65	10.58	10.52	10.47	10.42	10.37	10.34	10.30	10.27	10.24	10.21	10.19	10.17	10.15
3/4	11.48	11.34	11.22	11.11	11.01	10.92	10.85	10.78	10.72	10.67	10.62	10.58	10.54	10.51	10.47	10.45	10.42	10.40	10.38	10.36
11	11.66	11.52	11.40	11.30	11.20	11.12	11.04	10.98	10.92	10.87	10.82	10.78	10.75	10.71	10.68	10.66	10.63	10.61	10.59	10.58
1/4	11.84	11.71	11.59	11.49	11.39	11.31	11.24	11.18	11.12	11.07	11.03	10.99	10.95	10.92	10.89	10.87	10.84	10.82	10.81	10.79
1/2	12.03	11.90	11.78	11.68	11.59	11.51	11.44	11.38	11.32	11.27	11.23	11.19	11.16	11.13	11.10	11.08	11.06	11.04	11.02	11.01
3/4	12.21	12.08	11.97	11.87	11.78	11.70	11.64	11.58	11.52	11.48	11.43	11.40	11.37	11.34	11.31	11.29	11.27	11.25	11.23	11.22
12	12.40	12.27	12.16	12.06	11.98	11.90	11.83	11.78	11.72	11.68	11.64	11.60	11.57	11.55	11.52	11.50	11.48	11.46	11.45	11.43
1/4	12.58	12.46	12.35	12.25	12.17	12.10	12.03	11.98	11.93	11.88	11.84	11.81	11.78	11.75	11.73	11.71	11.69	11.68	11.66	11.65
1/2	12.77	12.65	12.54	12.45	12.37	12.30	12.23	12.18	12.13	12.09	12.05	12.02	11.99	11.96	11.94	11.92	11.90	11.89	11.89	11.86
3/4	12.96	12.84	12.73	12.64	12.56	12.49	12.43	12.38	12.33	12.29	12.26	12.22	12.20	12.17	12.15	12.13	12.12	12.10	12.09	12.08
13	13.14	13.03	12.92	12.84	12.76	12.69	12.63	12.58	12.54	12.50	12.46	12.43	12.41	12.38	12.36	12.34	12.33	12.31	12.30	12.29

SEMI-ANNUAL PAYMENTS MADE IN ARREARS

A table of the constant annual percent which is needed to amortize a principal amount calculated on a semi-annual basis figured in arrears. Divide by 2 to determine the semi-annual payment.

Interest Rate	2 YEARS	3 YEARS	4 YEARS	5 YEARS	6 YEARS	7 YEARS	8 YEARS	9 YEARS	10 YEARS	11 YEARS	12 YEARS	13 YEARS	14 YEARS	15 YEARS	16 YEARS	17 YEARS	18 YEARS	19 YEARS	20 YEARS
7	56.46	37.54	29.10	24.05	20.70	18.32	16.54	15.17	14.08	13.17	12.46	11.85	11.33	10.88	10.49	10.16	9.86	9.60	9.37
1/8	56.54	37.62	29.18	24.13	20.78	18.40	16.62	15.25	14.16	13.27	12.54	11.93	11.41	10.96	10.58	10.24	9.95	9.69	9.46
1/4	56.62	37.69	29.25	24.21	20.85	18.47	16.70	15.33	14.24	13.35	12.62	12.01	11.49	11.05	10.67	10.33	10.04	9.78	9.55
3/8	56.70	37.77	29.33	24.28	20.93	18.55	16.78	15.41	14.32	13.43	12.71	12.10	11.58	11.14	10.75	10.42	10.13	9.87	9.64
1/2	56.78	37.85	29.40	24.36	21.01	18.63	16.85	15.48	14.40	13.52	12.79	12.18	11.66	11.22	10.84	10.51	10.22	9.96	9.74
5/8	56.86	37.92	29.48	24.43	21.08	18.71	16.93	15.56	14.48	13.60	12.87	12.26	11.75	11.31	10.93	10.60	10.31	10.05	9.83
3/4	56.94	38.00	29.56	24.51	21.16	18.78	17.01	15.64	14.56	13.68	12.96	12.35	11.84	11.40	11.02	10.69	10.40	10.15	9.92
7/8	55.02	38.08	29.63	24.59	21.24	18.86	17.09	15.72	14.64	13.76	13.04	12.43	11.92	11.48	11.11	10.78	10.49	10.24	10.02
8	55.10	38.16	29.71	24.66	21.32	18.94	17.17	15.80	14.72	13.84	13.12	12.52	12.01	11.57	11.19	10.87	10.58	10.33	10.11
1/8	55.18	38.24	29.79	24.74	21.40	19.02	17.25	15.88	14.80	13.93	13.21	12.60	12.09	11.66	11.28	10.96	10.67	10.42	10.20
1/4	55.27	38.31	29.86	24.82	21.47	19.10	17.33	15.96	14.88	14.01	13.29	12.69	12.18	11.75	11.37	11.05	10.77	10.52	10.30
3/8	55.35	38.39	29.94	24.89	21.55	19.17	17.41	16.05	14.97	14.09	13.38	12.78	12.27	11.84	11.46	11.14	10.86	10.61	10.39
1/2	55.43	38.47	30.02	24.97	21.63	19.25	17.49	16.13	15.05	14.18	13.46	12.86	12.36	11.92	11.55	11.23	10.95	10.71	10.49
5/8	55.51	38.55	30.10	25.05	21.70	19.33	17.57	16.21	15.13	14.26	13.55	12.95	12.44	12.01	11.64	11.32	11.04	10.80	10.58
3/4	55.59	38.62	30.17	25.13	21.78	19.41	17.65	16.29	15.21	14.35	13.63	13.03	12.53	12.10	11.73	11.42	11.14	10.89	10.68
7/8	55.67	38.70	30.25	25.20	21.86	19.49	17.73	16.37	15.30	14.43	13.72	13.12	12.62	12.19	11.83	11.51	11.23	10.99	10.78
9	55.75	38.78	30.33	25.28	21.94	19.57	17.81	16.45	15.38	14.51	13.80	13.21	12.71	12.28	11.92	11.60	11.33	11.09	10.87
1/8	55.83	38.86	30.40	25.36	22.02	19.65	17.89	16.53	15.46	14.60	13.89	13.30	12.80	12.37	12.01	11.69	11.42	11.18	10.97
1/4	55.92	38.94	30.48	25.44	22.02	19.73	17.97	16.62	15.55	14.68	13.98	13.38	12.89	12.46	12.10	11.79	11.52	11.28	11.07
3/8	56.00	39.02	30.56	25.51	22.25	19.81	18.05	16.70	15.63	14.77	14.06	13.47	12.98	12.56	12.19	11.88	11.61	11.37	11.17
1/2	56.08	39.09	30.64	25.59	22.25	19.89	18.13	16.78	15.72	14.85	14.15	13.56	13.07	12.65	12.29	11.98	11.71	11.47	11.26
5/8	56.16	39.17	30.72	25.67	22.33	19.97	18.21	16.86	15.80	14.94	14.24	13.65	13.16	12.74	12.38	12.07	11.80	11.57	11.36
3/4	56.24	39.25	30.79	25.75	22.41	20.05	18.30	16.95	15.88	15.03	14.32	13.74	13.25	12.83	12.47	12.17	11.90	11.67	11.46
7/8	56.33	39.33	30.87	25.83	22.49	20.13	18.38	17.03	15.97	15.11	14.41	13.83	13.34	12.92	12.57	12.26	12.00	11.76	11.56
10	56.41	39.41	30.95	25.91	22.57	20.21	18.46	17.11	16.05	15.20	14.50	13.92	13.43	13.02	12.66	12.36	12.09	11.86	11.66
1/4	56.57	39.57	31.11	26.06	22.73	20.37	18.62	17.28	16.22	15.37	14.68	14.10	13.61	13.20	12.85	12.55	12.29	12.06	11.86
1/2	56.74	39.72	31.26	26.22	22.89	20.53	18.79	17.45	16.40	15.55	14.85	14.28	13.80	13.39	13.04	12.74	12.48	12.26	12.06
3/4	56.90	39.88	31.42	26.38	23.05	20.70	18.95	17.62	16.57	15.72	15.03	14.46	13.98	13.58	13.23	12.94	12.68	12.46	12.27
11	57.06	40.04	31.58	26.54	23.21	20.86	19.12	17.79	16.74	15.90	15.21	14.64	14.16	13.77	13.42	13.13	12.88	12.66	12.47
1/4	57.23	40.20	31.74	26.70	23.37	21.03	19.29	17.96	16.91	16.08	15.39	14.83	14.36	13.96	13.62	13.33	13.08	12.86	12.67
1/2	57.39	40.36	31.89	26.86	23.53	21.19	19.46	18.13	17.09	16.25	15.57	15.01	14.54	14.15	13.81	13.53	13.28	13.07	12.88
3/4	57.56	40.52	32.05	27.02	23.70	21.36	19.63	18.30	17.27	16.43	15.76	15.20	14.73	14.34	14.01	13.72	13.48	13.27	13.09
12	57.72	40.68	32.21	27.18	23.86	21.52	19.80	18.48	17.44	16.61	15.94	15.39	14.92	14.53	14.21	13.92	13.68	13.48	13.30
1/4	57.89	40.84	32.37	27.34	24.02	21.69	19.97	18.65	17.62	16.80	16.13	15.57	15.12	14.73	14.40	14.13	13.89	13.68	13.51
1/2	58.05	41.00	32.53	27.50	24.18	21.86	20.14	18.82	17.80	16.98	16.31	15.76	15.31	14.93	14.60	14.33	14.09	13.89	13.72
3/4	58.22	41.16	32.69	27.66	24.35	22.02	20.31	19.00	17.98	17.16	16.50	15.95	15.50	15.12	14.80	14.53	14.30	14.10	13.93
13	58.39	41.32	32.85	27.83	24.52	22.19	20.48	19.18	18.16	17.34	16.68	16.14	15.70	15.32	15.00	14.74	14.51	14.31	14.14

Interest Rate	21 YEARS	22 YEARS	23 YEARS	24 YEARS	25 YEARS	26 YEARS	27 YEARS	28 YEARS	29 YEARS	30 YEARS	31 YEARS	32 YEARS	33 YEARS	34 YEARS	35 YEARS	36 YEARS	37 YEARS	38 YEARS	39 YEARS	40 YEARS
7	9.16	8.98	8.82	8.67	8.53	8.41	8.30	8.20	8.11	8.03	7.95	7.88	7.81	7.75	7.70	7.65	7.60	7.56	7.52	7.48
1/8	9.26	9.07	8.91	8.76	8.63	8.51	8.40	8.30	8.21	8.13	8.05	7.98	7.91	7.86	7.80	7.75	7.71	7.67	7.63	7.59
1/4	9.35	9.17	9.00	8.86	8.72	8.61	8.50	8.40	8.31	8.23	8.15	8.08	8.02	7.96	7.91	7.86	7.82	7.77	7.74	7.70
3/8	9.44	9.26	9.10	8.95	8.82	8.70	8.60	8.50	8.41	8.33	8.25	8.19	8.12	8.07	8.02	7.97	7.92	7.88	7.85	7.81
1/2	9.54	9.36	9.19	9.05	8.92	8.80	8.70	8.60	8.51	8.43	8.36	8.29	8.23	8.17	8.12	8.07	8.03	7.99	7.96	7.92
5/8	9.63	9.45	9.29	9.15	9.02	8.90	8.80	8.70	8.61	8.53	8.46	8.40	8.33	8.28	8.23	8.18	8.14	8.10	8.07	8.03
3/4	9.72	9.55	9.39	9.24	9.12	9.00	8.90	8.80	8.72	8.64	8.57	8.50	8.44	8.39	8.34	8.29	8.25	8.21	8.18	8.14
7/8	9.82	9.64	9.48	9.34	9.22	9.10	9.00	8.90	8.82	8.74	8.67	8.61	8.55	8.49	8.45	8.40	8.36	8.32	8.29	8.26
8	9.91	9.74	9.58	9.44	9.32	9.20	9.10	9.01	8.92	8.85	8.78	8.71	8.65	8.60	8.55	8.51	8.47	8.43	8.40	8.37
1/8	10.01	9.83	9.68	9.54	9.41	9.30	9.20	9.11	9.03	8.95	8.88	8.82	8.76	8.71	8.66	8.62	8.58	8.54	8.51	8.48
1/4	10.10	9.93	9.78	9.64	9.52	9.40	9.30	9.21	9.13	9.06	8.99	8.93	8.87	8.82	8.77	8.73	8.69	8.66	8.62	8.59
3/8	10.20	10.03	9.88	9.74	9.62	9.51	9.41	9.32	9.24	9.16	9.09	9.03	8.98	8.93	8.88	8.84	8.80	8.77	8.74	8.71
1/2	10.30	10.13	9.97	9.84	9.72	9.61	9.51	9.42	9.34	9.27	9.20	9.14	9.09	9.04	8.99	8.95	8.91	8.88	8.85	8.82
5/8	10.39	10.22	10.07	9.94	9.82	9.71	9.61	9.52	9.45	9.37	9.31	9.25	9.20	9.15	9.10	9.06	9.03	8.99	8.96	8.93
3/4	10.49	10.32	10.17	10.04	9.92	9.81	9.72	9.63	9.55	9.48	9.42	9.36	9.31	9.26	9.21	9.18	9.14	9.11	9.08	9.05
7/8	10.59	10.42	10.27	10.14	10.02	9.92	9.82	9.74	9.66	9.59	9.52	9.47	9.42	9.37	9.33	9.29	9.25	9.22	9.19	9.16
9	10.69	10.52	10.37	10.24	10.13	10.02	9.93	9.84	9.76	9.70	9.63	9.58	9.53	9.48	9.44	9.40	9.37	9.33	9.31	9.28
1/8	10.79	10.62	10.47	10.34	10.23	10.12	10.03	9.95	9.87	9.80	9.74	9.69	9.64	9.59	9.55	9.51	9.48	9.45	9.42	9.39
1/4	10.88	10.72	10.58	10.45	10.33	10.23	10.14	10.06	9.98	9.91	9.85	9.80	9.75	9.70	9.66	9.63	9.59	9.56	9.54	9.51
3/8	10.98	10.82	10.68	10.55	10.44	10.33	10.24	10.16	10.09	10.02	9.96	9.91	9.86	9.82	9.78	9.74	9.71	9.68	9.65	9.63
1/2	11.08	10.92	10.78	10.65	10.54	10.44	10.35	10.27	10.20	10.13	10.07	10.02	9.97	9.93	9.89	9.85	9.82	9.79	9.77	9.74
5/8	11.18	11.02	10.88	10.76	10.64	10.54	10.46	10.38	10.30	10.24	10.18	10.13	10.08	10.04	10.00	9.97	9.94	9.91	9.88	9.86
3/4	11.28	11.12	10.98	10.86	10.75	10.65	10.56	10.48	10.41	10.35	10.29	10.24	10.20	10.15	10.12	10.08	10.05	10.02	10.00	9.98
7/8	11.38	11.23	11.09	10.96	10.85	10.76	10.67	10.59	10.52	10.46	10.40	10.35	10.31	10.27	10.23	10.20	10.17	10.14	10.12	10.09
10	11.48	11.33	11.19	11.07	10.96	10.86	10.78	10.70	10.63	10.57	10.52	10.47	10.42	10.38	10.34	10.31	10.28	10.26	10.23	10.21
1/4	11.69	11.53	11.40	11.28	11.17	11.08	10.99	10.92	10.85	10.79	10.74	10.69	10.65	10.61	10.57	10.54	10.52	10.49	10.47	10.45
1/2	11.89	11.74	11.61	11.49	11.39	11.29	11.21	11.14	11.07	11.02	10.96	10.92	10.88	10.84	10.81	10.78	10.75	10.72	10.70	10.68
3/4	12.10	11.95	11.82	11.70	11.60	11.51	11.43	11.36	11.30	11.24	11.19	11.15	11.11	11.07	11.04	11.01	10.98	10.96	10.94	10.92
11	12.30	12.16	12.03	11.92	11.82	11.73	11.65	11.58	11.52	11.47	11.42	11.37	11.34	11.30	11.27	11.24	11.22	11.20	11.18	11.16
1/4	12.51	12.37	12.24	12.13	12.03	11.95	11.87	11.81	11.75	11.69	11.65	11.60	11.57	11.53	11.51	11.48	11.45	11.43	11.41	11.40
1/2	12.72	12.58	12.46	12.35	12.25	12.17	12.10	12.03	11.97	11.92	11.88	11.84	11.80	11.77	11.74	11.71	11.69	11.67	11.65	11.64
3/4	12.93	12.79	12.67	12.57	12.47	12.39	12.32	12.26	12.20	12.15	12.11	12.07	12.03	12.00	11.98	11.95	11.93	11.91	11.89	11.88
12	13.14	13.01	12.89	12.78	12.69	12.61	12.54	12.48	12.43	12.38	12.34	12.30	12.27	12.24	12.21	12.19	12.17	12.15	12.13	12.12
1/4	13.35	13.22	13.11	13.00	12.92	12.84	12.77	12.71	12.66	12.61	12.57	12.53	12.50	12.47	12.45	12.43	12.41	12.39	12.37	12.36
1/2	13.57	13.44	13.32	13.23	13.14	13.06	13.00	12.94	12.89	12.84	12.80	12.77	12.74	12.71	12.69	12.67	12.65	12.63	12.62	12.60
3/4	13.78	13.65	13.54	13.45	13.36	13.29	13.22	13.17	13.12	13.08	13.04	13.00	12.97	12.95	12.93	12.91	12.89	12.87	12.86	12.85
13	14.00	13.87	13.76	13.67	13.59	13.52	13.45	13.40	13.35	13.31	13.27	13.24	13.21	13.19	13.17	13.15	13.13	13.11	13.10	13.09

QUARTERLY PAYMENTS MADE IN ADVANCE

A table of the constant annual percent which is needed to amortize a principal amount calculated on a quarterly basis figured in advance. Divide by 4 to determine quarterly payment.

Interest Rate	2 YEARS	3 YEARS	4 YEARS	5 YEARS	6 YEARS	7 YEARS	8 YEARS	9 YEARS	10 YEARS	11 YEARS	12 YEARS	13 YEARS	14 YEARS	15 YEARS	16 YEARS	17 YEARS	18 YEARS	19 YEARS	20 YEARS
7	53.09	36.61	28.39	23.47	20.21	17.88	16.15	14.82	13.75	12.89	12.18	11.58	11.07	10.64	10.26	9.94	9.65	9.40	9.17
1/8	53.15	36.67	28.45	23.54	20.27	17.95	16.22	14.89	13.83	12.96	12.25	11.66	11.15	10.72	10.35	10.02	9.73	9.49	9.26
1/4	53.20	36.73	28.51	23.60	20.34	18.02	16.29	14.96	13.90	13.04	12.33	11.74	11.23	10.80	10.43	10.10	9.82	9.57	9.35
3/8	53.26	36.79	28.57	23.66	20.40	18.09	16.36	15.03	13.97	13.11	12.41	11.81	11.31	10.88	10.51	10.19	9.90	9.65	9.43
1/2	53.32	36.85	28.64	23.73	20.47	18.16	16.43	15.10	14.05	13.19	12.48	11.89	11.39	10.96	10.59	10.27	9.99	9.74	9.52
5/8	53.37	36.91	28.70	23.79	20.54	18.23	16.50	15.17	14.12	13.26	12.56	11.97	11.47	11.04	10.67	10.35	10.07	9.83	9.61
3/4	53.43	36.97	28.76	23.86	20.60	18.29	16.57	15.25	14.19	13.34	12.64	12.05	11.55	11.12	10.76	10.44	10.16	9.91	9.70
7/8	53.48	37.03	28.82	23.92	20.67	18.36	16.64	15.32	14.27	13.41	12.71	12.13	11.63	11.20	10.84	10.52	10.24	10.00	9.78
8	53.54	37.09	28.89	23.99	20.74	18.43	16.72	15.39	14.34	13.49	12.79	12.20	11.71	11.29	10.92	10.61	10.33	10.09	9.87
1/8	53.59	37.15	28.95	24.05	20.81	18.50	16.79	15.46	14.41	13.57	12.87	12.28	11.79	11.37	11.01	10.69	10.42	10.17	9.96
1/4	53.65	37.21	29.01	24.12	20.87	18.57	16.86	15.54	14.49	13.64	12.95	12.36	11.87	11.45	11.09	10.78	10.50	10.26	10.05
3/8	53.71	37.27	29.08	24.18	20.94	18.64	16.93	15.61	14.56	13.72	13.02	12.44	11.95	11.53	11.17	10.86	10.59	10.35	10.14
1/2	53.76	37.33	29.14	24.25	21.01	18.71	17.00	15.68	14.64	13.80	13.10	12.52	12.03	11.62	11.26	10.95	10.68	10.44	10.23
5/8	53.82	37.39	29.20	24.31	21.08	18.78	17.07	15.76	14.71	13.87	13.18	12.60	12.11	11.70	11.34	11.03	10.76	10.53	10.32
3/4	53.87	37.45	29.26	24.38	21.14	18.85	17.14	15.83	14.79	13.95	13.26	12.68	12.20	11.78	11.43	11.12	10.85	10.62	10.41
7/8	53.93	37.51	29.33	24.44	21.21	18.92	17.21	15.90	14.86	14.03	13.34	12.76	12.28	11.87	11.51	11.21	10.94	10.71	10.50
9	53.98	37.57	29.39	24.51	21.28	18.99	17.29	15.98	14.94	14.10	13.42	12.84	12.36	11.95	11.60	11.29	11.03	10.80	10.59
1/8	54.04	37.63	29.45	24.58	21.35	19.06	17.36	16.05	15.02	14.18	13.50	12.92	12.44	12.03	11.68	11.38	11.12	10.89	10.68
1/4	54.10	37.69	29.52	24.64	21.41	19.13	17.43	16.12	15.09	14.26	13.57	13.01	12.53	12.12	11.77	11.47	11.21	10.98	10.78
3/8	54.15	37.75	29.58	24.71	21.48	19.20	17.50	16.20	15.17	14.34	13.65	13.09	12.61	12.20	11.85	11.56	11.29	11.07	10.87
1/2	54.21	37.81	29.64	24.77	21.55	19.27	17.57	16.27	15.24	14.41	13.73	13.17	12.69	12.29	11.94	11.64	11.38	11.16	10.96
5/8	54.26	37.87	29.71	24.84	21.62	19.34	17.65	16.35	15.32	14.49	13.81	13.25	12.78	12.37	12.03	11.73	11.47	11.25	11.05
3/4	54.32	37.93	29.77	24.91	21.69	19.41	17.72	16.42	15.40	14.57	13.89	13.33	12.86	12.46	12.12	11.82	11.56	11.34	11.15
7/8	54.38	37.99	29.83	24.97	21.76	19.48	17.79	16.50	15.47	14.65	13.98	13.41	12.94	12.54	12.20	11.91	11.65	11.43	11.24
10	54.43	38.05	29.90	25.04	21.82	19.55	17.87	16.57	15.55	14.73	14.06	13.50	13.03	12.63	12.29	12.00	11.75	11.52	11.33
1/4	54.54	38.17	30.02	25.17	21.96	19.69	18.01	16.72	15.71	14.89	14.22	13.66	13.20	12.80	12.47	12.18	11.93	11.71	11.52
1/2	54.66	38.29	30.15	25.30	22.10	19.84	18.16	16.87	15.86	15.05	14.38	13.83	13.37	12.98	12.64	12.36	12.11	11.90	11.71
3/4	54.77	38.41	30.28	25.44	22.24	19.98	18.31	17.02	16.02	15.21	14.54	14.00	13.54	13.15	12.82	12.54	12.29	12.08	11.90
11	54.88	38.53	30.41	25.57	22.38	20.12	18.45	17.18	16.17	15.37	14.71	14.17	13.71	13.33	13.00	12.72	12.48	12.27	12.09
1/4	54.99	38.65	30.54	25.70	22.52	20.27	18.60	17.33	16.33	15.53	14.87	14.33	13.88	13.50	13.18	12.90	12.67	12.46	12.28
1/2	55.10	38.78	30.66	25.84	22.66	20.41	18.75	17.48	16.49	15.69	15.04	14.50	14.06	13.68	13.36	13.09	12.85	12.65	12.48
3/4	55.22	38.90	30.79	25.97	22.80	20.56	18.90	17.64	16.65	15.85	15.21	14.68	14.23	13.86	13.54	13.27	13.04	12.84	12.67
12	55.33	39.02	30.92	26.11	22.94	20.70	19.05	17.79	16.81	16.02	15.38	14.85	14.41	14.04	13.72	13.46	13.23	13.03	12.86
1/4	55.44	39.14	31.05	26.24	23.08	20.85	19.20	17.95	16.97	16.18	15.54	15.02	14.58	14.22	13.91	13.64	13.42	13.23	13.06
1/2	55.55	39.26	31.18	26.38	23.22	20.99	19.35	18.10	17.13	16.35	15.71	15.19	14.76	14.40	14.09	13.83	13.61	13.42	13.26
3/4	55.66	39.39	31.31	26.51	23.36	21.14	19.51	18.26	17.29	16.51	15.88	15.37	14.94	14.58	14.28	14.02	13.80	13.61	13.45
13	55.78	39.51	31.44	26.65	23.50	21.29	19.66	18.42	17.45	16.68	16.05	15.54	15.12	14.76	14.46	14.21	13.99	13.81	13.65

Interest Rate	21 YEARS	22 YEARS	23 YEARS	24 YEARS	25 YEARS	26 YEARS	27 YEARS	28 YEARS	29 YEARS	30 YEARS	31 YEARS	32 YEARS	33 YEARS	34 YEARS	35 YEARS	36 YEARS	37 YEARS	38 YEARS	39 YEARS	40 YEARS
7	8.97	8.79	8.63	8.49	8.36	8.24	8.13	8.04	7.95	7.86	7.79	7.72	7.66	7.60	7.55	7.50	7.46	7.41	7.38	7.34
1/8	9.06	8.88	8.72	8.58	8.45	8.33	8.23	8.13	8.04	7.96	7.89	7.82	7.76	7.70	7.65	7.60	7.56	7.52	7.48	7.45
1/4	9.15	8.97	8.81	8.67	8.54	8.43	8.32	8.23	8.14	8.06	7.99	7.92	7.86	7.80	7.75	7.71	7.66	7.62	7.59	7.55
3/8	9.24	9.06	8.90	8.76	8.64	8.52	8.42	8.32	8.24	8.16	8.09	8.02	7.96	7.90	7.85	7.81	7.77	7.73	7.69	7.66
1/2	9.32	9.15	8.99	8.85	8.73	8.61	8.51	8.42	8.33	8.25	8.18	8.12	8.06	8.01	7.96	7.91	7.87	7.83	7.80	7.76
5/8	9.41	9.24	9.09	8.95	8.82	8.71	8.61	8.51	8.43	8.35	8.28	8.22	8.16	8.11	8.06	8.02	7.97	7.94	7.90	7.87
3/4	9.50	9.33	9.18	9.04	8.92	8.80	8.70	8.61	8.53	8.45	8.38	8.32	8.26	8.21	8.16	8.12	8.08	8.04	8.01	7.98
7/8	9.59	9.42	9.27	9.13	9.01	8.90	8.80	8.71	8.63	8.55	8.48	8.42	8.37	8.31	8.27	8.22	8.18	8.15	8.12	8.08
8	9.68	9.51	9.36	9.23	9.10	8.99	8.90	8.81	8.72	8.65	8.58	8.52	8.47	8.42	8.37	8.33	8.29	8.25	8.22	8.19
1/8	9.77	9.60	9.45	9.32	9.20	9.09	8.99	8.90	8.82	8.75	8.69	8.62	8.57	8.52	8.48	8.43	8.39	8.36	8.33	8.30
1/4	9.86	9.70	9.55	9.41	9.29	9.19	9.09	9.00	8.92	8.85	8.79	8.73	8.67	8.62	8.58	8.54	8.50	8.47	8.44	8.41
3/8	9.95	9.79	9.64	9.51	9.39	9.28	9.19	9.10	9.02	8.95	8.89	8.83	8.78	8.73	8.69	8.65	8.61	8.58	8.55	8.52
1/2	10.04	9.88	9.73	9.60	9.49	9.38	9.29	9.20	9.12	9.05	8.99	8.93	8.88	8.83	8.79	8.75	8.72	8.68	8.65	8.63
5/8	10.14	9.97	9.83	9.70	9.58	9.48	9.38	9.30	9.22	9.16	9.09	9.04	8.99	8.94	8.90	8.86	8.83	8.79	8.76	8.74
3/4	10.23	10.07	9.92	9.79	9.68	9.58	9.48	9.40	9.33	9.26	9.20	9.14	9.09	9.04	9.00	8.96	8.93	8.90	8.87	8.84
7/8	10.32	10.16	10.02	9.89	9.78	9.67	9.58	9.50	9.43	9.36	9.30	9.24	9.19	9.15	9.11	9.07	9.04	9.01	8.96	8.95
9	10.41	10.25	10.11	9.99	9.87	9.77	9.68	9.60	9.53	9.46	9.40	9.35	9.30	9.26	9.22	9.18	9.15	9.12	9.09	9.06
1/8	10.51	10.35	10.21	10.08	9.97	9.87	9.78	9.70	9.63	9.56	9.51	9.45	9.41	9.36	9.32	9.29	9.25	9.23	9.20	9.17
1/4	10.60	10.44	10.30	10.18	10.07	9.97	9.88	9.80	9.73	9.67	9.61	9.56	9.51	9.47	9.43	9.40	9.36	9.33	9.31	9.29
3/8	10.69	10.54	10.40	10.28	10.17	10.07	9.98	9.90	9.83	9.77	9.71	9.66	9.62	9.58	9.54	9.50	9.47	9.44	9.42	9.40
1/2	10.79	10.63	10.50	10.37	10.27	10.17	10.08	10.01	9.94	9.87	9.82	9.77	9.72	9.68	9.65	9.61	9.58	9.55	9.53	9.51
5/8	10.88	10.73	10.59	10.47	10.36	10.27	10.18	10.11	10.04	9.98	9.92	9.87	9.83	9.79	9.75	9.72	9.69	9.66	9.64	9.62
3/4	10.97	10.82	10.69	10.57	10.46	10.37	10.29	10.21	10.14	10.08	10.03	9.98	9.94	9.90	9.86	9.83	9.80	9.77	9.75	9.73
7/8	11.07	10.92	10.79	10.67	10.56	10.47	10.39	10.31	10.25	10.19	10.13	10.09	10.04	10.00	9.97	9.94	9.91	9.88	9.86	9.84
10	11.16	11.01	10.88	10.77	10.66	10.57	10.49	10.42	10.35	10.29	10.24	10.19	10.15	10.11	10.08	10.05	10.02	10.00	9.97	9.95
1/4	11.35	11.21	11.08	10.96	10.86	10.77	10.69	10.62	10.56	10.50	10.45	10.41	10.37	10.33	10.30	10.27	10.24	10.22	10.20	10.18
1/2	11.55	11.40	11.28	11.16	11.07	10.98	10.90	10.83	10.77	10.71	10.67	10.62	10.58	10.55	10.52	10.49	10.46	10.44	10.42	10.40
3/4	11.74	11.60	11.47	11.36	11.27	11.18	11.11	11.04	10.98	10.93	10.88	10.84	10.80	10.76	10.74	10.71	10.68	10.66	10.64	10.63
11	11.93	11.79	11.67	11.57	11.47	11.39	11.31	11.25	11.19	11.14	11.09	11.05	11.02	10.98	10.96	10.93	10.91	10.89	10.87	10.85
1/4	12.13	11.99	11.87	11.77	11.68	11.59	11.52	11.46	11.40	11.35	11.31	11.27	11.24	11.20	11.18	11.15	11.13	11.11	11.09	11.08
1/2	12.32	12.19	12.07	11.97	11.88	11.80	11.73	11.67	11.62	11.57	11.53	11.49	11.46	11.43	11.40	11.38	11.36	11.34	11.32	11.30
3/4	12.52	12.39	12.27	12.18	12.09	12.01	11.94	11.88	11.83	11.78	11.74	11.71	11.68	11.65	11.62	11.60	11.58	11.56	11.55	11.53
12	12.72	12.59	12.48	12.38	12.29	12.22	12.15	12.10	12.05	12.00	11.96	11.93	11.90	11.87	11.84	11.82	11.80	11.79	11.77	11.76
1/4	12.92	12.79	12.68	12.59	12.50	12.43	12.37	12.31	12.26	12.22	12.18	12.15	12.12	12.09	12.07	12.05	12.03	12.01	12.00	11.99
1/2	13.11	12.99	12.89	12.79	12.71	12.64	12.58	12.53	12.48	12.44	12.40	12.37	12.34	12.31	12.29	12.27	12.26	12.24	12.23	12.22
3/4	13.32	13.19	13.09	13.00	12.92	12.85	12.79	12.74	12.69	12.65	12.62	12.59	12.56	12.54	12.52	12.50	12.48	12.47	12.45	12.44
13	13.52	13.40	13.30	13.21	13.13	13.07	13.01	12.96	12.91	12.87	12.84	12.81	12.78	12.76	12.74	12.72	12.71	12.69	12.68	12.67

QUARTERLY PAYMENTS MADE IN ARREARS

A table of the constant annual percent which is needed to amortize a principal amount calculated on a quarterly basis figured in arrears. Divide by 4 to determine quarterly payment.

Interest Rate	2 YEARS	3 YEARS	4 YEARS	5 YEARS	6 YEARS	7 YEARS	8 YEARS	9 YEARS	10 YEARS	11 YEARS	12 YEARS	13 YEARS	14 YEARS	15 YEARS	16 YEARS	17 YEARS	18 YEARS	19 YEARS	20 YEARS
7	54.02	37.25	28.88	23.88	20.56	18.20	16.44	15.08	13.99	13.12	12.39	11.78	11.27	10.83	10.44	10.11	9.82	9.56	9.33
1/8	54.10	37.32	28.96	23.95	20.63	18.27	16.51	15.15	14.07	13.20	12.47	11.87	11.35	10.91	10.53	10.20	9.91	9.65	9.42
1/4	54.17	37.39	29.03	24.03	20.71	18.35	16.59	15.23	14.15	13.28	12.55	11.95	11.44	11.00	10.62	10.29	10.00	9.74	9.51
3/8	54.24	37.47	29.10	24.10	20.78	18.42	16.66	15.31	14.23	13.36	12.63	12.03	11.52	11.08	10.70	10.37	10.09	9.83	9.61
1/2	54.32	37.54	29.17	24.17	20.86	18.50	16.74	15.38	14.31	13.44	12.72	12.11	11.60	11.17	10.79	10.46	10.17	9.92	9.70
5/8	54.39	37.61	29.25	24.25	20.93	18.57	16.82	15.46	14.39	13.52	12.80	12.20	11.69	11.25	10.88	10.55	10.26	10.01	9.79
3/4	54.46	37.68	29.32	24.32	21.00	18.65	16.89	15.54	14.47	13.60	12.88	12.28	11.77	11.34	10.96	10.64	10.35	10.10	9.88
7/8	54.54	37.76	29.39	24.39	21.08	18.72	16.97	15.62	14.55	13.68	12.96	12.36	11.86	11.43	11.05	10.73	10.44	10.20	9.98
8	54.61	37.83	29.47	24.47	21.15	18.80	17.05	15.70	14.63	13.76	13.05	12.45	11.94	11.51	11.14	10.82	10.54	10.29	10.07
1/8	54.68	37.90	29.54	24.54	21.23	18.88	17.13	15.78	14.71	13.84	13.13	12.53	12.03	11.60	11.23	10.91	10.63	10.38	10.16
1/4	54.76	37.97	29.61	24.62	21.30	18.95	17.20	15.86	14.79	13.92	13.21	12.62	12.12	11.69	11.32	11.00	10.72	10.47	10.26
3/8	54.83	38.05	29.68	24.69	21.38	19.03	17.28	15.94	14.87	14.01	13.30	12.70	12.20	11.77	11.41	11.09	10.81	10.57	10.35
1/2	54.90	38.12	29.76	24.76	21.45	19.11	17.36	16.01	14.95	14.09	13.38	12.79	12.29	11.86	11.50	11.18	10.90	10.66	10.45
5/8	54.98	38.19	29.83	24.84	21.53	19.18	17.44	16.09	15.03	14.17	13.46	12.87	12.38	11.95	11.59	11.27	11.00	10.75	10.54
3/4	55.05	38.27	29.90	24.91	21.61	19.26	17.52	16.17	15.11	14.25	13.55	12.96	12.46	12.04	11.68	11.36	11.09	10.85	10.64
7/8	55.12	38.34	29.98	24.99	21.68	19.34	17.60	16.25	15.19	14.34	13.63	13.05	12.55	12.13	11.77	11.45	11.18	10.94	10.73
9	55.20	38.41	30.05	25.06	21.76	19.42	17.67	16.34	15.28	14.42	13.72	13.13	12.64	12.22	11.86	11.55	11.28	11.04	10.83
1/8	55.27	38.49	30.13	25.14	21.83	19.49	17.75	16.42	15.36	14.50	13.80	13.22	12.73	12.31	11.95	11.64	11.37	11.13	10.93
1/4	55.35	38.56	30.20	25.21	21.91	19.57	17.83	16.50	15.44	14.59	13.89	13.31	12.82	12.40	12.04	11.73	11.46	11.23	11.02
3/8	55.42	38.63	30.27	25.29	21.99	19.65	17.91	16.58	15.52	14.67	13.97	13.39	12.90	12.49	12.13	11.83	11.56	11.33	11.12
1/2	55.49	38.71	30.35	25.36	22.06	19.73	17.99	16.66	15.61	14.76	14.06	13.48	12.99	12.58	12.23	11.92	11.65	11.42	11.22
5/8	55.57	38.78	30.42	25.44	22.14	19.80	18.07	16.74	15.69	14.84	14.15	13.57	13.08	12.67	12.32	12.01	11.75	11.52	11.33
3/4	55.64	38.85	30.50	25.51	22.22	19.88	18.15	16.82	15.77	14.93	14.23	13.66	13.17	12.76	12.41	12.11	11.85	11.62	11.42
7/8	55.72	38.93	30.57	25.59	22.29	19.96	18.23	16.90	15.86	15.01	14.32	13.75	13.26	12.85	12.50	12.20	11.94	11.71	11.52
10	55.79	39.00	30.64	25.66	22.37	20.04	18.31	16.99	15.94	15.09	14.41	13.83	13.35	12.95	12.60	12.30	12.04	11.81	11.62
1/4	55.94	39.15	30.79	25.82	22.52	20.20	18.47	17.15	16.11	15.26	14.58	14.01	13.54	13.13	12.79	12.49	12.23	12.01	11.82
1/2	56.09	39.30	30.94	25.97	22.68	20.36	18.64	17.32	16.28	15.44	14.76	14.19	13.72	13.32	12.98	12.68	12.43	12.21	12.02
3/4	56.24	39.44	31.09	26.12	22.84	20.52	18.80	17.48	16.45	15.61	14.94	14.37	13.90	13.50	13.17	12.88	12.62	12.41	12.22
11	56.39	39.59	31.24	26.27	22.99	20.68	18.96	17.65	16.62	15.79	15.11	14.55	14.09	13.69	13.36	13.07	12.82	12.61	12.42
1/4	56.54	39.74	31.39	26.43	23.15	20.84	19.13	17.82	16.79	15.96	15.29	14.74	14.27	13.88	13.55	13.27	13.02	12.81	12.63
1/2	56.69	39.89	31.55	26.58	23.31	21.00	19.29	17.99	16.96	16.14	15.47	14.92	14.46	14.07	13.74	13.46	13.22	13.01	12.83
3/4	56.84	40.04	31.70	26.74	23.47	21.16	19.46	18.16	17.14	16.32	15.65	15.11	14.65	14.27	13.94	13.66	13.42	13.22	13.04
12	56.99	40.19	31.85	26.89	23.62	21.32	19.62	18.33	17.31	16.50	15.84	15.29	14.84	14.46	14.14	13.86	13.63	13.42	13.25
1/4	57.14	40.34	32.00	27.05	23.78	21.49	19.79	18.50	17.49	16.68	16.02	15.48	15.03	14.65	14.33	14.06	13.83	13.63	13.46
1/2	57.29	40.49	32.15	27.20	23.94	21.65	19.96	18.67	17.66	16.86	16.20	15.67	15.22	14.85	14.53	14.26	14.04	13.84	13.67
3/4	57.44	40.64	32.31	27.36	24.10	21.81	20.13	18.84	17.84	17.04	16.39	15.86	15.41	15.04	14.73	14.47	14.24	14.05	13.88
13	57.59	40.79	32.46	27.52	24.26	21.98	20.30	19.02	18.02	17.22	16.57	16.05	15.61	15.24	14.93	14.67	14.45	14.26	14.10

Interest Rate	21 YEARS	22 YEARS	23 YEARS	24 YEARS	25 YEARS	26 YEARS	27 YEARS	28 YEARS	29 YEARS	30 YEARS	31 YEARS	32 YEARS	33 YEARS	34 YEARS	35 YEARS	36 YEARS	37 YEARS	38 YEARS	39 YEARS	40 YEARS
7	9.13	8.95	8.78	8.64	8.50	8.38	8.27	8.18	8.08	8.00	7.93	7.86	7.79	7.74	7.68	7.63	7.59	7.54	7.51	7.47
1/8	9.22	9.04	8.88	8.73	8.60	8.48	8.37	8.27	8.19	8.10	8.03	7.96	7.90	7.84	7.79	7.74	7.69	7.65	7.61	7.58
1/4	9.31	9.13	8.97	8.83	8.70	8.58	8.47	8.37	8.29	8.20	8.13	8.06	8.00	7.95	7.89	7.85	7.80	7.76	7.72	7.69
3/8	9.41	9.23	9.07	8.92	8.79	8.68	8.57	8.47	8.39	8.31	8.23	8.17	8.11	8.05	8.00	7.95	7.91	7.87	7.83	7.80
1/2	9.50	9.32	9.16	9.02	8.89	8.78	8.67	8.58	8.49	8.41	8.34	8.27	8.22	8.16	8.11	8.06	8.02	7.98	7.94	7.91
5/8	9.59	9.42	9.26	9.12	8.99	8.87	8.77	8.68	8.59	8.51	8.44	8.38	8.32	8.26	8.21	8.17	8.13	8.09	8.05	8.02
3/4	9.69	9.51	9.35	9.21	9.09	8.97	8.87	8.78	8.69	8.62	8.55	8.48	8.43	8.37	8.32	8.28	8.24	8.20	8.16	8.13
7/8	9.78	9.61	9.45	9.31	9.19	9.07	8.97	8.88	8.80	8.72	8.65	8.59	8.53	8.48	8.43	8.39	8.35	8.31	8.28	8.24
8	9.88	9.70	9.55	9.41	9.29	9.17	9.07	8.99	8.90	8.82	8.76	8.69	8.64	8.59	8.54	8.50	8.46	8.42	8.39	8.36
1/8	9.97	9.80	9.65	9.51	9.39	9.28	9.18	9.08	9.00	8.93	8.86	8.80	8.74	8.69	8.65	8.61	8.57	8.53	8.50	8.47
1/4	10.07	9.90	9.74	9.61	9.49	9.38	9.28	9.19	9.11	9.03	8.97	8.91	8.85	8.80	8.76	8.72	8.68	8.64	8.61	8.58
3/8	10.16	9.99	9.84	9.71	9.59	9.48	9.38	9.29	9.21	9.14	9.07	9.02	8.96	8.91	8.87	8.83	8.79	8.76	8.72	8.70
1/2	10.26	10.09	9.94	9.81	9.69	9.58	9.48	9.40	9.32	9.25	9.18	9.12	9.07	9.02	8.98	8.94	8.90	8.87	8.84	8.81
5/8	10.35	10.19	10.04	9.91	9.79	9.68	9.59	9.50	9.42	9.35	9.29	9.23	9.18	9.13	9.09	9.05	9.01	8.98	8.95	8.92
3/4	10.45	10.29	10.14	10.01	9.89	9.79	9.69	9.61	9.53	9.46	9.40	9.34	9.29	9.24	9.20	9.16	9.12	9.09	9.06	9.04
7/8	10.55	10.38	10.24	10.11	9.99	9.89	9.80	9.71	9.64	9.57	9.51	9.45	9.40	9.35	9.31	9.27	9.24	9.21	9.18	9.15
9	10.65	10.48	10.34	10.21	10.10	9.99	9.90	9.82	9.74	9.67	9.61	9.56	9.51	9.46	9.42	9.39	9.35	9.32	9.29	9.27
1/8	10.74	10.58	10.44	10.31	10.20	10.10	10.01	9.92	9.85	9.78	9.72	9.67	9.62	9.58	9.54	9.50	9.47	9.44	9.41	9.38
1/4	10.84	10.68	10.54	10.41	10.30	10.20	10.11	10.03	9.96	9.89	9.84	9.78	9.73	9.69	9.65	9.61	9.58	9.55	9.52	9.50
3/8	10.94	10.78	10.64	10.52	10.41	10.31	10.22	10.14	10.06	10.00	9.94	9.89	9.84	9.80	9.76	9.73	9.69	9.67	9.64	9.62
1/2	11.04	10.88	10.74	10.62	10.51	10.41	10.32	10.24	10.17	10.11	10.05	10.00	9.95	9.91	9.87	9.84	9.81	9.78	9.76	9.73
5/8	11.14	10.98	10.85	10.72	10.61	10.52	10.43	10.35	10.28	10.22	10.16	10.11	10.07	10.02	9.99	9.95	9.92	9.90	9.87	9.85
3/4	11.24	11.09	10.95	10.83	10.72	10.62	10.54	10.46	10.39	10.33	10.27	10.22	10.18	10.14	10.10	10.07	10.04	10.01	9.99	9.97
7/8	11.34	11.19	11.05	10.93	10.82	10.73	10.64	10.57	10.50	10.44	10.38	10.34	10.29	10.25	10.22	10.18	10.15	10.13	10.10	10.08
10	11.44	11.29	11.15	11.04	10.93	10.84	10.75	10.68	10.61	10.55	10.50	10.45	10.40	10.37	10.33	10.30	10.27	10.25	10.22	10.20
1/4	11.64	11.49	11.36	11.25	11.14	11.05	10.97	10.90	10.83	10.77	10.72	10.68	10.63	10.59	10.56	10.53	10.50	10.48	10.46	10.44
1/2	11.85	11.70	11.57	11.46	11.36	11.27	11.19	11.12	11.05	11.00	10.95	10.90	10.86	10.82	10.79	10.76	10.74	10.71	10.69	10.67
3/4	12.05	11.91	11.78	11.67	11.57	11.48	11.41	11.34	11.27	11.22	11.17	11.13	11.09	11.05	11.02	11.00	10.97	10.95	10.93	10.91
11	12.26	12.13	11.99	11.88	11.79	11.70	11.63	11.56	11.50	11.45	11.40	11.36	11.32	11.29	11.26	11.23	11.21	11.19	11.17	11.15
1/4	12.47	12.34	12.21	12.10	12.00	11.92	11.85	11.78	11.72	11.67	11.63	11.59	11.55	11.52	11.49	11.47	11.44	11.42	11.42	11.39
1/2	12.68	12.54	12.42	12.32	12.22	12.14	12.07	12.01	11.95	11.90	11.86	11.82	11.78	11.75	11.73	11.70	11.68	11.66	11.64	11.63
3/4	12.89	12.75	12.64	12.53	12.44	12.36	12.29	12.23	12.18	12.13	12.09	12.05	12.02	11.99	11.96	11.94	11.92	11.90	11.88	11.87
12	13.10	12.97	12.85	12.75	12.66	12.59	12.52	12.46	12.41	12.36	12.32	12.28	12.25	12.22	12.20	12.18	12.16	12.15	12.13	12.11
1/4	13.31	13.18	13.07	12.97	12.89	12.81	12.75	12.69	12.64	12.59	12.55	12.52	12.49	12.46	12.44	12.42	12.40	12.38	12.37	12.35
1/2	13.52	13.40	13.29	13.19	13.11	13.04	12.97	12.92	12.87	12.82	12.79	12.75	12.72	12.70	12.68	12.66	12.64	12.62	12.61	12.60
3/4	13.74	13.62	13.51	13.41	13.33	13.26	13.20	13.15	13.10	13.06	13.02	12.99	12.96	12.94	12.91	12.90	12.88	12.86	12.85	12.84
13	13.96	13.83	13.73	13.64	13.56	13.49	13.43	13.38	13.33	13.29	13.26	13.23	13.20	13.18	13.15	13.14	13.12	13.11	13.09	13.08

17

MONTHLY PAYMENTS MADE IN ADVANCE

A table of the constant annual percent which is needed to amortize a principal amount calculated on a monthly basis figured in advance. Divide by 12 to determine monthly payment.

Interest Rate	2 YEARS	3 YEARS	4 YEARS	5 YEARS	6 YEARS	7 YEARS	8 YEARS	9 YEARS	10 YEARS	11 YEARS	12 YEARS	13 YEARS	14 YEARS	15 YEARS	16 YEARS	17 YEARS	18 YEARS	19 YEARS	20 YEARS
7	53.42	36.84	28.57	23.63	20.35	18.01	16.27	14.93	13.86	12.99	12.27	11.67	11.16	10.73	10.35	10.02	9.73	9.48	9.25
1/8	53.48	36.91	28.64	23.70	20.41	18.08	16.34	15.00	13.93	13.07	12.35	11.75	11.25	10.81	10.43	10.11	9.82	9.57	9.34
1/4	53.54	36.97	28.71	23.76	20.48	18.15	16.42	15.07	14.01	13.14	12.43	11.83	11.33	10.89	10.52	10.19	9.91	9.66	9.43
3/8	53.61	37.04	28.77	23.83	20.55	18.23	16.49	15.15	14.08	13.22	12.51	11.91	11.41	10.98	10.60	10.28	9.99	9.74	9.52
1/2	53.67	37.10	28.84	23.90	20.62	18.30	16.56	15.22	14.16	13.30	12.59	11.99	11.49	11.06	10.69	10.36	10.08	9.83	9.61
5/8	53.73	37.17	28.91	23.97	20.69	18.37	16.64	15.30	14.24	13.38	12.67	12.08	11.57	11.14	10.77	10.45	10.17	9.92	9.70
3/4	53.79	37.23	28.97	24.04	20.76	18.44	16.71	15.37	14.31	13.46	12.75	12.16	11.66	11.23	10.86	10.54	10.26	10.01	9.79
7/8	53.86	37.29	29.04	24.11	20.84	18.51	16.78	15.45	14.39	13.53	12.83	12.24	11.74	11.31	10.94	10.63	10.35	10.10	9.88
8	53.92	37.36	29.11	24.18	20.91	18.58	16.86	15.52	14.47	13.61	12.91	12.32	11.82	11.40	11.03	10.71	10.44	10.19	9.98
1/8	53.98	37.42	29.17	24.24	20.98	18.66	16.93	15.60	14.55	13.69	12.99	12.40	11.91	11.48	11.12	10.80	10.52	10.28	10.07
1/4	54.04	37.49	29.24	24.31	21.05	18.73	17.01	15.68	14.62	13.77	13.07	12.48	11.99	11.57	11.20	10.89	10.61	10.37	10.16
3/8	54.11	37.55	29.31	24.38	21.12	18.80	17.08	15.75	14.70	13.85	13.15	12.57	12.07	11.65	11.29	10.98	10.70	10.46	10.25
1/2	54.17	37.62	29.37	24.45	21.19	18.88	17.15	15.83	14.78	13.93	13.23	12.65	12.16	11.74	11.38	11.07	10.79	10.56	10.35
5/8	54.23	37.68	29.44	24.52	21.26	18.95	17.23	15.90	14.86	14.01	13.31	12.73	12.24	11.83	11.47	11.16	10.88	10.65	10.44
3/4	54.29	37.75	29.51	24.59	21.33	19.02	17.30	15.98	14.94	14.09	13.40	12.82	12.33	11.91	11.55	11.24	10.98	10.74	10.53
7/8	54.36	37.82	29.58	24.66	21.40	19.09	17.38	16.06	15.01	14.17	13.48	12.90	12.41	12.00	11.64	11.33	11.07	10.83	10.63
9	54.42	37.88	29.64	24.73	21.47	19.17	17.45	16.14	15.09	14.25	13.56	12.98	12.50	12.09	11.73	11.42	11.16	10.93	10.72
1/8	54.48	37.95	29.71	24.80	21.55	19.24	17.53	16.21	15.17	14.33	13.64	13.07	12.58	12.17	11.82	11.52	11.25	11.02	10.82
1/4	54.54	38.01	29.78	24.87	21.62	19.32	17.61	16.29	15.25	14.41	13.73	13.15	12.67	12.26	11.91	11.61	11.34	11.11	10.91
3/8	54.61	38.08	29.85	24.94	21.69	19.39	17.68	16.37	15.33	14.49	13.81	13.24	12.76	12.35	12.00	11.70	11.44	11.21	11.01
1/2	54.67	38.14	29.92	25.01	21.76	19.46	17.76	16.45	15.41	14.58	13.89	13.32	12.84	12.44	12.09	11.79	11.53	11.30	11.10
5/8	54.73	38.21	29.98	25.08	21.83	19.54	17.83	16.52	15.49	14.66	13.98	13.41	12.93	12.53	12.18	11.88	11.62	11.40	11.20
3/4	54.80	38.27	30.05	25.15	21.91	19.61	17.91	16.60	15.57	14.74	14.06	13.49	13.02	12.61	12.27	11.97	11.72	11.49	11.30
7/8	54.86	38.34	30.12	25.22	21.98	19.69	17.99	16.68	15.65	14.82	14.14	13.58	13.11	12.70	12.36	12.07	11.81	11.59	11.39
10	54.92	38.41	30.19	25.29	22.05	19.76	18.06	16.76	15.73	14.90	14.23	13.67	13.19	12.79	12.45	12.16	11.90	11.68	11.49
1/4	55.05	38.54	30.33	25.43	22.20	19.91	18.22	16.92	15.89	15.07	14.40	13.84	13.37	12.97	12.64	12.34	12.09	11.88	11.68
1/2	55.17	38.67	30.46	25.57	22.34	20.06	18.37	17.08	16.06	15.24	14.57	14.01	13.55	13.15	12.82	12.53	12.28	12.07	11.88
3/4	55.30	38.80	30.60	25.72	22.49	20.21	18.53	17.24	16.22	15.40	14.74	14.19	13.73	13.34	13.01	12.72	12.48	12.26	12.08
11	55.43	38.93	30.74	25.86	22.64	20.37	18.68	17.40	16.38	15.57	14.91	14.36	13.91	13.52	13.19	12.91	12.67	12.46	12.28
1/4	55.55	39.07	30.88	26.00	22.79	20.52	18.84	17.56	16.55	15.74	15.08	14.54	14.09	13.70	13.38	13.10	12.86	12.66	12.48
1/2	55.68	39.20	31.01	26.15	22.93	20.67	19.00	17.72	16.72	15.91	15.26	14.72	14.27	13.89	13.57	13.29	13.06	12.86	12.68
3/4	55.81	39.33	31.15	26.29	23.08	20.82	19.16	17.88	16.88	16.08	15.43	14.90	14.45	14.08	13.76	13.49	13.26	13.06	12.88
12	55.93	39.47	31.29	26.43	23.23	20.98	19.32	18.05	17.05	16.26	15.61	15.08	14.64	14.26	13.95	13.68	13.45	13.26	13.09
1/4	56.06	39.60	31.43	26.58	23.38	21.13	19.48	18.21	17.22	16.43	15.79	15.26	14.82	14.45	14.14	13.88	13.65	13.46	13.29
1/2	56.19	39.74	31.57	26.72	23.53	21.29	19.64	18.37	17.39	16.60	15.97	15.44	15.01	14.64	14.34	14.08	13.85	13.66	13.50
3/4	56.32	39.87	31.71	26.87	23.68	21.44	19.80	18.54	17.56	16.78	16.14	15.62	15.19	14.83	14.53	14.27	14.05	13.87	13.71
13	56.44	40.00	31.85	27.02	23.84	21.60	19.96	18.71	17.73	16.95	16.32	15.81	15.38	15.03	14.73	14.47	14.26	14.07	13.91

Interest Rate	21 YEARS	22 YEARS	23 YEARS	24 YEARS	25 YEARS	26 YEARS	27 YEARS	28 YEARS	29 YEARS	30 YEARS	31 YEARS	32 YEARS	33 YEARS	34 YEARS	35 YEARS	36 YEARS	37 YEARS	38 YEARS	39 YEARS	40 YEARS
7	9.05	8.87	8.71	8.57	8.44	8.32	8.21	8.11	8.02	7.94	7.87	7.80	7.74	7.68	7.63	7.58	7.53	7.49	7.45	7.42
7 1/8	9.14	8.97	8.81	8.66	8.53	8.41	8.31	8.21	8.12	8.04	7.97	7.90	7.84	7.78	7.73	7.68	7.64	7.60	7.56	7.53
7 1/4	9.23	9.06	8.90	8.76	8.63	8.51	8.40	8.31	8.22	8.14	8.07	8.00	7.94	7.89	7.84	7.79	7.75	7.71	7.67	7.63
7 3/8	9.32	9.15	8.99	8.85	8.72	8.61	8.50	8.41	8.32	8.24	8.17	8.11	8.05	7.99	7.94	7.89	7.85	7.81	7.78	7.74
7 1/2	9.42	9.24	9.08	8.94	8.82	8.70	8.60	8.51	8.42	8.34	8.27	8.21	8.15	8.10	8.05	8.00	7.96	7.92	7.89	7.85
7 5/8	9.51	9.33	9.18	9.04	8.91	8.80	8.70	8.61	8.52	8.44	8.38	8.31	8.25	8.20	8.15	8.11	8.07	8.03	7.99	7.96
7 3/4	9.60	9.43	9.27	9.14	9.01	8.90	8.80	8.71	8.62	8.55	8.48	8.42	8.36	8.31	8.26	8.21	8.17	8.14	8.10	8.07
7 7/8	9.69	9.52	9.37	9.23	9.11	9.00	8.90	8.81	8.72	8.65	8.58	8.52	8.46	8.41	8.36	8.32	8.28	8.25	8.21	8.18
8	9.78	9.62	9.46	9.33	9.21	9.10	9.00	8.91	8.83	8.75	8.68	8.62	8.57	8.52	8.47	8.43	8.39	8.36	8.32	8.29
8 1/8	9.88	9.71	9.56	9.43	9.30	9.19	9.10	9.01	8.93	8.86	8.79	8.73	8.67	8.63	8.58	8.54	8.50	8.47	8.43	8.40
8 1/4	9.97	9.80	9.66	9.52	9.40	9.29	9.20	9.11	9.03	8.96	8.89	8.83	8.78	8.73	8.69	8.65	8.61	8.58	8.54	8.52
8 3/8	10.07	9.90	9.75	9.62	9.50	9.39	9.30	9.21	9.13	9.06	9.00	8.94	8.89	8.84	8.80	8.76	8.72	8.69	8.66	8.63
8 1/2	10.16	10.00	9.85	9.72	9.60	9.49	9.40	9.31	9.24	9.17	9.10	9.05	8.99	8.95	8.90	8.87	8.83	8.80	8.77	8.74
8 5/8	10.25	10.09	9.95	9.82	9.70	9.60	9.50	9.42	9.34	9.27	9.21	9.15	9.10	9.06	9.01	8.98	8.94	8.91	8.88	8.85
8 3/4	10.35	10.19	10.04	9.91	9.80	9.70	9.60	9.52	9.44	9.38	9.32	9.26	9.21	9.16	9.12	9.09	9.05	9.02	8.99	8.97
8 7/8	10.45	10.28	10.14	10.01	9.90	9.80	9.71	9.62	9.55	9.48	9.42	9.37	9.32	9.27	9.23	9.20	9.16	9.13	9.10	9.08
9	10.54	10.38	10.24	10.11	10.00	9.90	9.81	9.73	9.65	9.59	9.53	9.48	9.43	9.38	9.34	9.31	9.27	9.24	9.22	9.19
9 1/8	10.64	10.48	10.34	10.21	10.10	10.00	9.91	9.83	9.76	9.69	9.64	9.58	9.54	9.49	9.45	9.42	9.39	9.36	9.33	9.31
9 1/4	10.73	10.58	10.44	10.31	10.20	10.10	10.02	9.94	9.87	9.80	9.74	9.69	9.65	9.60	9.56	9.53	9.50	9.47	9.44	9.42
9 3/8	10.83	10.68	10.54	10.41	10.30	10.21	10.12	10.04	9.97	9.91	9.85	9.80	9.75	9.71	9.68	9.64	9.61	9.58	9.56	9.53
9 1/2	10.93	10.77	10.64	10.52	10.41	10.31	10.22	10.15	10.08	10.02	9.96	9.91	9.86	9.82	9.79	9.75	9.72	9.70	9.67	9.65
9 5/8	11.03	10.87	10.74	10.62	10.51	10.41	10.33	10.25	10.19	10.13	10.07	10.02	9.98	9.93	9.90	9.87	9.84	9.81	9.79	9.76
9 3/4	11.12	10.97	10.84	10.72	10.61	10.52	10.43	10.36	10.29	10.23	10.18	10.13	10.09	10.05	10.01	9.98	9.95	9.92	9.90	9.88
9 7/8	11.22	11.07	10.94	10.82	10.72	10.62	10.54	10.47	10.40	10.34	10.29	10.24	10.20	10.16	10.12	10.09	10.06	10.04	10.02	9.99
10	11.32	11.17	11.04	10.92	10.82	10.73	10.65	10.57	10.51	10.45	10.40	10.35	10.31	10.27	10.24	10.21	10.18	10.15	10.13	10.11
10 1/4	11.52	11.37	11.24	11.13	11.03	10.94	10.86	10.79	10.72	10.67	10.62	10.57	10.53	10.49	10.46	10.43	10.41	10.38	10.36	10.34
10 1/2	11.72	11.57	11.45	11.34	11.24	11.15	11.07	11.00	10.94	10.89	10.84	10.79	10.76	10.72	10.69	10.66	10.64	10.61	10.59	10.58
10 3/4	11.92	11.78	11.65	11.54	11.45	11.36	11.29	11.22	11.16	11.11	11.06	11.02	10.98	10.95	10.92	10.89	10.87	10.85	10.83	10.81
11	12.12	11.98	11.86	11.75	11.66	11.58	11.50	11.44	11.38	11.33	11.28	11.24	11.21	11.17	11.15	11.12	11.10	11.08	11.06	11.04
11 1/4	12.32	12.19	12.07	11.96	11.87	11.79	11.72	11.66	11.60	11.55	11.51	11.47	11.43	11.40	11.38	11.35	11.33	11.31	11.29	11.28
11 1/2	12.52	12.39	12.28	12.18	12.09	12.01	11.94	11.88	11.82	11.78	11.73	11.70	11.66	11.63	11.61	11.58	11.56	11.54	11.53	11.51
11 3/4	12.73	12.60	12.49	12.39	12.30	12.23	12.16	12.10	12.05	12.00	11.96	11.92	11.89	11.86	11.84	11.82	11.80	11.78	11.76	11.75
12	12.94	12.81	12.70	12.60	12.52	12.44	12.38	12.32	12.27	12.23	12.19	12.15	12.12	12.09	12.07	12.05	12.03	12.01	12.00	11.99
12 1/4	13.15	13.02	12.91	12.82	12.74	12.66	12.60	12.55	12.50	12.45	12.41	12.38	12.35	12.33	12.30	12.28	12.27	12.25	12.24	12.22
12 1/2	13.36	13.23	13.13	13.04	12.95	12.88	12.82	12.77	12.72	12.68	12.64	12.61	12.58	12.56	12.54	12.52	12.50	12.49	12.47	12.46
12 3/4	13.57	13.45	13.34	13.25	13.17	13.11	13.05	12.99	12.95	12.91	12.87	12.84	12.82	12.79	12.77	12.75	12.74	12.72	12.71	12.70
13	13.78	13.66	13.56	13.47	13.39	13.33	13.27	13.22	13.18	13.14	13.10	13.07	13.05	13.03	13.01	12.99	12.97	12.96	12.95	12.94

19

MONTHLY PAYMENT MADE IN ARREARS

A table of the constant annual percent which is needed to amortize a principal amount calculated on a monthly basis figured in arrears. Divide by 12 to determine monthly payment.

Interest Rate	2 YEARS	3 YEARS	4 YEARS	5 YEARS	6 YEARS	7 YEARS	8 YEARS	9 YEARS	10 YEARS	11 YEARS	12 YEARS	13 YEARS	14 YEARS	15 YEARS	16 YEARS	17 YEARS	18 YEARS	19 YEARS	20 YEARS
7	53.73	37.06	28.74	23.77	20.46	18.12	16.37	15.01	13.94	13.07	12.35	11.74	11.23	10.79	10.41	10.08	9.79	9.54	9.31
1/8	53.80	37.13	28.81	23.84	20.54	18.19	16.44	15.09	14.02	13.14	12.43	11.82	11.31	10.87	10.50	10.17	9.88	9.62	9.40
1/4	53.87	37.19	28.88	23.91	20.61	18.26	16.52	15.16	14.09	13.22	12.51	11.91	11.40	10.96	10.58	10.25	9.97	9.71	9.49
3/8	53.94	37.26	28.95	23.98	20.68	18.34	16.59	15.24	14.17	13.30	12.59	11.99	11.48	11.04	10.67	10.34	10.06	9.80	9.58
1/2	54.00	37.33	29.02	24.05	20.75	18.41	16.67	15.32	14.25	13.38	12.67	12.07	11.56	11.13	10.75	10.43	10.14	9.89	9.67
5/8	54.07	37.40	29.09	24.12	20.83	18.49	16.74	15.40	14.33	13.46	12.75	12.15	11.65	11.21	10.84	10.52	10.23	9.98	9.76
3/4	54.14	37.47	29.16	24.19	20.90	18.56	16.82	15.47	14.41	13.54	12.83	12.24	11.73	11.30	10.93	10.61	10.32	10.08	9.86
7/8	54.21	37.54	29.23	24.26	20.97	18.63	16.89	15.55	14.49	13.62	12.91	12.32	11.82	11.39	11.02	10.69	10.41	10.17	9.95
8	54.28	37.61	29.30	24.34	21.04	18.71	16.97	15.63	14.56	13.70	12.99	12.40	11.90	11.47	11.10	10.78	10.50	10.26	10.04
1/8	54.35	37.68	29.37	24.41	21.12	18.78	17.05	15.71	14.64	13.78	13.08	12.49	11.99	11.56	11.19	10.87	10.60	10.35	10.14
1/4	54.41	37.75	29.44	24.48	21.19	18.86	17.12	15.78	14.72	13.87	13.16	12.57	12.07	11.65	11.28	10.96	10.69	10.44	10.23
3/8	54.48	37.82	29.51	24.55	21.27	18.93	17.20	15.86	14.80	13.95	13.24	12.65	12.16	11.73	11.37	11.05	10.78	10.54	10.32
1/2	54.55	37.89	29.58	24.62	21.34	19.01	17.28	15.94	14.88	14.03	13.33	12.74	12.24	11.82	11.46	11.14	10.87	10.63	10.42
5/8	54.62	37.96	29.65	24.70	21.41	19.08	17.35	16.02	14.96	14.11	13.41	12.82	12.33	11.91	11.55	11.24	10.96	10.72	10.51
3/4	54.69	38.03	29.72	24.77	21.49	19.16	17.43	16.10	15.04	14.19	13.49	12.91	12.42	12.00	11.64	11.33	11.06	10.82	10.61
7/8	54.76	38.09	29.80	24.84	21.56	19.24	17.51	16.18	15.13	14.28	13.58	13.00	12.50	12.09	11.73	11.42	11.15	10.91	10.71
9	54.83	38.16	29.87	24.92	21.64	19.31	17.59	16.26	15.21	14.36	13.66	13.08	12.59	12.18	11.82	11.51	11.24	11.01	10.80
1/8	54.90	38.23	29.94	24.99	21.71	19.39	17.66	16.34	15.29	14.44	13.75	13.17	12.68	12.27	11.91	11.60	11.34	11.10	10.90
1/4	54.96	38.30	30.01	25.06	21.78	19.46	17.74	16.42	15.37	14.52	13.83	13.25	12.77	12.36	12.00	11.70	11.43	11.20	11.00
3/8	55.03	38.37	30.08	25.13	21.86	19.54	17.82	16.50	15.45	14.61	13.92	13.34	12.86	12.45	12.09	11.79	11.53	11.29	11.09
1/2	55.10	38.44	30.15	25.21	21.93	19.62	17.90	16.58	15.53	14.69	14.00	13.43	12.95	12.54	12.18	11.88	11.62	11.39	11.19
5/8	55.17	38.51	30.22	25.28	22.01	19.69	17.98	16.66	15.61	14.78	14.09	13.52	13.03	12.63	12.28	11.98	11.72	11.49	11.29
3/4	55.24	38.58	30.30	25.35	22.09	19.77	18.06	16.74	15.70	14.86	14.17	13.60	13.12	12.72	12.37	12.07	11.81	11.58	11.39
7/8	55.31	38.66	30.37	25.43	22.16	19.85	18.13	16.82	15.78	14.94	14.26	13.69	13.21	12.81	12.46	12.16	11.91	11.68	11.49
10	55.38	38.73	30.44	25.50	22.24	19.93	18.21	16.90	15.86	15.03	14.35	13.78	13.30	12.90	12.56	12.26	12.00	11.78	11.59
1/4	55.52	38.87	30.58	25.65	22.39	20.08	18.37	17.06	16.03	15.20	14.52	13.96	13.48	13.08	12.74	12.45	12.20	11.98	11.78
1/2	55.66	39.01	30.73	25.80	22.54	20.24	18.53	17.23	16.20	15.37	14.69	14.13	13.66	13.27	12.93	12.64	12.39	12.17	11.99
3/4	55.80	39.15	30.87	25.95	22.69	20.39	18.69	17.39	16.37	15.54	14.87	14.31	13.85	13.46	13.12	12.84	12.59	12.37	12.19
11	55.93	39.29	31.02	26.10	22.85	20.55	18.86	17.56	16.54	15.72	15.05	14.50	14.03	13.64	13.31	13.03	12.79	12.57	12.39
1/4	56.07	39.43	31.17	26.25	23.00	20.71	19.02	17.72	16.71	15.89	15.23	14.68	14.22	13.83	13.51	13.23	12.98	12.77	12.60
1/2	56.21	39.58	31.31	26.40	23.15	20.87	19.18	17.89	16.88	16.07	15.40	14.86	14.41	14.02	13.70	13.42	13.18	12.98	12.80
3/4	56.35	39.72	31.46	26.55	23.31	21.03	19.34	18.06	17.05	16.24	15.58	15.04	14.59	14.21	13.89	13.62	13.39	13.18	13.01
12	56.49	39.86	31.61	26.70	23.47	21.19	19.51	18.23	17.22	16.42	15.77	15.23	14.78	14.41	14.09	13.82	13.59	13.39	13.22
1/4	56.63	40.01	31.75	26.85	23.62	21.35	19.67	18.40	17.40	16.60	15.95	15.42	14.97	14.60	14.29	14.02	13.79	13.60	13.43
1/2	56.77	40.15	31.90	27.00	23.78	21.51	19.84	18.57	17.57	16.78	16.13	15.60	15.16	14.80	14.49	14.22	14.00	13.80	13.64
3/4	56.91	40.29	32.05	27.16	23.94	21.67	20.01	18.74	17.75	16.96	16.32	15.79	15.36	14.99	14.68	14.42	14.20	14.01	13.85
13	57.06	40.44	32.20	27.31	24.09	21.84	20.17	18.91	17.92	17.14	16.50	15.98	15.55	15.19	14.88	14.63	14.41	14.22	14.06

Interest Rate	21 YEARS	22 YEARS	23 YEARS	24 YEARS	25 YEARS	26 YEARS	27 YEARS	28 YEARS	29 YEARS	30 YEARS	31 YEARS	32 YEARS	33 YEARS	34 YEARS	35 YEARS	36 YEARS	37 YEARS	38 YEARS	39 YEARS	40 YEARS
7	9.11	8.93	8.76	8.62	8.49	8.37	8.26	8.16	8.07	7.99	7.91	7.85	7.78	7.72	7.67	7.62	7.58	7.54	7.50	7.46
1/8	9.20	9.02	8.86	8.71	8.58	8.46	8.36	8.26	8.17	8.09	8.02	7.95	7.89	7.83	7.78	7.73	7.68	7.64	7.61	7.57
1/4	9.29	9.11	8.95	8.81	8.68	8.56	8.46	8.36	8.27	8.19	8.12	8.05	7.99	7.93	7.88	7.84	7.79	7.75	7.72	7.68
3/8	9.38	9.21	9.05	8.90	8.78	8.66	8.55	8.46	8.37	8.29	8.22	8.16	8.09	8.04	7.99	7.94	7.90	7.86	7.82	7.79
1/2	9.47	9.30	9.14	9.00	8.87	8.76	8.65	8.56	8.47	8.40	8.32	8.26	8.20	8.15	8.10	8.05	8.01	7.97	7.93	7.90
5/8	9.57	9.39	9.24	9.09	8.97	8.86	8.75	8.66	8.58	8.50	8.43	8.36	8.31	8.25	8.20	8.16	8.12	8.08	8.04	8.01
3/4	9.66	9.49	9.33	9.19	9.07	8.96	8.85	8.76	8.68	8.60	8.53	8.47	8.41	8.36	8.31	8.27	8.23	8.19	8.16	8.12
7/8	9.76	9.58	9.43	9.29	9.17	9.06	8.96	8.86	8.78	8.71	8.64	8.58	8.52	8.47	8.42	8.38	8.34	8.30	8.27	8.24
8	9.85	9.68	9.53	9.39	9.27	9.16	9.06	8.97	8.88	8.81	8.74	8.68	8.63	8.57	8.53	8.49	8.45	8.41	8.38	8.35
1/8	9.94	9.78	9.62	9.49	9.37	9.26	9.16	9.07	8.99	8.91	8.85	8.79	8.73	8.68	8.64	8.60	8.56	8.53	8.49	8.46
1/4	10.04	9.87	9.72	9.59	9.47	9.36	9.26	9.17	9.09	9.02	8.95	8.90	8.84	8.79	8.75	8.71	8.67	8.63	8.60	8.57
3/8	10.14	9.97	9.82	9.69	9.57	9.46	9.36	9.28	9.20	9.13	9.06	9.00	8.95	8.90	8.86	8.82	8.78	8.75	8.72	8.69
1/2	10.23	10.07	9.92	9.79	9.67	9.56	9.47	9.38	9.30	9.23	9.17	9.11	9.06	9.01	8.97	8.93	8.89	8.86	8.83	8.80
5/8	10.33	10.16	10.02	9.89	9.77	9.66	9.57	9.48	9.41	9.34	9.28	9.22	9.17	9.12	9.08	9.04	9.00	8.97	8.94	8.92
3/4	10.43	10.26	10.12	9.99	9.87	9.77	9.67	9.59	9.51	9.45	9.38	9.33	9.28	9.23	9.19	9.15	9.12	9.09	9.06	9.03
7/8	10.52	10.36	10.22	10.09	9.97	9.87	9.78	9.69	9.62	9.55	9.49	9.44	9.39	9.34	9.30	9.26	9.23	9.20	9.17	9.15
9	10.62	10.46	10.32	10.19	10.08	9.97	9.88	9.80	9.73	9.66	9.60	9.55	9.50	9.45	9.41	9.38	9.34	9.31	9.29	9.26
1/8	10.72	10.56	10.42	10.29	10.18	10.08	9.99	9.91	9.83	9.77	9.71	9.66	9.61	9.56	9.53	9.49	9.46	9.43	9.40	9.38
1/4	10.82	10.66	10.52	10.39	10.28	10.18	10.09	10.01	9.94	9.88	9.82	9.77	9.72	9.68	9.64	9.60	9.57	9.54	9.52	9.49
3/8	10.92	10.76	10.62	10.50	10.39	10.29	10.20	10.12	10.05	9.99	9.93	9.88	9.83	9.79	9.75	9.72	9.69	9.66	9.63	9.61
1/2	11.01	10.86	10.72	10.60	10.49	10.39	10.31	10.23	10.16	10.10	10.04	9.99	9.94	9.90	9.86	9.83	9.80	9.77	9.75	9.73
5/8	11.11	10.96	10.82	10.70	10.59	10.50	10.41	10.34	10.27	10.20	10.15	10.10	10.05	10.01	9.98	9.95	9.92	9.89	9.86	9.84
3/4	11.21	11.06	10.93	10.81	10.70	10.60	10.52	10.44	10.38	10.31	10.26	10.21	10.17	10.13	10.09	10.06	10.03	10.00	9.98	9.96
7/8	11.31	11.16	11.03	10.91	10.80	10.71	10.63	10.55	10.48	10.43	10.37	10.32	10.28	10.24	10.21	10.17	10.15	10.12	10.10	10.08
10	11.41	11.26	11.13	11.01	10.91	10.82	10.73	10.66	10.59	10.54	10.48	10.44	10.39	10.36	10.32	10.29	10.26	10.24	10.22	10.19
1/4	11.62	11.47	11.34	11.23	11.12	11.03	10.95	10.88	10.82	10.76	10.71	10.66	10.62	10.58	10.55	10.52	10.50	10.47	10.45	10.43
1/2	11.82	11.68	11.55	11.43	11.34	11.25	11.17	11.10	11.04	10.98	10.93	10.89	10.85	10.81	10.78	10.75	10.73	10.71	10.69	10.67
3/4	12.03	11.88	11.76	11.65	11.55	11.46	11.39	11.32	11.26	11.21	11.16	11.12	11.08	11.05	11.02	10.99	10.96	10.94	10.92	10.91
11	12.23	12.09	11.97	11.86	11.77	11.68	11.61	11.54	11.48	11.43	11.39	11.35	11.31	11.28	11.25	11.22	11.20	11.18	11.16	11.14
1/4	12.44	12.30	12.18	12.08	11.98	11.90	11.83	11.77	11.71	11.66	11.62	11.58	11.54	11.51	11.48	11.46	11.44	11.42	11.40	11.38
1/2	12.65	12.51	12.40	12.29	12.20	12.12	12.05	11.99	11.94	11.89	11.85	11.81	11.77	11.74	11.72	11.69	11.67	11.65	11.64	11.62
3/4	12.86	12.73	12.61	12.51	12.42	12.35	12.28	12.22	12.16	12.12	12.08	12.04	12.01	11.98	11.95	11.93	11.91	11.89	11.88	11.87
12	13.07	12.94	12.83	12.73	12.64	12.57	12.50	12.44	12.39	12.35	12.31	12.27	12.24	12.22	12.19	12.17	12.15	12.13	12.12	12.11
1/4	13.28	13.16	13.05	12.95	12.87	12.79	12.73	12.67	12.62	12.58	12.54	12.51	12.48	12.45	12.43	12.41	12.39	12.38	12.36	12.35
1/2	13.50	13.37	13.26	13.17	13.09	13.02	12.96	12.90	12.85	12.81	12.78	12.74	12.71	12.69	12.67	12.65	12.63	12.62	12.60	12.59
3/4	13.71	13.59	13.48	13.39	13.31	13.24	13.18	13.13	13.09	13.05	13.01	12.98	12.95	12.93	12.91	12.89	12.87	12.86	12.85	12.84
13	13.93	13.81	13.71	13.62	13.54	13.47	13.41	13.36	13.32	13.28	13.25	13.22	13.19	13.17	13.15	13.13	13.11	13.10	13.09	13.08

2. — Residential Properties

BUY AT ALL COSTS

Standard advice to the person who does not own his own home is that he should have bought last year or five years ago.

As each new set of construction and land prices is issued, the dream of almost every American to hold title to his own castle seems to move closer to oblivion.

The percentage jumps in housing values from year to year are astounding, and it is clear that to hope for a general lowering of price tags on existing or new homes is just wishful thinking.

While housing costs move steadily upward, the price for borrowing money to buy homes fluctuates. Timing of financing, then, would seem to be just as important a key to getting a good buy as finding a house priced under the market.

Of course, if the buyer is a cash customer, he does not have to face the question of financing. But even if he has the cash to spend, he should ask himself if most of his dollars are best put to use in a home.

Many families regard a paid-for house a great asset, and no one can argue with that belief, at least on the surface. Everyone likes the security of outright ownership of a home, but the buyer should consider some alternative uses of his cash before he plunges into his savings and depletes it all for one purchase.

Suppose the total cost of his house is $35,000. Unless he is in an extraordinarily good cash position — and some so-called monied people can't raise that kind of cash quickly — spending this much on a home will divert earnings or funds that could otherwise be used to buy more income-producing real estate.

If he puts less cash into the purchase of his home, this leaves him more cash to buy real estate with mortgages, of course, that rent will be able to carry. In addition, he will be earning a return on his investment and be building equity holdings and his own personal net worth.

MAKING THE MOST OF PROPERTY DOLLARS

Yes, a house owned outright will probably increase in value, but spreading cash around for a home and other real estate will show greater overall assets and provide one with a stronger financial statement than will ownership of a single property. The home owner will be able to borrow money on these investments from refinancing, taking cash earned to put into still more properties or investments.

For example, with $10,000 as equity in a home and $25,000 invested in income property which has a $75,000 mortgage, a person is much further ahead financially because he owns a total of $135,000 worth of real estate rather than having the entire $35,000 cash invested in a home.

If an owner should decide to sell his home, the financing will be much more attractive to a prospective buyer if he can pay the seller a certain amount of cash and assume the mortgage, which carries the advantage of being already placed and reduces the closing costs and fees to the new owner.

If one owns his home and needs to sell and finds himself in a tight money market, this may mean he will have to take back the first mortgage or maybe a second. The first would probably be long term and that would bring him a comparative loss as dollars become cheaper in inflation. Even the interest he charges would not compensate the lent dollar.

To protect money over the long haul, it would be to the seller's advantage to arrange for a short-term mortgage whenever possible, say a 10-year mortgage as opposed to 20 or 25-year terms. Both buyer and seller can design mortgage arrangements that will be equally fair if they sincerely want to exchange dollars and property by equal measures.

MORTGAGES — GETTING A PERSPECTIVE

Property buyers are actually fortunate in seeking mortgages in today's market, no matter what the money supply. Until the 1930's, home ownership was a rarity. Mortgage loans came from private lenders and were based on the property as security and did not take into consideration the mortgagor's salary. Mortgages were very short term, running from two to five years.

The lenders had a strong upperhand, being able to demand full payment or renewal of the note. If he chose not to renew, the buyer had to find another lender to pay off the existing loan, or the borrower would lose the property.

With the devastating effects of the great depression on home owners and the demands for housing in the 1940's a new trend emerged for home buyers. The Homeowners Loan Corporation was established to help stabilize real estate and the Federal Housing Administration was born in 1934. Institutional lending was devised to expand and control credit.

FHA designed a mortgage calling for real estate loans over a long term paid in monthly installments which were to include taxes and insurance. A uniform system of real estate appraisal and credit analysis of the borrower was thus set up for operational soundness of this program.

If a buyer decides to use a mortgage to purchase his home, he is among the vast majority of home buyers. The mortgage is the most widely known and used vehicle for financing real estate. The mortgagor or borrower offers his land or property as security against a loan from the mortgagee or lender who holds either the legal title or has a lien on the property until the mortgage is paid in full.

This first mortgage carries an interest rate which varies with a number of factors, including the economic state of the country, inflation, and availability of money to banks and lending institutions or individuals.

In this country, we are fortunate in being able to shop for mortgages just as we shop for a house to get the best possible financial arrangement, rate of interest, length of mortgage, and other services or pluses which competing organizations may offer.

The home buyer has a number of choices of mortgages open to him, and he should consider and evaluate all of them before making that final commitment. He may have to live with his decision for 20 years, so an initial investment of time and effort will pay handsome tangible dividends.

A mortgage can be as highly customized as a tailor-made suit or dress. The mortgage will depend not only on economic conditions but on the borrower and his capability to meet mortgage payments, the term over which he spreads the loan, the amount of money he wants to borrow, his military background, qualifications for government insurance or other government assistance, the house and property itself, and the need for a second mortgage.

VARIETIES OF LOANS

First, the borrower should know that there are various kinds of mortgages he should familiarize himself with and then choose the one that best fits his needs.

Full service banks, savings and loan associations, mortgage companies, mutual savings banks, and the government generally either make or back these types of loans for dwellings.

Conventional Loans — These are offered by commercial banks, savings and loan associations, mortgage companies, and mutual savings banks. These loans are not secured by the government as are Veterans Administration and Federal Housing Administration-insured mortgages.

The conventional mortgage rates are determined by individual lenders within boundaries established by state laws. The rate one gets will depend on the supply of money, demand for mortgages, and the length of time the borrower wants his loan to run.

Farmers Home Administration Loans — Under this program the government makes loans available to farmers or rural residents who are unable to obtain financing from other sources. A variety of loans is available to those engaged in farming through this FHA.

Federal Housing Administration-Insured Loans — Mortgages of this kind are obtained from FHA-approved sources for building, buying, or refinancing a home, but FHA or the government does not make the actual loan. The FHA insures lending sources against a certain amount of loss from non-payment on mortgages accepted by FHA for insurance. The borrower pays for this insurance as part of his monthly installment.

Veterans Administration-Insured Loans — Again, the government does not make these types of loans, but the veteran receives his mortgage from a lending source and a portion of it is insured by the VA.

Although the foregoing are the most commonly used mortgage loans, they are not the only vehicles for financing homes. Others include:

The Second Mortgage — Suppose the basic application for a mortgage is approved, but the lender is conservative in its loan-to-value ratio, that is, in the percentage of the price or value that it will loan.

This means either the borrower must apply elsewhere in hopes of acquiring a greater portion of the mortgage money, accept the approved loan, or try to get a second mortgage. There are a number of sources open to him for seconds. He should start with the owner of the property, asking him if he will take back a small second. If he agrees, the borrower can expect the loan to be short term and the interest rate to be high, possibly as high as the usury laws of his state permit. Of course, the borrower should try to negotiate for as low interest as possible with as long a term as he can get. If an owner really wants to sell, he will give his customer an attractive second mortgage.

However, the borrower should consider that a long-term amortized loan will not provide the lender the kind of yield he can expect from other investments and his mortgage will be junior to the first. Should a foreclosure be necessary, he would receive his money only after the first mortgagee was satisfied, putting a greater risk in the path of the lender taking seconds.

There are a few pluses for such a lender and the borrower may need to remind him of these if he is a novice at such financing, and he might be if he is a home owner and has not dealt in any other real estate. The borrower should point out that by taking a second mortgage, the seller is better able to dispose of the property. The seller also will be spreading out his income over a longer period and this should help reduce his capital gains taxes.

If the owner of the property refuses to take back a second, the borrower should ask his attorney or real estate salesman or broker if he knows of individuals looking for mortgages to hold. Individuals are the largest group of lenders of second mortgages and are especially important sources for first mortgage and construction loans in tight money markets.

If the borrower cannot find an individual lender, another possibility might be the mortgage companies, which real estate brokers can usually recommend. These are as close as the phone directory yellow pages. In almost every city in the United States one will see large ads in the yellow pages seeking investments in second mortgages. The borrower can visit them to get quicker action.

Mortgage companies, too, will lend short term at high interest rates and points or costs for placing the loan. These firms should be approached just as the savings and loans. An application and all data about the property, including its age, construction type, and survey should be presented.

Still another source for a second is the real estate brokerage firm. Some salesmen or brokers will even take a second mortgage in lieu of a cash commission. They will be stretching their commission out over a few years and will be earning some interest. If they face tax problems, this arrangement can be quite beneficial.

Construction Loans — These are used to build new homes or for home improvements and may be arranged through institutions. VA, the Federal Housing Administration, or Farmers Home Administration programs may be utilized for these types. Money may be advanced directly to the borrower or to the builder.

Open-end Mortgages — The need to add to or improve a home after the original long-term mortgage has been placed has given rise to these loans. They allow the borrower to obtain additional funds on his mortgage without having to refinance or make a short-term, high-interest rate loan for his home project.

The borrower may receive the difference between the amount of the original sum and the amount by which he has reduced the mortgage.

If, for example, the original mortgage is for $50,000, and he has paid it down to $40,000, he may draw $10,000.

A closed-end mortgage, in contrast, makes no provisions for increasing the balance.

Package Mortgages — These loans are designed to cover land, building, and certain kinds of equipment, such as kitchen appliances. Lenders' policies vary on this type of loan. Opposition is based on the fact that equipment usually wears out before the loan can be reduced substantially. Such loans do strengthen the buyer's financial position, allowing him to spread his obligations over a longer term.

Purchase Money Mortgages — These are mortgages held by property owners. The seller-owner usually agrees to hold a mortgage for about the same length of time and rates as an institution. Using such a mortgage, the buyer saves certain closing costs which always accompany a new mortgage from an institution.

UNDERSTANDING LENDERS
AND THE LOAN PROCESS

Whether one is in the market to buy a home or a shopping center, a basic understanding of lending sources and procedures is essential before he charges off to make an application. This background will not only help him become more conversant with the lenders but will allow him to eliminate some source possibilities and get busy working with those he feels will most likely be able to meet his needs and with whom he will be able to deal.

How does one learn about lenders? A study of sources at the end of this text will help and some personal research, including phone calls and visits with lenders, will lay the foundation.

A borrower should always keep in mind that sources and their policies change from time to time, and it is always advisable to check directly with the prospective lender on its current status on funds, interest rates, loan limits, and types of mortgages available before counting on that source being able to consider a loan.

For example, one savings and loan association in a borrower's town may decide it has enough money loaned out on single-family houses, but it may have funds available for triplexes, while another savings and loan in the area has plenty to lend for houses but no money for condominiums or mobile homes.

Any lender will appreciate the fact that a borrower also knows the basics of the loan process. This knowledge will save both time, and in some cases, the borrower's embarrassment. For instance, suppose a borrower believes that all he has to pay at closing is a down payment. He may be shocked when he is called by the bank or his attorney and told to bring an additional sum to the closing for certain costs.

In some cases, he may not be informed in advance of these other charges and might not be prepared at closing to meet them. This might delay or postpone the closing.

A borrower is advised to study the following subjects even before he approaches a lender for the first time because they might help him in his selection of a mortgagee and will certainly help him communicate more efficiently with members of the lending world.

Principal — This is the amount of money used for the mortgage and on which interest is paid.

Interest Rate — The percentage of the principal amount that is charged for use of the mortgage money is the interest rate. It is determined by the availability of money, the economy, lender policy, the type of property mortgaged, risk, and other factors. Rate limits are set by state laws.

Term — The length of time that a lender will make money available is the term of the loan. Terms vary with mortgagees — savings and loans and insurance companies usually offer longer-term mortgages than commercial banks do. The type of property also helps establish terms. A newer property gets longer terms because of its increased economic expectancy.

It should be remembered that the shorter the term, the lower the interest rate usually is.

Let's look at how the term of a loan can affect the mortgage payments:

If Mr. Jones decides he cannot afford $240 a month for a mortgage, he could reduce his payment by asking the lender for a longer term.

Checking the amortization tables preceding this chapter, we note that the debt constant for 8-1/2 percent for 30 years, monthly in advance is 9.17. This will make the total annual payment ($30,000 x 9.17) equal $2,751. This is $229.25 a month which will reduce his payment by $10.75 a month or $129 a year.

Amortization — When a loan is spread out over a period of time, and it is paid back periodically in payments that include principal and interest, the loan is amortized, that is, the principal amount of the debt is gradually reduced.

The payment, made monthly, quarterly or semi-annually, is usually a fixed amount. Interest has first claim in the installments, and the balance is credited toward repayment of the debt, which is reduced with every payment. Because the debt is less than it was the time before, the amount of money paid each payment on interest decreases. The amount applied to the principal increases.

Although the payment combines two different amounts, only the payment of principal is amortization.

Interest is a deductible expense for income tax purposes, but there is not allowed deduction as an expense for the amount of amortization going on each payment.

Amortized loans are the most commonly used kinds by institutions for residential mortgages. However, another means of paying off a mortgage is to make one lump sum payment when the note comes due. Interest could be paid then, too, or in installments beforehand.

The balloon mortgage actually combines qualities of both amortization and payment of the total amount. With this approach the borrower uses an amortized loan and then the unpaid balance becomes due at the end of the debt term.

Constant — Elements that determine the amount of each payment on a mortgage are the interest rate, amount of the mortgage, and length of term. The annual constant tells the borrower how much he will have to pay per year for each $1,000 borrowed including principal and interest. A constant is expressed as a percentage.

Here's an example showing how to figure out the constant and the actual mortgage payment:

Assume Mr. Stanley contracts to buy a home for which he needs a $30,000 mortgage. The loan is for 25 years at 8-1/2 percent interest to be paid monthly. Checking the amortization table, he sees that the debt constant to be paid monthly in advance is 9.60.

He multiplies the amount he borrows, $30,000, by the debt constant, 9.60, to get the total amount he must actually pay each year including principal and interest. This is $2,880 per year. Now he divides by 12 and gets $240 which is the total of the monthly payment.

Points — For making mortgage money available to a borrower, the lender will add points, a bonus of sorts for himself, into the closing costs. This will be a percentage of the principal amount. A lender should also be questioned about point charges (called discounts in VA or FHA loans) before the mortgage application is submitted.

Closing Costs — These are expenses incurred by buyer and seller in executing the mortgage and are paid at the closing. The borrower's costs may be fees for an appraisal, an attorney, escrow, recording of the deed and mortgage, a survey, title insurance, and state stamps on notes. The lender adds his points to these costs. Pro-rated taxes and insurance may also be paid by the new owner at closing.

The seller usually pays for an attorney, abstracting, state stamps on the deed, the real estate commission, recording of mortgages, and an escrow fee. These items may vary with the transaction and the states where the mortgages are made.

Here is an example of a closing statement for a home:

CLOSING STATEMENT

Mortgage Loan From
MAIN FEDERAL SAVINGS AND LOAN ASSOCIATION
TO
James and Helen White, His Wife

Lots 12 and 13, Block 11, Pinecrest Plat
Monticello Sec. D, pb 25/74 Dade

LOAN NO _____

RECEIPTS:

Mortgage Principal	$28,800.00
Deposit by Mortgagor	_____
	_____
	_____
	_____
Total _____	$28,800.00

DISBURSEMENTS:

Association Mortgage Costs ___3___ %	$ 864.00
Insurance	_____
Abstracting _____ Escrow	40.00
Interest ___5/24/74 − 6/30/74	220.40
Recording ___Warranty Deed	2.25
Satisfaction of 1st Mortgage	_____
Satisfaction of 2nd Mortgage	_____
TO CONSTRUCTION FUND	_____
Escrow for taxes and insurance	512.00
Credit Report	10.00
Stamps on Warranty Deed Fla. $96/Surtax $35.20	131.20
Harry H. Smith and Ann B. Smith	$27,020.15
Total _____	$28,800.00
Balance _____	$ 0.00

May 24 _____, 1974

It is hereby certified that I (or we) authorize the above disbursements, approve this statement of account, acknowledge receipt of the balance shown above, to-wit: the sum of $0.00_____, also copy of this closing statement and copy of mortgage note.

For Association Records Only

Approved on _____		
Month	Day	Year

Special Clauses — The borrower should always inquire about the lender's policies on various clauses that can affect his mortgage. For instance, if the lender includes an alienation clause in the mortgage, the mortgagor could be prevented from selling the house and letting the new buyer take over the mortgage, and the lender could call the loan demanding full payment.

A seller should have the right to assign his mortgage if he needs to. Institutions always have that right.

If the lender writes an escalation clause into the mortgage, it has the right to raise the interest rate periodically. Some institutions use variable interest rates as a standard mortgage practice.

The borrower should also inquire about the lender's policy on late payments and the time he allows to lapse before starting foreclosure proceedings.

A property buyer should make sure in his purchase contract that the offer he makes is subject to obtaining a certain mortgage financing. This is an extremely important clause since it allows the prospective buyer out if he cannot arrange the mortgage he wants.

Truth in Lending — In order to allow prospective borrowers to make adequate comparisons of the charges of various lenders, the Truth in Lending Act, Title I of the Consumer Credit Protection Act, was enacted in 1969.

The law requires that those engaged in lending must disclose certain information to their borrowers.

Implemented by the Board of Governors of the Federal Reserve System as Regulation Z, the law is known as Truth in Lending or Regulation Z to those in the lending field. This regulation supplies lending institutions with information they need to comply with the law and tells them how to meet requirements.

Covered under the law are all who are involved in regular extensions of credit, including banks, savings and loans, stores, credit unions, and finance companies.

A disclosure statement applicable to real estate financing outlines:

(1) The total of prepaid finance charges such as origination fees, discount points, construction loan fee, and FHA loan insurance costs.

(2) Those items not included under finance charge — real estate transfer charges and filing and recording fees, for instance.

(3) The amount of any late charges.

(4) Prepayment privileges for paying off the loan before it reaches maturity.

(5) A list of any property in which the lender has brought security interest.

(6) Cost of life, health, and accident insurance and the fact that this insurance is not mandatory as a condition of issuing the loan.

(7) A statement that although fire insurance is a requirement the borrower can choose his own insurance agent or company.

(8) Admission that the disclosure statement does not reflect many of the borrower's closing costs, for example, title examination, legal, credit reporting, and other fees.

A GUIDE TO GETTING A LOAN

The loan process is rather simple, with the applicant querying lenders in his area about interest rates, terms, and availability of funds and then following through one at a time by filing an application for a loan.

After the lender does its appraisal of the property, the buyer's references and financials are checked, the loan committee meets and the borrower will get a yes or no.

If it's yes, a closing date is set and meanwhile the title and abstract are researched and the buyer or his attorney and the lender work on details of the mortgage.

In most institutions one loan officer will work with the borrower, and he is the best contact for questions.

The only departure in this procedure for FHA- and VA-insured loans is that the buyer will complete their special forms which will be supplied by the lender.

SOURCES FOR LOANS

The Savings and Loan Association — S and L's have traditionally been the largest lenders of loans for homes in this country. They make conventional mortgages as well as those insured by FHA and VA.

The borrower will find S and L's located in almost every city or area of the country.

These institutions specialize in long-term mortgages for residences and are active in the short-term loan market for home improvement construction.

Rates and terms vary among S and L's, so all of those within the borrower's vicinity should be queried.

The Commercial Bank — These institutions are involved in making short-term or interim loans for construction in most parts of the country.

They do get into the long-term home loan field when there is an absence of other lenders for such purposes in the area. They are FHA- and VA-approved lenders.

The borrower should talk with loan officers of commercial banks in his area to learn firsthand what funds, rates, and policies prevail for home buyers at the time.

Application and processing procedures will be the same as they are with the S and L's.

The Mortgage Company — These firms are the most active originators of home loans in this country. That is, they make mortgages with their own funds and then sell them off in the secondary mortgage market.

Although their mortgages are sold, they might continue to service the loan, collecting payments and doing basic paperwork.

They make long-term home loans as well as construction loans and are the largest volume sources for FHA- and VA-insured mortgages.

A real estate broker or an attorney or accountant specializing in real estate can usually point out which companies are in the market for home mortgages at any given time.

These companies can be approached directly by the borrower or, in some cases, the real estate firm making the property sale will work on the borrower's behalf with these lenders.

The Mutual Savings Bank — These banks specialize in home loans, both conventional and FHA- and VA-insured. Most of them are located in the Northeast, and their loans may be limited to their own geographical areas.

The nearest bank may be found in the phone directory or by inquiring of the National Association of Mutual Savings Banks, 1200 Park Avenue, New York, New York 10028.

The borrower can make direct contact with these banks and ensuing mortgage procedures are standard.

THE GOVERNMENT CAN HELP

If one qualifies, there is a variety of government or government-related resources to help the home buyer.

Federal Housing Administration-Insured Loans — The government established the FHA in the 1930's to insure loans of lenders so they would be willing to make home mortgages.

Through the years, FHA has grown to encompass a variety of functions all involving the operation of housing loan insurance programs "designed to encourage improvements in housing standards and conditions, to facilitate sound home financing on reasonable terms, and to exert a stabilizing influence in the mortgage market."

FHA does not lend money and it does not build homes, but it greatly affects lending terms, building plans and specifications, and selection of housing sites by conditions under which it allows its insurance to be issued.

Of most concern to a buyer of real estate are Title I and Title II of the FHA Act. Title I insures lenders against loss on loans covering alterations, repairs, improvements, or conversions of existing structures and construction of new, small non-residential structures. Under the terms of Title I, FHA's liability is 90 percent of loss on individual loans and up to 10 percent of all such loans made by any institution. Title I makes provisions for insuring mortgages or improvement loans for one-to-four-family dwellings.

Title II sets forth provisions for insuring loans on one-to-four-family dwellings. Under the various sections of these titles, the FHA has established high standards that must be met by the property, the borrower, and the lender.

FHA will also insure loans in those areas in which a riot has occurred or in which a riot is threatened.

FHA has set criteria that are applied to each property to evaluate all factors that may affect the property, including qualifications and credit of the buyer.

Basically, these factors determine the eligibility of the property in question:

(1)   The property must have a dwelling designed for residential use by not more than four families.

(2)   The structure's building and construction requirements are set by FHA.

(3)   The housing standards of the community must also meet FHA standards.

(4)   The real estate must be owned by the mortgagor, that is, the deed held by him or the property must be on leasehold for not fewer than 99 years, which is renewable, or under a lease for not fewer than 50 years to run.

(5)   The mortgagee must establish that no sale or occupancy restrictions as to race, color, or creed have been placed on the property as of record February 15, 1950.

(6)   A mortgage on property with a dwelling to be rented by the mortgagor is ineligible if the property is a part of or adjacent to a project or group of similar rental properties with eight or more living units in which the mortgagor has any financial interest.

(7)   No two-to-four-unit dwellings and no one-unit dwellings are eligible if part of a group of five or more single-family dwellings held by the same mortgagor may be rented or offered for rent for transient or hotel purposes.

The FHA appraiser will consider these factors in evaluating a property — general condition of the house and lot, kinds of kitchen, laundry and other equipment included, and serious defects which are visible and which obviously need fixing.

FHA charges $40 for existing home appraisals and $50 for proposed homes. FHA collects this fee from the lender and the lender collects from the buyer or seller.

An applicant for FHA insurance must establish his current dependable income exclusive generally of overtime, room rentals, wife's income — unless this has been established as part of the family earnings — return on capital investment, or other possible income.

In addition, his current expenses on his housing are compared with those he will incur as an owner such as maintenance, insurance, utilities. His total financial obligations, life insurance, and other factors are all considered in evaluating a prospect for FHA insurance.

Terms set by the FHA under Section 235 of the Housing Act establish the maximum loan limit, maximum income limit, and minimum down payment, allowing for a 30-year mortgage with a possible 40-year term, if necessary. The Housing and Community Development Act of 1974 increased the home mortgage limit from $33,000 to $45,000.

The 1974 act also increased home improvement loans from a $5,000 limit to $10,000.

To qualify for making FHA-insured loans, an institution must be a corporation with assets of more than $100,000 and must be accepted by the FHA as a qualified lender. The institution may, of course, make conventional mortgage loans as well as FHA-insured loans.

Risks as well as interest rates, which are set for FHA loans by the Secretary of Housing and Urban Development, decrease on FHA loans. A borrower will pay this interest, principal, and FHA insurance, which is one-half percent per annum. Also, the borrower is required to deposit monthly payments for real estate taxes and insurance.

A borrower can choose any FHA approved lender for making application for his mortgage.

Approved automatically are national mortgage associations, federal reserve banks, federal home loan banks, and any federal, state, or municipal agency authorized to hold mortgages insured under Title II as security or as collateral or for any other purpose.

Also eligible for approval are members of the Federal Reserve System, institutions whose accounts are insured by the Federal Savings and Loan Insurance Corporation, and those institutions whose deposits are insured by the Federal Deposit Insurance Corporation. Charitable and non-profit groups with permanent funds of $100,000 and with experience in mortgage investments also may be approved.

The lender will determine from this information if a borrower is eligible for the FHA-insured loan and submit the application to the regional FHA office. Then the FHA will study the application, appraise the property, and apply the mortgage pattern for the area. A commitment for insurance is then issued if the application meets all the requirements, and when the commitment is received by the lender, the loan is made.

Some firms originate loans and then sell them to other institutions in what is known as a secondary mortgage market. This process enables the originating company to have fluid funds to invest in mortgages. In some cases, a borrower will continue to make his mortgage payments to the originating firm which collects a small fee for servicing the loan.

Veterans Administration-Insured Loans — Like FHA, the VA enters into agreement with regular lending institutions to guarantee or insure loans up to a certain amount. These include banks, savings and loan associations, insurance and mortgage companies. The risk to the lender is reduced through the VA program, and he probably will not experience any loss should the veteran or subsequent owner fail to repay the loan.

VA is authorized to guarantee home and farm loans made to eligible post-Korean conflict veterans and certain servicemen by lending institutions and to guarantee or insure home, farm, and business loans made to

World War II or Korean conflict veterans by lending institutions. Direct loans may be made in certain areas for the purpose of purchasing or constructing a home or farm residence or for its repair or alteration or improvement.

More specifically, those eligible for a VA-insured or guaranteed loan are:

(1) A veteran who served any time between September 16, 1940, and July 25, 1947, and was discharged under conditions other than dishonorable after at least 90 days active service (or for service-incurred disability in less than 90 days).

(2) A veteran whose entitlement was derived from active service between June 27, 1950, and January 31, 1955, inclusive. The minimum term of active service for veterans of the Korean conflict is the same as that required for World War II veterans, i.e., 90 days or discharge by reason of a service-connected disability.

(3) Widows of men who served during either of the periods referred to above and who died as the result of service.

(4) Any member of the Women's Army Auxiliary Corps who served for at least 90 days and who was honorably discharged therefrom for disability incurred in the line of duty rendering her physically unfit to perform further service in the Women's Army Auxiliary Corps or in the Women's Army Corps. (This applies only to persons so discharged from the Women's Army Auxiliary Corps prior to the integration of that corps into the Women's Army Corps, pursuant to Public Law 110, 78th Congress.)

(5) Certain United States citizens who served in the Armed Forces of a government allied with the United States in World War II.

The following are eligible for guaranteed loans, but are not eligible for insured or business loans (unless they also were eligible based on World War II or Korean conflict service, and such entitlement has not been used):

(1) Veterans who served on active duty for 181 days or more, any part of which occurred after January 31, 1955, and who were discharged or released under conditions other than dishonorable, or were discharged or released from active duty after such date for a service-connected disability. (This includes Vietnam veterans.)

(2) Servicemen who have served at least 181 days in active duty status, even though not discharged, while their service continues without a break.

(3) Widows of the above-described eligible persons who died as the result of service.

(4) The wife of any member of the armed forces serving on active duty who is listed as missing in action, or is a prisoner of war and has been so listed for a total of more than 90 days. Children of deceased veterans are not eligible to obtain a VA-guaranteed or insured loan.

Those World War II and Korean veterans who used their loan guaranty entitlement before May 7, 1968, may have between $5,000 and $8,500 additional entitlement for use in obtaining another GI loan. The maximum loan insurance has shown increases over the years and was raised to $12,500 on May 7, 1968.

The amount of additional entitlement available can be computed by subtracting the amount of entitlement used on previously guaranteed loans from the current maximum available entitlement. For instance, if a borrower is a veteran of 1960 and obtained a $12,500 home loan, $7,500, the maximum then, was guaranteed and he had no remaining entitlement. But under the new maximum of 1968, he would have another additional entitlement of $5,000 ($12,500 minus $7,500). If a borrower is in doubt about current eligibility, he should contact the nearest VA office, and it will give him a Certificate of Eligibility indicating the amount of his entitlement. The VA will also supply a number of helpful booklets fully explaining the VA loan benefits.

Government law requires that the applicant's income must have a proper relation to the terms of repaying the loan and other expenses. This means that his income must be sufficient to meet the anticipated mortgage payments on the loan, take care of his other obligations and expenses, and have an adequate amount remaining to support himself and his dependents.

For a VA-insured loan a borrower will apply to a regular lending institution usually a mortgage banker or savings and loan association. The VA guarantees 60 percent or a maximum of $12,500 of the loss of the loan.

A borrower can expect to pay a rate of interest that reflects the current money market. In 1968 the Secretary of HUD was authorized to establish a rate of interest "to meet the mortgage market," so this is a fluctuating rate.

The VA makes no charge for guaranteeing or insuring a loan. No commission or brokerage fees may be charged to a veteran for securing a GI loan. However, the lender may charge reasonable closing costs usually paid by a borrower. In the case of a home loan, such closing costs generally include the appraisal, credit report, survey, title evidence, and recording fees. The lender, as provided in schedules issued by the VA, may also make a reasonable flat charge to cover all other loan origination costs. In home loan cases, the closing costs and originating charge may not be included in the loan.

The VA loan offers many advantages, including no down payment, unless required by the lender if the purchase price exceeds the reasonable value determined by the VA; lower monthly payments because of the moderate interest rate; the long period allowed on the mortgage, and the opportunity to pay off all or part of the loan in advance with no penalty. A borrower should keep in mind, though, that the VA must pay the guarantee on the mortgage should he default, and then the amount paid by the VA must be repaid by him.

A borrower should understand, too, that should he sell his home, he is still personally liable on the debt unless he should be released or his mortgage debt is canceled. His VA office can explain the release procedures if the purchaser takes over his GI loan. If the buyer pays all cash for the property or he obtains his own loan, he is automatically released from any further obligation on the original GI loan.

A borrower can apply to the VA for a number of types of loans, including those for a house; residential unit in a condominium; to build a home; to repair, alter, or improve a home; to refinance his existing home loan; to buy a mobile home; to buy a farm; to construct a farm house or other buildings on a farm or repair, alter, or improve farm land or equipment. Under certain circumstances, cooperatively owned apartments and businesses may be guaranteed, and he should consult VA for details.

A GI loan on a home or business may run for 30 years, on a farm for 40 years. The amount of the loan eligible for guarantee is limitless except that home loans must not exceed the reasonable value of the property as established by the VA.

For a home loan, the veteran is required under Title 38, U.S. Code, to reside in the home he buys, builds, repairs, or alters. He must declare that he is in compliance with this requirement when he applies for the loan and at the closing. For making false certification, he is subject to possible criminal prosecution.

The veteran has an alternative in the case of farm loans. He may live on the farm he is operating if he chooses, or he may utilize the loan and actively supervise the farming operations.

VA's direct loan program is geared for GI's who cannot find home financing in their areas. The VA calls these housing credit shortage areas and they are usually rural and small cities and towns not near the commuting areas of larger cities where GI loans from private institutions have not been and are not presently available to veterans.

Closing costs for a direct loan are about the same as they are for a regular VA-insured loan. The VA also charges an additional origination fee of $50 or one percent of the loan whichever is more (two percent for the construction of a new home). Out of these percentages come payments for the credit report, appraisal fees and the loan closer's fee.

The interest rate for direct loans varies with governing law and VA regulations.

The Farmers Home Administration — Since many Americans have increasing interest in locating in rural areas away from the urban sprawls, we note that there are a number of government loans available for those who want to buy rural or farm homes. The best source of information for details is the Farmers Home Administration, U.S. Department of Agriculture, Washington, D.C. 20250, but we will outline the programs here briefly.

This agency makes loans in rural areas to finance homes, building sites, and essential farm service buildings. These areas include open country and locales with populations of not more than 10,000 which are rural in character and are not closely associated with urban centers.

Applications for loans from eligible veterans are given preference, but veterans and non-veterans must meet the same requirements.

The borrower may use home ownership loans to improve, build, repair, or rehabilitate rural homes and related facilities, farm service buildings, and waste disposal systems and to provide water for household and farmstead use. Emphasis is on new construction, and homes may be built on individual tracts or in subdivisions. Funds may be used, too, to modernize homes and to enlarge or remodel farm buildings and make improvements that will enhance the value of the property.

Keep in mind that these loans are available to people who are without decent, safe, and sanitary housing or necessary farm service buildings, are unable to obtain financing from private lenders on terms and conditions that they can reasonably be expected to pay, and have sufficient income to repay the loans and insurance premiums, taxes, maintenance costs, and other living expenses. Those with inadequate repayment ability may obtain loans by using co-signers. Maximum length of the loans is 33 years. When families progress to a better financial status, they are obligated by the loan contract to refinance through a commercial lender.

These loans are tailored to give assistance to low and moderate-income families to buy their own homes. Home ownership loans are made by the Farmers Home Administration to provide decent homes in suitable environments for American families, to encourage people to live in rural communities, and to encourage urban families to live in the countryside.

If building, applicants supply detailed plans, and the Farmers Home Administration reviews these plans and inspects construction as it progresses to help the borrower obtain sound and acceptable housing.

Houses may be located on desirable sites with an assured supply of safe drinking water and suitable arrangements for sewage disposal.

Application for these loans may be made at the Farmers Home Administration county office serving the area where the house or farm buildings are or will be located in. Fees are not charged for the appraisal or loan processing but applicants do pay, as part of the loan, for legal services necessary to guarantee title and loan closing costs.

The Farmers Home Administration is a decentralized agency with 42 state offices covering all 50 states, Puerto Rico, and the Virgin Islands. All rural counties are served from more than 1,700 county offices usually located in county-seat towns. Information on all loans is available at the FHA office serving the county in which the farm or home is located.

The Cooperative Farm Credit System — This program is designed to improve the income and well-being of American farmers and ranchers by furnishing sound, adequate, and constructive credit and closely related services to them, their cooperative, and to selected farm related businesses necessary for efficient farm operations.

Three component parts of the system — the Federal Land Banks and Federal Land Bank Associations, Federal Intermediate Credit Banks and Production Credit Associations, and the Banks for Cooperatives — provide credit for rural homes, to producers and harvesters of aquatic products, and to associations of such producers.

The 12 Federal Land Banks may make loans with terms of from five to 40 years secured by the equivalency of first liens on real estate through more than 500 local Federal Land Bank Associations.

Loans may be made to farmers and ranchers, among other groups, for any agricultural purpose and for other requirements. Common purposes include the purchase of farms, farmland, equipment and livestock; refinancing existing mortgages, and paying other debts; constructing and repairing buildings and financing other farm, farm home, or family needs.

Rural residents may borrow from the land banks to build, buy, remodel, improve, refinance, or repair a rural home. Only sound loans can be made, and the amount of credit extended, based on credit worthiness of the applicant, cannot exceed 85 percent of the collateral taken as security. The land banks may make simultaneous loans with the Farmers Home Administration.

For those who devote only a part of their time to farming and supplement their farm income from other sources, loans are available to part-time farmers and rural landowners through local land bank associations.

These loans may be used for an agricultural purpose, including the purchase of land and construction or repair of buildings. Loans of this kind are made for long-term periods with repayment schedules geared to income.

Application for a land bank loan is made through the office of the Federal Land Bank Association serving the county in which the farmer is located. The applicant supplies information regarding his financial status, the purpose of the loan, and other pertinent data. Then the property is appraised and the credit worthiness of the borrower is checked.

The 12 Federal Intermediate Credit Banks provide loan funds to the local Production Credit Associations, with more than 1,500 offices, and discount the notes of eligible borrowers given to other institutions financing agricultural producers. The FICBs may also participate with the Production Credit Associations in making loans.

Production Credit Associations make loans with terms up to seven years to farmers and ranchers and others, and loans may be made for a variety of purposes related to the production of agricultural products, the purchase, repair or maintenance of rural homes, and for almost any farm or farm family requirement.

The total credit extended may not at any time exceed the value of assets devoted to agricultural or aquatic endeavors, and the total amount of credit extended home owners may not exceed 85 percent of the appraised value of the property. Production Credit Associations may participate with one another in making loans and may also participate with other institutions in financing agricultural producers, including commercial banks.

PCAs are owned by the farmers borrowing from them, and credit is provided by the 12 Federal Intermediate Credit Banks through sale of the banks' bonds to private investors. The first-time applicant for a PCA loan should contact the PCA in his county, discuss plans with a representative, and file a formal application with the PCA. He should determine how much money he will need and work out a repayment schedule and furnish a financial statement.

We mention the Banks for Cooperatives only as part of the Cooperative Farm Credit System. These 12 district Banks for Cooperatives make loans directly to eligible cooperatives. The Central Bank for Cooperatives participates with the district banks in loans which exceed their individual lending limits. These banks may also participate with one another and with other financing institutions in making loans. They do lend to individuals for purposes of buying homes or farms.

Fannie Mae — Although the Federal National Mortgage Association is not an institutional lender, a borrower, surely will want to understand its functions as they affect the availability of money for mortgages.

In an attempt to level off the peaks and valleys that occur in the supply of money for housing and home financing, the federal government developed Fannie Mae in 1938. In 1968, FNMA was converted to a private corporation, operating on its own funds and paying full federal corporate income taxes. The board of directors governing the corporation number 10 — five are elected by the shareholders and five are appointed by the President of the United States.

Fannie Mae puts money into the mortgage market when the supply of funds from other sources is limited, buying more mortgages when money is in short supply and buying fewer when more money is available.

This corporation borrows its funds in the capital market through the sale of short and long-term obligations. It is able to borrow at relatively favorable interest rates because it is a government-sponsored corporation and its securities are agency securities, even though neither the notes nor the debentures are guaranteed by the U.S. government. FNMA does have a line of credit with the government which enables the Secretary of the Treasury to buy up to $2.25 million of FNMA obligations if necessary.

FNMA also raises capital funds through the sale of stock and this is traded on the major U.S. exchanges. FNMA purchases acceptable FHA, VA, and conventional mortgages from lenders, including banks, savings and loan associations, mortgage companies, and other originators that qualify as eligible sellers and have executed an appropriate selling agreement with FNMA.

Providing commitments for mortgages up to $35,000 ($52,500 in Alaska and Hawaii), 95 percent of value, and 30-year terms, Fannie Mae seeks to help fund the housing needs of the nation in accord with its role as a private corporation with a public purpose. FNMA provides a continuous source of liquidity for mortgage investment for interim lenders, particularly in tight money markets, consequently, helping to smooth out the cycle in mortgage credit. It is the largest single private purchaser of residential mortgages in the United States.

Ginnie Mae — The Government National Mortgage Association, commonly known as GNMA or Ginnie Mae, has the authority to issue government-guaranteed mortgage-backed securities.

Mortgage lenders accumulate pools of FHA-insured and VA-guaranteed loans. GNMA guarantees these loans which in turn are guaranteed by the full faith and credit of the government.

In 1974, the basic GNMA mortgage limit was increased from the $22,000 limit in prior law to $33,000, with statutory language enabling $38,000 to be set as the limit in high-cost areas.

The federal government authorized GNMA, which began operations on February 19, 1970, in order to aid in leveling out the material supply of mortgage funds. The program allows for the sale of fractional interest in blocks of these mortgages to investors. These yields compare with high-grade corporate issues.

GNMA securities receive interest and principal payments on a monthly basis. The issuer can be any type of mortgage lender including a savings and loan, mortgage company, or bank. The originator is compensated by lending fees, servicing fees, and other benefits for his efforts.

MORTGAGES FOR DUPLEXES, TOWNHOUSES, CONDOMINIUMS, CO-OPS, AND VACATION HOMES

If a borrower is buying a house, a duplex, or a townhouse, he will probably use the mortgage channels discussed throughout this chapter. He will apply to the regular institutions and try to use FHA or VA programs if they are applicable.

The condominium, like the townhouse, is individually purchased and taxed, that is the owner must usually find his own financing, unless the developer is taking back the mortgage or arranging financing through an institution. Most often, however, the owner must seek a mortgage and he applies to the same lenders as does the prospective owner of a house.

Both FHA and VA are active in insuring mortgages for condominiums, and the lender to which he applies will determine if the projects and the borrower qualify for these insured mortgages.

The buyer of a cooperative apartment is actually purchasing stock in a building and the right to occupancy. In a co-op, a single mortgage is taken out on the entire building so the buyer must accept the terms of that mortgage. He also must invest a large down payment if the co-op into which he is buying is older and the mortgage has been paid down. The buyer cannot purchase his unit free and clear with cash, but he must take on the existing mortgage arrangement. When buying a co-op, it is best to check for loans with the sponsors of the co-op.

Often, the sponsor will make a loan of what amounts to a second mortgage to help the buyer meet his down payment. The corporation also may hold securities or other collateral for part of the down payment.

If a borrower is in the market for vacation home financing, he should ask the institutions in his permanent home area for references to banks or lenders in the area of his vacation property. The FHA can insure mortgages for seasonal or vacation homes and these need not meet the requirements of the regular FHA home programs.

One may buy a lot or acreage for a second home and after the land contract matures, the new owner will find that FHA financing is permitted for the A-frame or recreation house he wants to build. Provided a 25 percent down payment is made, FHA can insure a mortgage up to $18,000. It is not required that the borrower live in the mortgaged home for any specific part of the year.

To a limited extent, local savings institutions will lend money for second homes, though they are much less inclined to do so during times when there is a shortage of funds for primary housing loans. The terms are a maximum of $5,000 and for periods of ten years or less.

Lenders of *all* types are aware that in times of recession one of the first things a cash-short family can forgo is a vacation retreat home in the mountains or by the sea.

SPECIAL CONSIDERATIONS FOR BUYING A MOBILE HOME

There are a number of avenues for financing a mobile home open to a borrower.

Banks, savings and loan associations, company credit unions, and finance companies all make mobile home loans. There are also government-backed programs and conventional loans for a borrower to choose from.

For conventional loans, a down payment of 20 to 30 percent is usually required, and the mortgage term can be for as long as 10 years, with the average from five to seven years. Interest rates range from 11 to 15 percent and are usually computed by an add-on method, with the interest added to the principal amount of the loan when it is made and the interest cost remaining the same over the life of the loan.

Mobile homes loans insured by HUD are made by approved lending institutions. HUD insures qualified institutions against loss on loans made from their own funds to finance the purchase of mobile homes intended by the buyers as their principal residences.

A borrower who desires HUD backing must have sufficient funds to make a specified small down payment, must intend to use the mobile home as his principal home, and must have an acceptable site for it. This may be rented in a mobile home park or it may be owned by the borrower. This land must meet HUD standards, and there must be no violation of zoning or other regulations applicable to mobile homes.

The mobile home must also meet HUD construction requirements, be at least 10 feet wide and 40 feet long, and must be new, or if not, it must have been financed with a HUD-insured loan when it was new. The total price of the mobile home may include furnishings, appliances, and accessory items as well as transportation to the site where it will be occupied and the initial premium for mobile home insurance.

The maximum amount is $10,000 for single-unit mobile homes, $15,000 for double-width mobile homes (two or more units or modules) and the maximum term of the loan is 12 years for single units and 15 years for double-width homes.

Interest rates vary with the term and amount of the loan, and cash down payment is 5 percent up to $6,000, 10 percent on the amount if over $6,000. Loans are secured by conditional sales contracts or chattel mortgages on the mobile home. The HUD insurance premium is paid by the lender.

A borrower should apply at any HUD-FHA-approved lender, and there is no application fee for HUD-insured loans.

Eligible veterans can have their mobile homes financed with loans guaranteed by VA. The VA loans can cover both the mobile home and the land where it will be located. VA offices will provide full current details on loans of this kind. The 1974 Housing Act includes a new National Mobile Home Construction and Safety Standards Act, which protects buyers of such homes. The buyer should check these provisions with lenders.

Construction Loans — Construction loans for individuals vary with institutions and other lenders, but the basics offered here are common to most individual building loans.

Once a person has his land, either owned outright or held on mortgage, he will submit his building plans or sketches to the lender and a total cost will be decided for the loan project. The lender will pay out to the builder amounts at intervals as stages of the house construction are completed, or the contractor-owner may be issued funds to pay the contractor.

When the building is finished, the lender will make a permanent loan. Interest, of course, will have been charged on the monies paid in segments during the construction. Some lenders of building money will not make permanent loans so they must be obtained from a long-term lender such as a savings and loan or a mortgage banking firm.

Some builders and developers will arrange financing for the customer or will take back mortgages themselves. These points should be covered when one shops for a builder.

TRY SOME CREATIVE SHORTCUTS IN FINANCING PROPERTY

If one finds that none of the previously mentioned financing programs will work for him, he should not despair. There are other means of obtaining financing. In fact, he may have to start his search by-passing traditional methods and being creative, if he finds himself in a general market that is not yielding to buyers' needs.

The owner might agree to a lease of his property with an option to buy and some of the rent paid might be applied to a down payment or the purchase price of the home.

Arrangements might be worked out, too, for what is called a balloon mortgage, which means simply that the loan will not be paid in full in amortized payments but there will be a balance due at the end of the mortgage. This allows the buyer time to raise more funds, over a longer period, which, perhaps, he was not able to do when he applied for a loan. The lender feels quite certain that the loan may even be extended or renewed at the end of the mortgage term allowing the buyer to refinance for the cash due if he does not have it himself.

Wrap-around Mortgages In some situations, the owner might accept a wrap-around mortgage arrangement. The wrap-around mortgage is actually a long-term second or junior mortgage loan. The lender assumes responsibility of making payments under the first mortgage, and the new buyer pays the wrap-around. The mortgagor obligates himself under a debt instrument for the total amount of the first mortgage plus the sum lent to him by the wrap-around mortgagee.

The rate of interest on the wrap-around will be well above the prevailing rate in the current market. Interest is based on the sum of the balance under the first mortgage plus the amount advanced to him by the wrap-around mortgage. In some cases, no money is advanced, but terms are given the buyer which differ from the terms of the first mortgage. In any case, the borrower, makes his payments to the wrap-around mortgagee and does not deal with the original lender.

Purchase-and-Sale Agreement — The owner might also agree to a long-term purchase-and-sale agreement with an occupancy clause, allowing the prospective buyer to move into the property while the lender holds an approved application that is awaiting processing or funding by an institutional lender. Often, banks will tell the buyer and seller that monies will not be available for a certain period but the loan will be approved. The seller then receives his cash down payment and the buyer has a place to live on a temporary rental basis.

Trade — A buyer may also work a trade with an owner. Particularly in times of tight money, individuals who want to buy a dwelling may find that trading off some possession is the most economical way of achieving that goal. One may own a commercial lot, a farm, vacation acreage, even an expensive luxury car that may have trade possibilities for a home of some kind be it a mobile home, townhouse, or single-family home.

First one establishes the approximate value of his property and then offers the asset to the owner of the property he wants.

If he is not dealing with a specific owner but wants a home of some kind, he should advertise in the local newspaper or in the area where he hopes to purchase a residence.

In addition, he might want to contact his local real estate board for specialists in trading properties and work with realtors who probably have lists of clients looking for some kind of trade, too.

The buyer should think very creatively when considering a trade. He may wind up taking a mortgage for which he would need to involve a lender of some kind or he may decide on taking a mortgage himself and owning his home outright, if he trades down.

SPECIAL CONSIDERATIONS FOR THE INVESTOR IN SMALLER PROPERTIES

There are a number of ways a small investor can make money through wise investments in homes, condominiums, townhouses, and duplexes by using special financing techniques. Opportunities will vary based upon the rental market. The best opportunities can be found in a difficult market as well as in an easy financial environment. Some of the methods he can use are:

Buy, Remodel, Refinance, and Lease — Buy a home that has been abused. Put it in tip-top condition and seek a new mortgage. Sometimes such new mortgages will give an investor most of his investment back. He can rent the property and realize a continuing income.

Buy, Remodel, and Sell — Instead of keeping the property, he may decide to sell. In a tight money market he can make a nice profit since no one can get financing on homes, but demand is high. He can actually increase his sales price above the current market by taking a second mortgage thus giving himself a good income. If possible, write cost-of-living adjustment clauses into the second mortgage so that as inflation increases, interest income will also rise.

Buy, Rent, and Refinance Later — This is a good way for an investor to get his investment back. In times of inflation, real estate usually holds its value. If an investor buys a home, duplex, etc. now and leases it, chances are that later he can refinance the mortgage and get more than enough money back to pay for his original investment, plus he has earned income and will continue to receive it in the future.

To obtain mortgages on rental properties, the investor should use the same lending routes one uses for financing a home.

Other than equity, the advantage of investing in smaller rental properties is that an investor is providing himself with depreciation. Because his property grows older each year he can deduct a certain annual amount allowable by the government from his income tax, which means he gets to keep more of the income he receives.

When he re-sells the property at a profit, he receives capital gains. Capital gains are taxed at a much lower rate than funds he receives from income.

Here's an example of how depreciation allowances work for an investor. Suppose he buys a house for $50,000 and depreciates it over 30 years or at 3-1/3 percent a year (100 percent divided by 30). He estimates the building cost at $40,000, so his yearly deductible depreciation allowance is $1,332 ($40,000 times 3.33 percent). He may then use this deduction to his tax advantage.

He may also use interest charges on his mortgage as deductions against overall income.

REFINANCING PROPERTY

Many home owners and investors find that in good money markets they may be able to refinance properties they have held for a few years and get almost all of their cash investment back to reinvest in other projects.

For refinancing, the property owner will apply either at his current lending institution or at another that has funds and is willing to look favorably at refinancing his real estate.

In many cases, if he shops carefully, he can obtain a better rate of interest than was part of his original mortgage, with a longer period to run and lower mortgage payments.

Refinancing is an excellent way to make property more attractive to buyers, too, since they will probably be better able to meet a cash requirement under a new mortgage — the owner's equity is lowered in such cases, of course, and he requires less of a down payment.

For example, suppose he has a mortgage for $25,000 on his home, but real estate has shown sharp increases and now the home is worth $50,000. The bank is willing to write a new mortgage paying off the existing mortgage and giving the owner the net, after processing costs of $14,000.

If he decides to sell his home, the mortgage is placed, and the buyer will then simply have to come up with whatever the difference is between the mortgage and what the seller wants for the property. The buyer is saved closing costs and finding a mortgage. The seller could take some cash — if the asking price is high — and give the buyer a small second, increasing the seller's return on investment still further.

A LAST WORD

The mortgage money market, like any other facet of life, is ever changing. As we have stated before, the availability of money is always caught and carried along with the pendulum that swings between inflation and deflation and in between. It is clear that the mortgage market will continue to undergo many changes and take new turns in order to thrive and make home or dwelling ownership possible.

For many decades, we have consistently relied on patterns and variations of these patterns to finance our homes. It is apparent that future home ownership, or for that matter ownership of any real estate, will demand many innovations.

It is certain that we will face varying degrees of world-wide inflation for many years to come. We simply must learn to manage in such markets to achieve the financing that will lead us to ownership of property.

Tight money markets always tend to bring out man's most energetic spirit be he in the mortgage field or simply a consumer who wants to own his own home.

3. — Apartment Houses

AN OVERVIEW

With land in America rising in price and the costs of building and maintenance of single-family homes going up, there is a steady need for rental apartments.

Apartments will always be in demand. Singles usually rent, as do young marrieds, those with young children who are in transient positions or cannot afford to buy, older people who are retired or returning from suburbia, and perennial cliff dwellers who never buy houses.

If apartment houses should go out of style someday, the owner has the option of converting his units to condominiums or cooperatives.

The apartment house is not the type of investment that one moves swiftly in and out of or else he will not realize maximum profit and tax benefits. In general, an investor should plan to keep the apartment house for seven to 12 years unless he is a developer who builds, leases and takes a profit as soon as possible, and moves the cash into another building program.

Where does the beginning investor start in his apartment house ventures?

Like the rental house, duplex, or triplex, the small apartment house is an excellent first real estate investment.

One's risks are minimal in this kind of ownership. A buyer's or developer's own rent might be absorbed if he takes residence in the building, and he can offset maintenance and management costs by taking on those duties himself.

Vacancies are more easily filled in apartment houses than they are in other kinds of real estate, such as the shop or store, and empty apartments usually will not hurt an owner financially to the degree that unrented commercial property can.

Rent collections and maintenance can be more difficult in apartment houses than they are in other properties, but this can be overcome if an owner is a good manager or hires a competent resident manager.

The Best Buys — What are the best buys for those who want an apartment house investment? There are usually excellent opportunities to buy, remodel, and refinance old or abused apartment buildings, and they offer good tax benefits, income, and resale value. Banks and other institutions are usually willing to lend about 70 percent of the appraised value of an apartment house, although this is a fluctuating figure and can change from lender to lender. In good times a borrower may be able to obtain 90 or even 100 percent financing.

Of course, there are newer, thriving apartment houses which a buyer would not have to improve but simply buy and manage. He probably will not reap so great a profit on these when he sells, but his return on investments will be high.

While middle or high-rent units may appeal to one's pride of ownership, it should be remembered that in economic bad times these are poor investments.

The safest apartments to invest in are bread-and-butter types, those with relatively low rents that still show a good profit.

The basic investment rule for apartment house investments is to buy only those that show a healthy gross income and will yield a solid cash return, from eight to 20 percent. The cash-on-cash return varies according to the tax benefit which is inherent in any particular property.

ADVANTAGES OF CHOOSING AN EXISTING APARTMENT HOUSE

Unless one is patient, persistent, somewhat experienced or willing to learn through experience, and has a good financial position, buying an existing apartment house would be preferable to building one.

Consider in building that the new developer must find the land, get it rezoned in some cases, coordinate the loan with segments of construction, and then meet the hurdles of delayed, or lack of building materials, work that must be redone to satisfy inspectors, and possible construction workers' strikes — on top of everything he must lease the building.

Another disadvantage of building is that the developer is often unable to charge the kinds of rents he needs to make any substantial profit because building materials, labor and other costs have risen so drastically that they eat away his potential gains. Basically, on larger projects an owner can expect this kind of operating breakdown — 45 percent of gross for debt service or costs of loan, 35 percent for costs and 20 percent for profit and vacancies.

New apartment house projects will probably have to be viewed on the basis of their first 10 to 15 years with increased rentals and costs considered in order to justify investment.

If one plans to develop a new apartment house, he will face tenant demands for amenities of a type that has never been encountered before. In order to be competitive, he must offer all or some of these attractions — private meeting rooms, party areas, adult and children's pools, tennis courts, golf courses, gymnasiums, saunas, health centers, children's play areas, multi-parking spaces for tenants and guests, security, and on-the-premises medical aid.

Tenants will also be rating new buildings more keenly as to their units' living and entertaining areas, kitchens, storage space, variety of interiors, noise levels, natural light, services of janitors and cleaners, and good maintenance of buildings and grounds.

Look for tenants to demand convenience to doctors, dentists, churches, schools, libraries, recreational facilities, shopping centers, hospitals, transportation, and employment.

Steps to Take before Entering the Market — A prospective owner should look at the apartment house he wants to buy or build through the discerning eyes of an appraiser and in the same manner the lender will. They consider all of these factors:

(1) The stability of the neighborhood, including offerings of the environs, such as schools, churches and services, and the building's type and size in relation to the area's needs.

(2) The physical characteristics of the apartment house, such as materials and construction design, age, condition, square footage and layout of each unit, parking, equipment of the apartments, amenities and special facilities.

(3) What is the quality of the location if it is a proposed building? Is the apartment house the highest and best use of the land? Are all utilities available? Are there proper setbacks to allow lighting, privacy, and air? Will traffic, noise levels, and commercial activity adversely affect the tenants?

(4) What about sources of income besides rental units? These could include rental of garage and commercial space, fees for use of facilities, sale of gas and electricity.

(5) Rental history or a rental unit breakdown which is either figured on a per unit or room basis and compared with rentals in the neighborhood or by rental per square foot. For a planned building, projected rentals are based on comparable prices in the surrounding areas. On an existing complex, other neighborhood rentals must be comparable.

(6) Expenses to operate the building, covering all maintenance, taxes, insurance, management, replacement of equipment, allowances for increases in wages and real property taxes. Past years' expense reports should be studied carefully for these costs. Before buying or building, actual costs and estimates must be checked and rechecked for accuracy.

(7) Net income, out of which come the principal and interest and return on investment. The net income figure, compared with mortgage charges, shows the security of the loan. The lender's financial analyst or appraiser will use expenses, debt service, and income to find the break-even point for the apartment house.

In making an application for a mortgage, the borrower should include a feasibility study, a personal financial statement of the individual or company, and a pro-forma based on what the borrower feels the rents will be and how he plans to accomplish this or in the case of an acquisition, the owner's past two years' expenses and cash flow statement.

Conducting Marketing Research — The buyer should point out as many winning characteristics as he possibly can to encourage the lender to want to be the mortgagee. There are many consulting firms competent to make feasibility studies on larger projects where required.

The best advice one can follow before making a decision to buy or develop is actually to do a personal study — walk and drive around the neighborhood and ask tenants in other buildings what they pay for rent, find out about occupancy levels and factors that may affect vacancies such as seasonal declines or special employment factors in the vicinity, search for appealing features such as shopping or medical centers to be built, investigate growth expectancies, and offer any other data that will help build a case for a loan.

A borrower should make as full a presentation as possible and know his property so well that no question the lender asks will trip him up.

Tips for Seeking Long-term Financing — A borrower should realize when dealing in larger numbers of units that the lender is less interested in his ability to repay the loan, although the borrower's financials are reviewed. The lender is looking not for substantial income the borrower earns, but in the last analysis for rents coming from the property.

Mortgagees, both primary and secondary, for larger apartment houses seldom ask for the personal guarantee of the buyer, but a borrower should check to see if his mortgage deed or trust contains an exculpatory clause which absolves him of any personal liability in repayment of the loan. He should limit his personal liability to the down payment. If the lender will not grant the borrower this sole security clause, he can accept the risk or spread it out by taking on partners in the project.

All of the aforementioned factors are used to help determine the interest rate the borrower will pay on his loan. Interest will also be influenced by the availability of money, competition from lenders, other types of attractive investments open at the time, government policies affecting taxation on investment earnings, and the particular requirements of the lender involving his cash flow, security, and yield needs.

Most lenders of apartment house loans will spread them out over 20 to 30 years. The rate of amortization will depend on the age, location and condition of the building, and income or expected income.

Now, let's examine the various types of apartment houses and how they can be financed.

MONEY FOR THE SMALLER APARTMENT HOUSE

If a borrower is considering buying or building an apartment house of four to 100 units, he is looking at what is classified as a smaller project. The garden apartment house project can be in this range, too, but for purposes of this discussion, let's assume that garden types are larger.

Buyer's Cash Flow and Tax Benefits — In figuring out if a buyer can handle an apartment house mortgage of any kind, he should look carefully at cash flow. A buyer should not expect big cash flow advantages if the owner pays for management and maintenance. If the owner is responsible for both of these, the purchaser can expect a better cash flow.

As for tax benefits, an owner can depreciate the building, so the more units the better, and he can depreciate the furniture and other fixtures over a short period and obtain high depreciation allowances. His tax picture is even brighter if the mortgage is highly leveraged since interest rates are deductible.

Types of Loans — If one is buying a smaller apartment house, the loan will probably be made by the local savings and loan association, an insurance company, a commercial bank, a mutual savings bank, or an individual lender. These sources have all been active in financing smaller buildings. The most attractive feature is the low amount of money involved, and investors find they can frequently borrow with the property as security.

The Veterans Administration will insure mortgages on multi-family rental units with one veteran buying four units; two veterans, six units; three veterans, seven units and so on.

The Federal Housing Administration also will insure apartment house loans and provide financing for construction but sets up restrictions as to amounts of rents to be charged. FHA policies for financing new developments are reviewed in this chapter under construction loans. FHA can insure loans to finance improvements, repairs, and additions to multi-family rental projects financed with an FHA-insured mortgage with no refinancing required.

A borrower should ask his lender or mortgage broker about VA- and FHA-insured loans and financing and he will help him utilize these programs if the project qualifies.

The easiest way to buy an apartment house with a good mortgage already placed is to assume that mortgage, ask the owner to take a second, and put down as little cash as possible. If the owner says no to a second or similar agreement, a buyer can seek an individual secondary lender or ask the broker to take his commission as a second, in large monthly payments to run over a short term or in lump sums at a later time.

If the seller owns the building outright, the most economical way to buy it is to get him to take a purchase money mortgage. If this does not work, the buyer will have to get the project financed through the channels mentioned here. If he decides the project is too costly for him to handle alone, he might try a partnership in which two or three people will be joint venturers in providing equity funds for the acquisition. The title will be held in the names of all the partners.

The wrap-around mortgage might be the answer if the existing loan is already placed at a low interest rate, and it would not be feasible to refinance the entire mortgage. The buyer will obligate himself to the old mortgage, and a new mortgage will be wrapped around the first. Both the first and new mortgage are evidenced by a mortgage bond or note in the total amount and secured by a mortgage or deed of trust.

The buyer will pay the wrap-around mortgage as a total to include the amount of the original document and an added sum to amortize the advance and interest on the combined total outstanding.

As the mortgagee, the buyer has leverage over what is specified in the first agreement and still faces a lower cost over the mortgage term than he would have by refinancing.

MORTGAGES FOR THE GARDEN VARIETY

Typically, garden apartments are spread out with considerable open space surrounding them. They may range from one to four stories and have a horizontal look as opposed to the vertical lines of the high-rise development.

When one develops above four stories to six or so, he has what is known as the medium-rise, and here higher density is allowed. These apartment complexes command higher rents and, of course, are more expensive to operate since they require elevators and other services and amenities that the garden units do not.

Profits and Cash Flow — Cash flow for garden apartments is low when compared with that of high-rise apartments, large office buildings, or shopping centers but it will be stable, and this quality forces prices up for garden apartments. The rule is simply that the larger the project, the greater cash flow one can expect.

There are numerous advantages in owning the garden apartments such as relatively low operating costs as compared with those of the buildings offering a full range of amenities, opportunity for owners to manage the apartments, and a ready market for resale.

Garden apartments of all kinds are sought-after investments since the cost of land in relation to the cost of buildings is low and depreciation for taxes comes from the latter. The big profit often comes from proceeds of the eventual sale.

The owner can also realize substantial return on investment if he trades up, that is sells and moves on to a larger apartment complex or another bigger property.

How to Make the Purchase — Many apartment house sellers will take a low down payment, as little as five percent in some cases, and agree to a highly leveraged second mortgage.

Otherwise, a wrap-around or a balloon mortgage might be tried. There is always a chance, too, the broker might take his commission as a second since for this kind of sale commissions run high.

If a buyer must find mortgage money on his own, he should try insurance company home offices or regional headquarters near the project,
commercial banks — they have gotten into wrap-around mortgages —
savings and loans, mutual savings banks, pension funds, mortgage bankers
and brokers, and individuals.

Government-insured loans are available from the institutions, and
the government itself funds certain types of apartment projects for low
and moderate income housing and elderly groups. FHA, the Department
of Housing and Urban Development, and the Farmers Home Administration are quite involved in the development of housing projects.

The institutions do not as a rule provide secondary financing. Mortgage companies or individuals might be a borrower's best bet for a second.
The borrower will find in his search for money that as he moves up in
numbers of units, he will find fewer lenders with the kind of funds he will
need for financing, so he should consider alternate techniques as potential
routes to his destination.

Besides the partnership and joint venture, a buyer might explore
using participation or some form of syndication.

Participation — A borrower may decide on a participation mortgage
in which two or more people own portions or shares of a single mortgage.
The mortgage is made to a trustee who issues a certificate of ownership
to each principal. Sometimes one buys shares in a large mortgage or in a
group of smaller ones and thus spreads out his risk.

Syndication — If a buyer is investing in a number of apartment houses,
he may decide to take on a group of partners and form a syndicate, sometimes called a joint venture.

The syndicate is more sophisticated than a joint venture in that the
syndicate usually includes a real estate broker, a developer, an investor,
and another real estate specialist who will manage the properties of the
syndicate and the group itself. The person who puts the syndicate together
is the general partner and takes on the liability held by those in a regular
partnership. He may add capital or services or both, and he is compensated in some way by the syndicate.

Most syndicates and joint ventures pay no federal income taxes, but
the individual members do and depreciation losses go directly to the individual members on a pro-rata basis. Such a private syndicate is not subject
to the rules of the Securities and Exchange Commission if there are only a
few members of the syndicate.

SYNDICATION TYPES

A syndication can take any legal form that suits the parties involved
and their tax situations, the extent of liability they want to take, manage-

ment roles they want to assume, if any, and state and federal regulations they are willing to have control their transactions.

Basically, these instruments are used for syndications: — the general partnership, the limited partnership, the corporation, the real estate investment trust, the joint venture syndicate, and the co-partnership. Of these, only the first two are generally means to finance the garden-type apartments. The others are called on in financing for larger and more diversified real estate packages.

The General Partnership — This kind of group is formed simply by family members or friends who pool resources, usually in equal parts, to buy a building or land and share in operational profits and in resale gains.

The Limited Partnership — When a syndicate becomes a limited partnership, it usually falls under the regulation of the Securities and Exchange Commission or state rules, depending on the number of investors. Such a syndicate is composed of a general partner, who manages the group interests, and limited partners, who own interests but play passive roles. Duties of both the general and limited partners and their ranges of control should be spelled out in the syndicate agreement.

The general partner or syndicator is the person who brings the property and sponsors together. He may be of any occupation but most likely the general partner will be a real estate broker, an attorney, a developer, a securities broker, or even a company or a department of a financial institution. Above all, the syndicator should be highly reliable, experienced, and able to show an impressive and stable track record for these or similar types of investments.

The limited partnership is set up much like a mutual fund with its professional management, diversification, liquidity, and tax advantages. Partners are liable for business obligations held to a specific capital contribution. The partnership is not treated as a separate taxable entity, and losses are passed to partners in relationship to amounts of ownership.

Who should invest? In evaluating the syndicate as an investment it should be remembered that like any other form of real estate, ownership in the syndication is not quickly liquidated. The syndication of properties should be undertaken only by those with enough extra capital for a long-term investment, who are also equipped with staying power and ability to take a risk, and have faith in all members of the syndicate.

Overall, the investor should check many details about the particular syndicate's investment, asking about its economic soundness, financial resources available for the project, its ability to stand on its own, correctness of current income, and yardsticks used for projected profits.

The Terms of the Syndicate Agreement — These should be extremely explicit and understood by all members of the syndicate to avoid legal or other difficulties in operation and resale. Items such as responsibilities and payment of the manager, names and monies invested by each person, and corresponding profits should be obvious to all from the start.

It should be decided if the fund will hold one or more properties, if the syndicate will perish with the sale of original assets or will there be purchases of other real estate, how will liquidity be provided for, will there be various levels of interest in the partnership, will the properties be specified or will part of the syndicate funds be blank check or uncommitted at the onset.

As to the question of single versus multiple properties, it is important to consider that assembling diverse properties, such as garden-type apartments and shopping centers, in one partnership could mean that high-yield building profits might be watered down in the overall picture by a package that is not producing so favorably.

Also the individual investor can achieve diversity on his own by buying shares in a number of syndicates with different types of properties.

At the other side of the scale, the fund approach reduces the number of times the syndicator has to register with the SEC, property management can be systemized and costs reduced, lower cash reserves are required since all properties would not require the same amount of cash at the same time, and syndicators can appeal to a wider range of investors since more properties demand greater backing.

In structuring the partnership, it must be determined whether a specific property will be offered or whether the syndicator will raise funds and then find property. The difficulty with the former is in gaining control of the property and coordinating the fund raising.

Guidelines for Buying Properties — Syndicators should gather all data on proposed properties, single or multiple, covering:

(1) Tenants' economic levels, their lease renewal and cancellation rights, deposits on hand.

(2) Owner's responsibilities under the leases and any other data that will affect income.

(3) Expenses and operating costs, such as service agreements, equipment guarantees, a maintenance schedule and fees, payroll figures and factors that might bring decreases or increases in rents, how vacancies factors will affect cash flow.

(4) Schedule of rents, taxes, mortgage payments and mortgage history, special clauses in the mortgage agreement calling for balloons, rights of the mortgagee in case of fire or condemnation, taxes and tax considerations for the present and future, and building-to-land ratio for figuring depreciation.

Syndication Procedures — Here is a checklist of steps to be followed for arranging for the specified property syndicate after the garden apartments, for instance, have been found and evaluated:

(1) Structure the syndicate as to size since SEC requires registration of syndicates with more than 25 members, considering it after this figure a public offering. If the syndicator sells to residents of his own state, his offering will not have to have

SEC registration either, but he will have to meet state requirements. In defining the syndicate, it should be decided, too, what income groups and even which individuals will make up the syndicate.

(2) Get the property under purchase contract or option for as long as is thought necessary to raise funds through the partners.

(3) Arrange for primary and secondary financing and timing of payments to coincide with the flow of initial funds into the partnership account. Make sure cash reserves will cover unexpected expenses, closing costs, and first mortgage payments in case rents are not spaced to cover these at first.

(4) Contact the SEC or state agency for registration documents before the prospectus gets under way so that all data necessary for these agencies will be included.

(5) Write a highly detailed prospectus explaining the background of the syndicator, the project, regulations, risk factors, costs to the members, compensation for the syndicator, and all other information that a buyer will need to know. An attorney will need to help in preparing this material.

(6) Plan the marketing of the partnership either through an advertising agency or by an in-house marketing staff.

(7) Arrange for sale of shares through a firm specializing in this kind of investment or sell shares yourself as the syndicator.

(8) Deposit funds in a trust account, setting up bookkeeping on sales and ownership. Investors may make only one payment or cash may be spread over a longer period, depending on the particular tax requirements of the members. This should be determined in the syndicate agreement and offered as part of the sale.

(9) Close on and acquire the property and present certificates of limited partnership and certificates of interest to each partner.

The syndicator will then begin managing or contracting management of the property, reviewing rent rolls and internal and external conditions of the building, and making necessary appearance or operational changes in the building for overall improvement to increase rents and raise the value for resale.

The promoter or syndicator will keep all members informed of the financials and provide shares of profit periodically.

It is also the syndicator who negotiates for sale of the property and eventually dissolves the partnership and distributes profits if termination is the goal of the partnership.

If one property has not been selected and a fund is being sold, all of these steps are followed basically except that the property is selected after funds have been collected and documents are cleared.

Compensation for the Syndicator — Rewards for the syndicator are derived in a variety of ways, which the promoter himself establishes since he designs the deal. He may take his money on the front end in fees for managing the properties or as interest in the project or both.

Front-end money is a percentage of the funds raised or property yield, plus a reimbursement for expenses.

A manager may collect his fee from gross revenues or from a fee similar to a real estate commission — after all, he is performing a real estate buying function for the group.

The manager may take part in the deal without investing any of his own cash or he can invest as much as any other participant. He may also receive fees by acting as the provider of the second mortgage, holder of a wrap-around mortgage, as a lessee or lessor.

Here is an example of how a general partner might be active in a syndicate by adding no cash of his own:

Suppose the syndicator finds a multi-million-dollar garden apartment complex and $450,000 is required in cash. He creates 35 units to finance the project, but he keeps five and sells 30 at $15,000 each. The five that he holds back are his payment for syndicating and managing.

Another means of profit for him is to buy the property, resell it to the group of which he is part, and wait for his return of capital until profits from rents have accrued or the property is sold. By using this method, the syndicator gets his initial cash outlay back and shares in the profits as the general partner.

These financial arrangements would seem fair since the promoter forms the syndicate, finds the properties, supervises and coordinates building management and maintenance, and keeps all partners informed and paid for their share of income.

In structuring his profit role in the partnership, the manager must consider his tax situation. In assessing his income from the syndicate, the manager can take the same depreciation for taxes that any other shareholder does. Also for tax purposes, he can postpone his fees for services until the syndicate is terminated.

If the syndicator exchanges his services for property, then this interest is non-taxable. Partnership interest is regular income when it is taken for services to the syndicate.

HIGH-RISE AND LARGE APARTMENT COMPLEXES

When we look at projections for the future, high-rises become increasingly important as dwellings and work areas. By the year 2000, about 50 percent of the world's people will be living in metropolitan areas. National and state land use laws will limit the control of development. Federal and state laws are sure to control open land and require better utilization of developed land.

To meet the needs of the increasingly high densities, our landscape will become a megalopolis of high-rises that soar 100 or 200 stories. Megastructures, which will be self-contained cities, will offer residents places to live, to shop, to exercise, to attend school, and even to work, with populations running as high as 25,000 each. Understanding financing of high-rises as it functions today should serve as a base for raising funds for tomorrow's living centers.

Today's high-rise apartment houses are those towering edifices that seem to be cities unto themselves. They have become a way of life in many metropolitan areas of this country, especially where prices of desirable land have gotten out of sight. In such places, builders have had to increase density and the use of the land in order to justify their costs.

Buildings of this kind range from simply tall to mammoth, with some stopped only by the soaring funds required to build and maintain them.

Perhaps, the most distinguishing facet of the high-rise, except height, is the appeal of its amenities. Most high-rises offer a glamourous setting and a complete set of services including security, doormen, a switchboard operation, and complete beauty and exercise centers.

The high-rise owner must offer these and more to attract and keep the high-income tenants for whom such structures are built. There are high-rises built, of course, for low and moderate-income groups in big cities, but these are intended to house as many people as possible on minimum land, and bear a purpose far different from most high-rises.

In economic hard times, high-rise and expensive rental units may suffer. The rule of thumb is simple enough, the higher the rents, the fewer people on that economic rung.

Cash and Other Benefits — Since tenancies seem to be more stable in high-rises than in other apartment houses, the owner can realize a rather fixed cash flow.

Financing and terms of repayment must be considered, of course, in determining cash flow. These mortgages usually carry a smaller loan-to-value ratio, requiring more cash initially, and cash flow is not so attuned to changes in gross revenues.

Although the high-rise's ratio of building cost to land value is high, some of the resulting tax benefits are diminished because the newer high-rise will have a longer life span.

What is a good high-rise investment? Successful owners report that there are some basic guidelines to buying a winning high-rise. Those that can absorb rental increases are the best bets, and these are generally in areas that are older and established as well as in growth centers.

Light-colored buildings are more appealing than dark brick or buildings painted dark colors. Buildings that are situated on northerly or westerly streets leading out of the center of the city succeed over other locations. Buildings that have special eye appeal with fountains, gardens, or sculpture also do well.

Sources for Financing High-Rises — Financing for the larger projects is more difficult, and many times a group of lenders may participate in financing a single project. Here is a list of sources that finance high-rise complexes:

(1) Insurance Companies — These have become increasingly active in making large loans for high-rise and expansive apartment house projects and are excellent sources for such funding.

(2) Mutual Savings Banks — A few of these have funds vast enough to finance larger projects. It is best to check with those you have in mind before making application.

(3) Savings and Loans — These are regulated by the Federal Home Loan Bank which require that the maximum loan of a member be in proportion to the association's assets. This prohibits many S and L's from making larger loans. However, they often participate with one another in order to handle bigger loans.

(4) The Commercial Banks — Their limits are set by the size of loans in relation to their assets, and very few of these institutions can handle huge permanent loans. They are very active, however, in supplying short-term and construction money.

(5) Pension Funds — These groups have large sums of money to invest and are constantly looking for projects such as high-rises that show high cash flow and high rates of return.

(6) Individual Investors — Some individuals and groups of investors are always on the lookout for good investments and can make sizable loans.

(7) The Mortgage Banker — A few large mortgage bankers, those firms with funds of their own to invest, often take positions in or finance high-rises.

(8) The Real Estate Investment Trust — Some of these financial entities, which attract groups of small investors, have been formed solely to finance real estate through mortgages. Some specialize in apartment house developments.

Secondary Financing — Often for high-rise complexes, a second mortgage would logically come from the owner since most regular lending institutions are prohibited by law from making seconds. It is also possible to get second mortgage money through mortgage brokers or from mortgage bankers, usually on short term.

FORMS FINANCING CAN TAKE

The more a project costs in terms of dollars, the more sophisticated financing techniques have to become, and so we find in financing high-rises a variety of vehicles used to produce ownership.

Beyond outright purchase and mortgaging by an individual or a group of investors to form a simple partnership or joint venture, there is the syndicate, discussed earlier, the corporation, the trust, and equity financing.

Corporation — Often classified as another kind of syndicate, the corporation is as common as the partnership. The corporation, however, is much more formal than the simple partnership. Depending on the laws of the state, a corporation may be formed with the property in question as the principal asset for which stock is issued to raise money required for the purchase.

The life of the corporation can be perpetual, and if stockholders die, there is no interruption of the entity's continuity. Stockholders bear no personal liability for debts or obligations of the corporation. Only their interest or stock in the venture can be lost.

Stockholders are free of personal liability in case of accidents in the building, but if the building is owned by individuals their insurance will take care of any law suits, so the corporate advantage in such instances is questionable.

If an individual forms a corporation to buy certain property and to avoid certain liabilities, he may be required to sign as the co-maker with the corporation, so the lender should be checked as to its policies in these cases.

Perhaps, the major drawback to the corporate form is that individual property owners are allowed many tax exemptions which the corporation is not. Corporate taxes can include special income taxes, origination taxes to the state of incorporation, annual franchise taxes, stock transfer taxes, federal capital tax, and local property taxes.

As far as federal taxes go, these can be avoided by the payment of salaries to directors and officers of the corporation.

Often a lender in a large project will place a director on the board of the corporation it lends to in order to protect its own interest in the project.

An individual with enough capital to invest in and operate his project to benefit only himself and family does not really need the corporate structure, but those with great sums sometimes find the corporation useful for liability purposes.

The Trust — In this entity, ownership of the property is divided into two parts with the legal title taken in the name of the trustee for the benefit of beneficiaries who own the equitable title. The trustee is held liable for legal actions and is in charge of all operations, accounting, and payment of income to the beneficiaries. A trust deed or agreement holds such a form together legally. Certificates are issued for shares much like stock certificates.

The trust is in some ways preferable to a corporation since there is more permanent management — the corporation usually changes directors and officers more often — and the trust has more flexibility. Trusts are not held to the statutes that corporations are and are not generally taxed in the same way that corporations are unless the state deems that a trust is in fact a corporation and treats it that way.

Equity Financing — One way to entice institutions into lending money for purchasing and developing apartment houses is to offer them equity participation in the deal. In fact, many mortgage trusts and insurance companies insist on such involvement in times of tight money.

Those lenders asking for equity can be offered a fixed percentage of gross income, a larger percentage of adjusted gross income, leasebacks under which the lender shares in the net income, or an installment contract under which the borrower buys back the property and is entitled to the depreciation deductions.

LONG-TERM FINANCING

Most lenders prefer long-term mortgages on apartment buildings, usually 25 years for smaller buildings and 30 years for high-rises.

Evaluating properties for loans and processing them takes time and money, and lenders with large sums to invest must limit the frequency of their loan making. They are also better able to project their income over longer periods based on these mortgages.

Those loans insured by the Federal Housing Administration or the Farmers Home Administration for apartment houses may run in excess of 40 years.

Although most lenders usually have rather fixed maturities on apartment houses, there can be some room for negotiation.

Most lenders are limited to 75 percent of appraisal on apartment house mortgages, but the government-insured loan ratio may be as much as 100 percent. These ratios vary with the stability of the area, rent levels, and projected future of the project.

Interest rates are not usually so negotiable as other points involved in the mortgage transaction since the rate will depend on the money market and not so much on the project itself.

Second mortgages are usually for shorter periods, five, 10 or 15 years. Some secondary sources are more liberal, allowing up to 20 years for a second. The number of years will depend on the negotiating skills of the buyer, the lender's requirements, and the kind of building to be financed.

MORTGAGE AND LEASE INSURANCE

Sometimes mortgage insurance is used as an inducement to get lenders to participate in an investment. Insurance of this kind enables financing of major projects despite money conditions and high interest rates. It insures the lender against loss due to default on a wide variety of industrial and commercial properties. Apartment house developments figure prominently in this kind of insurance.

Companies that insure such loans include Commercial Loan Insurance Corporation (CLIC), a wholly-owned subsidiary of Mortgage Guarantee Insurance Corporation (MGIC).

TYPES OF AMORTIZATION

Apartment house mortgage payments are often made quarterly at a constant level. An equal amount is paid each quarter with interest computed on the declining principal balance and with amortization payments increasing.

As an example, if the borrowed amount is $300,000 for 20 years at 9 percent interest paid quarterly in advance, the quarterly payments including both principal and interest will be $7,942.50. This payment will remain constant throughout the life of the loan.

If the constant amortization payment is employed, a specified amount is paid in amortization at each quarter and interest is computed on the declining balance with quarterly payments decreasing.

To illustrate, using the same $300,000 as the borrowed amount for 20 years, the quarterly principal payments would be $3,750. This figure is obtained by dividing the total of 80 payments into the principal amount of $300,000.

The interest is computed by multiplying the 9 percent by the remaining principal balance which will be $6,750 on the first payment. The total first payment, therefore, is $10,500 and the amount of interest on subsequent payments will decrease.

STEPS IN APPLYING FOR THE LOAN

(1) Before getting involved in application procedures, the buyer should have completed all his homework which should include his financial statement, the apartment house income and expense reports for at least a year, all data about the apartment house itself including age, blueprints if available, aerial photos, photos of the exterior and interior, a feasibility study of the area, and any background information that might be available from the local press or magazines. In short, any material that will favorably influence the lender should be in the package.

(2) The selling broker or local realtors may know which lenders will consider the apartment house loan and which types of buildings they prefer. If not, phone queries should be made to the mortgage departments of institutions or other possible sources and the current interest rates and terms available should be recorded for analysis.

(3) One application at a time is the rule when asking for an apartment house loan. All pertinent data about the building mentioned earlier should be included with the application form. If the lender does not use the formal application form, a broker will supply one and a letter of application may be made.

Following through with the Lender — After the lender has had a chance to receive the proposal, the borrower should call or write to see if he wants any additional data. If he does, the applicant should act speedily in supplying the information needed.

If a no comes back, another application and packet of data should be sent out right away to the second lender on the borrower's list.

Negotiating the Loan — If the loan application is accepted on the first round, negotiations on the loans can be expected soon. The lender will tell the applicant the amount of the loan he is willing to make, the interest rate, maturity, and other details. This may be a counter offer, or it may be the best deal the lender is willing to make.

It is up to the broker or the buyer to negotiate what the lender has proposed and to reach certain compromises. Usually, after the negotiations have been completed and terms agreed on, the buyer is required to deposit a fee that will be a good faith deposit or cover appraisals and other front-end costs.

The loan's finalization is then up to the lender's finance committee.

The lender will then issue a commitment letter which pledges that it will make available funds agreed on. Sometimes this is subject to receiving a final appraisal. The letter is signed by the borrower and he is thus bound to the terms of the mortgage at this point. A closing is scheduled at the anticipated completion or rent-up date and essentially the financing transaction is complete.

THE CONSTRUCTION LOAN

Financing the construction of an apartment house is two-edged, and the approach depends on whether one uses conventional financing or the government-insured programs.

Conventional Method — Two forms of construction financing are available to builders and developers. They may obtain a loan secured by a mortgage or they may be given a line of credit by vendors and sub-contractors.

The types of conventional loans available for construction are:

(1) Straight Construction Loan — Lenders specializing in this kind of loan make funds available only for construction, and builders must seek permanent financing from other sources. It is advisable for the builder to get his permanent financing before firming up the construction loan.

(2) Straight Construction Loan with Builder Referral to the Lender — Under this arrangement, the lender will make a loan to the builder for a maximum of a year with the understanding that purchasers will be referred to the lender for permanent financing. Previously, the lender and the builder will have agreed on most of the terms of the mortgage. This agreement is not legally binding on either party, and the buyer may decide he wants to get his own financing.

(3) Construction and Permanent Loan Combination — Using this plan, the builder is both granted construction funds during the building and at the completion of the project has a permanent long-term mortgage under one loan agreement. The amortization schedule on the permanent mortgage does not begin until the building is finished and in some cases has met certain rental projections mutually agreed to by lender and developer.

This kind of financial arrangement is used both for apartment houses, office buildings, and other income-producing properties as well as for homes and residential developments.

Alternatives — There are other types of loans which may aid the builder or developer in his financing planning. These include:

(1) The Long-term Take-out Commitment for a First Mortgage — The lender under this plan agrees to place long-term financing when the building is completed and in some cases rented in varying percentages.

(2) Standby Commitment — A lender commits to a long-term mortgage but does not plan in reality to do so. He is giving the borrower a guarantee that he will provide long-term financing. These agreements are often made when interest rates are high and the borrower wants to wait it out for them to come down and needs this kind of commitment guarantee to obtain a short-term loan. A fee is paid the standby lender who is bound by this agreement. Some lenders actually have to go through with borrowing from the standby lender, but the rates are usually very high.

(3) Construction Loan without any Take-out — This arrangement can work when a developer has had successes and a lender has enough confidence in his project that he knows a long-term mortgage will be forthcoming. The take-out is granted by mortgage investment trusts, large finance companies, some diversified financing institutions, and mortgage bankers.

(4) Interim or Intermediate Take-out Commitments — These are similar to long-term take-outs except the term of the loan will be from three to seven years.

There are two instances when this arrangement can be applied — the developer expects a longer term rent-up schedule or if interest rates are high and are expected to drop.

(5) Personal Guarantee of the Individual Developer or Developing Corporation — This method is suggested when the borrower's collateral and financial strength are adequate. A construction lender will then provide the funds because he knows his investment is secure.

Sources for Construction Loans — The main lenders for construction loans are commercial banks, mortgage trusts, finance and credit companies.

The Land — If the developer has a substantial bit of cash for the apartment house venture, his first step is to find and finance the land. It is best to pick top-dollar land that will run about 20 percent of the total project cost.

A seller will often take a low down payment and agree to a long-term mortgage. In some cases, buyers have put down nothing or five to 10 percent if the buyer is paying a high enough price. The buyer will need to get subordination on the land or pay the seller off before building.

Most institutions will not lend money to builders unless the land is subordinated, that is, the loan on the land must be second to the loan on the construction and long-term mortgage. In case of foreclosure, the loan on the building would be satisfied first and the land mortgage second.

Sources for Apartment House Land Mortgages — Besides asking the owner of the property to take a mortgage, or including the land and building in one mortgage, the buyer can approach several lenders such as insurance companies and real estate investment trusts for the land mortgage.

Some real estate investment trusts specialize in making land sale leasebacks. Under such an arrangement, the trust will buy the land and offer the investor or developer a lease and subordinate the land lease to a first mortgage which is held by an institutional lender, usually an insurance company. The owner of the land might be approached with a similar type of leaseback.

The owner might lease the land to the builder or developer for a long term, ranging from 50 to 99 years. This lease, of course, would have to be subordinated to the construction of first mortgage.

The Land Contract — The buyer can obtain the land without any down payment on a land sales contract. The seller retains title but gives possession to the buyer, and the buyer continues to hold the property as long as he makes payments.

The seller can dispossess the buyer should he default on payments, and he can also sell the contract if he wants his cash out of the deal.

The land sales contract is most often held by an escrow agent who, when the final payment has been made, gives the title to the buyer, or if there is default, the agent delivers the title to the seller and he evicts the buyer. In many states, this is the common practice as opposed to giving fee title at the time a sale is consummated.

Stages of a Conventional Construction Mortgage — After the land has been tied down or acquired, it is time to begin formal steps for getting that conventional construction mortgage. These will include:

(1) Preparation of the application, which will include a leaflet describing the project, the neighborhood and its conveniences, architects' plans and specifications, an analysis of costs, projected rentals, appraised value of the land or its cost, the amount of the mortgage sought, and the applicant's financial statements. If the borrower is a group, information about the members and any other data will add support to the loan request.

(2) Study of the loan proposal by the lender encompasses a review of the applicant's credit and financial resources, appraisal of the site and plans, preparation of government forms if the applicant has asked for a VA guarantee commitment or FHA insurance and the government agency's response, the lender's committee approval or disapproval, which includes the amount it will loan, terms and conditions of the agreement with the buyer.

(3) If the developer wants to pre-sell the project subject to completion, he may need to offer the loan package to the buyer at which time the buyer may accept or decide he wants a government-insured loan rather than the conventional one offered by the lender. Often a builder or developer will pre-sell his project before or shortly after breaking ground. The buyer is then able to reap first-owner tax and other benefits.

(4) Processing of the loan by the lender to cover such steps as application for title insurance, obtaining the building contract signed by the applicant and the contractors, signing of the notes and mortgage or signature by the primary lender and mortgage recording.

Meanwhile, the buyer will sign the construction loan agreement covering the investment to be made by him, advances by the lender and other requirements for the construction phase, purchase fire and hazard insurance, sign pre-construction documents covering liens and other encumbrances on the property, and deposit construction funds with the lender for disbursement.

(5) Disbursing of a buyer's monies for the stages of construction in amounts that the lender and applicant have agreed to.

(6) Payment of construction loan funds by the lender during which time there are inspections of the construction progress, followed by advances, with the final payment made when there is proof there are no liens against the property. Unpaid expenses such as loan interest service charges and appraisal fees are subtracted from the final advance.

(7) After the building is completed, the builder or developer usually sells the building or pays the construction mortgage until the property is sold or his long-term loan is funded.

(8) The construction lender can aid the developer by:
   (a) Transferring the developer's mortgage to a buyer.
   (b) Refinancing a new loan for the buyer.
   (c) Holding the mortgage in its portfolio with the developer making periodic payments.
   (d) Servicing the loan for a primary lender.
   (e) Funding the buyer's long-term mortgage.
   (f) Selling the mortgage by discounting the original face amount of the loan. He could then service the loan for the buyer of the mortgage at a fee if the mortgage owner desired.

Coordinating the Construction Loan and the Long-term Financing — In expanding the steps relating to obtaining construction money, understand that it is usually after the permanent financing has been issued that the developer will look for a construction loan, unless the construction money will also come from the permanent lender.

Assembling building plans and pulling together the arrangements for mortgage financing can take from three to seven more months depending on the money market, the kind of project involved, and the caliber of professionals handling the mortgage financing.

The developer can hit another time snag if he plans to build on a site where a building stands, and the tenants' leases must run out or must be brought out. Sometimes, the developer runs into legal problems and expenses as a result of buying such land and must anticipate these costs as well as those for demolition, eviction, or buying out tenants.

The construction loan should be tied to the needs of the builder's subcontractors. Subcontractors do not always meet the needs of other subs and delivery of materials and completion of jobs fall behind schedule. There may be labor problems, bad weather, and other handicaps that will delay the job.

Because of these problems, interest, taxes, and other costs, the builder or developer should have liberal cash reserves even with construction loan financing. If not, he will probably run short of cash and have to make late payments to subcontractors.

The construction and the permanent financing lender will work together to coordinate the transition from short-term to long-term money, or the mortgage banker can provide this service. The point is that when the construction is finished and the contractors' money is due, the long-term lender will supply the developer with funds with which he pays the construction loan and then the long-term mortgage on that sum begins.

If the long-term lender specifies that the developer must have a certain occupancy level before the permanent loan begins, the lender may advance only a portion of the agreed-to mortgage until the occupancy levels are met.

As an example, if the loan is for $3 million, but the current rentals will not cover such a mortgage, the lender will advance only $2,250,000.

When occupancy meets projections, the lender will advance the loan holdback amount. This holdback along with percentages of rentals, where participations are involved, will be written into the original mortgage. When occupancy reaches 85 percent, for instance, then the other $750,000 will be advanced. The construction lender will usually work with the permanent lender in this kind of arrangement, taking his payback as the rent-up progresses.

Tieing loans to rental schedules is a way of pressuring the builder or developer to rent apartments speedily. Sometimes the developer will rent unwisely, taking lesser amounts than he should. Good financial backing is thus almost mandatory to the long-range financial success of the project.

Construction can take a year or two or longer, and it may take six months or more before the apartment house is rented up, so the developer's financial staying power is essential.

If the short-term lender wants all cash at completion of the project and the long-term lender enforces the holdback plan, then the developer must get a gap loan to cover the amount held back by the long-term lender.

Who will lend him this money? Sometimes the insurance company making the long-term loan, but it will be at higher rate than the permanent mortgage. Mortgage trusts, commercial banks and finance companies, mortgage bankers, and individuals also write this kind of loan.

Utilizing Government Insurance and Programs for Apartment House Construction — The federal government is heavily involved in real estate programs that provide rental housing in the form of multi-family projects for the elderly, low and moderate-income groups, rural residents, and members of the Armed Forces. Some of these programs follow:

Farmers Home Administration — This agency makes loans in rural areas to provide rental housing for persons with low or moderate incomes and for persons 62 or older. Rural areas include open country and communities not closely associated with urban areas.

The term, rural, was expanded by the Housing and Community Development Act of 1974 to include areas with a population in excess of 10,000 but less than 20,000, and not contained within a Statistical Metropolitan Sample Area and which has a serious lack of mortgage credit as determined by the Secretary of Agriculture and the Secretary of HUD.

Loans are made primarily to build apartment-style housing, usually consisting of duplexes, garden-type, or similar multi-unit dwellings. The housing must be modest in size, design, and cost and adequate to meet tenants' needs.

Rent charges must be within the limits that eligible tenants can afford. Borrowers are required to deposit rental income in special accounts and set up reserve funds to meet long-term capital replacement needs. Limited profit borrowers are allowed a six percent return on their initial investment in the project.

Anyone with the ability and experience to operate a rental housing project is eligible. Loans are made to individuals, trusts, associations, partnerships, and profit and nonprofit organizations. A nonprofit corporation may be organized on a regional or multi-county basis.

Borrowers must provide rental occupancy to eligible individuals or families. They must be unable to finance the project with personal resources and unable to obtain credit from other sources on conditions and terms which would permit them to rent units to eligible families. If the borrower is a profit-oriented group, assets of the individual members will be considered in determining whether other credit is available.

The repayment period may run as long as 50 years, and applicants will be limited to $750,000 per project, but they may obtain loans to build more than one project if the need for the housing is clearly shown. All applicants must provide initial operating capital to equal at least two percent of the cost of the project.

Loans to nonprofit organizations can be up to 100 percent of the appraised value of the development cost, whichever is less. Loans to all others are limited to not more than 95 percent of the appraised value or development cost, whichever is less.

When the financial position of the borrower reaches the point where he can repay or refinance through a commercial lender, the loan contract provides that he will do so.

Applicants must provide detailed plans, specifications, and cost estimates. The borrower provides architectural services which will include inspections during construction. The Farmers Home Administration will review plans and inspect construction as it progresses.

A builder-applicant may obtain a loan under the same conditions as any other borrower and be permitted a contractor's fee which is typical for the area.

All borrowers are encouraged to get interim construction funds from local lenders, and a borrower must show that local construction funds are not available before the agency will provide such funds.

The Farmers Home Administration requires that a builder must wait until the loan is closed and authorization given by the FHA to start building. If interim financing is used, construction will begin only after the loan is approved and funds obligated.

The local county supervisor of the Farmers Home Administration will provide data on how to complete and file applications. Applicants must furnish complete financial information, preliminary plans, specifications and estimated cost, a budget of anticipated income and expenses, and survey information supporting the need for housing in the area.

There are no fees for appraisals or loan processing, but the applicant pays for legal services necessary to guarantee that he has satisfactory title to the site and for other incidental loan closing costs. These expenses may be included as part of the loan.

Each loan must be adequately secured to protect the government's interest, and usually a first mortgage will be taken on the building and site. A tie-in or second mortgage will be required as security in the case of a subsequent loan to improve or extend a project at the same location.

Applications should be made at the Farmers Home Administration county office serving the area in which the housing is located. The Farmers Home Administration can be contacted directly at its headquarters at the U.S. Department of Agriculture, Washington, D.C. 20250.

Federal Housing Administration — First, it should be realized that under FHA-insured financing there are restrictions on the amount of rents to be charged. On the other hand, under FHA the lender is protected and can accept smaller down payments. FHA also limits the interest rate and other charges, and it must determine as far as possible that the transaction is sound. FHA may adjust the interest ceiling according to the market conditions for money.

Apartment house developers may utilize various FHA programs for insured mortgages on multi-family rental projects, housing for members of the Armed Services, and housing for the elderly.

Major HUD, FHA Sections for Multi-unit Developers — The following are specifics of programs under the National Housing Act that may be utilized by apartment builders, developers and operators. Many of the changes noted have been affected by the Housing and Community Development Act of 1974:

(1) Housing for the Elderly — The Secretary of HUD is directed to consult with the Secretary of Health, Education, and Welfare to insure that special projects for the elderly or handicapped authorized pursuant to the public housing statute meet acceptable design standards, provide quality services and management, contain such related facilities as may be necessary to accomodate special needs of

intended occupants, and are in support of and supported by applicable state and area plans.

The new act revises the Section 202 direct loan program for housing for the elderly and handicapped. Major changes include:

(a) Loans made at a rate equal to the Treasury borrowing rate plus adequate allowances for administrative costs and probably losses.

(b) Eligibility for occupancy is expanded to include developmentally-disabled individuals.

(c) Directions to the Secretary to seek to assure that housing and related facilities assisted under the program are in support of, and supported by, applicable state and local plans responding to federal requirements for provision of an assured range of necessary services for occupants.

(d) Authority for the Secretary to issue notes for purchase by the Secretary of Treasury in the aggregate amount of $800 million.

(e) Limiting lending to aid in development of 202 projects in any fiscal year to the limits on such lending authority established for such year in appropriation acts.

(f) Requiring the Secretary to consider the availability of assistance under the Section 8 program when determining Section 202 project feasibility.

(g) Requiring the Secretary to assure that projects aided under both Section 202 and the Section 8 program serve both low and moderate-income families in a mix appropriate for the area and viable project operation.

Under Section 231, FHA is authorized to insure mortgages on rental housing projects of eight or more living units for persons 62 or over.

(2) Rental Housing — Eight or More Family Units — Section 207 provides for FHA insurance of mortgages, including advances made during construction, on new or rehabilitated rental projects of eight or more units. The amount of the mortgage may not exceed any of specified limitations. The mortgage must have a maturity satisfactory to the FHA Commissioner, and the mortgagor is required to certify that in selecting tenants he will not discriminate against families with children.

Mortgages given to finance specified types of permanent housing owned by the Government and sold to the public, covering five or more units, may be insured under Section 207.

Projects can be built for about three percent equity if the builder will leave in the seven percent profit and overhead which the FHA allows. Builders are permitted to take the three percent equity out of the project in three years instead of having to lock it in for the life of the FHA loan.

FHA Section 207 loan is 90 percent of face value which includes overhead, and a profit of seven percent. Loans for eight or more units may run to as long as 40 years.

Ceiling rents to produce a net income of 93 percent occupancy are set by FHA, and the formula yields return of about 11 percent on equity.

In order to qualify for the FHA insurance program, the apartment venture project must be located on real estate held in fee simple, on a leasehold for not fewer than 99 years or having 75 years to run from the date the mortgage begins or on leasehold for 50 years provided the lessor is a government agency, an Indian or an Indian tribe.

(3) Replacement and Rehabilitation Housing — Section 220 provides for mortgage insurance to assist in financing the rehabilitation of existing salvagable housing and the replacement of slums with new housing in areas certified to the FHA by the Housing and Home Finance Administrator as eligible. It also provides for FHA insurance for home improvement loans. The Federal National Mortgage Association may make construction advances under this program.

One advantage provided by Section 220 is that it enables the sponsor to obtain mortgage financing in a locality not otherwise favored by mortgage lenders. The mortgage amount is generally high enough to leave the sponsor with a fairly small cash equity investment. Where regular lending institutions are not interested or in a tight money market when the institutions are not lending at FHA interest rates, FNMA can be approached to provide the mortgage financing under its program of advance commitments.

The procedure to follow is first to obtain the mortgage insurance commitment from FHA and arrange with a commercial bank for the mortgage loan. The bank will get a commitment from FNMA to buy the mortgage at a discount. The sponsor will not be able to mortgage out but he may be able to come close to it.

(4) Insurance of Low-cost and Rehabilitation Housing — Section 221 authorizes the FHA to insure mortgages on low-cost housing for sale or rent to low and moderate-income families and families displaced from urban renewal areas or as a result of governmental action.

The mortgage may have a term of 40 years.

The section also covers construction or rehabilitation of multi-family rental or cooperative housing.

If the mortgagor is a nonprofit organization, the mortgage may equal 100 percent of value or 90 percent for profit mortgagors. The maximum mortgage maturity is the lessor of 40 years or three-fourths of the remaining life of the property.

Under the 1974 Housing and Community Development Act, mortgage limits are increased about 20 percent for the lower income non-subsidized Section 221(d) (2) program and the per unit mortgage limits are increased also by about 20 percent for Section 221(d) (3).

Public housing agencies were also made eligible mortgagors of projects for which mortgages are insured under Section 221(d) (3). Interest on such a mortgage is taxable.

(5) Experimental Housing — Section 233 provides FHA insurance for housing using advanced technology or experimental neighborhood design, deemed significant in reducing cost or improving quality. Factory-built units may be included.

(6) Military Housing Insurance — Title VIII authorizes insurance of mortgages on housing built on or near military reservations for the use of personnel of the Armed Forces on certification by the Secretary of Defense, and homes built for sale to civilians employed at military research and development installations.

(7) Housing Assistance for Low-income Families — The Housing and Urban Development Act of 1968 provided for two programs to help lower income families buy homes (FHA Section 235) and rent apartments (FHA Section 236). Both programs are made possible by monthly payments made by the government to the mortgagee. These payments reduce the home owner's or apartment renter's costs.

The per unit mortgage limits are upped about 20 percent for Section 236 dealing with multi-family lower income subsidy rental programs under the 1974 act.

Under Section 236, under the provisions of the Housing Law added in 1969, surplus federal lands can be leased or purchased below market value for low or moderate income housing and the purchase may be financed through FHA-insured mortgages. Another provision of 236 and 235 permits federal S and L's to join in the National Corporation for Housing Partnerships. Here's how this agency works: Projects get 90 percent financing through FHA-insured mortgages. The partnership puts up 25 percent of the equity and private investors who join in the partnership supply the remaining 75 percent and get the tax advantages of their share of depreciation allowances, interest deductions, etc.

The 1974 legislation also amended 236 to provide:

(A) Additional assistance for tenants who cannot pay the basic subsidized rental charge with 25 percent of their income (i.e., rents for 20 percent of the units may be reduced to as little as the cost of utilities of the units).

(B) Authority for increased subsidies to meet higher operating costs resulting from increased taxes or utility costs.

(C) A requirement that at least 20 percent of funds be allocated to projects for elderly or handicapped.

(D) A requirement that at least 10 percent of funds be used for rehabilitation projects.

(E) Provision for reducing tenant contributions toward rent from 25 percent of income to as low as 20 percent where utilities are billed separately.

(F) Income limits set at 80 percent of median income for area.

(G) Removal of 10 percent project limitation on number of non-elderly single persons who may be subsidized.

(H) Authority for HUD to contract with state or local agencies to monitor the management of assisted projects.

One of the advantages of the 236 program is that a limited-dividend sponsor can sell the project to a nonprofit organization or a cooperative. The new owner can, in turn, obtain a new FHA-insured mortgage under 236 to cover the purchase price.

This has not been possible in the past under other FHA multi-family programs. This should encourage large-scale participation in the program by private enterprise since it provides a means by which a profit-motivated sponsor can dispose of his property. The profit-motivated sponsor can sell if his capital needs dictate or after the tax benefits derived from accelerated depreciation have run out.

A 236 project can be sold at 100 percent of financing so that the sponsor gets back his equity plus amortization. Under this program, a limited-dividend sponsor can also manage the project without there being a conflict of interest. Small builders are encouraged to participate in the project in that the bonding requirements for projects costing $250,000 is waived.

Other Programs — The Emergency Home Finance Act should be checked by builders of apartments.

One of the provisions pertains to reduced interest rate for low and middle-income housing and is applicable to apartment houses.

Co-insurance Demonstration Program — A new FHA co-insurance authority was established in 1974 and contains the following major features:

(1) Usage and Liability — Use is optional with lenders, who must assume at least 10 percent of any loss, subject to a limitation on overall liability for catastrophic losses.

(2) Expiration of Authority — June 30, 1977.

(3) Limits on Use — The aggregate principal amount of co-insured mortgages and loans may not exceed 20 percent of the aggregate dollar amount of all home mortgages insured and 20 percent of the aggregate dollar amount of all multifamily mortgages insured.

(4) Sharing of Premiums — The sharing of premiums between HUD and lenders is required to be on an actuarially sound basis.

(5) Consumer Protections — Construction under the demonstration program must be inspected to ascertain whether minimum standards applicable under the regular program are met. HUD must consult with the mortgage lending industry to determine that the demonstration does not disrupt the mortgage market or make 100 percent mortgage insurance unavailable to those who need it. HUD may not withdraw, deny, or delay insurance under other programs because of the availability of co-insurance.

(6) Reports — HUD is required to report annually, describing the results of co-insurance experiments and presenting recommendations.

A LOOK AT THE 1974 PUBLIC HOUSING AMENDMENTS

Any developer desirous of federal assistance for apartment houses should be completely familiar with new rulings within the Housing and Community Development Act of 1974.

The new measure revises the law governing the low-rent public housing program, eliminating some provisions and altering others, provides additional annual contributions contract authority, and authorizes a new lower-income housing assistance program under the revised law. Among the many changes from prior law are the following:

Eligibility and Occupancy — The measure continues the provision authorizing public housing agencies to fix, subject to approval by the Secretary, income limits for occupancy and rents in traditional public housing.

However, it deletes the requirements for a gap of at least 20 percent between the highest income limits for admission and the lowest unassisted rents and income limits for continued occupancy in projects.

Definition of Income — Family income is redefined. For families in units assisted under the new lower-income housing assistance program, income is defined as total family income. For families in regular public housing, income, for purposes of the Brooke I limitation, continues to be adjusted in accordance with a statutorily prescribed formula which has been revised by eliminating double deductions for secondary wage earner spouses, clarifying deductions for dependents, eliminating deductions for heads of households or their spouses, and adding a deduction for foster child care payments made to a family.

Definition of Family — The law makes eligible for occupancy two or more single elderly, disabled, or handicapped individuals living together, or one or more such individuals living with another person determined essential to their well-being.

Minimum Rents — A requirement is added under which every family in regular public housing is required, regardless of the size of its income, to contribute at least five percent of its gross income to rent. If the family receives a welfare payment a part of which is specifically designated for housing, the family's minimum rent is to be the higher of five percent of gross income or the amount so designated. However, increased rents for public housing tenants required as a result of amendments effected by the statutory revisions — other than the welfare payment provision — are to be phased in at a rate of not more than $5 every six months.

For families in the new program, the lowest possible contribution to rent is to be 15 percent of total family income, with the Secretary authorized to establish a higher required contribution level (up to 25 percent of total family income) for certain classes of families (see below).

Also, the aggregate minimum rental required to be paid in any year by families in any project administered by a public housing agency receiving operating subsidies is to be an amount at least equal to 20 percent of the sum of the incomes of all such families.

Management Practices — Public housing agencies are to be required to establish tenant selection criteria to assure an income mix in projects (but waiting for higher income tenants where lower income tenants are available is not to be permitted), procedures for prompt rent payments and evictions for nonpayment, effective tenant-management relationships to assure tenant safety and adequate project maintenance and viable home ownership opportunities.

Also, at least 20 percent of families in any project placed under annual contributions in any fiscal year beginning after the effective date of the requirement are required to have incomes not in excess of 50 percent of area median income.

Homeownership — Homeownership for public housing tenant families will be facilitated by authorizing the sale of projects to tenants (and the purchase and resale to tenants of structures under Section 8) and the continuation of up to debt service annual contributions with respect to units sold to tenants.

Lower-income Housing Assistance Program — The law authorized a new lower-income housing assistance program to replace existing authority for assistance with respect to low-income housing in private accomodations (Section 23). Major features of the new program (contained in Section 8 of the proposed revised U.S. Housing Act of 1937) are as follows:

(1) Assistance will be provided on behalf of eligible families occupying new, substantially rehabilitated, or existing rental units through assistance payments contracts with owners (who may be private owners, cooperative, or public housing agencies, which are broadly defined to include agencies assisting in the development or operation of low-income housing as well as those directly engaged in such activities).

(2) Eligible families are those who, at the time of initial renting of units, have total annual family incomes not in excess of 80 percent of area median income, with adjustments for smaller and larger families, but the Secretary of Housing and Urban Development may establish higher or lower income ceilings if he finds such variations necessary because of prevailing levels of construction costs, unusually high or low family incomes, or other factors.

(3) Major responsibility for program administration is vested in the Secretary of Housing and Urban Development, who can contract directly with owners or prospective owners that may be public housing agencies who agree to construct or substantially rehabilitate housing. In the case of existing units, public housing agencies will contract with owners, except that the Secretary may do so directly where no public housing agency has been organized or where he determines a public housing agency is unable to implement the program.

(4) Assistance payments contracts will specify the maximum monthly rent which may be charged for each assisted unit. Maximum rents may not exceed by more than 10 percent a fair market rent established by the Secretary periodically, but not less than annually, for existing or newly constructed rental units or various sizes and types suitable for occupancy by eligible families, except that maximum rents may exceed fair market rents by up to 20 percent where the Secretary determines that special circumstances warrant or that such higher rents are necessary to implement an approved housing assistance plan. Fair market rent schedules will be published for comment prior to being implemented by publication in the final form in the Federal Register.

(5) The amount of assistance provided with respect to a unit will be an amount equal to the difference between the established maximum rent for the unit and the occupant family's required contribution to rent.

(6) Aided families will be required to contribute not less than 15 percent, nor more than 25 percent, of their total family income to rent, with the Secretary authorized to establish required contribution levels, taking into consideration the family's income, the number of minor children in the household and the extent of medical or other unusual expenses incurred by the family, however, the required contribution level will be statutorily fixed at 15 percent of total income for very large families with total incomes of between 50 and 80 percent of area median income, large

families with total incomes not over 50 percent of area median income, and families with exceptional medical or other expenses.

(7) At least 30 percent of the families assisted with annual contract authority allocations must be families with gross incomes not in excess of 50 percent of area median income, subject to adjustment by the Secretary.

(8) Maximum rent levels will be adjusted annually or more frequently to reflect changes in fair market rentals established for the area for similar sizes and types of dwelling units or, if the Secretary determines, on the basis of a reasonable formula. Also, the Secretary will make additional adjustments to the extent he determines such adjustments are necessary to reflect increases in the actual and necessary expenses of owning and maintaining the units which have resulted from substantial general increases in real property taxes, utility rates, or similar costs which are not adequately compensated for by the annual adjustments. However, rent adjustments may not result in material differences between rents for assisted and comparable unassisted units.

(9) Up to 100 percent of the units in a structure may be assisted, upon application of the owner or prospective owner, but in cases involving projects containing more than 50 units which are designed for use primarily by non-elderly and non-handicapped persons, the Secretary may give preference to projects involving not more than 20 percent assisted units.

(10) Assistance payments for any unit may run for a minimum period of one month and for the following maximum periods. In the case of existing units, payments may be made for as long as 180 months. In the case of new or substantially rehabilitated units, payments may be made for up to 240 months (except that if the project is owned by, or financed by a loan or loan guarantee from, a state or local agency, payments may run for as long as 480 months).

(11) Owners of new or substantially rehabilitated assisted units will assume all ownership, management and maintenance responsibilities including the selection of tenants and the termination of tenancy, but the owner may contract for such services with any entity including a public housing agency approved by the Secretary for the performance of such responsibilities.

Owners of existing units also will select tenants, but selections are to be subject to annual contributions contract requirements, and public housing agencies will have the sole right to give notice to vacate, although owners will have the right to make representations to the agency. Also, maintenance and replacement with respect to existing units will be in accordance with standard practice for the building concerned and the owner and the public housing agency may carry out other terms and conditions upon mutual agreement.

(12) Assistance may be continued with respect to unoccupied units, but only for up to 60 days if a family vacates before its lease is up or where a good faith effort is being made to fill an unoccupied unit.

(13) The Secretary is directed to take such steps as may be necessary to assure that assistance payments are increased on a timely basis to cover increases in maximum monthly rents or decreases in family incomes. Such steps are to include the making of assistance payments contracts in excess of the amounts required at the time of the initial renting of units, the reservation of annual contributions authority to amend housing assistance contracts, or the allocation of part of new authorizations to amend such contracts.

(14) Newly constructed or substantially rehabilitated dwelling units to be assisted under the program are to be eligible for mortgage insurance under FHA programs; and assistance with respect to such units may not be withheld or made

subject to preferences because of the availability for such units of mortgage insurance on a co-insurance basis or by reason of the tax exempt status of the bonds or other obligations to be used to finance such construction or rehabilitation.

(15) Assistance is to be available with respect to units in cooperatives (occupancy charges are to be deemed to be rent for purposes of making assistance payments and in accordance with regulations of the Secretary, some or all of the units in a section 202 project for the elderly or handicapped).

(16) Davis-Bacon Act labor standards requirements will apply to new construction or substantial rehabilitation projects containing nine or more units.

Other provisions permit local housing authority bonds with flexible maturities and balloon payments to finance public housing projects and prohibit HUD from applying new administrative policies to projects in derogation of rights of an owner under a lease entered into prior to establishment of the policy.

Allocation of Housing Subsidies — The measure provides a mechanism for disbursement of housing assistance funds:

(1) Urban-rural Split — At least 20 percent but not more than 25 percent of funds go to non-metropolitan areas.

(2) Basic Allocation Criteria — HUD will allocate funds on the basis of objective criteria — population, poverty, housing conditions and vacancies — modified as necessary to fulfill approved local housing assistance plans submitted as part of community development application or otherwise.

(3) Local Approval — Localities with approved housing assistance plans will review applications for consistency with plan. HUD may disregard a local objection and approve the applications, if the Secretary finds that the application is consistent with the housing plan. Local approval will not be required where an application involves:

(a) Twelve or fewer units in a single project or development.
(b) Housing in approved new communities where HUD determines such housing is necessary to meet new community housing requirements or
(c) Housing financed by state loans or guarantees except if the local housing assistance plan contains an objection to their exemption. Where there is no local plan, HUD must consider any state plan.

HOW TO APPLY FOR AN FHA-INSURED LOAN

Under the Housing and Community Development Act of 1974, FHA and HUD aim at speeding up the approval process to 30 days. This can, however, take much longer. The borrower is advised to seek the aid of a qualified FHA-approved lender in obtaining a loan.

This is a procedural guide a borrower can use in preparing his project for approval and acceptance by FHA:

(1) Application — The approved lender or FHA will provide the borrower with a current application. These are lengthy and detailed and should be filled out with meticulous accuracy. They should be signed by all required parties.

(2) Exhibits — The application will require exhibits which should be prepared and signed as requested. Addresses, legal descriptions, lot sizes, easements and encumbrances should be included.

(3) Plans and Specifications — All plans, specs, and other drawings should be complete and have proper signatures.
   (a) Plans and specs should be relative to the materials and construction methods which are used.
   (b) If plans and specs show optional items, the application must indicate which alternatives apply.
   (c) Details of critical points of the construction and unusual combinations of materials must be described.
   (d) Plot plans must comply with the FHA Minimum Property Standards. The architect should run a double check on these ratios before the submittal is made.
   (e) Adequate allocation must be made for exterior storage.

(4) Reference — The proper section of the National Housing Act should be mentioned. A developer can lose valuable time if he applies for the wrong section. The proper number of copies should also be submitted.

(5) Special Calculations — The heat loss calculations required in all applications should be complete and accurate.

(6) Feasibility and/or Appraisal — A feasibility study and appraisal prepared by an independent and respected consultant who has experience with FHA procedures is extremely helpful.

Often it will be necessary for a borrower to request an increase in an existing loan commitment from FHA or a change in materials used. He will submit a change application and in so doing should again review items noted previously. In addition, he should:

(1) Include supporting data relative to changes in the recent marketplace such as recent sales of comparable properties.

(2) Double check the change request form for signatures and accuracy of material requested. This is Form 2577.

(3) Include and double check Form 2005 describing the changes, including descriptions of materials, and enclose applicable drawings.

FHA BONDING REQUIREMENTS

FHA must be assured that once a project is started it will be completed. Henceforth, the developer must provide a personal indemnity agreement or performance bond. Insurance and bond companies provide this service. As an exception, a cash deposit of the amount set by the FHA or a letter of credit will be accepted. Local statutory requirements also accept projects in California, Florida, Louisiana, and Texas where the states have their own bond requirements.

If the FHA estimate of the project is $200,000 or less, no corporate surety bond is required provided the personal indemnity agreement is executed by the principals. Rehabilitation projects of 11 units or fewer are not bound to this requirement either unless more than two such projects by the same person are under way at the same time.

Bonding requirements for different type FHA projects are:

For a walk-up garden-type, where estimated costs to build are $2 million or less, 10 percent performance bond and a 10 percent prepayment bond. Over $2 million, a 25 percent performance bond and a 25 percent payment bond are required.

For a high-rise elevator type — 50 percent performance bond and 50 percent payment bond must be provided.

The cash deposit or irrevocable letter of credit amounting to one-half of the performance bond, or 10 percent of the estimated cost, whichever is more, will be accepted instead of the bonds.

TURNKEY HOUSING

The turnkey program was established to provide housing to the lowest income groups including those on welfare and relief, the ill, the indigent, and the retired whose incomes are low enough to make them eligible for public housing.

The builder of such housing turns over a completely finished project to a local housing authority which now usually leases the property.

Nothing is left for the authority to do but turn the key, and thus the terminology. Prior to the 1974 act, it was more customary for the authority to actually buy the project.

Under turnkey, private developers may initiate a housing program by naking proposals to a local housing authority or by responding to a local authority's request for proposals. A Local Housing Authority will not select a developer until there has been a public advertisement to offer all developers the chance to bid. The housing authority and the HUD regional office evaluate the proposals on the basis of site, design, price, and the developer's background and standing.

The winning bidder receives a contract which is supported by HUD financial assistance to an LHA through which the LHA agrees to lease the development for a specified rent once the project is fully completed according to the approved plans.

After the project is leased by LHA, it can be managed by LHA or its agent, which may be from private industry.

Turnkey processing involves an accelerated program. The developer may prepare a complete package, including working drawings and specifications when he is the selected developer. There is no letter of intent or feasibility conference and all processing such as detailing plans are condensed.

HUD's financial commitment to the LHA and to the developer backs up the lease and assures the lender that if the LHA fails to meet obligations of the contract, HUD will take over the project.

4. — Condominium and Cooperative Projects and Individual Units

HISTORY OF AND DIFFERENCES BETWEEN THE CONDOMINIUM AND COOPERATIVES

The cooperative ownership of apartments thrived for many years in England and the Scandinavian countries before gaining attention in the United States in the 1920's. This form of ownership enjoyed popularity here until over-financing and abuse by developers and individual owners gave cooperatives a bad name.

After World War II, cooperative financing again came to the forefront and is prominent today because of the high cost of land. Rising land prices often make rental units uneconomical and there is a growing trend for individual ownership of dwelling units. Co-ops offer income tax and equity advantages that rentals do not. Location of these units is usually central to many services and some amenities are within the complexes.

Cooperative ownership takes the trust or corporate form which creates cooperative apartments, or the individual form, which sets the framework for condominium apartments.

In the corporate structure, shares are divided in relation to the value or sales price of the property and allocated to each of the apartment units with size and location of the apartment determining the assessment of each unit.

The corporation holds the title and the owner's occupancy rights to his apartment are set forth in a long-term proprietary lease. Costs of operation, taxes, and debt service are established against the owner's shares. The owners elect officers, usually with one vote per party regardless of size of the unit, and the building is operated according to majority rule. A manager, or firm, is usually hired by the corporation to handle the day-to-day concerns of the tenants and building.

In the trust co-op form the title is transferred to a trust company, and this firm issues a certificate of beneficial interest to each owner. Shares may be divided equally, one share per unit — or according to the value of each apartment.

Under the equal shares plan, each owner has a lease at the full rental value for his unit as determined by appraisal. Dividends can come from operational savings, and these are discounted against monthly bills for rent. If shares vary, operational charges are assessed on a pro-rata basis.

Individual trustees, who are separate from the trust holding title, are responsible for management and are advised by a tenant-owner appointed management group.

The cooperative participant has a dual role. He is both tenant and owner. As far as ownership is concerned, he is participant in the investment syndicate and as for tenancy, he is the same as an average tenant of a rental apartment. He has rights and responsibilities for each position.

As an owner, he has the right to share in profits from operations of the property but usually these are operational charges established on costs and if all cooperators agree to sell the project, then he may make a profit. If he sells individually, he should offer the unit to the corporation first and then to the public.

As a tenant, he contracts to rent at a certain rate which includes operating expenses and some money for reserve.

The condominium concept has found widespread acceptance here and abroad, and the Department of Housing and Urban Development expects one-half the population to live in condominiums in the next 20 years.

This form offers complete unit ownership and ownership in common with the other owners of the facilities and grounds, including landscaping, parking, maintenance, lobby, utilities, pool, and other amenities. The facilities can be good profit centers for the developer should he choose to retain management and ownership of these amenities. There have been developer abuses in this area with some investors selling off these corporations to those who do not meet obligations to the owners. A developer should check carefully into all laws pertaining to the operation and sale of these entities in his state.

Since condos and co-ops are a way of life today, and there have been some questionable procedures in their development and operation, the federal government has an investigation underway on problems, difficulties, and abuses and potential abuses, and its report to Congress will underlie expected legislation.

The individual owner can own his unit outright and sell it, rent it, or finance it independently as he would a single-family home. Taxes are levied on single units, and owners pay maintenance and other expenses assessed by an owner association.

There are a number of other differences in the cooperative and the condominium apartment house projects. For instance in financing, one mortgage is taken out on the entire cooperative building and buyers must accept this loan agreement. A buyer of an older co-op must accept the mortgage already placed and sometimes make a substantial cash outlay since the original mortgage has amortized considerably. A buyer cannot buy the apartment outright either but must agree to take the existing mortgage arrangement.

Because the condominium has an overall mortgage and individual owners have their own, they have a great deal of flexibility in doing with the unit what they wish in terms of selling or leasing.

There are usually no restrictions on the sale or lease of the condominium units, but other owners do want to know that only responsible, financially able people become buyers. In some cases, prior approval by the association is required as well as first refusal of sale.

Condominium buyers looking for mortgages either apply to local lending institutions that may be referred by the developer of the project or have the developer provide the long-term mortgage he already has committed.

Institutions have varying rules on loan-to-value ratios. Loans may range from 70 percent to 95 percent of value or asking price.

Property tax liability may be lower for both condo and co-op owners because the tax liability on the land is spread among many owners. The condominium owner can deduct the mortgage interest from his income tax returns since he pays them both directly. The co-op owner can deduct his proportionate share of the cooperatives interest and taxes. If more than 20 percent of the co-op's income is derived from other than stockholder leases, the co-op can lose its tax status, and the owners also lose. Sources of income may include stores, shops, or leased amenities in the co-op building.

Risk factors vary, too. The condo owner is responsible for his mortgages, taxes, and assessments and does lose by default of others in his building. The owner is liable for maintenance costs as long as he owns the unit and his liability may be forced by legal action if he abandons the unit or claims he is not using the common elements.

Should the co-op shareholder fail to meet his obligations, other stock owners must make up for his shortages. In this case, the other tenants may evict the defaulting tenant and resell his unit. Ultimately, it is the corporation that is liable on the mortgage debt.

THE CONDOMINIUM AS A PROJECT

The condominium dates back to the ancient Romans and the term is French in origin. A condominium is a statutory system of ownership in fee simple of separate units in multi-unit structures in which elements are held in common.

The concept is concerned with the division of real estate into horizontal layers. This stands in contrast to the theory of vertical ownership of real estate from the center of earth upward towards infinity.

The condominium venture can take many physical forms. It can be a high-rise, a single-family detached house project, garden units, townhouses, or converted apartments of any size.

Uses of the condominium have extended beyond the residential realm, and the condo arrangement is applied to office buildings, resort projects, and even to shopping centers with merchants owning their own shops.

Before the developer proceeds with the condominium project either by building or converting, he should be keenly aware of the law pertaining to this form of real property ownership, and he should know that such a complex requires involved legal documents spelling out all facets of the project and owner's rights and duties.

The developer must register and file a prospectus with the Securities and Exchange Commission if he intends to remain a part of the operation, renting units for owners while they are away.

Special condominium legislation may be needed in areas where there is none. The jurisdiction must recognize the division of ownership on a condominium basis, the state must permit instruments that record mortgage on condominium units, and taxes must be assessed separately according to individual unit values.

Documents Needed — The three basic condominium instruments are the declaration of condominium, the bylaws, and the deed. Here is a brief explanation of these documents:

(1) Declaration of Condominium — This is the basic legal instrument of the project and describes in great detail everything about it, including descriptions of what the units consist of, common elements, percentage of ownership and common expenses, the association, maintenance and repairs, assessments, interest liability, destruction, reconstruction and insurance, transfer of lease or occupation of unit, right of institutional first mortgages, termination, and amendments.

(2) Bylaws — This document sets forth the government of the condominium and spells out rules for operation along with member meetings, voting rights, officers, director, and fiscal management and procedural details.

(3) Deed to Individual Units — Fee titles are given owners for their units and warranty deeds are presented for undivided interest in the common areas.

Building a Condominium — It is best, if at all possible, to have the same lender do both the construction loan and the permanent financing since moving from one to the other can create problems.

Consider that the construction lender usually will not subordinate his loan to permanent financing so the units must be released as they are sold from the construction loan and then made subject to the new first mortgage.

Some lenders will agree to this plan to reduce their loans, and others will not since they object to the selling time that may be involved and they want to control the whole project until enough units have been sold to pay off the entire loan. The developer should work this out in his master plan and come to some amiable agreement with the short-term lender.

Most lenders will want provisions incorporated into the bylaws that will protect their security interest, requiring freedom from restrictions on resale of units it may foreclose, insisting on reserves for replacements, maintenance, and working capital, and voting on critical issues. These provisions may also be a part of the mortgage so that a breach would mean a default and the lender could take legal action.

Figuring out Construction Costs — In estimating the value of the property for construction loan purposes, total the value of the pre-sold apartment units ready for delivery to the owners and the unsold units as it they were sold.

Putting this formula into figures, it may look this way:

Assume there are 300 units to be sold, and a market survey indicates an average per-unit sales price of $37,000 each. Some have been pre-sold and some have not. The total value of the project if sold out would be $11,100,000.

The construction lender agrees to loan 75 percent of $11,100,000 which equals $8,325,000.

FINANCING THE CONDOMINIUM

There are two phases in condominium financing. The first involves the short-term mortgage for the developer who builds or rehabilitates a structure to be sold as a condominium, and the second is long-term financing for the individual owners.

As each apartment is sold and cash is put down, the unit is financed and the developer is paid. He in turn pays the construction lender, taking out his profit in so doing.

Amenities are figured into the whole construction loan, and prices of apartments reflect these costs as well as the construction of the unit itself.

Sources for the Developer — The developer can call on savings and loans, mortgage trusts, insurance companies, some finance companies, and mutual savings banks for short-term construction loans for condominiums.

Active in the short-term loan market for conversions have been real estate investment trusts, some commercial banks, savings and loans, and mortgage trusts.

Life insurance companies, some savings and loan's and mortgage bankers have been offering construction and end-loan financing so that the developer has only one source to deal with.

Some mortgage companies and other financial institutions will warehouse long-term loans and resell them in the secondary market. Lenders will be looking for sound credit, good loan-to value ratio, a certain percentage of units sold, common areas mostly wrapped up, and funds in escrow to assure the completion of the project.

Under Section 234 of the National Housing Act, FHA-insured mortgages are available for individual units. FHA will not insure a single unit, however, until the construction is finished and 80 percent of the units are sold to FHA-approved buyers.

Authorization under this section extends to leasehold as well as fee simple interests. It prescribes the FHA requirements, inspections and appraisals for both new buildings and rehabilitated structures. This amendment to the National Housing Act was aimed at making high-ratio mortgage financing possible for purchasers of condominium apartments and, hence, to make construction of these projects feasible for middle and low-income groups.

To qualify for mortgage insurance under this program, the project must consist of five units. The project's units may be detached or semi-detached. They may be row houses or multi-family structures, walk-up or elevator type and may include commercial space.

Eligible mortgagors are individuals, partnerships, corporations, or other HUD-approved legal entities.

SELECTING THE BEST LENDER FOR THE PROJECT

The best lender probably will be one who has made mortgages before in the condominium field. He is familiar with all requirements, risks, and procedures. He is also one who will work with the borrower if he is a novice in this field.

Rates, loan-to-value ratios, terms, and other offerings by various lenders should be reviewed carefully by the borrower.

It is simplest to arrange for conventional construction loans. The conventional vehicle is used by developers who cannot comply with the FHA policy. Even if a blanket FHA mortgage is planned under Section 234, it's wise to have a standby commitment for conventional permanent financing.

The condo developer usually pays more for his construction financing than the homebuilder and is often required to have a takeout as a condition of the construction.

Before institutional lenders can offer mortgages on condominium projects, they must have statutory authority to do so. The developer should check any laws in his state and locale that may affect the lender's capabilities for such mortgages.

Usually, state laws require that the lien against each unit for its share of common expenses is subordinate to the first mortgage and taxes. Otherwise, lenders might not be willing or able to finance a unit on which the owners' association held a lien for unpaid expenses by a former owner.

Preparation of the Proposal — For both short-term and long-term loans, there are certain materials required. These should include financial

88   CONDOMINIUM AND COOPERATIVE PROJECTS

projections, total cost breakdowns as well as amounts of the specific units and expense for land and for site improvements such as bringing in sewer lines and utilities, leveling land, landscaping, paving parking lots, and building amenities such as pools, tennis courts, and health care facilities.

Plans and specifications of the building, a city map locating the project, aerial photos pinpointing the site and surrounding areas, on-site photos, and an appraisal of the project upon completion should also be submitted.

Some consulting firms will do both the appraisals and the feasibility study for the developer or he may do his own.

The lender will supply the developer with an application which usually includes a list of the supplementary material needed. An application fee is usually required upon submission.

If applying for an FHA-insured loan, the developer can obtain FHA Form No. 3201 to cover Section 234, as well as other types of loans, from his lender and FHA Form No. 3280-A which is a schedule for 234 (c) and other sections. The lender or the FHA will inform the borrower of any other documents needed for FHA purposes.

Transacting the Loan — Once an application is submitted it is important that a borrower follow through with the lenders on a weekly basis in order to keep appraised of the progress of his loan.

In two weeks to one month, the lender should be able to give the developer a yes or no. If the answer is yes, the lender will issue a letter of commitment to include the following:

(1) The total amount the institution plans to commit to individual units for long-term loans.
(2) A loan amount limit for each of the individual units.
(3) A loan amount for an average unit.
(4) Requirements that each individual borrower must meet to buy a unit.

Finalizing the Loan — With the commitment letter in hand, the developer approaches short-term lenders and based on this letter, plans, and financials, he is able to obtain necessary financing for the construction.

All through these steps, there will be give-and-take negotiations between lender and borrower to arrive at the most beneficial terms for both parties.

If the developer is using the FHA programs, he will work with the lender, supplying all materials required and will follow the same pattern of making plans for construction money as he would for conventional financing.

Arranging for Individual Purchase of Units — The developer will normally get his commitment for permanent financing first. This is for the benefit of buyers who may use such financing for an individual mortgage.

If projects are smaller or built in times of easy money, the construction loan may be made without a permanent mortgage takeout. This can leave buyers on their own to arrange financing. Developers of smaller projects can own the building free and clear and take back mortgages from individual buyers.

SETTING UP AMENITY FEES AND FINANCES
FOR MAINTENANCE FACILITIES

In a condominium project, preparation must be made for organizing and administering necessary amenities and their upkeep. Either the owners, the developer, or an outside agent must be responsible for these services.

In what has been termed the pure condominium, the owners who are members of the association have authority over all finances and maintenance costs, excluding taxes which are individually assessed.

Often the association will hire a manager and he will be paid out of the regular fees assessed members. Another way to handle management is to have the developer form a corporation which undertakes all direction, maintenance, and operations of amenities. However, this method is frowned on in many states. It does allow the developer a profit center which he may choose to sell. The corporation may subcontract for maintenance and other services.

Fees for maintenance and amenities are prorated per apartment, and the corporation builds in its own profit for its services.

If there are commercial amenities such as shops, these may be sold as condos rather than paid for by assessments, or retained by the developer and made a part of his corporation.

THE LEASEHOLD CONDOMINIUM

In states that permit, condominiums may be built on leased land. There are advantages in leasing land for the developer and unit buyer.

For the developer, this arrangement can provide more leverage, and for the owner, it can mean a lower overall price and down payment and greater depreciation since the building is the total base for depreciation for tax purposes.

There are two types of leasehold plans for the condominium accepting a leasehold, which is leasing the land from the existing landowner or creating a leasehold, whereby the developer will buy or otherwise own the land. He then sells it and leases it back obtaining subordination which will enable him to put up his building.

The latter allows the developer to finance 100 percent of his land cost and if the land is worth more when he conducts the sale leaseback then it was when he originally bought it, he will obtain considerably more.

As an example, assume Mr. Smith wants to develop a condo which will cost $1 million. His land cost is $200,000 and his building estimate is $800,000. Normally, a 75 percent first mortgage would give the developer $750,000 and the developer would have to come up with $250,000 cash. If he gives a sale leaseback on the land for 100 percent financing on this portion of the project he will receive $200,000 on the subordinated land lease and get a 75 percent loan on the $800,000 building for $600,000. This gives him a total leverage of $800,000 and he has to come up with $200,000 cash.

Now, let's suppose Developer Smith has owned the land for some time and his original purchase price was $50,000. When he decides to build, the value has increased substantially to the $200,000 figure on which he bases the price and his land sale leaseback.

In this example, the developer will have only $50,000 in the project. Let's say that when all the condos units are sold, they will bring a total purchase price of $1,300,000. In this case, Mr. Smith will have financed his entire project for $50,000 cash and will have made $250,000 profit for his effort.

When a developer accepts a leasehold, it is usually a case in which the condo developer is not able to buy the land and land leasing is the only way to obtain the property he wants.

When a land lease is part of a condo project, the developer can pass on the rent to unit owners in a number of ways.

The most common method is to have the developer on the project retain the master project lease, and as units are sold, each purchaser receives a partial assignment of the master lease. It is also possible for the developer to retain the master lease and sub-ground lease, perhaps at an increased rental, to the buyers of the condo units.

The master lease could be terminated at the end of construction and separate leases substituted for each individual unit. Then new leases would pass on from the fee owner to the new purchasers of the units.

Using another method, the master lease can be terminated, and individual unit leases created which go from the developer to the fee owner. As units are sold, the developer then assigns the unit leases to the respective purchasers of the individual units.

THE CONDOMINIUM AS A RESIDENCE

Applying for a New Mortgage — If the developer has already arranged for long-term mortgages for the buyers, the prospective owner will not have to shop for a mortgage unless he thinks he can get better terms with lower cash down.

If he does, then he inquires of local sources that make loans on condos. Usually these are the same sources used by homebuyers — the savings and loans, mutual savings banks, mortgage bankers, commercial banks, and some individuals. The buyer can get a junior mortgage from an individual, a mortgage company, or, in some cases, a finance company.

FHA and VA loans are also available for individual condo units. Condo housing is also made possible for rural residents by the government under provisions of the Community Development Act of 1974. The Secretary of Agriculture is authorized to make and insure loans to low- and moderate-income persons and families to cover a one-family dwelling unit in a condominium located in rural areas.

The Secretary also is authorized to make or insure blanket loans to a borrower who certifies that upon completion of a multi-family housing project, (1) each family unit will be eligible for a loan or insurance and (2) each dwelling unit will be sold only on a condominium basis and sold only to purchasers eligible for a loan or insurance.

If the condominium buyer is purchasing an already built and owned unit, he simply arranges for a down payment with the owner and assumes his mortgage. In some cases, the owner may take a second mortgage. He can also apply to the institutions for refinancing just as he would in buying a home.

THE COOPERATIVE AS A COMPLEX

Financing the Project — Loans for co-ops may be financed conventionally or through FHA-insured loans. Institutional lenders make loans for co-ops and the FHA also insures mortgages through Section 213 of Title II of the National Housing Act.

If the developer is building a co-op, he will apply the same analysis to this project that he would to any condo property, as far as mortgage financing goes. There are, however, numerous other stages that the co-op must undergo before completion. The sponsor must form the corporation, find land, prepare a financial analysis, gather construction estimates, arrange for short and long-term financing, and sell the co-op to the potential tenants-owners.

Since organizational procedures are stumbling blocks to such ventures, they are often taken on by builders or promotional organizations that build and sell stock and thereafter remove themselves from the project with their profit.

In setting the price on the amount of the mortgage that will be placed on the co-op when it is taken over by the corporation, the builder or sponsor must establish a price per unit, which carries with it a certain number of shares, and at the same time prorate that unit's share of the maintenance charges.

Usually a rental schedule is prepared and values are placed on each apartment. This serves as a basis for assigning stock value.

Operating expenses, real estate taxes, mortgage interest and amortization, cash reserves, and increases should all be included in the loan data for the sale of the shares.

The developer should decide to arrange for long-term financing first and then get his construction loan, paying the latter off by the sale of the units. He may, however, choose to get a short-term loan first and then arrange for permanent financing. He may also want to stay involved in the project as a manager or head of a management group.

Fortunately for the real estate investor, the hazards to the tenant-owner of a cooperative apartment seem minimal during a booming prosperity. There might, however, come a time of general financial trouble when some tenant-owners would have to default, and getting another share-holder could be difficult. In such times, each tenant remaining in the project has to assume his share of the cost of the vacant apartments.

When planning a co-op, the chances are the promoter will work with other investors rather than do it alone. Others can make their investments in cash or in necessary services. It is not unusual to have an architect or a lawyer provide professional services in return for future profits. Nor is it unusual for the owner of the land to become a partner. The investor in a cooperative is called the sponsor.

A sponsor can contract to erect the building and later convey the property to the apartment-house corporation. He arranges for temporary construction financing and a permanent mortgage well in advance of actual building. The site must be acquired or optioned. Since the amount of cash the sponsor receives from selling stock in the apartment-house corporation is predetermined, he can accurately estimate his profits before the co-op becomes incorporated.

The cooperative apartment sponsor is in the admirable position of being able to get a return on his investment in a relatively short time. He starts selling stock to participants as soon as the plan of organization is consummated. Unlike conventional apartment houses, equity isn't tied up until the property is sold.

Buying Shares as a Resident — The larger the loan on a first mortgage, the less money tenant shareholders will have to be charged for the purchase of stock. A second mortgage may sometimes be advisable to reduce the purchase price of stock. Of course, the interest and amortization charges of all mortgages become part of the apartment house corporation's annual expenses and will affect the size of carrying charges that the tenant-shareholders have to pay.

FHA can insure cooperative apartments. The borrower will have to satisfy FHA that the mortgaged property will be free and clear of all liens other than the insured mortgage, that the payments required by the mortgage bear a proper relation to his present and anticipated income and expense, and that he has a satisfactory credit standing.

Investors are also entitled to FHA financing through Section 213 of the National Housing Act for up to 90 percent of the projects replacement cost.

Leasehold Cooperative — Sponsors of co-op apartment houses frequently have their deals fall through because the owner of well-located desirable land is unwilling to sell. One increasingly popular solution to this problem is the leasehold cooperative. The cooperative corporation takes a long-term ground lease (75 to 99 years), paying an annual rental for the land and relinquishing title to the building at the termination of the lease.

At first, prospective co-op tenants may object to giving up the title. This initial reaction can often be overcome by stating the advantages of the leasehold cooperative. The down payment is lower. The land is not included in the purchase price and so there's less front-end cost to the tenant.

Also, tenant-owners have no real reason to worry about losing possession of their property in 75 or 99 years. After 75 or more years, the present buyers and their children will be dead, and the building will probably be torn down.

It must be pointed out that a tenant-stockholder pays a lower down payment when the land is leased, but his carrying charges will be higher because of the ground rent. The landowner may insist on provisions for an increased rental as the value of the land rises. This can be done in one of several ways — the ground lease can run for a relatively short term — for example, 21 years with a renewal option at a figure either fixed in the original lease or tied to the market value of the land at renewal.

Planning Commercial Space — To qualify for tax advantages, Section 216 of the Internal Revenue Code requires that 80 percent of the corporation's gross income must be derived from tenant-stockholders in the year in which the tenants want to deduct their share of the real estate taxes and mortgage interest. The remaining 20 percent may come from any source, but it is not advisable to use the full 20 percent exemption as a matter of course. Several stockholders, or even one, could default in payment of carrying charges and then outside income would exceed the limit.

Outright leasing of commercial space is not the only way to get outside income for the corporation. New York City, for example, has a number of cooperative apartment-hotels that earn extra income from the dining rooms, functions in public rooms and, in some cases, rooms set aside for transients.

Sources for Co-op Financing — Mutual savings banks, large New York based insurance companies, and mortgage banking houses are the best source for funds for the developers or sponsor of co-ops.

5. —— Office Buildings

A GENERAL DISCUSSION AND EXPLANATION

Millions of Americans spend a great part of their lives in office buildings, whether single-story suburban cubes or huge glass giants set aloft in the clouds.

Raising funds to create or buy these structures can be as varied as the buildings themselves. This chapter is designed to provide a simplified guide to some financing techniques that have made thousands of offices possible.

The history of the American office building is unique. When our cities were founded, these small buildings were located in the heart of town. In the boom years of the 1920's, office buildings grew multi-story in city centers. These structures were built throughout the country with easy credit acquired by two types of investors, the speculator-developer and the user.

These office buildings were soon over supplied, and during the depression vacancies caused by bankruptcies were everywhere. This turn of events might well serve as a lesson in caution to the investor, today, who is considering an office building or construction of any kind.

It was not until almost 25 years after the depression that a better economy and population increases caught up with the overbuilding of 1920's.

Even in a cyclical economy, the need for office space, prompted by a society built on paperwork and managed by white-collar workers, has spurred the addition of hundreds of thousands of office buildings of all sizes for both private enterprise and government at all levels. Not only is there a greater office work force, but there is an increasing demand for more space per employee.

Offices are built today in every location, from cities to suburbs. Smaller towns and suburban areas are attracting more and more office centers since land and building costs are less expensive than in downtown locations and more parking facilities are available away from cities. Medical complexes, insurance and real estate branches, and other service offices are frequently situated closer to their patients and clients than they have been in years past.

Still there is the lure of the skyscraper in many larger cities since it can offer the tenant luxury, prestige, proximity to conveniences and transportation. At the same time, these complexes can make economical use of high land costs, command high rents, and enjoy a substantial cash flow and depreciation.

In financing office buildings, it should be remembered that developers have tended in modern history to overreact to demands for space, and consequently, have been burdened with empty offices and foreclosures. In flooded markets, top operational and management skills are mandatory.

It has been said that "excess profits breed ruinous competition," and this is exactly what happens when a community begins to reach 95 to 100 percent occupancy of its office buildings. Many developers, corporations, and lenders all rush to fill the same demand and end up overfilling it. In 1974, this trend was evident in many parts of the United States, including Los Angeles, Miami, and Manhattan.

The single most important factor in successful office-building financing and operating is keen management, one that is flexible enough to adapt to any economic hazard. It may be difficult to convince lenders that such potential talent exists, but it can be done if the developer has carefully planned his project.

The office-building loan is favored among most lenders over one for an apartment house, but it is usually less desirable than an industrial or commercial mortgage. There are many lenders who have become experts in office-building loans and prefer them above all else.

The normal term of this type loan is 25 to 30 years, and the interest rate varies depending on the market at the time. An owner will usually pay one-quarter to one-half percent more for an office-building loan than for a commercial mortgage on a retail building.

Loan-to-value amounts which can be borrowed range from a 50 to a 100 percent loan, varying with the borrower's circumstances, location, credit, and rental guarantees. If a bank makes the loan, the term may range from an interim period of three to five years or from 10 to 15 years, again depending on many factors to be discussed and evaluated in the pages ahead.

STEP-BY-STEP GUIDE FOR A NEW PROJECT

How does the investor go about financing a new office building? These basic guidelines should provide most of the answers:

(1) The Pre-acquisition Study — This should include a check of the zoning and restrictions of the land to be built on, expected growth in the area, access to transportation or main highway arteries, public parking, the suitability of the locale to the prospective tenants, and overall personality of the vicinity. If a thorough investigation supports a need for a building, the next steps are in order.

(2) Control of the Land — Of course, the easy way to accomplish this is to buy or own the land, but, there are other ways by which land can

be attained at minimum or no cost to the developer. He can option the property until the success of the project is assured, go into partnership with the owner of the property, or put together a joint venture or syndicate with friends and associates to buy or option the land.

It is strategically wise to maintain long-term control by use of option renewals if possible. Projects often take longer than anticipated, so in the preliminary process, the developer must give himself and his project ample time allowances.

(3) Zoning Data — The lender will want to be provided with a copy of the local zoning codes relative to the subject property or to proof that the site can be used for its intended purpose.

(4) Architect's Renderings, Plans, Specs, and Survey — The lender will want to see a complete set of plans and specifications before issuing a firm commitment letter. Many architects will work with a developer, taking a portion of their fees after financing has been obtained and funded.

In some cases, developers will offer an architect a piece of the action, and in this way limit his out-of-pocket start-up costs.

A survey of the property owned or optioned is an important part of the package for lenders. When the long-term mortgage is funded, the take-out lender will require an "as built survey."

(5) Legal Description — A complete and accurate legal description of the land must be furnished.

(6) Financial Information — The lender will want to see:

(a) Financial projections on the project when completed. This data should include an itemized rent roll, a list of tenants, tenants' businesses, designation of tenants' space by office number, the space occupied by each tenant, rental per square foot, lease expiration (if there is no lease, say so in each case), cancellation clauses (if any), renewal privileges (if any), and average rental per square foot of the entire building.

Store rentals should be noted as such and the number of front feet of store space alloted to each tenant as well as square footage should be indicated. Detailed operating expenses, average operating expense per square foot, assessed value, real estate taxes, and extraordinary costs incurred in the operation of the building should be provided.

(b) The lender wants to know about the developer's character, reputation and experience. He is not overly concerned with the borrower's personal financial standing since the borrower usually does not assume personal liability on the mortgage obligation, and ownership of the property generally is set up in a corporation. The lender will want to see a personal financial statement from the borrowers, however.

The borrower's business ability and his experience with this type of property are considered. The lender prefers an investor to a speculator, one who has owned property for a long period to a new owner. He also favors real estate investment companies and estates that own a number of office buildings.

(c) Annual reports and the latest earnings statements if a corporation is making a loan. In some cases, lenders will require an even more thorough breakdown of a company's finances.

(d) Financial statements and other pertinent financial data on the major tenants. Having strong tenants can lower the cost of money for the developer.

(7) Leases on Space — Lenders will want to see copies of bankable commitment letters or executed leases. Seldom will all the space be leased and a lender is expressly interested in the status of the major tenants.

In case office buildings are constructed on speculation and have no, or very few leases, prior to construction the developer will need to prove an adequate market exists or will exist once the project is finished.

The investor should try not to develop office buildings for which leases are not firmly executed for a substantial portion of the space. Many otherwise astute developers have found themselves in serious financial trouble building speculatively only to experience a weak market which may have emerged between groundbreaking and opening of the projects undertaken.

(8) Feasibility Study — In today's financial market, a well-thought-out and conceived feasibility study is extremely important in obtaining an office-building loan. A formal study can be made after land is optioned or bought or a developer without a specific location might commission a study to help him locate land for his building.

If a smaller project is planned, with the cost under $1 million but more likely in the range of $100,000 to $500,000, an investor can conduct his own feasibility study. Starting from the site of the planned project, he should visit similar office buildings to see what their rentals are and what space is available, keeping detailed records of all his research. Along with a profile of the city and locale, this information should be submitted in formal summary to lenders.

With larger office buildings and complexes, it is recommended that the developer commission a professional feasibility study. There are a number of firms specializing in these studies, and they will provide an engineering evaluation, market studies, and even architectural plans. The best way to find the most competent consultant of this kind is to check with lenders or with the developer's mortgage banker.

(9) Purchase Contract or Land Lease — The lender will need proof of land control in the form of a copy of the purchase contract, option agreement, ground lease, or if owned, some proof of ownership.

PROPERTY MANAGEMENT AND MAINTENANCE

The developer should assure the lender of his ability to properly manage or direct management of the project when it is completed, and in the initial presentation, it is advisable to include information on how this will be executed.

If the lender does not have in-house capabilities, he can contract with a prestigious and competent property management company. As an alternative, he can hire a manager with solid experience.

HOW TO CHOOSE A LENDER OR BROKER

There are a few developers who are large enough and have the in-house talent to work directly with major institutions without channeling their needs through a mortgage banker or broker. For most developers, however, it is to their advantage to rely on the services of a mortgage banker because:

(1) He is in touch with the ever-changing money market and knows best where money is available at the lowest rates.

(2) Whether he is representing the lender or the borrower, his livelihood depends on his knowledge of the industry, which can be used for the benefit of those he represents.

(3) He knows what the lender wants in the way of a presentation and can best aid the developer in preparing it.

(4) He can structure the deal to best fit the parameters of the lender.

Questions to Ask the Mortgage Banker or the Lender — In preparing for long-term financing, the developer should query his broker, banker, or lender on these points which will help him decide with whom he should place his loan:

(1) Has the lender made this type loan before?

(2) What is the amount per square foot usually loaned?

(3) What is the parking ratio required?

(4) What is the loan-to-value amount usually loaned?

(5) What is the size of the normal loan the lender makes?

Choosing the Lender — Answers to the previous questions will help provide the developer with a comparative guide in deciding the best lender suited to his project.

Attorneys, accountants, and consultants might use these subject areas in helping clients invest in office buildings.

Guidelines a Lender Uses — Here is an internal memorandum a lender might devise to advise his correspondents or field representatives on the types of office buildings he will finance:

MEMORANDUM

TO: Field Representatives

FROM: Home Office

SUBJECT: Current Guidelines for Office Building Financing

BORROWER: Can be an individual, partnership, or corporation (no liability-recovery limited to proceeds of security). Occasionally, personal or corporate liability required to improve risk.

AMOUNT: The loan can call for funding in one or more draws with the first draw based upon completion of the improvements as defined and later draws upon achievement of specified leasing.

TYPE OF PROPERTY: In suburban office locations, buildings will generally be of the low-rise variety of single story so-called garden-type buildings, in the near-downtown areas of major cities, we prefer to lend on new, good quality high-rise structures. We also consider good opportunities for loans on older buildings that have been modernized. In such cases, our loans will be underwritten on a more conservative basis.

OCCUPANCY AND INCOME: We normally will look for most leases to contain tax stops and operating expense escalation provisions but in the absence of such provisions the loan amount will be underwritten accordingly. Coverage of debt service by our stabilized net income will usually range between 1.20 and 1.35 times. We usually stabilize income based on lease rentals currently obtained for similar properties and/or on actual leasing in force. It is important to realize that upward or downward adjustments often will be made for differences in landlord services, location factors, and in other amenities between our subject and other properties. In the case of existing properties, recognition is also given to the current leasing schedule as well as to the rentals being obtained under the most recent leases. We also consider the extent that income might be improved from renewals of existing lease.

LOAN RATIO: Usually in the 70 percent to 75 percent of value range.

MORTGAGE LOAN REQUIREMENTS: Except for existing construction, our commitments will normally range from 18 to 36 months depending upon the size of the project, type of construction, location, and leasing requirements. Also:
  (1) A stand-by deposit of 1 percent
  (2) Approval of all leases to our satisfaction
  (3) 80 percent leased prior to closing with income adequate to cover debt service after allocation for sufficient expenses
  (4) Project must be completed and in accordance with final plans and free from all liens.

Lenders Available — Lenders give a high preference rating to a well-located office project. Mortgage bankers have access to many types of sources. Insurance companies, savings and loan associations, pension funds, and commercial banks all are capable of making long-term loans on these buildings.

Following through with the Lender-Broker — The mortgage banker will usually want an exclusive or will have the developer fill out an application which requires an application fee. The developer will then need to provide the mortgage banker with the information outlined earlier. A lender takes 30 to 60 days to process a loan. It is wise to check with the lender or mortgage banker weekly to be updated on progress.

Letter of Commitment — Once a loan is approved, the lender will issue a bankable letter of commitment which will allow the developer to obtain his construction financing. The commitment letter will cover the major business decisions and briefly list the more important clauses affecting the commitment. Here are some of the items it may cover:

(1) Prepayment Penalty — Most long-term lenders do not want the loan paid off at all for five or 10 years. Thereafter, they usually let the borrower pay it off with a penalty which decreases toward the end of the term.

(2) Non-recourse Provision — It is to the borrower's advantage to obtain from the lender a right for no recourse to the borrower in the case of default except for the property described in the note and mortgage. This clause will effectively protect the borrower's other assets from liability.

(3) Multi-lender Loan Participation — In larger financings, there may be more than one lender involved in the transaction, and if so the commitment letter should spell out the various lenders' terms and conditions of their roles in the loan.

Long-term Financing on a New Project — The straight first mortgage has the advantages of keeping the capital structure simple and of increasing the investors' equity by periodic amortization payments.

Office buildings with a few major tenants of excellent credit on long-term leases usually have no trouble qualifying for a maximum loan.

When the tenant mix is more varied or a new structure has not yet been fully rented, a step-up mortgage can be used. Here the lender commits himself to a floor plan of a minimum amount. The initial amount then can be stepped up at varying intervals, depending upon the number of the nationally rated tenants coupled with the length of the leases.

The step-up amounts may ask for lower interest and amortization charges in view of the smaller risk that is presumed. Sometimes, no amortization is required for an initial period so that a new building can complete its rent roll. At that time, the full amount of the mortgage can be determined and amortization will begin.

CONSTRUCTION FINANCING

How to Choose the Lender — The major short-term lenders are commercial banks, real estate investment trusts, savings and loan associations, and finance companies. Banks and real estate investment trusts have been the most active sources of funds for this purpose.

Once the developer has his long-term mortgage, it is usually best for him to contact his commercial bank for the short-term and construction loan. This is also a service the mortgage banker normally provides.

Construction Loans on a Speculatively Built Office — A speculative builder who develops an office building before any tenants are secured usually cannot obtain a permanent mortgage commitment before completion of the building.

How does he obtain a construction loan? If the developer is well known, he may be able to get a construction loan without the back-up of a permanent commitment from a commercial bank. Since the real estate in its undeveloped state is inadequate security for the loan, the bank in effect is relying on the credit of the individual who normally will have to sign personally.

Standby Commitment — Even if the developer is able to arrange a permanent commitment from an institutional lender before construction, he may be better off using one of the other alternatives and waiting to negotiate the permanent loan when long-term rates are lower or his tenants are committed. Then, an institutional lender may be willing to advance more money on better terms, since construction and renting risks have largely been eliminated.

One Lender for Both Short-term and Long-term Financing — More and more lenders are considering financing both the long-term and short-term loans in one simplified package. The best prospects for this type of lending are the large life insurance companies which also have short-term REIT's which they manage. Banks and S and L's also have these capabilities, although the banks are more hesitant to grant the long-term portion of combined loans.

In the first stages of loan-making, the developer should tell his mortgage broker or banker he wants one-stop financing.

(1) An Intermediate Loan — If the rent-up period is anticipated to be long or long-term rates to be high, this kind of loan may suffice. A three-to-seven year loan is suggested to give the lending environment time to improve.

(2) Joint Venture with a Major Corporation — During a period of rising construction and development costs, high interest rates and tight money, an office building developer may join with a major corporation-office space tenant in a joint venture arrangement by which the developer gives up a piece of the action to get the necessary financing and cut down on the front money he needs to start his project.

The developer is thus assured of obtaining the financing he needs to complete his structure on time. With a major corporation taking space in the building, he should be in a strong position to attract other heavy tenants to his building and at higher rentals than he gets from his partner.

The corporation has a sound investment which serves as a hedge against inflation and assures it of the space it needs at a favorable rental.

(3) **Syndicates** — Using this technique, the developer will sell participating interest in the building on the simple basis of dividing it among a group of his associates or forming a larger entity with a more complex structure of ownership.

(4) **The Standby** — This procedure calls for obtaining a bankable standby commitment from a reputable financial house at a cost of from one percent to four percent. The developer deposits or banks the standby commitment with a commercial bank which advances construction money. This approach can be used only where the financial firm issuing the standby is fully prepared to provide actual permanent financing if necessary.

(5) **Short-term without a Take-out** — As mentioned, if a developer signs personally or has a good track record, this is a good alternative, although it is risky. The bank can advance short-term money without a long-term commitment but if permanent money has not been placed by the end of construction, the bank will have to call its loan.

(6) **Land Sale Leaseback with a Leasehold Mortgage** — A developer can use this technique to minimize the amount of cash he needs to put into a project. In such a situation, the developer will negotiate a sale leaseback on the land with a lender obtaining the rights of subordination to a first mortgage lender. The first mortgage holder will have first lien against the property in case of default.

The developer then has obtained 100 percent financing on the land and usually 75 percent of the appraised value of the building. If he has bought the land at an attractive price, perhaps, he can sell it to the lender at an increased amount which will further decrease his cash outlay.

If the developer is prepared to offer the lender a kicker, the leasehold mortgage can be obtained at market rates equivalent to those for a fee mortgage.

These kickers include a percentage of any gross rentals or net profits above a certain minimum, an option to the lender to buy the building at a fixed price at a future date, or a forced buy-back of the land by the developer if the leasehold loan is refinanced at a later date, with a resulting profit on the land sale to the institutional lender.

(7) **Sale Leasebacks** — The institutional lender would buy both land and buildings simultaneously, with the developer receiving a long-term operating lease. The institution is then paying for the construction as well as the land acquisition cost. The developer pays a higher rental but has no

mortgage obligation. The developer may find he has lower costs in this situation since the institutional lender has a sweetener in the form of the depreciation deduction which is available to it as the owner of the improvements.

(8) Participations and Joint Ventures with Lenders — High-ratio financing can be obtained where the institutional investor participates in the ownership of the office building and in a portion of its profits. In a tight market, investors ordinarily insist on a sweetener or equity participation which allows them to do this.

A joint venture between the developer and an institutional investor makes it possible for the developer to acquire the capital to carry out several projects at the same time with maximum leverage and minimum risk. The institutional investor gets the benefit of interest payments and also the additional kicker of participating in the profits of the venture. The developer supplies his know-how and managerial skills, and the institutional investor supplies the capital.

As a rule, the developer has the land and has done the preliminary work before bringing his proposition to the institutional investor. The developer will want the deal to be set up so that he contributes the land along with his preliminary work at current value rather than at cost. In one type of arrangement, the institutional investor may be given the right to have its capital investment returned to it before the profits are shared between it and the developer. During the period in which the institutional investor is being paid back its capital investment, the developer may be paid fees for constructing and managing the project.

Generally, the deal will be set up so that the method by which the parties can break up the joint venture is outlined in sufficient detail to pave the way for a friendly settlement.

FINANCING EXISTING OFFICE BUILDINGS

There are often many potential advantages in buying existing buildings and refinancing them later. Briefly stated:

(1) If the space is rented at below market value, the owner can increase the rent roll and realize a greater loan.

(2) If the building is remodeled, rents again, can be raised substantially.

(3) Because some older buildings have excellent addresses, the owner often buys high land value when he purchases an existing older building. This value figures prominently in the new mortgage, in resale or in putting up a new building.

Lender Requirements — Anyone involved in the financing or refinancing of an existing office building should evaluate the property using criteria such as these:

(1) Location — The lender will want to know if the building is in a prime location. Office buildings should be close to parking or transportation, service facilities, financial institutions, restaurants, shops and stores. In addition, if the building caters to tenants in a particular type of business, it should be near conveniences that are especially important to those tenants. The community and surrounding areas should be evaluated in terms of stability, growth potential, transportation, and amenities.

(2) Tenants and Rent Roll — The lender should see a current and accurate rent roll including each individual lease. Naturally, the lender will be impressed by triple-A tenants since they offer the highest security. The higher the rental paid per square foot, the better the tenancies, and the longer the term of the lease, the higher the quality of the tenancy.

The lender should know about the number of vacancies and when and how they can be filled.

(3) Income Projections — These can be calculated by projecting the free-and-clear income for 10 years and for the full mortgage period, using a 30-year term. Then, recalculated on the basis of 10-year financing, each five years thereafter for a 30-year term. As a rule of thumb, a building with a 30-year mortgage is worth six percent more than one with 25-year financing.

Income estimates should include anticipated rent increases, adjustments by reason of escalator clauses, service charges, etc. To arrive at a realistic estimate of net return, a careful estimate of both income and expenses and probable fluctuations in each should be made. Allowances should be made for services the leases require without charge.

Growth in profits can come about in two ways — increased operating efficiency and increased rentals. A general rise in rents comes about only in periods when demand exceeds the supply of available space. Rents in a particular building can be increased when they are below those prevailing in the area, provided the reasons for the lower rents can be corrected. This kind of building represents an excellent real estate investment.

(4) Management and Operation — The performance of past management should be rated and ways to improve it offered. The building should be looked at in terms of management's achievement of tenant satisfaction, numerous tenant services, quality performance of a staff, cleanliness, and appearance.

All operational costs, including allowances for vacancies, increases in salaries and new union contract provisions, services and utilities, as well as hidden costs not appearing on the balance sheet, must be dealt with.

(5) Size, Physical Condition, Construction and Parking — Larger buildings are more economical to operate, but there is less risk potential in a small building, so the owner must decide what the ideal size building is for his means.

He should carefully scrutinize the condition of the structure, finding out everything he can about construction, materials, air conditioning and heating, plumbing, water systems, fire protection, electrical wiring, elevators, and needed repairs.

The building must comply with all local and state regulations in design, equipment, and structure and possible violations should be investigated and cleared up.

Parking facilities should be remeasured and nearby parking availability should be investigated and recorded.

(6) Financing — The present financing on the property is a good clue as to its value in the eyes of the lender. Institutions normally lend up to two-thirds of the appraised value of the property. Loans on office buildings will often be three to four-and-a-half times the gross rent income for older buildings and five to six times the rent income for new buildings.

It is best to avoid a building that has several mortgages on it which cannot easily be consolidated. The building should not be so heavily financed that no cushion remains after the debt service charges.

(7) Amortization and Depreciation — Ask the rate of mortgage retirement in relation to the real depreciation, as distinguished from depreciation for accounting or tax purposes, less estimated increase in land value.

(8) Insurance — Check existing insurance for adequacy of coverage, possible duplication, and premium costs.

It may be possible through careful analysis and selection to make insurance savings. Are alterations and repairs necessary to meet insurance requirements or to get a lower rate? Check into the Workmen's Compensation Insurance. See if employees are properly classified.

(9) Real Estate Taxes and Assessments — Great care should be taken in checking real estate taxes. Is the assessment a full one or is it based on partial occupancy? Was there a tax break granted the owner because he was operating in the red? Is the assessment expected to increase and why or why not?

MAKING A FINANCIAL APPRAISAL OF
THE OFFICE BUILDING

For the developer's own benefit he should evaluate the building he wants to buy. He might begin by:

(1) Determining the Building's Rent Income — The first chore for the appraiser is the accurate measurement of rentable area. This may be more difficult than it sounds since there can be various ways of measuring usable space. The particular method will usually depend on local custom. Under one frequently used system, the rentable area of an individual office is computed by measuring from the inside surface of the outer building wall to the finished surface of the corridor side of the corridor partition and from the center of the partitions that separate the premises from adjoining rentable area. No deductions are made for columns and projections necessary to the building. However, building stairs, elevator shafts, pipe shafts, toilets, air ducts, and similar utility space are excluded.

The appraiser multiplies the square foot figure by the rent per square foot which the building can command in its present condition. This is not necessarily the rent being received since some tenants may be under leases entered into when competitive conditions were different. The rental figure used by the appraiser will ordinarily approximate rental in the immediate area unless there are special considerations relating to the particular building.

(2) Subtracting Operating Expenses — The appraiser's expense figures may also differ from those being paid at the time of the appraisal because of the effect of changed circumstances since contracts were signed. In addition, a different breakdown may be made between repairs

and capital improvements. The present owner will usually seek to charge off expenses to deductible repairs.

(3) Capitalizing the Result — The resulting figure for net income will then be capitalized to indicate value. A new building may be capitalized 10 times which means a 10 percent yield; an old building, seven or eight times showing a yield of 12 to 14 percent.

The other two appraisal methods, the cost approach and comparison approach, are used to supplement the income approach.

The cost approach is used to fix the upper limit of value since at that figure it is frequently more worthwhile to construct a new building. In addition to the usual items of cost, the appraiser must include cost of alterations for tenants.

The comparison approach is useful if pertinent data are available. Office buildings vary greatly, and comparable sales are infrequent. Only properties with similar floor areas should be used for comparison purposes since larger areas often produce a lower rental income per square foot than divided smaller areas.

REFINANCING THE PACKAGE

In addition to those methods already mentioned under financing new projects, there are other ways to consider when structuring the best financial package on an existing building. These may include:

(1) A New Mortgage — In times of inflation, the owner can increase rents and apply for a new loan based on the new leases. The owner can get back all or almost all his cash from the project. If he has made an exceptional purchase and managed to push rents way up by remodeling or redecorating, he may reap a handsome cash profit besides.

(2) An Owner Junior Mortgage — In purchasing the property, the new owner may persuade the seller to take a second or third mortgage, thus reducing the initial cash required to buy the building. Later, the buyer can arrange a new mortgage and pay off the junior loans.

(3) The Wrap-around Mortgage — The present lender or a new lender might be willing to provide a new mortgage, assuming the existing one and giving the new lender the advantage of having the older mortgage at a lower rate. The new mortgage will include two different rates, but the borrower makes one payment.

CORPORATE OWNERSHIP OF OFFICE BUILDINGS

The corporation with good earnings and a solid net worth has additional alternatives available to it to finance its real estate. Here are some it should consider:

(1) Net Lease Financing or True Lease or Beneficial Lease — This type of financing is usually conducted through the land or private place-

ment departments of major insurance companies and other institutions. Often, an equity investor will own the properties or in some cases it will be the institution.

This type of lease financing usually provides the corporation with lower rates and 100 percent financing. In order to qualify, most lenders require a company to have a minimum of $10 million in net worth and over $1 million a year in after-tax earnings.

(2) Sale Leaseback — In this type of lease financing, the property is sold to an investor who leases it back to the corporation. The investor must then get his mortgage from the real estate department of insurance companies which often set the loan-to-value ratio limit at 75 percent, although this is not a rigid figure.

This method is used by companies of all sizes, but is best suited for growing corporations. Any corporation with a net worth of less than $50 million frequently uses this method.

(3) Traditional Mortgage — Going to a mortgage banker, insurance company, savings and loan, or other institution is, of course, a means of getting 70-80 percent of the funds needed on any office building if the corporation wants to own the property. The disadvantage here is that it is impossible to get 100 percent of the funds needed.

(4) Secured Mortgage Bond — Using this method, the corporation can obtain up to 100 percent of its cost and still own the building. The debt, however, must show on the balance sheet as opposed to the net lease which does not. Again, the net worth of a company and its after-tax earnings must be at least $10 million and $1 million, respectively, to utilize this vehicle.

6. —— Shopping Centers

INTRODUCTION

Financing shopping centers is an art. It has a language all its own. These projects involve appraising, leasing, building, designing, zoning, utilities, politics, psychology, demographics, urban planning, ecology, soil engineering, feasibility studies, and the best sense of timing.

Those who develop centers know a lot about financing and those who finance centers know a great deal about tenant mix, competition, and growth trends.

DESCRIPTION OF TYPES

There are three recognized types of shopping centers, based on size. The smallest is the neighborhood variety which serves a small population pocket and caters to necessities such as food and drugs. It is usually a strip of stores.

The community, or middle-sized type, attracts chain stores and may have branches of area department stores, a post office and banks, as well as drug and grocery stores. This type is generally not so convenient for shoppers as the neighborhood center, is too small to compete with the regional, and is more vulnerable to competition from discount stores.

Merchants depending on comparison shopping are inclined to avoid becoming tenants in a community operation.

The regional center creates a whole new business district, offering a huge expanse of parking, the dominant department stores as anchors, and often the pleasure and safety of controlled climate malls.

In an increasing number of instances they stimulate the nearby construction of medical plazas, libraries, motels, restaurants, auto repair shops, and offices if they do not offer some of these facilities under their roofs or as part of their complexes. High-density housing often follows the introduction of a big regional shopping center.

Some of the regionals are joint ventures between a developer and one or more of the major department stores.

UNDERSTANDING THE ECONOMICS OF A SHOPPING CENTER

Before delving into financing a center, it is advisable to comprehend the basic economic framework of such projects. The reader should study carefully the operating statement and supporting details offered here to gain such insight.

Although the statement is hypothetical, the figures used fall within guidelines that are basically the median figures gathered from more than 30 regional centers, well-distributed geographically. These figures are sufficiently realistic so that any significant difference with an actual case might call for re-checking the figures of that case or determining the cause for the variance. The reader should allow for the inflationary factors covering the period from 1964 to date.

Line Number

Line			
1.	OPERATING STATEMENT		
2.	FINANCEABLE PLAZA		
3.	Superville, Ohio		
4.	650,000 G.L.A. (Gross Leasable Area)		
5.	Regional Type, Built in 1964		
6.	INCOME:		
7.	Minimum Guaranteed Rents, AAA	$730,000	
8.	Overage Rent Paid, AAA	84,000	
9.	Minimum Guaranteed Rents, Locals	410,000	
10.	Overage Rent Paid, Locals	62,000	
11.	Miscellaneous Income	24,000	
12.	Total Rent; Gross Receipts		$1,310,000
	Deduct		
13.	EXPENSES:		
14.	Maintenance and Housekeeping	$114,000	
15.	Advertising and Promotion	30,000	
16.	Real Estate Taxes	171,000	
17.	Insurance	20,000	
18.	General Administrative	89,000	
19.	Total Expenses		$ 424,000
20.	Net Income		$ 886,000
21.	Net Income P.S.F. (Per Square Foot) $1.36		
22.	Sales in Center — $33,150,000		
23.	Sales; P.S.F. of G.L.A. $51.00		
24.	Rent; P.S.F. of G.L.A. $ 2.01		
25.	Expenses; P.S.F. of G.L.A. $ .65		
26.	Expenses; % of Gross Receipts $ .32		
	Cost		
27.	Land	$1,180,000	
28.	Buildings and Related Costs	8,020,000	
29.	Total Cost	$9,200,000	

Financing

30.	First Mortgage, Life Insurance Company	$8,000,000
31.	Twenty year, 7% interest	
32.	(9.31 constant) Annual debt service	744,800
33.	Net income after debt service	141,200
34.	Equity	1,200,000

35.   Return on investment $\dfrac{20}{29} = 9.6\%$

36.   Return on equity $\dfrac{33}{34} = 11.8\%$

37.   Loan; per square foot of G.L.A. $12.30

38.   Loan; as multiple Gross Rent   6x

A REVIEW OF THE STATEMENT

Let's discuss the statement starting at the top:

Line 1. Name of report.
2. Name of shopping center.
3. Location of shopping center.
4. Size of shopping center.
5. Date of construction and type.
6. Important heading — income.
7. Total of the annual rent payments guaranteed to be paid by tenants, with net worth over $1,000,000 to the landlord.
8. The rent, based on percentage of sales, over the minimum rent, paid by AAA tenants to the landlord.
9. Total of the annual rent payments guaranteed to be paid by local tenants to the landlord. These tenants are incorrectly referred to sometimes as "non-rated," but in fact many are definitely well rated by Dun and Bradstreet but to a lesser net worth than AAA.
10. The rent, based on percentage of sales, over the minimum rent, paid by local tenants to the landlord.
11. Miscellaneous income to landlord would be common area charges paid by tenants, receipts from stamp and vending machines, public charges, billboard space, etc. Sometimes classified simply as "other income."
12. Total rent, synonomous with Gross Receipts or Gross Income. All the money received by the landlord from all sources.
13. Important heading — Expenses.
14. Type of expenses, includes repairs and maintenance to the building, the parking areas, the common areas, services provided to office areas (if any).
15. The sums paid by landlord, directly or indirectly via a merchants'

association for advertising and promoting the shopping center.

16. Real estate taxes paid by the landlord, net of any part paid by the tenants.

17. All insurance costs paid by the landlord relating directly to the shopping center.

18. General administrative expenses including management, secretarial services, security, accounting, and supplies and incidentals required to operate the shopping center.

19. The total expenses paid by the landlord, necessary to own and operate the shopping center.

20. Net income. Derived by subtracting line 19 from line 12. This is defined by ULI (Urban Land Institute) as "balance after operating expenses" and by appraisal usage as "net income before depreciation." It is also called "cash flow," or the spendable amount available if the venture was free and clear of debt but before any provision for income tax.

21. Derive net income per square foot by dividing line 20 by line 4 (G.L.A.).

22. Sales in center. Sum of all sales, not including sales tax made by all tenants in the center. Obtained by annual reports required by the leases with tenants.

23. Sales per square foot of G.L.A. is derived by dividing line 22 by line 4.

24. The average rent P.S.F. of G.L.A. is derived by dividing line 12 by line 4.

25. Expenses per square foot of G.L.A. is derived by dividing line 19 by line 4.

26. Expenses as a percent of total rent is derived by dividing line 19 by line 12.

27. Assumed cost of land and costs to prepare it for construction.

28. The assumed cost of buildings erected and appurtenances.

29. The assumed total cost to create the shopping center.

30. The assumed first mortgage placed on the center shortly after it opened for business.

31. The length of the mortgage for full amortization and the interest rate.

32. The "constant annual percent to amortize a loan" can be determined by looking in an amortization table to see what figure appears under the 7 percent interest rate column where it intersects with the line for 20 years. In this case it is 9.31, meaning that the annual amount in dollars to be paid to liquidate a given loan in twenty years with interest at 7 percent can be found by multiplying 9.31 by the principal amount of the loan. Ans. 9.31 times $8,000,000 = $744,800.

33. Based on the mythical mortgage, the net income after debt service, meaning the annual payment of the interest and amortization of the loan, is derived by subtracting line 32 from line 20.
34. The equity in a shopping center means the net investment by the owner in his project or total cost (line 29) minus financing (line 30).
35. The return on investment (R.O.I.) is the ratio between the net income and the total cost, or line 20 divided by line 29.
36. The return on equity is the ratio between the net income after deducting the cost of borrowed money (interest and principal repayment) and the equity, and is derived by dividing line 33 by line 34.
37. To determine the loan as an expression of dollars borrowed for each square foot of G.L.A., divide line 30 by line 4. The general range in early days (1955-1965) was $10 to $20; since then it has increased to $15 to $30.
38. To find loan as a multiple of gross rent, divide line 30 by line 8.

If you clearly understand lines 1-38, let's proceed to study the financing technique.

STEP-BY-STEP METHOD OF FINANCING CENTERS

This example of the development of a shopping center is presented in hopes that it will serve as a how-to guide for those interested in pursuing this kind of real estate project:

Let's say a man inherited a 60-acre tract of land. Shortly thereafter, he was contacted by a reputable commercial leasing firm from a nearby city, and he learned that one department store had firm interest in his property and another had a milder interest.

The owner employed the broker to secure commitments from the two department stores, after a preliminary plot plan was prepared at no charge by an architect who hoped to be chosen as the architect for the entire project.

After the broker produced letters of intent from the two department stores, the plans were submitted to the city zoning board to support an application for a rezoning from agriculture to commercial. The rezoning was approved, and site plan approval was given.

At this point, a year had expired since the owner was contacted by the leasing firm. The owner's expenses during the first year totaled less than $10,000, the major items being a topographic survey, including a metes and bounds description, legal fees for processing the zoning change, and real estate taxes.

Within the next six months, the letters of intent for the department stores were converted to firm leases, and negotiations started with a contractor who had built several smaller shopping centers.

Construction Loan — The owner could go no further without a construction loan. With only a plot plan, two leases, and optimism, he contacted a large regional bank, which had a reputation for mortgage cooperation with major life insurance companies, whereby the same mortgage instruments were acceptable to both the temporary and permanent lenders.

The preliminary meeting was favorable. Had it not been so, the owner would have pursued either a different bank, since only one other in that city had the financial capability necessary, or gone to a different city several hundred miles away as the major commercial banks are not restricted geographically.

Checklist — The owner was given a loan checklist and found that the approval of his application was contingent upon submission of:

(1) A standby commitment from a permanent lender — the bank needed absolute assurance that its loan would be paid off in full within a short period after completion of the project with proceeds from a permanent or long-term loan.

(2) A resume of the owner covering his education, his background in business and any comparable projects he had completed.

(3) A bank reference in writing.

(4) A financial statement from the owner in great detail.

(5) A detailed projected pro-forma of the proposed shopping center.

(6) Feasibility study, sometimes called market analysis.

(7) Name and Dun and Bradstreet rating of the proposed general contractor.

(8) Name and resume of the architect.

(9) Detailed breakdown of costs on forms provided by the bank.

(10) Final plans and specifications.

The owner was advised that current unwritten requirements of the bank were to have the proposed debt service of about $750,000 per year be equaled by minimum rents of AAA tenants.

AAA Minimums — The owner's leases in hand, those from the two department stores, carried combined rents of $570,000. Therefore, the key to satisfying the first requirement of the lender was to obtain additional AAA income of $180,000 per year ($570,000 plus $180,000 is $750,000). This task was assumed by the commercial leasing broker.

The Permanent Loan — The owner then began negotiations with a permanent lender, a life insurance company, whose portfolio already included several hundred millions of dollars in shopping center mortgages, for his take-out, or long-term loan. This company required even more detailed information than the construction lender because its exposure or risk period would cover much more time. Among the items required were:

(1) Copies of all AAA leases for review and approval by house counsel or lawyers on the staff of the insurance company.

(2) An M.A.I. appraisal of both raw land and completed project.

(3) A more detailed market analysis, including a comparison of the proposed project with a designated existing center 40 miles distant.

(4) Aerial photographs, one vertical or looking straight down and four obliques looking north, south, east, and west with site in foreground.

(5) A plot plan locating all utilities, the drainage plan , number of square feet in buildings, number of square feet in total site, parking layout and conformance to zoning requirements, and an index required by major tenants.

(6) Vicinity map showing all commercial projects and most office/industrial developments on major thoroughfares within three miles of the site.

(7) An artist's rendering of the buildings, sometimes called a "bird's-eye view," as it would appear from a helicopter hovering at 1000 feet and looking at the buildings from an angle.

(8) A copy of the construction lending agreement.

In the real world today, both the temporary lender and permanent lender require the same support items, the rationale of the former being, although there is a take-out commitment, what happens if it falls through?

The individual who has participated in mortgaging, either as borrower or lender, will understand the necessity of all the documentation described. It is briefly referred to as the paperwork, and each item fills a specific need.

The borrower must remember that final decisions on his application are usually made hundreds or even thousands of miles from his site by executives who probably have not seen the property and who are relying on photographs, appraisals, drawings, and leases alone to support their conclusion.

The lender must understand that all projections made prior to construction are just that — projections. In addition to possible omissions, a constant error of inflation will probably make all cost estimates fall short of the actual amount.

A borrower should anticipate this and secure a loan with a floor/ceiling amount, perhaps with a possible increase of 10 percent in the amount, tied to a rentable factor.

If, say, 90 percent of the space is rented at a future time, he could draw down something more than at 80 percent or 85 percent. A similar arrangement should be made with the permanent loan amount.

Outlots — Our owner received and acted on a suggestion from his broker. Before the plot plan was submitted to the department stores for approval, two outlots were removed. Each parcel was 150 feet by 200 feet and simply marked "not included" on the survey. The sale of one of these small parcels to an oil company provided the front money for architect's fees, engineering costs, an advance on commissions to the broker, the standby fee for lenders, and many of the items to obtain financing.

If the owner had not been fortunate enough to obtain funds from the outlots, it might have been necessary to invest much more money as equity.

It can be assumed that the construction mortgage or first lien during building will be in the same amount or very close to the contractor's price. The contract price will be well known to the lender, who has agreed to advance a total of, say, $7,900,000 in a series of draws by the builder, roughly as follows:

(1) $100,000 upon clearing and grading of the site.

(2) $400,000 upon completion of all foundations, utility connection lines and retaining walls.

(3) $1,500,000 upon completion of walls, columns and rough closing in (roofing) of all structures.

(4) The remainder for miscellaneous and unexpected costs.

Until completion, the bank would have paid the contractor a total of $7,900,000. Actually, a portion of this amount; usually about five to 10 percent, by agreement, is not disbursed, at the end of the construction. This is called a holdback and is the incentive for the contractor to complete all his work, to obtain all the certificates of occupancy from the municipality, and to correct within some specified period of time the omissions or latent defects. In actuality, some work and/or equipment deficiencies exist for a reasonable time after completion. When itemized and described, this is called a punch list. When the construction mortgage is placed on this project, it will be for a short time, maybe two years, and will carry an interest rate of about two percent or three percent more than the permanent loan. It may also involve points, which, at two points for instance, means the borrower receives 98 percent of the borrowed amount but pays interest on 100 percent of the amount.

CREATIVE METHODS

Joint Ventures and Syndicates — Another way to make the deal proceed would be for the owner, instead of playing the role of entrepreneur alone, to take in one or more silent partners who would advance some of the money necessary as equity, and in return share in the ownership of the center and its future income.

This joint venture agreement can call for two or more people to pool their resources equally and participate the same way in profit taking.

Or it can work this way: Should an investor need a second mortgage to acquire a shopping center he wants, he might ask three or four of his friends to go together and put up the funds for this junior financing, offering the partners certain benefits proportionate to their investment.

A syndicate is similar to the joint venture, but it usually involves a number of investors and if large enough can call for a public underwriting. The various forms of syndication are discussed in Chapter 2.

Land Sale Leaseback and Leasehold — In order to increase leverage, a developer can sell his land and lease it back from a lender who usually provides him with subordination.

He then uses the same or another lender and obtains a first mortgage on the property. An astute developer can get close to 100 percent financing in this way, especially if the value of the land is greater than his original cost and if his rent roll is large enough to justify a first mortgage loan and adequately service the debt.

Sale Leaseback — Another way for a developer to work out 100 percent financing on a center is to sell it, lease it back, and operate it. Developers or real estate operators who are good managers can use this procedure in acquiring new centers, where there is sound potential, either by increasing rent or by additional development of the center.

As an example, let's suppose Adams Property Management Company knows of a shopping center it would like to buy. The center is partially empty and has been badly abused. The property can be bought at a very good price, and the potential for increased rental income and substantial appreciation is significant.

The Adams Company contracts to buy the property from Mr. Beverly, the current owner, at a price of $2 million.

The Adams firm determines it will take another $200,000 to remodel and bring the center up to par. Therefore, either before or after acquiring the property, the company contracts for a sale leaseback for $2.2 million with an institutional lender, Columbus Life Insurance Company, which will receive a guaranteed 10 percent return before Adams gets anything, plus a percentage of the overage rental.

There is also an option for Adams to buy back the center at a price of $2.7 million any time after the third year. Adams has, therefore, gotten all the money it needs to improve the center without using its own money.

In addition, if Adams performs as a creative property manager, the firm can make enormous profits.

Let's assume Adams remodels and manages the property for three years, increasing rentals and overages and adding leaseable space to the center.

Now the property is valued at $3.25 million based on these improvements so that Adams exercises his buyback option with Columbus and keeps the center or resells it at a profit of $550,000. The lender, Columbus, is also happy because he has had a guaranteed return, plus overages and a profit of $500,000, when Adams exercised its repurchase option.

Current owners of shopping centers can also use the leaseback route to obtain cash to develop or buy new projects.

Balloon Mortgage — A method of reducing debt service is the balloon principle. The annual repayment schedule is not sufficient to completely pay off the loan, and at expiration a balloon amount remains which is due and payable in a lump sum. This situation is not nearly so risky as it would appear since loans on shopping centers seldom run to maturity anyway.

Loan Holdback Provisions — Sometimes a center developer gets a commitment for his permanent loan which is not for a fixed amount but one which has a floor or low amount up to a ceiling or highest amount. The difference is the holdback provision, and a construction lender will limit his loan to the low figure.

The holdback is an incentive feature which stimulates the borrower to perform as he promises, relative to rent rolls, or receive a lesser amount of refinancing.

Here is a demonstration of the method of overcoming the loan deficit:

(1) A, the permanent lender, commits to a $5-million loan with a holdback provision of $500,000.

(2) B, the construction lender, commits to the floor amount, $4,500,000.

(3) C, the borrower, cannot complete his project as he is $500,000 short on construction funds and cannot get more money because he has not yet obtained enough rental income to satisfy A.

(4) D, the gap lender, provides the necessary $500,000 to B, who then pays the contractor. D then has a $500,000 lien behind A.

(5) Hopefully, C gets his rent roll up to the requirements of A, whose release of holdback pays D. If not, a reasonable time is allowed for C to do so, and if he fails he must sell, refinance his permanent loan, or obtain funds from a new source to satisfy D, whose position might enable him to look to either the property or the borrower's credit or both.

Combination Mortgages — The traditional approach to financing large projects has been the two-step technique. Approval of the first step requires that the construction lender be convinced that his short-term investment will be both safe and profitable.

Taking the second step involves satisfying an entirely separate group, often in a different region or economic climate, that a deal is soundly conceived and will be safe and profitable over the long term.

During recent years, this method is often replaced with a single lender providing both construction and long-term financing. Often, especially with the real estate investment trust, the lender may also provide second mortgages, gap loans, and numerous other types. Some finance companies will also consider this one-step financing method.

CORPORATE FINANCING OF SHOPPING CENTERS

If a substantial corporation specializing in development built the shopping center, referred to in the example in the first part of this chapter, it could save money and move faster.

First, the interest rates would probably be lower which reflects:

(1) The pledge of corporate net worth instead of just the single property alone.

(2) Astuteness or experience in the marketplace.

(3) In-house capabilities of design and construction.

(4) Greater knowledge of leasing techniques and, in some cases, the elimination of brokerage.

In combination, these factors could be called economies of scale or those inherent to size and repetition.

Equity Kicker — If a period of money crunch or a shortage of funds relative to the demand exists, the entrepreneur may have to take in an unexpected partner, the lender, who will require a sweetener or equity kicker as part of the inducement to make the loan. Under this agreement, the lender receives something over and above the specified interest, perhaps an outright two percent of all profits generated or 10 percent of the profits in excess of X amount of dollars per year. In return for this potential extra income, the lender might forego or reduce the points needed to bring interest to the status in the real world or increase the loan-to-value ratio above the normal range of 67 percent to 75 percent.

Depending on which side of the table one sits, the preceding system is called gouging, rape, a justifiable protection against inflation, or a reasonable inducement to provide a scarce and valuable commodity.

Problems in Financing — Suppose that the entrepreneur finds that a) his AAA rent roll does not come up to his projection and b) his construction costs exceed his estimates. This situation is quite normal and has caused leading mortgage brokers to say they would prefer making a 100 percent mortgage to a pro than a 75 percent mortgage to a neophyte.

The developer goes back to the well. Sometimes an acute financial squeeze can be cured by recasting the mortgage. In our example, a 25-year repayment schedule instead of 20 years would reduce the annual constant from 9.31 to 8.49 — an annual saving of $65,600 per year! (multiply .82 by $8,000,000). One can expect the lender to ask for something in return, but even increasing the interest to seven-and-a-quarter percent provides a net reduction in annual cost of $50,400 (multiply 9.31 — 8.68, or .63 by $8,000,000).

REFINANCING

Although it may appear in refinancing that much of the risk is eliminated by dealing with a reality instead of a projection, do not be fooled by the superficial. This type of financing presents the nth degree in challenges, competition, and sophistication.

Let's consider an example:

A regional shopping center in South Florida was built using a $6-million construction loan which was retired by a $7.5 million long-term mortgage with a large national life insurance company for 20 years at six percent. The constant for debt service was 8.60, and multiplied by $7.5 million principal called for $645,000 per annum.

The center was successful. After five years, the department store was in the $20 million sales range as compared with $15 million in proforma projections. Other tenants were generally in overage rent positions.

Ownership was held by two equal partners. One offered to buy the other's interest and a deal was made, with an extended closing date.

The surviving partner applied to the original lender to see if the principal balance could be increased to the original amount. About 15 percent of principal had been paid, so this recast would provide cash of about $1 million over the balance and provide more than the amount needed to buy out the selling partner.

Surprise! The lender declined the proposal, leaving the owner in trouble, but not for long. As a classic example of the constant imbalance of the demand and supply for money, within 30 days a different life insurance company committed to a new loan at the same six percent interest rate, a new 20-year term and at not $7.5 million but $8 million dollars, leaving the borrower not $1.1 million of new funds but $1.6 million.

Ready for the finish? Shortly thereafter, the owner, now in the 100 percent class, sold the center to a northeastern investment institution for more than $3 million *over* the existing mortgage. Best of all, the profit was at the capital gains rate.

Refinancing is also desirable when:

(1) Loan expenses can be reduced by paying off an existing mortgage and placing a new mortgage at a lower interest rate.

(2) Depreciation has been taken at an accelerated rate to shelter income and has been used up to the point where it appears better to sell so that another buyer can start the depreciation system anew.

(3) Equity can be recaptured and provide for new ventures.

(4) It will make a property more salable since less difference between price and mortgage attracts more prospective buyers.

Special Techniques — Other methods of refinancing include:

(1) The Sale Leaseback — the seller converts his fee position to one of leasehold interest. The seller raises cash, and the purchaser receives income and depreciation. The sticky point is to what extent, if any, the fee owner shares in overage rents, or if any escalator clauses are to be applied to rent.

(2) A Second Mortgage — this method raises cash and maintains the first mortgage which will be lower. The problem is the high interest rate associated with second liens.

(3) Wrap-around Mortgage — a new lender takes over the debt position with regard to the existing first and provides additional funds at a higher rate. You pay both mortgage payments to the new lender, who pays your first trust. Your overall rate remains lower than a refinancing would permit, but the difference between the two rates could lower the monetary savings considerably.

(4) Sale Buyback — If the owner does not want to lose control of his property, he can sell and simultaneously contract to buy it back. The cash raised is equal to

the selling price less the down payment on the land contract. High-ratio financing is possible. Upon payment of all installments, the title reverts to the original owner.

Putting the Package Together — Both refinancing and original financing demand the preparation of a great sum of supporting material. In the former, perhaps, there will be even more data needed since the existing center has a history to record.

The lender will be most interested in amounts of overage rents paid and the trends, upward or downward, of all rents, guaranteed and overage.

A center which is maturing and increasing in sales will show a healthy cash flow improvement, which will be even more impressive if it has met new competition along the way.

If the ratio of overage rents to total rent is substantial, it could mean that sales are very good or that minimum rents were low, or some combination. Only close analysis will establish the extent to which these overage rents can be capitalized in the income approach for an appraisal to support a refinancing amount.

Another item that the lender will study, and this must be based on actual records, is whether the operating statement has been improved by deferred maintenance. If so, it is logical to expect a substantial increase in repair charges soon and a consequent reduction in cash flow.

THE FUTURE OF SHOPPING CENTERS

Life insurance companies, REIT's, and pension funds can be expected to continue favoring shopping centers. In addition to the substantial physical collateral, land and buildings, the AAA tenants in effect co-sign the mortgage, and in combination their rents will provide funds for a systematic retirement of the debt, whether the center is a great success, an average deal, or a bomb or dud.

At an International Council of Shopping Centers convention, a seminar leader asked his group, "What makes a shopping center site *good*?" He expected a lengthy, academic answer, but from the back of the room a veteran developer replied, "Any site is good if two department stores will sign 20-year leases."

Current feeling by experts in the development field is that relatively few regional malls will be built in the near future and then only by the most astute and respected entrepreneurs.

New projects will be almost exclusively limited to those who have done them before and have a firm grasp of all the planning and support activities, often covering five or more years of lead time prior to opening.

These experts, with their track records, have developed liaison with one or more major lenders, and the bulk of the action will be in the field of refinancing at a time when money costs have dropped below current levels.

However, the neighborhood center program should present many opportunities for investments on a greatly reduced scale per project.

Developers of neighborhood centers will improve land of the sites which will be within the range of four to ten acres. Land costs will be about $50,000 to $125,000 per acre. Entrepreneurs find that tying up land under option for a year will require patience and risk capital.

Since a high proportion of financing for these projects is placed locally, the local economic base largely controls the availability of loanable funds although insurance companies are taking an increasingly active role in this field.

Most neighborhood centers have as an anchor a supermarket chain store, and these stores are highly sought after by developers of this size center. The AAA supermarket which wants a specific location generates enough interest for either the current owner, a purchaser, or a developer to get out and comb the market for a lender with money. However, in some cases, supermarket chains are finding they have greater sales potential by locating in established neighborhood centers rather than in regional or community projects.

Both developers and lenders generally feel the community shopping center is no longer viable. Its lead tenant has been the 60,000-square-foot junior department store, which is no longer competitive in size, selection, or pricing with discount stores. Satellites hesitate to join such a weak key tenant, knowing that insufficient foot traffic will be generated. This type center is also particularly vulnerable to competition from regionals.

7. — Industrial Properties

SPECIAL ASPECTS

Industrial properties are those used for distribution, manufacturing, storage, service, or warehousing. They are usually located in specially zoned areas of the community.

Often these properties are not owned by the companies that occupy them since they are more involved in their businesses than in real estate and often prefer to lease, writing off the lease costs as expenses.

In recent years there have been three trends in industrial properties — (1) to build them in the form of large complexes situated between two or three large cities or metropolitan areas for the purpose of more convenient distribution of products; (2) to locate large industrial parks in the suburbs of big cities. In both cases, the projects are usually well designed and beautifully landscaped and often enhance the general area; and (3) to move large operations to regions of the country that have, heretofore, lacked industry and to suburban areas where businesses are free to expand buildings and are closer to work forces. Many industries have found less expensive labor by shifting to different parts of the country.

Industrials are increasingly located near interstate highways and expressway exchanges to provide easier access for employees and for moving goods.

All of these changes have been dictated by congestion within downtown areas, soaring tax rates, high land costs, and the increase of crimes against employees, as well as vandalism and theft.

As these centers have been moved to greater land expanses, there has been an increasing swing away from multi-story buildings which are mandatory in big cities because of land costs. Plants, today, often are one or two stories and have room to sprawl across the countryside.

To some degree there probably will be a return to the multi-level structures as prices of land in the outskirts rise and businesses continue to grow.

The developer who is hoping to build an industrial complex or the executive who is searching for a new business location should check out the commercial plans, if any, for the area he has in mind with the U. S. Department of Commerce, state and local agencies, chambers of commerce, and local financial institutions.

There are usually two different types of industrial properties, single-tenant and multi-tenant buildings. Both are desired investments since they provide appreciation potential, good cash flow, mortgage amortization, and substantial tax shelter benefits.

In addition they have proved to be sound, secure investments and are preferred by some investors over residential realty because industrial tenants are usually fewer than in apartment complexes and are more sophisticated in business and obligations of leases and rents.

Maintenance on industrial buildings is less, and leases are for longer periods and more binding than those of residential contracts.

On the other hand, sometimes the industrial developer takes a greater risk with fewer tenants because if they vacate, he has to meet high mortgages and often industrial properties will not be leased so quickly as other types of real estate.

Another chance that the developer may take in constructing and owning a single-purpose building is its functional obsolescence. Since technology changes so rapidly, the most-up-to-date printing plant, for instance, may not retain its operational effectiveness over a long period. After some time, the business may have to move to a more modern facility, so the developer should get as long a lease as he can and keep in mind the changing patterns of areas, highways, and populations and adjust to the markets by updating his buildings or converting them if he has to attract new tenants. The developer should plan his building's long-haul potentials, including alternative uses, and offer them to his lenders with his application for a loan.

HOW CORPORATIONS CAN OBTAIN FINANCING

Because of its structure, the corporation has different alternatives available to it for financing its real estate or raising capital based on real property. These include:

(1) Sale Leaseback or Net Lease — These transactions involve the corporation's first buying property either with cash or with a mortgage and selling the property to an investor and then leasing it back from him. Two legal contracts are needed, the sale contract and the lease agreement. The sale is contingent upon that lease agreement.

(2) Mortgage — The corporation can usually obtain 50 to 85 percent of the cash needed to buy or build a plant by arranging for a mortgage from an institution. He has to provide only the cash difference between loan and price as a payment.

(3) Private Placement of Debt — For this loan the corporation works with an investment banker, private placement specialist, or investment counselor who can place a loan with institutions based on the full faith and credit of the borrowing company. Up to 100 percent financing is possible under this plan. In many cases, this loan will cover the land, buildings, and

equipment. In such cases, the land and building portion of the financing might be for a longer period than the equipment segment.

If a company's financials are strong enough, it can get a fixed rate of interest for a long term, and the contract will be free of escalator clauses. To obtain this kind of financing, the company must usually have a net worth of $50 million or more and a good earnings record. Even with the larger companies today, lenders are beginning to ask for some type of guarantee against inflation.

Occasionally, if a corporation has a net worth of $10 million and an exceptionally good earnings record, it may be able to negotiate a fixed rate. The ability of a firm to win this type of financing also varies with the availability of money as well as the popularity of the particular industry at the time. There are occasional fads among businesses, with some winning the spotlight for a given time. For instance, a few years back, discount stores were very much in demand by investors since they were viewed as an exciting new trend.

(4) Loans and Private Placements with Incentives — With continued inflation throughout the world, there will be added use of financing which carries some type of bonus for the investor offering a fixed rate. For smaller companies just beginning this is an excellent means to financing.

This category loan can provide inflation hedges of many types and variations for the lender, including cost-of-living increases, warrants, convertibles, purchase of part ownership in the business, or participation in the company's profits.

(5) Short-term and Interim Loans — These loans are especially prevalent during times of inflation since lenders do not want to commit their dollars for long periods and watch their money shrink over these years. In some parts of the world, industrial plants have built with five-year loans and within four or five years the loan is rolled over based on the then current rates. In times of tight money, this practice also allows the corporation to refinance at a later date when money might be cheaper.

(6) Tax Revenue Bonds — These can be used when a corporation is providing an economic benefit to the community such as employment and, consequently, payroll and revenues. These are sometimes known as tax-exempt industrial development bonds.

Many states permit the local governments to issue these bonds to finance construction and industrial facilities that will be leased to private industry. Interest and amortization payments on these bonds are met with the revenue from the project. The taxing power of the town cannot be used to secure and pay off the principal and interest due on the bonds. The lease guarantee insurance provides that monthly rentals due under the lease to the industry will be made.

The bonds can be backed by rentals or revenue from a particular facility or by the full credit of the issuer.

The lease guarantee insurance is an additional aid in obtaining financing as is mortgage guarantee insurance. Lease and mortgage insurance policies can be obtained from private companies as well as through the Small Business Administration's lease and mortgage guarantee programs. This type of insurance will allow an industrial that could not otherwise do so to obtain financing.

The insurance company guarantees payment of the lease or loan in case of non-payment of rent or default in the mortgage. The financial transaction could work this way: The Red Shoe Manufacturing Company agrees to move its plant to Bay City if the city will sponsor a $25 million tax-exempt revenue bond issue for construction. The town agrees to this proposal.

The company puts up its plant, sells it to the city (the city uses proceeds from the bonds for the purchase), and leases it back at a low tax-deductible rent since it is tied to the interest rate of the bonds which, being tax exempt, is lower than could be obtained by other private financing. Red Shoe has the option of buying back the facility or renewing the lease when the lease expires.

(7) ***Direct State Loans*** — Some states make loans available to industries for building facilities from appropriated state funds. Information on these loans may be obtained from development commissions in state capitals.

PROCEDURES FOR INDIVIDUALS AND DEVELOPERS

Depending on the type of financing sought, the procedures and methods will vary. Steps also differ with the corporation's decision to construct its own building or contract with a developer who will handle the loan and the construction.

If a corporation wants a net lease or private placement financing, he will need to submit the following data to the lender usually through the investment banker or counselor:

(1) A term sheet showing all specific business decisions involved in the financing such as amount of the loan and term desired. This sheet will also include the corporate name and the name in which title will be taken, parties to the transaction and what roles they play in the financing, approximate time of closing, type of property, location, what percentage of space will be allocated to offices, stability of income, and relation of lease amount to other rentals in the area.

(2) A copy of the company's 10K form which all public corporations must file with the Securities and Exchange Commission.

(3) Annual reports for the last three years.

(4) The most recent earnings statement and balance sheets.

(5) Financial projections showing expenses and cash flow of the project to be built.

(6) A feasibility study which includes an appraisal of the proposed project, aerial and city maps with the project pinpointed, and photos of surrounding properties.

(7) Plans and specifications of the project.

(8) Occasionally, a five-year growth plan.

When an individual investor or developer wants financing based on the lease to a corporation, he will need to provide substantially the same data that the corporation would for a mortgage, but in addition he will need a copy of the lease between himself and the corporation.

If he is building speculatively or to sell, he must supply copies of leases, if he has managed to prelease, a personal financial statement and supporting information from the area stating the need for his kind of rental space.

THE BEST SOURCES FOR INDUSTRIAL PROPERTY LOANS

Loans to industrial companies are much in demand by the lending communtiy. Why? Businessmen are seasoned planners, industries stay put for a number of years, and many industrial units are well designed and, should there be default, provide easy space to rent or resell.

Among the most active lenders in this field are insurance companies, mutual savings banks, pension funds, savings and loan associations, finance companies, and commercial banks.

Some states have established industrial finance authorities to pump state money and credit into local development corporations to help them build industrial operations. These authorities are of two types — one guarantees the repayment of all or part of a mortgage loan made by private sources on an industrial plant and the other makes direct loans of state funds to the corporation for financing industrial projects.

In some cases, the authority will hold title to the project until its sale or lease. Funds are obtained by the issuance of bonds, as has been pointed out in this chapter, and the other is through direct state appropriation.

State industrial commissions can be of great help in supplying those interested with an overview of a community's industrial needs and in offering special programs through the state level offices.

The Small Business Administration lends on its own or with other institutions. Whether a business is considered small or large depends on its industry category. Usually in manufacturing, a company is termed small if it has under 250 employees and large if it employs more than 1,000 people.

Those wholesale companies with annual sales of no more than $5 million qualify. Retail or service firms with annual sales of not more than $1 million also qualify.

SBA, established by Congress in 1953 and made a permanent agency in 1958, makes loans for as little as $1,000 and as much as $350,000 although a bank may exceed this amount if it participates with SBA on the loan. The agency will consider guaranteeing up to 90 percent of a bank loan.

The SBA loans are made to those who are unable to get financing from banks on their own or from other government agencies.

The purpose of these loans may be business construction, expansion or conversion, the purchase of machinery or equipment and supplies, or in some cases, working capital.

Loans are not made for gambling, speculative or lending activities, newspaper or magazine publishing, or radio or television broadcasting, or for the sale of alcoholic beverages.

Eligibility and other requirements for SBA loans are available from the agency's regional or branch offices. SBA addresses can be found in the government source directory at the end of this book.

OBTAINING THE BEST DEAL

Comparing Sources — The corporation borrowing funds for real estate should check with two or three private placement specialists or investment bankers about its loan and decide which one can offer the best service for its needs.

The individual investor or developer might consult mortgage bankers and select one in the same basic way.

It should be remembered that certain lenders specialize in mortgages and loans within particular industries, and these sources can be best pointed out by mortgage brokers and bankers and investment specialists.

Negotiating the Best Rate — There are a number of pluses the borrower can take with him to the negotiating table that might sway the lender to his side for the best terms and rates possible. These include the borrower's willingness to sign personally, the multiplicity and top location of his building so that if he vacated it could be leased easily, an attractive earnings record, an impressive executive portfolio, company background data, and well-thought-out, five-year corporate growth plans.

THE TRANSACTION

Procedures of the transaction will depend on whether the borrower is an individual or a corporation and the type of loan sought.

Using the sale leaseback, the corporation would negotiate with the lessor either for a letter of intent or a lease subject to the lessor's obtaining a mortgage. Once this has been negotiated, the lessor proceeds to obtain mortgage financing.

In a few cases, there are some lessors who, because they are large institutions, may buy for all cash and therefore will not need a loan.

Once initial agreement is signed, the corporation will need to provide the lessor with all the details of the specific properties so that he may proceed to obtain his mortgage.

When the mortgage financing is finished, a closing will be scheduled. At the closing the lessor will provide the equity funds and the mortgage lender will supply the mortgage funds so the lessee corporation has 100 percent financing. In some cases, if a corporation wants to keep rent at a minimum, it will sell the property at book value or at less than cost to the lessor.

To illustrate, suppose Hacket Corporation has $1 million invested in a plant, including land and building. The corporation sells the property and leases it back for $120,000 for 25 years for a total of $3 million in rent.

As an alternative, let's assume book value is $750,000 and the firm sells it at that price and leases it back for book value or about $90,000 a year.

The rental would then be $30,000 a year less for a total savings of $750,000 over the term of the lease. Hacket Corporation must decide whether it is better to have the extra $250,000 to use in its business or to have the lower rent. If Hacket took the extra $250,000, it would also be subject to capital gains taxes.

In the net lease transaction, the lessee will be dealing through an investment banker, private placement specialist, or directly with the lender. Usually, this net lease financing will carry covenants which require the corporation to have various ratios for debt coverage. The most important of these is the fixed charge coverage providing a means so that the lender can monitor a company's ability to pay its fixed charges which include long-term debts and lease expenses.

The first stage of this financing is to agree in principle to the basic business terms and conditions of the financing. The second stage is usually a visit by the lender to the corporation at which time he will meet with the chief financial officer.

During this conference, the lender will begin to satisfy himself regarding a number of areas which include competence of management, control systems, operational ability, position of the company within its segment of the industry, training programs, and marketing plans.

Lenders are quite concerned about these subjects since they are investing in the company for a very long period.

After this meeting, the lender will take the financing proposal to his loan committee. In the interim there might be more negotiations between the lender and the company to finalize business decisions or details of the loan.

Once the proposal is approved by committee, a firm commitment letter is issued by the lender. The corporation can bank the commitment letter to get construction financing. The transaction is then turned over to the lender's legal department, and leases are finalized with the corporation's attorneys.

In a mortgage transaction, the developer or the corporation will make application usually through a mortgage banker to an institutional lender. This application usually requires a fee ranging from one-half to two percent of the loan amount.

Once all the material is received, the lender will make a personal inspection of the property. Thereafter, he will present the deal to his loan committee. Once the loan has been approved, a long-term letter of commitment will be provided the borrower for takedown or funding when the project is completed.

With this commitment letter, the borrower will be able to obtain his construction loan.

In setting up the transaction for a private placement financing, a corporation will work directly with an investment banker or other private placement specialist. The same procedures will apply as those in the net lease financing, except that the corporation will own the real estate in the private placement financing.

A disadvantage of the private placement is that the debt must show on the balance sheet since it is a direct obligation of the corporation. A net lease transaction is contingent liability and does not have to appear on the balance sheet.

CONSTRUCTION FINANCING

Using the Package — Once the borrower, whether a corporation or an individual, has obtained the long-term mortgage or lease commitment, it is then relatively easy for the borrower to use this commitment package to get construction money.

Choosing the Lender and Negotiating the Rate — The borrower should first check with his own commercial bank as well as mortgage investment trusts and mortgage bankers to determine prevailing rates. These specialists will try to find a lender for him at rates he wants to pay. Sources for short-term construction money are commercial banks, S and L's, real estate investment trusts, and large finance companies, such as Ford Motor Credit Corporation.

If the borrower prefers, he can contact these sources directly, but the advantage of using a specialist is that he knows the current marketplace better than anyone else. A professional finance representative is also skilled at negotiating for the best rates and can use his contacts with competing lenders to put together the best deal for his client.

Closing the Deal — Once the borrower has his long-term commitment, he gives the construction lender virtual assurance that he will be
paid off when the project is completed. The construction lender's major
concern will be whether or not the builder can stay within his estimated
cost framework.

Many times the lender will require that the builder be bonded,
which assures the lender, through the builder's insurance, that the project will be finished. The lender will periodically check construction as
it is in progress and will fund money as stages are completed.

Corporate Techniques — Companies with large cash flow can frequently obtain very favorable construction financing from their commercial banks.

For instance, if a company needs a short-term loan for a $2-million
construction project, and its compensating bank balance is about $300,000,
the bank will tend to make it that short-term loan at rates which will lean
toward prime.

Sometimes, corporations use their existing lines of credit with banks
for construction loans.

SINGLE-TENANT INDUSTRIALS

Properties under the sale leaseback and net lease agreements with
single tenant industrial companies are highly popular with lenders and
investors.

The term of the lease is usually 25 to 30 years, and it is guaranteed
by the full credit of the company. The owner does not have to worry
about maintenance or upgrading since the tenant will carry on these
duties as part of his business operation. In many other types of commercial real estate investments, leases are for shorter terms and maintenance is costly.

REFINANCING INDUSTRIAL PROPERTIES

When the mortgage on an industrial facility has run for about five
years and inflation has made building and land costs high, it might be
advisable to consider refinancing to regain original investment plus, perhaps, a profit on top of that initial outlay.

Institutional lenders will consider refinancing if the rental schedule
has been increased substantially, in times of inflation, and if they can see
increased demand for remodeled facilities for which refinancing funds
might be used.

There are several techniques in refinancing that can be used if a new
mortgage is not the right answer for the owner of the industrial complex.

He might try to get a second mortgage from mortgage banks, large finance companies, real estate investment trusts, or individual investors.

The previously discussed wrap-around mortgage is available from mortgage bankers, individuals, real estate investment trusts, and finance companies.

Both kinds of mortgages will give the owner of a building more cash to invest, use business operations, or improve his property.

FINANCING INDUSTRIALS ON LEASED LAND

Buildings of this kind are constructed on leased property when the land cannot be bought or when the developer or the builder wants to obtain greater leverage and forego buying the land.

With subordination, that is with the owner of the land having a secondary position to the mortgage holder of the building, the borrower agrees to a sale leaseback.

This allows the borrower to obtain 100 percent financing on the land portion of the project.

He will then get a leasehold mortgage on the building. The lender of this mortgage will have first position in case of default.

When a developer or company must build on unsubordinated land, that is with the mortgage holder of the building taking second position, it is more difficult to obtain financing.

In the case of a company, it can use its corporate credit in order to provide additional security for either the mortgage or a private placement. A developer might obtain funds by pledging additional assets which he has in order to secure the loan on the building.

DEVELOPING INDUSTRIAL PARKS

The investor who has his eye on developing an industrial center or park should realize that enormous sums of money and massive research are required for such an undertaking. Often, the developer must even sponsor or participate in additional facilities such as shopping centers, housing, office buildings, and other facilities to help sell and support the industrial complex.

The developer is usually a group or a company, and there are various avenues open for financing such a property. It can be joint-ventured with the owners of the land to reduce the amount of capital involved. The property can be bought with a purchase money mortgage with release clauses, allowing the developer to sell off parcels as industrial units are completed.

Some backers of these parks will provide for the development and financing of build-to-suit facilities for individual participants, make ground lease arrangements, or exchange properties so the tenant acquires fee title to his site.

The investors may choose to develop and operate the park, to sell it to a large corporation and to retain its management, or to sell shares in a company created to operate the park.

Funds for such projects are usually available from mortgage trusts, commercial banks, and large finance companies.

Investment specialists and mortgage bankers can offer excellent advice and service in this kind of financing.

8. — Restaurants, Service Stations, and Other Free-Standing Properties

EVALUATING CREDIT OF A CHAIN

A lender judges the rates and terms he will grant a chain store by the size or net worth of the company, its earnings record, and the acceptance of its particular industry by the current lending community.

A lender's decision to make funds available to a particular company will be based on the preceding criteria plus competence of management, control systems, operational capabilities, the firm's particular positioning in the industry, its ability to service the loan, and its training and marketing programs.

Guidelines constantly change, but generally a company with $50 million in net worth and with good earnings records can make his financing structure a net lease, a private placement, or a mortgage loan.

If the net worth (with good earnings) exceeds $10 million in a reasonably good market, he can choose from among a sale leaseback, private placement of debt, or a mortgage loan. Average companies with net worths of less than $10 million can obtain a mortgage loan, sale leaseback, or interim corporate loan. These guidelines also vary with the amount of time a company has been in business and with other standards.

SOURCES FOR DIFFERENT TYPES OF CHAIN STORES

Sources will vary based on the type and size of loan sought. For a single loan on a special-purpose building, it is best to see a mortgage banker, commercial bank, or a savings and loan association. A single-purpose property can vary in size from $100,000 to $800,000 for the larger restaurants or bowling alleys.

Many different types of lenders will make loans to special-purpose and free-standing properties whether a single unit or a package of them, but they must be sought out aggressively.

These include finance, insurance, investment, and small business companies and pension funds.

HOW TO PACKAGE A GROUP OF SMALL PROPERTIES FOR A SINGLE FINANCING

A major problem for both small and large companies mass-producing buildings in widespread geographical areas is obtaining adequate

133

financing for expansion. Often it is possible to package a number of these properties in a single financing either as a net lease, sale leaseback, mortgage, or private placement of debt. As an example, let's say that Burger King Corporation plans to build 200 restaurants over the next 18 months. These properties will be located in 20 different states and 75 different cities. The simple logistics of obtaining a loan on each unit are difficult and time consuming. The process can be greatly simplified if a single lender can be found who can make loans on all of the properties in one transaction.

Real Estate Loans and Sale Leasebacks — Generally speaking, if a chain or a store owner-developer is seeking a 60-80 percent loan, he will do so through the real estate department of a major institution, such as an insurance company, either directly or through a mortgage broker.

If a sale leaseback is negotiated, there will be a three or four-party transaction — the lender, the chain store (lessee), developer or investor (lessor) and, perhaps, a real estate or mortgage broker.

In either type transaction, the lender will only agree to finance existing properties or properties being build. He will not commit for future delivery or for properties to be constructed in the future.

The company can get 60 to 80 percent, but usually 75 percent, of its cost or appraised value for a loan of the land, building, and site improvements using the real estate mortgage approach, or 100 percent by choosing the sale leaseback method.

If an investor or developer is seeking a mortgage dependent on the lease, he should attempt to get the lender to base the loan on the appraised value of the lease. This value would be figured on the income stream of the lease as well as the lessee's credit. By so doing, the investor or developer may be able to borrow more funds so his actual out-of-pocket cost may be less than it would be if he based the appraisal on actual cost.

Upon making application, it is to the borrower's advantage to get an MAI or other accredited appraisal to aid in supporting this method.

To illustrate: Suppose Big Auto Stores is willing to pay a 13 percent rental for 25 years. On a $1-million net lease this will produce an income of $130,000 a year.

Assume the financial strength of the company is sufficient to have the lease capitalized by the lender at 10-1/2 percent so that the value of the income stream is appraised at $1,238,090.

A loan based on 75 percent of the appraised value would give the developer $928,567. Henceforth, the cash he would have invested is $71,433. Had the developer obtained a commitment from a lender based on the actual cost, he would have had to invest $250,000 in the project.

Bond Financing and Net Leases — Through the private placement of mortgage debt, the loan-to-value ratio can be much higher, even as much as 100 percent since the loan is chiefly based on the credit of the company involved.

The direct debt obligation is usually processed through a private placement specialist or the corporate finance department of an investment banking house. For such loans, lenders usually require restrictive covenants giving the lender certain guarantees that the company will operate in such a manner that it will be able to continue to pay the debt.

Many lenders have been hesitant to finance a number of small units using the regular mortgage route, but with a private placement of debt the lender is more concerned with the credit of the company as security than with the bricks and mortar aspects.

STEP-BY-STEP GUIDE

In dealing with smaller free-standing or special-purpose properties, there are usually two types of transactions used — one covers a number of smaller commercial properties and the other is for one to three parcels. The first type can involve 10 to 50 pieces of real estate located in many states, and these can be wrapped up in one single financial deal. The latter is usually restricted to a few properties in one metropolitan area.

Assembling the Package — Whether a loan for a large package or a single property is under consideration, there is certain information that is needed by the lender. Here is a checklist to use in the preparing of various loan presentations:

For a mortgage loan these items are needed:

(1) An annual report or current financial statement of the company.
(2) The most recent earnings statement.
(3) A map of the city indicating the site.
(4) An aerial photo showing the property.
(5) On-site photos.
(6) An appraisal.
(7) If a lender requires it, a feasibility study.
(8) An individual financial statement if a developer or individual is operating or developing the restaurant himself.

In addition to the data outlined for a mortgage, the following are required for a private placement:

(1) Annual reports for the last three years.
(2) Earnings statements for the last three years.
(3) Often, operating statements on the individual existing units of the company.
(4) A copy of existing loan covenants.

Added to the information listed for mortgage and private placements, the following are needed for a net lease:

(1) A copy of the purchase contract.

(2) A copy of the lease.

Required for a sale leaseback in addition to items listed under mortgage loans the following are required:

(1) A copy of the purchase contract.

(2) A copy of the lease.

(3) A copy of the developer's or investor's financial statement.

Approaching the Lenders — The first step in contacting lenders is to find out who has a reputation for providing funds for these types of properties. Owners and operators of similar types of properties, as well as the borrower's commercial bank, can provide such information.

Since loan sources for this kind of real estate are scarce, it is usually best to work through an aggressive mortgage banking house with creative financing capabilities.

Once the representative has been selected, it is best to provide him as quickly as possible with all the material he needs to present the borrower in the best light. Newspaper articles and public information releases are often very helpful in introducing a lender to a company.

Negotiating a Rate — When making arrangements with mortgage bankers or lenders, the borrower should come to terms with them regarding the rate and term which are satisfactory with the borrower. It is best for both parties to have a written statement between them so there is no misinterpretation of these points. Most mortgage bankers and lenders will require an application and good faith deposit to bind the agreement.

Getting the Commitment Letter and Handling Final Negotiations — A commitment letter on the project from the lender is next on the agenda in the loan transaction. This letter must be negotiated between the borrower and the lender to their mutual satisfaction. The commitment letter is usually three to four pages long and covers the major business decisions.

At this point, there will be more talk about one of the most important factors of the loan, the prepayment penalty. Long-term lenders like to freeze loans from seven to ten years. Savings and loan associations are usually the most lenient and in some cases do not require the penalty.

A personal meeting between lender and borrower is usually the best way to conclude negotiations successfully before closing. Discussed will be date of contract signing, confirmation of the major business decisions such as term of the loan, interest rate, if there will be any balloon payments, and dates and covenants that might be in the loan agreement.

Closing the Transaction — The actual closing is the issuing of funds to the borrower and the payment of fees and commissions to all parties participating in the financing. The closing process is the culmination of all the administrative procedures needed before funds are disbursed.

For the closing, attorneys finalize legal documentation. The title insurance company evaluates the abstract and issues title insurance. All existing mortgages are brought up to date and paid off.

OBTAINING CONSTRUCTION FINANCING

Before signing the long-term commitment letter, the borrower should make sure the commitment is bankable with a construction lender. This is true whether a company or an individual is seeking the loan. With a bankable commitment letter, construction financing is assured.

How the Chain Store Can Aid the Investor or Developer — The chain store company can best aid the sale leaseback and net lease developer or investor in the following ways:

(1) Providing him with the information needed by his lenders. Fifty percent of all loans attempted, but lost, fail because the lender did not have an adequate and thorough presentation or because there were long delays in the lender's receiving needed materials.

(2) Suggesting lenders to the lessor who might know the company well and might have loaned money on their leases in the past.

(3) Having top management available to visit with the lessor's lenders and introducing them to the company and answering any questions they may have.

Sources and How to Utilize Them — It is more difficult to obtain combined long-term and construction loans on these types of properties than on more traditional real estate because they are special purpose and free standing, and if they fail, they fail 100 percent. There is no revenue to lean on as there is in shopping centers, for instance. If a borrower can show that his free-standing property has multiple uses, the lender will feel more secure since there would be alternatives for use of the real estate in case of foreclosure. The best sources for both long-term and construction loans are the S and L's and the combined short-term/long-term mortgage trusts.

Other sources for this type of financing include insurance companies, commercial banks, mutual savings bands, finance companies, and a few pension funds.

Making Application — The same procedures will be necessary for the construction loan as for the long-term mortgage with the exception that the commitment letter will provide for separate fundings as construction progresses.

If a company prefers to do its own building, it can frequently obtain its own construction funds by utilizing existing lines of credit with its commercial banks or establishing new credit. This greatly simplifies otherwise complicated take-down procedures on a number of small properties.

Rapidly growing companies usually have large cash flows through commercial banks providing higher than normal compensating balances.

For this reason, attractive rates can frequently be established with these institutions.

Closing the Transaction — Once a construction commitment letter has been issued, the borrower and lender will need to negotiate the final terms and conditions of the loan. The borrower should be sure to have the construction loan open for five or six months longer than he plans construction to take in order to allow for unpredictable delays. He should also make sure the loan amount is adequate to complete construction. It is advisable that the builder be bonded and that a firm contract is signed for the builder to construct the premises at a definite price. Provisions should be made in a construction loan in case of price overruns.

Coordinating the Loan with Long-term Financing — Loan officers for both short and long-term financing should be introduced and constant contact should be maintained between them so coordination of the two loans can be monitored to the benefit of all principals. The mortgage banker or borrower should be responsible for this function.

REFINANCING THE PROJECT

When negotiating his original lease, the developer or investor might consider a longer-term lease than is traditionally accepted. This would allow him in five to seven years to refinance his project and get back some of his initial cash investment.

As an example, a normal lease in the restaurant industry is 15 to 20 years. Assume developer Brown negotiates a 25-year lease with a cost-of-living provision or other incentive. In a five-year period, the rental income substantially exceeds that of the earlier years allowing him to refinance the existing lease based upon the increased rentals.

Since he originally negotiated the longer term lease (25 years), a lender would be receptive to writing a new mortgage because there still are 20 years of guaranteed rental remaining at the end of the fifth year. Using this method, Brown can take money out of the project to reinvest in other projects.

If refinancing is a goal, it is also advisable to obtain an easy prepayment in the original lease which is negotiated so that at a later date the old loan can be paid off and a new one placed.

CREATIVE WAYS TO FINANCE PROJECTS

Whether an established chain, a young growing company, a developer, or an investor is involved, there are some creative ways to finance individual plans to increase leverage or obtain sites that would otherwise be impossible. Here is a check list of some of these approaches:

(1) Owner Build-to-Suit — If a land owner will not sell, get him to construct the building and lease it to the company. If he is unfamiliar with the procedures, take him to lenders or mortgage bankers for an explanation and assistance.

(2) Purchase — If the chain or developer can buy outright, this is, of course, ideal.

(3) Purchase, Development and Leaseback — This method, which gives maximum control to the company, calls for use of the company's funds to buy the land and build the unit. Once completed, a sale leaseback or net lease can be negotiated which will allow the company to get 100 percent of its money back plus its out-of-pocket costs. There are also more buyers for completed projects which they can inspect.

(4) Land Lease with Subordination — If an owner will not sell because of increased taxes he might have to pay or other personal reasons, try to get him to lease the land and subordinate his position to an institutional first mortgage. His lawyer should be satisfied that the owner is given ample protection. With subordination in hand, the company, investor, or developer can then go to an institutional lender and obtain the mortgage money needed to handle the development.

(5) Land Lease without Subordination — If the land owner still refuses to sell, the company can consider grouping a number of buildings which are constructed on leased land into a direct debt obligation privately placed and secured not only by the buildings themselves, but also by the full faith of the parent corporation. A developer or investor can also consider pledging additional assets personally or taking a smaller loan-to-value mortgage.

(6) Land and Contract — Using this approach, the buyer purchases the land and the seller takes back a purchase money mortgage. The mortgage can be subordinated or unsubordinated, and the method of obtaining financing for the building would be exactly the same as described under subordinated and unsubordinated land leases.

(7) Developer Build-to-Suit — This plan requires a builder or developer to buy land with his own money, arrange his own construction loan, and build the unit according to the plans and specifications of the chain store. This method minimizes cash outlay by a company but lessens its control over scheduling of openings and monitoring a number of different developers in varying geographical areas.

9. — Mobile Home Parks

AN OVERVIEW

The building of a house without any modular construction is known in the industry as stick building. Because conventional stick-built, single-family housing has soared 50 percent in price since 1970, the mobile home is becoming the new American dream, by necessity if not by choice, of those who choose not to be stacked vertically in apartments or horizontally in townhouses.

The output of mobile homes in 1973 was 556,920 and for 1974 the best estimate is 440,000, or almost a million units in 24 months. The 1973 figure was 85 percent of all single-family homes sold under $20,000 and an estimated 92 percent for 1974.

Mobile homes have a median price of $9,000 versus median conventional prices of $35,500 for new homes and $32,860 for used homes.

Mobile homes in the United States cost about $9 per square foot against $17.50 for conventional houses. However, the advantage of the mobile home is reduced by its higher interest rates, 13 percent versus 9, and shorter repayment periods, ten years opposed to 20.

The larger, best built, double-wide mobile homes are now approaching $20,000 in cost, which is not too far under the price of the least expensive condominiums. In many areas, mobile homes are competing in markets overburdened with condominiums where the supply runs as high as 24 months ahead of demand.

Vacancy rates are low in the mobile home parks, generally about two to five percent, and there are statistics to support a lower vacancy experience in parks charging a higher rent and providing more amenities.

The larger parks are about 250 acres, and the trend is toward even bigger projects with many planned in the area of 3,000 acres.

These more expensive parks can achieve economies of production and operation because of size and can be built in phases over many years to match demand. They can even be segregated into compatible groups with special areas for retirees, people with children, and those with pets. Perhaps, a section for park-owned homes available for rent could be provided, too.

HOW TO COST OUT A PROJECT

General Comments — A good first-step would be to go to an FHA or HUD office to get copies of circulars Number 4545.1 dated May 24, 1973, and Number 4940.5 dated June 18, 1973. The first describes the mobile home park program, Section 207, and the latter sets forth the minimum design standards for mobile home parks.

No ideal-sized park is specified, although eight spaces are minimum, and reference is made that smaller, owner-operated projects of 30 spaces or fewer may prove economically feasible. FHA encourages the building of larger, better-designed parks with more of the customary neighborhood amenities.

This kind of real estate development does not lend itself properly to averages. There is a great difference between a 20-space park and one with 2,000 spaces. Comparisons widen further when one looks at a prestige operation in California with each of its 242 home sites offering an ocean view, requiring double-wide homes, and providing 24-hour guard service, a nine-hole golf course, underground utilities, 40-foot-wide streets — and then to a 15-year-old park built under the hit-or-miss philosophy.

The California project, with its country club atmosphere, was built by Sequoia Pacific Realco and embodies the best techniques of the industry. Covering 70 acres, it has fewer than four homesites per acre.

Many older trailer parks were built without any planning other than using a design for maximum permitted density or home stands per gross acre. These often contain 10 or more dwellings per acre, especially of the smaller mobile homes. As a rule, top density is coupled with low rents and the least investment in amenities such as landscaping and pools.

The increase in costs of developing and operating mobile home parks since 1970 has pulled the rental standard of $40 to $50 up to $70 to $80 per unit in recent times.

The reasons for the jump? Consider these illustrations: There is an actual 40-acre, three-and-a-half-year-old park, which has 301 spaces, or 7.5 dwellings per acre. Two projects planned in the same state are 1) 103 acres, 500 spaces or five per acre and 2) 130 acres, 755 sites or 5.8 an acre.

A declining density and increasing land and development costs simply require higher rentals or higher sale costs for the new projects which will give the existing unit an advantage in profitability.

The 40-acre park spent over $100,000 for landscaping when built and to duplicate it today would require about $25,000 more.

Let's be fair and compare apples to apples. Park developers, in increasing numbers, are providing larger lots, better landscaping and more recreational facilities, sometimes by choice and sometimes because the government requires it. Where septic tanks were formerly all right, sewage treatment systems are the rule of the day.

In view of the foregoing examples and increasing prices and demands for conveniences and attractiveness, a costing-out checklist should provide for design fees, plot plans, high-grade landscaping, underground utilities, fenced perimeter, black-top private drives, an impressive entrance gate, a building for washers and dryers, a social-recreation building with air conditioning; a kitchen, restrooms, television, Ping-Pong equipment, a swimming pool with lighting for night use, barbecue pits, picnic tables and benches, and children's slides and merry-go-rounds if youngsters live in the park.

An Example — A worksheet for total costs to improve each of the stands or pads which a developer plans to provide should follow this outline:

XYZ MOBILE HOME PARK

Development Cost Per Site

1.	Site clearing and preparation	$ 200
2.	Drainage	200
3.	Streets/drives/parking	375
4.	Sewerage	475
5.	Water	400
6.	Paving stands	250
7.	Electrical service	375
8.	Recreational facilities	300
9.	Landscaping	250
10.	Utility building	75
11.	Miscellaneous	100
	Total	$3,000

The above list does not include land which will vary greatly in cost depending on the developer's location in the country. Recreation and landscaping prices are also subject to geographical differences and the make-up of the residents.

Average Costs and Profits — Again, averages in any field involving extremes in size and differences in quality should be considered with caution. If a multiple is needed for quick calculating, it is reasonable to use $3,000 per stand or space as the cost of land improvements required, meaning one would invest $18,000 per acre to create a density of six units per acre above the cost of the land itself.

Let's do a quick problem to see if the formula works, based on the assumption that a return of 20 percent on invested capital before taxes is expected:

One Acre

Income	Outgo
6 spaces at $75.00 per month = $450 per month = $5,400 yearly	6 spaces at $3,000 development cost = $18,000 5,000 Land $23,000

$$\text{yield} = \frac{\text{Return}}{\text{Investment}} = \frac{5,400}{23,000} = 23.5\%$$

Since the industry experiences an overhead of about 25 percent, the 23.5 percent would drop to 18 percent as the return on investment. The example, for the purpose of simplicity, ignores financing and is considered free and clear of debt.

ASSEMBLING THE NECESSARY DATA

If a developer is planning to buy raw land, he should not until his attorney can assure him that the zoning does or will allow his intended use. Also, he should assure himself what concessions or buffer strips or other amenities will be necessary to obtain the building permit.

A feasibility study can be exhaustive and must be if the developer will need substantial financing of any sort, especially involving FHA.

Many very successful existing parks have resulted from the prospective developer's taking a Sunday afternoon drive through all the competitive parks within about five miles, noting the number of vacant slots and reading in the local paper that several hundred thousand new mobile homes will be built and sold in the current year. The investor then jumps into the mainstream of activity and stays afloat. His research method, though, is hardly recommended today.

PROVISIONS TO CHECK

The borrower should investigate each of these points and satisfy himself that he is protected under the terms of his loan agreement:

(1) Is there a lock-in provision under which for a specified period of time there will be no prepayment privilege?

(2) What penalties are provided for prepayment of installments of principal?

(3) Does the loan have an equity participation feature under which the lender receives payments in excess of his contracted debt-service payment, based on a formula geared to increases in the gross rents produced by the project?

(4) Some mobile home park loan documents provide that if the lender feels unsafe or unsure about a loan, the loan may be recalled so that the entire unpaid balance becomes due at that time. The borrower will find this type of provision one with which he will not want to contend.

(5) If the borrower has several loans with the same lender, he should look for a provision stating that when a borrower has more than one loan with the lender and one loan is in default, this is tantamount to all loans being in default so that all unpaid loan balances become due and payable immediately.

(6) Does the loan provide for the right of the borrower freely to transfer the loan? This is important since lack of transferability might prevent a sale of the property.

(7) Is there a substitution of liability clause? If the property is sold and the

loan is transferred to the buyer, will the lender release the original borrower from all obligations under the loan?

(8) Does the loan contain a holdback provision under which part of the loan proceeds will be funded only when the project achieves occupancy at a specified rent level and within a specified time limit? If the lender insists on it, the borrower should try to limit the amount of the holdback to a small percentage of the loan. The borrower should try for as low a rent achievement provision as possible to free up the funds early in the game.

SOURCES AND HOW TO FINANCE MOBILE HOME PARKS

Loans for these developments are more difficult to acquire since sources are not so numerous as they are for other more conventional mortgages. Improvements on these properties are rapidly depreciable and in case of default the lender could have a bad time recapturing his investment. Mortgages often do not run more than 60 percent of the selling price.

Financing of these parks by REIT's is limited to large projects, and the developer of small to medium-sized parks should look to other sources such as commercial banks, finance companies, and some savings and loan associations and insurance companies.

On sites which meet its criteria, FHA will guarantee loans up to $2,500 per space and for parks up to $1,000,000 total not to exceed 90 percent of the estimated value of the property after construction or improvements. A typical such loan is for 20 years, but it can extend up to 40 years if the park is in accordance with local comprehensive plans and other details.

Financing companies are interested in mortgages for mobile home parks, especially if there is a tie-in with a mobile home dealer who sells homes and owns or has a substantial participation in a park. Such firms as C.I.T., Aristar, G.E.C.C., and others are examples of finance companies that make such loans.

Savings and loan associations do not aggressively seek financing of mobile homes on a direct basis. They do buy packages from service companies or intermediaries, which screen out applicants, check credit, handle the accounts, sell credit insurance, and pursue delinquencies.

The intermediaries that place financing with S and L's derive the bulk of their income from the life insurance required from the borrower, in connection with the title retention contract.

Commercial banks are a good source. They avoid long-term conventional mortgages but are heavy investors in the relatively short-term, seven to 10-year, financing of mobile homes, where interest of 12 to 15 percent prevails.

FHA regulations permit interest charges up to a maximum of 12 percent on financing of mobile homes and a term of 10 to 12 years. On a double-wide home, the term can run to 15 years.

ALTERNATIVES AVAILABLE FOR CORPORATIONS

The public corporation that builds mobile home parks has additional financing alternatives available to it. The company may decide to use corporate credit to secure a loan rather than encumber the mobile home park.

Corporations with large cash flow or substantial net worth and earnings can use existing or expanded lines of credit to fund a mobile home park until it is sold out.

THE ROLE OF MANUFACTURERS

The large increase in the number of firms constructing mobile homes has created a system whereby a sizable inventory of units will be assigned to a dealer for sale. The display resembles the floor-plan arrangement used by auto dealerships, and the units are not paid for until after sale to the final owner.

The inventory might consist of the products of several manufacturers to offer customers a broad price and quality range, as firms tend to specialize in products.

The floor plan often involves commercial banks and an established retailer can sometimes get 90 to 100 percent of his cost financed, which reduces his overall investment sharply. Sometimes, these display sections are actually part of a park, and of course, are stiuated on the highway frontage where traffic visibility and noise would make the space less desirable for residential use. If the dealer requires purchase of his models as a condition of renting a space, it is called a captive or a closed park.

If a developer plans to build a park on a busy highway, his chances of making a dealership arrangement are quite good, and might even be the basis for a territory franchise. If not, lending institutions should be contacted to ascertain if they will handle both the inventory of units and the liens after sale.

LEGAL RAMIFICATIONS AND HOW TO DEAL WITH THEM

Many leases in mobile home parks contain all of the "rules and regulations." These rules are continually being tested in court. Unless they are reasonable and enforced uniformly, it makes no difference whether they are in the lease or not. Even the leases themselves are being restricted by law. Some states are adopting laws restricting rent increase, establishing the notice period before increases, and defining the eviction process which is generally more favorable to the tenant. A developer or operator should not be a pioneer in his park in this regard. He should use a lease which is as short as possible, clearly understandable, fair and enforceable. He can get better cooperation from tenants by having at least an annual meeting to consider jointly new rules or modifications.

Other items which generate friction between landlord and tenant are attempts by the landlord to charge a fee or commission to the seller of a mobile home in his park. He may provide no service for the charge and attempt to collect by refusal to lease to the new owner after expiration of the present lease, forcing an expensive move.

The best policy is to establish at the beginning of each tenant's occupancy the procedures which will apply and stick to them.

MAINTENANCE COSTS AND MANAGEMENT

A mobile home park of up to about 50 spaces can be managed by a couple. The man usually handles landscaping, repairs, painting, and routine services. The woman manages the office, taking care of rent collections, bookkeeping, paying bills, and handling complaints. Often the management is performed by semi-retired people, who receive only a modest salary plus rent and utilities.

For a park of 300 spaces, the staff should be about five people — the managers, husband and wife, plus three men who, in addition to landscaping and cleaning assignments, would provide services in plumbing, electrical work, and painting. At least one man should be capable in maintaining washer and dryer facilities because outside service work is expensive and constant.

PUBLICATIONS

Here is a list of publications which should aid the owner or developer of mobile home parks:

Mobile Home Park Management
    and Developer
Published: Every other month
Editorial and Business Office
6229 Northwest Highway
Chicago, Illinois 60631

Mobile Home and Trailer News
    (Florida)
Published: Weekly (Oct.-May),
    every other week remainder
P. O. Box 967, Kendall Branch
Miami, Florida 33156
305/233-3421

Woodall Publishing Company
    (Industry Guide) or Woodall's Park
    Development Services, Inc.
5000 Hyacinth Place
Highland Park, Illinois 60035

Indiana Manufactured Housing
    Association, Inc.
3210 Rand Road
Indianapolis, Indiana 46241

Mobile Home Manufacturers
    Association
Box 201, 14650 Lee Road
Chantilly, Virginia 22021
Publishes "Law of Mobile Homes"

Standards for Mobile Home Parks
N.F.P.A. No. 502-A, 1974 Edition
470 Atlantic Avenue
Boston, Massachusetts 02210

Mobile Home Owners News
c/o Federation of Mobile Home
    Owners of Florida, Inc.
3375 — 34th Street North, Suite 202
St. Petersburg, Florida 33713

Southeastern Manufactured Housing
    Institute
Suite 112, Emerson Center
2810 New Spring Road
Atlanta, Georgia 30339

Credit Insurers of America
Mortgage Banker, Mobile Home
    Industry

1320 South Dixie Highway, Suite 950
Coral Gables, Florida 33146

Mobile Homes; Housings Best Buy
    (Booklet)
Revised Edition by Carl Edwards
6229 Northwest Highway
Chicago, Illinois 60631

Leisure Life Style Corporation
    (Marketing Packages)
P. O. Box 666
Borrego Springs, California 92004

Florida Mobilehome & Recreational
    Vehicle Association, Inc.
4212 El Prado Boulevard
Tampa, Florida 33609

10. — Land Development — from Lots to Recreational Facilities

GENERAL COMMENTS

Big money can be made by investors in land, and fortunes can be lost the same way. Land values can change drastically, making this kind of speculation about the highest risk category in real estate.

The land developer's ship comes in when the commodity is sold, but before that golden event, he must face cash outlays for principal and interest if he pays by mortgage, and taxes regardless.

The purchase of raw land or acreage for future sale, either as a whole or after subdivision into lots, requires great knowledge and some luck for the speculator or investor.

People who buy land do so either to use, to develop, or to hold until its utilization will change and demand a high price. Their goals often determine how they will approach the financing of the land they purchase.

Land development has become so complicated that a new real estate specialist emerged in the 1970's, the land packager. He acquires undeveloped land and processes it for the construction of such projects as shopping centers or multi-family housing. His work often includes obtaining rezoning, site plans, and building and utility permits.

The packager negotiates the conditional purchase contract and the land packaging which includes coordination with government agencies that control various aspects of the land.

All raw land in this country has appreciated considerably in the past few decades, typically at an accelerated degree. Some land has increased in value by a thousand percent. Other land has tripled or quadrupled during the same period.

Many otherwise knowledgeable people refuse to participate in land buying at any time, always remembering back a few years when they could have bought at a cheaper price.

A prudent purchaser, after considering the relationship of nearby national parks or scenic vistas, transportation, competitive projects, direction of growth corridors, availability of water and electricity, and good financing has an excellent chance to make money if he buys early, at the beginning of a trend.

It is not necessary to learn how to design, build, or finance improvements. All the investor has to do is wait until he can sell at a higher price.

A real estate tycoon once attributed his considerable fortune to "selling out too soon." In other words, one cannot wait for the last dollar or overstay the market.

SOURCES AND TECHNIQUES

Optioning — Most investors in land want to get control of the property for as little cash as possible. The best way to accomplish this goal is to option the land for purchase, agree to sell when the price is right, and take a profit.

Of course, the speculator can lose his option money if he cannot find a buyer within the agreed option time and is not prepared to buy. He could, of course, exercise the option and buy the land, hoping for a big sale later.

The beauty of this straight option is that the investor is not obligated to taxes or any other cost for the option period and the option money can be applied against the price of the land.

If the speculator can find a buyer for the land he has optioned, he presents the property as his land until the purchase contracts are signed. The person optioning the land then makes the difference between the option price and the appreciated value of the land or whatever the new buyer is willing to pay.

The rolling option can also be used when control of a large tract of land has been acquired, and the tract will be subdivided into lots. The investor can retain his option on the whole and at the same time use part of his option money on a lot or pay for the lot in full and roll his option on to the next parcel. The option on the tract is maintained and the investor can buy only those parcels he wants.

The landowner also can use the option technique to raise tax-free cash. If he does not want to sell or refinance, he can sell an option to purchase his property. No taxes are paid until the option is exercised. If the owner does not get his asking price, he does not actually sell.

Interest Only — Another means of buying land is to pay interest only. Believe it or not, some people don't need money or at least have no pressing need for cash on the barrel. If they are satisfied with other facets of a deal, these sellers will accept interest only for some period of the purchase money mortgage. This allows the buyer to use his funds elsewhere that otherwise would be used for reduction of principal. This can be used, for instance, during the start-up period of development when money needs are acute.

Purchase Money Mortgage — If an investor has no other alternative open to him than to buy the land either by cash or mortgage he must either persuade the seller to become the financier or take in some partners who have money or do both. The seller can help effect the deal in financing by a regular purchase money mortgage. The negotiating points then are 1) how much down payment is needed, 2) the length of pay-out and interest rate and 3) release clauses, if the parcel is sizable.

The investor should offer as low a down payment as the seller will take and for as long a term as possible.

These factors can protect the buyer handsomely in times of inflation, reduce the debt constant, and bring him higher profits when he sells.

For instance, Mr. Johnson manages to get a long-term mortgage on 20 acres of land for a total of $20,000 and only pays $1,000 down. In two years, he sells the parcel for $30,000 and realizes a profit of about $8,000.

Mr. Wilson bought 20 acres at the same price and paid cash. His profit was $9,500 after a $30,000 sale. Johnson is the smarter investor since his return on investment is eight times his investment, while Wilson's is less than one-third of his original investment.

Parcels intended to be developed over a lengthy period often have a clause that states that for certain payments made to the seller he will release from his purchase money mortgage specific portions of land which are fully described in advance.

The developer then can sell outright the released parcels to obtain money to proceed with his plans or be able to place new or first financing loans on the land released from the seller's lien.

By use of the following clauses, the mortgagor or buyer can obtain releases on parcels by paying a sum which is 50 percent of the land per parcel:

The mortgagor shall be entitled to obtain releases from the lien of this mortgage of any of the parcels designated herein and separately described and identified as parcels XYZ upon payment of the consideration to be fixed as hereinafter mentioned, subject to the following conditions:

(a) The consideration to be paid by the mortgagor to the mortgagee, for releases shall be fixed and arrived at as follows:

The original amount of the purchase money mortgage shall be multiplied by 150 percent consideration to be paid for any area of land to be released shall be that proportion of said sum of 150 percent of the original amount of the mortgage as the area of the land to be released shall bear to the total area of the land encumbered by said mortgage.

(b) On each release obtained, accrued interest thereon shall be paid on the consideration paid for said release from the date to which interest was last paid to the date of said release and the principal sum paid for said release (excluding interest) shall be applied in reduction of the principal sum of this mortgage.

(c) The mortgagor will supply to the attorney for the holder of this mortgage the legal description to be incorporated in any release requested, together with a copy of a survey showing the dimensions of the premises and amount of area computed in square feet sought to be released.

(d) Each instrument of release shall be in statutory recordable form and shall include all of the right, title, and interest, if any, in and to any street, road, or avenue adjoining the released premises to the center lines.

(e) All releases shall be prepared by the attorney for the holder of this mortgage at the expense of the mortgagor, such attorney's fee to be one hundred dollars ($100.00) for each such release.

(f) The mortgagor shall not be entitled to demand or obtain any release while the default exists in the performance of the terms or provisions of this mortgage, or of the obligation secured thereby.

(g) No release shall be requested nor shall same be given, for any area less than for all of the mortgaged land in any one of the separately described mortgaged parcels herein.

(h) It is understood that the first release to be obtained shall be either Parcel A or B, and after the first release shall have been obtained subsequent releases shall be granted for contiguous parcels as herein separately described. It is further understood that Parcel 4 may be released at any time without regard to contiguity.

(1) Any consideration paid for releases shall be credited on account of any amortization payment required in this mortgage and any amortization payment made as required by the within mortgage shall be credited to the amount of the consideration to be paid for any releases which may thereafter be requested by the mortgagor.

The mortgagee agrees to execute, acknowledge, and deliver, without charge, any and all consents and subordinations that may be required for the installation in streets of any public utility facilities, including but not in limitation of the following: water, gas, electric, sewage and storm drainage, and any consents that may be required by any lending institution or the Federal Housing Administration insuring or placing mortgages on the subject premises requiring the imposition of covenants and/or restrictions.

The mortgagor shall have the privilege to prepay the entire unpaid principal amount remaining due at any time prior to maturity and subsequent to January 1, 1980, on ten (10) days' prior written notice to the holder hereof with interest to the date of payment.

It is expressly understood and agreed by and between the parties hereto, that in the event of the foreclosure of this mortgage, it will be desirable that the mortgaged premises be sold in one parcel; that it will be impractical to sell the mortgaged premises in separate parcels; that an effort to sell the mortgaged premises in separate parcels would seriously prejudice and impair the security of the mortgagee and depreciate the prospective price which might be realized upon a foreclosure sale. It is, therefore, expressly understood and agreed that in the event of a foreclosure, the entire mortgaged premises may be sold in one parcel, and the mortgagor, for itself, its successors and assigns hereby expressly waives any present or future provisions of law requiring that the mortgaged premises be sold in parcels, and hereby consents that the entire mortgaged premises, or so much thereof as may still be subject to the lien of this mortgage, may be sold in one parcel.

The mortgagee or any owner of the within mortgage acquiring title to the mortgaged premises or any portion thereof by foreclosure or otherwise shall have the right to extend or connect to any sewer or any other utility installations made by the mortgagor or owner of the mortgaged premises without the payment of any cost, charge or expense.

Use of the Land to Finance — Under this plan, the developer leases raw land from the seller and pays an annual rent based on a value per acre. The land is developed and deeded to individuals and the seller is thus paid for the land from proceeds of sale. Title of the land is usually held by a corporate trustee.

Using another method, the lease-purchase contract, there is no down payment made by the buyer but he pays a rental which is applied to the purchase price. At the end of the rental period, this sum plus another lump is applied to a down payment. Thereafter, the buyer pays a sum plus interest per year.

Other Channels — Beyond this normal method of financing is an approach calling for more sophisticated planning. The developer who uses other methods may be short on cash and long on enthusiasm, he may have an unblemished record of success in land deals, or he might even be a novice eager to get his start in this exciting field.

The key to making a deal might be to involve the seller in the venture by swapping a lower down payment and easier terms for his right to share in the rewards as the project progresses.

The contract for this type of operation should be carefully prepared to protect the capital gains tax status of the seller. It should specify that the seller is only that and not a partner.

To illustrate this approach:

Mr. Abner sells a 200-acre farm to Mr. Benson, who plans to sub-divide the tract into 150 lots of about one acre each. The purchase price is $150,000. The terms — $20,000 cash at closing, a purchase money mortgage for $130,000 at six percent, interest only for the first two years, then the balance is due in 10 equal annual payments with interest at eight percent for the first five years and 10 percent for the last five years. The seller is to release his lien on parcels of 10 acres each upon payment of $15,000 for each parcel. A rough guide to retail pricing would be about five times the raw price or each lot should bring about $5,000.

This example indicates the impossibility of sub-dividing a 200-acre farm into 200 lots of one-acre size. Normally, about one-quarter of the total acreage will be lost in streets, parks, school sites, or preservation of lakes and stream beds.

In many situations, the needs or wants of the seller will open up un-expected avenues of financing.

Liquidation of a farm that has been willed to heirs by their parents often requires all cash or so most people think when hearing of estate transactions. But this is not always true.

Often an estate situation involves several minors with future educa-tional expenses. Provision of income over years by a purchase money mortgage is sometimes as desirable as all cash, and surely it is more at-tractive to most investors.

Entering into a financing transaction, or not entering into one without full knowledge of what the seller really desires is to overlook possibilities that can accrue to the mutual advantages of the parties.

Only after this basic method has been tried, is it time to explore outside sources for funds, such as private lenders.

There are many deals made for a 50 percent down payment that upon careful study would have been more suitable for both buyer and seller at 29 percent down. The buyer would have conserved cash for his development and the seller would not have been required to pay his full tax in the year of the transaction.

In contracts for sale of acreage where no immediate plans for resale by the purchaser are contemplated, purchase money mortgage terms of five or even up to 10 years are not uncommon. In recent years, the going rate of interest on these agreements has tended to be less than the inflationary rate, which works to the advantage of the borrower.

This trend suffered a setback caused by the oil crisis in the winter of 1973-74, when the appreciation of land at some distance from metropolitan areas was sharply curtailed. Purchasers who would otherwise have had a definite interest in a second home or a vacation site abandoned the idea as gasoline supplies dwindled and prices increased.

To a lesser degree, this unexpected problem diminished activity in land closer in to cities, but in some areas prices held firm or even continued to increase under the influence of a movement to take vacations closer to home.

Factors running counter to the depressant effects of the energy situation are 1) completion of the interstate highway system, 2) a burgeoning commitment to back-to-nature living, 3) a need to escape from pollution and population, and 4) a feeling that land, like many other commodities, is or will be in short supply.

Syndicates — For the part-time real estate investor or speculator, buying small parcels of land for development or appreciation can be an interesting entrée into the fascinating world of land dealings. Often, only one or two thousand dollars will be required, and good leverage is usually available.

The opportunity to form a partnership or syndicate to swing a larger deal is a logical next step after the first venture is sold out. Remember that profit is made by selling out — not holding out.

If the investor wants to form a syndicate, it is not necessary for him to know a lot of wealthy people whose aspirations of making money coincide with his own. He could start with his brother, a neighbor, his doctor, or someone with a similar hobby. If the idea is sound and has some glamour, the investor will be surprised how fast the word about it gets around. This is more likely to happen *after* he already has at least one profitable deal under his belt.

The Institutions — While land speculators may not be able to finance land, except via partnerships or groups or by mortgages from owners, the land developer who has plans to subdivide or build has many other doors open to him.

The regular institutional lenders either are prohibited from providing mortgages on unimproved land by law or do not undertake this kind of loan as a policy.

Some savings and loan associations will lend on raw land as part of an overall program calling for the mortgage's conversion to a construction loan and permanent financing as the subdivision and building are progressing.

Commercial banks, finance companies, real estate investment trusts, and life insurance companies are other lenders of money on land development when the land is in the path of obvious progress and can be turned into high-yield use.

Some institutions are joining land developers who have bought large tracts and turning these into new communities. The projects take enormous capital not only to initiate, but to carry for the years needed to bring to completion and start selling the residences it includes.

Government Assistance — The Federal Housing Administration offers FHA mortgage insurance for land development loans made by private lenders up to $25 million for each such project. The mortgage cannot exceed 75 percent of FHA's estimated value of the property on completion of the land development or 50 percent of its estimate of land value before development plus 90 percent of the estimated cost of the development, whichever is less.

Maximum payoff is seven years except for water and sewer facilities, and these may be financed *separately*. Payments are made on the loan as lots are released. The amount of the payment is 110 percent of the mortgage amount attributable to the leased lot, and the mortgage will be paid off when 91 percent of the lots have been released.

FHA does not control the prices of lots.

The project can be new or an expansion of one that exists, but it cannot include any part of a project that already has major improvements.

Improvements that are eligible are roads, streets, curbs, gutters, sidewalks, water lines and water supply installations, sewer lines and sewage disposal installations, and other related facilities that prepare land for use.

The Farmers Home Administration provides direct loans to public and private nonprofit corporations that will sell the developed home sites to low-and moderate-income families who are eligible for single-family housing loans or to nonprofit organizations eligible for rural rentals or cooperative loans. The site must be developed on a nonprofit basis.

LAND DEVELOPMENT FINANCING

Subdividing — The process of cutting up large tracts of raw land into smaller parcels or lots and offering them for sale is called subdividing. Any further work done to improve the land such as filling, grading, road building, and provision of utilities is called developing. The developer coordinates the project with governmental officials, architects, engineers, utility companies, surveyors, and others.

Developer's Contracts — Developers assist in financing the sale of lots in their subdivisions by offering terms of as low as 10 percent and up to 10 years to small purchasers, under contract for deed installment plans.

Lots are sold under contracts prepared by and generally favorable to the seller. There is no point in having an attorney review the form and suggest changes more favorable to the buyer because many of these contracts will be sold to bulk lenders whose attorneys have approved the standard form. Deviations, no matter how reasonable, would complicate the salability of the contracts and create more problems than the developer would want to tackle.

If a buyer has unusual financing problems and needs terms tailor-made to his cash flow abilities, he would do well to negotiate for individually owned properties whereby a reasonable flexibility by the seller can be expected.

Pitfalls of Developing — The bulk of existing contracts is at rates of six percent to eight percent of the unpaid balance. Land development companies have recently found money hard to get at 12 to 14 percent which, when obtained, is spent on improvements required by installment contracts at costs up to double those envisioned when long-range projections were originally made.

SUGGESTIONS TO THE LAND BUYER

Before purchasing land for subdivision or outright resale, consider the following:

(1) If the land is close to a metropolitan area, it may already be priced at or near its potential worth. It may have been exposed to many knowledgeable developers and may have changed hands several times in a decade. If a check of the courthouse records indicates such recent transfers, the best part of the profit may have already been skimmed.

Profit possibilities may still exist, but selling a lot at $4,000 that the investor has held for four years at $3,000 cost, considering interest and real estate taxes, is not nearly so good a deal as buying more remote acreage at $300 per acre, holding for the same period, and selling for $600 an acre.

(2) The financing is often better in purchasing rural property directly from an owner or through a broker than in buying a resale lot. Good leverage is probable on the former, but one who has paid off an installment contract on land at 10 percent down and balance over five years is seldom willing to give similar terms to his successor in title.

(3) In financing the purchase of a lot in a large project, the buyer should take advantage of the most lenient terms available. In other words, make no more than the minimum down payment, unless building is planned in the near future. By this method, the investor keeps the resalable factor in his favor, for in an emergency he might want to sell his land contract and recover his equity.

If the development has hundreds or thousands of available lots at the moment the owner has to liquidate his holding, he has stiff competition. Also, in budgeting payments of, say $25.00 per month toward lot purchase, one should allow for about 13 payments per year to handle real estate taxes. Many projects today require the purchaser to pay these taxes during the entire payment period preceding actual transfer of title.

(4) The purchaser should recognize that many hard-sell techniques are used by salesmen in lot projects. It is not unusual to be inspecting a very remote recreation development with a salesman who is called back to his car, via radio, and told that the lot he is showing has just been sold to another party who looked at it earlier.

The salesman apologizes for the looker's loss and offers a comparable site around the bend, urging a quick decision so that he won't be robbed again of the opportunity to get on the bandwagon.

The investor should beware of constant use of the phrases such as "making money automatically," "extremely easy terms," "only a few left." For every potential, there is a pitfall in land schemes.

The Federal Trade Commission under Section 5 of the FTC Act, which prohibits unfair or deceptive trade practices, has the authority to probe land developers suspected of deceptive practices related to land sales. An issue of complaint and court proceedings follow if the company is guilty.

The FTC's entry into the area of land development has sprung out of various land company abuses and from a general need to protect consumers against the all too notorious selling of property which has not been marketed for what it really is, usually unimproved, inaccessible, and underwater.

PROJECT FINANCING

For large housing projects, a mortgage is used to cover a tract of land on which a builder plans to develop a subdivision and build homes. Without the use of this type of financing, the builder would have to supply his own cash or obtain temporary credit until the purchaser of a home could obtain permanent financing.

When project financing is utilized, the lender takes a blanket mortgage on the project and advances money as the improvements are completed. Some mechanism by which parcels sold by the mortgagor can be released from the lien of the overriding mortgage by the payment of some proportional amount is required. The mortgage, for example, may provide that the mortgagor may obtain releases for designated parcels by paying a sum which is in the proportion that the area of the land released bears to the total area of land covered by the mortgage, multiplied by a designated percentage, 150 percent for example, of the original mortgage amount. Another method is to require amortization of the mortgage over a fairly short period, such as two years.

The lender in this type of financing is frequently the seller of the land, and he extends credit to the extent of the value of the land by means of a purchase money mortgage. A large landowner can afford to do this and still set a relatively low price on original acreage if he thereby gets the developer to commit himself to carrying through costly pioneering which will build value into the surrounding acreage.

In addition to the purchase money mortgage, the following approaches can be used to give a developer control over a large tract of land without having to put up the capital to buy it:

(1) Purchase contracts covering relatively long periods of time.

(2) Long-term purchase commitments or options on which modest carrying charges are paid by the developer.

(3) Successive options which the developer may pick up, sometimes at successively higher prices. These rolling options require the builder to develop each parcel as he goes along and so minimize the risk of the seller. At the same time, the builder can quit at any time he feels further development will not be profitable.

Financing the construction of large housing projects is undertaken by commercial banks, mortgage trusts, large finance companies, insurance companies, some S and L's, and mutual savings banks.

Federal Housing Administration or Department of Housing and Urban Development assistance may be used for these large ventures.

Mortgage bankers or brokers who specialize in larger projects will be able to lead the way to lenders for such projects.

THEME PARKS

The phenomenon in recreational land development today is the theme park. Although amusement parks have been with us for many decades as a part of big city life, only in the past few years have pre-planned regional or national parks become a part of the American life style.

Beginning with Disneyland in California, which enjoyed a monopoly for many years, a proliferation of similar projects has sprung up to absorb the excess money available for fun and games in an affluent society. These projects are not for the small-time developer, but are reserved for corporations capable of raising the $15 to $40 million needed to open the gates for business at a park of several hundred acres or, in the case of Disney World in Orlando, 28,000 acres.

Options — The land for a theme park is usually taken under option in a straw name to prohibit the seller from knowing either the name of the purchaser or the intended use.

Financing after closing is seldom necessary as the seller usually gets all cash or is paid off within a year or two so that construction financing can go on a clear land position.

The seller, in all events, must accept a contingency period, a delay that could run as long as 24 to 36 months. This period, during which the purchaser normally pays a sum roughly equal to real estate taxes plus legal costs as consideration for the option, allows time for design plans to be refined to the point that application for a building permit can be made.

Concurrently, the prospective purchaser might get involved in provisions for adequate utilities, zoning exceptions, and a multitude of environmental concessions which limit land development. Title will not pass until the developer is satisfied that his permit to build is valid and rights of appeal, if any, have expired.

Good examples of these projects can be observed at Santa Clara, California (Marriott), Kings Dominion at Richmond, Virginia (Taft Broadcasting), and the Flags projects in Atlanta, Dallas, and St. Louis.

There are signs that the success of a multi-million-dollar, family-oriented theme park to serve a regional trade area of many millions of customers will depend almost exactly on the same factors which control the sub-division of a 10-acre farm into recreation lots. These include location, amenities, timing, financing, competition, and promotion.

MISCELLANEOUS RECREATIONAL PROJECTS

Since recreational interests in this country seem to follow trends, the prospective investor in the various leisure-time projects should proceed with caution.

If he does make an investment in a recreation center, a bowling alley, for instance, he should keep property conversion ideas in the back of his mind. Can the facility be turned into a restaurant, theater or store if bowling loses its appeal in the area.

Tennis courts, golf courses of all sizes, drive-in theaters, pools,

clubs, marinas, bowling alleys, gymnasiums, and other recreational facilities can be worthwhile projects if they are extremely well planned.

If the facility is for municipal use, it can be financed by general
obligation bonds or the developer can build and sell it to local government. The Small Business Administration will make direct or participating
loans on marinas.

Local banks and S and L's are usually the best sources for funding projects of this nature, or investors can form corporations, joint ventures, or
limited partnerships to underwrite these ventures.

11. — Nursing Homes, Hospitals, and Medical Facilities

INTRODUCTION

Major financing in the medical field is either for nursing homes or hospitals. They vary as to basic needs, and their financing differs somewhat, too.

Nursing homes are classified either as centers where doctors, professional nurses or licensed medical professionals are continuously on duty caring for residents, or as facilities for the aged. The latter are principally residential care centers, which do not fully provide skilled nursing and medical services.

Regardless of type, the nursing home is usually privately owned, operated for profit, and licensed and regulated in the state where it is located.

Hospitals and nursing homes can both be privately or publicly owned and operated. Over 80 percent of all nursing homes, for example, are, and there are a number of hospital and nursing home chains. Both kinds of facilities may be owned and operated by non-profit associations.

The Medicade and Medicare programs provided by the federal government have brought about vast changes in medical finance. These programs have increased the funds available for medical help to those who previously could not afford it and caused a boom in hospital and nursing home development.

However, this emergence of new facilities is not unbridled. For instance, legislation known as HRI requires that any new hospitals in order to obtain and retain eligibility of Medicare and medical aid reimbursements must, prior to being built, have regional planning agencies give approval for the hospital. These HRI requirements naturally slow down development of new hospitals and facilities.

These types of moves by the federal government have had a tendency to scare away investors from the medical industry, but at the same time aid the existing medical facilities to keep from having any unnecessary vacancies.

In recent years, the profiles of medical facilities have changed drastically. We have moved away from large complexes built in the central city to more modest developments situated in suburbs. These centers provide convenience to area patients, can be built at lesser costs, and offer more modern surroundings than the older big buildings.

There are more than 30 million people in this country who are 65 years of age or older, so there is a continuing need for medical and care facilities for them and for other segments of the population.

ASSEMBLING A PLAN FOR DEVELOPMENT

Checking Zoning — The first stage in building any medical facility is to check with local zoning authorities to find what areas of the city or county are zoned for this purpose. This will save an enormous amount of time and energy, since the developer will not have to go through the long and tedious process of applying for zoning and special easements to build the medical center he has in mind.

Negotiating for the Land — Once the ideal parcel of land is found, it is recommended that this property either be optioned for a long time or be purchased subject to a closing conditional upon the builder's, developer's, or owner's obtaining all the necessary building and operating permits to utilize the land according to plan. This is an extremely important condition to specify since otherwise an individual builder or developer could wind up owning land he is unable to use for his first goal.

Special Considerations — In building a hospital, it must be remembered that the HRI legislation requires approval by regional planning agencies, and forms and permits may be obtained directly from them.

If a hospital complex is planned, it is recommended that the developer work through a professional real estate consultant schooled in such building programs. He will prepare a feasibility study of the project and the surrounding community so that a need can be shown the agencies and the financier. Going through with the sale of the property which is under contract should be subject to obtaining these approvals.

In the case of a nursing home, a feasibility study is also quite supportive. It should describe the need for the facility in the community and cover such subjects as available financing possibilities, type of building demanded in the area, a preliminary estimate of construction and improvement costs, and projections of the rental income which can be derived from the property. Other factors might include the facility's positive environmental impact with its attractive landscaping and architecture.

Lenders and others involved will want to know the strong selling points offered the patient and his family, such as the absence of street noises, a noisy neighborhood, blinking lights, and other hazards to peace and quiet. They will be impressed by the presence of emergency vehicles, access to sunlight, parks and patios, recreational areas, and other amenities.

Costs to Expect — Before proceeding with either type project, the developer should do a complete cost breakdown of his land, site improvement, architectural plans, financing, feasibility study, and other items. A projection should be worked against this based upon the rental income for a period of at least five years.

Completing the Package — A completed presentation for financing should consist of a contract or option agreement showing that the land is under control, necessary approval or application approval which has been obtained from necessary regional authorities and governmental agencies if the developer is building a hospital, a project breakdown showing all costs, a projection indicating income and expenses, architectural plans, feasibility studies, and appraisals.

SOURCES OF FINANCING

The Small Business Administration — This agency is authorized to grant participating loans to finance construction and operation of nursing homes and medical facilities of a proprietary nature. Current information can be found at the developer's nearest Small Business Administration office.

Commercial Banks — The banks are sources of both nursing home and hospital financing, but, their loans are usually more short-term. They provide construction loans and in some cases will offer longer term loans of five to seven and sometimes 10 years. In some cases, it is possible to obtain a long-term loan from a commercial bank.

A commercial bank may suggest a balloon mortgage in five to seven years with a payout of, say, 20 years, which will reduce the debt constant.

Private Placements — Hospital financing for nursing home chains may come via private placements with major institutions such as pension funds, commercial banks, and insurance companies. Applications for this type of financing are made through investment bankers, as well as the private placement departments of various lending institutions.

Tax-Exempt Revenue Bonds — Substantial funds, especially for hospital financing, are gathered through the issuance of revenue bonds by local and state agencies, which utilize government-insured or subsidized programs.

Such bonds are bought by individuals and institutions that benefit from the tax nature of the issues. The investor usually receives 25 to 30 percent higher returns than those shown on the normal bond buyer index.

These are usually extremely complex issues requiring legal documents that must be prepared by state and local agencies, municipal bond attorneys, the investment banking firm, and the hospital board and its legal advisors.

Most of these private issues are in the form of mortgages with first claim on revenues and properties, although there are, occasionally, unsecured loans that carry negative covenants which assure there will be no senior debt.

The majority of this tax-exempt debt is raised by local and state authorities and by municipalities under the Internal Revenue Service ruling 63-20.

The investment banking firm of Kidder, Peabody & Company is probably the nation's foremost authority on this type of financing.

Mortgage Bankers and Mortgage Brokers — Mortgage bankers and brokers can frequently assist a developer of medical facilities, providing he wants a traditional mortgage loan. About half of the hospitals and nursing homes in this country are built using traditional real estate financing.

The mortgage banker either will use his own funds or obtain money needed for the financing through institutional lenders. He can usually raise from 50 to 80 percent of the cost of the project.

The broker is similarly adept at finding funds, but, of course, does not provide equity himself.

HOW TO APPROACH SOURCES

Evaluating Lenders — By 1980, the capital outlay for medical facilities will reach $8.5 billion. Such demand calls any existing financing techniques and new ones into play. Probably more federal aid and direction will be provided.

One of the best-known government plans was the Hill-Burton Act, which involves direct construction grants and loans. However, there are so many agencies involved in its use and so much bureaucratic red tape that this act is virtually unused today.

The Hill-Burton Act provides that there is a claim on all the assets of the hospital project constructed with the grant over a 20-year period. This claim can be enforced in the event the hospital is no longer a nonprofit institution or is no longer used as a hospital business. This is another reason the act has not been popular within the industry.

In evaluating lenders, it is necessary that the borrower first consider the alternative types of sources of financing mentioned previously. If the borrower contemplates a small project, he may be able to go directly to a lender or to a mortgage broker or investment banker. If a larger and more complicated project is planned, he might want to consider a major consultant who specializes in obtaining loans of this nature. There are a number of such consulting firms such as Cresap, McCormick and Paget, Inc., management consultants in New York, who have done many complex evaluations on hospitals and nursing homes. Earl J. Frederick of the firm lists the capital fund sources available through federal and state agencies:

CAPITAL FUND SOURCES

FEDERAL

Hill-Burton Act
National Housing Act
Community Mental Health Center Construction Grant Program
Alcoholism Grant Program
Narcotic Addiction and Drug Abuse Grant Program
Children's Mental Health Grant Program
Health Maintenance Organization Program
Experimentally Designated Health Facility Grant Program
Health Professions Teaching Facility Construction Grant and Loan Programs
Nursing School Construction Grant and Loan Program
Cancer Facility Construction and Cancer Research Grant Program
General Clinical Research Center Grant Program
Social and Rehabilitation Service Vocational Rehabilitation Construction
    Grant Program
Federal Housing Administration's Mortgage Insurance Programs for Group
    Practice Facilities and Nursing Homes
FHA's Public Facility Loan Program
Economic Development Administration's Public Works Construction Grant
    and Loan Program
Veterans Administration's State Nursing Home Construction Grant Program
Small Business Administration's Small Business Loan Program

STATE

Authorities in these states have issued tax-exempt hospital revenue bonds:
Connecticut, Maine, Massachusetts, New Hampshire, New York (Medical
Care Facilities Finance Agency and the New York State Dormitory Auth-
    ority), South Dakota, and Vermont.

These states, among others, permit local governments to issue tax-exempt
bonds:
Alabama, Georgia, Indiana, Kentucky, Nebraska, Ohio, Oklahoma, Penn-
    sylvania, Tennessee, and Virginia.

If the borrower decides that a private placement is best suited for
him, it is best that he deal through an investment banker or private
placement specialist. If he decides a mortgage or the sale leaseback route
is the right vehicle, he should consider a mortgage banker or some of the
experts in leaseback financing.

Here are brief descriptions of the various alternatives available to a
borrower for different types of medical projects:

(1) Sale Leaseback Projects — This method is becoming increasingly popular in the industry since it gives the borrower or developing entity
100 percent financing. The buyer of the project provides all the funds
necessary to build the nursing home or medical complex exclusive of
equipment and leases it back to the company or group which will be
operating the project. In many cases, the equipment can also be handled

on a sale-leaseback type transaction. Funds can often be obtained from bank leasing companies and other types of finance and leasing companies.

(2) Mortgages — Often a loan can be acquired at 50 to 80 percent of value through a mortgage banking firm which, in turn, will either use its own funds or obtain money from a lending institution such as an insurance company, pension fund, or savings and loan association. In such a financing, an application is made to the mortgage banking firm and a good will application is made to the mortgage banking firm and a good will application fee is included. In making this type of application, the mortgage lender will need the usual type of information. The only disadvantage here is that the borrower must supply substantial funds on his own for the equity portion of the financing. He, of course, will be able to own the property himself.

(3) Commercial Banks — Many commercial banks will consider making loans on hospitals. Their term is usually shorter, from five to seven years. They are very strong in making construction and short-term loans. In some cases, they will consider a long-term loan if the borrower is a good customer of the bank. Occasionally, they have been known to make 20-to-25-year payout loans with a balloon at the end of seven to 10 years. Finance companies also are a source of higher interest rate loans for this type of financing.

(4) Taxable Bond Issue — Bonds for this financing are usually sold through an investment banking house or private placement department of some of the larger commercial banks. They are sold to institutions or to the public. Interest on these bonds varies dramatically depending upon current national marketing conditions. The interest rate is usually higher than the non-taxable bonds. However, it is usually not quite so complicated and the investment bankers can usually move somewhat faster than the government bodies.

(5) Tax-exempt Bonds — For non-profit hospitals the tax-exempt method has proven to be the least expensive way to finance the property since tax-exempt bonds are sought by institutions which benefit from the tax advantages. The amount of the loan will be determined by an in-depth evaluation by the lenders as to the project's ability to service the debt. Term of the debt can range from 20 to 40 years. Certain state, local, and federal governments are allowed to issue these tax-exempt hospital bonds and a special authority is usually set up to handle the financing.

Negotiating Rates — The borrower should remember that rates vary substantially from time to time, depending upon interest in various types of financing vehicles by institutions and by individuals buying in the marketplace. Prior to moving ahead with any loan, the borrower should research all methods and sources of financing to determine which are advantageous to him in the prevailing environment.

In negotiating rates, it is most mandatory that the borrower understand what process the lender goes through in making a decision as to the creditability of the loan. If all of these questions are anticipated and answered thoroughly in the original presentation, the borrower will be in a strong position to negotiate the best rate on his terms.

For a hospital, nursing home, or other medical facility loan, the lender may evaluate the following:

(1) Cash-Flow Projection — This is needed to show if the project will support the requested debt.

(2) Plans and Specifications of the Building — These may be original or copies.

(3) A Feasibility Study — If this is applicable, it should be included.

(4) Appraisal — An MAI appraisal on the proposed or existing property should be supplied.

(5) A Formal Proposal — This statement to the lender will include all terms and conditions which the borrower is requesting, including the amount of loan, the desired interest rate, and the length of term as well as various clauses which are important to the borrower, such as prepayment penalties he desires, and the loan-to-value ratio.

In the case of a mortgage, it should be remembered that the mortgage lender will seek a first mortgage on all the assets of the borrower not then encumbered. Sometimes if this is not possible or practical, he will consider a direct obligation of notes with a negative pledge clause.

(6) Need — Any lender will want to be sure the community that the medical facility services needs that complex. Any information, background data, or other material such as newspaper articles, public information releases, and other data which will support the need factor will be helpful in the proposal. This subject is dealt with extensively in the feasibility study.

(7) Management — The borrower will usually find that one of the most significant factors to the lender is the management of the complex. They will want to be convinced that the doctors and the administrators are competent and well trained. Biographical information on the hospital staff and their experiences is extremely useful.

For substantial loans, it is also helpful if the major administrative staff and doctors are available to visit with lenders.

(8) Planning — Those financing projects will also be impressed if a five-year plan is presented along with the financial package. This management plan should show that the operators of the project have a definite plan and have thought through the alternative needs of management in the community during the next five to 10 years. This is especially true for chain hospitals or chain nursing home companies.

FHA-INSURED MORTGAGE LOANS

Under FHA 232, mortgages for a single health care facility or for a combination of related facilities may be insured. This program helps finance construction and improvement of nursing homes and related facilities providing rehabilitation, intermediate, and/or extended care services.

The nursing home or related facility may be either privately owned and operated for profit or owned by a private, nonprofit corporation or association. The facility may serve people who need skilled nursing care and medical service but do not require acute hospital care. It may also provide a protective living environment and routine personal and health services for those who do not need skilled nursing care. The appropriate agency for the area in which the facility is located must certify the need.

The mortgagor for a proprietary facility may be a corporation, trust, partnership, or an individual approved by FHA. The nonprofit mortgagor may be a private corporation or association but must be organized for purposes other than making a profit for itself or for its officers or members. Also, it must not be controlled or directed in any way by persons or firms seeking to derive profit from the facility. A mortgagor may lease the facility to an operator on terms approved by FHA, but whether the mortgagor directly operates or leases the facility to another, it must be operated under all necessary licenses and inspections required by federal, state, or local regulations.

Mortgage Conditions — The mortgage may cover costs of new construction or rehabilitation of existing buildings. It may not exceed a 20-year term.

The project must include at least 20 beds, and funds may be advanced during construction. The mortgage amount includes cost of equipment for operating the nursing home, intermediate care facility, or both. The maximum mortgage amount is $12.5 million per project. Within this limit, the highest insurable mortgage amount for proposed construction is 90 percent of the FHA estimate of value.

On most rehabilitation projects, the mortgage amount may not exceed 90 percent of the estimated value after rehabilitation.

Under the National Housing Act Section 242, FHA can also insure mortgages on properties in the financing of hospitals. This can be for new or existing profit or nonprofit hospitals. Loans can be for a term as long as 25 years and for as much as 90 percent of the appraised value.

DEPARTMENT OF HEALTH, EDUCATION, AND WELFARE

The Department of Health, Education, and Welfare has a loan guarantee program and a direct loan program which went into effect in January 1972. This is principally a mortgage type program as it relates to the loan guarantee. Most of these loans, which are guaranteed, are acquired by commercial banks and investment banking houses, and they in turn sell them to other institutions.

The HEW direct loan program involves the buying of loans by HEW from private non-profit institutions which are able to issue tax-exempt securities. In return, HEW sells these obligations to the Federal National Mortgage Association or to the private securities market.

TAX AND LEGAL CONSIDERATIONS TO AID PROFITS

One of the best ways to show how a small project can benefit from a number of different types of financing techniques is to consider this specific example:

Several investors asked a well-known attorney and financial consultant to work up a financing plan for the construction and operation of a nursing home and hospital, each with a 100-bed capacity.

The plan worked out was, of course, tailored to fit the needs of the investors in this particular project; but an examination of it should prove instructive to anyone planning a similar project. In fact, the tax-saving techniques used in this plan may be adapted to many other types of business ventures as well. Here's what the plan looks like —

The estimated capital requirements:

$700,000 to build the nursing home
900,000 to build the hospital
50,000 to furnish and equip the nursing home
300,000 to furnish and equip the hospital
250,000 working capital

The plan contemplates the formation of five corporations, one owning the hospital building, one owning the nursing home building, one operating the pharmacy, one leasing and operating the hospital, and one leasing and operating the nursing home. The plan stipulates that each of these corporations will start out with no more than 10 individual stockholders so that the depreciation, interest, and taxes during construction and start-up losses can be deducted on the personal tax returns of the shareholders. This will significantly reduce the net investment required. After the buildings are completed, this will no longer be possible for the corporations owning the real estate, but the stockholders in the corporations operating the hospital and nursing home can continue to take fast depreciation of furniture and equipment as deductions on their individual tax returns.

Financial Structure of Nursing Home Real Estate Corporation — This is based on 66 percent financing from an insurance company or S and L. The percentage of mortgage to cost may be increased to 75 percent based on good design and high value attributed to land and building in an appraisal. Equity capital needed could be reduced by going to an FHA mortgage at 90 percent of value.

Capital stock — 100 shares

51 shares issued to investor A for land
49 shares issued to nine others for $1,000 a share

Debentures

$132,300 of 5 percent, 10-year debentures sold in ratio to stock purchased by nine others who acquire 49 percent of stock. Stock and debentures sold in a package of 1 share of stock ($1,000)and a $2,700, 10-year, 5 percent debenture of $3,700.

The capital structure of the nursing home will shape up this way:

Land valued at $	51,000	— 51 shares common
Cash	49,000	— 49 shares common
Cash	132,300	— 5 percent, ten-year debentures
Cash	500,000	— First mortgage on real estate backed up by lease
Cash of	50,000	— Prepaid rent
Total	$782,300	

Financial Structure of Nursing Home Operating Corporation — This corporation will lease the nursing home on a 20-year lease with renewal options. It will prepay or post security for $50,000 of rent. It will equip the nursing home for an estimated cost of $50,000. Additional working capital will be $100,000.

Thus, it will need $200,000 capital which will be obtained by selling 100 shares at $2,000 a share to 10 stockholders, an average investment of $20,000 for each stockholder.

Financial Structure of Private Hospital Real Estate Corporation — It will be necessary to depend on conventional financing here. This facility is the generator of the entire project. To get the necessary financing with minimum burden on all participants, the corporation operating the hospital will equip it and get the tax benefit of fast depreciation of the equipment. To attain the major financing necessary, the equipment will probably have to be hypothecated by the operating corporation to secure the real estate mortgage. Subject to the preparation of plans and negotiation with an insurance company or savings and loan, a $675,000 mortgage on a 100-bed private hospital in the location is possible. The rest of the money would be raised this way:

51 shares to investor A for land
49 shares to nine other shareholders for $1,000 a share
$183,750 of 5 percent, 10-year debentures to these stockholders
on the basis of $3,750 of notes for each share of stock

The capital structure would look like this:

Land valued at $	51,000	— 51 shares
Cash	49,000	— 49 shares
Cash	183,750	— 5 percent, 10-year debentures
Cash	675,000	— First mortgage on building also secured by $300,000 of equipment pledged by tenant and by lease
Total	$958,750	

Financial Structure of Hospital Operating Company — This corporation will require $100,000 for operating capital and $300,000 for equipment for a total of $400,000. It will lease the hospital for a 20-year term with renewal options. As security for the lease obligation, it will pledge the equipment and furnishings to further secure the mortgage on the hospital buildings. Ten stockholders will put up an average of $40,000 for this corporation. Although this will represent the largest investment unit, it will be minimized by the opportunity to deduct almost half of the investment on personal tax returns against profits or outside income over the first two years. In a 50 percent tax bracket, this can cut the net investment back by 25 percent.

Financial Structure of Pharmacy — This can be set up separately or integrated with the hospital real estate corporation or the hospital operating company.

Rents Paid to Real Estate Corporations — The operating companies will pay real estate taxes and all maintenance costs plus a net rent equal to 10 percent of the initial mortgage debt plus 12 percent of the equity investment over and above the mortgage debt needed to build the building.

Investments Available:

> 100 units of $2,000 each — nursing home operation
> 100 units of $4,000 each — hospital operation
> 49 units of $4,750 each — hospital real estate
> 49 units of $3,700 each — nursing home real estate

1968 LAWS PROVIDING FINANCIAL BENEFITS
FOR NURSING HOMES

In 1968 Congress enacted provisions offering the following three major improvements in the financing of nursing homes:

(1) Long-term Financing for Equipment — The land, building, and all major items of equipment needed to operate a nursing home can be included in a single FHA-insured mortgage. Formerly, nursing homes had to resort to relatively expensive short-term financing for all the times of equipment they needed.

As it now stands, the law makes it possible to get the FHA interest rate for both the nursing home and its equipment, but, more importantly, perhaps, it also means that the total amortization payments will be smaller in the first years when most investors find it a struggle to make income and outgo meet.

(2) Supplemental Loans — An existing nursing home that has an FHA-insured mortgage can get a supplemental FHA-insured loan for improvements, repairs and additions, including equipment. The supple-

mental loan will be limited to 90 percent of the estimated value of the improvements.

(3) Availability of FHA Loans — Since the interest-rate ceiling for FHA-insured mortgage loans can be adjusted to meet the competitive requirements of the money market, lenders should be more willing to make FHA-insured loans.

What's more, to help operators and investors in nursing homes get off the ground, there's a special break available during the first two years of operation. If "operating losses" during the first two years exceed income, FHA may permit the difference to be added to the mortgage. Included in the expenses of operation are taxes, interest and mortgage insurance premiums, and all other expenses of operation and maintenance, not including depreciation.

Conventional financing for nursing homes is usually obtained through mortgage companies, insurance companies, or investment banks. Normally, the lenders will consider a loan approximating 50 percent of the cost of a patient bed. The FHA-insured nursing home program, under Section 232, aims at providing nursing homes that are economically sound and structurally adequate for the safety, as well as the proper care, of the occupants. Nursing homes developed under this program are constructed by private builders. They are owned and managed by private concerns or individuals and not by the FHA. They are financed with loans of private capital made by FHA approved lenders. These lenders in turn are insured by FHA against loss in making the loans.

FHA Processing — In processing applications for mortgage insurance, FHA determines adequacy by determining, through its mortgage credit analysis, that the anticipated net income (after operating expenses, taxes, allowances for reserves, and a reasonable return on the invested equity capital in the real estate, equipment and furnishings) is adequate to meet the debt service under the mortgage as well as any other obligations.

The FHA mortgage credit analysis also will include analysis of the sponsorship with respect to character and reputation, ability and experience for developing, operating and building, either directly or indirectly, a nursing home of the proposed size and type.

Also, the financial capacity to complete, equip, and furnish the proposed home in accordance with FHA administrative regulations and with the needs related to the intended occupancy are considered.

REFINANCING AND MODERNIZING NURSING HOMES, HOSPITALS, MEDICAL FACILITIES

Increasing needs for medical services, technological advances in the field of medicine and medical care, a general shortage of money, soaring construction costs, and a general hesitancy on the part of many traditional lenders to stay away from the lending in the medical field are conditions encircling all medical facilities today.

This composite of troubles makes refinancing and upgrading of facilities doubly difficult. Still it has been estimated that as much as two-thirds to three-fourths of the funds being sought for hospital and medical construction would be funneled into modernizing, refinancing, and adding to existing medical facilities.

There is a dwindling supply of funds for refinancing and modernizing of hospitals. The more traditional government and philanthropic sources of money have been shrinking in recent years. Most medical complex borrowers needing this type of financing will more and more have to turn toward placing of debt through private placements, commercial banks, mortgage banking houses and investment bankers, and other more traditional and institutional sources.

Because of this shortage of funds in the marketplace, the importance of planning on the part of hospital and medical staffs will become urgent in order to obtain the funds which are available.

In seeking a loan of this nature, a borrower should provide the lender with a financial history of the existing operation and projections showing that the projected cash flow will adequately retire the debt requested. The lender is, of course, interested in all those subjects mentioned in this chapter under initial financing requirements and such items as the manpower of physicians available and different planning agents' approval, information on projected construction costs, and description of the current facilities including existing parking and site information.

12. ── Hotels and Motels

UNIQUE CHARACTERISTICS

The development and the financing of hotels and motels present a unique phase of real estate because of the nature of the entities. They are single purpose in usage. They are extremely vulnerable to constantly changing patterns of optimum design, location, size, and competition.

Both hotels and motels are difficult to finance and some lenders will provide only 50 percent loans.

Hotels, originally called inns, have been a part of commercial history since its beginning, which indicates they fulfill a basic need. Coupled with food, they provide the traveler with a temporary home. If the sale of strong beverages is included, with or without music and dancing, a focal point for casual or planned entertainment is established.

If located on a beach, in a scenic mountain setting, or in a winter sports area, these complexes become destination points for vacations or conventions or both.

Their susceptibility to change is glaringly obvious in the scores of examples of downtown hotels that have failed because we have moved away from rail travel to the automobile.

Many of these older hotels, generally excellent in design and construction, have not been able to offer parking spaces for each room, and most have suffered severely.

An example of change and decline in value hotels in the resort field would be Atlantic City, where magnificent buildings are just no longer the "in" places to go.

SOURCES OF FINANCING

Financing a hotel today can be difficult. Lending institutions are aware of the profitability trend, which is closely correlated to occupancy rates. The occupancy rate for all hotels is in the range of 60 percent to 70 percent, and the margin of profit per dollar of total sales falls in the range of 12 percent to 17 percent. Some companies do much better than the average. One major chain today achieves an occupancy rate of better than 80 percent, even though its rates are quite high. But even this company now feels that the investment in buying land, designing, financing, and building a major hotel involves heavy capital costs and excessive risks and has announced that its future program will be limited to operating buildings that have been built by others.

This method of expansion permits a prestige company to capitalize on its reputation and its extensive facilities for reservations and convention packaging without extensive borrowing in a high-interest market.

As in the case of a shopping center, the decision to build should follow an objective feasibility study, although the hotel study is specialized, and not comparable in most ways with one for a shopping center. Hotels can deliberately go to far-away places, where their patronage in no way relates to the economic status or numbers of people in the trade area. Examples are Barbados, Acapulco, the Cayman Islands, and Tahiti.

The prime financial objective in hotel development is occupancy rate, similar to the overage rent income sought in shopping centers. It is reasonable to say that a good occupancy rate will overcome all problems. Hotels being built today almost invariably belong to one of the major chains — Hilton, Marriott, Hyatt, Sheraton, H.C.A., Knott, Holiday Inns, Ramada, or Travelodge, for examples. Their financing is internally generated from cash flow, new stock or mortgaging.

The motel industry is a different animal altogether. Venture capital has come easily to this industry. Starting from scratch in the late 1930's, they now enjoy over 50 percent of the revenues in the lodging industry, and this figure is climbing. They also show an occupancy rate generally about 10 points above hotels. Despite generally lower rates per day, motel profits, based on percent of gross receipts, are about five to 10 points higher than those of hotels.

The success records of motels via franchising on a geographical basis has created groups within groups, meaning simply that an individual or syndicate with territorial rights to operate a certain brand name motel may assemble investors in backing one or more of the motels opened. Individuals can share in profits without having any expertise in this field.

Insurance companies and REIT's are major sources of motel financing. Their evaluation of a project revolves around its estimated income per room.

Some REIT's, such as Hotel Investors, Washington, D.C., specialize in loans for hotels and motels.

HOW TO ASSEMBLE A PACKAGE

(1) Prepare a feasibility study — Before pursuing a hotel or motel venture, call or write several of the chains operating in the selected geographical area and ask them their candid opinion of the site selected. Don't expect them to be overwhelmed by the call. Good negotiating form is to express no more than lukewarm interest.

(2) Add to the feasibility study support items such as aerial photographs, a topographical survey, traffic counts, plus any pertinent data from the local or regional Chambers of Commerce.

(3) Find out as much as possible about competitors' occupancy rates. If calls are made regularly over an extended period and competitors say they are sold out, keep records of this.

(4) Prepare a projection of operating income using the following as a guide:

200 rooms x $15 x 80 percent occupancy =	$	2,400 daily
$2,400 x 365 days = annual income of	$	876,000
This figure is called Room Income		
Add: Food income	$	490,000
Beverage income	$	180,000
Estimated Total Income		$1,546,000

Deduct

Cost of goods and services:			
	Rooms	$280,000	
	Foods/Beverages	$550,000	$ 830,000
Gross Operating Income			$ 716,000

Deductions from Income

Administrative expenses	$ 90,000	
Advertising/Promotion	$ 36,000	
Utilities	$ 60,000	
Maintenance and repairs	$ 50,000	$ 236,000
Gross Operating Profit		$ 480,000

Deduct

Real estate taxes	$48,000	
Insurance	$ 3,000	$ 51,000
Profit (as if free and clear)		$ 429,000

We must now make an assumption that the $429,000 will produce a market value of say eight times earnings or $3,432,000. Now consider whether or not the 200-room venture, furnished, with restaurant can be built with land included, for about this amount.

If a discrepancy is obvious, then the project may have to be scaled down, and obviously if the investor and partners or the syndicate are not capable of providing an equity of approximately $1.8 million, the project is in trouble. The arithmetic used in the example would be typical of a submission to a lender to support a loan application in the range of $1.5 to $1.7 million or 50 to 55 percent of value.

If the property is to be leased for a long term on a net basis to an experienced nationally known chain, a higher percentage of loan-to-value would be possible, and the tenant might be able to steer the owner to a lending institution interested in this type of mortgage.

(5) If the investor's plans are for an independent operation, he is now ready to make formal application for a letter of commitment, which will be simpler than the one used for a shopping center because the borrower is not required to obtain the specified ratio of AAA tenants.

(6) With a loan commitment and a builder's contract, the investor is ready to go ahead with the project.

CLOSING THE FINANCING

Before going to closing on the construction loan, the developer will need a contract with a reputable builder, almost always with one who is experienced. This is very important when building to specifications for a major chain. It is best to ask for a recommended contractor.

Also needed is a take-out commitment with the permanent lender. Check to see if the permanent mortgage will be a new instrument, or a buy-sell agreement in which the construction mortgage is modified to reflect the difference in terms and is then assigned to the long-term lender.

As mentioned before, over the past few years, REIT's have been very active in motel financing, often using to an advantage their willingness to provide land development and construction loans and permanent financing. Their application procedures do not differ much from those of older conventional sources, but their greater aggressiveness has put them well ahead of their competition. Their loans in this industry have chalked up a higher degree of success than many of their other loans.

When the project is built, the investor will still face several important and expensive steps before closing the permanent loan. He should be prepared to provide a survey as built showing everything required by the lender.

An appraisal by an appraiser approved in advance or even designated by the lender should be made available.

A mortgagee policy of title insurance, a certificate of occupancy, insurance policies, a tenant's written acceptance of the premises, and all other documents required are further musts. The investor cannot get started too soon in lining up who is to do all the paperwork and when it will be ready.

ALTERNATE METHODS

In a tight money market, construction sometimes proceeds with a construction loan intended to continue one to two years beyond the date of completion.

The developer hopes to place financing during such period with a permanent lender at an interest rate lower than current costs. This procedure is not recommended for beginners, as only the most astute and substantial developers could survive a worsening situation.

To hedge against the possibility that the construction loan will be called when due, some developers are willing to pay the standby fee for an interim loan, for a short term, and look to commercial banks for this financing.

Both of these techniques are devices to buy time, to postpone the final big decision in the hopes that a greater supply of money at a lower rate of interest will be available in the near future.

The developer must balance the actual savings, in the future, versus the relatively high cost of short-term loans, traditionally at two to four percent above the long-term rate.

It is also possible to finance the land separately by using a sale leaseback. This sometimes produces a 100 percent financing of land, though not the improvements.

Suppose a developer needing a $5 million financing for a motel arranges for a $4-million interim loan for five years from a conventional source, such as an insurance company, plus a $1-million second mortgage from a finance company.

These in combination will make a $5 million construction loan possible.

During the first few years after opening, if the motel operates successfully, the mini-permanent lender will rewrite a larger amount for a term of 20-25 years, and this funding pays off the second loan in full.

REFINANCING

Refinancing a motel or hotel which has a steady or improving income stream, is much easier than undertaking a new project. This is especially true where the involved unit is part of a chain operation and located near an airport or is adjacent to convention facilities or a major shopping center.

In refinancing, the penalty for a speculative venture is reduced or eliminated, and the loan-to-value ratio is usually higher. The peripheral income has been established and can be considered on practically the same basis as room income.

A borrower who approaches his refinancing by preparing bar charts for the five years immediately preceding his application date and who can substantiate his figures will get favorable consideration if his information is similar to the following:

	1968 $	1969 $	1970 $	1971 $	1972 $
Average Room Rate	11.00	11.60	12.10	13.00	13.80
	000	000	000	000	000
Gross Room Income	$600	$638	$695	$752	$795
Occupancy Rate Percentage	72.0	74.5	78.0	81.0	82.5
	000	000	000	000	000
Food Income $	320	348	385	410	445
	000	000	000	000	000
Beverage Income $	85	130	180	215	260

Old time entrepreneurship, except for isolated exceptions in the resort industry, is disappearing as the major chains increase their dominance in the hospitality field. The advent of the package tour, the travel agency business, and interlocking reservations systems suggest that the mom-and-pop motel has had it. Franchising is the modern answer to entrepreneurship, especially in the motel industry. The advantages of a large corporate name and personal attention join together for material benefit of both the company and local owners.

More than 60,000 motels have been built in the past 30 years. In many areas, the supply of rooms has increased at about 150 percent of the rate at which demand has risen.

Under such conditions, it is inevitable that large arithmetic increases in rooms sold per day accompany a declining occupancy rate percentage wise.

The fact that the national economic climate relates so directly to motel and hotel activity has resulted in the preparation of good barometers in this field. There is the annual publication, *Trends in the Hotel/Motel Business,* published by Harris, Kerr, Forster and Company and available through its regional offices.

The prospective applicant for a motel or hotel loan should do considerable in-depth homework about the needs in the field in general and about those in his own city and state specifically.

13. — Community Development and Government Programs to Assist Housing

INTRODUCTION

The federal government serves as an integral part of the development and re-development of housing and communities in general, co-ordinating funding and policies with state and local governments and their agencies.

This role is most obviously seen in the sweeping legislation of 1974. Public Law 93-383, passed by the 93rd Congress, is known as the Housing and Community Development Act of 1974. This act is omnibus legislation which substantially alters the federal government's participation in the nation's housing and community development activities. Most of these changes are discussed elsewhere in this desk book under the type of real estate they affect. Community Development (Title I) and Assisted Housing (Title II) give new direction to the downtown and core city programs previously and commonly known as Urban Development or model city projects.

Under the new program, emphasis is placed on guaranteed leasing by the government rather than on outright ownership as in the previous plan.

Funds are channeled to the local and state development agencies by the federal government under Title I. Instead of the previous piece-meal or categorical method of allocating funds for selected projects or groups of projects, the federal government provides block grant money based on the local agency's three-year plan. This provides the local agencies with greater decision-making powers over the actual use of the funds.

The government hopes to generate a major rejuvenation of core city and other community blight areas through this new program.

Additional major areas of importance to the housing and cities:

(1) The act set up provisions for additional subsidies for housing for low-income families and authorized 37,500 units to be built during 1975 and 1976 alone.

(2) It provided for rent subsidies for up to 200,000 units for 1975 and 1976. Using this plan, a landlord agrees to rent a portion of his apartments to low-income families for an amount they can afford to pay. The difference between what they can afford to pay and the market value is paid by the government.

Only a part of the owner's apartment house is rented to low-income individuals, and the remaining portion of the apartment house is rented to people of moderate, middle, or higher income groups. The act also encourages maximum use to be made of existing buildings, but new and rehabilitated housing can also qualify under the act.

(3) Home loan limits were increased from $33,000 to $45,000 under the Federal Housing Administration and the Veterans Administration programs.

(4) Federally chartered S and L's were allowed to increase home loans to a maximum of $55,000 from the previous $45,000 limit.

(5) The FHA is allowed to insure larger loans to mobile home owners and can also insure them for longer periods of time.

(6) For the first time, the government was allowed the right to establish new safety standards for mobile homes.

(7) Also authorized was $500 million a year for operating subsidies in existing public housing projects and $440 million for other federal subsidy programs to be funded through local agencies.

(8) Home improvement loans were increased from the previous $5,000 limit to $10,000 under FHA.

(9) The act allowed for construction of 40,000 to 50,000 units of publicly owned and operated housing, including the financing of the administration's leasing program. Provisions permit HUD to pay the difference between the local fair market rents and 20 to 25 percent of the gross income of eligible low-income families for the apartments rented.

(10) It authorized a total of $8.6 billion nearing 1975, 1976, and 1977 for block grants.

(11) The act also provided for up to $800 million in loans to developers of housing for the edlerly along with new money for certain rural housing projects.

(12) The act also set up federal aid for state operated housing development agencies.

(13) Section 235 and Section 236 subsidy programs were continued through 1975 and 1976 for total outlays of $450 million on which $75 would be new money.

PURPOSE AND OBJECTIVES OF THE 1974 ACT

In Section 101 of Title I of the 1974 act, Congress outlines the purpose and objectives:

(A) The Congress finds and declares that the nation's cities, towns, and smaller urban communities face critical social, economic and, environmental problems arising in significant measure from the following:

(1) The growth of population in metropolitan and other urban areas and the concentration of persons of lower income in central cities.

(2) Inadequate public and private investment and reinvestment in housing and other physical facilities and related public and social services resulting in the growth and persistence of urban slums and blight and the marked deterioration of the quality of the urban environment.

(B) The Congress further finds and declares that the future welfare of the nation and the well-being of its citizens depend on the establishment and maintenance of viable urban communities as social, economic, and political entities and require:

(1) Systematic and sustained action by federal, state, and local governments to eliminate blight, to conserve and renew older urban areas, to improve the living environment of low and moderate-income families, and to develop new centers of population growth and economic activity.

(2) Substantial expansion of, and greater continuity in, the scope and level of federal assistance, together with increased private investment in support of community development activities.

(3) Continuing effort at all levels of government to streamline programs and improve the functioning of agencies responsible for planning, implementing, and evaluating community development efforts.

(C) The primary objective of this title is the development of viable urban communities by providing decent housing and a suitable living environment and expanding economic opportunities, principally for persons of low and moderate income. Consistent with this primary objective, the federal assistance provided in this title is for the support of community development activities which are directed toward the following specific objectives:

(1) The elimination of slums and blight and the prevention of blighting influences and the deterioration of property and neighborhood and community facilities of importance to the welfare of the community, principally persons of low and moderate income.

(2) The elimination of conditions which are detrimental to health, safety, and public welfare through code enforcement, demolition, interim rehabilitation assistance, and related activities.

(3) The conservation and expansion of the nation's housing stock in order to provide a decent home and a suitable living environment for all persons but principally those of low and moderate income.

(4) The expansion and improvement of the quantity and quality of community services, principally for persons of low and moderate income, which are essential for sound community development and for the development of viable urban communities.

(5) A more rational utilization of land and other material resources and the better arrangement of residential, commercial, industrial, recreational, and other needed activity centers.

(6) The reduction of the isolation of income groups within communities and geographical areas and the promotion of an increase in the diversity and vitality of neighborhoods through the spatial deconcentration of housing opportunities for persons of lower income and the revitalization of deteriorating or deteriorated neighborhoods to attract persons of higher income.

(7) The restoration and preservation of properties of special value for historic, architectural, or esthetic reasons.

It is the intent of Congress that the federal assistance made available under this title not be utilized to reduce substantially the amount of local financial support for community development activities below the level of such support prior to the availability of such assistance.

(D) It is also the purpose of this title to further the development of a national urban growth policy by consolidating a number of complex and overlapping programs of financial assistance to communities of varying sizes and needs into a consistent system of federal aid which:

(1) Provides assistance on an annual basis, with maximum certainty and minimum delay, upon which communities can rely in their planning.

(2) Encourages community development activities which are consistent with comprehensive local and area-wide development planning.

(3) Furthers achievement of the national housing goal of a decent home and a suitable living environment for every American family.

(4) Fosters the undertaking of housing and community development activities in a coordinated and mutually supportive manner.

The following programs were terminated by the act:

(1) Open-space urban beautification historic preservation grants.

(2) Public facility loans.

(3) Water and sewer and neighborhood facilities grants.

(4) Urban renewal and Neighborhood Development Program (NDP) grants.

(5) Model cities supplemental grants.

(6) Rehabilitation loans (program to be ended one year from enactment which was August 22. 1974.)

AMOUNT OF FEDERAL FUNDS TO BE COMMITTED EACH YEAR

As of January 1975, funds include $8.4 billion in contract authority for three years with annual disbursement limitations of $2.5 billion in fiscal year 1975, $2.95 billion in fiscal year 1976, and $2.95 billion in fiscal year 1977. To the extent not otherwise obligated, sums appropriated for open space, water and sewer, neighborhood facilities, and model cities supplemental grants can be used during the first program year to liquidate contracts entered into pursuant to the $8.4-billion authorization.

In addition, up to $50 million for each of fiscal years 1975 and 1976 and $100 million for fiscal year 1977 is authorized for transition grants to communities with urgent community development needs which cannot be met through the title's allocation provisions.

ELIGIBLE RECIPIENTS OF FUNDS

States, cities, counties and other units of general local government (including designated public agencies), and certain private "new community" developers and "new community" citizens associations are eligible to receive funds.

In other words, cities of all sizes are eligible to participate. The grants made under this program are supplemental grants, i.e., the money a city receives is in addition to other funds available under regular, existing federal aid programs. A massive, concentrated and coordinated attack on an area big enough to rebuild or restore entire neighborhoods is comtemplated.

HOW THE PROGRAM WORKS

First, the city designates its own Demonstration Agency to coordinate the program, either a new agency or an existing agency, such as an existing urban renewal agency, can be designated. Then, this agency applies for a grant to plan the program. The federal government pays up to 100 percent of the planning cost. Finally, when the plan is approved, the agency carries out the program.

The program takes different forms in different cities, depending on the problem the city or community has. Local agencies design their programs to suit the particular needs of the locality. Thus, when a city has a large proportion of homes in disrepair or in a dilapidated condition, the program might include a project for the rehabilitation of these homes. Part of the grant funds might be used for loans to help nonprofit sponsors of rehabilitation housing to get started or to expand the city's public housing program.

A city may have a large number of elderly people living in a run-down area. This city might convert well-built, large but run-down buildings into safe nursing home facilities; clear and develop areas for parks, a community center or other neighborhood facilities, or make loans and grants to help pay the cost of rehabilitating housing owned by low-income elderly people.

WHAT A COMMUNITY MUST DO TO SECURE FUNDING

Need for an Application — Applicants are required to submit an annual application for federal approval which must contain:

(1) A summary of a three-year plan which identifies community development needs and objectives developed in accordance with area-wide development planning and national urban growth policies and which demonstrates a comprehensive strategy for meeting those needs.

(2) Formulation of a program which:

(a) Includes activities to meet community development needs and objectives.
(b) Indicates resources other than assistance under the title expected to be available to meet such needs and objectives.
(c) Takes account of environmental factors.

(3) A description of a program to:

(a) Eliminate or prevent slums, blight and deterioration where such conditions or needs exist.
(b) Provide improved community facilities and public improvements, including supporting health and social services where necessary and appropriate.

(4) A housing assistance plan which:

(a) Accurately surveys the condition of the community's housing stock and assesses the housing assistance needs of lower income persons.
(b) Specifies a realistic annual goal for the number of units or persons to be assisted, including the mix of new, existing, or rehabilitated units, and the size and types of projects and assistance best suited to the needs of area lower income persons.
(c) Indicates the general locations of proposed lower income housing with a view to furthering revitalization, promoting greater housing choice, and avoiding

undue concentration of low-income persons and assuring availability of adequate public facilities and services for such housing.

In limited circumstances, requirements 1, 2, and 3 may be waived in the case of smaller communities.

Requirements applicants must meet compliance with Civil Rights Acts, adequate citizen participation, A-95 review of applications, and an annual performance report including an assessment of past activities' relationship to the title's and the recipient's stated objectives.

Time Allowed for Federal Action on Application — Applications from metropolitan cities and urban counties, if submitted after the date set for consideration of applications, will be deemed approved after 75 days unless HUD notifies otherwise.

Scope of Federal Review Application — Applications from metropolitan cities and urban counties must be approved unless the description of community development and housing needs and objectives is plainly inconsistent with generally available information, the activities proposed are plainly inappropriate to meeting stated needs and objectives, or the application does not comply with requirements of the title or other applicable law or proposes ineligible activities.

Federal Authority Review of Performance of Approved Applicants and Adjust Assistance Levels — Housing and Urban Development will review programs at least annually and can make adjustments in assistance amounts where the program carried out was not substantially that described in the application, the program did not conform to the requirements of the title or other law, or the recipient does not have the continuing capacity to carry out the program in a timely manner.

Environmental Impact Statements — Under regulations of the Secretary, impact statements will not be required at the time applications are reviewed. Instead, recipients will prepare statements on specific projects having major impacts on the environment before they commit funds to those projects and will have to certify compliance to HUD before funds are released.

PERMISSIBLE USES OF FUNDS

In general, funds received under this title may be used to assist the type of activities which were eligible under the prior community development program. Specific activities may include the acquisition of real property which is:

(A) Blighted, deteriorated, deteriorating, or inappropriately developed.

(B) Appropriate for rehabilitation and conservation activities.

(C) Appropriate for preservation or restoration of historic sites, urban beautification, conservation of open spaces, natural resources or scenic areas, provision of recreation, or the guidance of urban development.

(D) To be used for the provision of eligible public works, facilities, and improvements.

(E) To be used for other public purposes.

(1) Acquisition, construction or installation of public works, facilities and site or other improvements including neighborhood facilities, senior centers, historic properties, utilities, streets, street lights, water and sewer facilities, foundations for air rights sites, malls and walkways, and recreation facilities. Flood and drainage facilities are eligible only where assistance under other federal programs is unavailable. This also includes code enforcement in deteriorated or deteriorating areas expected, together with public improvements and services, to arrest area decline, clearance, demolition, removal, and rehabilitation of buildings and improvements, including interim assistance and financing, rehabilitation of privately owned properties when incidental to other activities, and payments to housing owners for losses of rental income while temporarily holding units to be used for relocation.

(2) A disposition or retention of acquired real property.

(3) A provision of public services not otherwise available in areas of concentrated activities if necessary to support such activities, if funding for such services was applied for under any federal program and denied, and if such services are directed toward improving public services (employment, economic development, crime prevention, child care, health, drug abuse, education, welfare or recreation needs), and coordinating public and private programs.

(4) Payment of non-federal share in connection with other federal programs undertaken as part of the development program.

(5) Relocation payments and assistance for those displaced by assisted activities.

(6) Activities necessary to develop a comprehensive plan and a policy.

(7) A payment of reasonable administrative costs and carrying charges.

LIMITATIONS ON USE OF FUNDS

Grants are conditional on a recipient's certification that its Community Development Program has been developed so as to give maximum feasible priority to activities which will benefit low and moderate-income families or help prevent or eliminate slums or blight. However, approval also may be given to applications describing activities which the applicant certifies and HUD determines are designed to meet other community development needs having a particular urgency as specifically described in the application.

In addition, not more than 10 percent of estimated activity costs can be for local option activities or contingency accounts.

DISTRIBUTION OF FUNDS

Eighty percent of funds will go to metropolitan areas (Statistical Metropolitan Sample Areas) and 20 percent to non-metropolitan areas.

Funds to Metropolitan Cities and Urban Counties — If they meet application requirements, cities with populations of 50,000 and more and central cities of SMSA's are entitled to funds. These funds are to be distributed directly to them according to their needs measured against those of other cities.

Formula funds may exceed prior program levels but, where there is an excess, the city will be "phased-in" up to its full formula level over a three-year period. Urban counties also are entitled to formula funding based on their relative needs if they have power to undertake essential community development and housing assistance activities, directly or by agreement, in areas excluding metropolitan cities and incorporated units of general local government that have a population of 200,000 or more, which elect to be excluded.

Funding Based on Prior Program Levels — In addition to formula entitlement which will be paid to all metropolitan cities and urban counties, those cities and counties which had been receiving a higher level of funding under the prior programs will continue to receive this higher level during the first three years. Over the last three years of the title, the excess over formula will be phased out by thirds. However, cities and counties which had been receiving model cities grants will receive a full model cities "hold-harmless" amount long enough to give each the equivalent of five action years under the program and additionally will receive a declining percentage (80, 60 and 40 percent) of the full amount for a three-year period following the community's fifth action year. Amounts released by phase-out of hold-harmless amounts will be available for discretionary funding.

Smaller communities which have been participating in model cities, urban renewal (including NDP), or code enforcement will receive the same "hold-harmless" treatment even though they have no formula entitlement.

Distribution of Funds to Communities Not Entitled — Communities which have no formula entitlement and which have not been participating in urban renewal, model cities, or code enforcement can apply for assistance out of funds not used for entitlement payments. These funds will be divided among SMSA's, and non-SMSA areas of the various states, based on relative needs as determined by formula. For each of fiscal years 1975 and 1976, $50 million from appropriations will be added to the funds available for use in SMSA's.

COMMUNITIES NOT COVERED

Up to $50 million in fiscal 1975 and 1976 and $100 million for fiscal 1977 will be authorized for transitional grants to assist communities with special needs that cannot be met from the allocation provisions described above. Also, two percent of funds for each year will be set aside for a national discretionary fund which can be used for grants.

Loans — HUD is authorized to guarantee obligations issued by grant recipients for public agencies designated by them to finance acquisition or assembly of real property and related expenses to serve or be used in carrying out eligible activities which are identified in the application and for which grants under this title have been or are to be made.

HUD will reserve out of grant funds for that recipient at least 110 percent of estimated difference between acquisition costs and disposition proceeds, receive a local pledge of full faith and credit or revenues for the replacement of excess over amount reserved, and receive local pledges of future grant proceeds of any additional sums not otherwise repaid.

Guarantee obligations are to be taxable or tax free at the option of the issuer. If taxable, HUD will make grants to the issuer for up to 30 percent of net interest cost.

Transitional Authorizations — "Such sums as may be necessary" are authorized for urban renewal and model cities programs for fiscal 1975. Amounts received pursuant to these authorizations will be offset against first year entitlement or "hold-harmless" amounts received by localities out of 1975 block grant funds.

Close-out of Urban Renewal Projects — The Secretary is authorized to apply up to 20 percent of the grants made or to be made to the locality under the title toward repayment of outstanding temporary urban renewal loans where he determines, after consultation with the local renewal agency and the chief executive officer of the locality, that an urban renewal project cannot be completed without additional capital grants or the local public agency makes an appropriate request. The Secretary may apply a higher percentage of a locality's allocation upon the request of the recipient.

In addition, upon application of the local renewal agency and approval of the locality, the Secretary may approve a financial settlement of an urban renewal project where he finds that there will be surplus of capital grants after payment of temporary loan indebtedness. He may authorize the locality to transfer any such surplus for use under the title.

Advances — HUD is authorized to make advances to metropolitan cities, urban counties and "hold-harmless" cities of up to 10 percent of their first year, fiscal 1975, entitlements for use in continuing urban renewal or model cities programs, or preparing for implementation of the block grant program.

RAISING EQUITY CAPITAL FOR COMMUNITY DEVELOPMENT PROJECTS

A major problem in raising equity capital for any government sponsored project is that a return may be delayed for some years until the construction is completed and leases are entered into. The problem is even more difficult for community development projects, which can get bogged down in administrative delays, to say nothing of political hazards. It is difficult to get the public to invest in such projects because of the absence of an immediate return. On the other hand, relying on secondary financing to supplement conventional mortgage commitments means incurring inordinately high interest charges.

Tax Advantages — High-bracket investors are often interested in government sponsored housing programs because they can offer them substantial tax deductions during construction and development.

As part-owners of projects, they may deduct their share of real estate taxes and mortgage interest against ordinary income. While taxes may be eliminated wholly or in part in a project, interest charges will ordinarily be substantial. On the other hand, they may capitalize such charges, under Internal Revenue Service Section 266, if this better meets their particular requirements.

COMPREHENSIVE PLANNING GRANTS
FOR STATES AND COMMUNITIES

The new law revises section 701 of the Housing Act of 1954 and amends title VIII of the Housing and Urban Development Act of 1964. Major features of the revised section 701 include the following:

Eligible Grantees — Grantees are states for planning assistance to local governments, states for state, interstate, metropolitan, district, or regional activities, cities of 50,000 or more, urban counties as defined in the community development title, metropolitan area-wide organizations, Indian tribal groups or bodies, or other governmental units or agencies having special planning needs.

Eligible Activities — Activities which may be undertaken with grant money include those necessary to develop and carry out a comprehensive plan, to improve management capability to implement the plan, and to develop a policy-planning evaluation capacity to determine needs and goals and develop and evaluate programs.

Program Requirements — Each recipient must carry out an on-going comprehensive planning process. Biennial review of the plan is required as well as provision for citizen participation where major plans, policies, or objectives are determined. All plans must provide at a minimum:

(1) A housing element which takes into account all available data so that the housing needs of the areas studied in the plan will be adequately covered in terms of existing and prospective population growth. Formulation of State and local goals pursuant to title XVI of the Housing and Urban Development Act of 1968 is required.

(2) A land use element which includes (a) studies, criteria, and procedures necessary for guiding major growth decisions and (b) general plans with respect to the pattern and intensity of land use for residential, commercial, and other activities.

These elements must specify broad goals and annual objectives, programs, and evaluation procedures and be consistent with each other and stated national growth policies. With the exception of Indian tribes and agencies qualifying for direct grants because of special planning needs, recipients will be ineligible for further grants after three years from the date of enactment if the planning being carried out by the recipients does not include the above elements.

Recipients are to be required to employ professionally competent persons to carry out assisted activities. To the maximum extent feasible, assisted activities must cover entire areas with related development problems; use of existing plans and studies is required. Recipients must make reasonable progress in the development of comprehensive planning elements.

Special-Purpose Activities — HUD also may make grants to certain recipients to develop and implement plans for controlling major growth decisions and to survey sites and structures of historical and architectural value; and to organizations of government officials to make studies and develop and implement area-wide plans.

Applications — After initial application, an applicant must submit annually a work program for the succeeding year (including intended changes) and biennially an evaluation of the prior two years' progress (including changes in objectives).

Local Contributions — With the exception of grants for developing and implementating plans for controlling major growth decisions, which can cover up to 80 percent of costs, grants may not exceed two-thirds of the estimated cost of the work for which the grant is made.

Authorization — $130 million for fiscal year 1975 and $150 million for fiscal 1976 are authorized.

Funds for Research and Demonstration Projects — Up to $10 million plus five percent of appropriations is available from amounts appropriated for research and demonstration projects.

Technical Assistance — HUD may provide technical assistance and make studies and publish information on planning and related management problems.

Interstate Agreements — The consent of Congress is given to two or more states to enter into agreements, cooperative efforts, and mutual assistance in comprehensive planning for growth and development of interstate, metropolitan, or urban planning.

Limitations on Use of Funds — Funds may not be used to defray the cost of acquisition, construction, or rehabilitation of or preparation of engineering drawings or detailed specifications for specific housing, capital facilities, or public works projects.

Consultation With Other Federal Agencies — HUD is directed to consult with other Federal agencies having responsibilities relating to comprehensive planning, with respect to general standards and procedures, and specific grant activities of interest to such agencies.

Joint Funding — The title provides for joint use of funds obtained under two or more federal assistance programs for approved planning and related management activities, subject to regulations prescribed by the President.

Comprehensive Planning Definition — The definition in prior law is expanded to include:

(1) Identification and evaluation of area needs and formulation of specific programs to meet these needs, and

(2) Surveys of structures and sites of historic or architectural value.

Extension of Program to the Trust Territory of the Pacific Islands — The Trust Territory of the Pacific Islands is made eligible to receive grants under the section.

Amendments to Title VIII of the Housing and Urban Development Act of 1964 (Training and Fellowships) — The following amendments are made to Title VIII of the HUD Act of 1964:

(1) Title VIII urban fellowship program is expanded to include not only urban and housing "specialists" but those with a "general capacity in urban affairs and problems."

(2) HUD is authorized to make grants directly to institutions of higher learning to assist them in developing, improving, and carrying out programs for preparation of graduate or professional students in city, regional planning and management housing and urban affairs, or in research into improving methods of education in such professions.

(3) Title VIII's annual appropriations limit was increased by $3.5 million on July 1, 1974, and by an equal amount on July 1, 1975.

NEW TOWN DEVELOPMENT FINANCING

The federal government, through the Urban Growth and New Community Development Act of 1970, has attempted to encourage the development of well-planned new towns. Through this act, the government will aid developers and corporations in financing these programs.

Under Title VII of The Housing and Urban Development Act of 1970, the government will guarantee bonds up to $50 million for these projects.

Other assistance to developers includes planning grants, public facilities loans, and supplemental grants to state and local public bodies and agencies as additions to federal assistance otherwise available for water, sewer, and open-space projects if needed.

Programs may include new self-sustained communities, expanded communities, developments within cities, and satellite towns which are near metropolitan areas.

Considered the most important provision of the act is the creation of the New Community Development Corporation to operate within HUD to administer the Title VII programs.

The act provides for guarantees of principal, interest, and premium payments due on obligations the developers issued to finance land acquisition and development and construction of some public facilities.

Title VII authorizes the corporation to make loans to developers to enable them to pay interest costs on obligation in the first years, and these loans are repaid as soon as cash flow makes it possible.

The processes surrounding these kinds of projects are long and involved and begin with the developer meeting with members of the New Community Staff in Washington to determine if the project he has in mind is sound.

Then the developer prepares a complete package of appraisals feasibility studies and documents. These can cost upward of half a million dollars. Many stages follow, including evaluation by the government, its commitment, and debenture funding by the developer.

Most developers choose to form a separate entity to undertake the developer's obligations.

The form of the developer entity can be the corporation, a general partnership, or a limited partnership.

New community developments are for major developers, and those with interest should contact HUD or the New Community Staff in Washington.

14. — Tax Planning

A GENERAL DISCUSSION OF TERMS

Taxation in real estate transactions embraces massive information. It will be meaningful in this text to discuss only those tax points which are relative to real estate financing.

Taxable entities include individuals; corporations; partnerships; subchapter S corporations, which are allowed special tax benefits; trusts, and estates. The following are the most important factors affecting all taxpayers who are involved in real estate projects:

(1) Interest — Points, prepaid interest, imputed interest, excess investment interest.
(2) Tax preference income.
(3) Minimum taxable income.
(4) Refinancing or mortgaging out.
(5) Tax-free exchanges.
(6) Sale leaseback transactions — gain or loss, current deductibility.
(7) Depreciation.
(8) Tax considerations related to mortgages.

Let's look at each of these closely and see what they mean in typical real estate financing transactions.

INTEREST

Section 163 of the Internal Revenue Code provides for the deductibility of interest in the year it is paid or incurred depending on the accounting method the taxpayer uses. This usually covers all interest paid in owning or developing property whether or not the loan is secured by a mortgage.

Points — A buyer often is required to pay a premium in order to get a mortgage. This is called a loan processing charge or points and is deductible as interest if paid to the lender solely for the use of money.

For example, suppose an individual borrows $500,000 from a bank on property that he owns. The terms of the loan provide for a nine percent interest rate and two points or $10,000 at closing. This fee is deducted from the mortgage proceeds along with the usual closing costs for title, attorneys, etc. This $10,000 is paid to the lender for the use of money and is deductible as interest.

These points are deductible by a taxpayer in the year of payment and do not need to be amortized over the term of the loan if the deduction does not produce a material distortion of income.

When the seller, instead of the buyer, pays these points or fees, they cannot be deducted as interest expense. The seller, however, may treat them as a selling expense thereby reducing his profit on the sale.

Prepaid Interest — Prior to 1968, the taxpayer was allowed to make deductions of prepaid interest in rather large amounts in any one year. By using a rigid cash-basis approach, he could take the position that it made no difference as to the number of years he prepaid interest so long as the interest was accounted for during the year he made payment. However, this has been restricted.

As an example, using the latest ruling, let's assume that Brown buys an apartment house for $4 million, and he makes a down payment of $724,000. As a buyer under normal circumstances, he would not receive any tax deductions except for depreciation.

However, if Mr. Brown negotiates with the seller to allow him to consider a portion of the down payment as interest, he would realize a substantial deduction — $400,000 could be applied on the mortgage and an additional $324,000 could be paid for the first year's interest (nine percent on the $3.6 million purchase money mortgage). He may deduct the full $324,000 as interest.

If he is in the 50 percent tax bracket, Mr. Brown will save $162,000 in taxes (one-half of the prepaid interest). If he is in the 70 percent tax bracket, he will save $226,800 (70 percent of the $324,000 prepaid interest).

In this case, the seller may have from $162,000 to $226,800 of ordinary income out of this pre-paid interest, but many sellers are willing to enter into this type of transaction especially where there is a strong desire to sell.

This, of course, would not be beneficial to the seller unless he had adequate losses against which he can offset this income or if he has a very low taxable income.

In the past, a taxpayer was permitted to deduct as much as three years' prepaid interest in one year. Now it is necessary to establish whether a prepaid interest deduction "materially distorts income" of a taxpayer.

Prepaid interest and mortgage points are combined in determining whether there has been a sufficient prepayment of interest in excess of 12 months so as to create a presumption of material distortion.

As a consequence, a taxpayer may risk disallowance where he deducts points in the same year he deducts a year's prepaid interest.

If the amount is later disallowed as a tax deduction in the year he claimed the deduction, the interest will have to be restructured on the accrual basis.

Imputed Interest — Internal Revenue Code 483 in dealing with imputed interest applies to situations in which property is sold by installment payments and either a low rate of interest or no interest at all is provided for in the transaction. The code, therefore, treats an appropriate portion of the deferred payment as interest for tax purposes.

Where this code is applicable, both the buyer's disbursements and the seller's receipts may be recomputed to reflect the changes.

The advantage here to a buyer is that he will have additional interest to deduct. In the case of the seller, this method reduces his capital gains exposure.

Excess Investment Interest — Let's apply this term to its use: In hopes of realizing a long-term capital gain, a taxpayer purchases real estate which produces little or no current income. He is incurring interest expense for the purpose of carrying this investment. This interest expense is used to offset his other income such as salary. The Tax Reform Act of 1969 imposes limitations on the amount of investment interest that can be deducted by non-corporate taxpayers.

Excess investment interest can also be a tax preference item, as will be discussed later. The preference item for excess investment interest applies only to individuals, tax-option corporations and personal holding companies.

The Act limits the amount of investment interest otherwise allowed as a deduction for noncorporate taxpayers to an amount equal to the following (in order):

(1) $25,000.
(2) Net investment income.
(3) Net long-term capital gain and
(4) Fifty percent of any excess.

Let's assume that Mrs. Green, a taxpayer, pays investment interest of $75,000 in excess of $25,000 plus net investment income during a taxable year.

Except for any capital gains, she would be allowed to deduct $37,500 or 50 percent of the excess investment interest and carry over the balance of $37,500.

Construction loan interest on projects which are used in a trade or business is not investment interest and could be free of the aforementioned limitations. Whether a property is an investment parcel or is used in a trade or business is a technical question and must be answered by using the particular details involved.

Mortgage interest on real estate will be considered investment interest subject to the limitations if the real estate is net leased, unless the owner's operational business expenses meet certain tests prescribed in the new law.

The rules mentioned do not apply to corporations but do apply to partnerships with some modifications.

Investment interest on partnerships is taken into account separately by each of the partners. The allowable deductions, as mentioned, will be computed separately by each partner. Each partner will get higher deductions or lower deductions, depending on the nature and amount of taxable income they have received as evidenced on their returns.

Deductions on interest on passive investments are treated as tax preference income and are subject to certain limitations.

If the Treasury Department can prove that a taxpayer's interest deduction is fictitious or a function of an adjustment of the purchase price, the taxpayer may lose a portion of that interest deduction.

The strength of the deductibility of a real estate transaction will depend on the facts of the transaction and how well the tax advisors are able to document the taxpayer's position.

TAX PREFERENCE INCOME

The Tax Reform Act of 1969 calls for a 10 percent tax (in addition to other taxes) on certain specified tax preference items. These tax preference items are applicable to taxable years ending after December 31, 1969.

The most important of these tax preference items as they apply to real estate financing are capital gains and accelerated depreciation on real property. The added 10 percent is imposed on the taxpayer's domestic source of income only. Some exceptions are made for foreign-source items.

In computing the tax, the total of tax preference items is reduced by a $30,000 exemption and by the income tax for the year. Specific rules apply to real estate investment trusts, regulated investment companies, tax-option corporations, estates and trusts, and common trust fund participants. One should consult his certified public accountant or tax attorney about the application of these rules in his particular situation.

Under the old law, corporations as well as individuals utilized special tax benefits such as depreciation and other special deductions and deferrals of tax liability. This situation was inequitable when compared with that of individuals who were salaried or who received regular income and were taxed on these earnings without sharing in any tax breaks.

The new law is designed to charge the extra tax to those individuals and corporations benefiting from capital gains and depreciation advantages as these relate to their income.

Tax preference items are those considered in the computation of the 10 percent minimum tax and include:

(1) Capital Gain — The sale or exchange of real estate can result in a capital gain. With individuals the tax preference is 50 percent of the net long-term capital gain that exceeds the net short-term capital loss.

With corporations the determination is slightly more complicated. The tax preference item for capital gains is the ratio of the difference between its special tax rate and the general corporate tax rate to the general corporate tax rate.

For example, suppose ABC Corporation had a net long-term capital gain exceeding the net short-term capital loss of $120,000. A sum of $45,000 would be a tax preference item as follows:

$$\$120,000 \times \frac{48\% - 30\%}{48\%} = \$45,000$$

(2) The Accelerated Depreciation on Personal Property Subject to a Net Lease — Accelerated depreciation on personal property in excess of straight-line depreciation on property subject to a net lease is a tax preference item. Property is considered subject to a net lease if total business deductions for property for the taxable year are less than 15 percent of the gross rental income produced by the real estate or if the lessor is either guaranteed a specified return or guaranteed in entirety or partially against loss of income. Corporations other than tax-option corporations and personal holding companies are not subject to this provision.

(3) Accelerated Depreciation on Real Property — One other tax preference item is accelerated depreciation on buildings and other depreciable property. Accelerated depreciation is defined as the amount allowable for the year in excess of depreciation that could have been claimed had the straight-line method been utilized for each tax year. A separate computation of the excess must be made for each property. The status of accelerated depreciation as a tax preference item is substantially diluted by provisions limiting the use of accelerated depreciation methods.

(4) Bad Debt Deduction for Financial Institutions — Commercial banks, S and L's, and other institutions are allowed to deduct the amount of difference between actual loss and reserve for bad debts. In other words, this tax preference item exceeds the addition that would have been made if the bad debt reserve was based on the actual loss experience.

(5) Amortization — The code permits special and rapid amortization of pollution control facilities, railroad rolling stock, and the cost of acquiring, constructing, reconstructing or rehabilitating facilities for on-the-job training of employees or child-care centers primarily for the children of employees. To the extent that these deductions exceed the depreciation which would otherwise be allowable under the code, the special amortization is a tax preference item.

(6) Minimum Taxable Income — Income includes gross income from interest, rents, royalties, dividends (other than from foreign subsidiaries), net short-term capital gain from investment property, and other gains unless derived from the conduct of a business. It does not include income from property under a net lease entered into prior to October 10, 1969. It does include income from net-lease property where the lease is entered into after October 9, 1969. If the net-leased property is mortgaged real estate, interest on the mortgage would also be a tax preference item.

Net investment income in any taxable year is derived by subtracting expenses such as bad debts, property taxes, depreciation, amortizable bond premium, and other expenses directly attributable to the investment from the investment income.

As an example, imagine that Mr. Wright acquired a mortgage on undeveloped acreage. In so doing, he pays interest of $100,000 on the mortgage. Let's assume his investment income for the year was $30,000 including rents, dividends, and interest.

The expenses applicable to his investment income are $20,000. Mr. Wright would then have a tax preference item of $90,000. This is computed by subtracting $10,000, which is the difference between the $30,000 of investment income and his expenses of $20,000, from the $100,000 interest.

Computing the 10 Percent Tax — If a taxpayer overuses the tax preference items, the Internal Revenue Service will make an additional charge which in essence will reduce the amount he would normally receive as a tax preference credit.

As an example, if an individual received a tax preference on $60,000 in one year, this might be reduced in actuality because the IRS determined he overused the tax preference items. This charge is called the 10 percent tax.

The IRS reduces the tax preference items by:

(1) A $30,000 exemption — The law states the tax applies only to the sum of tax preference items in excess of $30,000. In the case of a married person filing a separate return, the $30,000 exemption is reduced to $15,000. One $30,000 exemption is divided equally among members of a controlled group unless they agree to an unequal distribution.

(2) Income taxes for the taxable year other than the accumulated earnings tax and the personal holding company tax — The amount of income tax which reduces the tax preference items is the total tax for the year minus credits allowable for foreign taxes, retirement income, and investment in property covered by tax preference items.

For example, assume the following about a taxpayer:

(1) His total taxable income is $150,000.
(2) He files a joint return.
(3) His net long-term capital gain over net short-term capital loss is $100,000.
(4) His excess investment interest is $40,000.

50% of Capital Gain of $100,000		$50,000
Excess Investment Interest		40,000
Total Tax Preference		$90,000
Less:		
Exemption	$30,000	
Income Tax	57,680	87,680
Subject to 10% Tax		2,320
10% Tax		$ 232

REFINANCING OR MORTGAGING OUT

When a taxpayer reaches a point where his principal payment is greater than his interest payment on a property mortgage, it could be to his advantage to consider alternative ways to treat his mortgage or property to receive better tax advantages. These methods might include:

(1) Reducing the amount of annual amortization, even though the payments may remain constant.

(2) Refinancing the mortgage so that no amortization is involved.

(3) Buying another piece of property that would have enough depreciation to offset the loss of tax shelter in the older property.

(4) Selling or exchanging the property altogether.

One who has a sizable equity in his property through appreciation in value and mortgage amortization can cash out on that equity in a tax-free manner by refinancing or mortgaging the property. It is this tax consideration which often motivates the property owner to mortgage, rather than to sell, as a means of raising capital.

Borrowing money on existing real estate which is owned is not taxable, nor does it change the taxable status of the property.

Mortgage borrowing generates cash, especially where the amount of the loan is more than the purchase price or construction cost. This is known as mortgaging out.

To illustrate the mortgaging out method: If an investor bought a piece of property for $1.5 million, and there is an existing mortgage of $1.2 million and the value rises to $2 million, the owner might get a new mortgage for $1.7 million.

If the original purchase required $300,000 in cash over the $1.2-million mortgage, the investor might use the proceeds of the $1.7 million mortgage to pay off the existing mortgage, get back his original $300,000 down payment plus another $200,000 to reinvest.

That $200,000 is tax-free cash, although the investor may have to pay capital gains taxes later.

TAX-FREE EXCHANGES

Generally, a gain or loss is recognized as a result of a sale or exchange of property. This is determined by the difference between the cost or other basis (adjusting for depreciation and depletion) of the property held and the fair market value of the property plus any cash received.

However, some types of exchanges are merely a change in form and do not result in a taxable gain or loss. The following paragraphs illustrate some of these exchanges:

Exchange for Property of Like Kind — No gain or loss is recognized where property used in a trade or business or held for investment is exchanged for property used in a trade or business or for investment. This rule does not cover stock in trade or other property held primarily for sale, or stocks, bonds or other securities but it does cover trade-in allowances.

An exchange of real property for personal property is not a like-kind exchange. However, the exchange of city real estate for a ranch or farm involves property of like-kind as does also an exchange of a fee interest in real estate for a leasehold with 30 years or more to run.

Exchange for Property of Like-Kind Plus Cash or Other Property — As mentioned above, if an exchange of property for property of like-kind qualifies and other (unlike) property or money is also received on the exchange, a gain is recognized to the extent of the sum of the money and the fair market value of the other property received. However, a loss from a similar exchange may not be deducted.

For example, if Mr. Taxpayer owns real estate with a basis of $20,000, and he exchanges it for real estate valued at $23,000 plus $6,000 cash, his total gain on the transaction would be $9,000. However, he would only recognize $6,000, the amount of cash received. This $6,000 is a capital gain. His basis for the new property would be $20,000.

If the property exchanged is encumbered by a mortgage, the amount of mortgage relieved is treated as other (unlike) property or cash. If both properties are mortgaged, the net reduction of the mortgage is treated as money.

Suppose Mr. Taxpayer owns real estate with a basis of $50,000 (fair market value of $75,000) on which he has a $65,000 mortgage. He exchanges it for real estate with a fair market value of $40,000 and a $30,000 mortgage. The taxable gain is computed as follows:

Fair market value of property received		$40,000
Less mortgage		30,000
		10,000
Mortgage on property transferred		65,000
		75,000
Basis of property transferred		50,000
Gain realized		25,000
Mortgage relieved	65,000	
Mortgage acquired	30,000	
	35,000	

The entire realized gain is taxable because it is less than the $35,000 net mortgage reduction.

It is immaterial whether a mortgage is assumed by the purchaser or whether the property is acquired subject to a mortgage.

Tax-free Transfer of Property to Controlled Corporation — No gain or loss is recognized if property of any kind is transferred to a corporation by one or more individuals, trusts or estates, partnerships or corporations — solely in exchange for stock or securities (not including stock rights or stock warrants) of the same corporation and if immediately after the exchange the same person or persons are in control of the transferee corporation, that is, they own 80 percent of the voting stock and 80 percent of all other stock of the corporation. However, gain on swap-fund transfers is taxed.

The Supreme Court does not require the restoration to income of a bad debt reserve when stock, equal in value to net accounts receivable, is received in exchange for a partnership's accounts receivable.

If, in addition to securities, the transferor-stockholder receives other property or cash, the gain, but not a loss, is recognized, but then only in an amount not in excess of the cash or the fair market value of the other property received.

SALE LEASEBACK TRANSACTIONS

Usually, if two unrelated parties contract for a sale leaseback, the agreement is given full effect for tax purposes. The term, unrelated, refers to those people who are not joined by family or business ties.

Gains or losses of the seller are recognized, that is, in the absence of a tax-free exchange, and rents of the seller-lessee are deductible business expenses.

If this kind of agreement is made between related parties, conditions are stricter. Only if a fair, reasonable price is set on the property and fair, reasonable rent is charged will the sale leaseback be eligible for tax purposes.

A sale leaseback contract can be struck down completely by courts if sale and rental are out of line with the market, or the agreement can be ordered readjusted to meet going rates of sales and rentals.

Should related parties be included in classes set forth in the Internal Revenue Code, losses on the sale of their property would be dissallowed. Losses on sales between related parties are dissallowed by statute to include sales:

(1) Made directly or indirectly to a member of the seller's family, spouse, whole or half brothers or sisters, ancestors or lineal descendants.

(2) To a corporation owned directly or indirectly by the seller to the extent of one-half or more of the total value of the outstanding stock.

(3) Between two corporations, both owned directly or indirectly by the same

person, if either corporation was a personal holding company, foreign or domestic, in the year before the sale.

(4) Between the grantor and a fiduciary of the grantors.

(5) Between two trusts if created by the same grantor.

(6) Bringing together a fiduciary and beneficiary of the same trust or of another trust created by the same grantor.

(7) Between a fiduciary of a trust and a corporation owned directly or indirectly by the grantor of the trust.

(8) To an exempt organization controlled directly or indirectly by the seller or his family.

If the property sold for leaseback consists in part of depreciable property, the gain on the sale is treated as ordinary income if the sale is made, directly or indirectly, between a husband and wife or between a stockholder and his corporation if more than 80 percent in value of the outstanding stock is owned by the stockholder, his spouse and his minor children and grandchildren.

DEPRECIATION

Applied properly, depreciation can keep cash flow from a property high and taxable income from that real estate low. Depreciation methods used on a property may change from time to time and may vary according to the type and age of the real estate owned.

These types of depreciation are used widely:

(1) Straight-line is utilized for all types of real estate, new and used. This method is where the depreciable amount is written off in equally annual amounts over the life of the depreciable item. As an example, assume a property is purchased at a price of $100,000. Land cost is $16,000 and average value at the end of the depreciable term of 30 years is estimated at $4,000. The amount to be depreciated is therefore $80,000 and can be written off in equal amounts over the 30 year term for a yearly amount of $2,666.67.

(2) One hundred twenty-five percent declining balance used for residential rental properties with a remaining useful life of 20 years or more.

(3) One hundred fifty percent declining balance is the fastest method available for new nonresidential rental properties.

(4) The sum-of-the-years-digits method is available only for new residential rental properties.

(5) Two hundred percent declining balance is used only for new residential rental properties.

(6) The straight-line approach using short useful life is designed for rehabilitation expenses for low or moderate income residential rental properties only (expenditures are depreciated on a straight-line basis utilizing a 60-month useful life).

TAX CONSIDERATIONS RELATED TO MORTGAGES

A Borrower's Tax Advantages — An ability to borrow substantial sums of money provides the real estate operator with a most important tax advantage. Borrowed money is received tax free by the borrower since it is not income and carries the duty of repayment. When dissected, borrowing on business real estate is withdrawing appreciation in value without selling and paying a capital gains tax on the amount received. The money can be used to buy other real estate or spent any way the borrower likes.

Placing a mortgage on real estate has no effect upon the owner's cost basis for his property unless a purchase money mortgage is involved. However, if the proceeds of the mortgage are re-invested in the property, the cost basis will rise with the amount of re-investment. The cost basis increases only when the owner raises his investment in the real estate.

Mortgage Expenses — Expenses incurred in placing a mortgage are considered non-deductible capital expenditures, and must be amortized over the life of the mortgage. Such expenses are finders' fees, title charges, attorney's fees, bonuses, mortgage placement fees, and normal bank charges which do not amount to the payment of interest.

A 10-year mortgage with placement expenses of $10,000 would result in a write-off of $1,000 per year. If the property is sold, or the mortgage satisfied after three years, write-off would be $7,000 (total placement costs, $10,000, less write-off for three years, $3,000).

Existing Mortgage Reduction — When an individual pays off his existing mortgage, he is discharging an existing monetary obligation. If a mortgage is involved, the owner receives a cost basis for the full purchase price including the amount of the mortgage when he originally purchased the property. It must be remembered that for tax purposes a mortgage can be paid off either by total cash, gradual amortization, by compromise, or forgiveness.

Treatment of Mortgage Payments — The mortgage interest is deductible during the year it is paid, and prepayment penalties on a mortgage are also deductible as interest in the year paid. Deductible also are point charges made by a bank for placement of the mortgage. This is true if the points are called placement fees or origination fees but does not hold for legitimate expense items such as the bank's attorney's fee or a title search.

Mortgage amortization payments are non-deductible items. They are treated in the same manner as the prepayments. Amortization payment is nothing more than a partial repayment of a loan, which does not have a tax effect.

Buying Mortgaged Property — An assumed or purchase money mortgage is added to the purchaser's cost and is part of the total purchase price of the property. For tax purposes, it is immaterial which way the mortgage is acquired. Of course, it is this principle which accounts for substantial depreciation deductions in real estate even if a small amount of equity is actually involved.

Qualifications relating to this principle are that if purchase money mortgage is artificially inflated, the IRS has indicated it will not recognize the price as a basis for computing depreciation. Second, a special rule not allowing the inclusion of the mortgage in the depreciation base of certain acquisitions by partnerships. If the limited partners plan to avoid personal liability on the mortgage and at the same time include the mortgage in the partnership's depreciation basis, it is important that they insure themselves that the partners, including the general partners, do not have any personal liability on the mortgage.

Foreclosures — If a mortgage is satisfied below its adjusted basis, the result is a bad debt loss to the lender. The loss is the difference between the adjusted basis or mortgage loan and the amount received for it.

A lender's basis for mortgage obligation is the original amount of the loan decreased by payments and partial write-offs and increased by additional advances to the borrower. The amount received on the sale or foreclosure of the mortgage is reduced by the lender's expenses in providing for the sale, as attorney's fees, filing fees, and commissions.

No loss is realized by a seller if he acquires the property, and potential loss can be postponed until resale of the property. The seller is not entitled to claim a bad debt loss on the buyer's note. This is tabled pending resale.

A gain is recognized to the seller on repossession only for the amount of cash or other property received less the gain on the original sale which has already been included in income. However, under limitations of the gain ruling, the taxable gain cannot exceed the gain on the original sale less the gain which has already been reported and repossession costs.

The basis of real property repossessed equals the basis of the note, including unsatisfied obligations, plus the repossession gain and expenses. So, the loss which was disallowed at the time of reacquisition is usually recognized when the repossessed real estate is sold.

In case of a compromise or forgiveness on a purchase money mortgage, the owner is relieved of the obligation to make an investment, for which he was credited at the time of purchase.

Distribution of Mortgage Proceeds — A corporation is a separate taxable entity, and money passing from it to stockholders creates another taxable form, usually a dividend. If a corporate owner of real estate borrows on a mortgage, the funds cannot be given to shareholders unless a tax is paid. The only exception would be if the corporation had no accumulated earnings and profits and the distribution would not exceed the stockholder's cost basis for his shares in the company.

How Corporate Distribution Affects Taxes — Assuming the amount of stock distributed by the company is not more than the shareholder's original cost of his stock, the distribution will not produce tax until it exceeds his cost basis. Even then the overage will be a capital gain to the shareholder unless the corporation is collapsible.

If the distribution from the corporation came from an FHA-guaranteed loan, the distribution is ordinary income by a special statutory provision.

Contributing Mortgaged Property to a Corporation — If an individual contributes property to a corporation in exchange for the company's stock, a good bit of the same rule for partnerships applies. It differs with a corporation, however, where the transfer of property will be a taxable exchange unless the person or persons contributing the property have controlling interest in the corporation. In this case, the transfer is tax-free, and the shareholder receives a cost basis for his shares on the same basis as the property transferred.

If the mortgage obligation exceeds the shareholder's cost basis for the real estate contributed, the excess will be a gain to the shareholder at the time of transfer.

Making a Gift of Mortgaged Property — A gift of mortgaged property to charity results in a charitable deduction equal to the equity in the property at the time of the gift or the amount by which the property's market value exceeds the mortgage. The donor's cost basis, past depreciation, and original cost are irrelevant.

In the case of a mortgage in excess of basis, the IRS will scrutinize the transaction in an attempt to find that the placing of the mortgage and the gift to charity were really part of a single plan whereby the property was actually sold to the charity for the amount of the mortgage. The IRS has proved this argument in the case of personal property, and it might do the same in real estate. If the mortgage was recently placed, the donor might find he sold the parcel for the amount of the mortgage and then gave the remaining equity to charity.

15. —— How the Specialists Aid in Real Estate Financing

There are four agents of production; land, labor, capital, and the entrepreneur.

Everything rests on land. Nothing can be built without labor nor can crops be grown or animals be raised. No one will work without being paid out of a reservoir of capital, and nothing happens automatically. An entrepreneur or manager must force and guide components toward an objective.

In real estate transactions, more than these four vital ingredients are involved to bring a deal to its conclusion. Actually, the single element of capital includes those who produce money for investment, the savers, those who lend it, the bankers, those who find it, mortgage brokers, those who research its potential, investment analysts, those who estimate its relative value, appraisers, and those who keep track of it, accountants.

Attorneys are also directly related to the capital function since they supply advice about the legalities of the use of investment dollars, provide an understanding of and execute contracts and if all else fails, bring suits to retain or recover capital.

THE ROLE OF THE BROKER OR SALESMAN

The person most visible in real estate sales is the man who brings buyer and seller together, the broker. He attempts to have his client and his customer reach a meeting of the minds. By an accepted definition of his duties, he has earned his commission when he presents to the owner a ready, willing, and able buyer. Such an accomplishment usually does not come from one meeting. It is normal to have a series of negotiations before the deposit receipt is executed.

If both buyer and seller want to wrap up a deal, the paper work is only a formality.

If either party wishes to minimize his risk, the paper work will be modified to provide escape clauses covering such items, for instance, as financing or zoning. These clauses help the buyer get out of contract if he cannot accomplish what he wishes to make the transaction right for him.

A broker should be up to the minute on the availability and cost of borrowing money. His knowledge can help make a deal, especially if his clients lack such information.

The training a broker or salesman must exhibit to the licensing authority to become registered seldom, if ever, requires demonstration of ability to act as a mortgage broker. For this reason, it is highly unusual for a broker to earn separate fees for consummating the deal and arranging financing. His assistance to his client or to the other party in obtaining funds via a mortgage is regarded as part of his normal duties unless specifically agreed otherwise.

It is best to keep in mind that the broker is required to act in a fiduciary manner with his client, and his primary loyalty must be to the party who is to pay his commission.

THE ACCOUNTANT

The accountant is needed in transactions in which the buyer or seller is in a substantially high financial bracket. Many people in real estate, partnerships, and even syndicates use only a bookkeeper or combination bookkeeper-secretary to perform accounting duties.

The primary function of the accountant in real estate projects is to keep the client fully advised of his capabilities in meeting future obligations and the tax consequences and especially benefits of a given transaction.

An ideal accountant has some legal training or background, a library of tax laws, rulings and practices, and solid experience in the market place.

THE ATTORNEY

It is true that on many occasions attorneys wander outside their defined responsibility, which is to act as legal advisors or protectors of their clients interest and not to move into the realm of financial advisors unless they are trained in that field.

The attorney can advise his client on local, state, and federal law as it effects real estate and real estate finance. He handles closings of all types of real estate transactions. He usually has many contacts that can help his client and is well respected in the community.

Many attorneys have an excellent background in banking, especially in mortgage practice, and often are the most highly educated participants in a transaction. In some states, attorneys are allowed to act as real estate brokers by virtue of their admission to the bar.

THE MORTGAGE BROKER

The mortgage broker's role is of variable importance in real estate financing. In smaller deals he usually is not involved at all. In medium-sized projects his function is often assumed by the real estate broker, the accountant, or the attorney.

In times of a plentiful supply of loanable funds, developers find it is possible to deal directly with many major lenders or even choose from among various sources. In this situation, a mortgage broker must convince lenders that he should be employed to find the best possible outlets for funds.

Conversely, in times of tight money, prospective borrowers are more likely to seek out the broker to perform difficult, if not impossible, feats of finding scarce money.

The broker may be paid by either lender or borrower, or his fee may be split between them if this is part of the agreement.

The income derived from mortgage brokerage usually is between one and two percent of the amount of the loan. This percentage is called a finder's fee or origination charge. If the originator remains in a servicing capacity after selling the mortgage to an investor, he is compensated at about one-half of one percent annually for collecting and accounting for the payments and transmitting funds to the long-term lender.

A mortgage broker's earnings are extremely sensitive to cyclical changes in the financial market, and he can maintain greater stability if he is employed as a correspondent for one or more major institutions to find and evaluate mortgage loans in his area.

THE MORTGAGE BANKER

The mortgage banker is a mortgage broker who invests for his own account, using his firm's equity money and lines of short-term credit from commercial banks.

His two main sources of income are construction loans, which are avoided by long-term institutional lenders, and warehousing, which refers to the practice of temporarily maintaining a position in mortgage transactions or funding these and then selling mortgages at a profit to institutions or investors when the market is ripe.

Construction loans are profitable because they pay a higher interest rate than is normally available. Profit from selling a mortgage by take-out agreement or speculation depends on wise and correct analysis of trends and projections. This is not a business for the inexperienced or uninformed, and at times the most experienced and informed wonder what they are doing in this tough, volatile area of finance.

THE BANKER

The banker's involvement in financing real estate is usually limited to construction loans. Traditionally, and often by law, the length of the term precludes his becoming engaged in the long-term mortgage business.

Bankers can be a good source of front or option money or loans which can safely be anticipated for liquidation in the near term, particularly in times of high interest when the borrower expects a lower rate to prevail at the time he places a permanent mortgage.

THE INVESTMENT ANALYST

In the context of real estate the term, investment analyst, is loosely used to describe the businessman in an institution who evaluates and recommends acquisition of stocks and bonds, properties, and mortgages or the private placement of corporate debt secured by real estate.

He may also negotiate purchases and agreements for the institution.

THE REAL ESTATE APPRAISER

An appraisal is an informed opinion of value which may or may not be accurate. A high-grade appraisal is prepared by a professional and submitted in writing after proper consideration of these criteria for estimating worth of real estate:

(1) Cost, less depreciation.
(2) Income produced.
(3) Comparison of property to similar parcels sold in the area.

A secondary level of appraising consists of estimates made by real estimate brokers, investors, or lenders whose opinions are usually quite accurate and market-oriented, but these individuals are not prepared with the skill and experience of the full-time professional appraiser.

The third-level appraisal is the "guestimation" of the layman and is normally limited to one's own property or real estate in the neighborhood.

An appraisal applies only at a specified date, and it loses credibility if it is stored away for future reference or decision-making. It can, however, be up-dated for a reasonable fee.

The appraisal usually sought is the one based on market value. There are a variety of other values, those for insurance, for taxation, and for liquidation, for instance. The appraiser must understand the purpose of the appraisal in every case.

CONSULTANTS

Real estate consultants are called on when management recognizes that expert advice is necessary or desirable and personal knowledge or in-house capabilities are inadequate.

The size and complexity of real estate financing transactions some-times strains even large financial institutions or corporations. This could occur when an isolated or one-time deal exposes either party to undue risk or when numerous deals are to be consummated within a limited time or in a geographical area requiring adaptation to different or even unknown ground rules.

CORPORATE REAL ESTATE SPECIALISTS

Corporations which are not primarily in the real estate business tend to consider real estate as a staff function and a necessary expense. Top management in these departments is seldom recruited from the field, certainly not in the ratio that it is for positions in operations, finance, or law. Perhaps this situation exists because real estate is not yet regarded as a true profession. The practicioner often enters this field with a limited education or late in life after passing an examination which, until recent years, was perfunctory.

The industry itself is being upgraded by higher educational criteria and stiffer examinations preceded by apprenticeship periods with the objective of weeding out part-timers or moonlighters and the semi-retired.

Corporations are beginning to realize that often a multi-million-dollar deal originates with a single location specialist in their real estate depart-ment and that corporate profits and growth can hinge on the integrity, accuracy, knowledge, experience, education, and determination displayed in his selection process and negotiating techniques.

This is true not only for real estate acquisitions, but for conversions, enlargements and disposals of surplus, non-productive real assets, and most especially for the financing sought or granted by his company.

PART 2 — SOURCES OF FINANCING AND HOW TO USE THEM

The Savings and Loan Associations

DEFINITION AND CHARACTERISTICS

Savings and loan groups began as cooperatives for the purpose of financing homes of the members with those members subscribing to shares and making payments on these shares.

Borrowing was permitted by the members after sufficient payments were made into the group and dividends were paid by the savings and loan to the members on the funds invested. Dividends were based on profits which often fluctuated widely.

Today, savings and loans are quite different in make-up as they cater to a wide spectrum of investors. Savings and loans are basically of two types, depending on whether they are organized under state or federal law.

Most savings and loans are mutual associations with depositors as shareholders who elect the board of directors. These directors determine investment policies as well as govern affairs of the association. In a few states, S and L's function as stock associations. These differ in that individuals buy stock providing equity capital to the association and, therefore, own the institution through their shares.

The word, federal, in a title indicates that the S and L is chartered under the Federal Home Loan Bank Board, and those which do not carry this designation may be known as savings and loan associations, cooperative banks, or building and loan associations, depending on the state in which the association is located.

The Federal Home Loan Bank Board, the basic regulatory body for federal S and L's, has 12 Regional Home Loan Banks, which provide reserve credit for savings and loan associations and lend money to them based on their mortgages as security, among other services.

The S and L has traditionally been the largest lender for homes but also makes loans to small and medium-sized investors on apartments, office, commercial, and industrial properties.

In considering the S and L's for mortgages these generalities will usually apply:

(1) The bulk of their loans are for residential mortgages of the conventional type. However, almost all federal and state S and L's can make VA and FHA loans free of their normal restrictions and limitations on asset allowances.

(2) Loans are made on properties within 100 miles from the S and L's home office or within the state where the home office is located. In some cases, S and L's cooperate with one another and loan outside of those areas so long as they participate with the local association in the loan transaction.

(3) Installment loans on homes or combination home and business properties may extend to 30 years in monthly payments and may go as high as 95 or 100 percent of value under the Housing Opportunity Allowance Program.

(4) Often the S and L will use the FHA rating criteria to appraise your property with consideration given to such points as its economic stability from adverse influences; freedom from special hazards; adequacy of civic social and commercial centers; adequacy of transportation; sufficiency of utilities and conveniences; level of taxes and special assessments; appeal of the neighborhood.

(5) Some S and L's ask that the borrower become a nominal depositor before obtaining a mortgage.

STATE AND FEDERAL REGULATIONS

It must be remembered that state and federal regulations are constantly being changed. There is a trend toward more liberal federal regulations for S and L's. In some states, Ohio as an example, S and L's structured through holding companies can make many types of loans almost anywhere in the United States.

MORE RECENT LEGISLATION

Under the Housing and Community Development Act of 1974, and more specifically the new Consumer Home Mortgage Assistance Act of 1974, lending and investment powers of Federal S and L's are changed as follows — as they relate to the federal government's involvement in housing and community development activities.

Construction Loans — S and L's are authorized to make line of credit loans on residential real estate relying on the borrower's general credit rating or other security. Such loans may not exceed the greater of (a) the sum of surplus, undivided profits and reserves or (b) three percent of assets.

Single-Family Dwellings Limitations — The maximum loan amount for single-family dwellings is increased from $45,000 to $55,000. The Federal Home Loan Bank Board is authorized to increase loan limits on dwellings in Alaska, Guam and Hawaii by up to 50 percent above the present $45,000 limit.

Increased Lending Authority — S and L's are authorized to invest, subject to FHLBB conditions, in loans, advances of credit and interests therein for primarily residential purposes without regard to limitations in existing law. Such investments may not exceed five percent of an association's assets.

Property Improvement Loans — The maximum amount for property improvement loans is increased from $5,000 to $10,000.

Loans from State Mortgage Finance Agencies — S and L's are authorized to borrow funds from state mortgage finance agencies and to reloan such borrowings at an interest rate which exceeds by not more than one-and-three-quarters percent the rate paid to mortgage finance agencies. The authority is subject to FHLBB regulations and is limited to the same extent as state law permits state-chartered S and L's to borrow from mortgage finance agencies.

OTHER NEW REGULATIONS

The Emergency Home Purchase Assistance act passed in 1974 allows the Government National Mortgage Association to buy conventional home mortgages from S and L's for the first time. During 1975, '76, and '77 alone, $8 billion in new funds will be channeled into the economy in this fashion. There is a $42,000 ceiling on each loan. Interest rates will vary depending on the current market.

MISCELLANEOUS LENDING POLICIES

Title XVII of the Housing and Urban Development Act of 1968 greatly expanded the financing and investment powers of federal S and L's and authorized them to use methods that formerly were not available for raising funds. Federal S and L's can make mortgage loans on one-to-four-family homes or combination home and business property within 100 miles of their home office, with a maximum of $42,000 loan limit. The loans can go up to 80 percent of appraised value and with maturities up to 30 years.

On single-family homes, under certain conditions, they may lend up to 90 percent of appraised value. Subject to certain limitations, Federal S and L's can invest in mortgage loans on improved non-residential real estate. They can have a limited portion of their assets invested in unamortized first mortgage loans and can make loans that depart from their general lending authority in the case of urban renewal loans.

A qualified federal S and L may invest up to 15 percent of its assets in loans on apartments. Federal S and L's can also make loans of up to $5,000 for vacation homes even though not secured by a first mortgage. Also, they are empowered to finance mobile homes without limitation as to amount so that the highest priced units are eligible. They can make unsecured loans for a large range of equipment items needed by home buyers.

A Federal S and L may, with HLBB blanket approval, make loans on short-term leaseholds in counties where lending on leaseholds extending or renewable automatically for fewer than 50 years is a local practice. In counties approved for short-term leasehold lending, a federal S and L may make this type of loan where the lease or sublease extends or is automatically renewable or is renewable at the option of the holder or of the association for a period of at least 10 years beyond maturity. Loans secured by such leaseholds created after October 12, 1968, carry additional conditions.

The Federal S and L may, subject to some conditions make loans secured, or guaranteed as to principal and interest, by the United States or by the Federal National Mortgage Association, a bank for cooperatives, a federal land bank or federal home loan bank, a federal intermediate credit bank, the Tennessee Valley Authority, or the Export-Import Bank of Washington. It may make unlimited loans and investments guaranteed under the New Communities Act of 1968. It may invest up to one percent of its assets in Agency for International Development-guaranteed housing projects under the Foreign Assistance Act of 1961.

In addition, a federal S and L may, subject to limitation, invest in time deposits, including certificates of deposit, in a home loan bank or Federal Deposit Insurance Corporation-insured bank.

STATE-CHARTERED S AND L's

As for state-chartered S and L's, these associations can, in the main, make the same kinds of loans as federal S and L's and on terms generally comparable to those made by the Federal S and L's. However, while some state-chartered associations are allowed to make equity investments in real estate, Federal S and L's ordinarily acquire equity interests in real estate only through foreclosure proceedings. Also, there usually is a greater emphasis on single-family home mortgages with state associations.

KINDS OF FINANCING TRANSACTED

S and L's have the capabilities to place long and short-term loans on all kinds of real estate although their major interest is in homes. Here is a checklist of the type loans S and L's will consider:

(1) Construction and long-term loans on homes, duplexes, condominiums, cooperatives, and townhouses.

(2) Home improvement loans on existing properties.

(3) Development, construction, and long-term financing for housing project developers.

(4) Short and long-term loans for multi-family structures (if the S and L is large enough), if not, it may be able to participate with another larger S and L.

(5) Smaller commercial, office, industrial, and shopping center properties, although this kind of financing depends on the size of the institution. Most average-sized S and L's keep their loans under $1 million. The larger S and L's and S and L holding companies can, of course, make large loans ranging into the millions of dollars.

(6) Mobile homes.

(7) Second homes and vacation homes.

Step-by-Step Procedures in Dealing with S and L's —

(1) Apply through your own mortgage broker or;

(2) Make a list of S and L's within 100 miles of your selected property and call or write until you find two or three that will consider making you a loan.

(3) Upon contact, cover the following with the loan officer in the mortgage department:

(a) Are loans being made on your type of property and if they are, give him specifics such as age of the property, location, size, lot size, price or estimated cost, and what you want to borrow.

(b) Ask about the amount of discounts, closing and other costs, escrow accounts for your insurance and taxes.

(c) Is a savings account required at the S and L before a mortgage is granted?

(d) Ask how long it will take to process the loan.

After you have gathered this information from all the S and L's, then sit down and analyze and pick the one best suited to your situation.

You will find a variety of programs offered so expeditious inquiries can save you money and time. Once you have selected what you consider the best buy, ask for an application from that S and L.

You can apply at your top two or three choices, but this practice is in some areas considered unfair to all prospective lenders. It is best to apply at one institution at a time. If you are turned down by the first, try the second, and so on down the line. Should you get a reputation for shopping loans through the multi-application process, lenders will grow sour about dealing with you in the future.

The next step on the lender's part will be an appraisal of the property you have chosen to buy. This analysis and appraisal is then turned over with information you have provided to the loan committee and that body makes a decision on a mortgage and how much will be provided as a loan to you. You may not receive the amount you asked for and in this event you might have to obtain a second mortgage or provide more cash as a down payment if you choose to.

Some loan officers will tell you that the amount you applied for will probably not be granted, and you will need a second so you might try to arrange another mortgage as part of your purchase contract.

After the committee's decision is offered to you and you accept, a closing date is set up at which time your bank representative, the Realtor, the seller, and attorneys for both you and the seller and any other principal holder of present mortgages complete the purchase transactions. The interim time, which can range from a month to three months, is used for acquiring deed information, title, abstract, title insurance, loan documents, and other pertinent data.

The deposit you made with your purchase contract is held in escrow usually by the Realtor until time of closing when it is applied to the down payment. The bank may provide you with its attorney so this is an expense you will not have to meet. It is usually advisable that you have your own attorney present to review the contract and be present at the closing. In many states, a title company will handle the closing for you.

THE OUTLOOK

With a changing, interdependent, international economic environment, we can expect further pressures to create continued changes in S and L regulations. In 1974, the 13th Annual World Congress was held in Rio de Janeiro, Brazil, and great interest was shown among members in an indexing system for counter-balancing the effects of inflation.

The United States is one of the few countries in the world still operating with fixed-rate, long-term loans. The indexing system, as used in Brazil, works by annually adjusting dividend equalization rates paid to depositors based on the cost of living. They also charge interest on loans based on the same cost-of-living indexing formula.

SAVINGS AND LOAN ASSOCIATIONS
WITH ASSETS IN EXCESS OF $100 MILLION

ALABAMA

City Fed. Savings & Loan Assn.
2030 Second Ave. North
Birmingham, Alabama 35203

Guaranty Savings & Loan Assn.
2012 2nd Ave. North
Birmingham, Alabama 35201

Jefferson Fed. Savings & Loan Assn.
215 N. 21st Street
Birmingham, Alabama 35203

ALABAMA (*Continued*)

First Fed. Savings & Loan Assn.
851 Beltline Highway
Mobile, Alabama 36601

ALASKA

First Fed. Savings & Loan Assn.
305 Fifth Ave.
Anchorage, Alaska 99501
*Over $88 million

ARIZONA

First Fed. Savings & Loan Assn.
3003 N. Central Ave.
Phoenix, Arizona 85012

Greater Arizona Savings
& Loan Assn.
122 N. Central Avenue
Phoenix, Arizona 85004

Southwest Savings & Loan Assn.
2933 N. Central Ave.
Phoenix, Arizona 85012

Western Savings & Loan Assn.
3443 N. Central Ave.
Phoenix, Arizona 85012

Pima Savings Assn.
151 N. Stone St.
Tucson, Arizona 85702

Tucson Fed. Savings & Loan Assn.
32 N. Stone Ave.
Tucson, Arizona 85702

ARKANSAS

First Fed. Savings & Loan Assn.
Garrison at 6th
Fort Smith, Arkansas 72901

First Fed. Savings & Loan Assn.
312 Louisiana St.
Little Rock, Arkansas 72201

Pulaski Fed. Savings & Loan Assn.
Third & Spring Streets
Little Rock, Arkansas 72201

CALIFORNIA

Republic Fed. Savings & Loan Assn.
2246 N. Lake Ave.
Altadena, California 91001

Anaheim Savings & Loan Assn.
187 W. Lincoln Ave.
Anaheim, California 92803

Central Calif. Fed. Savings
& Loan Assn.
Fed. Savings Bldg.
Auburn, California 95603

American Savings & Loan Assn.
9535 Wilshire Blvd.
Beverly Hills, California 90212

CALIFORNIA (Continued)

Beverly Hills Fed. Savings
& Loan Assn.
9401 Wilshire Blvd.
Beverly Hills, California 90212

Gibraltar Savings & Loan Assn.
9111 Wilshire Blvd.
Beverly Hills, California 90213

Great Western Savings
& Loan Assn.
8484 Wilshire Blvd.
Beverly Hills, California 90211

Perpetual Savings & Loan Assn.
9720 Wilshire Blvd.
Beverly Hills, California 90212

Community Savings & Loan Assn.
477 E. Compton Blvd.
Compton, California 90224

Downey Savings & Loan Assn.
8630 E. Florence Ave.
Downey, California 92041

Fresno Guarantee Savings
& Loan Assn.
1177 Fulton Mall
Fresno, California 93721

Imperial Savings & Loan Assn.
of Central Calif.
2150 Tulare St.
Fresno, California 93721

Sequoia Savings & Loan Assn.
1857 Fulton St.
Fresno, California 93720

Fidelity Fed. Savings & Loan Assn.
225 E. Broadway
Glendale, California 91209

Glendale Fed. Savings
& Loan Assn.
401 N. Brand Blvd.
Glendale, California 91209

Hawthorne Savings & Loan Assn.
13001 S. Hawthorne Blvd.
Hawthorne, California 90250

Hemet Fed. Savings & Loan Assn.
445 E. Florida Ave.
Hemet, California 92343

First Fed. Savings & Loan Assn.
6801 Hollywood Blvd.
Hollywood, California 90028

CALIFORNIA *(Continued)*

Mercury Savings & Loan Assn.
7812 Edinger Ave.
Huntington Beach, California 92647

AVCO Savings & Loan Assn.
2650 Zoe Avenue
Huntington Park, California 90255

Peoples Federal Savings
& Loan Assn.
150 S. Market Street
Inglewood, California 90306

Laguna Fed. Savings & Loan Assn.
260 Ocean Avenue
Laguna Beach, California 92651

Allstate Savings & Loan Assn.
800 Wilshire Blvd.
Los Angeles, California 90017

Atlantic Savings & Loan Assn.
5301 Whittier Blvd.
Los Angeles, California 90022

Brentwood Savings & Loan Assn.
12001 San Vicente Blvd.
Los Angeles, California 90049

California Fed. Savings
& Loan Assn.
5670 Wilshire Blvd.
Los Angeles, California 90054

Cost Fed. Savings & Loan Assn.
855 S. Hill Street
Los Angeles, California 90014

Home Savings & Loan Assn.
3731 Wilshire Blvd.
Los Angeles, California 90010

Lincoln Savings & Loan Assn.
630 W. Sixth Street
Los Angeles, California 90017

Los Angeles Fed. Savings
& Loan Assn.
1 Wilshire Bldg.
Los Angeles, California 90017

Marina Fed. Savings & Loan Assn.
8750 S. Sepulveda Blvd.
Los Angeles, California 90045

Pacific Savings & Loan Assn.
5401 Whittier Blvd.
Los Angeles, California 90022

CALIFORNIA *(Continued)*

Southern Calif. Savings
& Loan Assn.
431 W. 5th Street
Los Angeles, California 90013

State Mutual Savings & Loan Assn.
626 Wilshire Blvd.
Los Angeles, California 90017

Union Fed. Savings & Loan Assn.
426 S. Spring Street
Los Angeles, California 90013

Uslife Savings & Loan Assn.
5220 Wilshire Blvd.
Los Angeles, California 90036

Western Fed. Savings & Loan Assn.
600 S. Hill Street
Los Angeles, California 90014

World Savings & Loan Assn.
11170 Long Beach Blvd.
Lynwood, California 90262

Midvalley Savings & Loan Assn.
317 4th Street
Marysville, California 95901

Monterey Savings & Loan Assn.
449 Alvarado St.
Monterey, California 93940

Constitution Savings & Loan Assn.
1200 W. Riggin Street
Monterey Park, California 91754

North Hollywood Fed. Savings
& Loan Assn.
4455 Lankershim Blvd.
North Hollywood, California 91603

Golden West Savings & Loan Assn.
20th & Broadway
Oakland, California 94612

Oceanside Fed. Savings
& Loan Assn.
810 Mission Ave.
Oceanside, California 92054

Orange Savings & Loan Assn.
230 E. Chapman
Orange, California 92666

Coachella Valley Savings
& Loan Assn.
499 S. Palm Canyon Drive
Palm Springs, California 92262

CALIFORNIA (*Continued*)

Northern Calif. Savings
& Loan Assn.
300 Hamilton Avenue
Palo Alto, California 94301

Mutual Savings & Loan Assn.
315 E. Colorado Blvd.
Pasadena, California 91109

Pasadena Federal Savings
& Loan Assn.
199 N. Lake Ave.
Pasadena, California 91109

Provident Fed. Savings
& Loan Assn.
3756 Central Ave.
Riverside, California 92506

Pomona First Fed. Savings
& Loan Assn.
399 N. Garey Ave.
Pomona, California 91766

Redlands Fed. Savings
& Loan Assn.
10 N. Fifth St.
Redlands, California 92373

Provident Fed. Savings
& Loan Assn.
3756 Central Ave.
Riverside, California 92506

Sacramento Savings & Loan Assn.
424 L. Street
Sacramento, California 95814

Santa Fe Fed. Savings & Loan Assn.
701 North E. Street
San Bernardino, California 92403

Central Fed. Savings & Loan Assn.
640 C. Street
San Diego, California 92138

First Fed. Savings & Loan Assn.
1200 4th Avenue
San Diego, California 92101

Home Fed. Savings & Loan Assn.
7th & Broadway
San Diego, California 92112

Imperial Savings & Loan Assn.
2320 5th Avenue
San Diego, California 92101

CALIFORNIA (*Continued*)

San Diego Fed. Savings
& Loan Assn.
1265 6th Ave.
San Diego, California 92112

Silver Gate Savings & Loan Assn.
701 "C" Street
San Diego, California 92112

Bay View Fed. Savings
& Loan Assn.
2501 Mission Street
San Francisco, California 94110

California Savings & Loan Co.
800 Market Street
San Francisco, California 94102

Citizen's Savings & Loan Assn.
700 Market Street
San Francisco, California 94102

Eureka Fed. Savings & Loan Assn.
4610 Mission Street
San Francisco, California 94112

Fidelity Savings & Loan Assn.
260 California Street
San Francisco, California 94111

Imperial Savings & Loan Assn.
of the North
Columbus Green & Stockton Streets
San Francisco, California 94133

San Francisco Fed. Savings
& Loan Assn.
Post & Kearny Streets
San Francisco, California 94104

Security Savings & Loan Assn.
239 Grant Avenue
San Francisco, California 94108

Prudential Savings & Loan Assn.
526 W. Las Tunas Dr.
San Gabriel, California 91776

Bell Savings & Loan Assn.
400 El Camino Real
San Mateo, California 94402

West Coast Fed. Savings
& Loan Assn.
444 El Camino Real
San Mateo, California 94402

CALIFORNIA (*Continued*)

Mission Fed. Savings & Loan Assn.
936 State Street
Santa Barbara, California 93102

Santa Barbara Savings
& Loan Assn.
1035 State Street
Santa Barbara, California 93102

Century Fed. Savings & Loan Assn.
1347 5th Street
Santa Monica, California 90406

First Fed. Savings & Loan Assn.
401 Wilshire Blvd.
Santa Monica, California 90401

First Fed. Savings & Loan Assn.
1000 Fair Oaks Avenue
South Pasadena, California 91030

San Joaquin First Fed. Savings
& Loan Assn.
240 N. San Joaquin Street
Stockton, California 95202

State Savings & Loan Assn.
222 N. El Dorado Street
Stockton, California 95201

Empire Savings & Loan Assn.
6750 Van Nuys Blvd.
Van Nuys, California 91405

San FernandoValley Fed. Savings
& Loan Assn.
6842 Van Nuys Blvd.
Van Nuys, California 91405

Quaker City Fed. Savings
& Loan Assn.
7021 S. Greenleaf Ave.
Whittier, California 90608

COLORADO

Capital Fed. Savings & Loan Assn.
2625 S. Colorado Blvd.
Denver, Colorado 80222

Colorado Fed. Savings
& Loan Assn.
200 16th Street
Denver, Colorado 80202

Columbia Savings & Loan Assn.
Sixteenth at Broadway
Denver, Colorado 80202

COLORADO (*Continued*)

Empire Savings & Loan Assn.
1654 California Street
Denver, Colorado 80202

First Fed. Savings & Loan Assn.
3460 W. 38th Ave.
Denver, Colorado 80211

Majestic Savings & Loan Assn.
2420 W. 26th Avenue
Denver, Colorado 80211

Midland Fed. Savings & Loan Assn.
444 17th Street
Denver, Colorado 80202

Western Fed. Savings & Loan Assn.
700Seventeenth Street
Denver, Colorado 80202

World Savings & Loan Assn.
400 16th Street
Denver, Colorado 80202

CONNECTICUT

Danbury Savings & Loan Assn.
158 Main Street
Danbury, Connecticut 06810

First Fed. Savings & Loan Assn.
1137 Main St.
East Hartford, Connecticut 06108

Hartford Fed. Savings & Loan Assn.
50 State Street
Hartford, Connecticut 06103

First Fed. Savings & Loan Assn.
20-22 Church St.
Meriden, Connecticut 06450

First Fed. Savings & Loan Assn.
80 Elm Street
New Haven, Connecticut 06503

DISTRICT OF COLUMBIA

American Fed. Savings
& Loan Assn.
300 Penna. Ave., S. E.
Washington, D. C. 20003

Capital City Fed. Savings
& Loan Assn.
4301 Connecticut Ave. N. W.
Washington, D. C. 20008

DISTRICT OF COLUMBIA (*Continued*)

Columbia Fed. Savings
& Loan Assn.
730 — 11th St. N. W.
Washington, D. C. 20001

Eastern-Liberty Fed. Savings
& Loan Assn.
336 Penna. Ave. S. E.
Washington, D. C. 20003

First Fed. Savings & Loan Assn.
610 — 13th St. N. W.
Washington, D. C. 20005

Home Fed. Savings & Loan Assn.
1500 K St., N. W.
Washington, D. C. 20005

Interstate Building Assn.
15th & New York Ave. N. W.
Washington, D. C. 20005

Jefferson Fed. Savings & Loan Assn.
1680 K St., N. W.
Washington, D. C. 20006

National Perm Fed. Savings
& Loan Assn.
1400 G St., N. W.
Washington, D. C. 20005

Perpetual Building Assn.
500 — 11th St., N. W.
Washington, D. C. 20004

Washington Perm. Savings
& Loan Assn.
1421 F St., N. W.
Washington, D. C. 20004

FLORIDA

First Fed. Savings & Loan Assn.
415 — 10th St. West
P. O. Box 1969
Bradenton, Florida 33506

Clearwater Fed. Savings
& Loan Assn.
Cleveland Plaza
P. O. Box 4608
Clearwater, Florida 33518

First Fed. Savings & Loan Assn.
14 S. Fort Harrison Ave.
Clearwater, Florida 33516

FLORIDA (*Continued*)

Coral Gables Fed. Savings
& Loan Assn.
2501 Ponce de Leon Blvd.
P. O. Box 1488
Coral Gables, Fla. 33134

Daytona Beach Fed. Savings
& Loan Assn.
230 N. Beach Street
P. O. Drawer Y
Daytona Beach, Florida 32015

First Fed. Savings & Loan Assn.
501 N. Grandview Ave.
P. O. Box 1270
Daytona Beach, Florida 32015

First Fed. Savings & Loan Assn.
645 E. Atlantic Ave.
Delray Beach, Florida 33444

Atlantic Fed. Savings & Loan Assn.
1750 E. Sunrise Blvd.
P. O. Box 8608
Fort Lauderdale, Florida 33310

First Fed. Savings & Loan Assn.
of Broward County
301 E. Las Olas Blvd.
P. O. Box 781
Fort Lauderdale, Florida 33302

United Federal Savings
& Loan Assn.
3600 N. Fed. Highway
Fort Lauderdale, Florida 33306

First Fed. Savings & Loan Assn.
2200 Main Street
P. O. Box 940
Fort Myers, Florida 33902

First Fed. Savings & Loan Assn.
100 S. 2nd Street
P. O. Box 249
Fort Pierce, Florida 33450

Citizens Fed. Savings & Loan Assn.
400 Hialeah Dr.
P. O. Box 730
Hialeah, Florida 33011

Hollywood Fed. Savings
& Loan Assn.
1909 Tyler St.
P. O. Box 89
Hollywood, Florida 33022

FLORIDA *(Continued)*

Home Fed. Savings & Loan Assn.
1720 Harrison St.
P. O. Box 2166
Hollywood, Florida 33022

First Fed. Savings & Loan Assn.
300 W. Adams Street
P. O. Box 748
Jacksonville, Florida 32201

First Fed. Savings & Loan Assn.
Orange & Tennessee St.
P. O. Box 1527
Lakeland, Florida 33802

First Fed. Savings & Loan Assn.
200 Lake Avenue
P. O. Box 471
Lake Worth, Florida 33460

First Fed. Savings & Loan Assn.
100 Clearwater-Largo Rd.
P. O. Box 1960
Largo, Florida 33540

Biscayne Fed. Savings
& Loan Assn.
1790 Biscayne Blvd.
Miami, Florida 33132

Dade Fed. Savings & Loan Assn.
101 E. Flagler Street
P. O. Box 3981
Miami, Florida 33131

First Fed. Savings & Loan Assn.
One S. E. 3rd Avenue
Miami, Florida 33131

Flagler Fed. Savings & Loan Assn.
101 N. E. 1st Avenue
Miami, Florida 33132

Greater Miami Fed. Savings
& Loan Assn.
101 S. E. 2nd Ave.
Miami, Florida 33131

American Savings & Loan Assn.
of Florida
1655 Washington Ave.
Miami Beach, Florida 33139

Chase Fed. Savings & Loan Assn.
1100 Lincoln Road
P. O. Drawer X
Miami Beach, Florida 33139

FLORIDA *(Continued)*

Financial Fed. Savings
& Loan Assn.
401 Lincoln Road
Miami Beach, Florida 33139

Washington Fed. Savings
& Loan Assn.
1701 Meridian Ave.
P. O. Bin I
Miami Beach, Florida 33139

American Fed. Savings
& Loan Assn.
455 S. Orange Ave.
Orlando, Florida 32801

First Fed. Savings & Loan Assn.
145 Magnolia Ave.
P. O. Box 2073
Orlando, Florida 32802

Orlando Fed. Savings & Loan Assn.
77 E. Livingston
P. O. Box 2673
Orlando, Florida 32802

Century Fed. Savings & Loan Assn.
100 E. Granada Ave.
P. O. Box 7
Ormond Beach, Florida 32074

Palmetto Fed. Savings & Loan Assn.
600 — 8th Ave.
P. O. Box 337
Palmetto, Florida 33561

Mutual Fed. Savings & Loan Assn.
70 N. Baylen
P. O. Box 1969
Pensacola, Florida 32502

Southern Fed. Savings
& Loan Assn.
225 N. Fed. Highway
P. O. Box 879
Pompano Beach, Florida 33061

Community Fed. Savings
& Loan Assn.
2600 Broadway
P. O. Box 9847
Riveria Beach, Florida 33404

Florida Fed. Savings & Loan Assn.
Florida Fed. Bldg.
P. O. Box 1509
St. Petersburg, Florida 33731

FLORIDA (*Continued*)

Home Fed. Savings & Loan Assn.
1901 Central Ave.
P. O. Box 12288
St. Petersburg, Florida 33733

St. Petersburg Fed. Savings
& Loan Assn.
33 — 6th St. South
P. O. Box 13562
St. Petersburg, Florida 33733

Coast Fed. Savings & Loan Assn.
1718 Main Street
P. O. Box 2199
Sarasota, Florida 33578

First Federal Savings & Loan Assn.
1390 Main St.
P. O. Box 1478
Sarasota, Florida 33578

First Fed. Savings & Loan Assn.
500 Franklin St.
Tampa, Florida 33602

Tampa Fed. Savings & Loan Assn.
425 Florida Ave.
P. O. Box 2231
Tampa, Florida 33601

First Fed. Savings & Loan Assn.
101 Federal Pl.
P. O. Box 1577
Tarpon Springs, Florida 33589

First Fed. Savings & Loan Assn.
2045 — 14th Ave.
Box 1209
Vero Beach, Florida 32960

Fidelity Fed. Savings & Loan Assn.
218 Datura St.
P. O. Box 989
West Palm Beach, Florida 33402

First Fed. Savings & Loan Assn.
215 S. Olive Avenue
Drawer F
West Palm Beach, Florida 33401

Winter Park Fed. Savings
& Loan Assn.
200 E. New England Ave.
P. O. Box 1060
Winter Park, Florida 32789

GEORGIA

Atlanta Fed. Savings & Loan Assn.
20 Marietta Street
P. O. Box 1723
Atlanta, Georgia 30301

First Fed. Savings & Loan Assn.
40 Marietta St. N. W.
Atlanta, Georgia 30303

Fulton Fed. Savings & Loan Assn.
21 Edgewood Ave. N. E.
Atlanta, Georgia 30303

Standard Fed. Savings
& Loan Assn.
44 Broad St. N. W.
Atlanta, Georgia 30303

First Federal Savings & Loan Assn.
985 Broad St.
P. O. Box 1332
Augusta, Georgia 30903

Decatur Fed. Savings & Loan Assn.
250 E. Ponce de Leon Ave.
Decatur, Georgia 30030

DeKalb Fed. Savings & Loan Assn.
116 Clairmont Ave.
P. O. Box 460
Decatur, Georgia 30031

Macon Fed. Savings & Loan Assn.
337 — 3rd St.
P. O. Box 958
Macon, Georgia 31202

First Fed. Savings & Loan Assn.
132 E. Broughton St.
Savannah, Georgia 31401

HAWAII

First Fed. Savings & Loan Assn.
851 Fort St. Mall
P. O. Box 3346
Honolulu, Hawaii 96801

Honolulu Fed. Savings
& Loan Assn.
182 Merchant St.
P. O. Box 539
Honolulu, Hawaii 96809

International Savings
& Loan Assn, Ltd.
36 S. King St.
Honolulu, Hawaii 96813

HAWAII *(Continued)*

Pioneer Fed. Savings & Loan Assn.
926 Fort St.
P.O. Box 20
Honolulu, Hawaii 96810

Territorial Savings & Loan Assn.
900 Bishop St.
P. O. Box 1481
Honolulu, Hawaii 96806

IDAHO

First Fed. Savings & Loan Assn.
900 Jefferson St.
P. O. Box 2268
Boise, Idaho 83701
*Over $95 million

ILLINOIS

Germania Fed. Savings
  & Loan Assn.
543 East Broadway
Alton, Illinois 62002

Arlington Heights Fed. Savings
  & Loan Assn.
25 East Campbell Street
Arlington Heights, Illinois 60005

Aurora Savings & Loan Assn.
101 North Lake Street
Aurora, Illinois 60507

Home Savings & Loan Assn.
  of Aurora
77 South Broad
Aurora, Illinois 60507

Citizens Savings & Loan Assn.
100 East Washington Street
Belleville, Illinois 62220

Lincoln Fed. Savings & Loan Assn.
6655 West Cermak Road
Berwyn, Illinois 60402

Olympic Savings & Loan Assn.
6201 West Cermak Road
Berwyn, Illinois 60402

Bloomington Fed. Savings
  & Loan Assn.
115 East Washington Street
Bloomington, Illinois 61701

Avondale Savings & Loan Assn.
2965 Milwaukee Avenue
Chicago, Illinois 60618

ILLINOIS *(Continued)*

Bell Fed. Savings & Loan Assn.
Cor. Monroe & Clark Street
Chicago, Illinois 60603

Chesterfield Fed. Savings
  & Loan Assn. of Chicago
10801 S. Western Avenue
Chicago, Illinois 60643

Chicago Fed. Savings & Loan Assn.
100 North State Street
Chicago, Illinois 60602

Cragin Savings & Loan Assn.
5200 West Fullerton Avenue
Chicago, Illinois 60639

Fairfield Savings & Loan Assn.
1601 Milwaukee Avenue
Chicago, Illinois 60647

First Fed. Savings & Loan Assn.
  of Chicago
1 South Dearborn Street
Chicago, Illinois 60603

Home Fed. Savings & Loan Assn.
201 South State Street
Chicago, Illinois 60604

Hoyne Savings & Loan Assn.
4786 Milwaukee Avenue
Chicago, Illinois 60630

Liberty Fed. Savings & Loan Assn.
  of Chicago
5700 North Lincoln Avenue
Chicago, Illinois 60659

North West Fed. Savings
  & Loan Assn. of Chicago
4901 West Irving Park.Road
Chicago, Illinois 60641

Northwestern Savings & Loan Assn.
2300 North Western Avenue
Chicago, Illinois 60647

St. Paul Fed. Savings & Loan Assn.
  of Chicago
6700 West North Avenue
Chicago, Illinois 60635

Standard Federal Savings
  & Loan Assn.
4192 Archer Avenue
Chicago, Illinois 60632

ILLINOIS (*Continued*)

Talman Fed. Savings & Loan Assn.
of Chicago
5501 South Kedzie Avenue
Chicago, Illinois 60629

Unity Savings Assn.
4242 North Harlem Avenue
Norridge, Illinois 60634

Uptown Federal Savings
& Loan Assn.
430 North Michigan Avenue
Chicago, Illinois 60611

Mid America Fed. Savings
& Loan Assn.
5900 West Cermak Road
Cicero, Illinois 60650

Mutual Home & Savings Assn.
135 East Main Street
Decatur, Illinois 62523

First Fed. Savings & Loan Assn.
of Des Plaines
749 Lee Street
Des Plaines, Illinois 60016

Home Fed. Savings & Loan Assn.
16 North Spring Street
Elgin, Illinois 60120

Evergreen Savings & Loan Assn.
9950 South Kedzie Avenue
Evergreen Park, Illinois 60642

Illinois Fed. Savings & Loan Assn.
6550 North Illinois Street
Fairview Heights, Illinois 62208

Joliet Fed. Savings & Loan Assn.
120 North Scott Street
Joliet, Illinois 60431

Kankakee Fed. Savings
& Loan Assn.
310 South Schuyler Avenue
P. O. Box 552
Kankakee, Illinois 60901

LaGrange Fed. Savings
& Loan Assn.
1 North LaGrange Road
LaGrange, Illinois 60525

First Fed. Savings & Loan Assn.
of Peoria
111 North Jefferson Avenue
Peoria, Illinois 61602

ILLINOIS (*Continued*)

Security Savings & Loan Assn.
200 N E Adams Street
Peoria, Illinois 61602

Gem City Savings & Loan Assn.
636 Hampshire Street
P. O. Box 249
Quincy, Illinois 62301

Quincy-Peoples Savings
& Loan Assn.
730 Maine Street
Quincy, Illinois 62301

First Fed. Savings & Loan Assn.
of Rockford
612 North Main Street
Rockford, Illinois 61105

First Fed. Savings & Loan Assn.
of Wilmette
1210 Central Avenue
Wilmette, Illinois 60091

INDIANA

First Savings & Loan Assn.
of Central Indiana
33 West 10th Street
P. O. Box 191
Anderson, Indiana 46015

Union Fed. Savings & Loan Assn.
of Evansville
501 Main Street
Evansville, Indiana 47708

First Fed. Savings & Loan Assn.
of Fort Wayne
719 Court Street
Fort Wayne, Indiana 46801

First Fed. Savings & Loan ssn.
545 Broadway
Gary, Indiana 46402

First Fed. Savings & Loan Assn.
1 North Pennsylvania Street
Indianapolis, Indiana 46204

Railroadmen's Fed. Savings
& Loan Assn.
21 Virginia Avenue
Indianapolis, Indiana 46204

Union Fed. Savings & Loan Assn.
45 North Pennsylvania Street
Indianapolis, Indiana 46204

INDIANA *(Continued)*

Mutual Home Fed. Savings
& Loan Assn. of Muncie
110 East Charles Street
Muncie, Indiana 47305

Tower Fed. Savings & Loan Assn.
216-218 West Washington Avenue
South Bend, Indiana 46601

First Fed. Savings & Loan Assn.
Washington at Lincolnway
Valparaiso, Indiana 46383

IOWA

Citizens Fed. Savings & Loan Assn.
216 Brady Street
Davenport, Iowa 52801

Des Moines Savings & Loan Assn.
210 Sixth Avenue
Des Moines, Iowa 50307

Home Fed. Savings & Loan Assn.
601 Grand Avenue
Des Moines, Iowa 50307

United Fed. Savings & Loan Assn.
of Des Moines
4th and Locust Streets
Des Moines, Iowa 50308

KANSAS

Anchor Savings Assn.
8200 State Avenue
Kansas City, Kansas 66112

Railroad Building Loan
& Savings Assn.
129 East Broadway
Newton, Kansas 67114

American Savings Assn. of Kansas
1035 Topeka Avenue
Topeka, Kansas 66612

Capitol Fed. Savings & Loan Assn.
700 Kansas Avenue
Topeka, Kansas 66603

Mid Kansas Fed. Savings
& Loan Assn. of Wichita
230 South Market
Wichita, Kansas 67202

Wichita Fed. Savings & Lon Assn.
340 South Broadway
Wichita, Kansas 67202

KENTUCKY

Avery Fed. Savings & Loan Assn.
515 West Market Street
Louisville, Kentucky 40202

Greater Louisville First Fed.
Savings & Loan Assn.
417 West Market Street
Louisville, Kentucky 40202

Louisville Home Fed. Savings
& Loan Assn.
150 South Fifth Street
Louisville, Kentucky 40202

Portland Fed. Savings & Loan Assn.
200 West Broadway
Louisville, Kentucky 40202

LOUISIANA

Capital Building & Loan Assn.
258 North Fourth Street
P. O. Box 1389
Alexandria, Louisiana 70821

Calcasieu Savings & Loan Assn.
1155 Ryan Street
Lake Charles, Louisiana 70601

Fidelity Homestead Assn.
222 Baronne Street
New Orleans, Louisiana 70112

First Homestead & Savings Assn.
300 Baronne Street
New Orleans, Louisiana 70112

Security Homestead Assn.
221 Carondelet Street
New Orleans, Louisiana 70130

MAINE

Sun Fed. Savings & Loan Assn.
561 Congress Street
Portland, Maine 04101

MARYLAND

First Fed. Savings & Loan Assn.
2024 West Street
P.O. Box 1911
Annapolis, Maryland 21401

American National Building
& Loan Assn.
Lexington & Liberty Streets
Baltimore, Maryland 21201

MARYLAND (*Continued*)

Baltimore Fed. Savings
& Loan Assn.
Fayette & St. Paul Streets
Baltimore, Maryland 21202

Loyola Fed. Savings & Loan Assn.
Charles & Preston Streets
Baltimore, Maryland 21201

Vermont Fed. Savings
& Loan Assn.
25 West Fayette Street
P. O. Box 1916

Government Services Savings
& Loan, Inc.
7200 Wisconsin Avenue
Bethesda, Maryland 20014

Chevy Chase Savings & Loan, Inc.
8401 Connecticut Avenue
Chevy Chase, Maryland 20015

First Fed Savings & Loan Assn.
141 Baltimore Street
P. O. Box 1089
Cumberland, Maryland 21502

Maryland State Savings
& Loan Assn.
3505 Hamilton Street
Hyattsville, Maryland 20782

Citizens Building & Loan Assn., Inc.
8485 Fenton Street
P. O. Box 71
Silver Spring, Maryland 20907

Equitable Savings & Loan Assn.
11501 Georgia Avenue
Wheaton, Maryland 20902

MASSACHUSETTS

Boston Fed. Savings & Loan Assn.
30 Federal Street
Boston, Massachusetts 02110

First Fed. Savings & Loan Assn.
of Boston
50 Franklin Street
Boston, Massachusetts 02110

Home Owners Fed. Savings
& Loan Assn.
21 Milk Street
Boston, Massachusetts 02109

MASSACHUSETTS (*Continued*)

Merchants Co-Op Bank
125 Tremont Street
Boston, Massachusetts 02108

Workingmens Co-Op Bank
30 Congress Street
Boston, Massachusetts 02109

Hyannis Co-Op Bank
Main Street & Scudder Avenue
Hyannis, Massachusetts 02601

Lexington Fed. Savings
& Loan Assn.
1840 Massachusetts Avenue
Lexington, Massachusetts 02173

First Fed. Savings & Loan Assn.
of Lowell
15 Hurd Street
Lowell, Massachusetts 01852

Union Fed. Savings & Loan Assn.
48 North Street
Pittsfield, Massachusetts 01201

Middlesex Family Co-Op Bank
577 Main Street
Waltham, Massachusetts 02154

Waltham Fed. Savings
& Loan Assn.
716 Main Street
Waltham, Massachusetts 02154

Northeast Fed. Savings
& Loan Assn.
75 Main Street
P. O. Box 400
Watertown, Massachusetts 02172

First Fed. Savings & Loan Assn.
22 Pearl-Elm Street
Worcester, Massachusetts 01608

Home Fed. Savings & Loan Assn.
of Worcester
419 Main Street
Worcester, Massachusetts 01608

MICHIGAN

Ann Arbor Fed. Savings
& Loan Assn.
401 East Liberty Street
P. O. Box 1227
Ann Arbor, Michigan 48106

MICHIGAN (*Continued*)

Mutual Savings & Loan Assn.
623 Washington Avenue
Bay City, Michigan 48706

First Fed. Savings & Loan Assn.
1001 Woodward Avenue
Detroit, Michigan 48226

Peoples Fed. Savings & Loan Assn.
of Detroit
751 Griswold Street
Detroit, Michigan 48226

Metropolitan Savings Assn.
31550 Northwestern Highway
Farmington, Michigan 48024

First Fed. Savings & Loan Assn.
of Flint
460 South Saginaw Street
Flint, Michigan 48502

Mutual Home Fed. Savings
& Loan Assn.
88 Market Avenue, NW
Grand Rapids, Michigan 49502

Colonial Fed. Savings & Loan Assn.
20247 Mack Avenue
Grosse Pointe Woods, Mich. 48236

Detroit & Northern Savings
& Loan Assn.
400 Quincy
Hancock, Michigan 49930

First Fed. Savings & Loan Assn.
346 West Michigan Avenue
Kalamazoo, Michigan 49006

Capitol Savings & Loan Assn.
112 East Allegan
Lansing, Michigan 48901

Peoples Fed. Savings & Loan Assn.
602 South Monroe Street
P. O. Box 648
Monroe, Michigan 48161

Muskegon Fed. Savings
& Loan Assn.
880 First Street
P. O. Box 568
Muskegon, Michigan 49443

First Fed. Savings & Loan Assn.
of Oakland
761 West Huron Street
Pontiac, Michigan 48053

MICHIGAN (*Continued*)

First Savings & Loan Assn.
124 South Jefferson Avenue
Saginaw, Michigan 48607

Saginaw Savings & Loan Assn.
5145 Gratiot Road
Saginaw, Michigan 48603

American Savings Assn.
24700 Northwestern Highway
Southfield, Michigan 48075

Down River Fed. Savings
& Loan Assn.
20600 Ereka Road
Taylor, Michigan 48180

Standard Fed. Savings
& Loan Assn.
2401 West Big Beaver Road
Troy, Michigan 48084

MINNESOTA

First Fed. Savings & Loan Assn.
of Minneapolis
634 Nicollet Mall
Minneapolis, Minnesota 55402

Home Fed. Savings & Loan Assn.
730 Marquette Avenue
Minneapolis, Minnesota 55402

Midwest Fed. Savings
& Loan Assn.
801 Nicollet Mall
Minneapolis, Minnesota 55402

Twin City Fed. Savings
& Loan Assn.
801 Marquette Avenue
Minneapolis, Minnesota 55402

First Fed. Savings & Loan Assn.
of St. Paul
360 Cedar Street
St. Paul, Minnesota 55101

Minnesota Fed. Savings
& Loan Assn.
355 Minnesota
St. Paul, Minnesota 55101

Northern Fed. Savings
& Loan Assn.
395 Wabasha Street
St. Paul, Minnesota 55102

MISSISSIPPI

Bankers Trust Savings
& Loan Assn.
120 North Congress Street
P. O. Box 918
Jackson, Mississippi 39205

First Fed. Savings & Loan Assn.
P. O. Box 1818
525 East Capitol Street
Jackson, Mississippi 39205

MISSOURI

First Fed. Savings & Loan Assn.
325 Broadway
Cape Girardeau, Missouri 63701

Clayton Fed. Savings
& Loan Assn.
135 North Meramec
Clayton, Missouri 63105

Blue Valley Fed. Savings
& Loan Assn.
6515 Independence Avenue
Kansas City, Missouri 64125

First Fed. Savings & Loan Assn.
919 Walnut
Kansas City, Missouri 64106

Home Savings Assn.
1000 Grand Avenue
Kansas City, Missouri 64106

Safety Fed. Savings & Loan Assn.
910 Grand Avenue
Kansas City, Missouri 64106

Hamiltonian Fed. Savings
& Loan Assn.
9818-20 Clayton Road
La Due, Missouri 63124

Farm & Home Savings Assn.
221 West Cherry
P. O. Box 1893
Nevada, Missouri 64772

Carondelet Savings & Loan Assn.
7321 South Lindberg
St. Joseph, Missouri 63125

Community Fed. Savings
& Loan Assn.
8944 St. Charles Road
Overland, Missouri 63114

MISSOURI (*Continued*)

Home Fed. Savings & Loan Assn.
of Overland
8890 Lackland Road
Overland, Missouri 63114

Jefferson Savings & Loan Assn.
355 Manchester Road
Ballwin, Missouri 63011

Lafayette Fed. Savings
& Loan Assn.
9987 Manchester Road
Warson Woods, Missouri 63122

Missouri Savings Assn.
10 North Hanley
Clayton, Missouri 63105

Prudential Savings & Loan Assn.
6 South Brentwood Boulevard
Clayton, Missouri 63105

Roosevelt Fed. Savings
& Loan Assn.
825 Locust Street
P. O. Box 204
St. Louis, Missouri 63101

MONTANA

First Fed. Savings & Loan Assn.
of Great Falls
601 First Avenue North
P. O. Box 2547
Great Falls, Montana 59401

NEBRASKA

State Fed. Savings & Loan Assn.
201 North Sixth Street
P. O. Box 130
Beatrice, Nebraska 68310

First Fed. Savings & Loan Assn.
of Lincoln
1235 North Street
Lincoln, Nebraska 68501

Commercial Fed. Savings
& Loan Assn.
4501 Dodge Street
P. O. Box 1103
Omaha, Nebraska 68101

Nebraska Savings & Loan Assn.
1625 Farnam Street
Omaha, Nebraska 68102

NEVADA

First Western Savings Assn.
118 Las Vegas Boulevard South
Las Vegas, Nevada 89101

Nevada Savings & Loan Assn.
4800 West Charleston Boulevard
Las Vegas, Nevada 89102

Union Federal Savings
& Loan Assn.
2330 South Virginia Street
Reno, Nevada 89505

NEW HAMPSHIRE

Manchester Fed. Savings
& Loan Assn.
156 Hanover St.
Manchester, New Hampshire 03105

NEW JERSEY

First Savings & Loan Assn.
568 Broadway
Bayonne, New Jersey 07002

Ocean Fed. Savings & Loan Assn.
321 Chamber Bridge Rd.
Brick Town, New Jersey 08723

Inter-Boro Savings & Loan Assn.
Rt. 70 & Springdale Rd.
Cherry Hill, New Jersey 08034

Collective Fed. Savings
& Loan Assn.
202 Philadelphia Ave.
Egg Harbor City, New Jersey 08215

City Fed. Savings & Loan Assn.
East Jersey St. at Jefferson
Elizabeth, New Jersey 07201

Suburban Savings & Loan Assn.
100 Broadway
Elmwood Park, New Jersey 07407

ColumbiaSavings & Loan Assn.
25-00 Broadway
Fair Lawn, New Jersey 07410

Spencer Savings & Loan Assn.
34 Outwater Lane
Garfield, New Jersey 07026

Oritani Savings & Loan Assn.
321 Main Street
Hackensack, New Jersey 07601

NEW JERSEY (Continued)

First Savings & Loan Assn.
70 Sip Ave.
Jersey City, New Jersey 07306

Shadow Lawn Savings
& Loan Assn.
600 Broadway
Long Branch, New Jersey 07740

Berkeley Savings & Loan Assn.
521 Millburn Ave.
Millburn, New Jersey 07041

Investors Savings & Loan Assn.
249 Millburn Ave.
Millburn, New Jersey 07041

Crestmont Savings & Loan Assn.
22 Park Place
Morristown, New Jersey 07960

Barton Savings & Loan Assn.
1166 Raymond Blvd.
Newark, New Jersey 07102

Carteret Savings & Loan Assn.
866 Broad St.
Newark, New Jersey 07102

Mohawk Savings & Loan Assn.
40 Commerce St.
Newark, New Jersey 07102

North Jersey Savings & Loan Assn.
625 Main Ave.
Passaic, New Jersey 07055

Alexander Hamilton Savings
& Loan Assn.
1 Colt St.
Paterson, New Jersey 07505

United Savings & Loan Assn.
136 Market St.
Paterson, New Jersey 07505

Queen City Savings & Loan Assn.
107 Park Ave.
Plainfield, New Jersey 07060

Jersey Shore Savings & Loan Assn.
36 Washington St.
Toms River, New Jersey 08753

Lincoln Fed. Savings & Loan Assn.
of Westfield
30 East Broad Street
Westfield, New Jersey 07090

First Jersey Savings & Loan Assn.
392 Main Street
Wyckoff, New Jersey 07481

NEW MEXICO

Albuquerque Fed. Savings
& Loan Assn.
423 Copper Ave., N. W.
Albuquerque, New Mexico 87101

NEW YORK

Beacon Fed. Savings & Loan Assn.
2303 S. Grand Ave.
Baldwin, New York 11510

Colonial Fed. Savings
& Loan Assn.
300 East Main St.
Bay Shore, New York 11706

Bayside Fed. Savings & Loan Assn.
214-01 Northern Blvd.
Bayside, New York 11361

Tremont Savings & Loan Assn.
3445 Jeromc Ave.
Bronx, New York 10467

Equitable Fed. Savings
& Loan Assn.
356 Fulton Street
Brooklyn, New York 11201

Hamilton Fed. Savings
& Loan Assn.
413 86th St.
Brooklyn, New York 11209

Nassau Savings & Loan Assn.
2815 Atlantic Ave.
Brooklyn, New York 11207

Homestead Savings-Div. of
First Fed. Savings & Loan-
Rochester
360 Pearl St.
Buffalo, New York 14202

Century Fed. Savings & Loan Assn.
of Long Island
466 Central Ave.
Cedarhurst, New York 11516

Suffolk County Fed. Savings
& Loan Assn.
2100 Middle County Rd.
Centereach, New York 11720

Sunrise Fed. Savings & Loan Assn.
312 Conklin St.
Farmingdale, New York 11735

NEW YORK (*Continued*)

Flushing Fed. Savings
& Loan Assn.
136-21 Roosevelt Ave.
Flushing, New York 11354

Suburbia Fed. Savings & Loan Assn.
1000 Franklin Ave.
Garden City, New York 11530

Island Fed. Savings & Loan Assn.
196 Fulton Ave.
Hempstead, New York 11551

Heritage Fed. Savings
& Loan Assn.
Cor. New & Carver Streets
Huntington, New York 11743

Walt Whitman Fed. Savings
& Loan Assn.
1572 New York Ave.
Huntington Station, N. Y. 11746

Reliance Fed. Savings & Loan Assn.
162-04 Jamaica Ave.
Jamaica, New York 11432

Central Fed. Savings & Loan Assn.
249 E. Park Ave.
Long Beach, New York 11561

Astoria Fed. Savings & Loan Assn.
37-16 30th Ave.
Long Island City, New York 11103

Long Island City Savings
& Loan Assn.
37-10 Broadway
Long Island City, New York 11103

Maspeth Fed. Savings & Loan Assn.
56-18 69th St.
Maspeth, New York 11378

South Shore Fed. Savings
& Loan Assn.
4210 Sunrise Hwy.
Massapequa, New York 11758

Westchester Fed. Savings
& Loan Assn.
North Ave. at Huguenot St.
New Rochelle, New York 10802

Bankers Fed. Savings & Loan Assn.
24 John St.
New York City, New York 10038

Edison Savings & Loan Assn.
129 East 14th St.
New York City, New York 10003

NEW YORK (*Continued*)

Franklin Society Fed. Savings
& Loan Assn.
217 Broadway
New York City, New York 10007

Knickerbocker Fed. Savings
& Loan Assn.
722 Lexington Ave.
New York City, New York 10022

New York & Suburban Fed. Savings
& Loan Assn.
2438 Broadway
New York City, New York

Ninth Fed. Savings & Loan Assn.
1457 Broadway
New York City, New York 10036

Serial Fed. Savings & Loan Assn.
99 Church St.
New York City, New York 10007

Washington Fed. Savings
& Loan Assn.
1390 St. Nicholas Ave.
New York City, New York 10033

West Side Fed. Savings
& Loan Assn.
1790 Broadway
New York City, New York 10019

Niagara Permanent Savings
& Loan Assn.
800 Main St.
Niagara Falls, New York 14302

Home Fed. Savings & Loan Assn.
70-01 Forest Ave.
Ridgewood, New York 11227

Columbia Banking Savings
& Loan Assn.
31 Main St.
Rochester, New York 14614

Eastman Savings & Loan Assn.
377 State St.
Rochester, New York 14650

First Fed. Savings & Loan Assn.
320 Main St.
Rochester, New York 14604

County Fed. Savings & Loan
53 N. Park Ave.
Rockville Centre, New York 11571

NEW YORK (*Continued*)

Eastern Fed. Savings & Loan Assn.
160 Main St.
Sayville, New York 11782

Schenectady Savings & Loan Assn.
251-263 State St.
Schenectady, New York 12305

Empire State Fed. Savings
& Loan Assn.
188 E. Post Rd.
White Plains, New York 10601

Whitestone Savings & Loan Assn.
153-18 Cross Island Pkwy.
Whitestone, New York 11357

Columbia Savings & Loan Assn.
93-22 Jamaica Ave.
Woodhaven, New York 11421

Woodside Savings & Loan Assn.
60-20 Woodside Ave.
Woodside, New York 11377

NORTH CAROLINA

North Carolina Savings
& Loan Assn.
351 N. First St.
Albemarle, North Carolina 28001

Home Fed. Savings & Loan Assn.
139 S. Tryon St.
Charlotte, North Carolina 28202

Mutual Savings & Loan Assn.
330 S. Tryon St.
Charlotte, North Carolina 28202

Home Savings & Loan Assn.
315 E. Chapel Hill St.
Durham, North Carolina 27702

Gate City Savings & Loan Assn.
108 S. Greene St.
Greensboro, North Carolina 27402

Home Fed. Savings & Loan Assn.
113 N. Greene St.
Greensboro, North Carolina 27402

First Fed. Savings & Loan Assn.
300 S. Salisbury St.
Raleigh, North Carolina 27602

Raleigh Savings & Loan Assn.
219 Fayetteville St.
Raleigh, North Carolina 27602

NORTH CAROLINA (*Continued*)

First Fed. Savings & Loan Assn.
230 N. Cherry St.
Winston-Salem, N. C. 27102

Piedmont Fed. Savings
& Loan Assn.
16 W. 3rd St.
Winston-Salem, N. C. 27102

NORTH DAKOTA

Gate City Savings & Loan Assn.
500 2nd Ave. N.
Fargo, North Dakota 58102

Metropolitan Savings & Loan Assn.
215 N. Fifth St.
Fargo, North Dakota 58102

OHIO

Akron Savings & Loan Co.
156 S. Main St.
Akron, Ohio 44308

First Fed. Savings & Loan Assn.
326 S. Main St.
Akron, Ohio 44308

First Fed. Savings & Loan Assn.
of Columbus & Bexley
2450 E. Main St.
Bexley, Ohio 43209

Citizens Savings Assn.
100 Central Plaza South
Canton, Ohio 44702

First Fed. Savings & Loan Assn.
200 Tuscarawas St. W.
Canton, Ohio 44702

Eagle Savings Assn.
580 Walnut St.
Cincinnati, Ohio 45202

Home Fed. Savings & Loan Assn.
of Cincinnati
128 E. 4th St.
Cincinnati, Ohio 45202

Broadview Savings & Loan Co.
4221 Pearl Rd.
Cleveland, Ohio 44109

Citizens Fed. Savings & Loan Assn.
1876 E. 6th St.
Cleveland, Ohio 44114

OHIO (*Continued*)

Cleveland Fed. Savings
& Loan Assn.
614 Euclid Ave.
Cleveland, Ohio 44114

Cuyahoga Savings Assn.
One Erieview Plaza
Cleveland, Ohio 44114

The First Fed. Savings
& Loan Assn. of Cleveland
5733 Broadway Ave.
Cleveland, Ohio 44127

Ohio Savings Assn.
515 Euclid Ave.
Cleveland, Ohio 44114

Park View Fed. Savings
& Loan Assn.
2618 N. Moreland Blvd.
Cleveland, Ohio 44120

St. Clair Savings Assn.
813 E. 185th St.
Cleveland, Ohio 44119

The Second Fed. Savings
& Loan Assn.
333 Eucid Ave.
Cleveland, Ohio 44114

Third Fed. Savings & Loan Assn.
of Cleveland
7007 Broadway
Cleveland, Ohio 44105

Union Savings Assn.
One Terminal Tower
Cleveland, Ohio 44113

United Savings Assn.
7050 Broadway
Cleveland, Ohio 44105

Women's Fed. Savings
& Loan Assn. of Cleveland
320 Superior Ave.
Cleveland, Ohio 44114

Buckeye Fed. Savings
& Loan Assn.
36 E. Gay St.
Columbus, Ohio 43229

Dollar Savings Assn.
Gay at High
Columbus, Ohio 43215

OHIO (*Continued*)

State Savings Co.
66 E. Broad St.
Columbus, Ohio 43215

Citizens Fed. Savings
& Loan Assn. of Dayton
110 N. Main St.
Dayton, Ohio 45402

Gem City Savings Assn.
6 N. Main St.
Dayton, Ohio 45402

State Fidelity Fed. Savings
& Loan Assn.
33 N. Main St.
Dayton, Ohio 45402

First Fed. Savings & Loan Assn.
of Defiance
Cor. Clinton at Fifth
Defiance, Ohio 43512

West Side Savings & Loan Assn.
21500 Lorain Rd.
Fairview Park, Ohio 44126

West Side Fed. Savings
& Loan Assn. of Hamilton
445 Main St.
Hamilton, Ohio 45013

First Fed. Savings & Loan Assn.
of Lakewood
14806 Detroit Ave.
Lakewood, Ohio 44107

Hunter Savings Assn.
400 Loveland-Madeira Rd.
Loveland, Ohio 45140

Citizens Savings & Loan Co.
132 Main St.
Painesville, Ohio 44077

Shaker Savings Assn.
20133 Farnsleigh Rd.
Shaker Heights, Ohio 44122

State Savings & Loan Co.
4065 Mayfield Rd.
South Euclid, Ohio 44121

Merchants & Mechanics Fed.
Savings & Loan Assn.
20 S. Limestone St.
Springfield, Ohio 45502

OHIO (*Continued*)

First Fed. Savings & Loan Assn.
of Toledo
333 Erie St.
Toledo, Ohio 43624

People's Savings Assn.
337 Huron St.
Toledo, Ohio 43604

Toledo Home Fed. Savings
& Loan Assn.
626 Madison Ave.
Toledo, Ohio 43602

United Savings & Loan Assn.
519 Madison Ave.
Toledo, Ohio 43604

Peoples Fed. Savings & Loan Assn.
Peoples Fed. Building
Wooster, Ohio 44691

The Wayne Savings & Loan Co.
151 N. Market St.
Wooster, Ohio 44691

First Fed. Savings & Loan Assn.
of Youngstown
124 W. Federal St.
Youngstown, Ohio 44503

The Home Savings & Loan Co.
275 W. Federal St.
Youngstown, Ohio 44503

OKLAHOMA

Local Fed. Savings & Loan Assn.
201 N. Robinson
Oklahoma City, Oklahoma 73102

Oklahoma City Fed. Savings
& Loan Assn.
300 Park Ave.
Oklahoma City, Oklahoma 73102

Ponca City Savings & Loan Assn.
120 S. 3rd St.
Ponca City, Oklahoma 74601

Sooner Fed. Savings & Loan Assn.
of Tulsa
404 S. Boston
Tulsa, Oklahoma 74103

OREGON

Benjamin Franklin Fed. Savings
& Loan Assn.
Franklin Blvd.
Portland, Oregon 97204

Equitable Savings & Loan Assn.
1300 S. W. 6th Ave.
Portland, Oregon 97201

Portland Fed. Savings
& Loan Assn.
444 S. W. 5th Ave.
Portland, Oregon 97204

PENNSYLVANIA

Main Line Fed. Savings
& Loan Assn.
44 E. Lancaster Ave.
Ardmore, Pennsylvania 19003

Pennsylvania Fed. Savings
& Loan Assn.
273 Montgomery Ave.
Bala Cynwyd, Pennsylvania 19004

First Fed. Savings & Loan Assn.
Castor & Cottman Aves.
Flourtown, Pennsylvania 19149

First Fed. Savings & Loan Assn.
234 N. 2nd St.
Harrisburg, Pennsylvania 17108

Harris Savings Assn.
205 Pine St.
Harrisburg, Pennsylvania 17105

State Capital Savings & Loan Assn.
108 N. 2nd St.
Harrisburg, Pennsylvania 17105

First Fed. Savings & Loan Assn.
300 E. 8th Ave.
Homestead, Pennsylvania 15120

Cambria Savings & Loan Assn.
225 Franklin St.
Johnstown, Pennsylvania 15907

First Fed. Savings & Loan Assn.
of New Castle
First Fed. Plaza
New Castle, Pennsylvania 16103

PENNSYLVANIA (Continued)

Commonwealth Fed. Savings
& Loan Assn.
104 W. Main St.
Norristown, Pennsylvania 19401

Community Fed. Savings
& Loan Assn.
7501 Ogontz Ave.
Philadelphia, Pennsylvania 19150

East Girard Savings Assn.
7048 Castor Ave.
Philadelphia, Pennsylvania 19149

Home Unity Savings & Loan Assn.
4806-12 Frankford Ave.
Philadelphia, Pennsylvania 19124

Liberty Fed. Savings & Loan Assn.
202 N. Broad St.
Philadelphia, Pennsylvania 19102

Metropolitan Fed. Savings
& Loan Assn.
2231 Cheltenham Ave.
Philadelphia, Pennsylvania 19150

Public Fed. Savings & Loan Assn.
800 Chestnut St.
Philadelphia, Pennsylvania 19107

Third Fed. Savings & Loan Assn.
4625 Frankford Ave.
Philadelphia, Pennsylvania 19124

Century Fed. Savings & Loan Assn.
5912 Penn Mall
Pittsburgh, Pennsylvania 15206

First Fed. Savings & Loan Assn.
of Pittsburgh
300 Sixth Ave.
Pittsburgh, Pennsylvania 15222

Franklin Fed. Savings
& Loan Assn.
5816 Forbes Ave.
Pittsburgh, Pennsylvania 15217

Friendship Fed. Savings
& Loan Assn.
217 N. Highland Mall
Pittsburgh, Pennsylvania 15206

Mt. Lebanon Fed. Savings
& Loan Assn.
733 Washington Rd. (Mt. Lebanon)
Pittsburgh, Pennsylvania 15228

PENNSYLVANIA (*Continued*)

Parkvale Savings Assn.
3530 Forbes Ave.
Pittsburgh, Pennsylvania 15213

Second Fed. Savings & Loan Assn.
335 5th Ave.
Pittsburgh, Pennsylvania 15222

Red Hill Savings & Loan Assn.
400 Main St.
Red Hill, Pennsylvania 18076

York Fed. Savings & Loan Assn.
30 East King St.
York, Pennsylvania 17401

PUERTO RICO

United Fed. Savings & Loan Assn.
of Puerto Rico
1508 F. D. Roosevelt Ave.
San Juan, Puerto Rico 00922

First Fed. Savings & Loan Assn.
of Puerto Rico
1519 Ponce de Leon Ave. Stop 23
Santurce (San Juan), P. R. 00909

RHODE ISLAND

Old Colony Co-operative Bank
58 Weybosset St.
Providence, Rhode Island 02901

SOUTH CAROLINA

First Fed. Savings & Loan Assn.
34 Broad St.
Charleston, South Carolina 29402

Home Fed. Savings & Loan Assn.
1500 Hampton St.
Columbia, South Carolina 29202

Security Fed. Savings
& Loan Assn.
1233 Washington St.
Columbia, South Carolina 29211

Standards Savings & Loan Assn.
1339 Main St.
Columbia, South Carolina 29201

Fidelity Fed. Savings
& Loan Assn.
101 East Washington
Greenville, South Carolina 29602

SOUTH CAROLINA (*Continued*)

First Fed. Savings & Loan Assn.
320 Buncombe St.
Greenville, South Carolina 29602

SOUTH DAKOTA

Home Fed. Savings & Loan Assn.
Main Ave. & 11th
Sioux Falls, South Dakota 57102
*Over $88 million

TENNESSEE

First Fed. Savings & Loan Assn.
of Chattanooga
901 Georgia Ave.
Chattanooga, Tennessee 37402

Home Fed. Savings & Loan Assn.
of Johnson
City & Greenville
331 E. Main St.
Johnson City, Tennessee 37601

Kingsport Fed. Savings & Loan
& Loan Assn.
110 E. Center St.
Kingsport, Tennessee 37660

Home Fed. Savings & Loan Assn.
of Knoxville
515 Market St.
Knoxville, Tennessee 37902

Leader Fed. Savings & Loan Assn.
of Memphis
158 Madison Ave.
Memphis, Tennessee 38101

Fidelity Fed. Savings & Loan Assn.
of Nashville
226 3rd Ave.
Nashville, Tennessee 37219

First Fed. Savings & Loan Assn.
of Nashville
236 4th Ave. North
Nashville, Tennessee 37219

Home Fed. Savings & Loan Assn.
of Nashville
L. & C. Tower
Nashville, Tennessee 37219

Security Fed. Savings & Loan Assn.
500 Union St.
Nashville, Tennessee 37219

TEXAS

Abilene Savings Assn.
402 Cedar St.
Abilene, Texas 79604

Austin Savings & Loan Assn.
1008 Lavaca St.
Austin, Texas 78701

First Fed. Savings & Loan Assn.
11th & San Jacinto
Austin, Texas 78767

Mutual Savings Institution
1005 Congress Ave.
Austin, Texas 78701

First Fed. Savings & Loan Assn.
304 Pearl St.
Beaumont, Texas 77704

First Savings Assn.
1660 S. Staples St.
Corpus Christi, Texas 78404

American Savings Assn.
1616 Commerce St.
Dallas, Texas 75201

Dallas Fed. Savings & Loan Assn.
1505 Elm
Dallas, Texas 75201

First Fed. Savings & Loan Assn.
1811 Commerce St.
Dallas, Texas 75201

Metropolitan Savings & Loan Assn.
1401 Main St.
Dallas, Texas 75202

Oak Cliff Savings & Loan Assn.
325 W. 12th St.
Dallas, Texas 75208

Equitable Savings Assn.
811 Lamar
Fort Worth, Texas 76102

Tarrant Savings Assn.
Taylor at W. Fifth
Fort Worth, Texas 76102

Guaranty Fed. Savings
& Loan Assn.
2121 Market St.
Galveston, Texas 77550

American Savings & Loan Assn.
P. O. Box 66609
Houston, Texas 77006

TEXAS (Continued)

Benjamin Franklin Savings Assn.
720 Travis St.
Houston, Texas 77002

Center Savings Assn.
7311 S. Main
Houston, Texas 77025

Gibraltar Savings Assn.
2302 Fannin St.
Houston, Texas 77002

Home Savings Assn.
819 Main St.
Houston, Texas 77052

Houston First Savings Assn.
One Shell Plaza
Houston, Texas 77002

Southwestern Savings Assn.
3300 Main St.
Houston, Texas 77002

University Savings Assn.
2500 Dunstan St.
Houston, Texas 77005

Security Fed. Savings
& Loan Assn.
211 N. Gray St.
Pampa, Texas 79065

Alamo Savings Assn.
3326 Fredericksburg Rd.
San Antonio, Texas 78201

First Fed. Savings & Loan Assn.
of San Antonio
800 Navarro St.
San Antonio, Texas 78286

San Antonio Savings Assn.
111 Soledad
San Antonio, Texas 78296

First Fed. Savings & Loan Assn.
Austin Ave. at 13th
Waco, Texas 76701

UTAH

American Savings & Loan Assn.
235 Main St.
Salt Lake City, Utah 84111

UTAH (Continued)

Prudential Fed. Savings
& Loan Assn.
115 S. Main St.
Salt Lake City, Utah 84111

State Savings & Loan Assn.
125 S. Main
Salt Lake City, Utah 84111

VERMONT

Vermont Fed. Savings
& Loan Assn.
150 Bank St.
Burlington, Vermont 05401

VIRGINIA

First Fed. Savings & Loan Assn.
119-121 N. Washington St.
Alexandria, Virginia 22313

Arlington-Fairfax Savings
& Loan Assn.
6711 Lee Hwy.
Arlington, Virginia 22207

First Fed. Savings & Loan Assn.
2050 Wilson Blvd.
Arlington, Virginia 22201

Home Fed. Savings & Loan Assn.
700 Boush St.
Norfolk, Virginia 23501

Life Fed. Savings & Loan Assn.
238 Main St.
Norfolk, Virginia 23514

Mutual Fed. Savings & Loan Assn.
451 Boush St.
Norfolk, Virginia 23510

First Fed. Savings & Loan Assn.
Broad & Third
Richmond, Virginia 23260

Franklin Fed. Savings
& Loan Assn.
626 E. Broad St.
Richmond, Virginia 23240

First Fed. Savings & Loan Assn.
36 W. Church Ave.
Roanoke, Virginia 24001

WASHINGTON

Great Northwest Fed. Savings
& Loan Assn.
500 Pacific Ave.
Bremerton, Washington 98310

Capital Savings & Loan Assn.
5th & Franklin Sts.
Olympia, Washington 98501

Citizens Fed. Savings
& Loan Assn.
1409 5th Ave.
Seattle, Washington 98101

Great Western Union Fed. Savings
& Loan Assn.
1501 4th Ave.
Seattle, Washington 98111

Metropolitan Fed. Savings
& Loan Assn.
1516 Westlake Ave.
Seattle, Washington 98101

Washington Fed. Savings
& Loan Assn.
1423 4th Ave.
Seattle, Washington 95101

Lincoln First Fed. Savings
& Loan Assn.
W. 818 Riverside Ave.
Spokane, Washington 99201

Pacific First Fed. Savings
& Loan Assn.
11th & Pacific
Tacoma, Washington 98401

Columbia Fed. Savings
& Loan Assn.
Mission Sq. Bldg.
Wenatchee, Washington 98801

Yakima Fed. Savings & Loan Assn.
118 E. Yakima Ave.
Yakima, Washington 98202

WEST VIRGINIA

Cabell Fed. Savings & Loan Assn.
508 Ninth St.
Huntington, West Virginia 25701

WISCONSIN

Kenosha Savings & Loan Assn.
5935 Seventh Ave.
Kenosha, Wisconsin 53140

Anchor Savings & Loan Assn.
25 West Main St.
Madison, Wisconsin 53701

First Fed. Savings & Loan Assn.
of Madison
202 State St.
Madison, Wisconsin 53703

First Fed. Savings & Loan Assn.
of Wisconsin
200 E. Wisconsin Ave.
Milwaukee, Wisconsin 53202

Great Midwest Savings
& Loan Assn.
432 E. Wells St.
Milwaukee, Wisconsin 53202

Mutual Savings & Loan Assn.
of Wisconsin
510 East Wisconsin Ave.
Milwaukee, Wisconsin 53202

WISCONSIN (*Continued*)

National Savings & Loan Assn.
829 W. Mitchell St.
Milwaukee, Wisconsin 53204

Security Savings & Loan Assn.
184 W. Wisconsin Ave.
Milwaukee, Wisconsin 53203

West Fed. Savings & Loan Assn.
5500 W. Capitol Drive
Milwaukee, Wisconsin 53216

St. Francis Savings & Loan Assn.
3545 S. Kinnickinnic Ave. (Mil.)
St. Francis, Wisconsin 53207

United Savings & Loan Assn.
604 N. 8th St.
Sheboygan, Wisconsin 53081

WYOMING

Cheyenne Fed. Savings
& Loan Assn.
208 W. 19th St.
Cheyenne, Wyoming 82001

*Over $71 million

Banks

A DESCRIPTION AND GOVERNING RULES

Although commercial banks do make loans for residential mortgages, their primary lending activities in the real estate field center around short-term temporary loans for construction. In fact, according to rigid law, national banks may lend no more than 50 percent of appraised value over five years maximum. In reality they make longer-term and higher-ratio loans.

On amortized loans they may lend up to 66-2/3 percent of appraised value for 10 years if the loan will be at least 40 percent amortized during its term, up to 66-2/3 percent for 20 years if the loan will be fully amortized in 20 years, and up to 80 percent of appraised value for 25 years on home loans if fully amortized. Both national and state commercial banks can make FHA- and VA-insured loans free of restrictions imposed by national and state rules regarding loan-to-ratio value and maturity.

Commercial banks are federally or state chartered, and lending powers differ widely among states, so it is best to check the banks in the borrower's area for their current rules for financing homes.

There are two types of commercial banks — national and state. The nationals are chartered by and subject to supervision by the Comptroller of the Currency and the Board of Governors of Federal Reserve Board. Deposits are insured and may be examined by the Federal Deposit Insurance Corporation, the insuring group for all national banks.

Mortgages and other loans come from commercial banks' time deposits or savings deposits or trustee funds in their trust departments. Depositors are sometimes required to leave monies in their accounts for 30 days, but usually their money is readily available for withdrawal. Certificates of Deposit (CD's) are receipts for money deposited for a specified period and yield a certain set interest.

State banks do not bear the word *national* in their titles since they are chartered, regulated, and supervised by laws of their states. They are also subject to rules and examination of the Federal Reserve System and the Federal Deposit Insurance Corporation if they are subscribers to this insurance.

The FRS acts as a central bank with various regional banks which perform as a bankers' bank. The reserve requirement can be increased or decreased so that money is taken out of the economy through the commercial banking system.

The entire economy is heavily dependent on borrowings from the banks, and even other financial institutions such as real estate investment trusts and finance companies. To a lesser extent, insurance companies and pension funds are affected.

The commercial banks can also borrow from the Federal Reserve Banks as the need arises. The FRS regulates the activities of the banks in many ways in order to protect the depositor and monitor and centralize the flow of funds through the economy in a wise and prudent manner.

Commercial banks' involvement in making mortgage loans really depends on the presence of other lenders in the area. It is possible that a commercial bank will be a prime mortgage lender if there is no other mortgage source in the vicinity. Overall, in times of tight money, commercial banks will cut off mortgage loans and confine lending to short-term construction loans.

TAPPING THE RIGHT DEPARTMENT

The borrower might decide to use a commercial bank for his mortgage depending on where he lives, the types of activities of his selected banks, and the rates and terms offered. It is always a good idea to do research when applying for a loan and not rule out one type of lender because of its reported lending policies. There are always exceptions, and these have to be discovered by the individual.

Usually it is best to make a first contact in person, although a loan officer will mail out applications and answer questions by phone.

The borrower should query not only the mortgage loan people, but also the trust investment department which might be making mortgage investments.

The prospective customer needs to supply the same information he would for an S and L.

TYPES OF LOANS

Commercial banks can provide these types of loans:

(1) Short-term and Construction Loans — These can run from six months to three years.

(2) Interim Loans — Most banks have the ability, which they use sparingly, to provide seven-to-10 year loans. Sometimes these can have a longer payout so that the debt service requirements can be reduced.

(3) Credit Loans — These are based on an individual's credit standing or his

company's. It is often possible to use personal guarantees to obtain funds for a worthwhile short or long-term loan for real estate.

(4) Long-term Mortgages — Depending on the area of the country, many commercial banks can make long-term mortgages similar to those of the S and L's.

These banks also:

(1) Buy Real Estate — Sometimes the trust investment departments buy or place mortgages for trusts, estates, or pension funds for which they invest.

(2) Are Sources for International Funds — Most of the larger banks have foreign or international departments which can provide information, contacts, and sometimes funds from foreign sources for different types of real estate financing in this country.

HOW BANK CREDIT WORKS

The largest part of the money supply in this country comes from the actual, and the creation of, demand deposits in commercial banks. The money the average individual and the American businessman use through their checkbook accounts makes up 90 percent of all the business conducted in commercial banks.

Since most people process the bulk of the money they use, earn, or borrow through banks, the institutions have a continuous flow of deposits which are the sources of their assets and wealth. These are directly related to hardworking people and successful businesses. If one American is out of work or a business fails, it directly cuts into the stability of the commercial bank. Either of these cases decreases the amount of the bank's normal deposits as well as the cash flow generated by checkwriting, borrowing, and regular deposits of money from income or business.

As only a small percentage of a bank's deposits is ever needed or actually paid out, the bank has large sums which may be loaned out. In turn, these amounts are usually redeposited in the bank, creating new deposits.

Loans, of course, are secured by assets of the borrower which in essence are the productivity and assets of people and business. Based on these products and services, the banks actually create new money.

It should be remembered by every American that money may be called by any name — peso, dollar, franc, or pound — and made of any substance — paper, gold, or silver. Names and materials make no difference really. The real wealth of a nation is in the productivity of its people and the wise use and re-use of natural resources or assets owned or acquired.

Experience has shown us that certain percentages of a bank's deposits are needed to pay depositors who from time to time want their money. The federal government has, therefore, required that banks keep amounts of funds in reserve for those depositors. This is called the Federal Reserve requirement since it is set up by the Federal Reserve System.

THE 300 LARGEST COMMERCIAL BANKS

	ASSETS
Bank of America National Trust and Savings Association Bank of America Center San Francisco, California 94120	$41,844,380,000
First National City Bank 55 Wall Street New York, New York 10015	34,950,857,000
Chase Manhattan Bank, N.A. One Chase Manhattan Plaza New York, New York 10005	29,818,496,984
Manufacturers Hanover Trust Company 40 Wall Street New York, New York 10015	16,977,018,954
Morgan Guaranty Trust Company 23 Wall Street New York, New York 10015	15,367,277,651
Chemical Bank 20 Pine Street New York, New York 10015	14,225,653,633
Bankers Trust Company 16 Wall Street New York, New York 10015	14,022,424,000
Continental Illinois National Bank and Trust Company 231 South La Salle Street Chicago, Illinois 60693	12,366,800,000
First National Bank of Chicago One First National Plaza Chicago, Illinois 60670	12,083,748,900
Security Pacific National Bank Sixth and Spring Streets Los Angeles, California 90013	11,403,764,491
Wells Fargo Bank, N.A. 464 California Street San Francisco, California 94120	9,034,328,215
Crocker National Bank One Montgomery Street San Francisco, California 94104	8,016,015,774
Mellon Bank, N.A. Mellon Bank Building 525 William Penn Place Pittsburgh, Pennsylvania 15230	7,350,839,000

Irving Trust Company One Wall Street New York, New York 10015	$6,970,013,624
United California Bank 707 Wilshire Boulevard Los Angeles, California 90054	6,855,024,724
Marine Midland Bank-New York 140 Broadway New York, New York 10015	6,655,445,000
First National Bank of Boston 100 Federal Street Boston, Massachusetts 02110	6,103,307,600
National Bank of Detroit Woodward Avenue at Fort Street Box 116 Detroit, Michigan 48232	5,423,351,722
First Pennsylvania Banking and Trust Company 15th and Chestnut Streets Philadelphia, Pennsylvania 19101	3,926,227,000
Franklin National Bank 189 Montague Street Brooklyn, New York 11201	3,732,241,332
Union Bank 445 South Figueroa Street Los Angeles, California 90017	3,615,915,000
First National Bank in Dallas Post Office Box 6031 Dallas, Texas 75222	3,094,460,000
Harris Trust & Savings Bank 111 West Monroe Street Chicago, Illinois 60690	2,981,704,746
Republic National Bank of Dallas Pacific & Ervay Streets Dallas, Texas 75222	2,968,647,762
North Carolina National Bank 200 South Tryon Street Charlotte, North Carolina 28201	2,960,917,900
Seattle-First National Bank 1001 Fourth Avenue Seattle, Washington 98124	2,919,718,631
Cleveland Trust Company 900 Euclid Avenue Cleveland, Ohio 44101	2,872,057,544
Philadelphia National Bank Broad and Chestnut Streets Philadelphia, Pennsylvania 19119	2,857,514,095

Northern Trust Company La Salle and Monroe Streets Chicago, Illinois 60690	$ 2,766,052,072
Girard Trust Company One Girard Plaza Philadelphia, Pennsylvania 19101	2,743,812,000
Wachovia Bank and Trust Company, N.A. 301 North Main Street Winston-Salem, North Carolina 27102	2,729,942,748
National Bank of North Carolina 44 Wall Street New York, New York 10005	2,484,804,203
Bank of California, N.A. 400 California Street San Francisco, California 94104	2,398,328,000
Valley National Bank of Arizona 241 North Central Avenue Phoenix, Arizona 85001	2,362,653,586
Manufacturers National Bank of Detroit 151 West Fort Street Detroit, Michigan 48226	3,354,731,000
Detroit Bank & Trust Company Fort and Washington Boulevard Detroit, Michigan 48231	2,340,716,127
First National Bank of Oregon 1300 S.W. 5th Avenue Portland, Oregon 97201	2,230,742,928
Fidelity Bank 1200 East Lancaster Avenue Rosemont, Pennsylvania 19010	2,103,992,490
Pittsburgh National Bank Fifth Avenue & Wood Street Pittsburgh, Pennsylvania 15230	2,075,235,915
United States National Bank of Oregon 309 Southwest 6th Avenue Portland, Oregon 97204	2,066,925,483
First City National Bank of Houston 1001 Main Street Houston, Texas 77002	2,009,943,556
First Wisconsin National Bank 777 East Wisconsin Avenue Milwaukee, Wisconsin 53201	1,992,934,982
Citizens & Southern National Bank 35 Broad Street,N.W. Atlanta, Georgia 30301	1,988,890,612

Bank of New York   1,952,971,587
48 Wall Street
New York, New York 10015

National Bank of Commerce at Seattle   1,935,740,667
Second Avenue at Spring Street
Seattle, Washington 98101

Marine Midland Bank-Western   1,851,965,484
One Marine Midland Center
Buffalo, New York 14240

Texas Commerce Bank N.A.   1,756,189,979
Post Office Box 2558
Houston, Texas 77001

National City Bank of Cleveland   1,755,157,662
623 Euclid Avenue
Cleveland, Ohio 44114

Hartford National Bank & Trust Company   1,523,816,622
777 Main Street
Hartford, Connecticut 06115

First National Bank of Arizona   1,519,097,687
First National Bank Plaza
Post Office Box 20551
Phoenix, Arizona 85036

Connecticut Bank & Trust Company   1,504,570,418
One Constitution Plaza
Hartford, Connecticut 06115

First Union National Bank of North Carolina   1,489,019,138
301 South Tryon Street
Charlotte, North Carolina 28201

Security National Bank   1,496,522,000
31 Main Street
Hempstead, Long Island, New York 11550

American Fletcher National Bank
    & Trust Company   1,474,754,859
101 Monument Circle-10 East Market Street
Indianapolis, Indiana 46204

Industrial National Bank of Rhode Island   1,452,004,000
111 Westminister Street
Providence, Rhode Island 02903

Indiana National Bank   1,440,085,850
One Indiana Square
Indianapolis, Indiana 46266

Equibank N.A.   1,394,392,680
Fifth Avenue & Smithfield Street
Pittsburgh, Pennsylvania 15222

Virginia National Bank   1,366,969,354
One Commercial Place
Norfolk, Virginia 23510

Provident National Bank Bryn Mawr, Pennsylvania 19010	$1,353,148,826
Central National Bank 800 Superior Avenue Cleveland, Ohio 44114	1,348,090,079
Maryland National Bank Baltimore and Light Streets Post Office Box 987 Baltimore, Maryland 21203	1,347,991,501
First National Bank of Atlanta Post Office Box 4148 Atlanta, Georgia 30302	1,288,659,568
Michigan National Bank Michigan National Tower 124 West Allegan Street Lansing, Michigan 48904	1,257,084,712
Bank of Tokyo Trust Company 100 Broadway New York, New York 10005	1,256,125,157
National Shawmut Bank of Boston 40 Water Street Boston, Massachusetts 02109	1,240,306,075
American National Bank and Trust Company of Chicago 33 North La Salle Street Chicago, Illinois 60690	1,230,419,746
Trust Company of Georgia One Pryor Street, N.E. Atlanta, Georgia 30303	1,229,525,976
Northwestern National Bank of Minneapolis 7th and Marquette Avenue Minneapolis, Minnesota 55480	1,225,843,867
First National Bank 100 South Biscayne Boulevard Miami, Florida 33131	1,200,714,154
Riggs National Bank 1503 Pennsylvania Avenue, N.W. Washington, D.C. 20005	1,194,974,277
First National Bank 165 Madison Avenue Memphis, Tennessee 38103	1,170,953,154
First National Bank of Minneapolis 120 South Sixth Street Minneapolis, Minnesota 55402	1,165,314,351
State Street Bank & Trust Company 225 Franklin Street Boston, Massachusetts 02101	1,161,477,912

Mercantile Trust Company N.A. Eight, Locust, Seventh and St. Charles Streets St. Louis, Missouri 63101	$1,159,103,859
Manufacturers & Traders Trust Company One M & T Plaza Buffalo, New York 14240	1,137,696,558
First Western Bank & Trust Company 548 South Spring Street Los Angeles, California 90013	1,132,561,155
First National Bank in St. Louis 510 Locust Street St. Louis, Missouri 63101	1,130,608,885
Union Commerce Bank 917 Euclid Avenue Cleveland, Ohio 44101	1,112,278,655
First National State Bank of New Jersey 550 Broad Street Newark, New Jersey 07102	1,077,120,846
New England Merchants National Bank Prudential Center Boston, Massachusetts 02199	1,039,209,351
Union Planters National Bank 67 Madison Avenue Memphis, Tennessee 38101	1,034,340,235
Ohio National Bank 51 North High Street Columbus, Ohio 43216	1,024,173,322
County Trust Company 235 Main Street White Plains, New York 10602	1,017,232,927
Lincoln First Bank of Rochester 183 East Main Street Rochester, New York 14603	1,014,175,725
First-Citizens Bank & Trust Company Post Office Box 1377 Smithfield, North Carolina 27577	1,009,167,721
First National Bank of St. Paul 332 Minnesota Street St. Paul, Minnesota 55101	978,365,799
Bank of the Southwest N.A. Post Office Box 2629 910 Travis Street Houston, Texas 77001	967,002,536
Society National Bank of Cleveland 127 Public Square Cleveland, Ohio 44114	957,884,070

Peoples Trust of New Jersey 210 Main Street Hackensack, New Jersey 07602	$957,268,000
American Security & Trust Company 15th Street & Pennsylvania Avenue, N.W. Washington, D.C. 20013	955,805,667
Banco Popular de Puerto Rico 7 West 51st Street New York, New York 10036	955,455,049
Continental Bank Main and Swede Streets Norristown, Pennsylvania 19401	933,975,502
First & Merchants National Bank of Richmond 9th and Main Streets Richmond, Virginia 23261	926,150,451
Bank of Hawaii Financial Plaza of the Pacific 111 South King Street, P.O. Box 2900 Honolulu, Hawaii 96813	920,258,950
First American National Bank Fourth Avenue and Union Street Nashville, Tennessee 37237	917,082,666
Michigan National Bank of Detroit 500 Griswold Street Detroit, Michigan 48226	882,920,604
First National Bank of Birmingham Birmingham, Alabama 35288	881,903,995
Equitable Trust Company Clavert and Fayette Streets Baltimore, Maryland 21203	881,131,468
Northwestern Bank Drawer 310 North Wilkesboro, North Carolina 28659	880,468,950
Bank of the Commonwealth Commonwealth Building Fort & Griswold Streets Detroit, Michigan 48226	877,925,873
First National Bank of Maryland 25 St. Charles Street Baltimore, Maryland 21203	864,220,726
Midlantic National Bank 744 Broad Street Newark, New Jersey 07101	861,657,234
Whitney National Bank 228 St. Charles Avenue New Orleans, Louisiana 70161	854,548,129

Commerce Union Bank 400 Union Street Nashville, Tennessee 37219	$848,304,614
American Bank & Trust Company of Pennsylvania 35 North Sixth Street Reading, Pennsylvania 19601	836,016,000
Fidelity Union Trust Company 765 Broad Street Newark, New Jersey 07101	819,913,365
Bank of Tokyo of California 58 Sutter Street San Francisco, California 94120	811,745,753
First National Bank of Commerce Baronne and Common Streets New Orleans, Louisiana 70112	809,413,547
First National Bank of Nevada One East First Street Reno, Nevada 89501	807,060,852
Southern California First National Bank 530 B Street San Diego, California 92112	803,575,549
City National Bank 645 Griswold Street Detroit, Michigan 48226	798,010,248
National Commercial Bank & Trust Company 60 State Street Albany, New York 12207	796,159,390
First National Bank of Denver 633 17th Street Denver, Colorado 80202	792,333,503
South Carolina National Bank Columbia, South Carolina 29402	787,803,235
Industrial Valley Bank & Trust Company York Road & West Avenue Jenkintown, Pennsylvania 19046	787,505,375
Third National Bank 201 Fourth Avenue North Nashville, Tennessee 37219	783,056,692
First Hawaiian Bank King & Bishop Streets Honolulu, Hawaii 96847	782,711,630
Idaho First National Bank Boise, Idaho 83707	776,987,423
Suburban Trust Company 6495 New Hampshire Avenue Hyattsville, Maryland 20783	773,442,480

Arizona Bank 44 West Monroe Street Phoenix, Arizona 85003	$ 770,059,274
Union National Bank of Pittsburgh Wood Street and Fourth Avenue Pittsburgh, Pennsylvania 17604	767,863,209
Old Kent Bank & Trust Company One Vandenberg Center Grand Rapids, Michigan 49502	766,840,205
National Central Bank 23 East King Street Lancaster, Pennsylvania 17604	763,062,407
First National Bank 111 East Fourth Street Cincinnati, Ohio 45202	752,476,969
First Security Bank of Utah N.A. 79 South Main Street Salt Lake City, Utah 84110	747,701,474
Mercantile National Bank at Dallas 1704 Main Street Dallas, Texas 75201	745,910,306
Citizens Fidelity Bank & Trust Company Fifth and Jefferson Streets Louisville, Kentucky 40201	735,814,669
Pacific National Bank of Washington 1215 Fourth Avenue Seattle, Washington 98111	726,607,718
Merchants National Bank of Indiana 5243 Hohman Avenue Hammond, Indiana 46235	714,005,214
Banco Credito y Ahorro Ponceno One Union Square 70 Pine Street (Bond Dept.) New York, New York 10005	708,555,752
First National Bank of Louisville Fifth and Court Place Louisville, Kentucky 40201	707,943,880
United Virginia Bank Ninth and Main Streets Richmond, Virginia 23214	701,912,811
Republic National Bank of New York 452 Fifth Avenue New York, New York 10018	699,961,428
Fort Worth National Bank Fort Worth National Bank Building Post Office Box 2050 Fort Worth, Texas 76101	671,769,070

Union Trust Company of Maryland Baltimore and St. Paul Streets Baltimore, Maryland 21203	$665,936,170
Rhode Island Hospital Trust National Bank 15 Westminister Street Providence, Rhode Island 02903	657,978,625
New Jersey National Bank One West State Street Trenton, New Jersey 08603	656,986,626
Sumitomo Bank of California 365 California Street San Francisco, California 94104	647,919,530
Deposit Guaranty National Bank 200 East Captial Street Jackson, Mississippi 39205	645,706,460
Central National Bank in Chicago 120 South La Salle Street Chicago, Illinois 60603	643,276,000
Liberty National Bank & Trust Company 100 Broadway Oklahoma City, Oklahoma 73125	640,811,186
National Community Bank 24 Park Avenue Rutherford, New Jersey 07074	638,449,416
New Jersey Bank N.A. 1184 Main Avenue Clifton, New Jersey 07015	632,493,987
Central Trust Company Fourth and Vine Streets Cincinnati, Ohio 45202	632,065,134
Marine Midland Bank-Central 360 South Warren Street Syracuse, New York 13202	631,833,786
United Bank of Denver N.A. 1740 Broadway Denver, Colorado 80202	630,672,840
Huntington National Bank of Columbus 17 South High Street Columbus, Ohio 43215	630,338,452
State Bank of Albany 69 State Street Albany, New York 12201	630,035,342
Union Trust Company 300 Main Street Stamford, Connecticut 06904	624,107,307

Fifth Third Bank 38 Fountain Square Plaza Cincinnati, Ohio 45202	$ 608,476,001
First National Bank & Trust Company 120 North Robinson Oklahoma City, Oklahoma 73125	605,170,950
National State Bank 68 Broad Street Elizabeth, New Jersey 07207	604,780,007
First Security Bank of Idaho N.A. 905 Idaho Street Boise, Idaho 83702	602,568,162
Marine Midland Bank-Rochester One Marine Midland Plaza Rochester, New York 14639	600,030,005
First National Bank & Trust Company of Tulsa Box 1, 5th and Boston Streets Tulsa, Oklahoma 74193	594,316,900
First National Bank of Fort Worth One Burnett Plaza Fort Worth, Texas 76102	593,634,111
First National Bank 248 East Capitol Street Jackson, Mississippi 39205	591,646,156
Citizens Commercial & Savings Bank 328 South Saginaw Street Flint, Michigan 48502	587,504,604
Commerce Bank of Kansas City N.A. Tenth and Walnut Kansas City, Missouri 64141	583,414,000
Central Penn National Bank One Belmont Avenue Bala-Cynwyd, Pennsylvania 19004	581,999,554
First National Bank of Akron Main and Mill Streets Akron, Ohio 44308	577,687,803
Wilmington Trust Company 10th and Market Streets Akron, Ohio 44308	575,232,381
First National Exchange Bank of Virginia 201 South Jefferson Street Roanoke, Virginia 24011	573,665,788
LaSalle National Bank 135 South LaSalle Street Chicago, Illinois 60690	568,137,831

Peoples National Bank of Washington 1400 Fourth Avenue Seattle, Washington 98111	$564,763,728
Winters National Bank & Trust Company Winters Bank Tower Second and Main Dayton, Ohio 45401	553,769,356
Frost National Bank Main at Commerce San Antonio, Texas 78296	549,500,606
Banco de Ponce 2552 Broadway Manhattan, New York 10025	549,440,611
City National Bank & Trust Company 100 East Broad Street Columbus, Ohio 43216	545,512,165
Fulton National Bank 55 Marietta Street Atlanta, Georgia 30302	544,530,155
National Bank of Westchester 31 Mamaroneck Avenue White Plains, New York 10601	519,357,000
M & I Marshall & Ilsley Bank 770 North Water Street Milwaukee, Wisconsin 53201	518,651,470
Liberty National Bank & Trust Company Main, Court and Pearl Streets Buffalo, New York 14240	508,243,955
City National Bank 400 North Roxbury Drive Beverly Hills, California 90210	507,718,697
First National Bank 10th and Baltimore Post Office Box 38 Kansas City, Missouri 64141	499,009,401
Birmingham Trust National Bank 112 North 20th Street Birmingham, Alabama 35202	497,489,533
First National Bank of New Jersey 515 Union Boulevard Totowa, New Jersey 07512	493,763,879
Commonwealth National Bank 10-16 South Market Square Harrisburg, Pennsylvania 17108	489,233,831
Hibernia National Bank in New Orleans Carondelet, Gravier and Union Streets New Orleans, Louisiana 70112	487,116,000

Zions First National Bank South Main Street Salt Lake City, Utah 84111	$ 482,626,203
Bank of Virginia-Central Eighth and Main Streets Richmond, Virginia 23260	479,136,549
Toledo Trust Company 245 Summit Street Post Office Box 1628 Toledo, Ohio 43607	478,439,028
Omaha National Bank 1700 Farnam Street Omaha, Nebraska 68102	477,199,490
First Jersey National Bank One Exchange Plaza Jersey City, New Jersey 07303	477,118,936
Citizens & Southern National Bank of South Carolina Post Office Box 1039 Charleston, South Carolina 29402	469,261,708
European-American Bank & Trust Company 10 Hanover Square New York, New York 10005	467,470,037
Garden State National Bank 170 Main Street Hackensack, New Jersey 07601	466,632,000
Genesee Merchants Bank & Trust Company One East First Street Flint, Michigan 48502	466,478,972
South Jersey National Bank Cherry Hill, New Jersey 08034	466,244,899
National Bank of Tulsa 320 South Boston Street Tulsa, Oklahoma 74102	465,494,552
Empire National Bank 135 North Street Middletown, New York 10940	462,472,125
United Missouri Bank of Kansas City, N.A. 10th and Grand Avenue Kansas City, Missouri 64106	461,587,756
Exchange National Bank 130 South LaSalle Street Chicago, Illinois 60690	461,051,890
First National Bank of Tampa First Financial Tower Post Office Box 1810 Tampa, Florida 33601	458,153,766

Bank Leumi Trust Company of New York 579 Fifth Avenue New York, New York 10017	$457,442,776
Security Trust Company of Rochester One East Avenue Rochester, New York 14638	456,614,043
Long Island Trust Company 1401 Franklin Avenue Garden City, New York 11530	453,994,354
Bank of New Jersey Broadway at Market Street Camden, New Jersey 08101	452,502,650
Albuquerque National Bank Post Office Box 1344 Albuquerque, New Mexico 807103	449,671,811
United States Trust Company of New York 45 Wall Street New York, New York 10005	445,975,518
Colorado National Bank 17th & Champa Streets Denver, Colorado 80217	444,847,590
Brown Brothers, Harriman & Company 59 Wall Street New York, New York 10005	437,008,402
Old National Bank of Washington West 428 Riverside Avenue Spokane, Washington 99201	427,353,866
Worcester County National Bank 446 Main Street Worcester, Massachusetts 01608	424,443,112
Northeastern Bank of Pennsylvania Wyoming Avenue and Spruce Street Scranton, Pennsylvania 18501	421,704,824
Bankers Trust of South Carolina, N.A. Bankers Trust Tower Post Office Box 448 Columbia, South Carolina 29202	421,189,584
Hamilton National Bank 701 Market Street Chattanooga, Tennessee 37401	421,050,644
Connecticut National Bank 888 Main Street Bridgeport, Connecticut 06602	420,893,687
First Valley Bank 535 Main Street Bethlehem, Pennsylvania 18018	417,453,069

Houston National Bank Tenneco Building 1010 Milam Street Houston, Texas 77001	$ 416,949,623
State National Bank of Connecticut State National Tower 10 Middle Street Bridgeport, Connecticut 06604	408,148,784
First Virginia Bank 6400 Arlington Boulevard Falls Church, Virginia 22046	406,735,199
National Bank of Washington 14th and G Streets, N.W. Washington, D.C. 20005	405,986,966
Sterling National Bank & Trust Company 540 Madison Avenue New York, New York 10022	404,314,738
First National Bank of South Jersey 1100 Black Horse Pike Pleasantville, New Jersey 08232	403,266,580
American National Bank & Trust Company of New Jersey 225 South Street Morristown, New Jersey 07942	396,222,023
City National Bank of Connecticut 961 Main Street Bridgeport, Connecticut 06602	395,343,601
First National Bank Hamilton Mall at Seventh Street Allentown, Pennsylvania 18101	386,086,462
Southeast National Bank 401 Avenue of the States Chester, Pennsylvania 19013	385,136,641
Liberty National Bank & Trust Company 416 West Jefferson Street Louisville, Kentucky 40201	383,554,236
First National Bank of South Carolina Post Office Box 11 Columbia, South Carolina 29202	383,363,715
Central Jersey Bank & Trust Company Route 9 Freehold, New Jersey 07728	379,599,216
United Penn Bank 8-18 West Market Street Wilkes-Barre, Pennsylvania 18701	376,953,810
Walker Bank & Trust Company 175 South Main Street Salt Lake City, Utah 84110	375,233,474

First National Bank of Pennsylvania 940 Park Avenue Meadville, Pennsylvania 16335	$374,683,911
Continental-Bank of Texas 800 Rusk Street Houston, Texas 77052	374,204,608
Lincoln National Bank & Trust Company of Fort Wayne 116 East Berry Street Fort Wayne, Indiana 46802	372,892,084
National Bank of Commerce One Commerce Square Memphis, Tennessee 38150	370,930,471
Oneida National Bank & Trust Company of Central New York 268 Genesee Street Utica, New York 13503	370,093,497
City National Bank 25 West Flagler Street Miami, Florida 33101	368,660,668
Bank of Delaware 300 Delaware Avenue Wilmington, Delaware 19899	367,137,311
Iowa-Des Moines National Bank 6th and Walnut Des Moines, Iowa 50304	366,266,810
Central Bank of Alabama N.A. 247-251 Johnston, S.E. Decatur, Alabama 35601	363,867,961
First Trust & Deposit Company 201 South Warren Street Syracuse, New York 13202	361,891,739
Provident Bank One East Fourth Street Cincinnati, Ohio 45202	361,360,828
Central Trust Company 44 Exchange Street Rochester, New York 14603	357,753,513
National Bank of Commerce of San Antonio Post Office Drawer 121 San Antonio, Texas 78291	356,117,427
Security Bank & Trust Company 16333 Trenton Road Southgate, Michigan 48192	355,419,972
Farmers Bank of the State of Delaware Wilmington, Delaware 19889	354,611,186

Sun First National Bank of Orlando 200 South Orange Avenue Orlando, Florida 32802	$353,110,054
Marine National Exchange Bank One Marine Plaza Milwaukee, Wisconsin 53201	352,092,806
Central Bank & Trust Company 15th & Araphoe Streets Post Office Box 5548, Terminal Annex Denver, Colorado 80217	351,259,618
American National Bank & Trust Company 736 Market Street Chattanooga, Tennessee 37401	350,621,880
First National Bank in Albuquerque Albuquerque, New Mexico 87103	350,322,366
Union Bank & Trust Company N.A. Union Bank Building Grand Rapids, Michigan 49502	348,958,788
Southern Arizona Bank & Trust Company 150 North Stone Avenue Tucson, Arizona 85702	346,947,524
Fourth National Bank & Trust Company 200 East Douglas Wichita, Kansas 67202	346,440,217
Fidelity National Bank 901 Main Street Lynchburg, Virginia 24505	345,945,435
Atlantic National Bank of Jacksonville 121 Hogan Street Jacksonville, Florida 32202	341,649,266
Central Bank N.A. 301, 20th Street Oakland, California 94612	340,261,535
Exchange National Bank of Tampa Tampa, Florida 33601	338,865,964
National Boulevard Bank of Chicago 400-410 North Michigan Avenue Chicago, Illinois 60611	338,731,723
Branch Banking & Trust Company 223 West Nash Street Wilson, North Carolina 27893	338,696,830
United Counties Trust Company 142 Broad Street Elizabeth, New Jersey 07207	335,507,511
Dauphin Deposit Trust Company 213 Market Street Harrisburg, Pennsylvania 17105	334,991,281

El Paso National Bank El Paso, Texas 79999	$334,666,183
Colonial Bank & Trust Company 81 West Main Street Post Office Box 2149 Waterbury, Connecticut 06720	331,853,809
Boatmen's National Bank in St. Louis Post Office Box 236 St. Louis, Missouri 63166	330,971,349
Gary National Bank 504 Broadway Gary, Indiana 46402	326,659,850
Citizen's Bank & Trust Company of Maryland Riverdale, Maryland 20840	323,844,151
Lake View Trust & Savings Bank 3201 North Ashland Avenue Chicago, Illinois 60657	322,553,832
First National Bank & Trust Company of Michigan 108 East Michigan Avenue Kalamazoo, Michigan 49001	320,580,899
Norfolk County Trust Company 1319 Beacon Street Brookline, Massachusetts 02146	311,435,574
Hibernia Bank Market, McAllister and Jones Streets San Francisco, California 94102	311,306,509
Peoples National Bank of New Jersey Post Office Box 300 Westmont, New Jersey 08108	310,364,468
Merchants National Bank of Allentown 702 Hamilton Street Allentown, Pennsylvania 18101	309,931,002
Lincoln First Bank—Central N.A. One Lincoln Center Syracuse, New York 13201	309,680,019
Pioneer Trust & Savings Bank 4000 West North Avenue Chicago, Illinois 60639	309,630,051
Delaware Trust Company 900 Market Street Wilmington, Delaware 19899	308,688,277
Marine Midland Bank-Southern 150 Lake Street Elmira, New York 14902	305,449,962
American Bank & Trust Company 2531 Plank Road Baton Rouge, Louisiana 70821	304,986,537

State National Bank One State National Plaza El Paso, Texas 79901	$302,886,223
Texas Bank & Trust Company One Main Place Dallas, Texas 75250	302,850,000
Valley Bank of Nevada 113 South Fourth Street Las Vegas, Nevada 89114	299,245,584
Worthen Bank & Trust Company N.A. 200 West Capitol, P.O. Box 1681 Little Rock, Arkansas 72203	298,584,724
Colonial First National Bank 303 Broad Street Red Bank, New Jersey 07701	297,042,729
Merchants National Bank of Mobile 106 St. Francis Street Post Office Box 2527 Mobile, Alabama 36622	296,844,420
Wayne Oakland Bank 400 South Main Street Royal Oak, Michigan 48067	296,629,186
First National Bank of Eastern Pennsylvania 11 West Market Street Wilkes-Barre, Pennsylvania 18701	296,293,971
First National Bank of Omaha 16th and Dodge Street Omaha, Nebraska 68102	296,130,383
National Bank of Commerce National Bank of Commerce Building/ LTV Tower Dallas, Texas 75221	295,648,842
Bank of New Orleans & Trust Company BNO Building, 1010 Common Street New Orleans, Louisiana 70112	295,588,257
Southern National Bank of North Carolina 500 North Chestnut Street Lumberton, North Carolina 28358	295,480,742
Bank of Louisville-Royal Bank & Trust Company Broadway at Fifth Louisville, Kentucky 40202	293,833,964
Marine Midland Bank of Southeastern New York, N.A. 347 Main Street Poughkeepsie, New York 12602	293,714,793
Mercantile-Safe Deposit & Trust Company Two Hopkins Plaza Baltimore, Maryland 21203	293,331,605

Community National Bank of Pontiac 30 North Saginaw Street Pontiac, Michigan 48056	$ 293,021,912
Franklin State Bank Somerset, New Jersey 08873	292,219,284
Austin National Bank 501-11 Congress Avenue Austin, Texas 78781	290,442,600
Bank of North Carolina, N.A. New River Shopping Center Jacksonville, North Carolina 28540	290,424,820
Louisiana National Bank 451 Florida Boulevard Baton Rouge, Louisiana 70801	290,079,857
First National Bank Market at Milam Shreveport, Louisiana 71154	289,897,374
First National Bank of Mobile 31 North Toyal Street Mobile, Alabama 36621	288,821,033
Bank of Idaho, N.A. 700 West Idaho Street Boise, Idaho 83705	288,804,991
Capital National Bank in Austin 7th & Colorado Austin, Texas 78701	288,269,289
Third National Bank & Trust Company 34 North Main Street Dayton, Ohio 45202	287,273,432
National Bank of South Dakota Main Avenue at 9th Street Sioux Falls, South Dakota 57101	286,636,358
Commercial National Bank in Shreveport Market Street at Milam Street Shreveport, Louisiana 71152	286,611,803
First National Bank & Trust Company 13th and M Lincoln, Nebraska 68501	286,120,131

Insurance Companies

EXPLANATION OF THE INSURANCE COMPANY

In September, 1974, *Forbes* magazine called insurance companies "those marvelous money machines." *Forbes* estimated $91 billion was logged as premiums during 1973. In addition, the industry earned $22 billion in investments and other income. Some $79 billion went toward expenses, benefits and other costs, and the remaining $34 billion was channeled back into the industry's capital base.

The insurance industry now boasts more than $336 billion in assets. About 40 percent of this sum is invested in real estate either as mortgage loans or outright ownership.

The life insurance companies have established rather liberal lending patterns with large amounts invested in all types of real estate, from homes to apartments to industrial properties. The larger companies prefer minimum single investments of from one to three million dollars.

Liquidity is of less importance to life insurance companies than to other types of lenders. It is fairly easy for these concerns to plan and determine claims as well as operating expenses.

The average borrower will pay the mortgage off in 12 to 13 years even though terms for most mortgages range from 15 to 30 years, depending on the type of real estate and the borrower's credit.

Many insurance companies have begun also to buy and hold real estate for their own portfolios.

GENERAL LENDING GOALS AND POLICIES

Here are some of the general lending policies of insurance companies:

(1) State laws and those of the Security and Exchange Commission govern all life insurance companies, with states setting such regulations as to type of investments companies may make, percentage of assets that can be put into types of investments, and maximum loan-to-value ratios for mortgages made. Lending powers, however, are much greater among these companies than among previously discussed sources.

(2) Life insurance companies are either mutuals, completely owned by policyholders, or stock companies, privately owned by stockholders who receive dividends. Both kinds of companies make similar types of loans.

(3) Loan-to-value ratios are from about 66-2/3 to 90 percent for conventional mortgages and for FHA-and VA-insured loans are exempted.

(4) Insurance companies are not generally required to amortize real estate loans or limit them to maximum maturity.

(5) Mortgage loans may be made by life insurance companies anywhere in the United States, and some state laws extend the boundary into Canada. Large companies particularly are quite expansive in national mortgage loans; smaller firms usually concentrate on local needs in the area of conventional mortgages.

(6) Insurance companies are the nation's major lenders of funds for apartment houses, office buildings, and other commercial real estate. They are excellent sources of government-insured loans and are not subject to many of the restrictions placed on other mortgage makers.

APPLYING FOR A LOAN

Application for mortgages from an insurance company should be made through its local office or the home office if that is close. The company's real estate loan department will need all details of the property to be mortgaged. When first querying the company, these points should be covered — lending policies on the type of property to be financed, loan-to-value ratio, percentage of interest usually charged, length of term of mortgages offered, the advisability of making application, and front-end interest points charged.

The application may be processed at the branch office, where the mortgage is negotiated and finalized. In other cases, the company may work with mortgage bankers in the borrower's own town who act as representatives of the insurance firm. In a few cases, brokers will handle transactions exclusively for the insurance company, carrying out all the details of servicing the mortgage. It is advisable for those seeking mortgages to contact mortgage bankers since they are highly capable of presenting mortgage proposals to lenders in the most advantageous manner.

MAKE-UP OF THE INVESTMENT DEPARTMENTS

Insurance company investments are usually divided among:
(1) Publicly traded stocks and bonds (securities).
(2) Private placements with corporations.
(3) Real estate including mortgages and ownership.

The amount of funds available to any one department depends on where the higher returns are being earned at the time. During recent years, the private placement and real estate departments have often been in competition within their own firms.

There is somewhat of a trend toward private placements because:
(1) Many national, industrial and retail chains find it easier to get 100 percent financing for expansion. Also, they do not have the cumbersome procedural problems such as obtaining appraisals that traditional real estate financing requires.

(2) Industrial and manufacturing firms are finding plant development and expansion easier to do for some of the same reasons — as stated in the preceding sentences.

(3) Rates of return have tended to be higher in private placements.

HOW TO ESTABLISH RELATIONS WITH THE HOME AND LOCAL OFFICES

Mortgage loan officers of insurance companies are quite aware of the importance of good relations with the public and are helpful in answering inquiries from those hoping to conduct business with them.

A letter or a phone call to the home office will put one in touch with the local representative of any insurance company, whether he is a correspondent with a mortgage banking house or an employee of the insurance company.

HOW TO MAKE APPLICATION FOR A MORTGAGE

Most insurance applications for mortgages are similar. They are available through the company's main or branch offices or through mortgage brokers. In addition to the application, one must usually submit the following:

(1) A check (usually one percent) as an application fee which is usually credited to the loan at closing.

(2) Financial statements of the borrower, whether a corporation or an individual.

(3) Plans and specifications of the building.

(4) If a corporation, the latest 10K form.

(5) If a corporation, the latest annual report and earnings statement.

(6) Information on the background of the developer.

(7) A project feasibility study which is very important for a new project.

(8) An appraisal of the property.

(9) A city map on which the property is indicated.

(10) An aerial photograph showing the project.

(11) An on-site photograph.

(12) Background information on the community.

HOW A CORPORATION CAN MAKE APPLICATION FOR A PRIVATE PLACEMENT

It is usually best to have an investment banker or private placement specialist experienced in such matters make application on behalf of a corporation.

The investment banker will visit the firm and spend a good deal of time evaluating the company. He will prepare a private placement memorandum and corporate information brochure to present to lenders. Usually more than one lender will participate in the offering. If real estate is involved, the financing will usually be structured as a secured private placement. The security is the real estate and the parent company fully guarantees the loan. This is a good method of financing if existing buildings on leased land are involved.

The author's firm, Property Resources Company, South Miami. Florida, specializes in this type financing as do a number of the prominent New York investment banking houses.

If the corporation wishes to apply for a loan on its own, the financial officer responsible should write or call the insurance company directly to query it on lending policies and availability of funds. The insurance firm that the borrower talks with may recommend its regional or local office or its mortgage correspondents.

NEGOTIATING THE LOAN

Before the loan application is submitted to the insurance company's loan committee, representatives may negotiate with the borrower, setting forth parameters that the committee will probably accept.

After the committee approves the loan and issues the letter of commitment, there will be further negotiations before the loan is finalized. A major area for discussion concerns prepayment of the loan. The lender's position generally is against prepayment. The company puts considerable money into each loan transaction and cannot afford the time or dollars to make reinvestments at short intervals.

The lender usually will want to freeze the loan for five to 10 years. Thereafter there is usually a prepayment penalty which decreases annually until there is no prepayment penalty.

As an example, consider a million-dollar loan at 10 percent interest for 20 years. The lender sets a prepayment penalty which will not allow the loan to be paid off for seven years. Beginning in the eighth year, the borrower is allowed to pay the loan in full at 10 percent of the remaining principal balance.

The penalty will decrease by one percent a year until it reaches 100 percent and there would be no prepayment penalty thereafter. Assume at the end of the 11th year, there is a $700,000 principal balance. If the loan were prepaid at that time, it would take $728,000 to pay off the loan or a $28,000 penalty, which is figured at 104 percent of the principal balance.

MAJOR LIFE INSURANCE COMPANIES

Aetna Life Insurance Company
151 Farmington Avenue
Hartford, Connecticut 06115

Alabama National Life
  Insurance Company
P. O. Box 15197, Broadview Station
Baton Rouge, Louisiana 70815

American Bankers Life Assurance
  Company of Florida
600 Brickell Avenue
Miami, Florida 33131

The Baltimore Life Insurance Co.
Baltimore Life Building
Mt. Royal Plaza
Baltimore, Maryland 21201

Atlas Life Insurance Co.
415 South Boston Avenue
Tulsa, Oklahoma 74103

American Amicable Life
  Insurance Co.
Alico Center
Waco, Texas 76703

American Benefit Life
  Insurance Co.
1500 American Bank Building
New Orleans, Louisiana 70130

American Family Life
  Insurance Co.
3099 East Washington Avenue
Madison, Wisconsin 53701

American Founders Life
  Insurance Co.
6937 North Interregional
P. O. Box 2068
Austin, Texas 78767

American General Life
  Insurance Co.
2727 Allen Parkway
Houston, Texas 77019

American Guaranty Life
  Insurance Co.
1433 S. W. Sixth Avenue
Portland, Oregon 97201

American Health and Life
  Insurance Co.
300 Saint Paul Place
Baltimore, Maryland 21202

American Heritage Life
  Insurance Co.
11 East Forsyth Street
Jacksonville, Florida 32202

American Hospital & Life
  Insurance Company
Pecan and St. Mary's Streets
San Antonio, Texas 78206

American Income Life Insurance Co.
609-611 North 25th Street
Waco, Texas 76703

American Life & Accident
  Insurance Company of Kentucky
431 West Main Street
Louisville, Kentucky 40202

American Life Insurance Co.
827 Washington Street
Wilmington, Delaware 19899

American Mutual Life
  Insurance Co.
Liberty Building
Des Moines, Iowa 50307

American National Insurance Co.
Moody Avenue and Market Street
Galveston, Texas 77550

American Republic Insurance Co.
6th and Keosauqua
Des Moines, Iowa 50301

American States Life
  Insurance Co.
542 North Meridian Street
Indianapolis, Indiana 46206

American United Life
  Insurance Co.
30 West Fall Creek Parkway
Indianapolis, Indiana 46206

Atlanta Life Insurance Co.
148 Auburn Avenue, N. E.
Atlanta, Georgia 30303

Acacia Mutual Life
  Insurance Company
51 Louisiana Avenue, N. W.
Washington, D. C. 20001

Aid Association for Lutherans
222 West College Avenue
Appleton, Wisconsin 54911

Alexander Hamilton Life Insurance
  Company of America
Village of Quakertown
Farmington, Michigan 48024

All American Life
  & Casualty Company
O'Hare Plaza
8501 West Higgins Road
Chicago, Illinois 60631

Alliance-Mutual Life
  Insurance Company
680 Sherbrooke Street, West
Montreal, Quebec, Canada

Allstate Life Insurance Company
Allstate Plaza
Northbrook, Illinois 60062

The Amalgamated Life
  Insurance Company, Inc.
15 Union Square, West
New York, New York 10003

Bankers Life and Casualty Company
4444 Lawrence Avenue
Chicago, Illinois 60630

Bankers Life Company
711 High Street
Des Moines, Iowa 50307

Bankers Life Insurance Company
  of Nebraska
Cotner and O Streets
Lincoln, Nebraska 68501

Bankers Mutual Life Insurance Co.
500 West South Street
Freeport, Illinois 61032

Bankers National Life Insurance Co.
1599 Littleton Road
Parsippany, New Jersey 07054

Bankers Security Life
  Insurance Society
1701 Pennsylvania Avenue, N. W.
Washington, D. C. 20006

Bankers Union Life Insurance Co.
200 Josephine Street
Denver, Colorado 80206

Ben Hur Life Association
Main and Water Streets
Crawfordsville, Indiana 47933

Beneficial Life Insurance Co.
47 West South Temple Street
Salt Lake City, Utah 84101

Beneficial Standard Life
  Insurance Co.
3700 Wilshire Boulevard
Los Angeles, California 90005

Benefit Trust Life Insurance Co.
1771 Howard Street
Chicago, Illinois 60626

Berkshire Life Insurance Company
700 South Street
Pittsfield, Massachusetts 01201

Boston Mutual Life Insurance CO.
156 Stuart Street
Boston, Massachusetts 02116

Brotherhood of Railroad Trainmen
  Insurance Department, Inc.
666 Euclid Avenue
Cleveland, Ohio 44114

Business Men's Assurance Company
  of America
One Penn Valley Park
Kansas City, Missouri 64141

Cal-Farm Life Insurance Co.
2855 Telegraph Avenue
Berkeley, California 94705

California-Western States Life
  Insurance Company
2020 L Street
Sacramento, California 95814

The Canada Life Assurance Co.
330 University Avenue
Toronto 1, Ontario, Canada

Capital Reserve Life Insurance Co.
428 East Capitol Avenue
Jefferson City, Missouri 65101

The Capitol Life Insurance Co.
1600 Sherman Street
Denver, Colorado 80203

Central Life Assurance Co.
611 Fifth Avenue
Des Moines, Iowa 50309

Century Life Insurance Co.
Century Life Building
Fort Worth, Texas 76102

Charter National Life Insurance Co.
8301 Maryland Avenue
St. Louis, Missouri 63105

Chicago Metropolitan Mutual
Assurance Company
4455 Dr. Martin Luther King Drive
Chicago, Illinois 60653

Citizens Life Insurance Co.
of New York
1180 Avenue of the Americas
New York, New York 10036

Coastal States Life Insurance Co.
1459 Peachtree N. E.
Atlanta, Georgia 30309

The College Life Insurance Company
of America
College Square at Central Court So.
Indianapolis, Indiana 46206

Colonial Life & Accident
Insurance Company
1612 Marion Street
Columbia, South Carolina 29201

The Colonial Life Insurance
Company of America
11 Prospect Street
East Orange, New Jersey 07019

Colonial Penn Life Insurance Co.
Colonial Penn Building
Philadelphia, Pennsylvania 19102

Columbian Mutual Life
Insurance Co.
Vestal Parkway East
Binghamton, New York 13902

The Columbus Mutual Life
Insurance Co.
303 East Broad Street
Columbus, Ohio 43215

Combined American Insurance Co.
2909 Oak Lawn Avenue
Dallas, Texas 75219

Commonwealth Life & Accident
Insurance Company
3500 Lindell Boulevard
St. Louis, Missouri 63103

Commonwealth Life Insurance Co.
Commonwealth Building
Broadway at Fourth Street
Louisville, Kentucky 40201

Community National Life
Insurance Co.
Community Center
Third & Boston Streets
Tulsa, Oklahoma 74101

Companion Life Insurance Co.
230 Park Avenue
New York, New York 10017

Confederation Life Association
321 Bloor Street, East
Toronto 285, Canada

Connecticut General Life
Insurance Co.
Hartford, Connecticut 06115

Connecticut Mutual Life
Insurance Co.
140 Garden Street
Hartford, Connecticut 06115

Constitution Life Insurance Co.
4423 West Lawrence Avenue
Chicago, Illinois 60630

Continental American Life
Insurance Co.
11th and King Streets
Wilmington, Delaware 19899

Continental Assurance Co.
310 South Michigan Avenue
Chicago, Illinois 60604

Co-Operative Life Insurance Co.
1920 College Avenue
Regina, Saskatchewan, Canada

Country Life Insurance Company
1701 Towanda Avenue
Bloomington, Illinois 61701

Crown Life Insurance Company
120 Bloor Street, East
Toronto 285, Canada

Cuna Mutual Insurance Society
5910 Mineral Point Road
Madison, Wisconsin 53705

Diamond State Life Insurance Co.
P. O. Box 2210, Main Post Office
Miami, Florida 33101

The Dominion Life Assurance Co.
111 Westmount Road
Waterloo, Ontario, Canada

Durham Life Insurance Co.
Durham Life Building
Raleigh, North Carolina 27602

Eastern Life Insurance Company
of New York
355 Lexington Avenue
New York, New York 10017

Educators Mutual Life Insurance Co.
2490 Lincoln Highway East
Lancaster, Pennsylvania 17604

The Employer's Life Insurance Co.
of America
110 Milk Street
Boston, Massachusetts 02107

The Equitable Life Assurance Society
of the United States
1285 Avenue of the Americas
New York, New York 10019

Equitable Life Insurance Co.
3900 Wisconsin Avenue
Washington, D. C. 20016

Equitable Life Insurance Co.
of Canada
Waterloo, Ontario
Canada

Equitable Reserve Association
116 South Commerical Street
Neenah, Wisconsin 54947

The Excelsior Life Insurance Co.
20 Toronto Street
Toronto 1, Ontario, Canada

Executive Life Insurance Co.
Executive Life Building
9777 Wilshire Boulevard
Beverly Hills, California 90212

Farm Bureau Life Insurance Co.
Farm Bureau Building
Tenth and Grand Avenue
Des Moines, Iowa 50307

Farm Bureau Life Insurance Co.
of Michigan
4000 North Grand River Avenue
Lansing, Michigan 48904

Farm Family Life Insurance Co.
Route 9W
Glenmont, New York 12077

The Farmers and Bankers Life
Insurance Co.
200 East First Street
Wichita, Kansas 67202

Farmers New World Life
Insurance Co.
9611 Sunset Highway, S. E.
Mercer Island, Washington 98040

Farmers and Traders Life
Insurance Co.
960 James Street
Syracuse, New York 13201

Federal Life and Casualty Company
78 West Michigan Avenue
Battle Creek, Michigan 49016

Federal Life Insurance Company
6100 North Cicero Avenue
Chicago, Illinois 60646

Fidelity Bankers Life Insurance Co.
Ninth and Main Streets
Richmond, Virginia 23218

Fidelity and Guaranty Life
Insurance Co.
Calvert and Redwood Streets
Baltimore, Maryland 21203

Fidelity Life Association
110 Tenth Avenue
Fulton, Illinois 61252

The Fidelity Mutual Life
Insurance Co.
The Parkway at Fairmount Avenue
Philadelphia, Pennsylvania 19101

Fidelity Union Life Insurance Co.
1511 Bryan Street
Dallas, Texas 75201

Fireman's Fund American Life
Insurance Company
3333 California Street
San Francisco, California 94120

First National Life Insurance Co.
P. O. Box 969
Austin, Texas 78767

The First Pyramid Life Insurance
Company of America
Pyramid Life Building
Little Rock, Arkansas 72203

Franklin Life Insurance Co.
Franklin Square
Springfield, Illinois 62705

General American Life
Insurance Co.
N. W. corner 15th and Locust Streets
St. Louis, Missouri 63166

General United Life Insurance Co.
2015 Grand Avenue
Des Moines, Iowa 50312

Georgia International Life
Insurance Co.
615 Peachtree Street, N. E.
Atlanta, Georgia 30308

Giant Oak Life Insurance Co.
211 N. Ervay Building
Suite 1310
Dallas, Texas 75201

Girard Life Insurance Company
of America
Exchange Park
Dallas, Texas 75235

Gleaner Life Insurance Society
1600 North Woodward Avenue
Birmingham, Michigan 48012

Global Life Insurance Co.
480 University Avenue
Toronto, CANADA

Globe Life and Accident
Insurance Company
311 West Sheridan Avenue
Oklahoma City, Oklahoma 73102

Globe Life Insurance Co.
223 West Jackson Boulevard
Chicago, Illinois 60606

Golden State Mutual Life
Insurance Co.
1999 West Adams Boulevard
Los Angeles, California 90018

Government Personnel Mutual Life
Insurance Company
505 East Travis Street
San Antonio, Texas 78205

Great American Reserve
Insurance Co.
2020 Live Oak Street
Dallas, Texas 75201

Great Commonwealth Life
Insurance Co.
1309 Main, 1600 Davis Building
Dallas, Texas 75202

The Empire Life Insurance Co.
243 King Street
East Kingston, Ontario, CANADA

Empire Life Insurance Co.
of America
1712 Commerce Street
Dallas, Texas 75201

Empire State Mutual Life
Insurance Co.
315 North Main Street
Jamestown, New York 14701

Great Southern Life Insurance Co.
3121 Buffalo Speedway
Houston, Texas 77006

Great National Life Insurance Co.
Harry Hines at Mockingbird
Dallas, Texas 75235

The Great-West Life Assurance Co.
60 Osborne Street North
Winnipeg 1, Manitoba, CANADA

Guarantee Mutual Life Company
8721 Indian Hills Drive
Omaha, Nebraska 68114

Guarantee Reserve Life
Insurance Co.
128 State Street
Hammond, Indiana 46320

Guaranty Income Life Insurance Co.
929 Government Street
Baton Rouge, Louisiana 70821

Gulf Life Insurance Company
1301 Gulf Life Drive
Jacksonville, Florida 32207

Hartford Life Insurance Company
Hartford Plaza
Hartford, Connecticut 06115

Home Beneficial Life Insurance Co.
3901 West Broad Street
Richmond, Virginia 23230

Home Life Insurance Company
253 Broadway
New York, New York 10007

The Home Life Insurance Co.
of America
506 Walnut Street
Philadelphia, Pennsylvania 19105

Home Security Life
Insurance Company
505 West Chapel Hill Street
Durham, North Carolina 27702

Horace Mann Life Insurance Co.
216 East Monroe Street
Springfield, Illinois 62701

ITT Hamilton Life Insurance Co.
212 South Central Avenue
Clayton, Missouri 63105

The Imperial Life Assurance Co.
of Canada
95 St. Clair Avenue, West
Toronto 7, Ontario, CANADA

The Independent Life and Accident
Insurance Co.
233 West Duval Street
Jacksonville, Florida 32202

The Independent Order of Foresters
789 Don Mills Road
Don Mills, Ontario, CANADA

Indianapolis Life Insurance Co.
2960 North Meridian Street
Indianapolis, Indiana 46208

Industrial Life Insurance Co.
1080 St. Louis Road
Sillery, Quebec, CANADA

Inter-Ocean Insurance Company
2600 Victory Parkway
Cincinnati, Ohio 45206

Interstate Life & Accident
Insurance Co.
Interstate Life Building
Chattanooga, Tennessee 37402

Investors Syndicate Life
Insurance Co.
Investors Building
Eighth and Marquette
Minneapolis, Minnesota 55402

Jefferson National Life Insurance Co.
241 North Pennsylvania Street
Indianapolis, Indiana 46204

Jefferson Standard Life
Insurance Co.
Jefferson Square
Greensboro, North Carolina 27420

Kansas Farm Life Insurance Co., Inc.
2321 Anderson Avenue
Manhattan, Kansas 66502

Kennesaw Life and Accident
Insurance Co.
1447 Peachtree Street, N. E.
Atlanta, Georgia 30309

Knights of Columbus
71 Meadow Street
New Haven, Connecticut 06507

Lafayette Life Insurance Co.
2203 South 18th Street
Lafayette, Indiana 47902

The Lamar Life Insurance Co.
317 East Capitol Street
Jackson, Mississippi 39201

Liberty National Life Insurance Co.
301 South 20th Street
Birmingham, Alabama 35202

Life and Casualty Insurance Co.
of Tennessee
Life and Casualty Tower
Nashville, Tennessee 37219

Life Insurance Co. of Georgia
600 West Peachtree Street, N. W.
Atlanta, Georgia 30308

Life Insurance Company
of North America
1600 Arch Street
Philadelphia, Pennsylvania 19101

Lincoln American Life Insurance Co.
60 North Main Street
Memphis, Tennessee 38103

Lincoln Income Life Insurance Co.
6100 Dutchmans Lane
Louisville, Kentucky 40205

Lincoln Liberty Life Insurance Co.
11th and "O" Streets
Lincoln, Nebraska 68501

The Lincoln National Life
  Insurance Co.
1301-27 South Harrison Street
Fort Wayne, Indiana 46801

London Life Insurance Co.
London Life Building
London, Ontario, CANADA

Loyal Protective Life Insurance Co.
11 Deerfield Street
Boston, Massachusetts 02215

Lutheran Brotherhood
701 Second Avenue, South
Minneapolis, Minnesota 55402

Lutheran Mutual Life Insurance Co.
201-211 First Street, S. E.
Waverly, Iowa 50677

Mammoth Life and Accident
  Insurance Co.
606-608 West Walnut Street
Louisville, Kentucky 40203

The Manhattan Life
  Insurance Company
111 West 57th Street
New York, New York 10019

Massachusetts Mutual Life
  Insurance Co.
1295 State Street
Springfield, Massachusetts 01101

The Mercantile & General
  Reinsurance Company, Ltd.
34 King Street East
Toronto 1, Canada

Mid-Continent Life Insurance Co.
1400 Classen Drive
Oklahoma City, Oklahoma 73101

Midland National Life Insurance Co.
104 South Maple Street
Watertown, South Dakota 57201

The Midwest Life Insurance
  Company of Lincoln, Nebraska
500 South 16th Street
Lincoln, Nebraska 68509

Midwestern United Life
  Insurance Co.
7551 U. S. Highway 24 West
Fort Wayne, Indiana 46804

The Monarch Life Assurance Co.
333 Broadway Avenue
Winnipeg, Manitoba, CANADA

Monumental Life Insurance Company
Charles and Chase Streets
Baltimore, Maryland 21202

The Mutual Life Insurance Company
  of New York
1740 Broadway at 55th Street
New York, New York 10019

Mutual Service Life Insurance Co.
1919 University Avenue
St. Paul, Minnesota 55104

Mutual Trust Life Insurance Company
77 South Wacker Drive
Chicago, Illinois 60606

National Farmers Union Life
  Insurance Company
1575 Sherman Street
Denver, Colorado 80203

The National Investors Life
  Insurance Company
Second and Broadway
Little Rock, Arkansas 72203

National Liberty Life Insurance Co.
150 Allendale Road
Valley Forge, Pennsylvania 19481

The National Life & Accident
  Insurance Company
301 Seventh Avenue, North
Nashville, Tennessee 37219

The National Life Assurance
  Company of Canada
522 University Avenue
Toronto 2, Ontario, CANADA

National Mutual Benefit
119-121 Monona Avenue
Madison, Wisconsin 53701

National Travelers Life Company
820 Keosauqua Way
Des Moines, Iowa 50308

National Trust Life Insurance Co.
2701 Union Avenue Extended
Memphis, Tennessee 38112

National Western Life Insurance Co.
1302 Guadalupe Street
Austin, Texas 78767

Nationwide Life Insurance Co.
246 North High Street
Columbus, Ohio 43216

Navy Mutual Aid Association
Navy Department
Washington, D. C. 20370

North American Company for Life
 & Health Insurance
209 South La Salle Street
Chicago, Illinois 60604

North American Reassurance Co.
245 Park Avenue
New York, New York 10017

The North Atlantic Life Insurance
 Company of America
Robbins Lane,
Jericho, L. I., New York 11753

North Carolina Mutual Life
 Insurance Co.
411 West Chapel Hill Street
Durham, North Carolina 27702

Northern Life Assurance Company
 of Canada
291 Dundas Street
London, Ontario, CANADA

Northern Life Insurance Company
Third Avenue at University Street
Seattle, Washington

The Old Line Life Insurance
 Company of America
707 North Eleventh Street
Milwaukee, Wisconsin 53233

Old Republic Life Insurance Co.
307 Michigan Avenue North
Chicago, Illinois 60601

Pacific Standard Life Insurance Co.
1766 El Camino Real
Burlingame, California 94010

Patriot Life Insurance Company
575 Madison Avenue
New York, New York 10022

The Paul Revere Life Insurance Co.
18 Chestnut Street
Worcester, Massachusetts 01608

Peninsular Life Insurance Co.
645 Riverside Avenue
Jacksonville, Florida 32204

Pennsylvania Life Insurance Co.
3130 Wilshire Boulevard
Santa Monica, California 90406

Peoples-Home Life Insurance
 Company of Indiana
3637 North Meridian Street
Indianapolis, Indiana 46208

The Philippine American Life
 Insurance Company
870 Market Street
San Francisco, California 94102

Piedmont Life Insurance Co.
1197 Peachtree Street, N. E.
Atlanta, Georgia 30309

Pierce National Life Insurance Co.
3807 Wilshire Boulevard
Los Angeles, California 90005

The Pilgrim Health and Life
 Insurance Co.
1143 Gwinnett Street
Augusta, Georgia 30903

Pilot Life Insurance Co.
Greensboro, North Carolina 27420

Pioneer American Insurance Co.
6401 Camp Bowie Boulevard
Fort Worth, Texas 76116

John Hancock Mutual Life
 Insurance Company
200 Berkeley Street
Boston, Massachusetts 02117

Kansas City Life Insurance Co.
3520 Broadway
Kansas City, Missouri 64111

Kentucky Central Life Insurance Co.
200 East Main Street
Lexington, Kentucky 40507

Kentucky Home Mutual Life
Fifth and Jefferson Streets
Louisville, Kentucky 40202

League Life Insurance Co.
P. O. Box 5010
Detroit, Michigan 48235

Liberty Life Insurance Co.
Wade Hampton Boulevard
Greenville, South Carolina 29602

Life Assurance Co. of Pennsylvania
230 South 15th Street
Philadelphia, Pennsylvania 19102

Life Insurance Company of Alabama
302 Broad Street
Gadsden, Alabama 35901

Life Insurance Company of Kentucky
231 West Main Street
Louisville, Kentucky 40202

The Life Insurance Company
of Virginia
Capitol & 10th Streets
Richmond, Virginia 23209

Life Insurance Company of America
375 Collins Road, N. E.
Cedar Rapids, Iowa 52406

Maccabees Mutual Life
Insurance Co.
25800 Northwestern Highway
Southfield, Michigan 48075

The Manufacturers Life
Insurance Co.
200 Bloor Street, East
Toronto 5, Ontario, CANADA

The Marine Life Insurance Co.
5435 Spring Garden Road
Halifax, Nova Scotia, CANADA

Massachusetts Indemnity & Life
Insurance Company
100 William Street
Wellesley, Massachusetts 02181

Massachusetts Savings Bank
Life Insurance
120 Tremont Street
Boston, Massachusetts 02108

Metropolitan Life Insurance Co.
One Madison Avenue
New York, New York 10010

Michigan Life Insurance Co.
3101 North Woodward Avenue
Royal Oak, Michigan 48068

The Midland Mutual Life
Insurance Co.
250 East Broad Street
Columbus, Ohio 43216

The Ministers Life
& Casualty Union
3100 West Lake Street
Minneapolis, Minnesota 55416

The Minnesota Mutual Life
Insurance Company
Victory Square
St. Paul, Minnesota 55101

Modern Woodmen of America
1701 First Avenue
Rock Island, Illinois 61201

Monarch Life Insurance Co.
1250 State Street
Springfield, Massachusetts 01101

Montreal Life Insurance Co.
630 Sherbrooke Street West
Montreal, Quebec, CANADA

Mutual Benefit Life Insurance Co.
520 Broad Street
Newark, New Jersey 07101

The Mutual Life Assurance Company
of Canada
227 King Street South
Waterloo, Ontario, CANADA

Mutual Security Life Insurance Co.
3000 East U. S. 30 By-Pass
Fort Wayne, Indiana 46805

National Bankers Life Insurance Co.
Commerce & Ervay Streets
Dallas, Texas 75201

National Catholic Society
of Foresters
59 Van Buren Street
Chicago, Illinois 60605

National Educators Life
Insurance Co.
205 Northwest Seventh Street
Fort Worth, Texas, 76106

National Fidelity Life Insurance Co.
National Fidelity Life Building
1002 Walnut Street
Kansas City, Missouri 64106

New England Mutual Life
501 Boylston Street
Boston, Massachusetts 02117

New York Life Insurance Co.
51 Madison Avenue
New York, New York 10010

New York Savings Bank Life
Insurance Co.
200 Park Avenue
New York, New York 10017

North American Benefit Association
1338 Military Street
Port Huron, Michigan 48060

North American Life Assurance
105 Adelaide Street West
Toronto 1, Ontario, CANADA

North American Life & Casualty Co.
1750 Hennepin Avenue
Minneapolis, Minnesota 55403

North American Life Insurance
  Company of Chicago
35 East Wacker Drive
Chicago, Illinois 60601

The Northwestern Mutual Life
720 East Wisconsin Avenue
Milwaukee, Wisconsin 53202

Northwestern National Life
20 Washington Avenue, South
Minneapolis, Minnesota 55440

Occidental Life Insurance Co.
  of California
12th Street at Hill
Los Angeles, California 90054

Occidental Life Insurance Company
  of North Carolina
Cameron Village
Raleigh, North Carolina 27605

Ohio National Life Insurance Co.
Wm. Howard Taft Rd at Highland Ave
Cincinnati, Ohio 45219

Ohio State Life Insurance Co.
100 East Broad Street
Columbus, Ohio 43215

Old American Insurance Co.
4900 Oak Street
Kansas City, Missouri 64141

Olympic National Life Insurance Co.
Olympic National Building
Seattle, Washington 98104

Pacific Fidelity Life Insurance Co.
1150 South Olive Street
Los Angeles, California 90015

Pacific Mutual Life Insurance Co.
Pacific Mutual Building
Los Angeles, California 90054

Pacific National Life Assurance
215 Market Street
San Francisco, California 94105

Palmetto State Life Insurance Co.
1310 Lady Street
Columbia, South Carolina 29202

Pan-American Life
2400 Canal Street
New Orleans, Louisiana 70119

Pioneer Mutual Life Insurance Co.
205 Tenth Street North
Fargo, North Dakota 58102

Protective Life Insurance Co.
2027-29 First Avenue North
Birmingham, Alabama 35202

Provident Life and Accident
  Insurance Company
Fountain Square
Chattanooga, Tennessee 37402

Provident Life Insurance Co.
Provident Life Building
Bismarck, North Dakota 58501

Polish Roman Catholic Union
  of America
984 Milwaukee Avenue
Chicago, Illinois 60622

The Reliable Life Insurance Co.
231 West Lockwood Avenue
Webster Groves, Missouri 63119

Royal Neighbors of America
230 — 16th Street
Rock Island, Illinois 61201

Rural Security Life Insurance Co.
801 West Badger Road
Madison, Wisconsin 53701

Seaboard Life Insurance Co.
  of America
5783 S. W. 60th Court
Miami, Florida

Security Life and Trust Co.
420 North Spruce Street
Winston-Salem, North Carolina 27102

The Security Mutual Life
  Insurance Co.
200 North 15th Street
Lincoln, Nebraska 68508

Sentry Life Insurance Co.
1421 Strongs Avenue
Stevens Point, Wisconsin 54481

Shenandoah Life Insurance Co.
2301 Brambleton Avenue, S. W.
Roanoke, Virginia 24015

Southern Farm Bureau Life
  Insurance Co.
515 East Amite Street
Jackson, Mississippi 39205

Southern Life Insurance Company
330 South Green Street
Greensboro, North Carolina 27420

Southland Life Insurance Co.
Southland Center
Dallas, Texas 75221

The Sovereign Life Assurance Co.
  of Canada
1320 Yonge Street
Toronto 7, CANADA

Standard Life Insurance Co.
Standard Life Building
Pearl and Roach Streets
Jackson, Mississippi 39205

State Capital Life Insurance Co.
2620 Hillsborough Street
Raleigh, North Carolina 27602

The State Life Insurance Co.
15 East Washington Street
Indianapolis, Indiana 46204

Stockman National Life
  Insurance Co.
1823-25 West St. Joe Street
Rapid City, South Dakota 57701

Sun Life Assurance Company
  of Canada
Dominion Square
Montreal 110, CANADA

Sun Life Insurance Company
  of America
Sun Life Building, Charles Center
Baltimore, Maryland 21201

Sunset Life Insurance Company
  of America
3200 Capitol Boulevard
Olympia, Washington 98501

Supreme Life Insurance Co.
  of America
3501 So. Dr. Martin Luther King, Jr.
Chicago, Illinois 60653

Surety Life Insurance Co.
1935 South Main Street
Salt Lake City, Utah 84115

Teachers Insurance and Annuity
  Association of America
730 Third Avenue
New York, New York 10017

Texas Life Insurance Co.
Texas Life Bldg., 526 Austin Avenue
Waco, Texas 76701

Time Insurance Company
735 North Fifth Street
Milwaukee, Wisconsin 53203

The Travelers Insurance Co.
One Tower Square
Hartford, Connecticut 06115

The Union Labor Life Insurance Co.
850 Third Avenue
New York, New York 10022

Union Life Insurance Company
Union Life Building
Little Rock, Arkansas 72201

United American Life Insurance Co.
1717 California Street
Denver, Colorado 80202

United Family Life Insurance Co.
494 Spring Street, N. W.
Atlanta, Georgia 30308

United Fidelity Life Insurance Co.
1025 Elm Street
Dallas, Texas 75202

United Founders Life Insurance Co.
5900 Mosteller Drive
Oklahoma City, Oklahoma 73112

United Home Life Insurance Co.
54 Monument Circle
Indianapolis, Indiana 46204

United Insurance Co. of America
One East Wacker Drive
Chicago, Illinois 60601

United Services Life Insurance Co.
1701 Pennsylvania Avenue, N. W.
Washington, D. C. 20006

The Unity Mutual Life Insurance
  Company of New York
636 South Warren Street
Syracuse, New York 13201

Universal Life and Accident
Insurance Company
901 Ross Avenue
Dallas, Texas 75202

The Victory Life Insurance Co.
300 West Eighth Street
Topeka, Kansas 66603

Wabash Life Insurance Co.
2929 North Meridian Street
Indianapolis, Indiana 46208

Washington National Insurance Co.
1630 Chicago Avenue
Evanston, Illinois 60201

Western Bohemian Fraternal
Association
1900 First Avenue, N. E.
Cedar Rapids, Iowa 52402

Western Reserve Life Assurance
Company of Ohio
335 Euclid Avenue
Cleveland, Ohio 44114

The Western and Southern Life
Insurance Company
400 Broadway
Cincinnati, Ohio 45202

Western States Life Insurance Co.
700 Seventh Street, South
Fargo, North Dakota 58102

William Penn Fraternal Association
429 Forbes Avenue
Pittsburgh, Pennsylvania 15219

Woodman Accident and Life Co.
1526 "K" Street
Lincoln, Nebraska 68508

World Insurance Company
203 South 18th Street
Omaha, Nebraska 68102

National Guardian Life
Insurance Company
2 East Gilman Street
Madison, Wisconsin 53703

National Life Insurance Co.
National Life Drive
Montpelier, Vermont 05602

National Producers Life
Insurance Co.
2300 North Central Avenue
Phoenix, Arizona 85004

The Penn Mutual Life
530 Walnut Street
Philadelphia, Pennsylvania 19105

Peoples Life Insurance Co.
601 New Hampshire Avenue, N. W.
Washington, D. C. 20037

Philadelphia Life Insurance Co.
111-115 North Broad Street
Philadelphia, Pennsylvania 19107

Phoenix Mutual Life
1 American Row
Hartford, Connecticut 06115

Polish National Alliance of U. S.
of North America
1514-20 West Division Street
Chicago, Illinois 60622

Presbyterian Ministers Fund
1809 Walnut Street
Philadelphia, Pennsylvania 19103

Praetorian Mutual Life Insurance Co.
1607 Main Street
Dallas, Texas 75201

Protected Home Mutual Life
30 East State Street
Sharon, Pennsylvania 16146

Provident Mutual Life
4601 Market Street
Philadelphia, Pennsylvania 19101

The Prudential Insurance Co.
of America
Prudential Plaza
Newark, New Jersey 07101

Puritan Life Insurance Co.
245 Waterman Street
Providence, Rhode Island 02901

Pyramid Life Insurance Co.
Eighth & State Streets
Kansas City, Kansas 66101

Reliance Standard Life
Insurance Co.
4 Penn Center Plaza
Philadelphia, Pennsylvania 19103

Republic National Life
3988 North Central Expressway
Dallas, Texas 75204

Reserve Life Insurance Co.
403 South Akard Street
Dallas, Texas 75222

Rockford Life Insurance Co.
526-532 West State Street
Rockford, Illinois 61101

Safeco Life Insurance Co.
4347 Brooklyn Avenue
Seattle, Washington 98105

La Sauvegarde Life Insurance Co.
152 Harrison Street
Topeka, Kansas 66603

Security Benefit Life Insurance Co.
700 Harrison Street
Topeka, Kansas 66603

Security Life and Accident Co.
Security Life Building
Denver, Colorado 80202

South Coast Life Insurance Co.
Harry Hines at Mockingbird Lane
Dallas, Texas 75235

Southern Life and Health
    Insurance Company
2121 Highland Avenue
Birmingham, Alabama 35205

Southwestern Life Insurance Co.
Southwestern Life Building
Dallas, Texas 75201

Standard Insurance Company
1100 S. W. Sixth Avenue
Portland, Oregon 97204

Standard Life Insurance Company
    of Indiana
300 East Fall Creek Boulevard
Indianapolis, Indiana 46205

State Farm Life Insurance Co.
State Farm Insurance Building
Bloomington, Illinois 61701

State Reserve Life Insurance Co.
301 West First Street
Ft. Worth, Texas 76102

Stuyvesant Life Insurance Co.
1105 Hamilton Street
Allentown, Pennsylvania 18101

Tennessee Life Insurance Co.
Chamber of Commerce Building
Houston, Texas 77001

Union Bankers Insurance Co.
2551 Elm Street
Dallas, Texas 75226

The Union Central Life
    Insurance Co.
P. O. Box 179
Cincinnati, Ohio 45201

Union Mutual Life
400 Congress Street
Portland, Maine 04112

United Benefit Life Insurance Co.
3316 Farnam Street
Omaha, Nebraska 68131

United Farm Bureau Family Life
    Insurance Company
130 East Washington Street
Indianapolis, Indiana 46204

United Life & Accident
2 White Street
Concord, New Hampshire 03301

Western Life Insurance Co.
385 Washington Street
St. Paul, Minnesota 55102

Wisconsin National Life
    Insurance Co.
220-222 Washington Avenue
Oshkosh, Wisconsin 54901

Woodman of the World Life
    Insurance Society and/or Omaha
    Woodmen Life Insurance Society
1700 Farnam Street
Omaha, Nebraska 68102

World Service Life Insurance Co.
Service Life Center
309 West Seventh Street
Fort Worth, Texas 76102

The United States Life Insurance
    Co. in the City of New York
125 Maiden Lane
New York, New York 10038

Valley Forge Life
310 South Michigan Avenue
Chicago, Illinois 60604

The Variable Annuity Life
  Insurance Co.
2727 Allen Parkway
Houston, Texas 77001

West Coast Life Insurance Co.
605 Market Street
San Francisco, California 94105

Western Farm Bureau Life
  Insurance Co.
1200 Lincoln Street
Denver, Colorado 80203

Zurich Life Insurance Co.
  of Canada
188 University Avenue
Toronto 1, Ontario, CANADA

Mutual Savings Banks

INTRODUCTION TO THE BANKS

There are about 500 such mutual banks with 1,354 branches, and they may be found in the phone directory or by writing the National Association of Mutual Savings Banks, 1200 Park Avenue, New York, N.Y. 10028. The association lists all banks, addresses and resources.

USING THE RIGHT APPROACH

Before applying to a mutual savings bank, these points should be reviewed:

(1) Home loans, on one-and-two-family dwellings, make up about 75 percent of the mutual savings banks' combined total assets.

(2) Mutual savings banks are chartered under their state laws and a commissioner of banks or someone with a similar title of the state banking department supervises them. Those banks whose deposits are insured by the Federal Deposit Insurance Corporation are subject to some examination, but not regulation, by that agency.

(3) In times of tight money, these banks, like other savings banks, hold back on loans since deposits in this situation may be channeled to other higher yielding investments, leaving these institutions with fewer deposits. In some states, the usury laws prohibit the mutual banks from raising interest rates above a fixed percentage on home loans. In times when money is flowing evenly, the mutual banks seek home and other traditional mortgages.

(4) Mutual banks' loan-to-value ratio (on non-government-insured mortgages) ranges from 50 to 90 percent according to state law. There are also restrictions in some states restricting the maximum amount in dollars on any individual loan. The percentage of assets or deposits that may be placed in mortgages is restricted, and states decide maximum terms, amortization, and other loan factors.

(5) There are no real geographic boundaries where the mutuals make government-insured loans, but for conventional mortgages the limits are within the state or within adjoining states. Some mutuals go beyond their usual geographic confines when their communities' needs are met, and then they may move into the national market working with mortgage brokers as correspondents.

(6) With all their specifications, the mutual savings banks are still excellent sources for those buying single-family dwellings, since trustees usually prefer these loans. Only the larger banks are likely to extend significant loans to apartment house, commercial, or industrial projects.

(7) In considering a loan, the mutual banks will take these factors into account — higher risk of loss with a higher loan-to-value ratio; loss would probably be greater on older properties as opposed to newer real estate; proximity to the

lender reduces loss ratio; properties occupied by owners carry less risk than those leased by tenants; straight loans carry greater risk than those amortized.

(8) Some of the larger banks make direct placement loans for corporations.

Like the S and L's, these mutual savings banks are organized to serve the communities in which the branches are located.

For a loan, contact should be made with the nearest mutual savings bank by telephone or visit.

The Institutional Securities Corporation, 200 Park Avenue, New York, N.Y. 10017, is also a valuable source of information. It is owned by the New York mutual savings banks and offers nationwide facilities for servicing of mortgages, inspection and appraisal of real estate, examination of mortgage servicing agents, mortgage tabulating service, purchase and management of Federal Housing Administration and Veterans Administration-insured mortgages under trust or agency agreements, and servicing of and administration of mortgages under participation agreements. A subsidiary corporation offers pension funds collateral trust notes secured by mortgages.

100 OF THE LARGEST MUTUAL SAVINGS BANKS

These mutual savings banks are listed in graduated order according to their total assets:

	ASSETS
The Bowery Savings Bank 110 East 42nd Street New York, New York 10017	$3,427,144,612
The Dime Savings Bank of New York 9 DeKalb Avenue Brooklyn, New York 11201	3,037,683,864
The Philadelphia Saving Fund Society Coulter & Anderson Avenues Ardmore, Pennsylvania 19003	3,023,348,361
The New York Bank for Savings 1230 Avenue of the Americas New York, New York 10020	2,611,515,319
Emigrant Savings Bank 5 East 42nd Street New York, New York 10017	1,913,666,838
Dollar Savings Bank of New York 2530 Grand Concourse Bronx, New York 10458	1,861,077,936
The Greenwich Savings Bank 1356 Broadway at 36th Street New York, New York 10018	1,597,817,727

The Williamsburgh Savings Bank One Hanson Place Brooklyn, New York 11243	$1,535,173,687
The Lincoln Savings Bank 531 Broadway Brooklyn, New York 11206	1,478,688,562
Buffalo Savings Bank 545 Main Street Buffalo, New York 14203	1,363,093,893
The Seamen's Bank for Savings 30 Wall Street New York, New York 10005	1,331,351,188
Dry Dock Savings Bank 742 Lexington Avenue New York, New York 10022	1,265,746,108
The Howard Savings Institution 768 Broad Street Newark, New Jersey 07101	1,262,751,730
The Greater New York Savings Bank 449 5th Avenue Brooklyn, New York 11215	1,188,412,488
Washington Mutual Savings Bank Second Avenue at Spring Street Seattle, Washington 98101	1,163,995,100
The Western Saving Fund Society of Philadelphia Lancaster Avenue & Station Road Haverford, Pennsylvania 19041	1,119,120,685
Jamaica Savings Bank 161-01 Jamaica Avenue Jamaica, New York 11406	1,091,542,148
Union Dime Savings Bank 1065 Avenue of the Americas New York, New York 10018	1,079,410,427
Franklin Savings Bank of New York Eighth Avenue & 42nd Street New York, New York 10036	1,066,261,283
East River Savings Bank 26 Cortlandt Street New York, New York 10007	1,058,094,840
Erie County Savings Bank One Main Place Buffalo, New York 14202	1,037,732,810
The Manhattan Savings Bank 385 Madison Avenue New York, New York 10017	988,833,969

Society for Savings $916,203,040
31 Pratt Street
Hartford, Connecticut 06101

People's Savings Bank-Bridgeport   903,354,078
Main & State Streets
Bridgeport, Connecticut 06602

The Brooklyn Savings Bank   859,559,224
Corner of Fulton & Montague Streets
Brooklyn, New York 11201

Anchor Savings Bank   845,886,362
Fifth Avenue at 54th Street
Brooklyn, New York 11220

The Provident Institution for Savings
    in the Town of Boston   793,412,347
30 Winter Street-36 Temple Place
Boston, Massachusetts 02105

Farmers & Mechanics Savings Bank
    of Minneapolis   783,830,225
90 South Sixth Street
Minneapolis, Minnesota 55402

The East New York Savings Bank   778,441,161
2644 Atlantic Avenue
Brooklyn, New York 11207

The Long Island Savings Bank   755,213,922
Bridge Plaza North
Long Island City, New York 11101

The Boston Five Cents Savings Bank   751,369,607
10 School Street
Boston, Massachusetts 02108

Metropolitan Savings Bank   735,038,553
189 Montague Street
Brooklyn, New York 11201

Central Savings Bank in the City of New York   701,183,355
Broadway & 73rd Street
New York, New York 10023

The Community Savings Bank   700,712,482
235 East Main Street
Rochester, New York 14604

The Green Point Savings Bank   672,304,446
807 Manhattan Avenue
Brooklyn, New York 11222

United Mutual Savings Bank   659,614,796
1370 Avenue of the Americas
NewYork, New York 10019

Beneficial Mutual Savings Bank   657,285,897
1200 Chestnut Street
Philadelphia, Pennsylvania 19107

Ridgewood Savings Bank 71-02 Forest Avenue Ridgewood, New York 11227	$647,261,185
Dollar Savings Bank 4th Avenue & Smithfield Street Pittsburgh, Pennsylvania 15230	643,946,702
Eastern Savings Bank Tremont and Park Avenue Bronx, New York 10457	643,327,955
Harlem Savings Bank 205 East 42nd Street New York, New York 10017	635,824,523
Old Stone Savings Bank 86 South Main Street Providence, Rhode Island 02901	618,904,702
Germantown Savings Bank GSB Building City Line & Belmont Avenues Bala-Cynwyd, Pennsylvania 19004	617,271,173
Charlestown Savings Bank 55 Summer Street Boston, Massachusetts 02110	606,175,057
South Brooklyn Savings Bank Atlantic Avenue & Court Street Brooklyn, New York 11202	588,625,903
Prudential Savings Bank 390 Avenue of the Americas New York, New York 10011	566,261,287
Rochester Savings Bank 40 Franklin Street Rochester, New York 14604	536,788,575
Schenectady Savings Bank 500 State Street Schenectady, New York 12301	533,366,306
Onondaga Savings Bank 101 South Salina Street Syracuse, New York 13201	526,446,722
The Western New York Savings Bank 438 Main Street Buffalo, New York 14202	521,895,605
Empire Savings Bank 221 West 57th Street New York, New York 10019	515,342,097
Albany Savings Bank 20 North Pearl Street Albany, New York 12201	514,875,686

The Queens County Savings Bank 38-25 Main Street Flushing, New York 11352	$513,214,594
The Savings Bank of Baltimore Baltimore & Charles Streets Baltimore, Maryland 21203	501,487,563
Suffolk Franklin Savings Bank 45 Franklin Street Boston, Massachusetts 02110	489,229,925
Syracuse Savings Bank One Clinton Square Syracuse, New York 13201	466,220,519
Hamburg Savings Bank 1451 Myrtle Avenue Brooklyn, New York 11237	465,646,241
Wilmington Savings Fund Society 838 Market Street Wilmington, Delaware 19899	449,446,562
Roosevelt Savings Bank of the City of New York 1024 Gates Avenue Brooklyn, New York 11221	424,486,187
The New Haven Savings Bank 170 Orange Street New Haven, Connecticut 06502	417,069,927
Provident Savings Bank of Baltimore 240 North Howard Street Baltimore, Maryland 21201	413,048,211
Springfield Institution for Savings 1459 Main Street Springfield, Massachusetts 01101	410,780,057
American Savings Bank 335 Broadway New York, New York 10013	380,601,089
United States Savings Bank of Newark 772 Broad Street Newark, New Jersey 07102	378,977,851
Provident Savings Bank Washington & York Streets Jersey City, New Jersey 07302	378,452,489
Connecticut Savings Bank 47 Church Street New Haven, Connecticut 06501	375,676,295
Hudson City Savings Bank 587 Summit Avenue Jersey City, New Jersey 07306	373,984,020

North Side Savings Bank 185 West 231st Street Bronx, New York 10463	$366,279,143
The Dime Savings Bank of Williamsburgh 209 Havemeyer Street Brooklyn, New York 11211	361,374,485
Richmond Hill Savings Bank 115-20 Jamaica Avenue Richmond Hill, New York 11418	359,738,851
Newton Savings Bank 1188 Centre Street Newton, Massachusetts 02159	349,539,001
Waterbury Savings Bank 60 North Main Street Waterbury, Connecticut 06720	348,067,796
The Roslyn Savings Bank 1400 Old Northern Boulevard Roslyn, New York 11576	338,857,329
Home Savings Bank 69 Tremont Street Boston, Massachusetts 02108	333,211,388
The Savings Bank of Utica 233 Genesee Street Utica, New York 13501	329,604,063
Fidelity Mutual Savings Bank 524 West Riverside Avenue Spokane, Washington 99201	329,049,640
Fulton Savings Bank of Kings County 395 Jay Street Brooklyn, New York 11201	326,330,161
The Morris County Savings Bank 21 South Street Morristown, New Jersey 07960	325,697,536
Citizens Savings Bank 870 Westminister Street Providence, Rhode Island 02902	324,222,146
Eastchester Savings Bank 22 East First Street Mount Vernon, New York 10551	316,063,741
Monroe Savings Bank 300 Main Street East Rochester, New York 14604	306,607,283
The Binghamton Savings Bank 62-68 Exchange Street Binghamton, New York 13902	300,555,105

Worcester County Institution for Savings 365 Main Street Worcester, Massachusetts 01608	$ 299,191,448
Yonkers Savings Bank 16 South Broadway Yonkers, New York 10701	295,687,259
Peoples Savings Bank of Yonkers 12 South Broadway Yonkers, New York 10701	285,526,371
Union Warren Savings Bank 216 Tremont Street Boston, Massachusetts 02116	278,363,198
The Poughkeepsie Savings Bank 21 & 23 Market Street Poughkeepsie, New York 12602	275,184,918
Staten Island Savings Bank 81 Water Street Stapleton, New York 10304	274,638,025
Bloomfield Savings Bank 11 Broad Street Bloomfield, New Jersey 07003	267,341,887
Peoples Savings Bank 450 Main Street Worcester, Massachusetts 01608	265,421,874
Cambridge Savings Bank 1374 Massachusetts Avenue Cambridge, Massachusetts 02138	264,259,686
Community Savings Bank 200 Main Street Holyoke, Massachusetts 01040	264,055,542
Amoskeag Savings Bank 875 Elm Street Manchester, New Hampshire 03105	250,261,991
Mechanics & Farmers Savings Bank 930 Main Street Bridgeport, Connecticut 06601	247,524,480
South Boston Savings Bank 460 Broadway Boston, Massachusetts 02127	247,218,850
Troy Savings Bank 32 Second Street Troy, NewYork 12180	239,435,148
Mechanics Savings Bank 80 Pearl Street Hartford, Connecticut 06101	233,494,172

The Home Savings Bank $ 233,330,331
One Mamaroneck Avenue
White Plains, New York 10601

Maine Savings Bank   230,865,615
15 Casco Street
Portland, Maine 04104

Dorchester Savings Bank   227,010,057
572 Columbia Road
Boston, Massachusetts 02125

Mortgage Bankers

HOW THE MORTGAGE BANKING HOUSE OPERATES

Mortgage bankers are most often the best sources for loans of any type or description. The reason is simple. They are constantly in touch with the changing financial market and know where the money is at any given time. They usually charge from one to three percent of the loan amount for their services, but they can find the lowest rates and terms for a loan, which the individual cannot usually do by himself.

There are a number of ways to contact a good mortgage banker. Real estate brokers as well as attorneys can guide the borrower to competent mortgage bankers and can aid in filing the loan applications with them.

The borrower can contact these sources directly, if he chooses, after gathering all information needed for the loan.

HOW TO RATE THE MORTGAGE BANKING
HOUSE AND BROKER

One of the best ways to determine the reputation of any mortgage banker is to request his references and verify them. Also, local banks, attorneys, or real estate brokers can offer advice.

If he is a member of the Mortgage Bankers Association of America, he is probably in good standing in the field.

SERVICES OFFERED BORROWER AND LENDER

Mortgage companies are ready sources for short-term construction loans as well as long-term mortgages of all types, be they conventional, Federal Housing Administration- or Veterans Administration-insured. They are particularly good sources during tight money markets since they are in touch with many types of lenders and know where funds are available. Since these companies are not under the direction of boards of trustees, they can offer almost immediate action on loan applications.

The mortgage banker will aid a borrower in evaluating his project and maximizing the amount and term of the loan he can obtain.

In addition to those mentioned, other services he provides the borrower are structuring the loan, contacting lenders best suited to the particular financial requirements, and negotiating the deal and carrying it to completion.

Some of the advantages a mortgage banker provides a lender are:

(1) Screening requests and submitting only those loans that meet the lender's requirements.

(2) Providing the lender with a local representative in market places far removed from the lender.

(3) Cutting overhead costs for lender by weeding through applications and setting up contacts with desirable clients.

(4) Offering the lender a continuous flow of quality applications.

(5) Keeping lenders abreast of local market conditions, loan demand, and growth plans.

These companies generally do not make loans to hold in their own portfolios, rather they originate mortgage loans and sell or broker them. This may change in tight money markets when the mortgage company may carry its own mortgages.

When they sell mortgages, it is usually to insurance companies, large commercial banks, and other sources. They borrow short-term funds from commercial banks and do not as a rule lend from their own business in originating loans.

Even though a mortgage might be sold, the mortgage company might still service the account, that is, collect the mortgage, keep tax records, handle refinancing, and arrange for mortgage loan extensions, extracting its fee from monthly mortgage payments. This is especially true of home loans. Servicing is an arrangement between the buyer of the mortgages and the mortgage company and does not in any way affect the amount an individual mortgages.

The best way to find the mortgage companies in any area is simply to look in the phone directory, call the companies, and ask them what kinds of loans they make. If their conditions are suitable, an application should be made.

For a mortgage transaction the broker will need the usual data supplied to any lender for an existing property owned or to be constructed. This information is outlined in preceding pages.

TRANSACTIONS FOR VA- AND FHA-INSURED LOANS

The mortgage banker is ideally trained to provide service whether for home loans or multi-family projects. He must be an FHA/VA-government approved lender in order to make FHA/VA-loans.

He will fill out all forms and process them for the borrower. Fees are very small in relation to the work he does and the services he performs.

MORTGAGE BANKERS

ALABAMA

Charter Mortgage Company
Suite 600, Bank for Savings Bldg.
P.O. Box 10784
Birmingham, Alabama 35202

Cobbs, Allen & Hall Mortgage
Company, Inc.
602 Bel Air Boulevard
P.O. Box 6256 (Loop)
Mobile, Alabama 36606

Ballard Mortgage Company, Inc.
First National Bank Bldg.
P.O. Box 2068
Montgomery, Alabama 36103

Engel Mortgage Company, Inc.
806 Governor's Drive, S.W.
Huntsville, Alabama 35801

ALASKA

Coast Mortgage Company
700 G Street
P.O. Box 1200
Anchorage, Alaska 99501

ARIZONA

Marshall Mortgage & Trust Co.
5138 N. Central Avenue
Phoenix, Arizona 85011

Associated Mortgage &
Investment Co.
5133 North Central Avenue
Phoenix, Arizona 85012

Bankers Mortgage Company
Suite 206-C
4350 East Camelback Road
Phoenix, Arizona 85018

Western American Mortgage Co.
728 East McDowell Rd.
Phoenix, Arizona 85004

ARKANSAS

Modern American Mortgage
Corporation
712 West Third St.
Little Rock, Arkansas 72201

ARKANSAS (Continued)

First Mortgage Corporation
Suite 1555
Union National Plaza
Little Rock, Arkansas 72201

Texarkana Mortgage Company,
Inc.
316 East 4th St.
Texarkana, Arkansas 75501

Block Mortgage Co., Inc.
Markham and State Streets
Little Rock, Arkansas 72203

CALIFORNIA

Sequoia Mortgage Company
285 S. First Street
San Jose, California 95109

Colonial Mortgage Service Co.
of California
550 Kearny Street
San Francisco, Calif. 94108

Montgomery Street Mortgage
Corporation
235 Montgomery Street
San Francisco, California 94104

Amfac Mortgage Corporation
222 Front St.
San Francisco, California 94111

Southern Mortgage Company
Suite 136
Fifth Ave. Financial Centre
2550 Fifth Avenue
San Diego, California 92103

United California Mortgage
Company
245 South Los Robles Avenue
Pasadena, California 91109

Colonial Mortgage Service Co.
of California
110 West C Street
San Diego, California 92101

Westland Mortgage Service Co.
P.O. Box 1675
Sacramento, California 95808

McMillan Mortgage Co.
4211 Wilshire Boulevard
Los Angeles, California 90010

CALIFORNIA (*Continued*)

Heitman Mortgage Company
1900 Avenue of the Stars
Los Angeles, California 90067

Investor's Mortgage Service Co.
5900 Wilshire Boulevard
Los Angeles, California 90051

Larwin Mortgage Investors
9100 Wilshire Boulevard
Beverly Hills, California 90212

Keystone Mortgage Co., Inc.
Suite 808
Pierce National Life Building
3807 Wilshire Boulevard
Los Angeles, California 90010

CANADA

Cumberland Mortgage
Corporation Ltd.
567 Hornby Street Zone 1
Vancouver, B.C., Canada

COLORADO

Central Mortgage & Investment
Company
430 North Tejon
Colorado Springs, Colorado 80902

Advance Mortgage Corporation
165 Cook Street
Denver, Colorado 80206

First-American Mortgage Company
950 Capitol Life Center
Denver, Colorado 80203

First Denver Mortgage
P.O. Box 5341
Denver, Colorado 80217

CONNECTICUT

The McCue Mortgage Company
70 Grove Hill
New Britain, Connecticut 06050

DELAWARE

Continental Mortgage Company
1102 West Street
Wilmington, Delaware 19899

Russell Mortgage Co.
1012 Washington Street
Wilmington, Delaware 19801

DISTRICT OF COLUMBIA

Cafritz Mortgage Corporation
1825 K Street Northwest `
Washington, D. C. 20006

Colonial Mortgage Corporation
of D. C.
1101 17th Street, Northwest
Washington, D. C. 20036

FLORIDA

Associated Mortgage Investors
120 Giralda Avenue
P. O. Box 1998
Coral Gables, Florida 33134

Barnett Mortgage Trust
Barnett Bank Building
Jacksonville, Florida 32202

Adair Mortgage Company
of Florida
415 Mutual of Omaha Building
1201 Brickell Avenue
Miami, Florida 33131

Atico Mortgage Corporation
Suite 279, Kennedy Building
5200 W. Kennedy Boulevard
P. O. Box 22743
Tampa, Florida 33622

GEORGIA

Lynes Mortgage Company
120 St. Julian Street East
Savannah, Georgia 31402

Southeastern Mortgage
Corporation
116 North Jackson Street
Albany, Georgia 31701

Gulf States Mortgage Co., Inc.
1305 Second Avenue
Columbus, Georgia 31902

Bankers Mortgage Associates
830 Fulton National Bank Building
P. O. Box 1518
Atlanta, Georgia 30301

HAWAII

Heitman Mortgage Company
677 Ala Moana Boulevard
Honolulu, Hawaii 96813

HAWAII (Continued)

Realty Mortgage Corporation
320 Ward Avenue
Honolulu, Hawaii 96814

Honolulu Mortgage Co., Ltd.
235 Queen Street
Honolulu, Hawaii 96813

IDAHO

Utah Mortgage Loan Corporation
435 Shoup Avenue
P. O. Box 460
Idaho Falls, Idaho 83401

Mortgage-Insurance Corporation
323 Idaho Street
P. O. Box 639
Boise, Idaho 83701

Mortgage-Insurance Corporation
155 South Arthur Avenue
P. O. Box 1786
Pocatello, Idaho 83201

Utah Mortgage Loan Corporation
917 West Idaho Street
P. O. Box 1247
Boise, Idaho 83701

ILLINOIS

Quinlan and Tyson Mortgage
Corporation
1569 Sherman Avenue
Evanston, Illinois 60204

Mercantile Mortgage Company
1201 N. North Street
P. O. Box 386
Peoria, Illinois 61601

Johnson Mortgage Company
240 North Park Street
Decatur, Illinois 62523

Northern Illinois Mortgage Co.
506 Rockford Trust Building
Rockford, Illinois 61101

Great Lakes Mortgage Corporation
111 West Washington Street
Chicago, Illinois 60602

Advance Mortgage Corporation
120 West Madison
Chicago, Illinois 60602

ILLINOIS (Continued)

Combank Mortgage Funding Ltd.
208 South LaSalle Street
Chicago, Illinois 60604

Greenebaum Mortgage Company
33 North Dearborn Street
Suite 1919
Chicago, Illinois 60602

Republic Realty Mortgage
Corporation
111 West Washington Street
Chicago, Illinois 60602

Union Realty Mortgage Co., Inc.
100 West Monroe Street
Chicago, Illinois 60603

INDIANA

Colonial Mortgage Company
of Indiana, Inc.
3140 South LaFountain Street
Suite #6
Kokomo, Indiana 46901

Waterfield Mortgage
Company, Inc.
702 North Michigan Street
South Bend, Indiana 46601

Colonial Mortgage Company
of Indiana, Inc.
1815 North Meridian
Indianapolis, Indiana 46202

Lake Mortgage Company, Inc.
570 Washington Street
Gary, Indiana 46402

Meridian Mortgage Co., Inc.
129 E. Market Street
Indianapolis, Indiana 46202

Colonial Mortgage Company
of Indiana, Inc.
P. O. Box 969
Muncie, Indiana 47305

IOWA

Northland Mortgage Company
3601-03 Douglas Avenue
Des Moines, Iowa 50313

Northland Mortgage Company
2435 Kimberly Road
Bettendorf, Iowa 52722

KANSAS

J. C. Sargent Mortgage
& Investment Co., Inc.
2101 West 21st Street
Topeka, Kansas 66604

The Union Mortgage And
Investment Company
403 Commercial Building
Kansas City, Kansas 66101

KENTUCKY

Kentucky Mortgage Company
of Paducah
P. O. Box 1406
Paducah, Kentucky 42001

Lincoln Mortgage Corporation
278 Harrison Avenue
P. O. Box 1520
Lexington, Kentucky 40501

Louisville Mortgage Service
Company
101 West Building
101 West Broadway
P. O. Box 1053
Louisville, Kentucky 40202

American Fletcher Mortgage
Company, Inc.
1941 Bishop Lane
Louisville, Kentucky 40218

LOUISIANA

First Fidelity Mortgage Company
18th at Tower
Monroe, Louisiana 71201

First National Mortgage
Corporation
1111 South Jefferson Davis Pkwy.
P. O. Box 13766
New Orleans, Louisiana 70125

First National Mortgage
Corporation
1804 Dallas Drive
P. O. Box 15868
Baton Rouge, Louisiana

Security Mortgage Insurance
Company
4900 Government Street
P. O. Box 66357 Central City Sta.
Baton Rouge, Louisiana 70806

LOUISIANA (*Continued*)

Cosmopolitan Mortgage
Corporation
306 Milam Street, Suite 1107
P. O. Drawer 1446
Shreveport, Louisiana 71102

MARYLAND

Mortgage Investors of Washington
7316 Wisconsin Avenue
Bethesda, Maryland 20014

Capital Mortgage Investments
5530 Wisconsin Avenue
Chevy Chase, Maryland 20015

FirstMortgage Corporation
4700 Auth. Place, Suite 400
Camp Springs, Maryland 20023

Maryland Mortgage Company
6 South Calvert Street
Baltimore, Maryland 21202

Advance Mortgage Corporation
Scuderi Building, Suite 707
6101 28th Avenue
Marlow Heights, Maryland 20031

MASSACHUSETTS

Beacon Mortgage Co., Inc.
1425 Beacon Street
Brookline, Massachusetts 02146

Guaranty Mortgage Corporation
69 Winn Street
Burlington, Massachusetts 01803

Investors Mortgage Insurance
Company
100 Federal Street
P. O. Box 570
Boston, Massachusetts 02102

Western Mortgage Investors
10 High Street
Boston, Massachusetts 02110

MICHIGAN

Ann Arbor Mortgage Corporation
2512 Carpenter Road
P. O. Box 1044
Ann Arbor, Michigan 48106

MICHIGAN (Continued)

Standard Mortgage Corporation
201 Northland Towers
15565 Northland Drive
Southfield, Michigan 48075

Waterfield Mortgage
Company, Inc.
813 W. South Street
Kalamazoo, Michigan

Citizens Mortgage Corporation
2428 Burton S. E.
Grand Rapids, Michigan 49506

General Mortgage Corporation
1814 Genesee Towers
Flint, Michigan 48502

Consolidated Mortgage
Corporation
1400 Industrial Building
Detroit, Michigan 48226

Michigan Mortgage Corporation
139 Cadillac Square
Detroit, Michigan 48226

MINNESOTA

Northland Mortgage Company
630 Hamm Building
St. Paul, Minnesota 55102

Northland Mortgage Company
Southdale Office Centre
6750 France Avenue South
Minneapolis, Minnesota 55435

Conservative Mortgage Company
1200 Roanoke Building
Minneapolis, Minnesota 55402

Schumacher Mortgage
Company, Inc.
Deitrich Building
5300 Glenwood Avenue
Minneapolis, Minnesota 55422

MISSISSIPPI

IDS Mortgage Corporation
Room 150, Terrace Floor
656 North State Street
Jackson, Mississippi 39201

Carraway Mortgage
Company, Inc.
317 Electric Building
P. O. Box 891
Jackson, Mississippi 39205

MISSISSIPPI (Continued)

Bailey Mortgage Company
161 E. Amite Street
Jackson, Mississippi 39201

Bradley Mortgage Company
125 North State Street
P. O. Box 1286
Jackson, Mississippi 39205

MISSOURI

Mercantile Mortgage Company
1835 S. Stewart Street
Springfield, Missouri 65804

General Mortgage Company
of St. Louis
10449 St. Charles Rock Road
St. Ann, Missouri 63074

Mercantile Mortgage Company
7730 Forsyth Blvd.
St. Louis, Missouri 63105

Linwood Mortgage Company
One West Armour Boulevard
Kansas City, Missouri 64111

Tomahawk Mortgage
Company, Inc.
821 Dakota
Independence, Missouri 64056

NEBRASKA

Northland Mortgage Company
Pacific Plaza
7301 Pacific Street
Omaha, Nebraska 68114

NEW JERSEY

Jersey Mortgage Company
430 Westfield Avenue
Elizabeth, New Jersey 07207

Coolidge Mortgage Service Co.
525 Cooper Street
Camden, New Jersey 08102

Bond & Mortgage Company
of New Jersey
One Cherry Hill Mall
Cherry Hill, New Jersey 08034

J.I. Kislak Mortgage Corporation
581 Broad Street
Newark, New Jersey 07102

NEW JERSEY (*Continued*)

Alexander Summer Mortgage Co.
222 Cedar Lane
Teaneck, New Jersey 07666

Bankers Mortgage Company
1333 Broad Street
Clifton, New Jersey 07013

Mortgage Brokerage Services
30 Evergreen Place
East Orange, New Jersey 07018

NEW YORK

Dominion Mortgage
& Realty Trust
1410 Liberty Bank Bldg.
Buffalo, New York 14202

Inter-Island Mortgagee Corp.
176-60 Union Turnpike
Flushing, New York 11366

Associated Mortgage Companies,
Inc.
Suite 2110
509 Madison Avenue
New York, New York 10022

GIT Realty And Mortgage
Investors
280 Park Avenue
New York, New York 10017

The Leader Mortgage Company
70 Pine Street
New York, New York 10005

NEW MEXICO

J. Duval West Mortgage Company
8313 Menaul Boulevard, N.E.
P.O. Box 3527
Albuquerque, New Mexico 87110

NORTH CAROLINA

NCNB Mortgage Corporation
P.O. Box 10347
Suite 104
Friendly Center Office Bldg.
600 Green Valley Road
Greensboro, North Carolina 27408

Wachovia Mortgage Company
P.O. Box 2236
Asheville, North Carolina 28802

NORTH CAROLINA (*Continued*)

Commonwealth Mortgage
Company
3820 Merton Drive
Raleigh, North Carolina 27609

Atlantic Mortgage And
Investment Company
3034 Trenwest Drive
P.O. Box 15066
Winston-Salem, N.C. 27103

OHIO

The Leader Mortgage Company
808 Gwynne Building
600 Main Street
Cincinnati, Ohio 45202

C.C. Fletcher Mortgage Company
437 Carew Tower
Cincinnati, Ohio 45202

The Leader Mortgage Company
508 Akron Savings and Loan Bldg.
Akron, Ohio 44308

Citizens Mortgage Corporation
1010 East Ohio Building
E. 9th And Superior Avenue
Cleveland, Ohio 44114

Mortgage Securities, Inc.
1375 Euclid Avenue
Cleveland, Ohio 44115

The Galbreath Mortgage Company
101 East Town Street
Columbus, Ohio 43215

Advance Mortgage Corporation
601 Third National Building
Dayton, Ohio 45402

Mortgage Corp. of Ohio
1830 West High Street
Piqua, Ohio 45356

Mortgage Corp. of Ohio
616 North Limestone Street
Springfield,Ohio 45503

North Central Mortgage
Corporation
1520 Hulman Building
Dayton, Ohio 45402

OKLAHOMA

Midland Mortgage Co.
5529 South Lewis
Tulsa, Oklahoma 74105

OKLAHOMA *(Continued)*

Miller Mortgage Company
114 North Third
Ponca City, Oklahoma 74601

Harry Mortgage Co.
730 Hightower Building
Oklahoma City, Oklahoma 73102

Oklahoma Mortgage Company,
Inc.
Robinson At N.W. 3rd Street
P.O. Box 1768
Oklahoma City, Oklahoma 73101

OREGON

Mortgage Bancorporation
167 High Street, S.E.
Salem, Oregon 97308

Farwest Mortgage Company
700 Title & Trust Bldg.
321 S.W. 4th Avenue
Portland, Oregon 97204

National Mortgage Co.
305 S.W. 4th Avenue
Portland, Oregon 97204

PENNSYLVANIA

Republic Mortgage Company
226 South 16th Street
Philadelphia, Pennsylvania 19102

Crockett Mortgage Company
112 South 16th Street
Philadelphia, Pennsylvania 19102

Advance Mortgage Corporation
5006 Lenker Street
Mechanicsburg, Pa. 17055

The Galbreath Mortgage Company
of Pennsylvania
2940 U.S. Steel Building
600 Grant Street
Pittsburgh, Pennsylvania 15219

Housing Mortgage Corp.
535 Fifth Avenue
Pittsburgh, Pennsylvania 15219

PUERTO RICO

Consolidated Mortgage & Finance
Corporation
First Federal Building, Suite 918
Santurce, Puerto Rico 00910

PUERTO RICO *(Continued)*

International Charter Mortgage
Corporation
1401 Banco Economias Building
Hato Rey, Puerto Rico 00918

Berens Mortgage Bankers, Inc.
GPO Box 3529
1913 Ponce de Leon Avenue
San Juan, Puerto Rico 00936

Trust Mortgage Corporation
Pan Am Building
255 Ponce de Leon Avenue
Hato Rey, Puerto Rico

SOUTH CAROLINA

Carolina National Mortgage
Investment Co., Inc.
5420 Rivers Avenue
North Charleston, S.C. 29505

Carolina National Mortgage
Investment Co., Inc.
The Florence Mall
Florence, South Carolina 29501

Wachovia Mortgage Company
315 Calhoun Street, Suite 107
Charleston, South Carolina 29401

Southern Mortgage Company
136 Laurens Street, N.W.
P.O. Box 1136
Aiken, South Carolina 29801

TENNESSEE

Charter Mortgage Company
1232 Stahlman Building
Nashville, Tennessee 37201

Nashville, Mortgage And Realty
Company
Suite 210, Stahlman Building
Nashville, Tennessee 37201

National Mortgage Company
4041 Knight Arnold Road
Memphis, Tennessee 38118

Guaranty Mortgage Company
of Nashville
Downtowner Building
Shelby & Center Streets
P.O. Box 146
Kingsport, Tennessee 37662

TEXAS

Capitol Mortgage Bankers, Inc.
1901 North Lamar Blvd.
Austin, Texas 78701

Mortgage And Trust, Inc.
4445 Gollihar Road
P.O. Box 6818
Corpus Christi, Texas 78411

Grinnan Mortgage Company
710 Mercantile Bank Building
Dallas, Texas 75201

Charter Mortgage Company
4321 Alpha Road
Dallas, Texas 75240

Mortgage And Trust, Inc.
501 Mercantile Securities Building
1802 Main Street
Dallas, Texas 75201

Home Mortgage Company of
El Paso
307 Texas Avenue
El Paso, Texas 79901

Citizens Mortgage Company
2324 Fannin, Suite 200
Houston, Texas 77002

Loper Mortgage Company
206 San Pedro
San Antonio, Texas 78205

Modern American Mortgage
Corporation
520 West 12th
Texarkana, Texas 75501

UTAH

National Mortgage Company
203 East 21st South
P.O. Box 630
Salt Lake City, Utah 84110

Utah Mortgage Loan Corporation
15 South Main Street
P.O. Box 488
Logan, Utah 84321

Bettilyon Mortgage Loan Co.
333 West 21st South
Salt Lake City, Utah 84115

Western Mortgage Loan
Corporation
2464 Washington Boulevard
Ogden, Utah 84401

UTAH (*Continued*)

Tracy Mortgage Company
465 East Second South
Salt Lake City, Utah 84111

VIRGINIA

Commonwealth Mortgage
Company
9th & Bank Streets
Richmond, Virginia 23219

Finney Mortgage Corp.
626 N. Ridge Street
P.O. Box 1239
Danville, Virginia 24541

Mortgage Investment Corporation
101 Franklin Road, S.W.
Roanoke, Virginia 24011

First Mortgage Corporation
P.O. Box 1601
Petersburg, Virginia 23803

WASHINGTON

Olympic Mortgage Corporation
101 North 85th Street
Seattle, Washington 98103

Hamill Mortgage, Inc.
1107 A Street
Tacoma, Washington 98402

Seattle Mortgage Company
Arcade Plaza
2nd & University
Seattle, Washington 98101

Bankwest Mortgage Company
10116 N.E. 8th Street
Bellevue, Washington 98004

WISCONSIN

Mortgage Associates, Inc.
125 East Wells Street
Milwaukee, Wisconsin 53202

Continental Mortgage Insurance,
Inc.
2 East Gilman Street
Madison, Wisconsin 53701

Republic Realty Mortgage
Corporation
161 West Wisconsin Avenue
Milwaukee, Wisconsin 53203

Pension Funds, Foundations, and Money Managers

GENERAL DEFINITION OF PENSION FUNDS

Pension funds are one of the newest groups of major lenders to become active in the real estate financing field. They are more diverse in characteristics and were less regulated in investment policy than most other institutions until 1974. The Pension Reform Act of that year, officially designated the Employee Retirement Income Security Act of 1974, P.L. 93-406, adopted the most sweeping overhaul of pension plans and employee benefit rules in our history.

These rules, which are both tax and no-tax in scope, affect every pension or employee benefit plan. The law features tight fiduciary rules, audited financial statements for plans, and a Pension Benefit Guaranty Corporation insures plans against failure. The Treasury and Labor departments are responsible for administering the employee plan structure. In recent years the pension funds have experienced rapid growth and have become a powerful force in mortgage investments.

With their increasing assets, second only in volume to life insurance companies, the pension funds are moving steadily into the mortgage loan and real estate acquisition field. Through the years, pension funds have invested in government securities and stocks and bonds since their founding during the last quarter of the nineteenth century.

Checking with unions, government employee groups, or companies and industries in the local area is the best way to find out if their pension funds make mortgage loans. Real estate brokers, bankers, or attorneys also may know of available financing through pension funds.

These funds, however, usually delegate their investment management to professional portfolio managers and the trust and investment departments of major commercial banks and insurance companies. To contact portfolio managers, use the list in this chapter. To reach bank trust managers, refer to the list in this book on commercial banks and write to the manager of the trust investment department.

The insurance companies that invest for pension funds do so either through a special investment department or through their own investment departments which have long been organized and investing for the insurance company and its policy holders.

A BRIEF HISTORY

The American Express Agency brought out the first pension plan in 1875, and by 1905, railroads and public utilities were organizing their own pension funds which spread to other industries in the decade to follow.

In the 1920's, life insurance companies began to sell group annuity policies. The civil service retirement system was established in 1920, and the Old Age and Survivors Insurance Plan under the Social Security program laid the groundwork for the accelerated expansion of pension funds.

During the wage and price freezes of World War II, the pension fund programs were one of the few ways employees could be rewarded.

ADMINISTRATION OF THE FUNDS

The pension funds were among the least governed of the major financial institutions, although recent federal regulations, as mentioned earlier, have attempted to eliminate some of the abuses which occurred during the 1960's and early 1970's. These abuses ran the gamut from loss of individual benefits through bad fund management, to unleashed use of monies by top executives.

There are a number of different types of pension funds each of which has many variations of central, investment and administrative methods. The more important types are:

(1) Insured — These are sold and administered by the insurance companies. Funds are invested by the insurance firm exclusively.

(2) Federally-Administered Pension Funds — These are funds entirely managed by the federal government. Monies are principally invested in U. S. Treasury obligations.

(3) Local and State Government Pension Funds — These funds may be good sources for future investments in real estate since most of their current investments are in fixed-income investments. Most of the money they now have invested in real estate is in mortgages with FHA and VA guarantees.

(4) Non-insured Corporate Pension Funds — This group is the largest and most active of the pension funds. Most of these have been managed by a few of the larger banks for many years, but the trend is away from this type of management and investment since the success of many of the investments has been less than spectacular. So, portfolio managers and regional commercial banks are attracting an increasing amount of the funds' business. Trustees administer these pension funds,

they may handle the investments themselves. In most cases, they have one or more professional managers take on this assignment.

If trustees do invest, the group is called a self-administered pension fund. General Electric is one of the largest of these.

LENDING POLICIES AND RECENT TRENDS

Pension funds usually consider mortgages and real estate ownership as an alternative to investing in bonds. In the past, bonds have cost less to oversee and manage than properties. For this reason, there has been a trend toward setting up intermediary organizations which acquire and manage realty investments for the pension funds.

The largest amounts of these funds have traditionally gone into Federal Housing Administration- and Veterans Administration-insured mortgages.

It can be reasonably expected there will be a continuous flow of investments into mortgages, long-term sale leasebacks, and property acquisitions.

It is estimated that by 1980 there will be $215 billion in private non-insured pension funds. If present trends continue, seven to 10 percent of this money could be invested in real estate for a potential of $15 to $21.5 billion dollars.

This investment would be accomplished by the organization of commingled funds (those joined from multi-sources for investment strength and lower administrative costs) by money managers, Wall Street houses, insurance companies, and banks.

When there is a shortage of real estate funds from savings and loans, insurance companies and mortgage trusts, pension funds will tend to enter the field because of the higher returns which will be available to them.

FOUNDATIONS AND ENDOWMENT FUNDS

The larger foundations and endowment funds are sources of money for real estate financing, but they are more difficult to locate and develop working relationships with. Contact is usually best made through an investment banker, money manager, mortgage banker, or the trust department of a commercial bank.

Sometimes one will be successful in reaching these funds directly, especially if the fund chosen is in the same area as the property.

Since these sources are so widespread, diversified, and subject to changes in assets and policies, it is impractical to include them in this reference.

Detailed lists of endowment funds and foundations can be found in the reference section of any public, college or university library. Look in the card section under the subject, foundations. These are available for the United States, Canada, South and Latin America, Africa, and Asia.

MONEY MANAGERS

The following list consists of money managers who are either bank trust departments, corporations, or individuals specializing in managing funds for others. Most of these managers are responsible for investing large sums of pension fund, trust, endowment, and foundation money in private and public securities as well as in real estate ownership and mortgages. They can be contacted directly or through a mortgage banker or investment banker, depending upon the nature of the realty investment involved.

Post & Astrop
1500 Rhodes — Haverty Building
Atlanta, Georgia 30303

Templeton, Dobrow & Vance, Inc.
177 North Dean Street
Englewood, New Jersey 07631

Scudder, Stevens & Clark
345 Park Avenue
New York, New York 10022

Windsor Association, Inc.
954 1 Main Place
Dallas, Texas 75250

Professional Economics, Inc.
850 Boylston Street
Chestnut Hill, Massachusetts 02167

Trainer, Wortham & Company, Inc.
345 Park Avenue
New York, New York 10022

Standish, Ayer & Wood, Inc.
50 Congress Street
Boston, Massachusetts 02109

Pulsifier & Hutner, Inc.
14 Wall Street
New York, New York 10005

Securities Counsel, Inc.
408 Wildwood Avenue
Jackson, Michigan 49201

Stein, Roe & Farnham
150 South Wacker Drive
Chicago, Illinois 60606

Fayez Sarofim & Company
1405 First City National Bank Bldg.
Houston, Texas 77002

Aetna Life & Casualty Company
151 Farmington Avenue
Hartford, Connecticut 06115

American Express Asset
Management Company
550 Laurel Street
San Francisco, California 94120

Alliance Capital Management
Corporation
140 Broadway
New York City, New York 10005

Boyd Watterson & Company
1500 Union Commerce Building
Cleveland, Ohio 44115

Campbell, Henderson & Company
3100 First National Bank Building
Dallas, Texas 75202

David L. Babson & Company, Inc.
1 Boston Place
Boston, Massachusetts 02108

Cooks & Bieler, Inc.
Philadelphia National Bank Building
Broad & Chestnut Streets
Philadelphia, Pennsylvania 19107

Davidge & Company
1747 Pennsylvania Avenue N. W.
Washington, D. C. 20006

Eaton & Howard, Inc.
24 Federal Street
Boston, Massachusetts 02110

James Hotchkiss Associates, Inc.
208 South LaSalle Street
Chicago, Illinois 60604

Dale A. Lindsay
21 West Putnum Avenue
Greenwich, Connecticut 06830

McCuen & McCuen, Inc.
2020 Union Bank Building
San Diego, California 92101

Brundage, Story & Rose
90 Broad Street
New York, New York 10004

Hunter, Miller & Fleming, Inc.
120 Montgomery Street
San Francisco, California 94104

Douglas T. Johnson & Company, Inc.
460 Park Avenue
New York, New York 10022

Arthur H. Spiegel,
    Investment Counsel
504 Sunshine Building
Albuquerque, New Mexico 87101

Dodge & Cox, Inc.
3500 Crocker Plaza,
    Post at Montgomery Street
San Francisco, California

Neville, Rodie & Shaw, Inc.
100 Park Avenue
New York, New York 10017

Everett Harris & Company
550 South Flower Street, Room 719
Los Angeles, California 90017

Alexander, Van Cleef,
    Jordan & Wood, Inc.
National City Bank Building
Cleveland, Ohio 44114

Gofen & Glossberg
135 South LaSalle Street
Chicago, Illinois 60603

Clifford Associates
639 South Spring Street
Los Angeles, California 90014

Heber-Fuger-Wendin, Inc.
810 Ford Building
Detroit, Michigan

Franklin Cole & Company, Inc.
2 Wall Street
New York, New York 10005

Danforth Associates
384 Washington Street
Wellesley Hills, Massachusetts 02181

Mairs & Power, Inc.
West 2062 First National
    Bank Building
St. Paul, Minnesota 55101

Chase Investment
    Counsel Corporation
415 4th Street N. E.
Charlottesville, Virginia 22901

Paul, Armstrong & Tindall, Inc.
9601 Wilshire Blvd.
Beverly Hills, California 90210

John N. Blewer, Inc.
685 Fifth Avenue
New York, New York 10022

Argus Investors' Counsel, Inc.
140 Broadway
New York, New York 10005

Wentworth, Dahl & Belden
2900 Crocker Plaza
San Francisco, California 94104

Stephenson & Evers
220 Montgomery Street
San Francisco, California 94104

John G. Pell & Company
1 Wall Street
New York, New York 10005

T. Rowe Price & Associates, Inc.
1 Charles Center
Baltimore, Maryland 21201

Frederic Samuels
1747 Van Buren Street, Suite 950
Hollywood, Florida 33020

Loomis, Sayles & Company, Inc.
225 Franklin Street
Boston, Massachusetts 02110

Montag & Caldwell, Inc.
2901 First National Bank Tower
Atlanta, Georgia 30303

Lionel D. Edie & Company
530 Fifth Avenue
New York, New York 10022

Bridges Investment Counsel, Inc.
256 Swanson Building
8401 West Dodge Road
Omaha, Nebraska 68114

Neil F. Campbell, Inc.
10889 Wilshire Blvd., Suite 945
Los Angeles, California 90024

E. W. Axe & Company, Inc.
400 Benedict Avenue
Tarrytown, New York 10591

Beck, Mack & Oliver
6 East 43rd Street
New York, New York 10017

Dahlberg, Kelly and Wisdom, Inc.
803 Hibernia Bank Building
New Orleans, Louisiana 70112

Chemical Bank
20 Pine Street
New York, New York 10015

Citizens & Southern National Bank
35 Broad Street
N. W. Atlanta, Georgia 30301

City Bank & Trust Company
161-163 W. Michigan Avenue
Jackson, Michigan 49201

Cleveland Trust Company
900 Euclid Avenue
Cleveland, Ohio 44101

Colonial Management
 Associates, Inc.
75 Federal Street
Boston, Massachusetts 02110

Colorado National Bank
17th & Champa Streets
Denver, Colorado 80217

Connecticut Bank & Trust Company
One Constitution Plaza
Hartford, Connecticut 06115

Connecticut General Life
 Insurance Co.
900 Cottage Grove Road
Bloomfield, Connecticut 06002

Continental Illinois National Bank
 & Trust Co. of Chicago
231 South La Salle Street
Chicago, Illinois 60693

Criterion Capital Management
 Company
One Constitution Plaza
Hartford, Connecticut 06115

Crocker Investment
 Management Corporation
One Montgomery Street
San Francisco, California 94138

Crocker National Bank
One Montgomery Street
San Francisco, California 94138

Chase Investors
 Management Corporation
One Chase Manhattan Plaza
New York, New York 10005

Detroit Bank & Trust Company
Fort and Washington Blvd.
Detroit, Michigan 48231

Dreyfus-Marine Midland, Inc.
767 Fifth Avenue
New York, New York 10022

F. Eberstadt & Company, Inc.
61 Broadway
New York, New York 10006

Equitable Life Assurance
 Society of the U.S.
1285 Avenue of the Americas
New York, New York 10019

Farmers Bank of the State
 of Delaware
Dover, Delaware 19801

The Fidelity Bank
1200 E. Lancaster Avenue
Rosemont, Pennsylvania 19010

Fidelity Mutual Life
 Insurance Company
Fidelity Mutual Life Building
Philadelphia, Pennsylvania 19101

Fidelity Union Trust Company
765 Broad Street
Newark, New Jersey 07101

Fiduciary Trust Company
of New York
1 Wall Street
New York, New York 10005

Massachusetts Mutual Life
Insurance Company
1295 State Street
Springfield, Massachusetts 01111

Mathers & Company, Inc.
One First National Plaza
Chicago, Illinois 60670

Midlantic National Bank
744 Broad Street
Newark, New Jersey 07101

Mellon National Bank
& Trust Company
Mellon Bank Building
525 William Penn Place
Pittsburgh, Pennsylvania 15230

Morgan Guaranty Trust Company
of New York
23 Wall Street
New York, New York 10015

NN Investment Services, Inc.
731 N. Jackson Street
Milwaukee, Wisconsin 53202

National Bank of Detroit
Woodward Avenue at Fort Street
Box 116
Detroit, Michigan 48232

National Bank of Alaska
Fourth and E. Box 660
Anchorage, Alaska 99501

National Bank of Commerce
45 South Second Street
Memphis, Tennessee 38101

National City Bank of Cleveland
623 Euclid Avenue
Cleveland, Ohio 44114

National Boulevard Bank of Chicago
400-410 North Michigan Avenue
Chicago, Illinois 60611

National Bank of Commerce
of Seattle
Second Avenue at Spring Street
Seattle, Washington 98101

Oppenheimer & Company
One New York Plaza
New York, New York 10004

Northwestern National Bank
9th & Main Streets
Sioux Falls, South Dakota 57262

Northern Trust Company
La Salle and Monroe Streets
Chicago, Illinois 60690

National Shawmut Bank of Boston
40 Water Street
Boston, Massachusetts 02109

Republic National Bank of Dallas
Pacific & Ervary Streets
Dallas, Texas 75222

Pittsburgh National Bank
Fifth Avenue & Wood Street
Pittsburgh, Pennsylvania 15230

Pacific National Bank of Washington
1215 Fourth Avenue
Seattle, Washington 98111

Philadelphia National Bank
Broad & Chestnut Streets
Philadelphia, Pennsylvania 19119

The Prudential Insurance Company
of America
Prudential Plaza
Newark, New Jersey 07101

Seattle-First National Bank
1001 Fourth Avenue
Seattle, Washington 98124

Boston Company of the Southeast
One Boston Place
Boston, Massachusetts 02106

Smith, Barney and Company, Inc.
1345 Avenue of the Americas
New York, New York 10019

Wilmington Trust Company
10th and Market Streets
Wilmington, Delaware 19899

United Bank of Denver
1740 Broadway
Denver, Colorado 80202

Valley National Bank of Arizona
241 No. Central Avenue
Phoenix, Arizona 85001

Wachovia Bank & Trust Company
301 North Main Street
Winston-Salem, North Carolina 27102

Wells Fargo Bank, N.A.
464 California Street
San Francisco, California 94120

Western Asset Management Services
600 South Spring Street
Los Angeles, California 90054

U.S. Trust Company of New York
45 Wall Street
New York, New York 10005

United States National Bank
of Oregon
309 Southwest 6th Avenue
Portland, Oregon 97204

First City National Bank of Houston
1001 Main Street
Houston, Texas 77002

Fifth Third Bank
38 Fountain Square Plaza
Cincinnati, Ohio 45202

First National Bank in Dallas
P. O. Box 6031
Dallas, Texas 75222

Idaho First National Bank
10th & Idaho Streets
Boise, Idaho 83727

Indiana National Bank
One Indiana Square
Indianapolis, Indiana 46204

John Hancock Mutual Life Insurance
200 Berkeley Street
Boston, Massachusetts 02117

Industrial Bank of Rhode Island
111 Westminister Street
Providence, Rhode Island 02903

Irving Trust Company
1 Wall Street
New York, New York 10015

Kuhn Loeb & Company
40 Wall Street
New York, New York 10005

Lazard Freres & Company
1 Rockefeller Plaza
New York, New York 10020

Lehman Brothers Inc.
1 William St.
New York, New York 10004

Liberty National Bank
& Trust Company
100 Broadway
Oklahoma City, Oklahoma 73102

Lincoln First Banks, Inc.
183 Main Street E.
Rochester, New York 14603

Loeb Rhoades & Company
42 Wall Street
New York, New York 10005

Bank of Southwest N.A.
910 Travis Street
Houston, Texas 77002

M & I Investment Management
Corporation
770 N. Water Street
Milwaukee, Wisconsin 53202

Manufacturers National Bank
151 W. Fort Street
Detroit, Michigan 48226

IDS Advisory Corporation
IDS Tower
Minneapolis, Minnesota

Bankers Life Company
711 High Street
Des Moines, Iowa 50307

Bankers Life Insurance Company
of Nebraska
Cotner & O Streets
Lincoln, Nebraska 68501

Bernstein — Macaulay, Inc.
767 Fifth Avenue
New York City, New York 10022

Boatmen's National Bank of St. Louis
Box 236
St. Louis, Missouri 63166

The Boston Company Institutional
Investors, Inc.
One Boston Place
Boston, Massachusetts 02106

Boston Company Investment Council
One Boston Place
Boston, Massachusetts 02106

The Boston Company
of Louisville, Inc.
One Boston Place
Boston, Massachusetts 02106

Central National Bank of Cleveland
800 Superior Avenue
Cleveland, Ohio 44114

Central Trust Company
Fourth and Vine Streets
Cincinnati, Ohio 45202

Central Penn National Bank
One Belmont Avenue
Bala Cynwyd, Pennsylvania 19004

Bank of California
400 California Street
San Francisco, California 94104

American Fletcher National Bank
  & Trust Company
101 Monument Circle
10 E. Market Street
Indianapolis, Indiana 46204

BA Investment Management
  Corporation
Bank of America Center
San Francisco, California 94120

David L. Babson & Company, Inc.
301 West 11th Street
Kansas City, Missouri 64105

Bank of North Dakota
700 Main Street
Bismarck, North Dakota 58501

Bankers Trust Company
16 Wall Street
New York, New York 10005

Boston Company, Inc.
One Boston Place
Boston, Massachusetts 02106

Chemical Bank New York Trust
  Company
20 Pine Street
New York, New York 10005

National Detroit Corporation
Woodward Ave. at Fort Street,
  Box 116
Detroit, Michigan 48232

BankAmerica Corporation
Bank of America Center
San Francisco, California 94120

Mercantile Bankshares Corporation
Two Hopkins Plaza
Baltimore, Maryland 21203

First Pennsylvania Corporation
Packard Building,
15th & Chestnut Streets
Philadelphia, Pennsylvania

BanCal Tri-State Corporation
400 California Street
San Francisco, California 94104

Republic of Texas Corporation
Dallas, Texas

Fidelity Union Bancorporation
765 Broad Street
Newark, New Jersey 07101

First Union, Inc.
510 Locust Street
St. Louis, Missouri 63101

Northwest Bancorporation
1200 Northwestern Bank Building
Minneapolis, Minnesota 55480

Clevetrust Realty Investors
1525 Investment Plaza Building
Cleveland, Ohio 44114

The Bank of New York
48 Wall Street
New York, New York 10005

Bankers Trust Company
280 Park Avenue
New York, New York 10017

Chase Manhattan Corporation
One Chase Manhattan Plaza
New York, New York 10005

Manufacturers Hanover Corporation
229 South State Street
Dover, Delaware 19901

Continental Illinois Corporation
231 South La Salle Street
Chicago, Illinois 60693

Marine Midland Banks, Inc.
250 Park Avenue
New York, New York 10017

Wilmington Trust Company
10th and Market Streets
Wilmington, Delaware 19899

First Bank System, Inc.
14th Floor, First National
  Bank Building
Minneapolis, Minnesota 55480

Detroit Bank & Trust Company
Fort and Washington Blvd.
Detroit, Michigan 48231

Citizens & Southern Corporation
46 Broad Street
Charleston, South Carolina 29402

J. P. Morgan & Company, Inc.
23 Wall Street
New York, New York 10005

First Chicago Corporation
One First National Plaza
Chicago, Illinois 60670

Mellon National Corporation
P. O. Box 15629
Pittsburgh, Pennsylvania 15244

Harris Bankcorp, Inc.
111 West Monroe St.
Chicago, Illinois 60690

Nortrust Corporation
50 South LaSalle Street
Chicago, Illinois 60690

Western Bancorporation
600 South Spring St.
Los Angeles, California 90054

Girard Trust Bank
One Girard Plaza
Philadelphia, Pennsylvania

Charter New York Corporation
One Wall Street
New York, New York 10005

Wells Fargo & Company
420 Montgomery Street
San Francisco, California 94104

Security Pacific Corporation
561 South Spring Street
Los Angeles, California 90051

Fidelco Growth Investors
1200 E. Lancaster Avenue
Rosemont, Pennsylvania 19010

Wachovia Corporation
301 North Main Street
Winston Salem, North Carolina 27102

Crocker National Corporation
One Montgomery Street
San Francisco, California 94138

Manufacturers National Corporation
151 West Fort Street
Detroit, Michigan 48226

Mercantile Bancorp, Inc.
721 Locust Street
St. Louis, Missouri 63101

Provident National Corporation
Broad & Chestnut Sts.
P. O. Box 7648
Philadelphia, Pennsylvania 19101

CBT Corporation
One Constitution Plaza
Hartford, Connecticut 06115

State Street Bank & Trust Company
225 Franklin Street
Boston, Massachusetts 02101

Trust Company of Georgia
Pryor Street & Edgewood Avenue
Atlanta, Georgia 30303

Lincoln First Banks, Inc.
One Lincoln First Square
Rochester, New York 14643

National City Corporation
623 Euclid Avenue
Cleveland, Ohio 44114

Pittsburgh National Corp.
Fifth Avenue & Wood Street
Pittsburgh, Pennsylvania 15222

Fiduciary Trust Company
1 Wall Street
New York, New York 10005

Hartford National Bank
  & Trust Company
777 MainStreet
Hartford, Connecticut 06115

First National Bank
100 Federal Street
Boston, Massachusetts 02110

Citicorp Factors, Inc.
399 Park Avenue
New York, New York 10022

United States Trust Company
45 Wall Street
New York, New York 10005

First International Bancshares, Inc.
1401 Elm Street
Dallas, Texas 75222

Sarasota Bank & Trust Company
1601 Main Street
Sarasota, Florida 33578

First Pennsylvania Banking
  & Trust Company
15th & Chestnut Streets
Philadelphia, Pennsylvania 19102

First Seneca Bank
  & Trust Company
248 Seneca Street
Oil City, Pennsylvania 16301

First Trust Company of St. Paul
332 Minnesota Street
St. Paul, Minnesota 55101

First Union National Bank
301 S. Tryon Street
Charlotte, North Carolina 28201

First Wisconsin Trust Company
735 N. Water Street
Milwaukee, Wisconsin 53202

Goldman, Sachs & Company
55 Broad Street
New York, New York 10004

Mercantile-Safe Deposit
  & Trust Company
2 Hopkins Plaza
Baltimore, Maryland 21203

Mercantile Trust Company
8th E. Locust Street
St. Louis, Missouri 63101

Metropolitan Life
  Insurance Company
1 Madison Avenue
New York, New York 10010

Minnesota Mutual Life
  Insurance Company
10601 Wayzata Blvd.
Hopkins, Minnesota 55343

Harris Trust & Savings Bank
111 W. Monroe Street
Chicago, Illinois 60690

Hartford National Bank
  & Trust Company
777 Main Street
Hartford, Connecticut 06115

Houston National Bank
1010 Milam
Houston, Texas 77001

Security National Bank
115 Broad Hollow Road
Melville, L. I., New York 11746

Security Pacific National Bank
P. O. Box 2097 Terminal Annex
Los Angeles, California 90051

Security Trust Company
  of Rochester
One East Avenue
Rochester, New York 14638

Standard & Poor's Intercapital
  Dynamics Fund, Inc.
1775 Broadway
New York, New York 10019

State Street Research
  & Management Company
225 Franklin Street
Boston, Massachusetts 02110

Northwestern National Bank
  of Minneapolis
7th and Marquette Avenue
Minneapolis, Minnesota 55480

Old Stone Bank
Providence, Rhode Island 02901

Pacific Mutual Life
  Insurance Company
700 Newport Center Drive
Newport Beach, California 92663

Putnam Advisory Company, Inc.
265 Franklin Street
Boston, Massachusetts 02110

Rhode Island Hospital Trust
  National Bank
15 Westminster Street
Providence, Rhode Island 02903

Riggs National Bank
1503 Pennsylvania Ave. N. W.
Washington, D. C. 20005

St. Louis Union Trust Company
510 Locust Street
St. Louis, Missouri 63101

Brown Brothers Harriman
& Company
59 Wall Street
New York, New York 10005

Reich & Tang, Inc.
230 Park Avenue
New York, New York 10017

Rothschild L. F. & Company
99 William Street
New York, New York 10038

First National Bank
P. O. Box 38
Kansas City, Missouri 64141

First National Bank
42 N. Main Street
Mansfield, Ohio 44902

First National Bank
& Trust Company
P. O. Box 927
Augusta, Georgia 30903

First National Bank
& Trust Company
120 North Robinson Street
Oklahoma City, Oklahoma 73102

First National Bank
& Trust Company of Tulsa
Box 1
Tulsa, Oklahoma 74193

Trust Company of Georgia
Pryor Street and Edgewood Avenue
Atlanta, Georgia 30303

Union Trust Company
300 Main Street
Stamford, Connecticut 06904

Union National Bank of Pittsburgh
Wood Street & Fourth Avenue
Pittsburgh, Pennsylvania 15230

Toledo Trust Company
P. O. Box 1628
Toledo, Ohio 43607

Transamerica Investment
Management Company
600 Montgomery Street
San Francisco, California 94111

Travelers Insurance Company
One Tower Square
Hartford, Connecticut 06115

Society National Bank of Cleveland
127 Public Square
Cleveland, Ohio 44114

Schroder Naess & Thomas
One State Street
New York, New York 10004

Scudder, Stevens & Clark
10 Post Office Square
Boston, Massachusetts 02109

First Kentucky Trust Company
Fifth & Court Place
Louisville, Kentucky 40202

First National Bank of Atlanta
P. O. Box 4148
Atlanta, Georgia 30318

First National City Bank
399 Park Avenue
New York, New York 10022

The First National Bank of Boston
100 Federal Street
Boston, Massachusetts 02110

First National Bank of Birmingham
Birmingham, Alabama 35288

First National Bank of Chicago
One First National Plaza
Chicago, Illinois 60670

First National Bank & Trust Co.
of Racine
Racine, Wisconsin 53403

Girard Bank
One Girard Plaza
Philadelphia, Pennsylvania 19101

General American Investors
Company, Inc.
330 Madison Avenue
New York, New York 10017

First National Bank of Cincinnati
111 E. Fourth Street
Cincinnati, Ohio 45202

First National Bank of Memphis
165 Madison Avenue
Memphis, Tennessee

First National Bank of Minneapolis
120 South Sixth Street
Minneapolis, Minnesota 55402

First National Bank of Oregon
1300 S. W. 5th Avenue
Portland, Oregon 97201

First National Bank of Toledo
Madison at Huron Street
Toledo, Ohio 43604

First National Bank of Denver
621 17th Street
Denver, Colorado 80202

Manufacturers Hanover
  Trust Company
350 Park Avenue
New York, New York 10022

Marine Midland Bank
1 Marine Midland Plaza
Rochester, New York 14639

Marine National Exchange Bank
111 East Wisconsin Avenue
Milwaukee, Wisconsin 53202

Marine National Bank
111 East Wisconsin Avenue
Neenah, Wisconsin 54956

Clark, Dodge & Company, Inc.
140 Broadway
New York, New York 10005

Columbia Management Company
621 S. W. Morrison Street
Portland, Oregon 97205

Delaware Investment Advisers, Inc.
7 Pennsylvania Plaza
Philadelphia, Pennsylvania 19103

Drexel, Burnham & Company, Inc.
60 Broad Street
New York, New York 10004

Calvin Bullock, Ltd.
1 Wall Street
New York, New York 10005

Faulkner, Dawkins & Sullivan
One New York Plaza
New York, New York 10004

Valley Bank & Trust Company
1500 Main Street
Springfield, Massachusetts 01103

Wertheim & Company, Inc.
One Chase Manhattan Plaza
New York, New York 10005

Neuberger & Berman
120 Broadway
New York, New York 10005

Shareholders Asset
  Management Company
1888 Century Park E.
Los Angeles, California 90067

Finance Companies

AN OVERVIEW OF THIS KIND OF INSTITUTION

The finance company was originally created to make small loans to individuals for such items as automobiles, furniture, and appliances. As the commercial banks grew in this field, the small credit or finance companies began to diversify and become active in other areas of finance.

Over the years, many of them have grown into huge financial institutions with significant interests in real estate. Ford Motor Credit Corporation and C.I.T. Corporation, among others, have been most aggressive in various phases of real estate financing.

KINDS OF FINANCING CONDUCTED

The finance companies most desired loan is usually short-term construction; however, these firms are very creative. They buy or finance receivables for land development companies, make interim loans of various types and descriptions, and provide junior financing, including second mortgages, wrap-arounds, and others.

Some have also been known to make long-term loans, acquire sale leasebacks, issue standbys, and provide joint venture funds to developers of shopping centers, apartment houses, and other projects.

SHORT-TERM AND INTERIM LOANS

These companies underwriting policies for short-term and interim loans are similar to those of the mortgage trusts. They are extremely security-conscious and require meaningful collateral for loans. Often a loan will be granted based on security of different kinds.

As an example, a Miami-based restaurant chain sought a loan from a Midwestern diversified financial company. A commitment was issued for a $3.0 million, 15-year loan with a seven-year balloon. There was no prepayment penalty after the third year, but the security required for the loan included the guarantee of the company, pledging of the real estate, personal guarantees, the assignment of publicly traded stock, and other vacant land in Texas.

Since the funds allowed the young firm to begin a much-needed expansion program, no company equity was given up, and there was an easy prepayment penalty, management decided to accept the loan.

All loans made by finance companies on real estate are not always this demanding. These companies can be most creative and helpful in aiding a developer or investor who has a worthwhile project.

LONG-TERM LOANS

Occasionally, but not often, finance companies will make long-term loans. These are usually in conjunction with land acquisition and construction loans as opposed to outright long-term mortgages.

From time to time, they also buy long-term net leases or sale leasebacks and will consider, with proper security, the financing of buildings on leased land. They are also a good source for special-purpose properties such as hotels and motels, restaurant chains, and hospitals.

GENERAL REGULATIONS

Finance companies are not regulated by the federal government. They are subject to the usury laws in the individual states where they operate.

The borrower should investigate maximum percentages on loans and other standards established for finance companies in the state where he hopes to transact a loan.

HOW TO TRANSACT A LOAN

The companies may be contacted directly by calling or writing the real estate investment officer for the area of the country where the particular property is located. They also operate through mortgage bankers and brokers, so these may be queried.

Mortgage loans are processed much the same way as the mortgage investment trust does. An application is submitted with an application fee. If the application is approved, the borrower is required to make a further deposit assuring the lender he will not back out of the deal. The total fees to this point are from one to two percent of the loan requested. This amount is usually applied to the loan at closing. Lending policies may vary slightly from company to company.

ASSESSMENT OF THE COMPANIES

Finance and credit companies making loans in the real estate field move slowly and very deliberately.

They are concerned both with the bricks and mortar aspects of the loan as well as the credit of the borrower.

They look at the borrower's track record, the economic conditions of the community in which the projects are located, and projected costs compared with those of similar projects recently completed.

MAJOR FINANCE COMPANIES

General Motors Acceptance
Corporation
767 Fifth Avenue (58th Street)
New York, New York 10022

Ford Motor Credit Company
The American Road
Dearborn, Michigan 48121

C. I. T. Financial Corporation
650 Madison Avenue
New York, New York 10022

Household Finance Corporation
Prudential Plaza
Chicago, Illinois 60601

Commercial Credit Company
300 St. Paul Place
Baltimore, Maryland 21202

Beneficial Corporation
Beneficial Building
1300 Market Street
Wilmington, Delaware 19899

Chrysler Financial Corporation
16250 Northland Drive
Southfield, Michigan 48075

Sears Roebuck Acceptance
Corporation
919 Market Street
Wilmington, Delaware 19899

Associates Corporation of
North America
1 Gulf & Western Plaza
New York, New York 10023

General Electric Credit Corporation
570 Lexington Avenue
New York, New York 10022

Avco Financial Services, Inc.
620 Newport Center Drive
Newport Beach, California 92660

Walter E. Heller International
Corporation
105 West Adams Street
Chicago, Illinois 60690

International Harvester Credit
Corporation
401 North Michigan Avenue
Chicago, Illinois 60611

Transamerica Financial Corporation
1150 South Olive Street
Los Angeles, California 90015

Montgomery Ward Credit
Corporation
4 Denny Road
Wilmington, Delaware 19809

GAC Finance Inc.
1105 Hamilton Street
Allentown, Pennsylvania 18101

James Talcott, Incorporated
1290 Avenue of the Americas
New York, New York 10019

J.C. Penney Financial Corporation
3801 Kennett Pike
Wilmington, Delaware 19807

Westinghouse Credit Corporation
Three Gateway Center
Pittsburgh, Pennsylvania 15222

American Investment Company
8251 Maryland Avenue
St. Louis, Missouri 63105

American Finance System, Inc.
1100 Wilmington Trust Building
Wilmington, Delaware 19801

Liberty Loan Corporation
7711 Bonhomme Avenue
St. Louis, Missouri 63105

American Credit Corporation
American Building
201 South Tryon Street
Charlotte, North Carolina 28234

Allis-Chalmers Credit Corporation
Milwaukee, Wisconsin 53201

Boise Cascade Credit Corporation
Boise, Idaho 83701

Mack Financial Corporation
Allentown, Pennsylvania 18105

Family Finance Corporation
300 Delaware Avenue
Wilmington, Delaware 19899

Fruehauf Finance Company
10900 Harper Avenue
Detroit, Michigan 48232

Credithrift Financial Corporation
601 N.W. Second Street
Evansville, Indiana 47701

Borg-Warner Acceptance
Corporation
4001 West Devon Avenue
Chicago, Illinois 60646

ITT Thorp Corporation
Thorp, Wisconsin 54771

John Deere Credit Company
Suite 600, 1 East 1st Street
Reno, Nevada 89501

W.T. Grant Financial Corporation
3945 Kennett Pike
Wilmington, Delaware 19807

McDonnell Douglas Finance
Corporation
3855 Lakewood Boulevard
Long Beach, California 90846

General Finance Corporation
1301 Central Street
Evanston, Illinois 60201

J.I. Case Credit Corporation
700 State Street
Racine, Washington 53404

Capital Finance Corporation
100 East Broad Street
Columbus, Ohio 43215

ITT Aetna Corporation
1900 Hempstead Turnpike
East Meadow, New York 11554

Dial Financial Corporation
207 Ninth Street
Des Moines, Iowa 50307

Clark Equipment Credit Corporation
324 East Dewey Avenue
Buchanan, Michigan 49107

American Express Credit
Corporation
401 Hackensack Avenue
Hackensack, New Jersey 07601

White Motor Credit Corporation
3411 Silverside Road
Wilmington, Delaware 19810

Midland-Guardian Company
111 East 4th Street
Cincinnati, Ohio 45202

Allstate Financial Corporation
1601 Concord Pike
Wilmington, Delaware 19803

Gamble Aldens Finance Company
5000 West Roosevelt Road
Chicago, Illinois 60607

Honeywell Finance Inc.
2701 Fourth Avenue South
Minneapolis, Minnesota 55408

Interstate Securities Company
3430 Broadway
Kansas City, Missouri 64141

First Pennsylvania Financial
Services, Inc.
S.E. 15th and Chestnut Streets
Philadelphia, Pennsylvania 19102

Singer Credit Corporation
30 Rockefeller Plaza
New York, New York 10020

Massey Ferguson Credit Corporation
1901 Bell Avenue
Des Moines, Iowa 50315

Southwestern Investment Company
205 East 10th
Amarillo, Texas 79167

Aetna Business Credit, Inc.
111 East River Drive
East Hartford, Connecticut 06108

Allied Stores Credit Corporation
221 Bergen South Mall
Paramus, New Jersey 07652

Budget Capital Corporation
6436 Wilshire Boulevard
Los Angeles, California 90048

USI Credit Corporation
529 Fifth Avenue
New York, New York 10017

USLIFE Credit Corporation
125 Maiden Lane
New York, New York 10038

Macy Credit Corporation
c/o Macy's Roosevelt Field
Garden City, New York 11530

Standard Financial Corporation
277 Park Avenue
New York, New York 10017

Firstmark Financial Corporation
110 East Washington Street
Indianapolis, Indiana 46204

Mercantile Financial Corporation
69 West Washington Street
Chicago, Illinois 60602

Union Investment Company
First National Building
Detroit, Michigan 48226

Postal Finance Company
810-14 Pierce Street
Sioux City, Iowa 51102

Appliance Buyers Credit Corporation
200 Broad Street
St. Joseph, Michigan 49085

Amoco Credit Corporation
200 East Randolph Street
Chicago, Illinois 60601

May Department Stores Credit
  Company
6th 7th Olive & Locust
St. Louis, Missouri 63101

Ritter Financial Corporation
Church Road and Greenwood Avenue
Wyncote, Pennsylvania 19095

Carte Blanche Corporation
3460 Wilshire Boulevard
Los Angeles, California 90005

John P. Maguire & Co., Inc.
1290 Avenue of the Americas
New York, New York 10019

A.J. Armstrong Co., Inc.
850 Third Avenue
New York, New York 10022

Local Loan Company
105 West Madison Street
Chicago, Illinois 60602

Public Loan Company
Plaza Drive
Vestal, New York 13850

Commercial Alliance Corporation
770 Lexington Avenue
New York, New York 10021

Lane Wood, Incorporated
1309 Main Street
Dallas, Texas 75202

Sunoco Credit Corporation
1200 Philadelphia Pike
Wilmington, Delaware 19809

Associated Dry Goods Credit
  Corporation
417 Fifth Avenue
New York, New York 10016

Diners' Club, Inc.
10 Columbus Circle
New York, New York 10019

Stephenson Finance Company, Inc.
518 South Irby Street
Florence, South Carolina 29501

Fidelity Acceptance Corporation
910 Plymouth Building
Minneapolis, Minnesota 55402

International T & T Credit
  Corporation
1900 Hempstead Turnpike
East Meadow, New York 11554

Northwest Acceptance Corporation
310 N.E. Oregon Street
Portland, Oregon 97214

Mastan Company, Inc.
640 Fifth Avenue
New York, New York 10019

Kentucky Finance Company, Inc.
500 Kentucky Central Building
Lexington, Kentucky 40507

Signal Finance Corporation
Three Gateway Center
Pittsburgh, Pennsylvania 15222

Pacar Financial Corporation
Post Office Box 1518
Bellevue, Washington 98004

Sun Finance & Loan Company
1015 Euclid Avenue
Cleveland, Ohio 44115

Oxford Finance Companies, Inc.
6701 North Broad Street
Philadelphia, Pennsylvania 19126

Government Employees Corporation
7551 West Alameda Avenue
Denver, Colorado 80217

Rosenthal & Rosenthal, Inc.
1451 Broadway
New York, New York 10036

Government Employees Financial
    Corporation
7551 West Alameda Avenue
Denver, Colorado 80217

Century Acceptance Corporation
1003 Walnut Street
Kansas City, Missouri 64106

FBS Financial, Inc.
1400, First National Bank Building
Minneapolis, Minnesota 55480

Allied Finance Company
2808 Fairmont Street
Dallas 1, Texas 75201

Local Finance Corporation
State Road 3 North 2 Mile
Hartford City, Indiana 47348

Cessna Finance Corporation
5800 East Pawnee
Wichita, Kansas 67201

Local Finance Corporation
399 Westminister Street
Providence, Rhode Island 02903

American Standard Credit, Inc.
390 #8 Parkway Center Building
Pittsburgh, Pennsylvania 15220

Commercial Discount Corporation
105 West Adams Street, Room 300
Chicago, Illinois 60603

DAC Corporation
3974 Woodcock Drive
Jacksonville, Florida 32207

Koehring Finance Corporation
780 North Water Street
Milwaukee, Wisconsin 53201

Gamble-Skogmo Acceptance
    Corporation
5100 Gamble Drive
Minneapolis, Minnesota 55440

CNA Financial
310 South Michigan Avenue
Chicago, Illinois 60604

First Charter Financial
9465 Wilshire Boulevard
Beverly Hills, California 90212

Imperial Corporation of America
P.O. Box 631
San Diego, California 92112

Equimark
Fifth Avenue at Smithfield
Pittsburgh, Pennsylvania 15222

Chubb
100 William Street
New York, New York 10038

Gilbraltar Financial Corporation
    of California
9111 Wilshire Boulevard
Beverly Hills, California 90213

Mortgage Trusts

EXPLANATION AND BACKGROUND OF THE TRUSTS

The mortgage real estate investment trust was born as an offshoot of Sections 856-58 of the Internal Revenue Code which were passed under Public Law 86-779 on September 14, 1960.

Qualified real estate investment trusts can get special tax treatment whereby they do not pay any federal income or capital gains tax on income or gains which they distribute to their shareholders, provided they distribute annually at least 90 percent of their ordinary taxable income. In a loophole in the law, REIT's are now permitted to hold back the paying of dividends for as much as two years.

The shareholder pays for the cash he receives from the REIT at capital gains rates on the capital gains distributed, no tax at all on any distribution that does not constitute taxable income or capital gains, and at his normal income tax rate for that part of the distribution which constitutes ordinary income.

The purposes for which Congress extended this conduit tax treatment to qualified REIT's are to offer an opportunity for small investors to participate in large real estate investments with expert management and on a scale previously available only to a few wealthy individuals, and to encourage the growth of investment trusts, which increase the funds available for financing of the large real estate developments and redevelopments needed in metropolitan areas.

In the early years of the trusts' development, many professionals in the real estate industry stayed away from the new entity since the law seemed complicated. Managers or advisors were also unable to find adequate monetary rewards for their efforts through the REIT's.

With understanding and use in the late 1960's, mortgage trusts became very popular and now they are a significant force in the lending community.

Recently in one year, the investment banking community raised almost $900 million in new trust issues. The mortgage trusts now have billions of dollars invested in short-, long-term, and other types of mortgage instruments.

OPERATION OF THE TRUSTS

The trusts cannot be divided into groups since in practice they can usually invest in a wide range of types of real estate, and their lending

319

practices overlap considerably. REIT's are unincorporated associations that operate in the business trust form. They own interests in real estate or mortgages and can also own real estate.

Mortgage trusts make loans for construction, development, and long-term real estate financing. Their income is derived primarily from interest earned and discounts received. They can, and do, finance every step of a real estate enterprise, including the acquisition of land, development and construction, and completion of the building. This one-stop financing gives them the opportunity to make interim or construction loans from which they get high interest rates and a relatively fast turnover.

A mortgage REIT may invest in the following:

(1) Residential Mortgages — While mortgage trusts have the ability to invest in residential mortgages, they rarely do, since returns on these types are low. Thus, it is difficult for the trusts to leverage these investments.

(2) Multi-family Residence Loans — These would include short-term loans for condominium and cooperative projects.

(3) Commercial Mortgages — These probably represent the most common type of holding since they offer the best combination of return and safety. Holdings can be diversified geographically and functionally, as between office buildings, shopping centers, etc.

(4) Construction and Development Loans — These are attractive because they offer a substantially higher return than that on straight first mortgages. These loans provide financing for land development and for the construction and improvement of buildings. The loans ordinarily run for one year but are renewable.

(5) Interim-Purchase Mortgages — These are mortgages held for interest income by the REIT. The REIT agrees to sell the mortgage back to the original holder after a designated period at cost. This is known as warehousing. These offer the trust a source of short-term income. The seller of the mortgage often is one needing funds temporarily for another purpose but who doesn't wish to liquidate permanently his interest in the mortgage.

(6) Mortgages Purchased at a Discount — Many mortgages, particularly those insured by FHA and VA, are bought at a discount. These may create a problem for the REIT. If the discount income is regarded as capital gain, then it has to be included under the 30 percent test. This test says that gross income from the sale of mortgages held less than four years (plus income from sale of securities held less than six months) can't be more than 30 percent of the trust's total income.

(7) Any Type Loan Secured by Real Estate.

The mortgage trusts must adhere to certain federal regulations that affect the manner in which they loan out funds. A summary of the most important regulations is as follows:

(1) At least 75 percent of gross income must be from real estate sources.

(2) At least 90 percent of gross income must be from conventional investment sources (interest, dividends, rentals of real property, capital gains, and real estate tax abatements or refunds).

(3) No more than 50 percent of the trust can be owned directly or indirectly by five or fewer people.

(4) Ownership of a real estate investment trust must be held by not fewer than 100 persons.

(5) The trust cannot be engaged in the business of dealing in real estate for sale. It can earn capital gains. The holding period is four years, and these gains may not exceed 30 percent in any one year.

(6) At the close of each quarter of each taxable year, at least 75 percent of the value of total assets must be invested in real estate assets, cash, receivables, and government securities.

(7) The trust must distribute 90 percent of its taxable income for each taxable year.

(8) No one individual may own more than 35 percent of the trust.

THE LONG-TERM TRUST

The basic objective of the long-term mortgage trust is to develop a portfolio of high quality long-term mortgages.

Where possible, these mortgages will provide for additional income in the form of overages, participations or even warrants, convertibles or other kickers, depending on the capabilities of the borrower.

MAKING THE LOAN

Mortgage REIT's usually have their loans approved by the finance committee or the trustees or both. Field representatives usually originate the loans from mortgage bankers or in some cases directly.

The mortgage REIT's will require all the normal data which usually accompanies a mortgage application.

Loan approval takes from 30 to 45 days from receipt of the application.

THE TOP MORTGAGE TRUSTS

	ASSETS
Chase Manhattan Mortgage & Realty Trust One Boston Place Boston, Massachusetts 02108	$752,925,000
Continental Mortgage Investors 100 Federal Street Boston, Massachusetts 02110	642,894,000
First Mortgage Investors 30 Federal Street Boston, Massachusetts 02110	615,611,000
Great American Mortgage Investors Suite 2850, Equitable Life Building 100 Peachtree Street, N.W. Atlanta, Georgia 30302	413,353,178
Citizens & Southern Realty Investors 33 North Avenue, N.E. Atlanta, Georgia 30302	409,452,747
Diversified Mortgage Investors 100 Federal Street Boston, Massachusetts 02110	364,272,000
Lomas & Nettleton Mortgage Investors 2001 Bryan Tower Dallas, Texas 75201	350,149,039
Guardian Mortgage Investors 47 West Forsyth Street Jacksonville, Florida 32203	319,245,881
C.I. Mortgage Group One Boston Place Boston, Massachusetts 02108	303,813,432
MassMutual Mortgage & Realty Investors 1295 State Street Springfield, Massachusetts 01111	295,300,073
Fidelity Mortgage Investors c/o Fidelity Mortgage Advisors, Inc. Box 4214 Jacksonville, Florida 32203	277,237,986
The Equitable Life Mortgage & Realty Investors 100 Federal Street Boston, Massachusetts 02110	267,767,693
MONY Mortgage Investors 1740 Broadway New York, New York 10019	267,041,078
Cousins Mortgage and Equity Investments 300 Interstate North Atlanta, Georgia 30339	256,430,000

Alison Mortgage Investment Trust 1900 Avenue of the Stars Los Angeles, California 90067	$220,527,157
Security Mortgage Investors 28 State Street Boston, Massachusetts 02109	218,916,602
Wells Fargo Mortgage Investors Los Angeles International Airport Post Office Box 30015, Terminal Annex Los Angeles, California 90030	215,533,000
Tri-South Mortgage Investors 15 Dunwoody Park, Suite 100 Atlanta, Georgia 30341	215,033,411
Heitman Mortgage Investors 10 South La Salle Street Chicago, Illinois 60603	206,542,972
Continental Illinois Realty One Wilshire Building Los Angeles, California 90017	204,830,000
North American Mortgage Investors 294 Washington Street Boston, Massachusetts 02108	198,746,974
Wachovia Realty Investments 1100 South Stratford Road Winston, Salem, North Carolina 27103	190,831,138
American Century Mortgage Investors 11 East Forsyth Street Jacksonville, Florida 32202	185,412,753
Northwestern Mutual Life Mortgage & Realty Investors 720 East Wisconsin Avenue Milwaukee, Wisconsin 53202	179,180,000
Mortgage Trust of America 141 Battery Street San Francisco, California	177,305,000
Capital Mortgage Investments 5530 Wisconsin Avenue Chevy Chase, Maryland 20015	174,585,228
Independence Mortgage Trust Post Office Box 866 Atlanta, Georgia 30301	164,615,700
Barnett Mortgage Trust Barnett Winston Building 720 Gilmore Street Jacksonville, Florida 32204	154,042,429
BT Mortgage Investors 225 Franklin Street Boston, Massachusetts 02110	153,818,000

HNC Mortgage & Realty Investors 830 East State Street Westport, Connecticut 06880	$153,020,000
First Pennsylvania Mortgage Trust 28 State Street Boston, Massachusetts 02109	150,656,662
Realty Refund Trust 402 Capital National Bank Building 1101 Euclid Avenue Cleveland, Ohio 44115	147,317,822
Larwin Mortgage Investors 9100 Wilshire Boulevard Beverly Hills, California 90212	146,946,257
Unionamerica Mortgage & Equity Trust 9595 Wilshire Boulevard Beverly Hills, California 90212	143,354,807
PNB Mortgage & Realty Investors 7320 Old York Road Melrose Park, Pennsylvania 19126	135,613,139
IDS Realty Trust 2400 IDS Tower Minneapolis, Minnesota 55402	126,979,226
Midland Mortgage Investors Trust Post Office Box 26648 Oklahoma City, Oklahoma 73126	119,759,177
First Wisconsin Mortgage Trust 241 West Wisconsin Avenue Milwaukee, Wisconsin 53203	117,077,561
Fidelico Growth Investors 1200 East Lancaster Avenue Rosemont, Pennsylvania 19010	115,657,495
Hamilton Investment Trust 342 Westminister Avenue Elizabeth, New Jersey 07208	115,362,038
Institutional Investors Trust 140 Broadway New York, New York 10005	115,328,434
Colwell Mortgage Trust 3223 West 6th Street Los Angeles, California 90020	111,795,830
Atico Mortgage Investors 28 State Street Boston, Massachusetts 02109	111,520,630
Gulf Mortgage & Realty Investments 1301 Gulf Life Drive Jacksonville, Florida 32207	109,192,280

Clevetrust Realty Investors 1010 Investment Plaza Building Cleveland, Ohio 44114	$108,375,000
Cameron-Brown Investment Group 4300 Six Forks Road Raleigh, North Carolina 27609	106,111,726
First of Denver Mortgage Investors First National Bank Building Box 5311 Denver, Colorado 80217	103,568,045
Beneficial Standard Mortgage Investors 3700 Wilshire Boulevard Los Angeles, California 90010	102,156,245
State Mutual Investors 440 Lincoln Street Worcester, Massachusetts 01605	99,462,000
Associated Mortgage Investors c/o Associate Mortgage Managers (Ltd.) 120 Giralda Avenue, P.O. Box 1998 Coral Gables, Florida 33134	92,168,208
Republic Mortgage Investors 2401 Douglas Road Miami, Florida 33145	91,512,646
Sutro Mortgage Investment Trust 9200 Sunset Boulevard Los Angeles, California 90069	91,196,287
Justice Mortgage Investors 505 North Ervay Dallas, Texas 75201	86,812,423
Barnes Mortgage Investment Trust 100 Federal Street Boston, Massachusetts 02110	84,969,944
American Fletcher Mortgage Investors 225 Franklin Street Boston, Massachusetts 02110	84,573,524
Palomar Mortgage Investors 5348 University Avenue San Diego, California 92105	82,531,459
Mortgage Investors of Washington 7316 Wisconsin Avenue Washington, D.C. 20014	73,474,958
Indiana Mortgage & Realty Investors 10 Light Street Baltimore, Maryland 21202	73,264,915
The Hotel Investors 10605 Concord Street Kensington, Maryland 20795	73,096,397

Baird & Warner Mortgage & Realty Investors $70,338,418
10 South La Salle Street
Chicago, Illinois 60603

Galbreath First Mortgage Investments   69,832,892
246 North High Street
Columbus, Ohio 43216

National Mortgage Fund   69,128,569
1300 East Ninth Street
Cleveland, Ohio 44114

Barnett-Winston Investment Trust   67,896,549
720 Gilmore Street
Post Office Box 2720
Jacksonville, Florida 32203

Larwin Realty & Mortgage Trust   67,858,629
9100 Wilshire Boulevard
Beverly Hills, California 90212

Citizens Mortgage Investment Trust   64,678,803
24700 Northwestern Highway
Southfield, Michigan 48075

Texas First Mortgage REIT   63,964,768
Post Office Box 1413
1919 Allen Parkway
Houston, Texas 77019

Hanover Square Realty Investors   60,774,518
90 Park Avenue
New York, New York 10016

NJB Prime Investors   52,467,131
950 Clifton Avenue
Clifton, New Jersey 07013

Lincoln Mortgage Investors   50,706,000
609 South Grand Avenue
Los Angeles, California 90017

Mortgage Growth Investors   48,774,951
294 Washington Street
Boston, Massachusetts 02108

Northwestern Financial Investors   48,183,443
500 East Morehead Street
Post Office Box 10636
Charlotte, North Carolina 28231

Franklin Realty & Mortgage Trust   47,419,721
Two Penn Center Plaza
Philadelphia, Pennsylvania 19102

Atlanta National Real Estate Trust   47,184,966
2300 Peachtree Center-Cain Tower
229 Peachtree Street N.E.
Atlanta, Georgia 30303

Jim Walter Investors 1500 North Dale Mabry Highway Tampa, Florida 33622	$45,881,876
KMC Mortgage Investors 2060 Idle Hour Center Lexington, Kentucky 40502	44,123,424
American Fidelity Investments 501 West High Street Springfield, Ohio 45501	25,250,000
American Realty Trust 2000 Jefferson Davis Hwy. Arlington, Virginia 22202	56,900,000
Arlen Property Investors 84 State Street Boston, Massachusetts 02109	52,000,000
Atico Mortgage Investors 28 State Street Boston, Massachusetts 02109	155,000,000
Atlanta National Real Estate Trust 229 Peachtree Street N.E. Atlanta, Georgia 30303	48,600,000
BankAmerica Realty Investors Bank of America Center Suite 4545 San Francisco, California 94104	265,200,000
Berg Enterprises Realty Group 450 Park Avenue New York, New York 10022	27,800,000
BT Mortgage Investors 225 Franklin St. Boston, Massachusetts 02110	168,500,000
Builders Investment Group P.O. Box 848 Irwin Building, North Gulph Road Valley Forge, Pennsylvania 19482	423,500,000
Cabot, Cabot & Forbes Land Trust One Boston Place Boston, Massachusetts 02108	213,400,000
Central Mortgage & Realty Trust United Missouri Bank Building Kansas City, Mo. 64142	45,400,000
Chevy Chase Real Estate Trust 8401 Connecticut Avenue Chevy Chase, Maryland 20015	15,700,000
C.I. Realty Investors One Boston Place Boston, Massachusetts 02108	200,000,000

Cintinational Development Trust 400 North Roxbury Drive Beverly Hills, California 90210	$ 24,900,000
Citizens Mortgage Investment Trust 24700 Northwestern Highway P.O. Box 426 Southfield, Michigan 48075	100,000,000
CleveTrust Realty Investors 1010 Investment Plaza Cleveland, Ohio 44114	142,200,000
Commonwealth National Realty Trust 401 North Washington Street Rockville, Maryland 20850	26,500,000
Connecticut General Mortgage & Realty Investments 1500 Main Street Springfield, Massachusetts 01115	470,000,000
Continental Illinois Realty P.O. Box 2026 Santa Monica, California 90406	230,000,000
Corporate Property Investors 230 Park Avenue New York, New York 10017	258,000,000
Cumberland Equity Trust P.O. Box 432 Clarksville, Tennessee 37040	1,500,000
Delaware Valley Realty and Mortgage Investors 21 East Airy Street Norristown, Pennsylvania 19401	8,000,000
Derland Real Estate Investment Trust P.O. Box 9183 1815 North Fort Meyer Drive Arlington, Virginia 22209	2,100,000
Dominion Mortgage & Realty Trust Main Place Tower Buffalo, New York 14202	30,800,000
Financial Florida Investors 115 East Garden Street P.O. Box 12915 Pensacola, Florida 32576	3,900,000
First Commerce Realty Investors 821 Gravier Street New Orleans, Louisiana 70112	63,600,000
First Continental Real Estate Investment Trust 3693 Southwest Freeway Houston, Texas 77027	51,100,000

First Fidelity Investment Trust 12th and Walnut Streets Building 25 East 12th Street Kansas City, Missouri 64106	$28,500,000
First Memphis Realty Trust P.O. Box 1100 Memphis, Tennessee 38101	79,200,000
First Virginia Mortgage and Real Estate Investment Trust 6400 Arlington Blvd. Falls Church, Virginia 22042	107,100,000
Flatley Realty Investors 155 Wood Road Braintree, Massachusetts 02184	25,100,000
Fraser Mortgage Investments 1000 Union Commerce Arcade Cleveland, Ohio 44115	48,100,000
GIT Realty and Mortgage Investors 230 Park Avenue New York, New York 10017	37,600,000
Gould Investors Trust 245 Great Neck Road Great Neck, New York 11021	39,000,000
GREIT Realty Trust 5045 Township Line Road Drexel Hill, Pennsylvania	69,000,000
Gulf Mortgage and Realty Investments 222 Franklin Street Boston, Massachusetts 02110	158,600,000
Gulf South Mortgage Investors P.O. Box 25276 Oklahoma City, Oklahoma 73125	74,800,000
IDS Realty Trust IDS Center Minneapolis, Minnesota 55402	346,000,000
Independence Mortgage Trust P.O. Box 12098 San Diego, California 92112	175,000,000
Institutional Investors Trust One Boston Place Boston, Massachusetts 02108	182,800,000
Investors Realty Trust Third National Bank Building Nashville, Tennessee 37219	62,600,000

Investors REIT One 5900 Roche Drive Columbus, Ohio 43229	$14,400,000
Investors REIT Two 5900 Roche Drive Columbus, Ohio 43229	14,200,000
JMB Realty Trust 875 N. Michigan Avenue Chicago, Illinois 60611	44,100,000
Lomas & Nettleton Mortgage Investors 2001 Bryan Tower P.O. Box 5644 Dallas, Texas 75222	410,200,000
M & T Mortgage Investors 3100 Travis Street Houston, Texas 77006	42,700,000
Mid-Atlantic Mortgage Investors 9401 Indian Head Highway Oxon Hill, Maryland 20022	2,600,000
Henry S. Miller Realty Trust 2001 Bryan Tower Dallas, Texas 75201	31,000,000
Mortgage Trust of America 600 Montgomery Street P.O. Box 3795 San Francisco, California 94119	187,000,000
Nationwide Real Estate Investors 246 North High Street Columbus, Ohio 43215	65,000,000
Newport Equities Trust 2082 Michelson Drive Newport Beach, California 92664	4,000,000
NJB Prime Investors c/o Bingham, Dana & Gould 100 Federal Street Boston, Massachusetts 02110	105,700,000
Northern States Mortgage and Realty Investors 517 Diamond Shamrock Building 110 Superior Avenue Cleveland, Ohio 44114	36,000,000
Realty Investors 720 E. Wisconsin Avenue Milwaukee, Wisconsin 53202	244,300,000
Stone Mortgage and Realty Trust 86 South Main Street Providence, Rhode Island 02901	43,000,000
Pease & Elliman Realty Trust 919 Third Avenue New York, New York 10022	37,200,000

Pennsylvania Real Estate Investment Trust Cedarbrook Hill III Wyncote, Pennsylvania 19095	$ 77,300,000
Philadelphia Mortgage Trust One Decker Square Bala Cynwyd, Pennsylvania 19004	2,000,000
PNB Mortgage and Realty Investors 7320 Old York Road Melrose Park, Pennsylvania 19126	150,000,000
Property Capital Trust Three Center Plaza Boston. Massachusetts 02108	72,000,000
Property Trust of America Property Trust of America Bldg. 2211 E. Missouri El Paso, Texas 79903	44,400,000
Realty Growth Investors 401 Washington Avenue P.O. Box 5423 Towson, Maryland 21202	87,000,000
Realty Income Trust 40 Westminister Street Providence, Rhode Island 02903	78,500,000
Realty and Mortgage Investors of the Pacific 44 Montgomery Street San Francisco, California 94104	76,000,000
Realty ReFund Trust 1101 Euclid Avenue Cleveland, Ohio 44115	49,000,000
Republic Mortgage Investors c/o Mortgage Investment Services Inc. P.O. Box 3108 2401 Douglas Road Coral Gables, Florida 33134	91,000,000
Ryan Mortgage Investors 611 Ryan Plaza Drive Arlington, Texas 76012	20,000,000
F. Saul Real Estate Investment Trust 8401 Connecticut Avenue Chevy Chase, Maryland 20015	342,500,000
Security Mortgage Investors 28 State Street Boston, Massachusetts 02109	233,000,000
Southwest Mortgage & Realty Investors 5150 N. Shepherd Houston, Texas 77018	10,200,000
State Mutual Investors 440 Lincoln Street Worcester, Massachusetts 01605	157,900,000

Summit Properties 1129 Central Building Akron, Ohio 44308	$61,500,000
Sutro Mortgage Investment Trust 9200 Sunset Blvd. Los Angeles, California 90069	114,400,000
TMC Mortgage Investors 45 School Street Boston, Massachusetts 02108	76,500,000
Tri-South Mortgage Investors 15 Dunwoody Park, Suite 100 Atlanta, Georgia 30341	244,200,000
The UMET Trust 9595 Wilshire Blvd. Beverly Hills, California 90212	204,300,000
U.S. Bantrust P.O. Box 4387 421 S.W. 6th Avenue, Suite 615 Portland, Oregon 97204	79,600,000
U.S. Leasing Real Estate Investors 633 Battery Street San Francisco, California 94111	56,200,000
U.S. Realty Investments Terminal Tower Cleveland, Ohio 44113	145,000,000
Universal Mortgage & Realty Trust 640 Fifth Avenue New York, New York 10019	32,000,000
Virginia Real Estate Investment Trust 11 North Sixth Street P.O. Box 1218 Richmond, Virginia 23209	47,800,000
Western Mortgage Investors 93 Purchase Street Boston, Massachusetts 02110	28,000,000

Real Property Trusts and Limited Partnerships

SPECIAL FEATURES

When the REIT law was passed in September, 1960, its major objective was to provide the small investor with a public vehicle through which he could own real estate. Popularly known as the equity trust, the real property trust is the type REIT best suited to accomplish this goal.

The real property trust (RPT) offers the same tax advantages as the mortgage trust. In addition, the RPT offers the investor most of the same depreciation advantages as the landowner.

Limited partnerships are usually offered through specialized investment bankers who have real estate licenses. Usually the partnerships are geared to investors who have special tax problems. The most common are tax-shelter limited partnerships on new projects which offer "first-user tax advantages."

Other LP's buy properties that are older and more stable but do not have such good tax advantages.

A third group specializes in cash flow as well as potential capital gain opportunities which both LP's and equity trusts have in common.

ACQUISITION POLICIES AND TRENDS

The real property trusts are interested in long-term real estate ownership and are far more stable than the mortgage trusts. They can buy for all cash or they can buy subject to mortgages.

Usually they prefer buying high quality real estate with a minimum of $500,000 cash per investment.

The type real estate these trusts like include shopping centers, office buildings, commercial properties, and multi-family residential properties. They also buy high-grade sale leasebacks on industrial properties or good retail facilities.

They generally seek cash-on-cash returns ranging all the way from eight to 20 percent depending on the depreciation and tax advantages of the particular acquisition.

The limited partnership acquisition policies are more complicated since they usually must tie a property up from 90 to 120 days while the registration is processed through state and/or federal security agencies for approval and until the investment banking group is successful in selling the limited partnership's interest.

HOW TO APPROACH THE TRUST

The trusts may be contacted either through their representative mortgage bankers, real estate brokers, or directly.

The first step is to request their acquisition guidelines so the borrower will know what to submit to them.

The limited partnership groups should be approached in the same manner.

RATING THE TRUST

The real property trust as well as limited partnerships vary widely in their needs and requirements.

The RPT can best be rated by the total size of its assets. Size and success of recent underwritings are helpful in judging limited partnerships.

THE TOP EQUITY TRUSTS
AND LIMITED PARTNERSHIPS

	ASSETS
Builders Investment Group 750 East Swedesford Road Valley Forge, Pennsylvania 19481	$331,363,069
Connecticut General Mortgage & Realty Investments 1500 Main Street, Room 2518 Springfield, Massachusetts 01115	313,115,000
B.F. Saul Real Estate Investment Trust 8401 Connecticut Avenue Chevy Chase, Maryland 20015	301,680,882
Continental Illinois Properties 606 Wilshire Boulevard, Suite 500 Santa Monica, California 90406	227,267,000
C.I. Realty Investors One Boston Place Boston, Massachusetts 02108	222,340,126
Bank America Realty Investors 555 California Street, Suite 4545 San Francisco, California 94104	201,490,000

General Growth Properties 1055 Sixth Avenue Des Moines, Iowa 50306	$167,098,260
First Union Real Estate Equity & Mortgage Investments 55 Public Square, Suite 1650 Cleveland, Ohio 44113	146,100,738
Cabot, Cabot & Forbes Land Trust One Boston Place Boston, Massachusetts 02108	143,314,739
U.S. Realty Investments Suite 700, Terminal Tower Cleveland, Ohio 44113	141,955,796
Hubbard Real Estate Investments 125 High Street Boston, Massachusetts 02110	96,834,363
Realty & Mortgage Investors of the Pacific 44 Montgomery Street, Suite 2600 San Francisco, California 94104	78,287,159
ICM Realty 600 Third Avenue New York, New York 10016	73,946,869
Property Capital Trust Three Center Plaza Boston, Massachusetts 02108	73,357,210
First Memphis Realty Trust Post Office Box 1100 Memphis, Tennessee 38101	72,714,146
Realty Income Trust 40 Westminister Street Providence, Rhode Island 02903	66,213,220
GREIT Realty Trust 5045 Township Line Road Drexel Hill, Pennsylvania 19026	60,716,000
U.S. Bancorp Realty & Mortgage Trust 421 S.W. Sixth Avenue Portland, Oregon 97204	56,616,824
Prudent Real Estate Trust 245 Great Neck Road Great Neck, New York 11201	54,454,955
U.S. Leasing Real Estate Investors 633 Battery Street San Francisco, California 94111	53,486,262
Investors Realty Trust Third National Bank Building Nashville, Tennessee 37219	52,550,717

Summit Properties Second National Building Akron, Ohio 44308	$52,546,105
American Realty Trust 2000 Jefferson Highway Arlington, Virginia 22202	51,203,799
Wisconsin Real Estate Investment Trust Suite 1448, Marine Plaza Milwaukee, Wisconsin 53202	51,097,684
Virginia Real Estate Investment Trust 11 North 6th Street Richmond, Virginia 23219	50,482,100
Kavanau Real Estate Trust 757 Third Avenue New York, New York 10017	46,575,415
Real Estate Investment Trust of America 294 Washington Street Boston, Massachusetts 02108	42,691,601
Arlen Property Investors 888 7th Avenue New York, New York 10019	40,836,000
Mutual Real Estate Investment Trust 41 East 42nd Street New York, New York 10017	40,395,922
Gould Investors Trust 245 Great Neck Road Great Neck, New York 11021	39,606,388
Citizens Growth Properties 1300 East Ninth Street Cleveland, Ohio 44114	37,440,563
Washington Real Estate Investment Trust Suite 220, 7910 Woodmont Avenue Washington, D.C. 20014	33,233,446
Pennsylvania Real Estate Investment Trust Cedarbrook Hill III, Mezzanine 26 Glenwood Avenue and Limekiln Pike Wyncote, Pennsylvania 19095	29,534,723
First Fidelity Investment Trust 12th & Walnut Street Building 25 East 12th Street Kansas City, Missouri 64106	28,483,878
Property Trust of America 4301 Montana Avenue El Paso, Texas 79903	28,431,857
Northern States Mortgage and Realty Investors 517 Diamond Shamrock Building Cleveland, Ohio 44114	26,891,018

Flatley Realty Investors Mark 128 Office Park 150 Wood Road Braintree, Massachusetts 02184	$25,490,990
New Plan Realty Trust 369 Lexington Avenue New York, New York 10017	25,176,872
Henry S. Miller Realty Trust 2001 Bryan Tower Dallas, Texas 75201	25,086,955
JMB Realty Trust 875 North Michigan Avenue Chicago, Illinois 60611	20,986,069
Piedmont Real Estate Investment Trust 1110 American Building Charlotte, North Carolina 28202	20,799,309
Riviere Realty Trust 1832 M Street N.W. Washington, D.C. 20036	16,915,843
Terrydale Realty Trust 4005 Pennsylvania Kansas City, Missouri 64111	14,970,467
Riverside Real Estate Investment Trust 118 West Adams Street Jacksonville, Florida 32202	14,359,602
Home Investors Trust 85 Pondfield Road Bronxville, New York 10708	13,536,991
Commonwealth Realty Trust Wyncote House Office Building Wyncote, Pennsylvania 19095	11,721,187
United States Equity & Mortgage Trust Suite 1416; Glendon Avenue Los Angeles, California 90024	9,262,722
Monmouth Real Estate Investment Trust 125 Wyckoff Road Eatontown, New Jersey 07724	9,192,998
Hibbard, Spencer, Bartlett Trust 2201 West Howard Street Evanston, Illinois 60202	8,700,017
Indiana-Florida Realty Trust 3704 B South Reed Road Kokomo, Indiana 46901	8,145,746
Real Estate Investment Trust of California 2497 Harbor Blvd. — Suite 10 Ventura, California 93003	6,359,861

Western Investment Real Estate Trust 465 California St. No. 1118 San Francisco, California 94104	$ 6,839,467
Denver Real Estate Investment Assoc. 650 Seventeenth St. — Suite 701 Denver, Colorado 80202	31,153,357
Riverside Real Estate Investment Trust 228 North LaSalle St. Chicago, Illinois 60601	14,359,602
Bradley Real Estate Trust 250 Boylston Street Boston, Massachusetts 02116	17,148,029
Chicago Real Estate Trustees 250 Boylston Street Boston, Massachusetts 02116	4,061,460
National Realty Investors One Boston Place Boston, Massachusetts 02108	43,826,079
Pittsburgh Realty Investment Trust 1312 Frick Bldg. Pittsburgh, Pennsylvania 15219	15,495,422

LIMITED PARTNERSHIP GROUPS

Integrated Resources
295 Madison Avenue
New York City, New York 10017

MultiVest, Inc.
26300 Telegraph Road
Southfield, Michigan 48076

Larwin Realty & Mortgage
9100 Wilshire Boulevard
Beverly Hills, California 90212

Oppenheimer Fund, Inc.
1 New York Plaza
New York, New York 10004

Donaldson, Lufkin & Jenrette, Inc.
140 Broadway
New York, New York 10005

JMB Income Properties, Ltd.
875 North Michigan Avenue
Chicago, Illinois 60611

Piedmont Management Co.
177 North Dean Street
Englewood, New Jersey 07631

Buyers of Real Estate

**(Including Diversified Real Estate Corporations,
Investment Companies, Groups, Investors, and Syndicates)**

There are investors in the market continuously who desire to buy and own real estate. They range from the individual operator to the large institutions which are actively pursuing joint ventures, sale leasebacks, net leases, and outright purchase of diversified property portfolios.

The best way to contact these people is directly by phone or letter, or through real estate and mortgage brokers. One will usually find them very cooperative and candid regarding their investment parameters.

Among those listed here are individuals and joint venture real estate investors. A real estate investor, developer, or broker who has experience but who does not wish to invest his own capital can frequently turn to this type of investor-lender to finance all or a large portion of the equity cost of a project while he adds his time and knowledge and little, or no, cash of his own to the undertaking.

Characteristics of venture capital and joint venture groups vary. They range from very sophisticated institutions to fast-reacting entrepreneurs. It is best to contact them directly by phone or mail and request their criteria.

COMPANIES SPECIALIZING IN SALE LEASEBACKS AND NET LEASES

One way to get 100 percent real estate financing is through the sale leaseback or net lease method of financing.

The sale leaseback involves a company's selling of a property and leasing it back. The net lease is similar, but the company signing the lease must make certain guarantees to the lender or buyer of the property.

Usually, corporations utilize these types of loans, and often the mortgage banker is the best guide to sources if he is not a source of funds himself.

The borrower or seller will find a great mixture of sources for leasebacks and net leases including individuals, mortgage bankers, private and public companies, and investment trusts.

This field of financing is highly complicated, and some lenders and brokerage houses specialize in these kinds of transactions. The author's firm, Property Resources Company, of South Miami, Florida, is one of these, doing approximately $100,000,000 a year in leaseback and net lease financing.

INVESTORS

The following is a list of some of the most active buyers or equity investors in real estate:

BUYERS OF REAL ESTATE

(Including Diversified Real Estate Corporations,
Investment Companies, Groups, Investors and Syndicates)

Avco Community Developers
2223 Avenida de la Playa
Box 2348
La Jolla, California 92037

Atlanta Motor Lodges, Inc.
120 North Ave. N. W.
Atlanta, Georgia 30303

Apache Corp.
1800 Foshay Tower
Minneapolis, Minnesota 55402

All-State Properties, Inc.
52 Brompton Rd.
Great Neck, N. Y. 11021

Arlen Realty & Development Corp.
888 Seventh Ave.
New York, N. Y. 10019

Assurity Structures Corp.
P. O. Box 785
Camarillo, California 93010

Allied Properties
420 Taylor Street
San Francisco, California 94102

American Investment Co.
  Development Corp.
120 S. LaSalle St.
Chicago, Illinois 60603

All Realty Co.
6215 Greenbelt Rd.
College Park, Maryland 20740

Atlantic Corp.
55 Court Street
Boston, Massachusetts 02108

Artdale Investments
340 E. Diamond Lake Rd.
Minneapolis, Minnesota 55419

Alpha Equities, Inc.
1530 Palisade Ave.
Fort Lee, N. J. 07024

American Property Investors
c/o Integrated Resources, Inc.
295 Madison Avenue
New York, N. Y. 10017

Axlerod Management Co.
45 W. 139th Street
New York, N. Y. 10037

Avanti Equity Real Estate
248 Fairhaven Blvd.
Woodbury, N. Y. 11797

American Financial Corp.
3955 Montgomery Rd.
Cincinnati, Ohio 45212

Alliance Business Investment Co.
500 McFarlin Bldg.
Oklahoma City, Oklahoma 74103

Associated Securities Co.
Law & Finance Bldg.
Pittsburgh, Pa. 15219

Arden, M.E. Co.
2377 Greenfield Rd.
Southfield, Mich. 48075

Armstrong, A.J. Co., Inc.
850 Third Ave.
New York, N. Y. 10022

Arredondo & Co., Inc.
1110 E. 42nd St.
New York, N. Y. 10017

Associated Urban Finance
10880 Wilshire Blvd.
Los Angeles, California 90024

The Avemco Group
7315 Wisconsin Avenue
Bethesda, Md. 20014

American Furniture Mart
666 N. Lake Shore Drive
Chicago, Illinois 60611

American Cynamid Co.
Berdan Avenue
Wayne, N. J. 07470

American Standard Inc.
40 W. 40th Street
New York, N. Y. 10018

AVCO Corp.
1275 King Street
Greenwich, Conn. 06830

Big Boy Properties, Inc.
1001 E. Colorado St.
Glendale, California 91205

Boston Garden Arena Corp.
North Station
Boston, Mass. 02114

Baker Properties, Inc.
510 Baker Bldg.
Minneapolis, Minn. 55402

Bahamas Caribbean Corp. Ltd.
5008 Dodge St.
Omaha, Nebraska 68132

Bush Terminal Co.
48 43rd St.
Brooklyn, N. Y. 11232

Basic Properties
295 Madison Ave.
New York, New York 10017

Bookbinder Financial Corp.
5021 E. Exeter Blvd.
Phoenix, Arizona 85018

Bigelow, Ernest A.
737 Broad St. — Ext.
Waterford, Conn. 06385

Bellevue Holding Co.
1605 Pennsylvania Ave.
Wilmington, Delaware 19899

Berstein, Joseph F. Co., Inc.
P. O. Box 828
Palm Beach, Fla. 33480

Borg-Warner Equities Corp.
One IBM Place
Chicago, Ill. 60611

Bass & Weisberg, Realtors
3411 Bardstown Road
Louisville, Ky. 40218

Beacon Construction Co.
One Center Plaza
Boston, Mass. 02108

The Boston Co. —
  R. E. Counsel, Inc.
One Boston Place
Boston, Mass. 02106

Boston Financial Technology
  Group, Inc.
70 Federal Street
Boston, Mass. 02100

Bear Hill Investment Corp.
60 Hickory Dr.
Waltham, Mass. 02154

Baillon Co.
St. Paul Bldg.
St. Paul, Minn. 55102

Bankhalter, Manny
154 W. 70th St.
New York, N. Y. 10023

Bear, Stearns & Co.
One Wall St.
New York, N. Y. 10005

Beck, Flesher, & Vernon, Inc.
245 Park Ave.
New York, N. Y. 10017

Berger, Matthew P. & Co., Inc.
Ten E. 40th St.
New York, N. Y. 10016

Brause Realty
280 Madison Ave.
New York, N. Y. 10016

Breitbart Corp.
Two Park Ave.
New York, N. Y. 10016

Brown Brothers, Harriman & Co.
59 Wall St.
New York, N. Y. 10005

Burnet, W. E. & Co.
88 Pine St.
New York, N. Y. 10005

Butcher & Sherrerd
1500 Walnut St.
Philadelphia, Pa. 19105

Boyle Investment Co.
42 S. Second St.
Memphis, Tenn. 38103

Bonanza Corp.
P. O. Box 388
Conroe, Texas 77301

Brooks Investment Co.
408 N. Sylvania
Fort Worth, Texas 76111

Burton, L. R. Realtor
5700 Highland Dr.
Salt Lake City, Utah 84121

Baker, John S. Investment Co.
Washington Bldg.
Tacoma, Wash. 98401

Batter & Greenberg
182 Hillside Ave.
Williston Park, N. Y.

Barksdale Corp., Howard S.
2 West 45th St.
New York, N. Y. 10036

Bankers, Edward & Co.
P. O. Box 1223
Houston, Texas 77001

Bellavue Investors Co.
5151 Monroe St.
Toledo, Ohio 43623

Blum & Ross
389 Central Ave.
Lawrence, N. Y. 11559

Brooks, Harvey & Co.
of California, Inc.
44 Montgomery St.
San Francisco, Calif. 94104

Broadwell Investing Corp.
370 Seventh Ave.
New York, New York 10001

Buhl Realty Co.
1612 Buhl Bldg.
Detroit, Mich. 48226

Burton, Goldstein, Mendel & Sattele
1401 Paces Ferry Rd. N. W.
Suite D-110
Atlanta, Ga. 30327

Bruckner, Eric & Co.
800 Garden St.
Santa Barbara, Calif. 93101

Boston Fish Market Corp.
220 Northern Ave.
Boston, Mass. 02110

Bethlehem Steel
8th & Eaton Ave.
Bethlehem, Pa. 18016

Boise Cascade
One Jefferson Square
Boise, Idaho 83728

Building & Land Tech. Corp.
2440 Hwy. 9
Lakewood, N. J. 08701

Bloomfield Building Industries
100 N. Main Bldg.
Memphis, Tenn. 38103

Bankers Building Corp.
105 W. Adams St.
Chicago, Ill. 60603

Blaustein Industries Inc.
1 N. Charles St.
Baltimore, Md. 21201

Coldwell Banker
533 Fremont Ave.
Los Angeles, Calif. 90017

Coral Ridge Properties, Inc.
9500 W. Sample Ave.
Coral Springs, Fla. 33065

Cousins Properties Incorporated
300 Interstate North
Atlanta, Ga. 30339

Crawford Corp.
Village Green
Crofton, Md. 21113

C. I. Mortgage Group
One Boston Place
Boston, Mass. 02108

Commonwealth Equities, Inc.
Suite 205
5001 W. 78th St.
Minneapolis, Minn. 55437

Canal-Randolph Corp.
277 Park Ave.
New York, N. Y. 10017

City Lands Inc.
120 Broadway
New York, N.Y. 10005

Costain, Richard (Canada) Ltd.
3500 Dufferin St.
Downsview, Ontario
Canada

Cavanagh, Bert Realty
29 E. Camelback Rd.
Phoenix, Arizona 85012

Copper State Realty Co.
1230 E. Magee Rd.
Tucson, Arizona 85718

Capital Guaranty Corp.
280 S. Beverly Dr.
Beverly Hills, California 90212

Creative Funding, Inc.
Suite 617
9465 Wilshire Blvd.
Beverly Hills, Calif. 90212

California Land & Exploration Co.
6290 Sunset Blvd.
Los Angeles, Calif. 90028

Carlsberg Financial Corp.
1801 Century Park W.
Los Angeles, Calif. 90067

Colwell Diversified
  Financial Services
Suite 1024
3255 Wilshire Blvd.
Los Angeles, Calif. 90010

CGC Financial Corp.
Suite 617
2550 Fifth Ave.
San Diego, Calif. 92103

Coleman, Curtis Co.
Suite 2100
U. S. National Bank Bldg.
San Diego, Calif. 92101

Cohen, Burton I.
901 Farmington Ave.
W. Hartford, Conn. 06119

Castellani, V. B. & Co., Inc.
1826 Jefferson Place.
Washington D. C. 20036

Cross, C. J. & Assocs., Inc.
1120 Connecticut Ave. N. W.
Washington D. C. 20036

Capital Investment Co.
239 Merchant St.
Honolulu, Hawaii 96813

Capital Resources Corp.
307 N. Michigan Ave.
Chicago, Ill. 60601

Cumbest Enterprises
2833 Montebello Terr.
Baltimore, Md. 21214

Cardinal Properties, Inc.
One Boston Place
Boston, Mass. 02108

Continental Real Estate Equities, Inc.
100 Federal St.
Boston, Mass. 02110

Corcoran, John M. & Co.
1601 Blue Hill Ave.
Mattapan, Mass. 02126

Citrin, J. A. Sons Co.
Suite 1801
Travelers Tower
Southfield, Mich. 48076

Cohn, Teddy & Associates
300 Main St.
Orange, N. J. 07050

Carlyle Holding Corp.
340 E. 46th St.
New York, N. Y. 10017

C.A.V. Enterprises, Inc.
32 E. 57th St.
New York, N. Y.

Collins Tuttle & Co., Inc.
261 Madison Ave.
New York, N. Y. 10016

County Dollar Corp.
635 Madison Ave.
New York, N. Y. 10022

Colvin, Lowell Inc.
747 East Ave.
Rochester, N. Y. 14607

Commerce Investment, Inc.
Cascade Bldg.
Portland, Oregon 97204

Cynwyd Investments
191 Presidential Blvd.
Bala-Cynwyd, Pa. 19004

Commercial Realty Marketing, Inc.
Monroe Complex
Bldg. 1
Monroeville, Pa. 15146

Cook Investment Properties, Inc.
Box 16902
Memphis, Tenn. 38116

Corrigan, L. F.
211 N. Ervay
Dallas, Texas 75201

Crow, Trammell Co.
2001 Bryan St.
Dallas, Texas 75201

Courtney & Courtney
5280 Trail Lake Dr.
Fort Worth, Texas 76133

Charter Financial Group, Inc.
Suite 1870
2700 S. Post Oak Rd.
Houston, Texas 77027

Calbancor.Realty, Inc.
523 West 6th St.
Los Angeles, Calif. 90014

Capital Management Services, Inc.
611 W. 6th St.
Los Angeles, Calif. 90017

Centex Corp.
4600 Republic National Bank Tower
Dallas, Texas 75201

Central Investment Corp.
811 Central Bank Bldg.
Denver, Colorado 80202

The Charter Co.
47 W. Forsyth St.
Jacksonville, Fla. 32202

Colin, Fred
500 Old Country Rd.
New York, N. Y. 11530

Cox, W. T. Company
P. O. Box 1021
Orlando, Fla. 32802

Cranbrooke Realty Co.
Ottawa Hills Shopping Center
Toledo, Ohio

CNA Financial
310 S. Michigan Ave.
Chicago, Ill. 60604

Castle & Cooke Inc.
Financial Plaza Pacific
Honolulu, Hawaii 96802

Champion Int. Corp.
777 3rd Ave.
New York, N. Y. 10017

Citizens Financial
1300 E. 9th St.
Cleveland, Ohio 44114

City Investing
767 5th Ave.
New York, N. Y. 10022

Chase Enterprises (David Chase)
999 Asylum Ave.
Hartford, Conn. 06105

Christiana Securities
3046 Du Pont Bldg.
Wilmington, Delaware 19898

Corning Glass
Walnut St.
Corning, N. Y. 14830

Cantor, Edward A.
408 E. Elizabeth Ave.
Linden, N. J. 07036

Canada Southern Railway
466 Lexington Ave.
New York, N. Y. 10017

Disc, Inc.
Suite 700
L St. N. W.
Washington, D.C. 20036

Dexter Horton Realty Co.
19 W. 44th St.
New York, N. Y. 10036

Doric Properties, Inc.
450 Park Ave.
Alameda, Calif. 94501

Draper Financial Corp.
Ross Bldg.
San Francisco, Calif. 94104

Dutcher & Co.
2545 W. Eighth Ave.
Denver, Colorado 80204

Donatelli & Klein, Inc.
Suite 708
1666 "K" St. N. W.
Washington, D. C. 20006

Diversified Investment Assocs., Inc.
25 S. Charles St.
Baltimore, Md. 21201

Doran, Harold
500 Brisbane Bldg.
Buffalo, N. Y. 14203

Dunlop Real Estate Equities, Inc.
230 Cedrus Ave.
E. Northport, N. Y. 11731

Dilliard, John A.
1650 Broadway
New York, N. Y. 10019

Drexel Firestone, Inc.
60 Broad St.
New York, N. Y. 10004

Dunlop Realty Inc.
330 Madison Ave.
New York, N. Y. 10017

DuPont, Glore, Forgan, Inc.
One Wall St.
New York, N. Y. 10005

The Durst Organization
1133 Ave. of the Americas
New York, N. Y. 10036

Dusco Inc.
345 Park Ave.
New York, N. Y. 10022

Delta Organization Corp.
475 Montauk Hwy.
West Islip, N. Y. 11795

Davis Realty Investments, Inc.
1815 Wm. Howard Taft Rd.
Cincinnati, Ohio 45206

Dicker, Edward T. Investments
2600 Fairmont
Dallas, Texas 75201

Dusco Inc.
7122 Aberdeen St.
Dallas, Texas 75230

Driskell, Joe Real Estate
4117 W. Rosedale
Fort Worth, Texas 76107

The Drummond Co. Realtors
2400 E. Belknap
Ft. Worth, Texas 76111

Duddlesten, Wayne Interests
P. O. Box 22348
Houston, Texas 77027

Dement, Jim Investments
Suite 100
2446 Cee Gee
San Antonio, Texas 78217

Dominion Assocs.
Massey Bldg.
4th & Main Sts.
Richmond, Va. 23219

David, Stanley M. & Associates
Suite 203
8609 N. W. Plaza Dr.
Dallas, Texas 75225

Davos Inc.
420 Lexington Ave.
New York, N. Y. 10017

Dreyfus Corp.
767 5th Ave.
New York, N. Y. 10022

Dattel Realty Co.
100 No. Main St.
Memphis, Tenn. 38103

Denver Real Estate Invest.
1755 Glenarm Pl.
Denver, Colorado 80202

Equity Capital Co.
430 First Ave. N.
Minneapolis, Minn. 55401

Equity Research Corp.
16055 Ventura Blvd.
Encino, Calif. 91316

Elkay Investment & Management Co.
1615 Bonanza St.
Walnut Creek, Calif. 94596

Ellms, Ruth, Real Estate
P. O. Box 264
Saugatuck Station
Westport, Conn. 06880

Economic Development Corp.
1309 Rand Rd.
Arlington Hts., Ill. 60004

Eaton & Howard Inc.
24 Federal St.
Boston, Mass. 02110

Eastman Dillon, Union Securities
    & Co., Inc.
One Chase Manhattan Plaza
New York, N. Y. 10005

The Ellman Group, Inc.
One Penn Plaza
New York, N. Y. 10001

Eliokum Investment Corp.
334 W. 6th St.
Cincinnati, Ohio 45202

Eastern States Investment Co.
2424 Far Hills Ave.
Dayton, Ohio 45419

Einkelstein Realty Co.
Third National Bank Bldg.
Nashville, Tenn. 37219

Executive Investors Inc.
1215 Pinckney
Madison, Wisconsin 53703

Essex Co.
Suite 828
1180 Raymond Blvd.
Newark, N. J. 07102

Englander Associates
2800 First National Bank Bldg.
Denver, Colorado 80202

Equity Planning Corp.
33 Public Square
Suite 1010
Cleveland, Ohio 44113

Environmental Systems
3030 S. Bundy Dr.
Los Angeles, Calif. 90066

Evans Products
1121 S. W. Salmon St.
Portland, Oregon 97205

First Hartford Realty Corp.
390-R W. Middle Tpke.
Manchester, Conn. 06040

First Realty Investment Corp.
801 41st Street
Miami Beach, Fla. 33140

Federal Shell Homes, Inc.
225 W. Carolina St.
Tallahassee, Fla. 32301

Financial Resources Group
110 Main St.
Hackensack, N. J. 07601

First General Resources Co.
505 Park Ave.
New York, N. Y. 10022

Franchard Corp.
640 Fifth Ave.
New York, N. Y. 10019

First American Equity Corp.
1974 Sproul Rd.
Broomall, Penn. 19008

Frisbie & Co.
Suite 202, 245 Columbine St.
Denver, Colo. 80206

The First Republic Corp.
of America
302 Fifth Ave.
New York, N. Y. 10001

First Investment Corp.
N. Washington at Princess St.
Alexandria, Va. 22314

Forest Lawn Mtge. & Investment Co.
1600 S. Glendale Ave.
Glendale, Calif. 92105

Farnow, Dale Co.
2636 Ocean Ave.
San Francisco, Calif. 94108

Feder, Jack M.
 & Jack M. Feder Jr.
333 Kearney Street
San Francisco, Calif. 94108

Fisher, Jess & Co.
1000 Connecticut Ave. N. W.
Washington D. C. 20036

Fine Realty Co.
3737 E. 116th St.
Carmel, Indiana 46032

Fletcher Oil Co., Inc.
800 Marquette
Bay City, Mich. 48706

Fenton Assocs.
16591 Meyers Rd.
Detroit, Mich. 48235

Fox & Lazo Inc.
2101 Route 70 E.
Cherry Hill, N. J. 08003

Fane, Jason
410 College Ave.
Ithaca, N. Y. 14850

First Boston Corp.
20 Exchange Place
New York, N. Y. 10005

French, Fred F. Mgmt. Co.
551 Fifth Ave.
New York, N. Y. 10017

First Empire Realty Credit Corp.
235 Mamaroneck Ave.
White Plains, N. Y. 10605

Frates Properties Inc.
5800 E. Skelly Dr.
Tulsa, Oklahoma 74135

Frank, R. J. & Assocs.
6625 N. E. 82nd Ave.
Portland, Oregon 97218

Friedland, George
123 S. Broad St.
Philadelphia, Pa. 19109

Frank, Jerome J.
2115 S. Harwood
Dallas, Texas 75215

Forney, Bill Enterprises
Suite 204
1800 St. James Place
Houston, Texas 77027

First Investment Corp.
N. Washington at Princess St.
Alexandria, Va. 22314

Far West Securities Co.
West 825 Riverside Ave.
Spokane, Washington 99201

"First" Realty Co.
7211 Burleigh St.
Milwaukee, Wisc. 53210

Feinberg, Peter
60 East 42nd St.
New York, N. Y. 10017

Farber Commercial Corp.
370 7th Ave.
New York, N. Y. 10001

Fingerhut, Jack
5883 S. W. 20th St.
Miami, Fla.

First General Resources Co.
505 Park Ave.
New York, N. Y. 10022

Frisch, Reuben
3000 Diplomat Parkway
Apt. 802
Hallandale, Fla.

Florida Mortgage Funding Corp.
1441 Brickell Ave.
Miami, Fla. 33131

Forest City Enterprises Inc.
10800 Brookpark Rd.
Cleveland, Ohio 44130

Fikes, Leland Estate
325 N. St. Paul
Dallas, Texas 75201

Ferro Corp.
1 Erieview Plz.
Cleveland, Ohio 44114

Fischback & Moore
545 Madison Ave.
New York, N. Y. 10022

Flagg Industries
702 Forest Ave.
Pacific Grove, Calif. 93950

Furehauf Corp.
10900 Harper Ave.
Detroit, Mich. 48232

Furman-Wolfson Corp.
1440 Broadway
New York, N. Y. 10018

First Union Realty
33 Public Sq. Bldg.
Cleveland, Ohio 44113

Garden Land Co. Ltd.
17315 Sunset Blvd.
Pacific Palisades, Calif. 90272

Giant Food Inc.
P. O. Box 1804
Washington, D. C. 20013

Gotham Investment Corp.
1707 "H" St. N. W.
Washington, D. C. 20006

Gulf American Land Corp.
557 N. E. 81st St.
Miami, Fla. 33138

Gould Investors Trust
245 Great Neck Rd.
Great Neck, N. Y. 11021

General Realty & Utilities Corp.
111 W. 40th St.
New York, N. Y. 10018

Great American Realty Corp.
440 W. 34th St.
New York, N. Y. 10001

Grant Bldg. Inc.
1701 Grant Bldg.
Pittsburgh, Penn. 15219

Grosvenor Inter. Holdings Ltd.
19th Floor
777 Hornby St.
Vancouver, British Columbia
Canada

The Galaxy Organization
224 Luhes Center Bldg.
Phoenix, Arizona 85003

Grubb & Ellis Co.
1333 Broadway
Oakland, Calif. 94612

Gaetani Investment Corp.
4444 Geary Blvd.
San Francisco, Calif. 94118

Goodin Realty
4990 Mission St.
San Francisco, Calif. 94112

Grant, M. Inc.
Suite 8L,
407 Lincoln Rd.
Miami Beach, Fla. 33139

GGV Associates Ltd.
One Pine Valley Ct.
Ormond Beach, Fla. 32074

Grandoff Investments Inc.
915 Ashley Dr.
Tampa, Fla. 33602

Gil Investment Co.
10515 W. McNichols
Detroit, Mich. 48221

Griffin Investment Corp.
8200 Humboldt Ave. S.
Minneapolis, Minn. 55431

Greenberg Development Co.
Room 309
11906 Manchester
St. Louis, Missouri 63131

Greenberg, David
Suite 200
1135 Clifton Ave.
Clifton, N. J. 07013

Gavey & Co., Inc.
80 Park Ave.
New York, N. Y. 10016

Giller & Stein
521 Fifth Ave.
New York, N. Y. 10017

Glickman, Louis J.
565 Fifth Ave.
New York, N. Y. 10017

Goldman Sachs Realty Corp.
55 Broad St.
New York, N. Y. 10004

Grant, Eugene M./Lionel
R. Bauman
Two W. 45th St.
New York, N. Y. 10036

Gordon, J. Realty Corp.
3400 Monroe Ave.
Rochester, N.Y. 14618

The Gateside Corp.
150 White Plains Rd.
Tarrytown, N. Y. 10591

Gree, Harrison & Son
4318 Montgomery Rd.
Cincinnati, Ohio 45212

Gutin, Harry B. Inc.
4115 Edwardo Rd.
Cincinnati, Ohio 45209

Golden, Louis M. Jr.
843 Western Savings Fund Bldg.
Philadelphia, Pa. 19107

Goldstein, Raymond & Co.
17th and Samson Sts.
Philadelphia, Pa. 19103

Griffin, Ben Enterprises Inc.
3511 N. Hall St.
Dallas, Texas 75219

The Gustafson Group, Inc.
2034 Houston Natural Gas Bldg.
Houston, Texas 77002

Gable, Kenneth Real Estate
300 St. Paul Place
Baltimore, Maryland 21202

Gomez, Serge
1790 Coral Way
Miami, Fla. 33145

Goodrich Investors Group
40 Court St.
Boston, Mass.

Grolier Development Corp.
575 Lexington Ave.
New York, N. Y. 10022

Guaranty Investment Co.
1800 Citizens Tower
P. O. Box 1748
Oklahoma City, Oklahoma 73101

Gulf Oil
439 Seventh Ave.
Pittsburgh, Pennsylvania 15230

Georgia Railroad
4 Hunter St. S. E.
Atlanta, Ga. 30303

Great Northern Iron Ore Prop.
1481 First National Bank
St. Paul, Minn. 55101

Gould Enterprises
370 Lexington Ave.
New York, N. Y. 10017

Grant Bldg. Inc.
330 Grant St.
Pittsburgh, Pa. 15219

Horizon Corp.
4400 E. Broadway
Tucson, Arizona 85703

Helix Land Co.
4825 Avion Way
San Diego, Calif. 92115

Hawaiian Pacific Industries, Inc.
914 Ala Moona Blvd.
Honolulu, Hawaii 96814

Hilton Hotels Corp.
720 S. Michigan Ave.
Chicago, Ill. 60605

Hotel Corp. of Israel
1 N. LaSalle St.
Chicago, Ill. 60602

Hotel Corp. of America
390 Commonwealth Ave.
Boston, Mass. 02215

Helmich Investment Corp.
307 Luhrs Bldg.
Phoenix, Ariz. 85003

Harvey Capital Corp.
9570 Wilshire Blvd.
Beverly Hills, Calif. 90212

Herman, Lawrence
328 S. Oakhurst Dr.
Beverly Hills, Calif. 90212

Harbor Properties Ltd.
Box 1799
San Pedro, Calif. 90733

Hirsch Feld Press
Speer Blvd. & Acoma St.
Denver, Colo. 80204

Housman, S. Real Estate
Suite 304
19 W. Flagler St.
Miami, Fla. 33130

Hemisphere Equity Investors Inc.
999 S. Bayshore Dr.
Miami, Fla. 33131

Home Investment Co. Inc.
230 Guaranty Bldg.
Cedar Rapids, Iowa 52401

Hubbard Real Estate Investments
125 High St.
Boston, Mass. 02110

Hamilton Investment Trust
342 Westminister Ave.
Elizabeth, N. J. 07208

The Hammerson Property Corp.
100 Park Ave.
New York, N. Y. 10017

Hayden Stone, Inc.
767 Fifth Ave.
New York, N. Y. 10022

Heller, Stanley & Co.
44 Wall St.
New York, N. Y. 10005

Hermann, Henry H.
1st National Bank Bldg.
Utica, N. Y. 13501

Harkavy, Franklin Investments, Inc.
6252 Joyce Lane
Cincinnati, Ohio 45237

Harsh Investment Corp.
811 N. W. 19th Ave.
Portland, Oregon 97209

Healy Realty
1100 Langhorne-Newton Rd.
Langhorne, Pa. 19047

Howard Realty Co.
10 Dorrance St.
Providence, Rhode Island 02903

Hill-Elliott Inc.
2101 Mercantile Bank Bldg.
Dallas, Texas 75201

The Howard Corporation
1000 Republic Bank Bldg.
Dallas, Texas 75222

Hendricks, Alan B.
2030 Kearns Bldg.
Salt Lake City, Utah 84101

Hines, Gerald D. Interests
2100 Post Oak Tower
Houston, Texas 77027

The Hartman Group
Capital Development Division
1720 Travelers Tower
26555 Evergreen Rd.
Southfield, Mich. 48076

Harrison Factors Corp.
18 East 41st St.
New York, N. Y. 10017

Income Invested Funds, Inc.
Box 203
Anchorage, Alaska 99501

International Airport
    Hotel Systems, Inc.
Miami International Airport
Miami, Fla. 33148

Investment Corp. of Fla.
Box 7126
Ft. Lauderdale, Fla. 33304

Insurance Exchange Bldg.
175 W. Jackson Blvd.
Chicago, Ill. 60604

Investors Funding Corp. of N. Y.
630 Fifth Ave.
New York, N. Y. 10020

Interstate Equity
450 Seventh Ave.
New York, N. Y. 10001

Inland Investor Inc.
Lowe Bldg.
Sheridan, Wyoming 82801

Insured Investment Co.
P. O. Box 90777
Los Angeles, Calif. 90009

Investcal Realty Corp.
1200 S. Calif.
    First National Bank Bldg.
San Diego, Calif. 92101

International Equities, Inc.
Box 331
Coconut Grove, Fla. 33133

Intervest, Inc.
714 E. Colonial Drive
Orlando, Fla. 32803

Inner City Industries
2400 S. Michigan Ave.
Chicago, Ill. 60616

Investment Brokers Corp.
200 W. Douglas St.
Wichita, Kansas 67202

ICI Resources, Inc.
Suite 204
Travelers Tower
Southfield, Mich. 48076

Integrated Resources, Inc.
295 Madison Ave.
New York, N. Y. 10017

Interstate Investors Inc.
866 United Nations Plaza
New York, N. Y. 10017

I.S.I. Investment Corp.
P. O. Box 20527
Greensboro Airport Interchange
Greensboro, N. C. 27420

Investors Group Ltd., Inc.
5900 Roche Dr.
Columbus, Ohio 43229

Indeas Corp.
Box 87
Glenolden, Pa. 19036

Inge Investments Inc.
314 Meadows Bldg.
Dallas, Texas 75206

Inland Diversified
Suite 1000
United Virginia Bank Bldg.
Norfolk, Va. 23510

Investors Central Management
600 Third Avenue
New York, N. Y. 10016

Investors & Developers Services Inc.
Suite 1610
5530 Wisconsin Ave.
Chevy Chase, Md.

Inland Steel
315 W. Gorham St.
Madison, Wisc. 53703

International Basic Econ. Corp.
1271 Avenue of the Americas
New York, N. Y. 10020

International Paper
220 E. 42nd St.
New York, N. Y. 10017

International Telephone & Telegraph
320 Park Ave.
New York, N. Y. 10022

Jacobson, Jack Co.
41 Sutter St.
San Francisco, Calif. 94104

Judelson & Assoc.
150 E. Palmetto Park Rd.
Boca Raton, Fla. 33432

Jen-Rentals, Inc.
Box 18301
Wichita, Kansas 67218

Jobel Realty Corp.
24 Deborah Rd.
Newton Center, Mass. 02159

The Jacobson Cos.
Suite 712
One New York Avenue
Atlantic City, N. J. 08401

Jaffe, J. H.
20 Evergreen Place
E. Orange, N. J. 07018

Jefferson National Corp.
One Huntington Quadrangle
Huntington Station, N. Y. 11746

Jemal, Ralph D.
94 Percheron Lane
Roslyn Heights, N. Y. 11577

Komarek, H. R. Real Estate
   Investments
6638 E. Kiami
Tucson, Arizona 85715

Jones, Alan I. Investments, Inc.
3128 Lemmon Ave. E.
Dallas, Texas 75204

Jordan Financial Corp.
8700 King George Drive
Dallas, Texas 75235

Johnson-Loggins, Inc.
1601 First City East Bldg.
Houston, Texas 77002

Janis, Edward
30 East 42nd St.
New York, N. Y. 10017

Johnston, Lemon, & Co.
1425 "H" St. N. W.
Washington, D. C. 20005

Kreedman Realty &
   Construction Corp.
9601 Wilshire Blvd.
Beverly Hills, Calif. 90212

Kennedy Mgmt. Corp.
Rt. 1
1159 Poquonnock Rd.
Groton, Conn. 06340

Kaufman & Broad Bldg. Co.
18610 W. Eight Mile Rd.
Southfield, Mich. 48075

Knott Hotels Corp.
575 Madison Ave.
New York, N. Y. 10022

Kenney, Michael K. & Assocs.
Drawer 1598
Beverly Hills, Calif. 90213

Kay Properties
Suite 201
17071 Ventura Blvd.
Encino, Calif. 91316

Khan, J. & Co.
65 Via Chepairo
Greenbrae, Calif. 94904

Kilroy Industries
626 Wilshire Blvd.
Los Angeles, Calif. 90017

Kendrick, Maurer & Smith, Inc.
P. O. Box 1129
San Diego, Calif. 92112

Kato Enterprises, Inc.
7580 W. 20th Ave.
Denver, Colo. 80215

Keyes National Investors
2525 S. W. Third Ave.
Miami, Fla. 33129

Kent Investment & Realty Co.
695 E. Wesley Rd. N. E.
Atlanta, Ga. 30324

Kessler Co.
P. O. Box 6301
Louisville, Ky. 40206

Katzenberg, Herbert M.
707 N. Calvert St.
Baltimore, Md. 21202

Kao, Henry S.
340 Darby Lane
Mountainside, N. J. 07092

Kislak, J. I. Inc.
581 Broad St.
Newark, N. J. 07102

Kramer, Albert R. Syndications
1758 E. 54th St.
Brooklyn, N. Y. 11234

Kay & Co.
60 E. Hartsdale Ave.
Hartsdale, N. Y. 10530

The Kempner Corp.
60 E. 42nd St.
New York, N. Y. 10017

Kenney, Charles
60 East 42nd St.
New York, N. Y. 10017

Klausner Associates
280 Madison Ave.
New York, N. Y. 10016

Koeppel & Koeppel
26 Broadway
New York, N. Y. 10004

Kreitman, Richard
128 Court St.
White Plains, N. Y. 10601

Kling, Harold G. Inc.
310 Tri State Bldg.
Cincinnati, Ohio 45202

Knox & Reilly
401 Wood St.
Pittsburgh, Pa. 15222

Kaplan, Melvin
155 Montgomery St.
Suite 240
San Francisco, Calif. 94104

Kelly, Tim
755 New Ballas Rd.
St. Louis, Mo. 63141

KPK Corp.
100 S. Wacker Dr.
Chicago, Ill. 60606

Killearn Properties
Tallahassee Bank Bldg.
Tallahassee, Fla. 32303

Larwin Mortgage Investors
16255 Ventura Blvd.
Encino, Calif. 91316

Life Investment Planning Co.
130 Bush St.
San Francisco, Calif. 94104

Lincoln Cos.
2648 S. York
Denver, Colo. 80210

The Lendorff (U.S.A.) Group
   of Companies
2841 Greenbriar Parkway S. W.
Atlanta, Ga. 30331

Ladson Investments
Box 338
Vidalia, Ga. 30474

Lee, Herbert
1005 Kaimoku Place
Honolulu, Hawaii 96821

Logan, Seymour N. Associates
29 S. La Salle St.
Chicago, Ill. 60603

The Earle Lipchin Co.
530 St. Paul Place
Baltimore, Md. 21202

Landahl, Brown, & Weed Assocs.
8605 Cameron St.
Silver Springs, Md. 20910

Lexton-Ancira
4901 Main
Kansas City, Missouri 64112

Link Investment Realty
Suite 1106
1st National Bank Bldg.
Reno, Nevada 89591

Low & Low
66 Hawley St.
Binghamton, N. Y. 13901

Lambert Brussels Real Estate Corp.
280 Park Ave.
New York, N. Y. 10017

Lavergene, Mel Interests
Suite 306
900 Town & Country Lane
Houston, Texas 77024

Lawrence, Sylvan Co.
100 William St.
New York, N. Y. 10038

Lehman Brothers
One William St.
New York, N. Y. 10004

Levy, Sydney
575 Lexington Ave.
New York, N. Y. 10022

Lipstein, Michael
425 Park Ave.
New York, N. Y. 10022

Loeb, Rhoades & Co., Inc.
42 Wall St.
New York, N. Y. 10005

Lyman, G. Realty Corp.
641 Lexington Ave.
New York, N. Y. 10022

The Lynford Organization Inc.
Suite 3502
375 Park Ave.
New York, N. Y. 10022

Land Mortgages Co.
Gem City Sugs. Bldg.
Dayton, Ohio 45402

Lomma International, Inc.
305 Cherry St.
Scranton, Pa. 18505

Lakeway
1200 Lakeway Dr.
Austin, Texas

Luedecke Co., Realtors
4305 Marathon Blvd.
Austin, Texas 78756

Lomar Properties
Box 19932
Dallas, Texas 75219

Landmark Equities Corp.
Suite 700
600 Jefferson St.
Houston, Texas 77002

The Lehndorff (U.S.A.) Group
of Companies
6401 Banyan Glen
Houston, Texas 77027

Lane, Ernest W. & Co.
2266 N. Prospect Ave.
Milwaukee, Wisc. 53202

Lee & Waxer, Inc.
2040 W. Wisconsin Avenue
Milwaukee, Wisc. 53233

Liska Investment Co., Inc.
Box 7002/7600 Harwood Ave.
Milwaukee, Wisc. 53213

Lozoff, Shelby
1840 N. Farwell Ave.
Milwaukee, Wisc. 53202

Luljack Inc.
7211 W. Fond duLac Ave.
Milwaukee, Wisc. 53218

Lambrecht Realty Co.
3300 Penobscot Bldg.
Detroit, Mich.

Land Investment Research Co.
1801 Century Park W.
Los Angeles, Calif. 90067

Lariver, Marvin
100 Ashley Drive
Tampa, Fla. 33602

Ludlow Corp.
145 Rosemary St.
Medham Hts., Mass. 02194

McDowell Enterprises, Inc.
P. O. Box 149
Nashville, Tenn. 37202

McNeil Real Estate Fund, Ltd.
c/o Pacific Plan of California
2200 Sand Hill Road
Menlo Park, Calif. 94025

McCormick Investments, Inc.
Two First National Plaza
Chicago, Ill. 60670

McKinney & Co.
Suite 5016
1717 Penn Avenue
Pittsburgh, Pa. 15221

McDowell Enterprises, Inc.
P. O. Box 149
Nashville, Tenn. 37202

Metropolitan Development Corp.
8447 Wilshire Blvd.
Beverly Hills, Calif. 90211

Midwestern Mortgage Investors
1630 Welton St.
Denver, Colo. 80202

Mobile Home Communities
A-360 Prudential Plaza
Denver, Colo. 80202

Mott, Don Assoc., Inc.
120 S. Court Ave.
Orlando, Fla. 32801

Multivest, Inc.
222255 Greenfield Rd.
Southfield, Mich. 48075

Magna Investment &
  Development Corp.
2015 S. 2nd St. East
Salt Lake City, Utah 84102

Markborough Properties Ltd.
50 Holly Street
Toronto, Ontario
Canada

Metric International Realty
3740 E. Seventh
Long Beach, Calif. 90804

Meadows, Inc.
6053 Expressway
Jacksonville, Fla. 32211

Mills, J. B. Co.
420 Lincoln Rd.
Miami Beach, Fla. 33139

Marcus, Elton D. Developers
10912 56th St.
Tampa, Fla. 33617

Maryland Industrial Enterprises
Box 5381
Baltimore, Md. 21209

The March Co.
225 Franklin St.
Boston, Mass. 02110

Moskow, Michael B. & Co.
Two Park Square
Boston, Mass. 02116

Mansour Developments
1009 Detroit St.
Flint, Mich. 48503

Muellee, J. C. Investment Co.
7301 Natural Bridge Road
St. Louis, Missouri 63121

Manufacturers & Traders Trust Co.
One M & T Plaza
Buffalo, N. Y. 14240

Maidman, Irving
1465 Broadway
New York, N. Y. 10036

Matrock Equities
48 W. 21st Street
New York, N. Y. 10010

Merrill Lynch, Pierce, Fenner &
  Smith
70 Pire St.
New York, N. Y. 10801

Mortgage Advisory Service Co.
700 Terminal Tower
Cleveland, Ohio 44113

Manhattan Investment Co.
935 E. Broad St.
Columbus, Ohio 43205

Murnen, Ray A. Co.
1314 Madison Ave.
Toledo, Ohio 43624

Merriam, John W.
123 S. Broad St.
Philadelphia, Pa. 19109

MCI Properties, Inc.
Suite 2400
2001 Bryan Tower
Dallas, Texas 75201

Murchison Brothers
First National Bank Bldg.
Dallas, Texas 75202

Maxwell, Jack Investments
2525 Ridgmar Blvd.
Fort Worth, Texas 76116

Murphree, Dennis E. Interests
707 River Oak Bank Bldg.
Houston, Texas 77019

Munz Investment Real Estate, Inc.
Suite 913
110 E. Main
Madison, Wisconsin 53703

Murray Director Affiliates, Inc.
16 West 46th St.
New York, N. Y. 10036

Monogram Industries
10889 Wilshire Blvd.
Los Angeles, Calif. 90024

Monumental Corp.
N. E. Corner Charles & Chase
Baltimore, Md. 21202

Mountain States Financial Corp.
2808 Central S. E.
Albuquerque, N. M. 87106

Madison Square Garden Corp.
410 Park Ave.
New York, N. Y. 10022

Northern California Developers Inc.
2026 K Street
Sacramento, Calif. 95814

North Washington Land Co.
1160 Rockville Pike
Rockville, Md. 20852

Northampton Corp.
9823 Central Ave.
Upper Marlboro, Md. 20870

N. Y. Equities Inc.
280 Broadway
New York, N. Y. 10007

National Funding Corp. of America
301 Almeria Ave.
Miami, Fla. 33134

Norwood-Edison Realty
6063 Northwest Hwy.
Chicago, Ill. 60631

Northland Capital Corp.
402 W. First St.
Duluth, Mich. 55802

Norman Holding Company
926 Phelps Rd.
Teaneck, N. J. 07666

Nationwide Equities, Inc.
505 Park Ave.
New York, N. Y. 10022

Nationwide Real Estate Co.
200 W. 57th St.
New York, N. Y. 10019

Nelson Co.
103 Park Ave.
New York, N. Y. 10017

New York Securities Co.
One N. Y. Plaza
New York, N. Y. 10004

Northern Union Holdings Corp.
3665 W. 117th St.
Cleveland, Ohio 44111

North Central Mortgage Corp.
Hulman Bldg.
Dayton, Ohio 45402

Nordlinger Realty Co.
6824 Shawnee Rd.
Richmond, Va. 23225

Nielson Realty Inc.
4225 W. North Ave.
Milwaukee, Wisc. 53208

National Homes
Earl Ave. & Wallace St.
Lafayette, Ind. 47902

National Realty Investments
31 Milk St.
Boston, Mass. 02109

National Equities
200 Park Ave.
New York, N. Y. 10017

Noyes, Charles F. Co.
42 Broadway
New York, N. Y. 10004

Orr, F. W. Inc.
P. O. Box 238
Summit, N. J. 07901

Ornstein, J. Alan Assoc.
295 Madison Ave.
New York, N. Y. 10017

O'Keefe & Eisenberg, Inc.
646 Tuckahoe Rd.
Yonkers, N. Y. 10710

Olimol Realty, Inc.
2510 West Eighth St.
Erie, Pa. 16505

Overton, W. W. & Co., Inc.
One Main Place
Dallas, Texas 75250

Owen Realty Co.
3136 W. Sixth
Fort Worth, Texas 76107

Occidental Petroleum
10889 Wilshire Blvd.
Los Angeles, Calif. 90024

Pacific Coast Properties, Inc.
1633 26th St.
Santa Monica, Calif. 90404

Prel Corp.
Park 80 Plaza West-One
Saddle Brook, N. J. 07662

Prescott-Lancaster Corp.
18 Lancster Rd.
Union, N. J. 07083

Presidential Realty Corp.
180 S. Broadway
White Plains, N. Y. 10605

Puget Park Corp.
904 Seventh Ave.
Seattle, Wash. 98104

Peel Village Developments Co., Ltd.
170 Kennedy Rd. S.
Brampton, Ontario
Canada

Palo Verde Investment Co.
1800 N. Central Ave.
Phoenix, Ariz. 85004

Panorama International Real Estate
810 18th St. N. W.
Washington, D. C. 20006

Philipsborn Equities, Inc.
2121 Ponce De Leon Blvd.
Coral Gables, Florida 33124

Property Resources Co.
7799 S. W. 62nd Ave.
South Miami, Florida 33143

Property Research & Investment
Suite 924
57 Forsyth St. N. W.
Atlanta, Ga. 30303

Pivar, Alvin R. Real Estate
10065 Wind Stream
Wilde Lake
Columbia, Md. 21043

P & L Assoc.
76-09 172nd St.
Hillcrest, N. Y. 11366

Paine, Webber, Jackson
  & Curtis, Inc.
140 Broadway
New York, N. Y. 10005

Presidential Realty Corp.
180 S. Broadway
White Plains, N. Y. 10605

Pearson, Charles C. Co.
Leader Bldg.
Cleveland, Ohio 44114

Priemer, Barnes & Assoc.
2829 Euclid Ave.
Cleveland, Ohio 44115

Perrault, Ainslie Co.
728 S. Boulder Ave.
Tulsa, Oklahoma 74103

Properties Diversified, Inc.
3207 N. Front St.
Harrisburg, Pa. 17110

Prudential Bond & Mortgage Co.
4149 East Thompson St.
Philadelphia, Pa. 19137

Pennsylvania Real Estate
  Investment Trust (PREIT)
Cedarbrook Hill
Wyncote, Pa. 19095

Palmetto Corp.
Box 20027
Houston, Texas 77025

Perssion, Sidney Investment Co.
1910 W. Wells St.
Milwaukee, Wisc. 53233

Property Capital Trust
3 Center Plaza
Boston, Mass. 02108

Paxton, Frank Corp.
6311 St. John Ave.
Kansas City, Mo. 64123

Perinin Corp.
71-73 Mount Wayte Ave.
Framingham, Mass. 01701

Philip Morris
100 Park Ave.
New York, N. Y. 10017

Prosher Corp.
1900 Ave. of the Stars
Los Angeles, Calif. 90067

Pangles Master Markets
1100 A Prosperity Rd.
Lima, Ohio 45802

Pick Hotels Corp.
20 N. Wacker Dr.
Chicago, Ill. 60606

Perry, A. W. Inc.
44 Bromfield St.
Boston, Mass. 02108

Royal Palm Beach Colony, Inc.
8101 Biscayne Blvd.
Miami, Fla. 33138

Riker Delaware Corp.
La Gorce Sq.
Burlington, N. J. 08016

The Richards Group, Inc.
107 Northern Boulevard
Great Neck, N. Y. 11021

Realty Equities Corp. of New York
375 Park Ave.
New York, New York 10022

Real Estate Equities Corp.
Suite 315
Paulsen Bldg.
Spokane, Washington 99201

Revenue Properties Co. Ltd.
12 Sheppard St.
Toronto, Ontario
Canada

Real Estate Capital Corp.
1185 Roberto Lane
Los Angeles, Calif. 90024

Rossco, Incorporated
Suite 1600
1900 Ave. of the Stars
Los Angeles, Calif. 90067

Real Property Consultants
2390 El Camino Real
Palo Alto, Calif. 94306

Realty Systems Inc.
Suite A- 360
Prudential Plaza
Englewood, Colorado 80110

Rose, Irwin R. & Co.
1840 N. Meridian St.
Indianapolis, Ind. 46202

Riggs Realty Co.
4 Woodsend Place
Potomac, Md. 20854

Ramsac Corp.
21001 Van Born Rd.
Taylor, Mich. 48180

Ryan Co.
1158 S. Glenstone
Springfield, Mo. 65804

Roberts Realty Investment
   & Development Co.
913 E. Charleston Blvd.
Las Vegas, Nevada 89104

Rachlin & Co.
17 Academy St.
Newark, N. J. 07102

Rosen, Robert A.
8529 Wicklow Place
Jamaica Estates, N. Y. 11432

Rappoport, Simon & Stanley
41 E. 42nd St.
New York, N. Y. 10017

Rafaco Enterprises, Inc.
60 E. 42nd St.
New York, N. Y. 10017

Rei Properties, Inc.
375 Park Ave.
New York, N. Y. 10022

Ritter, Leo & Co.
Suite 1700
1776 Broadway
New York, N. Y. 10019

Rosenthal & Rosenthal Inc.
1451 Broadway
New York, N. Y. 10036

Rosen Bros.
731 James St.
New York, N. Y. 13203

Rabkin, Sig Realty Co.
515 Melish Ave.
Cincinnati, Ohio 45229

Ramonoff, Milford M. Inc.
2616 W. Central Ave.
Toledo, Ohio 43606

Raskin, Edwin B. Co.
15th Floor
Third National Bank Bldg.
Nashville, Tenn. 37219

Rogers, Lyman David
2123 First National Bank Bldg.
Dallas, Texas 75202

Ragland, Inc.
P. O. Box 852
Houston, Texas 77001

Real Estate Equities Corp.
Suite 315
Paulsen Bldg.
Spokane, Wash. 99201

Rhodes Investment Co.
Broadway Terrace Bldg.
Tacoma, Wash. 98401

Republic Housing Corp.
1700 Main
Dallas, Texas 75201

Rouse Co.
American City Bldg.
Ellicott City, Md. 21043

Realty Investment Co.
P. O. Box 747
Hilo, Hi. 96720

Southern Realty & Utilities
15450 N. W. 27th Ave.
Miami, Fla. 33054

Statler Hotels Delaware Corp.
208 S. La Salle St.
Chicago, Ill. 60604

Sheraton Corp. of America
470 Atlantic Ave.
Boston, Mass. 02210

Smokler, Bert L & Co.
Northland Towers W.
Southfield, Mich. 48075

Shelter Corp. of America, Inc.
1550 E. 78th St.
Minneapolis, Minn. 55423

Seaway Shopping Centers, Inc.
275 Madison Ave.
New York, N. Y. 10016

Sea Pines Co.
Hilton Head Island,
South Carolina 29928

Sears Enterprises, Inc.
Eight Paseo Redondo W.
Tucson, Ariz. 85705

SMK Investments
P. O. Box 12766
Tucson, Arizona 85711

Shreiber, Howard E. Realty
Investment Co.
9300 Wilshire Blvd.
Beverly Hills, Calif. 90212

Stuart Schwab & Co.
Suite 700
9701 Wilshire Blvd.
Beverly Hills, Calif. 90212

Stein, Darling & Co., Inc.
Suite 300
11440 San Vicente Blvd.
Los Angeles, Calif. 90049

Synergised Real Estate, Inc.
6222 Wilshire Blvd.
Los Angeles, Calif. 90048

Starkey Investment Co.
332 B St.
San Diego, Calif. 92101

Spectrum Financial Cos.
1700 S. El Camino Real
San Mateo, Calif. 94402

Summit County Investment Co.
P. O. Box 188
Breckenridge, Colorado 80424

Schuchat, David G.
Investment Bldg.
Washington, D. C. 20005

Stevens, Howard B. Inc.
P. O. Box 2024
Miami Beach, Fla. 33140

Shidler & Petty
21st Floor
745 Fort St.
Honolulu, Hawaii 96813

Sampson, Bogeaus & Shafer
799 Elm St.
Winnetka, Ill. 60093

S-G Securities, Inc.
Suite 1050
One Boston Place
Boston, Mass. 02108

State Properties of New England
59 Temple Place
Boston, Mass. 02111

Sarko, Harold Inc.
8701 E. Seven Mile Rd.
Detroit, Mich. 48234

Smith Finance Corp.
1555 Penobscot Bldg.
Detroit, Mich. 48226

S & A Realty Co.
7755 Carondelet Ave.
St. Louis, Missouri 63105

Small Business Investment
  Corp. of America
One W. Main St.
Hackensack, N. J. 07602

Stirling, Don Inc.
1518 Old Country Rd.
Elmsford, N. Y. 10523

Schneider, Walter J.
185 Great Neck Rd.
Great Neck, N. Y. 11021

Smolen, Michael H.
82 Hanson Lane
New Rochelle, N. Y. 10804

Segal, Ken
41 E. 57th St.
New York, N. Y. 10022

Shearson Realty & Development
14 Wall St.
New York, N. Y. 10005

Silverstein, Harry G. & Sons
801 2nd Ave.
New York, N. Y. 10017

Smith, Barney Real Estate Corp.
1345 Ave. of the Americas
New York, N. Y. 10019

Society Realty Inc.
243 E. 39th St.
New York, N. Y. 10016

Storper & Co.
663 Fifth Ave.
New York, N. Y. 10022

Swig, Weiler & Arnow
437 Madison Ave.
New York, N. Y. 10022

Spaulding Securities Corp.
201 Chamber of Commerce Bldg.
Syracuse, N. Y. 13202

Schulman Investment Co.
Four Corporate Park Dr.
White Plains, N. Y. 10604

Standard S & L Assn.
10 W. Third St.
Winston Salem, N. C. 27101

Stein, David
4752 Reading Rd.
Cincinnati, Ohio 45237

Schottenstein Investment Corp.
37 N. Third St.
Columbus, Ohio 43215

Sylvania Realty & Investment Co.
5808 Monroe St.
Sylvania, Ohio 43560

Swartz, Seymour
1920 Collingwood Blvd.
Toledo, Ohio 43624

Sanditen, Wilfred Investments
3314 E. 51st St.
Tulsa, Oklahoma 74135

The Seltzer Partnership
100 Presidential Blvd.
Bala Cynwyd, Pa. 19004

Shannon Associates
Suite 304
One Fairway Plaza
Huntingdon Valley, Pa. 19006

Shott Realty Co., Inc.
Box 6116
Salt Lake City, Utah 84106

Saracino, Tony Inc.
3324 S. State
Salt Lake City, Utah 84115

Stendig Development Corp.
2500 Riverside Drive.
Danville, Va. 24541

Santa Anita Consolidated Inc.
1 Wilshire Blvd.
Los Angeles, Calif. 90017

Thunderbird International Corp.
525 N. Sepulveda Blvd.
El Segundo, Calif. 90245

Texmar Realty Co.
19 W. 44th St.
New York, N. Y. 10036

Tishman Realty & Construction
Co., Inc.
666 Fifth Ave.
New York, N. Y. 10019

Terry, William E. & Co., Inc.
Hall Bldg.
Little Rock, Arkansas 72201

Thom, Sidney M. & Co., Inc.
233 Louisiana St.
Little Rock, Ark. 72201

Transcontinental Heritage Inc.
9025 Wilshire Blvd.
Beverly Hills, Calif. 90211

Tamkin, Jeffrey H.
10960 Wilshire Blvd.
Los Angeles, Calif. 90024

Transamerican Investment
Properties, Inc.
260 North Rock Rd.
Wichita, Kansas 67206

Transamerican Properties
Suite 237
1500 N. Woodward Bldg.
Birmingham, Mich. 48011

Two Trees Inc.
Ten E. 53rd St.
New York, N. Y. 10022

Third Western Realty Co.
230 Concord St.
Dayton, Ohio 45408

Time, Inc.
Rockefeller Center
New York, N. Y. 10020

Tomerlin Properties
6418 Fisher Rd.
Dallas, Texas 75214

The Scott A. Taggert Co.
430 E. 2nd St.
Salt Lake City, Utah 84111

Tenneco Inc.
1010 Milam
Houston, Tx. 77002

Triester, S. L. Investment
& Financial Corp.
1700 Market St.
Philadelphia, Pa. 19103

The Titan Group
529 5th Ave.
New York, N. Y. 10017

Transcontinental Investment
201 E. 42nd St.
New York, N. Y. 10017

Timber Products Co.
523 W. 6th St.
Los Angeles, Calif. 90014

Union America Mortgage
Banking & Real Estate Group
2700 Wilshire Blvd.
Los Angeles, Calif. 90057

United Investors
1721 K Street N. W.
Washington, D. C. 20006

Unisource Corp.
6700 France Ave.
Minneapolis, Minn. 55435

United Equities Ltd.
367 Ellece Ave.
Winnipeg, Manitoba
Canada

Unionamerica Advisors, Inc.
9595 Wilshire Blvd.
Beverly Hills, Calif. 90212

U. S. Financial Pacific
1250 Sixth Ave.
San Diego, Calif. 92101

Universal Realty Corp.
2198 E. Main St.
Bridgeport, Conn. 06610

United Properties Ltd.
1309 Rand Road
Arlington Heights, Ill. 60004

United National Corp.
745 Fifth Ave.
New York, N. Y. 10022

Univest Inc.
500 W. Wilson Bridge Rd.
Worthington, Ohio 43085

United Investors Realty Corp.
Bon Accord Farm Rd. 3
Boyertown, Pa. 19512

Uris Bldgs. Corp.
850 3rd Ave.
New York, N. Y. 10022

U. S. Realty Investments
Terminal Tower
Cleveland, Ohio 44113

U. S. Financial
1298 Prospect St.
La Jolla, Calif. 92037

Valley Forge Corp.
P. O. Box 855
Valley Forge, Penn. 19482

Victoria Ward Ltd.
Room 601
1240 Ala Moana
Honolulu, Hawaii 96814

Viking Investment Corp.
Box 123
Lawrence, Kansas 66044

The Vantage Companies
2525 Stemmons Twy.
Dallas, Texas 75207

Western Pioneer Co.
3243 Wilshire Blvd.
Los Angeles, Calif. 90005

Wollack, Richard
1131 Ingraham Bldg.
Miami, Fla. 33131

Walter, Jim Corp.
1500 N. Dale Mabry Hwy.
Tampa, Fla. 33607

W L K P Realty Corp.
60 E. 42nd St.
New York, N. Y. 10017

The Wolf Corp.
10 E. 40th St.
N. Y., N. Y. 10016

Wallace Investments Inc.
Hartford Bldg.
Dallas, Texas 75201

Willis M. Allen Co.
1127 Wall St.
La Jolla, Calif. 92037

Williams-Bowker Co.
2233 Watt Ave.
Sacramento, Calif. 95825

Winski, Louis R. & Co.
5475 Pire Ave.
San Diego, Calif. 92122

Westminister Investing Corp.
1511 K St. N. W.
Washington, D. C. 20005

Westcoast Realty
1890 S. Ocean Dr.
Hallandale, Fla. 33009

Wietor, Michael G.
6031 Hollywood Blvd.
Hollywood, Fla. 33024

Werner, Wollack & Co.
25 S. E. 2nd Ave.
Miami, Fla. 33131

Wilfred Wolfson Properties
800 National Bldg.
Minneapolis, Minn. 55402

Ward, Raymond E.
12213 E. 39th Terr.
Independence, Mo. 64052

Weintraub, Robert G.R.I.
37 Washington St.
Binghamton, N. Y. 13901

Walker, G. H. & Co.
45 Wall St.
New York, N. Y. 10005

Walter & Samuels
342 Madison Ave.
New York, N. Y. 10017

Weis, Voison, & Co., Inc.
111 Broadway
New York, N. Y. 10006

White, Weld & Co.
20 Broad St.
New York, N. Y. 10005

Wolfson, Theodore
1472 Broadway
New York, N. Y. 10036

The E. Laurence Weisman Co.
414 Brook Ford Rd.
Syracuse, N. Y. 13224

Warr Realty Co.
315 N. Harvey
Oklahoma City, Ok. 73102

Westminster Properties, Inc.
85 Westminster St.
Providence, R. I. 02903

Wichita Investment Co.
Republic Bank Tower
Dallas, Texas 75201

Weatherby, Lester C.
1306 Trans-American Bldg.
Fort Worth, Texas 76102

Wallace-McConaughy Corp.
Walker Bank Bldg.
Salt Lake City, Utah 84111

Weil-McClain
10400 N. Central Expressway
Dallas, Texas 75231

Weyerhauser Real Estate Co.
2525 S. 336th St.
Federal Way, Wash. 98002

Wickes Corp.
110 W. "A" St.
San Diego, Calif. 92101

Weingarten Markets Realty
600 Lockwood
Houston, Texas 77011

Weaver Bros. Inc.
1446 New York Ave. N. W.
Washington, D. C. 20005

Ziegelman, Aaron
200 W. 57th St.
New York, N. Y. 10019

Other Groups of Lenders and Brokers

Although a number of major lenders for mortgage loans have been discussed, these by no means corner the market. In times of economic changes, significant shifts in mortgage trends occur. Many sources should be considered before the borrower makes a decision on what institution or group or person will carry his mortgage. Some of the most important groups and lenders not yet discussed follow.

BANK HOLDING COMPANIES

The bank holding companies, like the S and L holding companies, have more liberal lending capabilities than banks themselves. They can own other financing institutions of all types and descriptions including finance companies and mortgage banking companies. This is a list of the most important bank holding companies, listed by regions of the country they usually serve.

	ASSETS
NORTHEASTERN UNITED STATES	
The Bank of New York Company, Inc. 48 Wall Street New York, New York 10015	$3,811,045,625
Charter New York Corporation One Wall Street New York, New York 10005	7,448,752,595
Financial General Bankshares, Inc. 1701 Pennsylvania Avenue, N.W. Washington, D.C. 20006	1,827,817,912
Lincoln First Banks, Inc. One Lincoln First Square Rochester, New York 14643	2,544,480,000
WESTERN UNITED STATES	
Bank of America National Trust & Savings Assn. Bank of America Center San Francisco, California 94120	40,845,476,000

WESTERN UNITED STATES *(Continued)*

Crocker National Bank One Montgomery Street San Francisco, California 94138	$ 7,180,286,923
Security Pacific National Bank 561 South Spring Street Los Angeles, California 90051	11,688,925,468
Wells Fargo Bank, NA 464 California Street San Francisco, California 94120	8,924,671,000
Western Bancorporation 600 South Spring Street Los Angeles, California 90054	15,214,508,129

CENTRAL UNITED STATES

BancOhio Corporation 51 North High Street Columbus, Ohio 43216	2,531,760,067
Cleveland Trust Company 900 Euclid Avenue Cleveland, Ohio 44101	3,097,437,101
Continental Illinois National Bank & Trust Company 231 South LaSalle Street Chicago, Illinois 60693	12,287,965,000
First Bank System, Inc. 14th Floor, First National Bank Building Minneapolis, Minnesota 55480	433,762,345
First National Bank of Chicago One First National Plaza Chicago, Illinois 60670	11,061,130,000
First Wisconsin Bankshares Corp. 735 North Water Street Milwaukee, Wisconsin 53202	2,909,428,240
Michigan National Corp. 1700 North Woodward, P.O. Box 589 Bloomfield Hills, Michigan 48013	2,657,012,000
Northwest Bancorporation 1200 Northwestern Bank Building Minneapolis, Minnesota 55480	447,618,000

SOUTH-SOUTHWESTERN UNITED STATES

Citizens & Southern National Bank 35 Broad Street, N.W. Atlanta, Georgia 30301	2,499,246,262

SOUTH-SOUTHWESTERN UNITED STATES *(Continued)*

First City Bancorporation of Texas, Inc.   2,638,436,000
1001 Main Street, P.O. Box 2557
Houston, Texas 77001

First International Bancshares, Inc.   3,485,188,000
First National Bank Building, P.O. Box 6031
Dallas, Texas 75202

Republic National Bank of Dallas   3,649,182,235
Pacific and Ervary Street
Dallas, Texas 75222

SAVINGS AND LOAN HOLDING COMPANIES

General Characteristics — The S and L holding company is a corporation set up under federal and state law by an S and L, the major stockholders of an S and L, or an individual who has controlling interest in the S and L.

This company is allowed more latitude in type, size, and geographic spread of loans than is the S and L itself.

Most of these are organized as stock companies and have, in addition to the S and L, other subsidiaries such as finance, business investment, and leasing companies. Some may even own real estate.

Kinds of Loans — How to Apply — Through associate subsidiaries, holding companies can make short-term and interim loans, standby and gap loans, wrap-around mortgages, participation loans with other S and L's, and many other types of financings.

Normal loan procedures would follow if the holding company showed interest in financing the project.

SAVINGS AND LOAN HOLDING COMPANIES

American Financial Corporation
1 East Fourth Street
Cincinnati, Ohio 45202

California Financial Corporation
11 Tillman Place
San Francisco, California 94108

Empire Financial Corporation
6750 Van Nuys Boulevard
Van Nuys, California 91405

Far West Financial Corporation
626 Wilshire Boulevard
Los Angeles, California 90017

Financial Corp. of Santa Barbara
7 West Figueroa Street
Santa Barbara, California 93104

Financial Federation Inc.
615 South Flower
  at Wilshire Boulevard
Los Angeles, California 90017

First Charter Financial Corporation
9465 Wilshire Boulevard
Beverly Hills, California 90212

First Lincoln Financial Corporation
640 West Sixth Street
Los Angeles, California 90017

First S&L Shares Inc.
1630 Welton Street
Denver, Colorado 80202

First Surety Corporation
237 East Olive Avenue
Burbank, California 91503

First Western Financial Corp.
112 Las Vegas Boulevard South
Las Vegas, Nevada 89101

Gibraltar Financial Corporation
of California
9111 Wilshire Boulevard
Beverly Hills, California 90213

Golden West Financial Corporation
1970 Broadway
Oakland, California 94612

Great Western Financial Corporation
8484 Wilshire Boulevard
Beverly Hills, California 90211

Hawthorne Financial Corporation
13005 South Hawthorne Boulevard
Hawthorne, California 90250

Imperial Corporation of America
2320 Fifth Avenue
San Diego, California 92101

Trans-World Financial Company
9601 Wilshire Boulevard
Beverly Hills, California 90210

Union Financial Corporation
One Terminal Tower
Cleveland, Ohio 44113

United Financial Corporation
of California
9800 South Sepulveda Boulevard
Los Angeles, California 90045

Warner National Corporation
136 East Sixth Street
Cincinnati, Ohio 45202

Wesco Financial Corporation
315 East Colorado Boulevard
Pasadena, California 91109

CREDIT UNIONS

Corporate credit unions are known from time to time to finance homes and other projects for employees as well as outside investors, developers, and owners of real estate. Examples of these groups are the various public school teacher credit unions.

Credit Unions may be located by checking with companies in any locale or through mortgage banking companies.

If secured private placements on corporate realty are involved, contact would be made through investment bankers or counselors.

INVESTMENT CLUBS

There are thousands of investment clubs in this country, some of which invest in real estate.

One of the best ways to get information on these clubs is through the National Association of Investment Clubs, 1515 East 11 Mile Road, Royal Oak, Detroit, Michigan 48068. The executive director is Thomas O'Hara. The association has over 13,000 member clubs.

INVESTMENT BANKERS

Services — Many investment banking houses have excellent realty capabilities. They can be a very important source of aid to one seeking funds for traditional or corporate realty.

Depending on the house and its particular interest, here are some of the services it may provide:

(1) Public underwriting of a company, REIT, limited partnership, or other public vehicles.

(2) Private placements of secured mortgage bonds or unsecured notes.

(3) Public mortgage bond underwriting.

(4) Mortgage financing, usually through real estate subsidiaries.

(5) Net lease financing.

(6) Realty consulting, usually through a real estate subsidiary.

(7) Research.

Developing the Proper Contact — Investment bankers can be approached directly, but it might be a better idea to ask commercial bankers, attorneys, or accountants for a proper introduction to the investment banking house that can best fulfill the inquirer's financing needs.

A specialist in the house is assigned to projects, and it is best when meeting with him to evaluate his and the house's expertise in any particular area.

Costs — The person seeking funds usually pays most of the initial expenses for the project. In addition, the house gets a percentage of the venture when it is sold. In the case of an underwriting, this could mean many thousands of dollars.

CORPORATE BOND TRUSTS AND MUTUAL FUNDS

Some of the publicly traded mutual funds invest in real estate, for the most part, through the private placement of securities with corporations and occasionally through mortgages as well as real estate ownership.

Corporate bond trusts are interested in public or private placements only. Private placements involving real estate of both the mutual funds and corporate bond funds are usually secured not only by direct debt but also by a mortgage on the land and building improvements. This may also include financing of the fixtures and equipment.

How to Make Application — Mutual funds are approached best through the investment banker, if private placement is sought, and through an astute mortgage banker in the case of mortgages. REITS are essentially mutual funds; however, some diversified mutual funds make real estate investments directly or indirectly. The borrower can, of course, make

direct contact with the investment officer either in charge of private placements or real estate loans and acquisitions.

CORPORATE BOND TRUSTS

The following is a list of corporate bond trusts and investment companies that invest to some degree in private placements:

American General Bond Fund
3910 Keswick Rd.
Baltimore, Maryland 21211

Drexel Bond-Debenture
   Trading Fund
1500 Walnut Street
Philadelphia, Pennsylvania 19102

Federated Income & Private
   Placement Fund
450 Penabscot Bldg.
Detroit, Michigan 48226

John Hancock Investors
200 Berkley
Boston, Massachusetts 02117

Lincoln National Direct Placement
   Fund
1301 S. Harrison St.
Ft. Wayne, Indiana 46802

Mutual of Omaha
3205 Dodge St.
Omaha, Nebraska 68131

CNA Larwin Investment
9100 Wilshire Boulevard
Beverly Hills, California 90212

The REIT Income Fund
294 Washington Street
Boston, Massachusetts 02108

St. Paul Securities
385 Washington Street
St. Paul, Minnesota 55102

Transamerica Income Shares
701 Montgomery Street
San Francisco, California 94111

INDIVIDUALS

Individuals who want to invest their money in mortgages usually
make themselves known to bankers, real estate and mortgage brokers and
often advertise in the press. In tight money days, it is individuals who make
many loans, of course, at higher interest rates but at the same time at greater risk to themselves.

Individual lenders are usually looking for shorter-term mortgages
than would be made by an institution, and terms and arrangements of these
loans by individuals are in no way standardized. Details are worked out
between the lender and borrower.

A real estate buyer should always consider asking a seller to take back
a purchase money mortgage. This is also a means by which a seller can
turn idle real estate equities into income for himself. Individual owners
can be very creative and are often willing to take high risks. They will
consider first, second or third mortgages, gap loans, wrap-arounds, piggy-
backs, land mortgages, and others.

Making Application — Your local newspaper real estate classified and display advertising sections carry names and addresses of people who want to invest their funds in mortgages and, as has been mentioned, real estate brokers and bankers usually have clients who want to put some of their money to work in good real estate loans.

ESTATES

Those acting as executors of estates may take back mortgages on property being liquidated from an estate or seek mortgages in which to invest funds on behalf of an estate.

Estates can be reached through attorneys specializing in estate and probate work, through commercial bank trust officers responsible for the management of estates, or through money management firms such as investment banking houses.

SMALL BUSINESS INVESTMENT COMPANIES AND MINORITY ENTERPRISE SMALL BUSINESS INVESTMENT COMPANIES

An SBIC is a Small Business Investment Corporation licensed and regulated by the Small Business Administration. SBIC's are intended to be profit-making firms and are either privately or publicly owned and operated. They exist to aid small businesses in many ways, ranging from furnishing equity capital to offering advisory services.

Some SBIC's will loan from $3,000 to well over $1,000,000 in construction and development and, in some cases, long-term mortgages.

The loans may be secured by real estate or unsecured with the proper credit and are available to the small businessman. In order to obtain a loan, it often helps to offer the small business investment company incentives through participation, warrants, convertibles, or outright sale of some of the company's stock to them.

SBIC's often participate with one another if loans are too large for one alone to undertake. The SBIC that assembles the package can be entitled to what is similar to a commission for this service.

Many commercial banks are establishing operating SBIC's. Additional information and aid through SBIC's can be obtained from the National Association of SBIC's, 512 Washington Building, Washington, D.C. 20005.

The Application — Loan preferences and varying investment policies differ substantially from firm to firm. They usually prefer to loan in their own geographical area, but may participate in other area loans if a local SBIC originates and services the loan. Application information is available from anyone of the SBIC's listed below. Loans are long term and usually must be made to a company with a net worth under $2.5 million and after-tax earnings of under $250,000 annually.

Submission requirements vary but one must usually submit financial statements including balance sheets and earning statements, projections for future income, background information on management, a statement on the use of funds, competitive position of the company, and a feasibility study of the real estate project to be purchased or built.

It should be remembered that SBIC and MESBIC lenders are primarily interested in financing real estate as it pertains to the operation and growth of a small business.

These SBIC's are listed by state. All of them will consider investments of $500,000 or greater on each application.

SMALL BUSINESS INVESTMENT COMPANIES

ALASKA

Alaska Business Investment
Corporation
P. O. Box 600
Anchorage, Alaska 99501

CALIFORNIA

Continental Capital Corporation
555 California Street, Suite 2690
San Francisco, California 94104

First Small Business Investment
Company of California
621 South Spring Street, Suite 505
Los Angeles, California 90014

First Southern Capital Corporation
1615 Cordova Street
Los Angeles, California 90007

Foothill Venture Company
8383 Wilshire Blvd.
Beverly Hills, California 90211

Unionamerica Capital Corporation
445 Figueroa Street
Los Angeles, California 90017

Wells Fargo Investment Company
475 Sansome Street
San Francisco, California 94111

COLORADO

Central Investment Corporation
of Denver
811 Central Bank Building
Denver, Colorado 80202

CONNECTICUT

Connecticut Venture Capital Corp.
37 Lewis Street
Hartford, Connecticut 06114

Connecticut Capital Corp.
488 Whalley Avenue
New Haven, Connecticut 06511

Conresco Corporation
10 River Street
Stamford, Connecticut 06901

The First Connecticut Small
Business Investment Company
177 State Street
Bridgeport, Connecticut 06603

First Miami SBIC
293 Post Road
Orange, Connecticut 06477

Hartford Community Capital
Corporation
777 Main Street
Hartford, Connecticut 06115

Investors Capital Corporation
955 Main Street
Bridgeport, Connecticut 06603

Manufacturers SBIC
of Connecticut
1488 Chapel Street
New Haven, Connecticut 06511

Marwit Capital Corporation
19 West Elm Street
Greenwich, Connecticut 06830

Northern Business Capital
Corporation
79 Isaac Street
Norwalk, Connecticut 06850

DELAWARE

Delaware Investment Company
200 West 9th Street
Wilmington, Delaware 19801

DISTRICT OF COLUMBIA

Allied Capital Corporation
1625 I St., N. W.
Washington, D. C. 20006

Capital Investment Company
of Washington
1001 Connecticut Ave., N. W.
Washington, D. C. 20006

Columbia Ventures, Inc.
1701 Pennsylvania Ave. N. W.
Washington, D.C. 20006

Distribution Services Inv.
Corporation
1725 K Street, N. W.
Washington, D. C. 20006

Greater Washington Industrial
Inv., Inc.
1015 18th Street, N. W.
Washington, D. C. 20036

North American Corporation
637 Washington Bldg.
Washington, D. C. 20005

Small Business Investment
Company of New York, Inc.
1701 Pennsylvania Avenue, N. W.,
Suite 960
Washington, D. C. 20006

FLORIDA

Arlington Florida Fund Inc.
6201 22nd Street, North
St. Petersburg, Florida 33702

Atlantic Investment Fund, Inc.
150 S. E. Third Avenue
Miami, Florida 33131

Equilease Capital Corp.
3200 Ponce de Leon Blvd., Rm. 218
Coral Gables, Florida 33134

First Florida Funding Corporation
110 South Orange Avenue
Sarasota, Florida 33577

FLORIDA *(Continued)*

First Miami SBIC
420 Lincoln Road, Rm. 235
Miami Beach, Florida 33139

First North Florida SBIC
107 North Madison Street
Quincy, Florida 32351

Gold Coast Capital Corp.
1451 North Bayshore Drive
Miami, Florida 33132

Gulf States Capital Corp.
3605 North Davis
Pensacola, Florida 32503

Market Capital Corp.
1102 N. 28th Street
Tampa, Florida 33605

Small Business Assistance Corp.
of Panama City, Florida
6704 West Highway 98
Panama City, Florida 32401

Southeast SBIC, Inc.
100 S. Biscayne Boulevard
Miami, Florida 33131

GEORGIA

Citizens & Southern Cap. Corp.
P. O. Box 4899
Atlanta, Georgia 30303

CSRA Capital Corporation
914 Georgia Railroad Bank Bldg.
August, Georgia 30903

Dixie Capital Corporation
2400 First National Bank Bldg.
Atlanta, Georgia 30303

Equilease Capital Corp.
1720 Peachtree Street, N. W.
Atlanta, Georgia 30309

Fidelity Capital Corporation
290 Interstate North
Atlanta, Georgia 30339

First American Investment
Corporation
300 Interstate North
Atlanta, Georgia 30339

Investors Equity Inc.
11 Pryor Street, Suite 920
Atlanta, Georgia 30303

GEORGIA *(Continued)*

Mome Capital Corporation
912 Main Street
Thomson, Georgia 30824

SBI Corp. of Georgia
22 Marietta Street, N. W.
Atlanta, Georgia 30303

Southeastern Capital Corporation
3715 Northside Parkway, N. W.
Atlanta, Georgia 30327

Transamerica Capital Corp.
1 South Oakwood Drive
Savannah, Georgia 31404

HAWAII

Small Business Investment
  Company of Hawaii, Inc.
1575 South Beretania Street
Honolulu, Hawaii 96814

ILLINOIS

Advance Growth Capital Corp.
LaGrange, Illinois

Atlanta/La Salle Capital
  Corporation
150 S. Wacker Drive, Suite 575
Chicago, Illinois 60606

Continental Illinois Venture
  Corporation
231 S. LaSalle Street, Suite 1738
Chicago, Illinois 60604

First Capital Corporation
  of Chicago
One First National Plaza
Chicago, Illinois 60670

IOWA

Mor-America Capital Corporation
200 American Building
Cedar Rapids, Iowa 52401

MASSACHUSETTS

Federal Street Capital Corporation
75 Federal Street
Boston, Massachusetts 02110

UST Capital Corporation
40 Court Street
Boston, Massachusetts 02108

MINNESOTA

Minnesota Small Business Inv. C.
2338 Central Avenue N. E.
Minneapolis, Minnesota 55418

Northwest Growth Fund, Inc.
960 Northwestern Bank Building
Minneapolis, Minnesota 55402

Westland Capital Corporation
705 First National Bank Bldg.
Minneapolis, Minnesota 55402

NEBRASKA

Mor-America Capital Corporation
One First National Center
Omaha, Nebraska 68102

NEW JERSEY

Monmouth Capital Corp.
First State Bank Bldg.
Tom's River, New Jersey 08753

NEW YORK

Bonan Equity Corporation
60 East 42nd Street
New York, New York 10017

Chase Manhattan Capital
  Corporation
1 Chase Manhattan Plaza
New York, New York 10005

CMNY Capital Company, Inc.
77 Water Street
New York, New York 10005

Creative Capital Corporation
99 Park Avenue
New York, New York 10016

15 Broad Street Resources
  Corporation
15 Broad Street
New York, New York 10005

The First Connecticut Small
  Business Investment Company
60 Wall Street
New York, New York 10005

FNCB Capital Corporation
399 Park Avenue
New York, New York 10022

The Franklin Corporation
1410 Broadway
New York, New York 10018

NEW YORK *(Continued)*

The Hanover Capital Corporation
485 Madison Avenue, Suite 804
New York, New York 10022

M. & T. Capital Corporation
One M. & T. Plaza
Buffalo, New York 14240

Midland Capital Corporation
110 Williams Street
New York, New York 10038

North River Securities Co.
595 Madison Avenue
New York, New York 10022

Royal Business Funds Corporation
250 Park Avenue
New York, New York 10017

Struthers Capital Corporation
630 Fifth Avenue
New York, New York 10020

OHIO

Commerce Capital Corporation
11 West Sharon Road
Cincinnati, Ohio 45246

OKLAHOMA

Alliance Business Investment
Company
500 McFarlin Building
11 East Fifth Street
Tulsa, Oklahoma 74103

PENNSYLVANIA

Alliance Enterprise Corporation
1616 Walnut Street
Philadelphia, Pennsylvania 19103

RHODE ISLAND

Industrial Capital Corporation
111 Westminister Street
Providence, Rhode Island 02903

Narragansett Capital Corporation
40 Westminister Street
Providence, Rhode Island 02903

TEXAS

Alliance Business Investment
Company
4850 One Shell Plaza
Houston, Texas 77002

TEXAS *(Continued)*

Capital Southwest Corporation
1800 Mercantile Dallas Bldg.
Dallas, Texas 75201

CSC Capital Corporation
750 Hartford Building
Dallas, Texas 75201

First Dallas Capital Corporation
714 First National Bank Bldg.
Dallas, Texas 75222

Texas Capital Corporation
2424 Houston Natural Gas Bldg.
Houston, Texas 77002

VIRGINIA

Virginia Capital Corporation
515 Ross Building
Richmond, Virginia

WASHINGTON

Washington Capital Corporation
1417 Fourth Avenue
Seattle, Washington 98101

WISCONSIN

Capital Investments, Inc.
735 N. Fifth Street
Milwaukee, Wisconsin 53203

Commerce Capital Corporation
6001 North 91st Street
Milwaukee, Wisconsin 53225

Commerce Capital Corporation
(Branch)
106 West Second Street
Ashland, Wisconsin 54806

Commerce Capital Corporation
(Branch)
9 South Main Street
Fond du Lac, Wisconsin 54935

Commerce Capital Corporation
(Branch)
126 Grand Avenue
Wausau, Wisconsin 54401

Mor America Capital Corporation
122 West Washington Avenue
Madison, Wisconsin 53703

Foreign Funds

GENERAL TRENDS IN LENDING AND INVESTING
BY PEOPLE FROM OTHER NATIONS

The economies of all nations have become vastly more interdependent over the past two or three decades, and real estate investments have taken on an international character as we have moved toward a world economy.

Foreign investment in the United States has always existed, but large funds were channeled this way first in the nineteenth century when the British helped finance the transcontinental railroad.

In the mid-1960's, foreign money began flowing in as equity capital for construction projects, and with the rise in interest rates this area of financing heated up considerably.

During the early 1970's when the dollar was cut by eight percent and then by 10 percent, the level of foreign investment rose rapidly since it was to the advantage of those who held U.S. dollars to bring them to the shores where their purchasing power would not be decreased. Inflation abroad also pushed investors to this country. Lower land prices here and tax treaties were further motivations for the foreigner to put his money to work in the United States.

Foreign funds have been greatly attracted to the United States, too, because of our long-term political and economic stability. In most recent years, foreign interests have streamed into American real estate projects at unprecedented rates.

In addition to all the other advantages of backing American realty, foreign buyers are exempt from capital gains on the appreciation of their money here. They have a lead over domestic investors because they can usually pay more for real estate than U.S. citizens since the decrease in the value of American currency. Foreign speculation has often caused prices of properties to shoot up out of proportion and out of reach of some U.S. buyers.

Dollars from abroad are invested not only in existing buildings but in new construction, particularly through joint ventures and limited partnerships. The Securities and Exchange Commission makes it indirectly less expensive for builders to obtain equity abroad. Even though the SEC has tightened disclosure requirements for registering limited partnerships, it provides that if a security is sold exclusively to citizens of another country, the registration requirements and filing of the prospectus could be overlooked.

There are strong arguments for and against heavy foreign investments here. On one hand, some Congressmen and officials see the trend as stimulating to the economy, producing more jobs, offering us a change to utilize foreign talents and technology, and providing short-term balance of payments benefits.

Others view the situation with alarm particularly if ownership of farmland, mineral rights, and plant sites are involved, since investors could export all products from such lands leaving the American market lacking.

With continuing Congressional investigations of foreign investments, some kind of government action can be expected — to both pinpoint and regulate the range of foreign monies in our land.

SPECIAL INTEREST FROM INVESTORS
ALL AROUND THE WORLD

Among major investors in America are semi-private Arab investment companies, Japanese trading companies, British land companies, Dutch and German trusts, rich Latin Americans, and Swiss and European pension funds.

Recently, the Arabs have been investing most heavily in U.S. real estate and some financial experts say that more than a billion dollars from these Middle East states will probably be spent on our realty over the next few years alone.

Americans and Arabs are joint-venturing shopping malls, various commercial buildings, hotels, resorts, islands, office complexes, and apartment houses.

Industrialization will probably absorb much of these states' newer oil money, but great sums of capital will continue to be earmarked for U.S. and European real estate. Japan is closed to foreign investments in land. Since Arab states do not practice unity, investing in their neighboring countries is not wise, and the poorer nations do not offer security.

Arabs see strong prospects for the American economy compared with those of Japan or Europe, since inflation in these areas is greater than that in the United States. Also, the European and Japanese have a higher dependency on energy sources than the United States does.

Real estate is the Arabs' favored investment as they see it as the best hedge against inflation, and real estate is cheaper here than in Europe. U.S. construction costs are lower and, in general, real estate investments hold more security and promise in America.

This is not to say that the Arabs are making loans or buying real estate right and left in the United States. The Arabs are aware that their assets could be frozen as Egyptian assets were when, in 1957, the Suez Canal was nationalized by Egypt.

To curb such fears, however, and to promote good relations with the Arabs, the United States has in recent years appointed full-fledged ambassadors for more Arab states, and diplomatic relations have been improved.

Like the Arabs' companies, the Japanese trading companies have expanded their wealth through investments around the world, including substantial real estate acquisitions and loans in the United States.

Investments were held back somewhat in 1974 when the Bank of Japan put restrictions on the outflow of cash from Japan to offset higher oil prices. The purchase of second homes, which had become a practice among Japanese, in such places as Hawaii was discouraged then, too.

Citizens of Japan, the Nationalist Chinese, and people of Hong Kong have tremendous real estate holdings in this country. They have invested heavily in Florida, Texas, New York, Hawaii, and California. The Japanese are involved in residential construction, operating extensions of their own construction companies in Japan. They are financing and building huge condominium projects and apartment house complexes as well as housing projects. In some cases, they are joint-venturing these kinds of projects with American firms.

The Japanese are also joint-venturing in large commercial construction programs for warehouses and industrial buildings. They have been drawn quite naturally to agricultural and timber land operations since they are in short supply in both areas. In hopes of recapturing Japanese tourist money, they have invested in resort hotels in this country.

The British have been extremely active in real estate investments here, over the last few years, concentrating on income-producing properties. Not only are they discouraged by the British economy, but clamps have been put on their investments in Australia and Canada.

Older, well-situated buildings will eventually bring higher returns than rents from newer buildings that cost such great sums to build, the British feel. They see an upsurge in rental markets similar to their own, and so they have recently bought existing buildings, both residential and commercial, in larger cities in the United States. In fact, they are buying millions of dollars worth of urban properties, including hotels, motel chains, and shopping centers.

Small foreign investors have also planted their dollars in American soil for solid yield. They first invested in offshore funds in the late 1960's, and when these ran into trouble through faulty management and other difficulties, they began to move their cash into American real estate investment trusts and the German and Dutch trusts. Some of these smaller investors also started buying land plots through American companies marketing in Europe.

Some of the largest U.S. real estate investment trusts have borrowed from the Eurodollar market and have many foreign shareholders. Europeans view the REIT's as low-risk investments.

A number of American land development companies sell land to wealthy Swiss, German, and Latin American professionals. These tracts and lots are for the most part located in Florida and Texas.

HOW TO UTILIZE CONTACTS, BANKS AND OTHER CHANNELS FOR FINANCING

The individual foreign investor is far more cautious with his real estate investments than the average American. In some countries of the world, especially in South and Latin America, it is against the law to take funds outside the country. For this reason, foreign investors in U.S. real estate and mortgages often invest through close friends here or indirectly through funds and institutions usually, but not always, located outside of the United States.

Making these contacts takes persistence and patience. It can be done through the international departments of commercial banks here or in other countries or through U.S. investment bankers, European merchant bankers, attorneys specializing in international law, or accounting firms with departments or divisions specializing in international taxation or business.

Wall Street brokerage houses have real estate departments that can put builders and foreign money suppliers together for a percentage fee, which can run high.

Foreign embassies or officials based in the United States also can provide information on their countries' investment sources and policies.

FOREIGN INVESTORS IN UNITED STATES REAL ESTATE

The following are lenders that from time to time may invest in mortgages or real estate here and abroad:

JAPANESE TRADING COMPANIES

Mitsubishi
Marunorichi Bldg.
4-1, Marinouchi
2-Chome
Chiyoda-ku
Tokyo, Japan 100

Yamazen Co. Ltd.
5, 1-Chome
Higashi-Azabu
Minato-ku
Tokyo, Japan

Kintetsu Enterprises
1520 Webster Street
San Francisco, California 94115

Mitsui & Co. USA, Inc.
200 Park Avenue
New York, New York 10017

Mitsui & Co.
2-9 Nishi Shi-Mboshi
It-Chome
Minato-ku
Tokyo, Japan

Kanematsu-Gosho, Inc.
Suite 4811
1 World Trade Center
New York, New York 10048

Tokyo Investment Services
International, Inc.
c/o Bank America Realty Services,
Inc.
Bank of America Center
San Francisco, California 94120

EUROPEAN PROPERTY COMPANIES

Capital & Counties Property
Company, Ltd.
St. Andrew's House
40 Broadway
London SWIH OBT, England

The Land Securities Investment
Trust Limited
1 Frederick's Place, Old Jewery
London EC2R 8DB, England

St. Martins Property Corporation
Limited
St. Martin's House
16 St. Martins 1e-Grand
London EC1 4EL, England

Stock Conversion and Investment
Trust Limited
130 Jermyn Street
London SW1Y 4UP, England

The Hammersons Property &
Investment Trust Ltd.
100 Park Lane
London W1Y HAR, England

MEPC, Ltd.
Brook House, 113 Park Lane
London W1Y HAY, England

Trafalgar House Investments Ltd.
Cleveland House, 19 St. James Square
London SW1Y 4JG, England

Societe Generale Immobilaire
DiLavori Di Utilita Pubblica
Piazzale dell 'Agricoltura 24
Rome, Italy 00144

Trizec Corporation, Ltd.
5 Place Dille Marie
8th Floor
Montreal, Quebec, Canada

Hammerson Property Corporation
100 Park Avenue
New York,New York 10017

Lex Service Group, Ltd.
5 Burlington Gardens
London W1X2QQ, England

Trust House Forte
166 High Holborn
London, WC1Z6PS, England

C Itoh & Co., Ltd.
68, 4-Chome, Kitokyutaromachi
Higashi-ku-Osaka

British Land Co., Ltd.
104 Westbourne Terrace W2
London, England

EUROPEAN REAL ESTATE INVESTMENT TRUSTS

Witan Company, Limited
28 Austin Friars
London EC2N 2ED, England

Cable Trust Limited
Electra House, Victoria Embankment
London WC2R 3HP, England

Foreign & Colonial Investment
Trust Co., Ltd.
Winchester House, 77 London Wall
London EC2N 1DD, England

Robeco
Rotterdamsch Belagginsconsortium,
N.V.
Heer Bokelweg 25, P. O. B. 973
Rotterdam, The Netherlands

British Assets Trust Limited
1 Charlotte Square
Edinburgh EH2-4DZ, Scotland

The Alliance Trust Co., Ltd.
Meadow House, 64 Reform Street
Dundee DD1, TJ, Scotland

Globe Investment Trust Ltd.
Electra House, Victoria Embankment
London WC2R 3HP, England

The Industrial & General Trust
  Limited
Winchester House
77 London Wall
London EC2N 1BH, England

The Mercantile Investment
  Trust Ltd.
Winchester House, 77 London Wall
London EC2N 1BY, England

Rolinco N.V.
Heer Bokelweg 25
Rotterdam 1, Netherlands

EUROPEAN INSURANCE COMPANIES

Allianz Versich
Allianz Versicherungs -AG
7 Stuttgart 1, Reinsburgstrasse 19
Postfach 534, West Germany

C. T. Bowring & Co., Limited
The Bowring Building, Tower Place
London EC3P3BE, England

Commercial Union Assurance Co.,
  Ltd.
P. O. Box 420, St. Helens, 1
Undershaft, London EC3P 3DQ
England

Eagle Star Insurance Co., Ltd.
1 Threadneedle Street
London EC2R 8BE, England

General Accident Fire & Life
  Assurance Corp., Ltd.
Gen. Bldgs.
Perth, PH 1 5TP, Scotland

Generali
Assicurazioni Generali S.p.A.
2 Piazza Duca degli Abruzzi
Rome, Italy 34100

Gdn. Royal Exchange Assurance, Ltd.
Royal Exchange
London EC3P 3DN, England

Legal & General Assurance
  Society, Ltd.
Temple Court,
11 Queen Victoria Street
London EC4N 4TP, England

Nationale-Nederlanden N.V.
15 Prinses Beatrixlaan
The Hague & 130, Schiekade
Rotterdam, The Netherlands

Pearl Assurance Co., Ltd.
252 High Holborn
London WC1V 7EB, England

Phoenix Assurance Co., Ltd.
Phoenix House
4-5 King William Street
London ECHP 4HR, England

The Prudential Assurance Co., Ltd.
142 Holborn Bars
London EC1N 2NH, England

Royal Insurance Co., Ltd.
1 North John Street
Liverpool L69 2AS, England

Royale Belge Vie
Societe Anonyme Assurances
Blvd. du Souverain 25
1170 Bruxelles, Belgium

Tokio Marine & Fire Insurance
  Co., Ltd.
1-1 Marunouchi 3 Chome Chiyoda-Ku
Tokyo, Japan 100

Zurich Insurance Company
(Zurich Compagnie d'Assurances)
Mythenquai 2, 8022
Zurich, Switzerland

Equity & Law Life Assurance
  Society, Ltd.
20 Lincoln's Inn Fields
London WC2A 3ES, England

Sedgwick Forbes Holdings, Ltd.
Regis House, 43-6 King William Street
London EC4R 9AP, England

Sun Alliance and London Insurance,
Ltd.
1 Bartholomew Lane
London EC2N 2AB, England

Taisho Marine and Fire Insurance
Ltd.
5, 1-Chome, Kyobashi, Chuo-Ku
Tokyo, Japan

Aetna Life and Casualty Company
151 Farmington Avenue
Hartford, Connecticut 06115

WORLD BANKS

Mercantile Bank and Trust
Company, Ltd.
P. O. Box F 2558
Freeport, Bahamas

Canadian Imperial Bank
of Commerce
Toronto, Ontario, Canada

The Royal Bank of Canada
32 Market Street, Box 247
Montreal, Quebec, Canada

Toronto Dominion Bank
Toronto, Ontario, Canada

Wirtschaftsbank Zurich
P. O. Box 3294
Zurich, Switzerland

Banco Atlantico
Av. Generalisimo 407 bis
Barcelona, Spain

Bank of Finland
Suomen Pankki-Finland Banks
P. O. Box 160 00101
Helsinki, Finland 10

The Bank of Canton Ltd.
6 Des Voeux Rd. Central
P. O. Box 133
Hong Kong

Bank of New Zealand
P. O. Box 2392
Wellington, C.I., New Zealand

Bankhaus Deak & Co. Ltd.
(Bankkommanditgesellschaft)
Rathaustrasse 20 Postfach 306
1011 Wien, Austria

Neue Bank Nuova Banca
Talstrasse 41 CH 8022
P. O. Box 507
Zurich, Switzerland

Banco Do Brasil S.A.
New Kokusai Building
4-1 Marunouchi-3 Chome
P. O. Box 1726
Brazil, S.A.

Bank Negra Indonesia 1946
Tokyo Branch
Kokusai Building 3-1-1
Marunouchi
Chivoda-ku, Tokyo 100 Japan

The Bank of Tokyo, Ltd.
6-3, Nihombashi Honguku-cho,
Chuo-ku
Tokyo, Japan

The Industrial Bank of Japan, Ltd.
3-3 Marunouchi 1-Chome, Chiyvda-ku
Tokyo 100, P. O. Box 8 4, Japan

The First National Bank
of Chicago (Lebannon)
59 Riad Solh Street, P. O. Box 162
Beruit, Lebannon

Barclays Bank of Zambiu, Ltd.
P. O. Box 1936
Cario Road
Lusaka, Zambia, Africa

Banque Commerciale Zairoise
SARL
8-10, Avenue Wagenia
Kinashasa P. O. Box 2798
Republic of Zaire, Africa

Barclays National Bank
Limited SouthWest Africa
P. O. Box 95, Kaiser Street
Winhock, SouthWest, Africa

Sanwa Bank
Tokyo, Asaka, Africa

U D C Bank
10th Floor Unicorn House
Marshall & Sauer Streets
P. O. Box 1115
Johannesburg, South Africa

The Taiyo Kohe Bank Ltd.
56 Naniva-cho, Ikuta-ku
Kobe 650, Japan

Clydesdale Bank Ltd.
30 St. Vincent Place
Glasgow G1 2HL, Scotland

Bank of Nova Scotia
Wismo Nusantara Building
Jolan M. H. Thamrin, 14th Floor
Jokarata, Indonesia

Chase Manhattan Bank, N.A.
Bombay Representative Office
P. O. Box 1961
Bombay, India

Bank of America
Calcutta Branch
P. O. Box 518
Calcutta 1, India

British Bank of the Middle East
Branch of London
P. O. Box 57
Manamia, Bahrain

Deak & Co. (Far East, Ltd).
406 Shell House
Hong Kong

Arawak Trust Company, Ltd.
36 Queen Street, P. O. Box N1447
Freeport, Bahamas

The Hanil Bank Ltd.
130-2 Ka Namdaimoon-Ro
Chung-ku, Seoul, Korea

Bank of Canada
Ottawa, Ontario, Canada

Banco Nacional de Mexico, S.A.
Isabel la Catolica 44-3er
Piso, Mexico 1, D.F.

RoyWest Banking Corporation
Limited
P. O. Box N 4889
Nassau, Bahamas

Banco Nacional de Nicaragua
Managua, D. N.

Pacific Atlantic Bank, Inc.
Ave. Fredrica Boyd y Calle 51
P. O. Box 8639
Panama 5, Panama

Banco Nacional de Panama
P. O. Box 5220
Panama, 5, Republic of Panama

The First National Bank of Boston
Avenida General Bartolome Mitre 570
Avellaneda, Buenos Aires, Argentina

First National City Bank
Avenida Colon y Luis Maria Drago
Bahia Blanca, Argentina

Banco de Comercio
Esquina de San Jacinto
Edif. Banco de Comercio
Caracas, 101 — Venezuela, S.A.

Standard Bank of South Africa
Limited
P. O. Box 3862
Johannesburg 2000, Africa

The HongKong Bank Group
1 Queen's Road Central
Hong Kong, Asia

Bank of New South Wales
60 Martin Place
Sydney 2000, N.S.W., Australia

Bank Pars
Pars Building
193 Takhte Jamshid Avenue
Tehran, Iran

Societe Generale
29 Boulevard Haussmann
75009 Paris, France

Societe Generale de Banque
Generale Bankmaatschappij
29 Rue Rovenstein
R-1000
Brussels, Belgium

Pohjoismaiden Yhdyspankki
Nordiska Foreningsbanken
Helsinki, Finland

Credit Lyonnais
19, boulevard des italiens-75
Paris, France

Allgemeine Deutsche Credit-Anstalt
6000 Franfurt am Main, Lindenstr. 27
Frankfurt, Germany

Allied Irish Banks
Lansdowne House
Ballsbridge, Dublin 4, Ireland

Banca Nazionale del Lavoro
Via V. Veneto
119-Rome, Italy

Banca Totta & Acores
Rua do Ouro
88-Lisbon 2, Portugal

Banco de Bilbao
Barcelona Branch
Plaza de Cantelina, 5
P. O. Box 819
Barcelona, Spain

Svenska Handelsbanken
11, Arsenalsgatan, Box 12128
S-10224 Stockholm, Sweden, Europe

Barclays World of Banking
54 Lombard Street
London EC3P 3AH

PART 3 — DEFINITIONS

This glossary covers the most important nomenclature of real estate financing used both in this book and generally in the field. It is intended to aid those in real estate and related areas, attorneys, bankers, teachers, investors, researchers, appraisers, officials, students, and others with specialized needs in their association with the financing of real property.

Hopefully, the definitions will enrich the user's understanding of terms most often used in business transactions and will improve his ability to read and grasp the literature in this segment of the real estate industry.

AAA (Triple A) Tenant — A well-known tenant, usually with a net worth in excess of a million dollars. Sometimes, if large and important, called an *Anchor.*

Abatement Clause (Lease) — A provision releasing tenant from its obligation to pay rent in the event the leased premises become unusable as a result of fire, flood, explosion, or other specified events.

Absolute Title — A title which is exclusive and complete.

Abstract of Title — A summarized chronological history of the title, consisting of a synopsis of the various links in the chain of title, together with a statement of all liens, charges, or encumbrances affecting a particular parcel of land.

Acceleration Clause — A clause generally found in mortgages or installment contracts requiring payment of the indebtedness to be made in full in the event of a default of any of its covenants. Other instruments, such as leases and notes, may also contain acceleration clauses.

Accessory Building — Any building other than the main one; an out-building, such as a detached garage.

Accrued Interest — Interest that has already been earned; accumulated interest that is due and payable.

Acquisition Cost — The total sum paid to obtain title to property, including closing expenses, such as stamps on deeds and mortgages, survey charges, appraisal fees, title insurance, legal fees, mortgage origination bank charges, and any other costs necessary to obtain ownership.

Acre — A measure of land, 160 square rods (1,840 square yards; 43,560 square feet).

Action Price — A price which will initiate serious negotiations toward a sale — something lower than asking price.

Adjustments — In financing, the credits and debits of a closing statement including such matters as taxes, insurance, rent prorations, escrowed funds, etc. when property is sold.

Administrator — A person appointed by court to administer the estate of a deceased person who left no will; that is, who died intestate.

Administrator's Deed — A form of deed used by the administrator of an estate to convey the property of one who has died leaving no will or executor.

Administratrix — A female administrator.

Ad Valorem — Real estate taxes proportionate to the value of the property.

Adverse Possession — The right of an occupant of land to acquire title against the real owner, where possession has been actual, continuous, hostile, visible, and distinct for the statutory period which varies between states.

Adverse Usage — Utilization of land that is detrimental to its value, or to nearby properties, or both.

Affidavit — A declaration reduced to writing, and sworn or affirmed to before some officer who has authority to administer an oath or affirmation.

Agent — One who represents another from whom he has derived authority.

Agents of Production — (1) Land; (2) Labor; (3) Entrepreneur; (4) Financing.

Agreement of Sale — A written agreement whereby the purchaser agrees to buy certain real property and the seller agrees to sell upon terms and conditions set forth therein.

Agreement for Deed — A contract requiring an owner to convey real property provided specific future payments are made by purchaser, and other terms of the agreement are met. Sometimes called *Contract for Deed.*

Air Rights — The rights to the use of the open space above land or buildings. Normally refers to space over highways, railroad tracks, or existing buildings. Also, the right to control the air space by not building, thereby assuring light and ventilation.

Alienation — The act of transferring real property from one person to another.

Allowance — In commercial leasing, the sum agreed to be paid by landlord to tenant for leasehold improvements within tenant's premises. Usually expressed in dollars per square foot.

Amortization — The liquidation of a debt on an installment basis.

Anchor Tenant — A Triple-A Tenant, such as a large department or discount store, or a nationally-known chain that forms the nucleus of a modern-day shopping center. The anchor tenant is a mainstay that draws the public and stabilizes the center by assuring a profitable operation for all the other tenants. Anchor tenants are sought out first and they are often given leases amounting to a subsidy.

Annuity — A sum of money or its equivalent that constitutes one of a series of periodic payments.

Appraisal — An estimate of quantity, quality, or value. The process through which conclusions of property value are obtained; also refers to the report setting forth the estimate and conclusion of value reached by correlation, unless a single technique is used.

Appraisal by Capitalization — An estimate of value by capitalization of productivity and income.

Appraisal by Comparison — Comparability to the sale prices of other similar properties, more accurate if many nearby recent transfers have occurred.

Appraisal by Summation — Adding together of parts of a property separately appraised to form the whole; for example, value of the land considered as vacant added to the cost of reproduction of the building, less depreciation. Sometimes called *Cost Approach.*

Appreciation — An increase in value.

Appurtenance — That which belongs to something else; something which passes as an incident to land, such as a right of way.

Aquatic Rights — The rights of abutting owners to use rivers, seas, oceans, and watercourses, as well as the land beneath the water.

Assemblage — Process of acquiring several parcels of land to create a larger parcel with more value or usefulness. Sometimes called plottage.

As Is — Words to indicate that no warranty or guarantee is intended, and that purchaser should use caution in inspecting for possible defects in condition.

Asking Price — The listed price of real estate; the price that it is initially offered in a sale. The term sometimes denotes flexibility from which negotiations can begin.

Assessed Valuation — Assessment of real estate by a unit of government for taxation purposes.

Assignee — The person or corporation to whom an agreement or contract is assigned.

Assignment — The method or manner by which a right, a specialty, or contract is transferred from one person to another.

Assignment of Lease — An assignment which occurs when a tenant transfers all his interest in a leasehold to another. This distinguishes it from a sublease in which some portion of the lease is retained. Grantor is sublessor and grantee is sublessee.

Assumption of Mortgage — Taking title to property that has an existing mortgage, and becoming personally liable for its payments.

Attornment — Acknowledgment by tenant of a new landlord.

Bad Title — A defective title. A title that, with reason, a purchaser may lawfully refuse to accept. (See *Unmarketable Title.*)

Balloon Mortgage — A mortgage that provides for periodic payments which do not completely amortize the loan at the end of the term. As a consequence, a larger final payment becomes due. Some states now require that a balloon mortgage be clearly identified as such on the mortgage instrument in order for it to be enforceable. Florida, for example, requires the following wording: "This is a balloon mortgage and the final payment of the balance due upon maturity is $____ together with accrued interest, if any, and all advancement made by the mortgagee under the terms of this mortgage."

Bargain and Sale Deed — A deed in which the seller, for a valuable consideration, "grants, bargains, and sells" specific property to a purchaser. The purchaser receives possession "unto himself and his heirs in fee simple forever." A bargain and sale deed can be with or without covenants against grantor's acts.

Basis Point — A measurement of fluctuations in the current yield equal to 1/100 of one percent bonds or bills.

Basket Loan — A loan of the type not primarily made by a lender in its normal routine. Proceeds are called "Basket Money."

Bearish Outlook — Expecting a decline.

Bill of Sale — An instrument used in a real estate transaction to transfer items other than real property. Furniture, fixtures, appliances, merchandise, motor vehicles, and similar chattels are found in a bill of sale.

Binder — An agreement to cover a down payment for the purchase of real estate as evidence of good faith on the part of the purchaser; in insurance, a temporary agreement given to one having an insurable interest, and who desires insurance subject to the same conditions which will apply if, as, and when a policy is issued.

Blanket Mortgage — A single mortgage which covers two or more pieces of real estate.

Blighted Area — One declining in value; approaching slum conditions.

Blue Sky Laws — Laws designed to regulate companies for the protection of the public and aimed at fly-by-night firms selling securities, land, gold mines, etc.

Boilerplate Language — Detailed or voluminous contract language not involving essentials.

Boiler Room Operation — Unethical and, often, illegal, high-pressure tactics that generally begin with an unsolicited telephone sales pitch. Continual pressure is put on the prospect to buy. Though the term is usually associated with the selling of questionable stocks, it has been carried over into real estate by way of land sale companies that maintain telephone crews to create leads.

Bomb — A bad deal, poor investment, white elephant. Also called (if based on ego) a *Monument*.

Bona Fide — Anything done with sincere, good intentions. Honestly and openly done. Without fraud.

Bond — Any obligation under seal. A real estate bond is a written obligation, usually issued on security of a mortgage or a trust deed.

Bond Type Lease — A lease which is with a tenant whose credit rating is very high with non-cancellable clause, absolutely net and for a long term.

Book Depreciation — The amount that can be deducted for depreciation purposes from the cost of an asset on the books of the owner of a business. Book depreciation, for income tax purposes, has no relationship with depreciation, as used in appraising.

Book Value — The dollar value of an asset as carried on the records of a company, and not necessarily what it would bring in the open market. Book value is the cost of the asset plus additions and improvements, minus accrued depreciation.

Bounds — The limits of property lines. Boundaries; enclosures; borders. See *Metes and Bounds*.

Broker — One employed by another, for a fee, to carry on any of the activities listed in the license law definition of the word, which varies between states.

Building and Loan Association — An incorporated, mutual organization with the prime purpose of investing a member's funds in residential mortgages and repaying him in the form of stocks or periodic dividends.

Building Code — Regulating the construction of buildings within a municipality by ordinance or law.

Building Lien — A builder's charge or encumbrance upon property.

Building Line — A line fixed at a certain distance from the front and/or sides of a lot, beyond which no building can project.

Building Loan — A loan for the duration of the construction of a building, usually providing for periodic payments for specified phases. Also called *Construction Loan* or *Interim Loan*.

Bullish Outlook — Expecting an increase.

Bundle of Rights — All the legal rights that go with ownership of property. The rights to sell, lease, mine, build, mortgage, improve, will to another, etc. that one possesses with ownership of real estate. Rights within the framework of the law to control one's property are now being diminished by a variety of governmental processes.

Buyer's Market — A period in the business cycle in which a type of property for sale is plentiful. Consequently, sellers must lower their prices and make concessions in their terms or both in order to make a sale.

C.B.D. — Abbreviation for Central Business District.

Call Loan — A loan payable on demand.

Cancellation Clause — A provision written into some contracts and leases giving one or both of the parties the right to cancel the agreement in the event of a specified occurrence. As to rated tenants in commercial projects, lenders view these clauses with repugnance.

Capital Gain — Profit gained from the sale of a capital asset in excess of its acquisition cost or appraised value or appreciation in value, over a period of time, on money invested in an asset.

Capitalization Method — A means of appraising real property by subtracting expenses from income on an annual basis, and multiplying the result by an accepted factor (the cap rate) to determine value. Also called *"Income Approach."*

Cap Rate — A rate of return derived after considering amount, quality, and durability of income.

Carryover Clause — The clause, found in an exclusive listing, that protects the broker for a short specified time (beyond the expiration date of the listing) in the event someone who was shown the property when the exclusive listing was in force later became a purchaser.

Cash Flow — Amount of usable cash from income-producing property after all expenses are paid.

Caveat Emptor — "Let the buyer beware." Under the theory of this legal maxim, the buyer is expected to judge and evaluate property carefully before purchasing. Unless there is misrepresentation, a person buys at his own risk.

Center Productivity (Shopping Centers) — Divide total sales in center by gross leaseable area.

Certificate of No Defense — An instrument, executed by the mortgagor, upon the sale of the mortgage, to the assignee, as to the validity of the full mortgage debt.

Certified Check — A check guaranteed to be good by the bank upon which it is drawn. Upon issuance it is immediately debited against the drawer's account and the bank will honor it upon presentation.

Chattel — Personal property, such as household goods or fixtures.

Chattel Mortgage — One which encumbers personal property.

Clear Title — Good, or marketable title; one free from encumbrances.

Clearing Title — The process of checking the recorded and unrecorded instruments affecting a property and taking whatever action is required to clear any defects, in order that it may become good, marketable, or insurable.

Client — One who employs a broker, lawyer, appraiser, etc. and is responsible for payment of their commissions or fees.

Climate — All current relevant factors, for example, the "tax climate" in a certain city.

Cloud on the Title — An outstanding claim or encumbrance which, if valid, would affect or impair the owner's title; a mortgage or judgment.

Close — To complete a transaction; when real estate formally changes ownership. The transaction is called a closing on a settlement.

Closed Mortgage — A mortgage that cannot be paid off until maturity.

Closed-end Mortgage — A mortgage that has no provisions for increasing the balance. Opposite from an *Open-End Mortgage* which permits the mortgagor to continue borrowing from it, in amounts up to the original sum.

Closing Costs — The numerous expenses buyers and sellers normally incur in the transfer of ownership of real estate, such as:

Buyer's Expenses at Closing	*Seller's Expenses at Closing*
Recording Deed & Mortgage	State Stamps on Deed
State Stamps on Notes	Abstracting
Attorney's Fee	Recording Mortgages
Escrow Fees	Real Estate Commission
Title Insurance	Survey Charge
Survey Charge	Attorney's Fee
Appraisal & Inspection Fees	Escrow Fee

Closing Statement — A detailed financial account of all the credits and debits that the buyer and seller receive at the closing of a real estate transaction.

Cluster Developing — The construction of homes or buildings in close proximity to one another. As a result, the open space around the buildings can be utilized to best advantage. Result: convenience, extra and closer parking facilities, overall efficiency and economy of operation, better landscaping, etc.

Coinciding Indicator — An activity whose rise or fall coincides with the overall economy.

Collateral — Anything of value that a borrower pledges as security.

Commercial Paper — Funds loaned by corporations directly to other corporations.

Commercial Property — Income property such as office buildings, hotels, motels, apartment houses, parking lots, warehouses, lofts, gasoline stations, shopping centers and stores zoned for business purposes, as distinguished from residential, industrial, or agricultural properties.

Commingling Funds — The illegal practice of combining escrow money with personal or business funds in a common account.

Commission — Sum due a real estate broker for services in that capacity.

Commitment — A pledge or promise to do something in the future. Lending institutions generally give written commitment letters containing specific terms of mortgage loans they will give. Commitments can be either "firm" or "conditional." Conditional commitments may be contingent upon such factors as the borrower's credit, completion of construction, or that a certain percentage of occupancy be obtained. Often a charge, "the stand-by fee" is made by the lender.

Commitment Fee — A charge by a lender for reserving funds for future disbursements.

Common Law — Body of law that grew up from custom and decided cases (English law) rather than from codified law (Roman law).

Community Property — Property owned jointly by husband and wife. Though the law differs in various states, it generally refers to property obtained during their marriage.

Community Shopping Center — Defines size of an area served. It is larger than a neighborhood center, but smaller than a regional center.

Comparison Approach — A technique in appraising. (See *Appraisal.*) Sometimes called *Market Approach.*

Completion Bond — A bond posted by a contractor as a guarantee that he will satisfactorily complete a project and that it will be free of any liens. Sometimes called a *Performance Bond.*

Condemnation — Taking private property for public use, with compensation to the owner, under the right of eminent domain.

Condemnation Appraisal — An estimate of the value of property that is undergoing condemnation proceedings.

Conditional Sales Contract — (See *Agreement For Deed* and *Contract For Deed.*)

Condominium — Individual ownership of a portion of a building that has numerous other units similarly owned. Each owner possesses a deed and a good and marketable title to it. He pays his taxes independently of the other owners and may buy, sell, mortgage, lease, or will the portion that he holds.

Consideration — Something of value given to induce a person to enter into a contract. It usually is money, but need not be. Personal services, merchandise, or nothing more than love and affection are sufficient consideration.

Constant — The ratio of the annual repayment to each thousand dollars borrowed is the annual constant.

Construction Loan — (See *Building Loan.*)

Constructive Eviction — Breach of a covenant of warranty of quiet enjoyment; for example, the inability of a purchaser or lessee to obtain possession by reason of a paramount outstanding title.

Contract for Sale — (See *Agreement For Deed.*)

Constructive Notice — Notification by the recording of documents in public records or by publication; by so doing the public is presumed to have notice.

Continuance (of Abstract) — Bringing an Abstract up to date by searching the public records, noting any changes in ownership, new liens and encumbrances, etc. The abstract is continued to the present time.

Contract — A binding agreement between competent parties, with sufficient consideration given, to do or abstain from doing something. An agreement, written or oral, that is enforceable by law.

Contract for Deed — (See *Agreement For Deed.*)

Contract Rent — Rent specified in a lease.

Conventional Loan — That type of mortgage loan normally granted by a bank or savings and loan association. A loan based on real estate as the security, as distinguished from one guaranteed or insured by an agency of the government.

Conversion — The act of changing a property from one use to another, as for example, when a residence is renovated and partitioned into offices. The illegal converting of funds or appropriating another's assets for one's own use.

Convertible Debt — That which the lender has the option to change from straight debt to an equity (stock) position.

Conveyance — The means or medium by which title to real estate is transferred.

Cooperating Brokers (Co-Brokers) — Two or more brokers working together on one real estate transaction. Their shared efforts, if successful, will result in a shared commission.

Cooperative Apartment — In a cooperative type of ownership the tenants of the building are stockholders in a corporation that owns and operates the real estate.

Correlation — In appraising real property it is standard practice for professional appraisers to take separately the three accepted appraisal methods (Comparison, Cost, and Capitalization), evaluate the property from each standpoint and, by correlating these conclusions, arrive at a knowledgeable single estimate of value.

Cost Approach — A method of estimating the value of property by deducting depreciation from the replacement cost, then adding the value of the land to the remainder. Depreciation, as used in the cost approach, is the difference between replacement cost and the market value of the improvements.

Counteroffer — A new offer as to price, terms, and conditions, made in reply to a prior unacceptable one. The counteroffer supersedes the original offer.

Covenant — An agreement between two or more persons, by deed, whereby one of the parties promises the performance or non-performance of certain acts or that a given state of things does or does not exist.

Crunch — A period of "tight money"; when demand for loans is in excess of available funds.

Cubage — Width of building multiplied by depth of building and by the height, figured from basement floor to the outer surfaces of walls and roof.

Cumulative Attraction, Law of — Stores grouped draw more customers than stores apart.

Curable Depreciation — Depreciated property that is nevertheless economically sound. Property in which the cost to repair or remodel would sufficiently enhance its value to justify the expenditure. The opposite of *Incurable Depreciation.*

Curing the Title — (See *Clearing Title.*)

Dealer — One who buys and sells real estate regularly. Has tax implications.

Debenture — A bond given as evidence of a debt, but unsecured by a specific asset. The security a debenture holder has is the credit standing and worth of the company. Debentures usually are long-term obligations.

Debt Instrument — The document creating the debt. In the case of mortgaged property, it is the note or bond that the borrower signs, and not the mortgage itself, which only pledges the property as collateral. Other examples of debt instruments are promissory notes and stock certificates.

Debt Service — The sum of money required periodically to make the payments necessary to amortize a debt and interest charges; the principal and interest payments.

Declaratory Judgment — A binding legal decree.

Declining Balance Depreciation — A method wherein the owner of improved property can deduct more for depreciation in the early years of a building, than would normally apply if distributed over the life of the asset. If the title holder is the original owner, he can elect to deduct up to double the regular depreciation the first year, and slightly lesser amounts each succeeding year. When acquiring resale property, one can begin by deducting no more than one and one-half times the Straight Line Depreciation.

Dedication — An appropriation of land by an owner to some public use together with acceptance for such use by or on behalf of the public.

Deed — A writing by which lands, tenements, and hereditaments are transferred, which writing is signed, sealed, and delivered by the grantor.

Default — The non-performance of a duty, whether arising under a contract, or otherwise; failure to meet an obligation when due.

Defeasance — An instrument which nullifies the effect of some other deed or of an estate. If a clause, it applies to the instrument of which it is a part.

Deficit Financing — Spending more than current income, by borrowing.

Defective Title — A flaw in the title. For example, if an otherwise good title is illegally obtained, or an illegal consideration was used, it is a defective title.

Deferred Maintenance — Maintenance to a building which should be done but is postponed. The decline in physical condition permits a temporary increase in cash flow.

Deferred Payments — Provisions in a mortgage allowing for the postponment of principal or interest payments. Mortgages on new commercial buildings or apartment houses often need a grace period in which to obtain tenants, in order to build up the income stream.

Deficiency Judgment — The difference between the indebtedness sued upon and the sale price of the real estate at the foreclosure sale. Also called *Deficiency Decree*.

Demand Note or Mortgage — A note or mortgage that can be called in for payment at any time upon the demand of the holder, without prior notice.

Demographics — External factors affecting a site, including population, visibility, economic base, traffic, neighborhood characteristics, per capita income, topography, etc.

Deposit — The sum of money placed in trust as evidence of good faith for the future performance of a real estate transaction. Money given as a pledge to do something at a later time. Earnest Money; down payment.

Deposit Receipt — An instrument used to submit a written offer for the purchase of property. It serves as a receipt of money deposited. Upon acceptance by seller, it becomes a binding contract.

Depreciation — Loss in value, brought about by deterioration through ordinary wear and tear, action of the elements, or functional or economic obsolescence.

Depth Table — A schedule for valuing various portions of a parcel of land having street frontage, with the greatest value applying to frontage and declining value applied to the central and rear portions. This method is often used by tax assessors.

Deterioration — (of value) Opposite of appreciation. Degeneration can be by internal or external forces, or both.

Developed Land — Land which has had additions to enhance its value or usefulness.

Developer — A person who, to put land to its highest and best use, subdivides it into homesites or builds roads, houses, and shopping centers as well as all other facilities.

Directional Growth — The direction in which a community can reasonably be expected to grow.

Discharge — In contracts it refers to cancelling the obligation. If all terms and conditions of a contract were met, it would be completed or discharged by performance.

Disclaimer — (A) Renunciation or rejection of an estate; refusal to acknowledge an interest in it. Denial of ownership. (B) A statement denying legal responsibility of the accuracy or correctness of the presented facts.

Discount — (A) That which can be taken off the established amount. Mortgages, for example, are frequently discounted when paid in advance of maturity. (B) A sum paid to obtain certain preferred mortgages, as the payment of points to a lending institution for FHA and VA mortgages when market interest rates are higher than established ceilings.

Disintermediation — The shift of savings into investments or institutions offering a higher return.

Dispossess — To deprive one of the use of real estate, as to force one to vacate.

Distressed Property — Property that for any reason is bringing an inadequate return to the owner, or is in difficulty for other reasons. For example, in a blighted area, where market values are declining.

Down Payment — (Earnest Money) (Deposit) (Good Faith) Payment made by a purchaser of real estate as evidence of good faith.

Drawing Area — Distance to which customers will be attracted. (Shopping Centers).

Earned Increment — A gain, growth, or increase resulting from actions taken or work performed.

Earning-Price Ratio — A ratio of the net income of property to the selling price. As an example, if a building nets $100,000 profit and is sold for $80,000, the earning-price ratio is 8 (8 times the income). (See *Net Multiplier.*)

Easement — The right, liberty, advantage or privilege which one individual or the public has in lands of another (a right of way).

Economic Life — The period over which a property may be profitably utilized.

Economic Obsolescence — A decline in the market value of property due to any external influence.

Economic Rent — An estimate of rent that could be obtained in the current market. It could be more or less than the contract, or actual, rent being obtained. Usually calculated by comparison with similar properties. Also called *Fair Market Rent.*

Effective Age — A building's physical condition, not its actual age, determines its effective age. For appraisal purposes, it is an assumed age that would be equivalent to the physical condition of the structure; the better the condition, the lower the effective age. For example, some well-maintained 35-year-old buildings may be assigned an effective age of 20 or 25 years. It is used to indicate to the prospective purchaser or appraisal client that the structure is in better or worse condition that the average building of similar vintage.

Ejectment — A form of action to regain possession of real property, plus damages for the unlawful retention.

Eminent Domain — The right of the people or government to take private property for public use upon payment of compensation. Expropriation.

Encroachment — A building, part of building, or improvement which intrudes upon or invades a highway or sidewalk or trespasses upon property of another.

Encumbrance — A claim, lien, charge, or liability attached to and binding upon real property, such as a judgment, unpaid taxes, or a right of way; defined in law as any right to, or interest in, land which may subsist in another to the diminution of its value, but consistent with the passing of the fee.

Entrepreneur — A sole proprietor of a business. An individual who builds a commercial enterprise taking all the risks and responsibilities, suffering any loss or enjoying any profit that may result. (See *Agents of Production.*)

Equal Dignity — A reference to mortgages, liens or other legal obligations that are equally ranked in status, so that one does not take precedence over the other.

Equity — The interest or value which an owner has in real estate over and above the mortgage against it; system of legal rules administered by courts of chancery.

Equity of Redemption — Right of original owner to reclaim property sold through foreclosure proceedings, by payment of debt, interest, and costs.

Equity Kicker — A participation in the equity position of a development by the lender as an inducement to lend funds. Used in periods of tight money or lenders' market.

Equity R.E.I.T. — One formed for the purpose of purchasing equities in real estate. (See *Mortgage R.E.I.T.*)

Escalation Clause — Provides for rent increases.

Escape Clause — (See *Cancellation Clause.*)

Escrow — A deed or something of value delivered to a third person for the grantee to be held by him until the fulfillment or performance of some act or condition.

Estate — Quantity of interest a person has in land and the improvements upon it.

Estate — (At Sufferance)(At Will) (For Life) (In Remainder) (In Severalty) (In Fee Simple) — various types of interest in real property.

Estate in Reversion — The residue of an estate left in the grantor, to commence in possession after the termination of some particular estate granted by him. In a lease, the lessor has the estate in reversion after the lease is terminated.

Estoppel Certificate — An instrument used when assigning a mortgage to another, setting forth the exact remaining balance of the indebtedness on a certain date. It can be signed by the mortgagor or mortgagee, but the one so doing is held responsible for the representation made.

Et Al — (Latin) And another or and others.

Et Ux — (Latin) And wife.

Eviction — A violation of some covenant in a lease by the landlord, usually the covenant for quiet enjoyment; also refers to process instituted to oust a person from possession of real estate.

Examination of Title — A search of the records relating to a property to determine the status of the title as to its marketability and insurability. Also called *Searching the Title.*

Exception to Title — Any defect or insufficiency in the title brought to light as a result of an examination of title or through other research.

Excess Rent — Difference between contract rent and economic rent.

Exchange of Real Estate — A real estate transaction in which two or more properties are traded either at equal (par) value or when a sum of money is used to balance the exchange. Both principals simultaneously become buyers and sellers.

Exclusive Agency — The appointment of one real estate broker as sole agent for the sale of a property for a designated period of time.

Exclusive — (Commercial Leasing) Lease provision giving a tenant protection against direct competition within a project or within a distance usually described as a radius from a point.

Exclusive Right of Sale — An agreement (usually written) employing a broker for a specified period of time to the exclusion of all others, including the owner, to sell a property.

Exculpatory Clause — A clause often included in leases that clears or relieves the landlord of liability for personal injury to tenants as well as for property damages.

Executory Contract — A contract where something remains to be done by either party before title can pass. A contract not completely performed. When that which remains to be done is completed, it becomes an "executed" contract and the transfer of title may then take place.

Express Easement — Written in a deed or contract. More definite than implied. (See *Eminent Domain.*)

Expropriate — (See *Eminent Domain.*)

Extended Coverage — Additional insurance at an extra premium for coverage not generally found in the normal insurance contract. Insurance for the coverage of certain specified risks, such as smoke damage, windstorm, hail, lightning, vehicle damage, riots, aircraft accidents, explosions, civil disorders, etc.

Extension Agreement — An agreement to extend the terms of an instrument. An extension agreement in a mortgage, for example, grants additional time to perform one or more of its provisions.

F.A.R. — Abbreviation for floor area ratio — the ratio allowed by existing zoning of floor area to lot area.

Failure of Consideration — When the consideration given in a contract or other instrument has dropped in value from what it was originally. For example, a check given as a deposit that is returned marked "insufficient funds."

Failure to Perform — Failure of one of the parties to a contract to perform that which was agreed upon. This can occur by a deliberate act or because of subsequent circumstances beyond control.

Fair — Equitable; reasonable; impartial; just. Free from favoritism; unbiased. This word is much used in real estate in such forms as Fair Consideration, Fair Contract, Fair Dealings, Fair Market Value, Fair Rent, Fair and Equitable Settlements, Fair Compensation, Fair Housing, Fair Description, etc.

Fannie Mae — A common name for the Federal National Mortgage Association (FNMA).

Feasibility — (Study, Report) An analysis of a specific site or described area to determine all possibilities for putting it to its highest and best use.

Federal National Mortgage Association — More popularly known as Fannie Mae, this is a branch of the U.S. Department of Housing and Urban Development (HUD). Its prime function is to purchase mortgages from banks, trust companies, mortgage companies, savings and loan associations, and insurance companies to provide funds for additional mortgage lending.

Federal Land Bank System — The purpose of this government agency is to make available long-term mortgage loans, at equitable terms, to farmers, so they may own their own farms.

Federal Savings and Loan Association — A financial institution that is federally chartered and privately owned either by stockholders or by depositors. Federal Savings and Loan Associations' prime functions are twofold: 1. Financing homes and, to a more limited degree, commercial properties, through conventional loans and FHA and VA mortgages. 2. Providing interest-bearing savings accounts which are government insured to $40,000. All Federal Savings and Loan Associations are required to be members of their regional Federal Home Loan Bank.

Fee; Fee Simple; Fee Simple Absolute — These three terms are synonymous and mean that the owner has absolute, good, and marketable title to the property conveyed to him. It is complete ownership without condition.

Fee Appraiser — A professional appraiser whose services are available to the general public for a fee.

Fiduciary — A position of trust and confidence. One who transacts business for another and by so doing establishes a relationship of great faith. A broker is automatically put in such a position when he is employed to act for his principal, or employer.

Financial Statement — A written statement of an individual's or company's assets, liabilities, and net worth as of a specified date.

Finder's Fee — Money paid to another for furnishing a buyer, seller, listing, borrower, lender, or property.

Firm Contract — One which is executed and binding on all parties.

Firm Price — One stated by owner as the minimum acceptable to him; indicates little or no interest in offers or negotiations.

Fiscal Policy — Governmental actions on taxes and spending.

Fiscal Year — The business year as distinguished from the calendar year. A 12-month period in which accounts of a business are calculated and income taxes computed. The most commonly used period is one, which is also used by the Federal Government, ending June 30.

First Deed of Trust — A lien on property that is first in dignity by virtue of being first recorded.

First Mortgage — A lien on property that is superior to any other. Sometimes called senior mortgage, *First Lien* or *First Loan*. Takes precedence over a junior or second mortgage, if any.

First Refusal — The right given a person to have the first privilege to purchase or lease real estate, or the right to meet an offer made by another.

Fixed Asset — Assets necessary for the general operation of a business. Assets that are permanent in nature and have an economic life covering many years.

Fixture — Any fittings or furnishings that are attached to a building and considered a part of it. That which is annexed to real property and legally goes with spouts, etc. for waterproofing.

Float — A banking term describing checks in process of collection but not cleared. Within a local area, checks may float for approximately three days before clearance, with out-of-town and out-of-state checks taking as long as ten days or more.

Flyspecking — The careful scrutiny of a document, particularly in reference to an abstract of title, to uncover every technical defect; the inference being that even a flyspeck will be detected and examined by the diligent searcher. "Same as Nit-picking."

Forced Sale — A forced sale occurs when one sells or loses his property without actually wanting to dispose of it, as in bankruptcy proceedings or to satisfy unpaid taxes or liens. Involuntary alienation.

Force Majeure Clause — Provision in a contract which excuses one or both parties in the event an act of God or similar circumstance.

Forces Affecting Value — Physical, social, economic, geographic.

Foreclosure — A court process instituted by a mortgagee or lien creditor to defeat any interest or redemption which the debtor-owner may have in the property; follows default by mortgagor (borrower).

Forfeit — To give up the right to, or physical possession of, something. Loss of anything of value because of failure to act or otherwise do that which was agreed upon.

Formal Contract — A contract that is in writing and signed under seal.

Fraud — Deceiving; misrepresenting. An untruth in order to obtain an illegal advantage of, or something of value from, another.

Free and Clear — A reference to ownership of property that is free of all indebtedness. Property that never had a mortgage encumbering it, or in which the mortgage has been paid in full.

Freedealer — In some states, a married woman dealing in real estate on her own behalf must register with the state as a freedealer. After being declared as such, she no longer needs her husband's signature or consent to buy, sell, or lease property.

Freehold — An estate in fee simple or for life; applies to land or an interest that is derived from land.

Freeholder — A person holding legal or equitable title to property.

Front Foot — (Value) The value of property expressed in dollars per linear feet of frontage on a street, to the entire depth unless otherwise specified.

Front Man — A person acting as a front or dummy for another. Also called a "straw man."

Front Money — Money required to get a project under way. Funds used for such matters as the down payment, feasibility study, preliminary plans, appraisal, survey, test borings, etc. "Sometimes called Seed Money."

Functional Obsolescence — Defects in a structure that detract from its marketability and value. When a building begins to outlive its usefulness through antiquated equipment, such as inadequate electrical wiring, outmoded elevator service, lack of, or poor, air-conditioning, impractical design, faulty heating plant, etc., it becomes functionally obsolete. (See *Economic Obsolescence.*)

Gap Financing — A loan to a developer or builder when construction funds are not sufficient to complete a project, or to overcome restrictions in holdback in the permanent loan commitment.

General Lien — A lien against a person rather than his real property. This lien gives the right to detain personal property until a debt is satisfied.

General Mortgage — (See *Blanket Mortgage.*)

General Warranty — A covenant in the deed whereby the grantor agrees to protect the grantee against all claims.

Ginnie Mae — Colloquial for Government National Mortgage Association (GNMA).

Good Faith Money — (See *Down Payment.*)

Good Record Title — Title to property that is free of recorded encumbrances.

Grace Period — A period when a mortgage payment or other debt becomes past due, and before it goes into default. Most mortgages provide for a specified period of time when it can be paid without penalty or default. Commonly 30 days.

Grant — The act of transferring property. To bestow an interest in real property upon another.

Grantee — A person to whom real estate is conveyed; the purchaser.

Grantor — A person who conveys real estate by deed; the seller.

Gross — The whole amount with nothing taken out; total. The word is often used in matters related to real estate, with terms such as gross estate, gross profit, gross revenue, gross sales, gross loss, gross lease, gross income, gross earnings, etc.

Gross Income — The total of money received from income property or a business, before operating expenses, taxes, depreciation, commissions, salaries, fees, etc. are deducted.

Gross Lease — One in which landlord, or owner, or lessor pays all property charges regularly incurred through ownership, such as repairs, maintenance, real estate taxes. Seldom used in a commercial transaction (office buildings excepted) today, having been succeeded by the opposite type, or *Net Lease,* in which the costs mentioned above are borne by tenant, or lessee.

Gross Multiplier — The number, usually between 6-10, which multiplied by the cash income, or gross income, will produce an estimate of property value.

Ground Lease — A contract for possession and use of land. May be *fixed* (at a constant figure) or *variable* (subject to index adjustments) or *stepped* (including charges at specified intervals).

Guarantee (Clause) — A provision in, or attached to, a contract in which a parent company agrees to meet the obligations assumed by its subsidiary, sometimes with limiting conditions.

Habendum Clause — The "To Have and To Hold" clause which defines or limits the quantity of the estate granted in the premises of the deed.

Handshake Deal — A deal closed or sealed by a handshake. Sometimes called a gentlemen's agreement.

Heirs and Assigns — Part of the phraseology found in deeds, contracts, and other documents when transferring title. Heirs are recipients of an inheritance; assigns are parties who may be subsequently designated by the assignor.

Hidden Amenities — The favorable features of a property that may not always be noted at first inspection, but nevertheless are present and serve to enhance its value. High quality of workmanship, superior materials, and good maintenance are examples.

Highest and Best Use — When land is being put to its most logical and productive use. Such factors as beauty and utility to the surrounding community should be considered, as well as the highest income it can bring the owner.

High-Rise (Hi-Rise) — An indefinite term, but generally understood to mean an apartment house or other structure higher than three or four stories and requiring heavy construction methods. When referring to large office buildings, the term "skyscraper" is more applicable; when referring to apartment buildings, it designates those requiring elevators.

Holdback — Contingency provisions in a loan commitment reducing the amount disbursed if certain conditions are not met.

Holdover Tenant — A tenant who remains in possession of leased property after the expiration of the lease term. Also called a *Tenant at Sufferance.*

Hold Period — A time established by a bank to allow for clearance of a check before permitting withdrawal against it.

Homestead — Real estate occupied by the owner as a home; the owner enjoys special rights and privileges.

Illegal Contract — A contract made for an unlawful purpose. It may be correctly drawn and executed, but its illegality renders it void.

Immoral Contract — A contract in which the consideration or the purpose itself is based on something morally wrong and not in keeping with accepted concepts of human behavior. The contract is automatically void.

Implied Contract — A contract that is deduced or inferred by the actions and conduct of the principals. Not in writing.

Implied Easement — An encroachment upon property that has been left unchallenged for a long period of time. One that is apparent by long and continued use.

Implied Listing — A listing obtained without the owner's oral or written consent, but with his knowledge. Apprising by implication.

Improved Land — Man-made additions to and on real property that enhance its value. Made to land or grading, roadbuilding, irrigating, draining, installing water lines, cultivating farmland, building sidewalks, bringing in electricity, etc. Made on land by the construction of buildings, bridges, structures of all kinds, fencing, etc.

Income — The financial benefits from business, labor, capital invested, or property. The monetary return or other advantageous benefits of an investment. The amount of gain received in money, goods, or services over a period of time.

Income Approach to Value — A method of appraising property basing the estimate of value upon the net amount of income produced by the property. It is calculated by subtracting the expenses of the property from the gross income and multiplying the result by a factor or multiple.

Income Property — Property owned or purchased primarily for the monetary return it will bring. It may be classified as commercial, industrial, or residential.

Incurable Depreciation — Depreciation of property that is beyond rehabilitating. Property in which the cost to repair or remodel would be uneconomical and unjustified.

Incurable Title — A cloud or other encumbrance on the title to property that cannot be removed, consequently preventing the transfer of ownership.

Indenture — A formal written instrument made between two or more persons in different interests; name comes from practice of indenting or cutting the deed on the top or side in a waving line. Many contracts begin with the words "This Indenture," followed by date and names of parties, Witnesseth — — —.

Industrial Park — A planned development of industrial plants, warehouses, factories, and wholesale distributing firms. Adequate public utilities, wide streets, ample railroad sidings, professional landscaping, and the modern plants themselves contribute to attractive, carefully conceived and coordinated industrial areas. May be under single or many ownerships.

Inflation Hedge — Investments made in the hope that income or appreciation will equal or exceed loss of value due to inflation.

Infringement — (See *Encroachment.*)

Ingress — Entrance or access to property.

Innocent Purchaser — One who obtains title to property in good faith believing there are no hidden title defects.

Installment Sales Contract — A contract for the sale of property in which the buyer receives possession of the property, but not title to it, upon signing the contract. The buyer makes regular installment payments until the contract is fulfilled and then receives the deed and title.

Institutional Lenders — Banks, Federal Savings and Loan Associations, and life insurance companies that invest depositors' and clients' funds in mortgages and other loans are called institutional lenders. Individual or private lenders invest their own money. Also called Conventional Lenders.

Instrument — A written legal document, such as a deed, bill of sale, contract, option, bond, lease, affidavit, will, mortgage, acknowledgment, or any other formal document.

Insurable Title — Land that a title insurance company will issue a policy for, after making a thorough search of the abstract.

Insurance — A method of guaranteeing or indemnifying an individual or company against loss from a specified hazard. For the payment of an agreed sum (premium), the insurer or underwriter issues a policy to the insured that gives financial protection for a stated period of time.

Insurance on Mortgage Property — An insurance policy on mortgaged property that is generally made mandatory by the lender to protect his equity in the property in the event of a fire or other loss.

Insured Loan — A loan in which the lender is assured partial or full payment in the event of a default by the borrower.

Interest Location — A site located between a residential area and the regular marketplace for that area.

Interest — (A) A portion, share, or right in something. A partial but not complete ownership. Having an interest does not necessarily indicate possessing title, as for example, in a leasehold interest or mortgage. (B) The charge or rate paid for borrowing money; the compensation received for loaning it.

Interim Financing — Short-term, temporary financing that is generally in effect during a building's construction or until a permanent, long-term loan can be obtained. (See *Building Loans.*)

Intermingling Funds — (See *Commingling Funds.*)

Investor — One who puts money into a business or real estate venture with the intention of realizing a satisfactory financial return on the capital invested. (See *Speculator* for difference in objective.)

Ironclad Agreement — An agreement that cannot be broken or evaded by the parties to it. The term applied to precisely worded written agreements. (See *Cancellation Clause.*)

Joint and Several Liability — The term is used when compensation for liability may be obtained from one or more parties either individually or jointly, whichever may be most advantageous. Example: Partners are responsible for their own and the others' actions in business.

Joint Tenancy — Property held by two or more persons together with the distinct character of right of survivorship.

Joint Venture — The joining of two or more people to carry out a specific business venture; a cooperative endeavor. Sometimes called a Joint Adventure.

Judgment — Decree of court declaring that one individual is indebted to another and fixing the amount of such indebtedness.

Judgment d.s.b. — D.s.b. is the abbreviation for the Latin *debitum sine brevi,* which means "Debt without writ." It is a judgment confessed by authority of the language in the instrument.

Judgment by Default — A judgment given when a defendant fails to appear in court, to file necessary pleadings or otherwise to take proper legal steps.

Judgment Lien — A lien that binds the land of a debtor so that its proceeds can be used to satisfy a debt. The holder of the lien may prevent the owner from using the property, or cause it to be sold at a public auction and the proceeds applied toward satisfaction of the lien.

Judicial Sale — A sale of real or personal property ordered by a court or other authorized legal body.

Junior Mortgage — A mortgage second in lien to a previous mortgage. Also called *Subordinate Mortgage.*

Just Compensation — Impartial, legitimate, fair compensation. See *Eminent Domain.*

Key Lot — A lot strategically located so as to increase its value, usually with regard to an abutting lot.

Key Money — A sum paid to obtain a leasehold interest; to buy the KEY to the premises.

Kick-Back — The unauthorized, secret payment of money to an individual or group in return for a favorable decision, information, or assistance.

Laches — Neglect or an unreasonable delay in bringing about a legal claim or asserting a right.

Lag Indicator — An activity whose rise or fall follows the trend in the overall economy.

Land — In the general sense, land encompasses the entire solid portion of the earth's crust. It means all real property and includes everything that is permanently affixed to it.

Land Contract — A contract for the purchase of real estate upon an installment basis; upon payment of last installment, deed is delivered to purchaser. See *Agreement for Deed.*

Land Economics — Branch of the science of economics which deals with the classification, ownership, planning, and utilization of land and buildings erected thereon.

Land Grant — A gift of government land to a university, public utility, railroad, or the like that would be in the best interest and benefit of the general public.

Landlocked — A piece of land not abutting a public road.

Landlord — One who owns leased property; the lessor.

Land Poor — One who owns land but, because of taxes, assessments, interest payments on a mortgage, or other obligations, is continually short of money.

Land Usage — The use being made of land or the uses permitted under zoning ordinances.

Late Charge — A charge stated in the instrument of debt as a penalty for installment loans and mortgage payments when not paid on time.

Lead Bank — A bank which commits to a large loan, then arranges for other banks to participate, or furnish some of the money.

Lead Indicator — An activity whose rise or fall precedes a similar trend in the overall economy.

Lease — A contract, written or oral, for the possession of lands and tenements on the one hand and a recompense of rent or other income, on the other.

Leaseback — A transaction in which a seller remains in possession as a tenant after completing the sale and delivering the deed.

Lease Insurance — A lease guarantee policy that protects the landlord against a default in rental payments by the tenant.

Lease-Purchase Agreement — An agreement which provides that all or a portion of a tenant's rent be applied to the purchase price at a future time.

Lease Renewal — By an extension agreement or endorsement, the terms of a lease may be renewed. A typical lease renewal reads as follows:

By mutual consent, this lease is hereby extended for a term of _____ years beginning _____ and ending _____ for a total rental of $_____ payable $_____ per month. All terms and conditions in the original lease shall remain in full force and effect.

Leased Department — A portion of a store rented by an outside firm or individual; a concession.

Leased Fee Interest — The owner's interest in a leased property.

Leasehold Interest — An estate in realty held under a lease.

Leasehold Value — As economic conditions change, a lease may be worth more or less with the passing of time. Leasehold value is that increase in the market value of a lease over what is being paid. See *Excess Rent, Contract Rent* and *Economic Rent.*

Legal Descriptions — Methods of identifying with exactness the location of land and defining its boundaries.

Legal Notice — See *Constructive Notice.*

Legal Rate of Interest — The maximum rate of interest that can be charged for the use of money as specified in state laws or regulations of federal agencies. "A violation is called *Usury.*"

Lessee — A person to whom property is rented under a lease. A *Tenant.*

Lessor — A person from whom property is rented under a lease. A *Landlord.*

Letter of Credit — A letter, from a company or bank in one area of the country to a similar business establishment in another, introducing the person named and vouching for him and specifying a sum of money to be extended to him.

Level Payment Mortgage — A mortgage payment schedule in which the same amount is paid periodically. The amount of the payment credited to the interest gradually decreases while the amount for amortizing the principal gradually increases as each payment is made. "Also called *Constant Payment Mortgage.*"

Leverage — In real estate, the term means the effective use of money by investing the least amount of capital possible when acquiring property in order that it may bring the maximum percentage of return by mortgaging to the highest amount that is practical.

Lien — A charge or claim upon property which is an encumbrance until discharged, or paid off. The property itself is the security.

Lien Affidavit — An affidavit stating there are no liens or other encumbrances against a particular property other than those itemized and described.

Lien Theory (See Title Theory States) — States offering more legal protection to the mortgagor than the mortgagee. Lien-theory states hold that the lender has only a lien on property and possesses no title interest whatsoever.

Life Estate — An estate or interest held during the term of some certain person's life, not necessarily the life of the holder. May be less in duration than actual life, as contingency termination provisions can be included by grantor.

Limited Partnership — A partnership arrangement which limits certain of the partner's liability to the amount invested and likewise places a limitation on the amount of profit he can make.

Liquid Assets — Cash on hand or other assets that can be readily turned into cash.

Liquidated Damages — The sum agreed upon as payment for a breach of contract.

Liquidation Value — The amount of cash that could be raised if an asset was sold at a forced sale.

Listing — A broker's authority to sell or lease real property for an owner.

Littoral Rights — Belonging to shore as of sea or great lakes; corresponds to riparian rights.

Loan Closing Costs — Those expenses charged against the borrower, or mortgagor, by the lender.

Loan-to-Value Ratio — The percentage derived by dividing the loan by the appraised value of the property being mortgaged.

Lock, Stock, and Barrel — In real estate, an expression used in contracts for the sale of businesses indicating that everything on the premises is included in the sale.

Locked-in Clause — The provision in a mortgage prohibiting prepayment of installments, or coupled with penalty provisions for such prepayment.

Long Form Mortgage Clause — This clause in a mortgage provides for the mortgagor to assume responsibility for its satisfaction when he takes title and not just acquire the property subject to it, which carries no personal responsibility in the event of defaulting. (See *Assumption of Mortgage.*)

Long-Term Lease — A lease of long duration. What is considered "long," however, is relative. A three- or four-year lease for an apartment would be considered of long duration, while for a business lease it would not, as terms for ten- to twenty-five year leases for commercial purposes are considered long.

Long-Term Loan — In banking, mortgage loans for real estate made for 20 years or more are considered long-term loans.

Loophole — "See *Escape Clause.*" An unintentional, or deliberate insertion, omission, or vague wording which would permit one party to a contract to avoid his legal responsibility, or to litigate in an attempt to do so.

Lot, Block and Subdivision — In subdividing land, the tract is first assigned a name, and each block and lot within that subdivision is numbered or lettered on a map of the subdivision after being recorded with the proper governmental (usually county) authority; it then becomes officially recognized when legally describing property. (See *Legal Descriptions.*)

Management Agreement — A contract between an owner and agent for the management of property.

Marginal Land — Land that is of little economic value due to such factors as inaccessibility, poor quality of soil, steep terrain, lack of rainfall, etc.

Marginal Loan — One involving higher than normal risk.

Marketable Title — Good title; clear title. Title to property that is free of significant defects and which a purchaser will accept without objections.

Market Data Constraints — The time, location, and physical characteristics of the transactions analyzed in the comparison approach to value in appraising.

Market Value — The highest price which a buyer, willing but not compelled to buy, would pay, and the lowest a seller, willing but not compelled to sell, would accept.

Master Lease — The original lease. Also called *Base Lease* and *Prime Lease.* Any sublease or assignment of lease must be based on the master lease.

Master Plan — A long-range, overall concept of an area's development generally proposed by the planning department of a city or other community for adoption by the governing body. By projecting population changes and growth trends, it becomes possible to prepare plans for adequate highways, parks, housing, and the overall highest and best usage of the land.

Mechanic's Lien — A lien created by statute which exists in favor of persons who have performed work or furnished materials in the erection or repair of a building.

Meeting of Minds — A mutual intention of two persons to enter into a contract affecting their legal status based on agreed-upon terms.

Megalopolis — A large, heavily populated urbanized area, sometimes extending over hundreds of miles. A region which contains cities and suburbs in huge industrial centers merging into other cities and their suburbs. "See *Standard Metropolitan Statistical Area.*"

Memorandum of Agreement — An informal, written agreement outlining the essentials of a transaction which is binding upon both parties and remains in force until a more formal contract is drawn.

Metes and Bounds — A description in a deed of the land location, in which the boundaries are defined by directions and distances. Starts at P.O.B. (Point of Beginning). Then circumscribes all boundaries, returning finally to P.O.B.

Middleman — When applied to real estate, an agent employed by both buyer and seller. It is an ethical and legal business arrangement provided both principals are aware of the dual employment. The practice is not common today.

Millage — For real estate taxes, it is the factor generally used to state the rate of taxation and compute the taxes. One mill per thousand is equivalent to $1 of taxes per thousand of assessed value. The assessed value multiplied by the millage rate will equal the tax bill for a given year.

Mix — (Commercial Leasing) The type, size, number, and locations of tenants in a given project. Formerly based on superficial ideas, the process of selection and negotiation has become quite sophisticated.

Mixed Estate — Ground Rent for ninety-nine years that is renewable forever. Though a leasehold in form, in reality it has more of the characteristics of fee ownership.

Monetary Policy — Federal actions taken to control the supply of money.

Money — The medium of exchange. A storehouse of value. A claim, now or later, on goods and services.

Money Market — The current availability of loanable funds and the rate of interest being charged to borrow it. Like any commodity, the money market fluctuates with its availability and the demand. When in short supply, the interest rates become higher, and vice versa.

Month-to-Month Tenancy — A tenant for one month. Also, when a tenant with an expired lease, a month-to-month lease, or no lease at all continues paying rent and remains in occupancy from one month to another.

Moratorium — An authorized postponement in meeting an agreed obligation during a period of financial distress; an officially controlled waiting period for permission to do something. For example, sewer connection.

Mortgage — A conditional transfer of real property as security for the payment of a debt or the fulfillment of some obligation.

Mortgagee — A person to whom property is conveyed as security for a loan made by such person (the creditor).

Mortgagee in Possession — A mortgagee creditor who takes over the income from the mortgaged property upon a default on the mortgage by the debtor.

Mortgagor — An owner who conveys his property as security for a loan (the debtor).

Mortgage Banker — A firm that furnishes its own funds for mortgage loans, which are normally sold later to permanent investors. Usually, they continue to service the loans at a specified fee.

Mortgage Broker — An individual or company that obtains mortgage loans for others by finding lending institutions, insurance companies, or private sources that will lend the money.

Mortgage Correspondent — An agent of a lending institution authorized to handle and process loans.

Mortgage Debt — An indebtedness created by a mortgage and secured by the property mortgaged. Personal liability may or may not be a part of the obligation.

Mortgage Investment Company — A company that buys mortgages for investment purposes, such as insurance companies, trust companies, banks, savings and loan associations, and private organizations formed expressly for investing their funds in mortgages.

Mortgage Note — A note, secured by a mortgage, that serves as evidence of an indebtedness and states the manner in which it shall be paid.

Mortgaging Out — Borrowing *all* the cost of purchase.

Mortgage Premium — A charge for placing or originating a mortgage; points. This is an expense in addition to normal closing costs and comes about when: (1) the legal interest rate (as in the case of FHA and VA mortgages) is less than the prevailing mortgage market rate; and (2) there is a scarcity of readily available mortgage money.

Mortgage R.E.I.T. — One formed for the purpose of purchasing mortgages and lending money on real estate. (See *Equity REIT.*)

Multiple Listing — The arrangement among real estate board or exchange members whereby each broker brings his listings to the attention of the other members so that if a sale results, the commission is divided between the broker bringing the listing and the broker making the sale.

Municipal Lien — A lien, created by a local government, against a property owner to obtain funds in order to make improvements to his and immediately surrounding   properties.

Neighborhood Shopping Center — The smallest of the three recognized types of centers. It serves the basic needs in its vicinity, and is usually of the *strip* or *row* design, with all stores facing toward the street, with parking in front and side exposures.

Net Income — The money remaining after all expenses are subtracted from the gross income. The profit.

Net Net Income — In real estate dealings the word "net" is sometimes repeated for emphasis, stressing actual profit after all expenses are paid, including mortgage reduction payments (principal and interest). What remains is cash flow, or money available for use.

Net Lease — A lease requiring the tenant to pay all the costs of maintaining the leased premises including taxes, insurance, and normal repairs. Structural repairs are a normal exception, payable by landlord. Opposite of *Gross Lease.*

Net Listing — A price, which must be expressly agreed upon, below which the owner will not sell the property and at which price the broker will not receive a commission; the broker receives the excess over and above the net listing as his commission.

Net Multiplier — A more accurate factor than *Gross Multiplier* in roughly calculating value because some major variables (taxes, etc.) have been deducted. (See *Earning-Price Ratio.*)

Nonconforming Use — The lawful use of land or improvements upon it that does not comply with current zoning regulations. It is allowed to remain as it was before the zoning ordinance was passed. Generally, such properties cannot be replaced, remodeled, or enlarged, hence purchasers should exercise caution.

Nondisclosure — Courts have described nondisclosure as "misrepresentation by silence." When certain material facts of a property are withheld from the buyer and are later discovered, he may sue for nondisclosure.

Note — Written evidence of a debt, specifying amount and terms of repayment.

Obsolescence — (See *Economic* and *Functional Obsolescence.*)

Occupancy Map — Locations of retail stores plotted on a map of a central business district. Useful in determining 100 percent locations, or where maximum pedestrian traffic occurs.

Occupancy Rate — Ratio of square footage leased to gross square footage in a building.

Open-end Mortgage — A mortgage which permits the borrower to reborrow the money paid on the principal, usually up to the original amount.

Open Listing — A listing made available to more than one broker. The first broker who procures a buyer Ready, Willing, and Able for the price and terms of the listing is the one who receives the commission.

Open Market Operations — Sales and purchases of U.S. obligations by the Federal Reserve to increase or decrease the money supply in banking.

Open Mortgage — A mortgage that can be paid off at any time before maturity without penalty.

Operating Expenses — The actual expenses necessary to maintain a property in usable or rentable condition, to protect it against hazards and to pay taxes, including management, maintenance, repairs, utilities, furniture replacement, taxes, and insurance. Excluded as operating expenses are principal and interest mortgage payments, depreciation, and interest on money invested.

Operating Ratio — The ratio of the expenses of running commercial property or a business to its gross income.

Opinion of Title — An attorney's opinion as to the status of the title to a specified piece of property after studying the abstract. He concludes whether the seller has good and marketable title, defective title, or any title at all.

Option — The right to purchase or lease a property at a certain price for a certain designated period, for which right a consideration is paid by the optionee, or prospective buyer.

Optionee — The prospective tenant or buyer.

Optioner — The prospective landlord or seller.

Origination Fee — A charge for establishing and processing a new mortgage loan.

Outlot — In shopping centers, small parcels excluded from temporary and permanent mortgages to permit developer to sell or lease, capitalizing on the earned increment possibilities.

Overage Rent — Retail store leases are usually established at a guaranteed minimum figure, plus a percentage of the volume of business the store does over a specified amount going to the landlord as additional rent. This amount is referred to as "the overage." Normally this is paid annually.

Over-Improvement — An improvement to land that is more extensive or costly than justified by current or foreseeable conditions. Sometimes called a *Monument,* or *White Elephant* or *Ego Trip.*

Owners Affidavit of No Liens — An affidavit which states that all work done to the subject property has been completed, that the owners are in undisputed possession, and that there are now no liens or chattel mortgages encumbering it.

Package Mortgage — A type of mortgage used in home financing that covers both the realty and certain appliance and equipment items such as air conditioner, kitchen range, laundry machine, garbage disposal unit, refrigerator, dryer, and carpeting.

Parking Ratio — For office buildings, it is a required number of off-street parking spaces for a designated floor area. For apartments, a minimum of about one to one-and-a-half parking spaces per dwelling unit. For shopping centers, it usually requires that about 3/4 of gross land area be devoted to parking and drives.

Partial Release Clause — A clause found in some mortgages and deeds providing for the release of a portion of the property when certain prescribed stipulations are met.

Participation Loan (A) — One in which the "lead" lender arranges for other lenders to furnish part of the funds required.

Participation Loan (B) — One in which the lender obtains a "piece of the action," or participation in profits of the project being mortgaged as an inducement to provide the funding. Used in "tight money" periods.

Parties — The participants in a transaction. The principals. In contracts and other instruments, the "party of the first part" refers to the seller or lessor; the "part of the second part" to the buyer or lessee.

Party Wall — A wall erected on the line between two adjoining properties, belonging to different persons, for the use of both properties. It cannot be removed without consent of both owners.

Pension Funds — Trust funds belonging to union, corporate, or governmental pension programs. These funds are often invested in large, well-secured mortgages.

Percentage Lease — A lease in which the rental includes a percentage of the volume of sales, usually in addition to a guaranteed minimum.

Performance Bond — A bond posted to guarantee that the builder will satisfactorily complete a construction contract and that it will be free of liens.

Permanent Financing A long-term loan in the form of a mortgage. Usually extends over 15, 20 or more years with a fixed interest rate.

Personal Liability — The personal responsibility to repay a debt, in addition to the pledge of the collateral.

Personalty — All articles or property that are not real estate. A contraction of "Personal Property"; also called "Chattels."

Physical Depreciation — The decline in property value due to the action of time and the elements, as well as through usage; deterioration.

Piggyback Loan — A loan where there is a smaller loan tied onto a larger, conventional loan to provide more money than the usual loan-to-value ratio would permit.

P.I.T.I. — An abbreviation used in describing total monthly carrying charges of a mortgage; i.e., principal, interest, taxes, insurance.

Plat Book — A public record of various recorded plans in the municipality or county.

Plottage — (See *Assemblage.*)

Point — The term is frequently used when referring to mortgage premiums and is 10 percent of the principal amount. It is a method used by lenders to obtain additional revenue over the legal interest rate. (See *Basis Point.*)

Police Power — The inherent rights of a government to pass such legislation as may be necessary to protect the public health and safety and/or to promote the general welfare. The foundation for ordinances pertaining to zoning and land planning.

Portfolio — A collective word; describes the total investments owned by an institution or individual.

Possession — The act or state of possessing; the holding and peaceful enjoyment of property.

Power of Attorney — A written authority for one to act as another's agent. The extent of the authority is limited to that stated in the instrument.

Power of Sale — The authority given by an owner for another to sell real property or other assets. The legal power to produce a change in ownership.

Preliminary Sales Agreement — An agreement made before a more formal and detailed sales contract is drawn; a binder. A memorandum of agreement; a letter of intent.

Prepayment Clause — A clause in a mortgage permitting the mortgagor to pay all or part of the unpaid balance before it becomes due, thereby saving the interest or clearing the way for a new mortgage.

Prepayment Penalty — A penalty imposed upon a mortgagor for paying the mortgage before it becomes due, when there is no Prepayment Clause.

Present Worth Tables — Tables showing the present value of the right to receive future payments. Figured at various interest rates.

Primary Trade Area — The geographic limits encompassing population logically expected to do convenience and comparison shopping at a given site.

Principal — Has three distinct meanings: 1. One of the main parties in a real estate transaction; the purchaser or the seller. 2. In the law of agency, the one giving the authority to another to act for him. The employer of a real estate broker; the broker's client; the one responsible for paying his commission. 3. The basic amount of money as distinguished from interest. The capital sum; the amount upon which interest is paid.

Private Lenders — A term used to distinguish individuals who lend money from institutional lenders: banks, insurance companies.

Procuring Cause — In a real estate transaction, it is the broker or his salesman, who produces a Ready, Willing, and Able buyer for the agreed-upon price and terms, who is the procuring cause of the transaction and, therefore, entitled to receive a commission.

Pro Forma — A projection of future income and expense. If actual, would be called *Operating Figures.*

Progress Payments — Periodic payments made to a contractor as construction of a project advances.

Project Financing — In single family or condominium projects, overall financing is often accomplished by the use of blanket mortgages. Release clauses are provided for in the mortgage and put into effect upon payment of a pro rata share by the developer. As each home or condominium unit in a section is completed, it can immediately be sold off. The purchaser of the home receives a new, permanent mortgage. In this manner a project helps finance itself as it progresses toward completion.

Promoter — (See *Entrepreneur.*)

Property — That which is legally owned by an individual or group and which may be kept and enjoyed or disposed of as the owner sees fit. The unrestricted rights to something owned which are guaranteed and potected by the government. Property is divided into two classes, Real and Personal.

Property Management — A part of real estate activity defined as renting, supervising, collecting, paying, and the overall maintaining and managing of real estate for others.

Prorate — Proportion according to one's interest. In real estate contracts, for example, taxes, insurance, rents, interest, and certain other annual expenses of the property are generally prorated at the time of closing and charged to buyer or seller.

Punch List — Itemized list of incomplete work and parts, usually prepared near end of construction.

Purchase Money — The sum of money paid to obtain ownership to property. The financial consideration given.

Purchase Money Mortgage — A mortgage given by a grantee to the grantor in part payment of the purchase price of real estate.

Quality of Estate — The manner in which an estate is to be owned as to type of possession (sole, jointly, tenancy-in-common, etc.) and time (present or future). Value or physical characteristics of the estate have no connection.

Quality of Income — A determination of the probability of receiving future payments of rent based on the financial strength of the tenant(s).

Quiet Enjoyment — The right of an owner to the use of property without interference of possession. The right of reasonable privacy.

Quiet Title Suit — A suit to remove a defect, cloud, or any questionable or conflicting claims against the title to property.

Quit-Claim Deed — The instrument used to remove any and all claims or interest in ownership that an individual may have, without his warranting the quality or validity of the title.

Rationalized Report — A feasibility report which justifies an action or decision already taken, made, or planned.

Ready, Willing, and Able — The phrase means that a buyer is completely agreeable and fully qualified to enter into and consummate a transaction. "Ready" means that he is prepared at this time to enter into a contract. "Willing" refers to a person's own free choice and that he is of a mind to buy. "Able" has to do with his ability to meet the financial requirements of the agreement.

Real Estate — The land itself and everything below, growing upon, or attached to it.

Real Estate Investment Trust — A group of real estate investors consisting of one or more trustees who hold title to the assets for the trust and control its acquisitions, management, and sale. Though unincorporated, the trust must be owned in the form of shares by 100 or more people (no five of whom are to possess over 50 percent interest). The major advantage of a business structure of this nature is the tax benefits, as no corporation income tax need be paid. (See *Equity* and *Mortgage R.E.I.T.*)

Real Estate Market — The buying and selling of real property that creates supply and demand resulting in the setting of market values and prices. Also used to describe related activities: financing, managing, leasing, etc.

Real Estate Rate — The cost of borrowed money after allowing for the loss in value caused by inflation.

Realtor — A coined word used to designate an active member of a local real estate board affiliated with the National Association of Real Estate Boards.

Realty — Contraction of "Real Property."

Reassessment — A re-evaluation; a change in the assessed value of property; a reappraisal.

Recapture Clause — A clause in leases giving the landlord the right to terminate the lease if certain conditions or standards are not maintained, such as may occur in a percentage lease, where the landlord has the right to cancel if a specified minimum volume of business is not maintained. Another definition: a clause found in ground rents providing an option for the outright purchase of the land for a specific price and at a specified time in the future. (See *Ground Rent.*)

Recasting a Mortgage — The act of reconstructing an existing mortgage by increasing its amount, interest rate, or length of time.

Receiver — A court-appointed, neutral party who takes possession and manages the property of a bankrupt or of property being otherwise litigated.

Reconveyance — To convey or return ownership of real estate to one who previously had title to it. The transfer of title back to its former owner.

Record — 1. A written statement; to officially commit to writing; to transcribe for future use or reference. 2. Placing a document on the public records by recording it in the proper county office where the general public may examine it.

Redemption — The right of a mortgagor to redeem the property by paying the debt after the expiration date; the right of an owner to reclaim his property after a sale for taxes.

Rediscount Rate — The rate charged by the Federal Reserve Bank for loans made to member banks.

Reduction of Mortgage Certificate — (See *Estoppel Certificate.*)

Refinance — To renew or extend existing financing or obtain another source, usually for an amount larger than the original loan.

Reformation of Deed — Modification of a deed by court order when a spelling or other mechanical error has been made in preparing it, a fraud has been perpetrated by one of the parties, or for any other reason wherein the true intentions of the deed have not been fulfilled. Also called "Correction Deed."

Refunding Mortgage — (See *Refinance.*)

Regional Shopping Center — The largest type recognized. Serves an extensive "drawing area." Minimum of two department stores (anchors). Current construction leans toward EMAC design; i.e., enclosed mall air-conditioned.

Release Clause — 1. A clause found in blanket mortgages providing for the payment of a portion of the indebtedness so that a proportionate part of the property can be released. (See *Project Financing.*) 2. Any clause that releases a party from an agreement when a specified contingency arises.

Release of Lien — Instrument(s), signed by subcontractors, material men and anyone else who may have a lien on the property, stating satisfaction of debt. It affords only limited protection for a new owner, as other lien holders who have not signed the release can sue. A new owner's best safeguard is to obtain title insurance covering Mechanic's Liens.

Relet — Leasing the premises again, as occurs following an expired lease or when a lease is broken allowing the landlord to attempt immediately to rerent the property. The first tenant who abandoned the lease is still liable, though generally to a lesser degree, for the unexpired term of the lease.

Renewal Costs — Costs charged by the lender to extend a loan. Usually higher if a new owner (borrower) is involved.

Rentable Area — (Shopping Centers) The standard definition is called *Gross Leaseable Area* and includes all that area for which tenants pay rent. It is only the area producing income to the landlord, and excludes the common area, which is used by all tenants and customers; for example, malls, sidewalks, parking areas, landscaped areas, public restrooms, truck, and other service facilities.

Rental Multiple — The number currently used to multiply annual gross rent to arrive at a rough indication of value.

Rent Roll — A complete, accurate roster of the tenants that includes such information as the term of the lease, the security being held on deposit, and the amount of the rental.

Replacement Cost — 1. The amount of money that would be needed to replace the equivalent of a building, furnishings, or other asset. 2. In appraising it is the estimated current cost to replace an asset similar or equivalent to the one being appraised. (See *Cost Approach.*)

Reproduction Cost — (See *Replacement Cost.*)

Right of Redemption — A reserved right, granted by statute, to free a property from foreclosure by paying the debts, fees, and other accumulated charges that are causing it to be encumbered.

Right of Survivorship — A right held by a surviving joint owner giving him sole title to the property. This right is found in Joint Tenancies and Tenancies by the Entirety.

Right of Way — The right to pass over another's property. It is an easement that can be either private or public; i.e., for one person or for the public at large.

Rolling Option — A series of options encumbering a parcel of land, exercisible separately, which can be terminated by buyer (optionee) at intervals.

Run with the Land — When covenants or restrictions regarding a property become incumbent upon each succeeding owner, it is said to "run with the land."

Sale and Leaseback — A transaction in which the seller remains in occupancy by simultaneously signing a lease (usually of long duration) with the purchaser at the time of the sale. By so doing, the seller receives cash for the transaction, while the buyer is assured a tenant and thus a fixed return on his investment.

Sale, Leaseback, Buyback — A Sale-and-Leaseback transaction in which a further provision is made for the leaseholder to have the option to buy back his original property after a specified period of time as the lessee. This type of transaction has tax-shelter and profit benefits for both parties. Usually ten or more years of lease term precedes the option of the lessee to repurchase.

Sandwich Lease — In subleasing property, when the holder of a sublease in turn sublets to another, his position is that of being "sandwiched" between the original lessee and the second sublessee.

Satellite Community — A separate community situated near a large city that is closely tied economically, politically, and socially to the metropolitan area it borders. If mainly residential, may be called "bedroom" community.

Satellites (Shopping Centers) — Tenants who are compatible with, and who thrive on proximity to, the anchor or "major" tenants. Inelegantly called "parasites."

Satisfaction of Lien — The instrument which certifies that a lien has been fully paid. Same meaning applies to *Loans* and *Mortgages*.

Savings and Loan Association — A financial institution that is state or federally chartered and privately owned by the depositors or stockholders. Its prime functions are to furnish first-mortgage loans on improved real estate and to provide government-insured, interest-bearing savings accounts.

Seasoned Mortgage — A mortgage in which periodic payments have been made, for a relatively long period of time, and the borrower's pattern of punctuality is well established.

Secondary Mortgage Market — The process of lenders selling their mortgages in bulk, with continually fluctuating interest rates, comprises the Secondary Mortgage market. F.N.M.A. buys huge blocks of mortgages, providing liquidity for primary lenders.

Secondary Trade Area — An area outside of a primary trade area in which the population could logically be expected to do comparison shopping at a given site.

Second Lien — A lien which is second to, junior to, or subordinate to the first lien.

Security — A deposit or personal pledge to guarantee payment of an obligation, to insure against damages, or to guarantee the faithful performance of an agreement.

Seller's Lien — A mortgage or note held by the seller and commonly called a purchase money mortgage.

Seller's Market — When any commodity, including real estate, is in short supply, the seller is in a more commanding position. Within reason, an owner can generally name his price and terms. He can sometimes choose the best of several offers. When supply and demand are not balanced, it is referred to as a seller's market.

Senior Mortgage — (See *First Mortgage.*)

Servicing — Activities connected with collecting payments on mortgages and transmitting to mortgagee, and accounting, insuring, inspecting, foreclosing, etc.

Setback Line — A zoning regulation prohibiting the construction of a building, beyond a prescribed distance from the property line. Sometimes called *Building Line.*

Severalty — Sole ownership. An estate held by one person only.

Shell and Allowance (Shopping Centers) — A common practice wherein the developer builds only the primary (Shell) portion of a building, giving a monetary allowance to the tenant to be used to complete the finished space.

Shopping a Deal — The practice of negotiating an agreement, then attempting to improve on the terms with alternative suppliers, lenders, tenants, etc.

Short Form — A condensation of a lengthy instrument, containing the essential features, usually for recording purposes.

Short-Term Loan (or Financing) — A loan of short duration. In real estate financing, it is generally considered that a mortgage of 10 years or less is a short term. Mortgage loans for 20 years or more are referred to as long-term loans. Loans between 10 to 20 years are medium-term loans.

Short Rate — When an insurance policy is cancelled, the rate for the time that it was in force will increase, as the premium originally charged was calculated on the full period of the policy. This increased premium is known as the "short rate."

Silent Partner — An inactive partner in a business. One who has a monetary interest but does not participate in operation of the company.

Simple Interest — Interest that is computed on the principal amount of a loan only. No provision for interest on interest, as occurs with a loan containing Compound Interest.

Single-Purpose Improvement — An improvement not easily or economically convertible to another use.

Sinking Fund — A gradually accumulated fund created to reduce and extinguish a debt. At the end of a given period, the fund will have a sufficient amount, including interest earned, to replace loss or satisfy an obligation that has fallen due. A method of retiring or paying off a bond issue.

Social Obsolescence — (See *Economic Obsolescence.*)

Specific Performance — A. Performing exactly, or as nearly so as possible, the terms of a contract. B. After a default by one of the parties, it is the name given the lawsuit brought for failure to perform as stated in the agreement.

Speculator — An individual engaged in speculating in real property. An intuitive, knowledgeable party who studies the real estate market, anticipates its trends, and invests for his own account. If he foresees a rise in prices, he will acquire properties and hold them for the most opportune time to sell. Often becomes wealthy by "selling out too soon." Seldom waits for last increment of profit. (See *Investor.*)

Split Financing — Financing the fee (land) separately from the improvements thereon.

Spot Zoning — Nonconforming zoning that differs from the general pattern of the surrounding area, or the action taken to create this condition.

Spread — The difference between the interest paid to depositors in a savings institution, and interest collected from borrowers.

S.M.S.A. — Standard Metropolitan Statistical Area. A federally designated geographically described urban area with cohesive patterns of trade/communication/employment/transportation.

Statute of Frauds — This early English statute was founded to prevent frauds and perjuries, and has been enlarged to become a basic concept and foundation of real estate and contract law; i.e., to be in writing and duly executed to be enforceable.

Statute of Limitations — A statute placing a time limit on the right of action in certain cases where a remedy is sought in a court of law. (See *Laches.*)

Statutory Lien — A lien that arises under the rules of a statute. Tax Liens and Judgment Liens are examples.

Straight Line Depreciation — A method of calculating an allowance for depreciation of a building by deducting a constant amount annually over the anticipated life of the building. It allows the owner to regain his investment in the property during its useful life. The amount is calculated by dividing the total cost of the building by its estimated economic life.

Straight Loan — A loan in which only interest payments are periodically made with the entire principal amount becoming due at maturity.

Subject to Mortgage — The term subject to means limiting, qualifying, or subordinate to. When used in mortgages it refers to taking title to property which has an existing mortgage, but without assuming personal liability for its payment. If liability is to be assumed, it must be so stated and agreed upon.

Subordination — A lien holder consenting to place his interest in lesser rank than another. This frequently occurs when the seller of vacant land, in order to make the sale, takes back a purchase money mortgage and agrees to lower its rank to a position inferior to a construction or permanent loan, or, if lessor of land, subordinates his fee position to similar financing.

Subrogation — Substitution of one person for another in regard to a legal right, interest, or obligation, such as a mortgage holder's selling his rights and interest to another.

Substantial Performance — When virtually all the provisions of a contract are met, with the possible exception of minor technicalities or inadvertent omissions.

Summary Proceedings — Short legal proceedings without a jury, indictments, subpoenaed witnesses, or the usual and often lengthy and expensive requirements of a regular course of law.

Summation Appraisal — (See *Cost Approach*.)

Surety — A personal guarantee to fulfill an obligation. One who has legally committed himself to the fidelity, obligations or debts of another, should that party fail to perform as agreed.

Syndicate — A group of investors who undertake to pursue a limited objective for a limited period of time. A short-term partnership. Individuals who combine abilities and finances in a business venture.

Take Back a Mortgage — A reference, found in contracts, to an owner taking back a Purchase Money Mortgage to facilitate a sale of property.

Takeout Commitment — A commitment by a lending institution to assume or liquidate a short-term construction loan and issue a more permanent mortgage.

Tangible Property — Property that is material in form. Real or personal property that can be perceived or touched such as a house, furnishings, or the land itself. The opposite of intangible.

Tax Deed — The form of deed used when land is sold for non-payment of taxes, deemed to pass Fee Simple title to the holder.

Tax Participation Clause — A clause in a lease providing for the pro rata payment by the tenant of any increase in taxes during the term of the lease, often limited to increases after first or second year thereof. Also called a Tax-Stop clause.

Taxable Income — Add amortization to cash flow, then subtract depreciation.

Taxpayer — Typically, a one-story inexpensive store, originally so called because the revenue from it was sufficient only to pay the taxes on the property. Though still called taxpayers, stores as income-producing real estate are now often highly profitable forms of investment, bringing far greater returns to the owner than just the taxes.

Tenancy in Common — Form of estate held by two or more persons, each of whom considered as possessing the whole of an undivided part.

Tenant — A person who holds real estate under a lease (lessee).

Tenant at Sufferance — One who comes into possession of lands by lawful title and keeps it afterwards without any title at all.

Term Mortgage — A mortgage having a stipulated duration, usually under five years, in which only interest is paid. At the expiration of the term, the entire incipal amount becomes due. (See *Long-Term Loan.*)

Thin — A financial status which is marginal or shaky.

Thrift Institution — (See *Savings and Loan Association.*)

Time is the Essence Clause — The clause in a contract that places great importance on completing the terms and conditions exactly when specified. It means the specific date is an essential element of the agreement.

Title — Evidence of ownership, which refers to the quality of the estate.

Title by Adverse Possession — Acquired by occupation and recognized as against the paper title owner.

Title Insurance — A policy of insurance which indemnifies the holder for any loss sustained by reason of defects in the title.

Title Theory States — States in which legal emphasis is placed on protecting the lender of mortgage money should a mortgage go into default. In these states, he is assumed to have some lawful title to the mortgaged property. Having a title interest, it is easier for him to recover the property should there be a default. (See *Lien Theory States.*)

Traffic Generator — Describes the major tenant(s) in a shopping center or C.B.D. — usually chain or prestige department stores. (See *Anchor Tenant.*)

Treasury Bill — A short term obligation of the United States.

Trustee — A party who legally holds property in trust for others.

Turnkey Job — A building term indicating completeness of construction with nothing to be done but turn the key and move in. Also called Key Job.

Unaccrued — Without periodic accumulation; not developing or continuing to grow. Not yet due.

Underimproved Land — A. Land needing further development in order to realize its highest and best usage. B. Land that has improvements upon it that are incompatible with its highest and best use.

Underwriter — A. An expert who evaluates insurance policies that have been solicited and accepts or rejects insurance risks. B. A firm which guarantees the sale of a security issue with the intention of distributing it to the public directly or via other dealers.

Unearned Increment — An increase in value of real estate due to no effort on the part of the owner; often due to increase in population, or to improvements on nearby properties.

Unilateral Contract — A contract in which only one party expressly agrees to something. Unlike a fully executed (bilateral) contract, just one principal is bound by the terms of the agreement.

Uninsurable Title — Property that a title insurance company will not insure.

Unmarketable Title — Title that is not necessarily bad, but one in which sufficient doubt is found to render it unsalable until the defects are cured.

Unrecorded Instrument — Any document that has not been publicly recorded.

Unrecorded Plat — A land survey that has not been made a part of the public record.

Urban Sprawl — The uncoordinated growth of residential development outward from center of a city, especially applies to extensive single-family subdivisions.

Utility Easement — A right-of-way easement granted to utility companies for the use of another's land. For example, telephone poles, electric lines, sewer, water and gas mains on and under private property.

Useful Life — The period of time during which an asset will have economic value and be usable.

Vacancy Factor (or Rate) — The percentage of a building's unrented space during a given period.

Vacated Street — A street that has been officially abandoned by a public agency. Normally, dedicated streets revert one half to each abutting owner.

Value — The worth of one thing in comparison with another. The market value. Something desirable and therefore having worth.

Value, Elements of — 1. Demand. 2. Scarcity. 3. Utility. 4. Transferability.

Variance — As applied to real estate, it is a special request to do something with property which is an exception to the existing zoning laws. Involves a distinct change or an enlargement of current usage.

Vendee — The purchaser of real estate under an agreement. The buyer. The grantee.

Vendor — The seller of real estate, usually referred to as the party of the first part in an agreement for sale. The grantor.

Venture Capital — Risk capital. Money invested that is unsecured. Usually offers the highest percentage of return because of the uncertainty involved.

Vested — Placed in possession and control. Given or committed to another.

Voluntary Alienation — The normal transfer of interest and title when real estate changes ownership. Involuntary, the opposite, means done under duress.

Waiver — The renunciation, abandonment, or surrender of some claim, right, or privilege.

Warranty Deed — One that contains a covenant that the grantor will protect the grantee against any claimant.

Wear and Tear — Depreciation, or wearing out, from normal usage.

Wheeler-Dealer — A speculator who rapidly buys and sells properties. A knowledgeable investor always seeking fast, profitable deals. Sometimes called *In and Outer,* or *Wheel.*

Windfall — (See *Unearned Increment.*)

With Prejudice — In law, when the judge issues an adverse decision "with prejudice," it means that the court has issued a final decision and no further appeal to that court will be heard.

Without Prejudice — In general, when a decision is handed down "without prejudice," it means that an individual's right to amend his appeal or seek a different verdict or file a new application is still open.

Without Recourse — This term is most frequently found in endorsements of negotiable instruments, and means that the endorser does not assume responsibility or liability for its collection.

Wrap-around Mortgage — A refinancing technique used in times of increasing or higher interest rates in which the lender assumes payment of the existing mortgage and gives a new, increased mortgage to the borrower at a higher interest rate. As defined by its name, the new mortgage "wraps around" the original one. The increased amount is always second to the existing lien.

Writ of Execution — A writ which authorizes and directs the proper offices of the court (usually the sheriff) to carry into effect the judgment or decree of the court.

Writ of Mandamus — A court order directing that a specific thing be done. X — In signing legal documents, individuals who cannot write should affix an "X" where the signature would ordinarily go. A witness writes the person's name around the mark as follows:

his
Robert (X) Jones
mark

Yield — The profit or income that an investment or property will return. The money derived from any given business venture, usually expressed as a percentage on the investment.

Zoning — The division of land into separate classifications for different usages such as business, residential, light, medium or heavy industry, etc. as well as regulating the type and density of the improvements upon it.

Zoning Ordinance — Exercise of police power of a municipality in regulating and controlling the character and use of land and improvements.

INDEX